3ds Max 7.5 Projects

Helping Designers Do More with Less

Boris Kulagin

BPB PUBLICATIONS
B-14, CONNAUGHT PLACE, NEW DELHI-110001

FIRST INDIAN EDITION 2006

Distributors:

MICRO BOOK CENTRE
2, City Centre, CG Road,
Near Swastic Char Rasta,
AHMEDABAD-380009 Phone: 26421611

COMPUTER BOOK CENTRE
12, Shrungar Shopping Centre, M.G. Road,
BANGALORE-560001 Phone: 5587923, 5584641

MICRO BOOKS
Shanti Niketan Building, 8, Camac Street,
KOLKATTA-700017 Phone: 22826518, 22826519

BUSINESS PROMOTION BUREAU
8/1, Ritchie Street, Mount Road,
CHENNAI-600002 Phone: 28410796, 28550491

DECCAN AGENCIES
4-3-329, Bank Street,
HYDERABAD-500195 Phone: 24756400, 24756967

MICRO MEDIA
Shop No. 5, Mahendra Chambers, 150 D.N. Road,
Next to Capital Cinema V.T. (C.S.T.) Station,
MUMBAI-400001 Ph.: 22078296, 22078297

BPB PUBLICATIONS
B-14, Connaught Place, **NEW DELHI-110001**
Phone: 23325760, 23723393, 23737742

INFO TECH
G-2, Sidhartha Building, 96 Nehru Place,
NEW DELHI-110019
Phone: 26438245, 26415092, 26234208

INFO TECH
Shop No. 2, F-38, South Extension Part-1
NEW DELHI-110049
Phone: 24691288, 24641941

BPB BOOK CENTRE
376, Old Lajpat Rai Market,
DELHI-110006 PHONE: 23861747

NOTE: THE CD-ROM INCLUDED WITH THE BOOK HAS NO COMMERCIAL VALUE AND CANNOT BE SOLD SEPARATELY.

Original ISBN : 1-931769-43-5

Printed in India by arrangement with
A-LIST, LLC, USA.

Price : Rs. 270/-

ISBN 81-8333-087-8
Published by Manish Jain for BPB Publications, B-14, Connaught Place, New Delhi-110 001 and Printed by him at Akash Press, New Delhi-110020.

III

Contents

Preface

The Goals of This Book

As the title suggests, this book concentrates on the practical applications of the latest version of the 3ds Max v.7.1 3D modeling and animation software package from Autodesk, with extensions to version 7.5 5. The book is also dedicated, as the name suggests, to solving the problems associated with three-dimensional modeling and rendering using the most efficient state-of-the-art methods.

Ten years ago, high-level three-dimensional graphics were the domain of only the largest companies, but the steady growth in computer performance and fall in the price of the associated hardware since then has made them available to even the smallest of companies, as well as to freelancers. 3ds Max is used more and more frequently in combination with software products intended for three-dimensional modeling of engineering problems — computer-aided design and computer-aided modeling (3D CAD/CAM). These products are well suited to the creation of three-dimensional models. As a rule, however, they lack the tools necessary to achieve high-quality, photorealistic rendering. Thus, modeling using AutoCAD (ADT, Revit, ArchiCAD) is often combined with rendering (3ds Max) for modeling and rendering interior and exterior surroundings.

Significant attention is paid to modeling in this book because building a model properly is half the battle. Although 3ds Max allows you to import models from engineering software products, while Autodesk constantly emphasizes how quick and easy this is, it is much more expedient in most cases to recreate the model anew in 3ds Max.

Unfortunately, the main modeling techniques utilized in CAD/CAM software products — Boolean operations with objects and modeling using NURBS surfaces, are not good enough for modeling in 3ds Max. I even know the case where a hollow hemisphere in 3ds Max was modeled by means of sequential subtractions of a cube and a sphere of a smaller diameter than the initial sphere. I have no objections to this method but, at the same time, I am not one of its fans. As a matter of fact, 3ds Max provides a large number of more efficient ways of producing the same result.

Modeling will be considered here using examples that are easy enough to understand from the modeling point of view, and the most suitable and convenient method is used with every model, accounting for further texturing, rendering and, in many cases, animation.

All of the models considered in the first chapter are the creations of students and design beginners, developed under the guidance of experienced instructors. I tried to re-create these works in 3ds Max, without considerable deviations from the author's ideas. The skill required to achieve your intended result, without letting the software product push you around, is one of the abilities you will have to master.

However, creating a model properly is only half way to success. The rest of the process involves materials, lighting, and final rendering.

Practically every state-of-the-art product, including 3ds Max, provides rendering tools that employ contemporary and physically accurate algorithms for computing phenomena such as global lighting, reflections, and refractions. Thanks to the power of contemporary computers, rendering results of a satisfactory quality can be done in a reasonable amount of time. We will pay considerable attention to these issues throughout the book. Some "unfair" tricks that will help you achieve the desired results in a minimum of time will also be covered.

Intended Audience

This book is intended mainly for designers that are well-acquainted with computer graphics and accustomed to working with two-dimensional editors and, possibly, even with CAD/CAM products. As a rule, these people have lots to do and are short of time. Thus, they cannot afford to master all of the available capabilities of specific software product. With this fact in mind, I have done my best to avoid overloading the book with the description of showy functions that weren't particularly germane to the case in point. The functions of this type are numerous, but they represent a topic for a different book.

I am in no way trying to belittle traditional 2d designers and artists. Their work and talents will always be needed. I am sure that your drawing skills are excellent and that you are capable of creating perfect illustrations. I hope that this book will help you to introduce new features into your works.

The Book Structure

The book is divided into three chapters.

Chapter 1 briefly formulates the main principles for organizing your work with 3ds Max, as well as the main techniques involved in working with this software product. This chapter is intended to help you understand the basic principles of 3ds Max. Under no circumstances should it be considered as a reference. If you intend to master 3ds Max at a higher level, you can't do without reference literature.

The title of *Chapter 2*, "*Modeling and Graphic Presentation of Industrial Design Objects*," speaks for itself. This chapter has five simple models for you to create step by step. Note that the term "presentation" should be interpreted as obtaining images that can be considered realistic, as an addition to the main presentation portfolio. I won't go so far as to declare that traditional presentation methods have become obsolete. As for this chapter, it covers lots of theoretical and practical issues related to working with 3ds Max in the context of specific model.

Chapter 3 concentrates fully on the design of interiors from scratch. It isn't loaded with theoretical issues and considerations because it is assumed that you have already read the preceding two chapters.

Certain conventions are used for the presentation of materials throughout this book.

Instructions explaining what should be done are given in list format, such as the following:

- ❐ Open the scene.max file.

To simplify the process of searching for the required command for beginners who may not know how to do this, the following formatting convention is used:

Main menu → File → Open

Finally, the text contains a large number of notes, explanations and tips, formatted as follows:

The text formatted as follows, can be skipped, if you wish. As a rule, this would have no effect on the results achieved in the current example. However, if you are a beginner user of 3ds Max, I strongly recommend that you pay attention to the information contained in these notes.

Innovations That Have Appeared in Version 7.5

This version of 3ds Max is an extension of version 7.0 and is available to subscribers only. I am sure that all of these innovations will become part of 3ds Max 8. Version 7.5 includes the following three extensions, which can be installed individually.

A brief list of main innovations used in this book is provided below.

Autodesk VIZ Extension contains several innovations transferred from Autodesk VIZ 2006:

- The Sweep modifier and Extended splines, which simplify the creation of various profiles
- The use of physically scaled textures, which simplify the texturization process
- A scene state in combination with Batch render feature, which optimizes the process of final rendering
- The radiosity adaptive subdivision method, which speeds up the process of computing indirect lighting and improves the final result

The Mental ray 3.4 Extension with an improved Final Gather algorithm, among other improvements, considerably speeds up rendering when this module is used.

Hair and Fur Extension, based on the popular Shave and a Haircut package, allows for the creation realistic hair, fur, grass, prickles, etc. Although this extension hasn't found an application in this book, it would be unfair to pass over it without mention.

In addition to the latter extension, the book uses Cloth Extension, the module for creating clothes. This module is not supplied as part of Version 7.5, and must be loaded individually. This extension also is available to 3ds Max subscribers as a free download.

Hardware Requirements

In contrast to other high-grade products for working with three-dimensional graphics, 3ds Max is generally capable of running on computers that might be considered less than powerful in the context of the latest processors and memory. However, to work comfortably, your computer should at least be based on an Intel Pentium 4 chip with a clock frequency of no less than 2 GHz, and be equipped with no less than 512 MB RAM, a video adapter supporting Direct3D or OpenGL at the hardware level, and equipped with no less than 128 MB RAM. It is recommended to install either the MS Windows 2000 SP 4 or the Windows XP SP 2 operating system. It is also best to work with a monitor that is at least 17 inches.

Acknowledgments

First of all, I would like to thank Alexander Steshenko, the art director of the Panzar studio, for the idea for this book, which he came up with a few years ago during a private conversation.

Further development of this topic was suggested by Olga Yatshuk, head of the New Information Technologies Faculty of the National Design University (Moscow).

Special thanks go to Ann Zhyiryakova, Mary Malinina, Michael Morozov and Valery Kuleshov, all of whom are professors of engineering graphics and design at the Moscow State University of Electronics, — for their consultation and help in choosing objects for modeling. Special thanks is also in order for Valery Kuleshov, who was so kind as to allow me to use his custom model of an interior.

I deeply appreciate the kind permission from students and graduates of the Moscow State University of Electronics — Alina Morozovskaya, Yulia Cherepneva, Alyona Makhankova, Inna Arkhipova, Helen Perminova and Mary Guergel — to use their term papers for some of the examples provided in this book.

Special appreciation is also due to the following colleagues and friends:

- Igor Sivakov, Paul Ledin (aka Puppet), and Gennady Afonin, for their help in getting to bottom of the truth with regard to mental ray
- Andrew Koslov, for his kind permission to use and publish his IES Generator program on the companion CD
- The specialists at Realtime Studio, for their help in modeling interiors and permission to use one of their works on the cover of this book
- My students from the Realtime School, who were the first to test out the examples published in this book
- Alex Duka, for his important ideas in the field of interior rendering.
- Elisabeth Tarasova, for her critical notes and ideas, which made this book much better than it would have been otherwise

I would also like to thank all of my friends and my family — in particular, my wife Marina — for their patience, understanding, and support. Much of what is good in this volume is the result of their contribution. Whatever shortcomings there may be are my responsibility alone.

Chapter 1

Introduction to 3ds Max

3ds Max is a large universal software package with numerous features. A description of these features would require a voluminous book, perhaps, difficult to read. However, a common user who isn't crazy about 3D graphics would hardly use all these features even if he or she knew them. In addition, many buttons don't always allow you to understand the essence. In this chapter, I'll try to give you only the necessary information about the 3ds Max interface and manipulations with objects and the modifier stack. I'll also tell you about the logical structure of 3ds Max. Without knowing this, you could fail to understand the response of 3ds Max to your actions.

This chapter describes only briefly the issues of modeling, mapping, illumination, rendering, and animation. These are addressed when describing examples throughout this book. Many theoretical issues are also discussed when applied to practical projects.

The First Start

When you start 3ds Max for the first time after its installation, it displays a window that instructs you to select a graphics driver (Fig. 1.1), which determines how objects are displayed in the viewports. The first selection (**Software**) doesn't use features of modern 3D accelerators. It makes sense to use it only if you have a very old video card such as S3 Trio. You might be surprised, but 3ds Max knows how to work with this video card. However, you should install Direct 3D 9 in your system, and it isn't likely to work in a system with such an old video card.

It makes little difference whether you select OpenGL or Direct3D. However, the developers of 3ds Max obviously prefer the latter. For example, in the Direct3D mode you can use FX files (Direct3D shaders) as materials for real-time rendering. However, if you aren't a developer of computer games, it makes no difference for you, which driver you select. You should be guided only by the features of your video card and its performance in various modes.

After you start 3ds Max, it's wise to configure the driver.

Menu bar → Customize → Preferences → the Viewports tab →Configure Drivers

If the line next to the **Configure Driver** button reads something like "Microsoft OpenGL/Direct3D" rather than the video card manufacturer's name, 3ds Max is most likely in the software simulation mode. Either select another mode or locate a problem with the graphics driver.

Settings for Direct3D (Fig. 1.2, *a*) and OpenGL (Fig. 1.2, *b*) are slightly different and depend greatly on the video card. I'd like to draw your attention to a few points.

- The checkboxes (pointed to by arrows with ones) allow you to display all edges in the viewports regardless of whether the edges are visible. As a rule, this is undesirable, so uncheck the checkboxes. (For OpenGL, the checkbox is unchecked by default; however, it is checked for Direct3D).
- If your video card supports the Dual Planes mode for OpenGL, uncheck the appropriate checkbox (pointed to by an arrow with a two). When there are few objects in a scene, this mode slows drawing objects in the viewports.
- Select the maximum numbers for the texture quality values in the viewports (highlighted by rectangles with threes). If you encounter problems, select the values one step lower.

Set the other parameter as you like.

Remember that the display in the viewports directly depends upon the configuration of the graphics driver. If you find that 3ds Max works slowly, displays the viewport names in too small letters, or doesn't display certain elements (e.g., Bezier handles), change the driver settings so that the system's performance increases; for example, disable anti-aliasing.

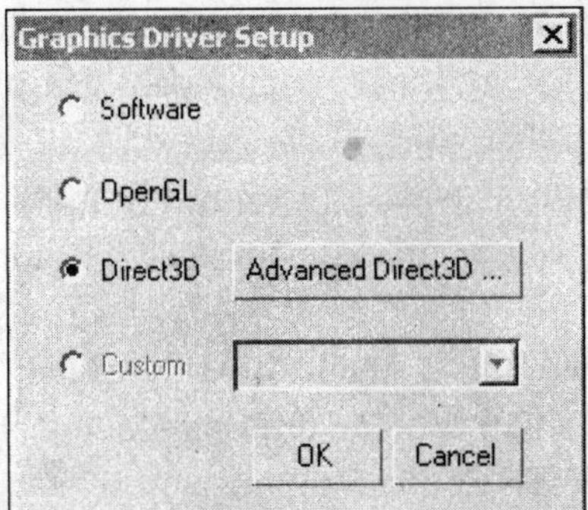

Fig. 1.1. The graphics driver selection window

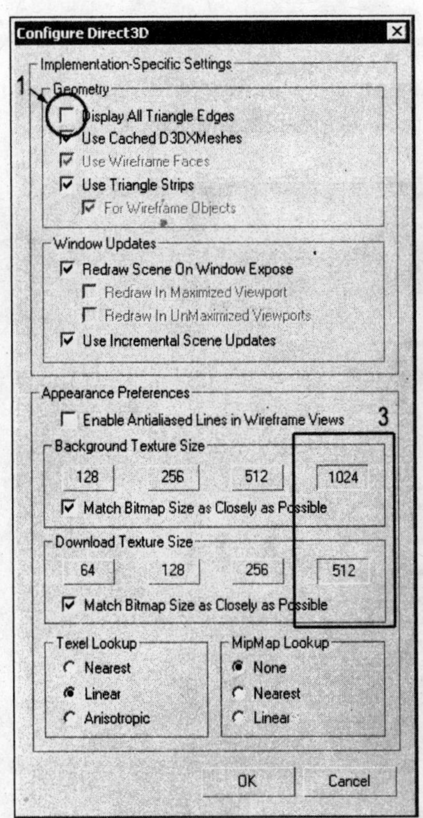

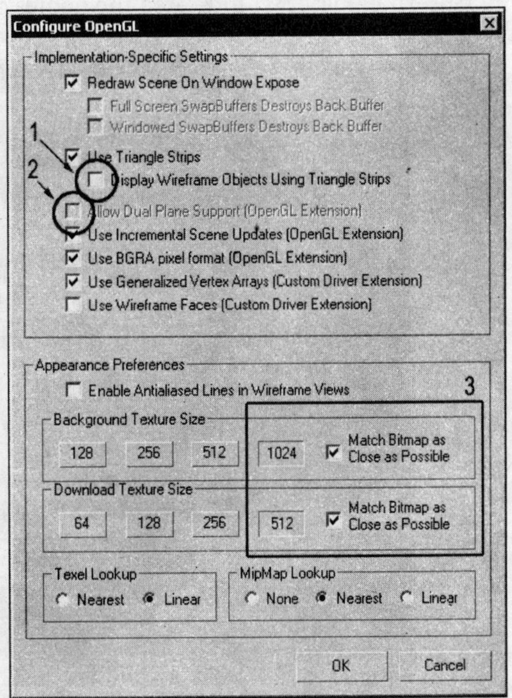

a *b*

Fig. 1.2. Configuring Direct3D (*a*) and OpenGL (*b*)

To work with 3ds Max comfortably, change the following settings. First, select the best scheme for the user interface (Menu bar → **Customize** → **Load custom UI Scheme**). I recommend that you use **discreet-dark.ui**. It is more convenient than the standard scheme in that it provides more contrast, but less bright, so it doesn't tire the eyes. For figures in this book, I'll use the **discreet-dark.ui** scheme because it looks better when printed.

If your display resolution is small (lower or equal to 1280 × 1024 pixels), I recommend that you use small toolbar buttons (Menu bar → **Customize** → **Preferences** → the **General** tab; uncheck the **Use Large Toolbars Buttons** checkbox). However, it's up to you. In the book, I'll use small buttons.

Use Large Toolbar Buttons

The 3ds Max Interface

If you followed my advice, the 3ds Max interface on your computer should appear as shown in Fig. 1.3. I indicated the names of the most important interface elements.

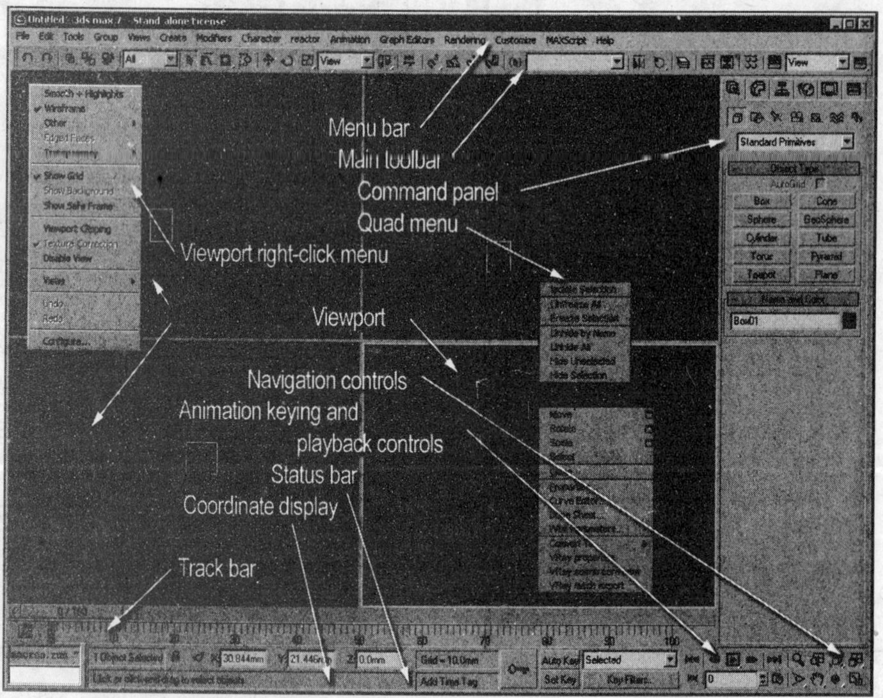

Fig. 1.3. The 3ds Max interface

Viewports. These display your models as you create and animate them.

Command Panel. This panel consists of a few subpanels tabs. To switch among them, click the appropriate tab.

- **Create.** This subpanel contains commands that allow you to create objects. They are arranged by the types of objects (Geometry, Shapes, etc.). Each division has subdivisions implemented as drop-down menus that contain necessary buttons. This panel is somewhat obsolete because it is most convenient to create objects using the **Create** menu in the menu bar or using the <Ctrl>+Quad menu combination. However, you'll eventually get into the **Create** panel.

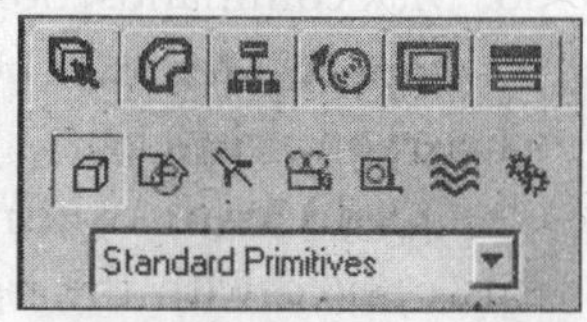

- **Modify.** After you create an object, you edit it on this panel. The panel contains the modifier stack and all commands available in this mode. Remember that you can edit only the selected object and the parameters of only one modifier for the selected object. The exceptions are objects and modifiers that are linked using the Reference or Instance relationships, or if a modifier is applied to multiple objects simultaneously.
- **Hierarchy.** This panel is divided into three subpanels. The **Pivot** subpanel edits pivot parameters for the selected objects, such as their location. A description of the other two subpanels (**IK** and **Link Info**) is beyond the scope of this book.

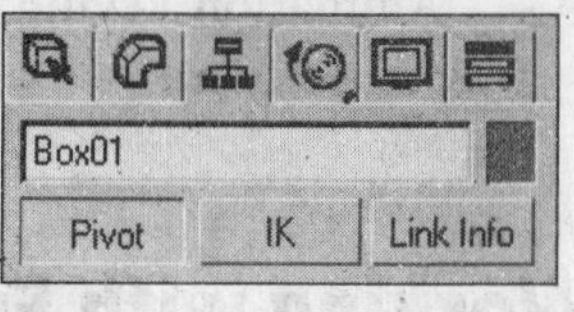

- **Motion.** This panel is used for setting parameters of animation controllers. I'll describe these tools later, using practical examples.
- **Display.** The tools on this panel are used for controlling how objects are displayed. Because most of the tools are available in the pop-up menu and the **Display Floater** window (Menu bar → **Tools**), this panel is used rarely. In addition, it is inconvenient.
- **Utilities.** This panel contains many interesting commands and tools, which will be used in examples later in this book.

The command panel can be scrolled vertically. Click it anywhere with the left mouse button and drag up or down. You can also arrange the command panel into multiple columns. Move the mouse pointer to the border of the panel and drag it to the right or to the left while keeping the left mouse button pressed. Finally, you can remove this panel and turn it into a floating window. This could be convenient if your system supports two or more monitors. You would place the viewports on one monitor, and all the other components including the command panel on the other monitor.

Menu Bar and **Main Toolbar**. These interface components contain general 3ds Max commands. Some of the commands are available on both bars.

Pop-up Menus. These are opened with right clicks. Their contents depend on where you right-click.

Quad Menu. As its name implies, this menu consists of four submenus. Generally, it is opened with the right mouse button. However, there are a few menus that are opened with the right mouse button when keeping the <Ctrl>, <Alt>, or <Shift> key pressed. Some other menus are opened with shortcuts such as the <V> key, which opens the view selection menu.

Navigation Controls. These are used for navigation in the viewports. They are seldom used because navigation can be done using the middle mouse button, and many navigation commands are executed using shortcuts. I'll describe this later.

Status bar. This bar displays the current status, such as grid spacing.

Coordinate Display. This panel allows you to enter or edit the coordinates of an object, rotation angles, and the zoom level.

Animation keying and playback controls. This panel allows you to record and play animation.

Working with Files

All commands necessary to work with files are available in the **File** menu on the Menu bar. I'll concentrate on specific commands and features rather than describe well-known commands such as **File Open.**

- The dialog box of the **Save As** command contains a button labeled with a plus. This button allows you to save files with consecutive numbers appended to their names, such as Scene01.max, Scene02.max, etc. It is a very useful feature, and I recommend that you use it to save intermediate variants of the scene.
- The **Save Selected** command allows you to save only the selected objects. It can be useful when you create your object library.
- Adding objects stored in MAX files is usually done with the **Merge** command. After you select the desired file, you'll see a dialog box that allows you to select the objects needed (Fig. 1.4, *a*).

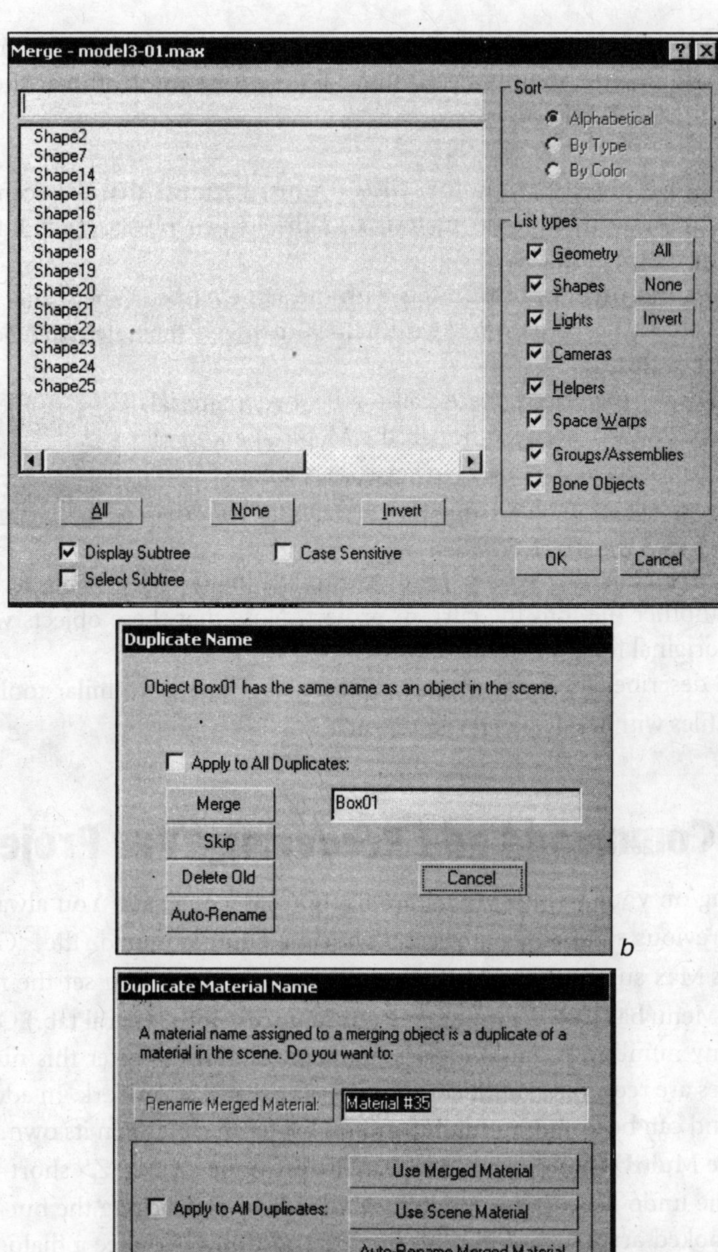

Fig. 1.4. The **Merge** dialog box (*a*), the **Duplicate Name** warning windows for objects (*b*) and materials (*c*)

- To load objects stored in files with other formats, use the **Import** command. Each file type requires special import settings. I'll describe some of them when discussing projects later in this book.

When you load objects from other files, it often happens that the scene contains objects with the same names and materials as the loaded objects (Fig. 1.4, *b* and *c*). What should you do in this case?

It is strange, but there can be objects with the same name in the scene. Of course, you should avoid such a situation. Avoid names such as Rectangle01112 because this would be very confusing.

With regard to materials, there cannot be two materials with the same name in a scene although the Material editor allows you to select the same names. However, as soon as you try to apply the material, 3ds Max displays a warning window so that you can avoid the name conflict.

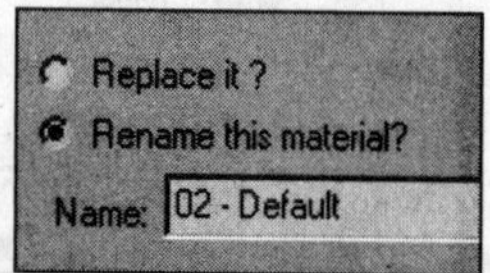

The **Xref Objects** and **Xref Scenes** commands allow you load objects and entire scenes from another file into the current project. Note that these objects will remain linked to the original files.

Chapter 3 describes these features in more detail. There is a similar tool, File Link Manager, for files with the DXF/DWG format.

The *Undo* Command and Recovering Your Project

When working on your project you, are likely to make mistakes. You always can return to the previous state of the project with the **Undo** command (the <Ctrl>+<Z> shortcut). 3ds Max supports the **MultiUndo** feature, and you can set the number of undo levels. (Menu bar → **Customize** → **Preferences** → the **General** tab.) On this tab, you can set any number of undo levels. Remember that the greater this number, the more resources are required and, therefore, less effective is your work. In addition, not every command can be undone, and the undo list often clears up on its own.

To execute **MultiUndo**, you can repeatedly press the <Ctrl>+<Z> shortcut or open the undo list (Main toolbar → **Undo**) by right-clicking the button with a crooked arrow pointing to the left and down. You'll see a dialog box with your previous actions listed. Find the action, to which you want to return, and click the **Undo** button. If you undo too many actions, don't worry. There is the **Redo** button (with a crooked arrow pointing to the right and down) that redoes the undone actions.

Sometimes, 3ds Max fails to work. This can be caused by its internal or external problems; for example, there may be a problem in the operating system. In these cases, a dialog box appears that instructs you to save your project under the Project_name__recover.max name. When you start 3ds Max next time, this file will be at the top of the **Open Recent** list. If you don't find it there, look for it in the 3DSMax\Autoback\ folder.

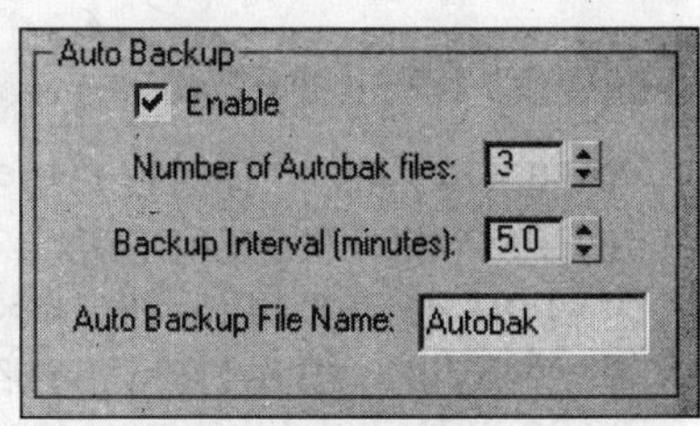

Sometimes (e.g., when the power supply fails), 3ds Max cannot create a backup copy of your project. In these cases, the auto backup feature comes in handy. (Menu bar → **Customize** → **Preferences** → the **Files** tab → **Auto Backup**). When this feature is enabled, 3ds Max periodically saves the current file in the Autoback folder under the name Autoback<number>.max. By default, this is done every five minutes. If the project is large, saving it can take much time. In this case, you might want to disable this option.

When you start 3ds Max after a failure, load the automatic backup copy first! Remember, the backup files are rewritten periodically.

3ds Max allows you to save its current state so that you can recover it later (the **Hold** and **Fetch** commands). I recommend that you execute the **Hold** command prior to any important action that can introduce irrevocable changes into the scene.

Menu bar → **Edit** → **Hold** or the <Ctrl>+<Alt>+<H> shortcut

Menu bar → **Edit** → **Fetch** or the <Ctrl>+<Alt>+<F> shortcut

The **Fetch** command cannot be undone. In fact, 3ds Max saves the current state in the Autoback\Maxhold.mx file with the **Hold** command and loads the file with the **Fetch** command.

The simplest and most effective way involves saving your project periodically. I recommend that you save intermediate states using the **Save Copy As** command.

Working with the Viewports

The effectiveness of your work with 3ds Max depends greatly upon how well you use the viewports. In the following subsections, I describe the main manipulations with the viewports.

Setting the Layout

When you start 3ds Max for the first time, you see the standard layout of the viewports that displays the top, front, left, and perspective viewports. You can maximize any viewport at any time by pressing the <Alt>+<W> shortcut (W stands for *wide*). 3ds Max also allows you to resize any viewport. To do this, move the mouse pointer to the boundary of a viewport (the pointer will take the shape of four arrows) and resize the viewport by dragging the boundary while keeping the left mouse button pressed. To return to the previous size of the viewport, right-click any boundary and select the only menu item, **Reset Layout**.

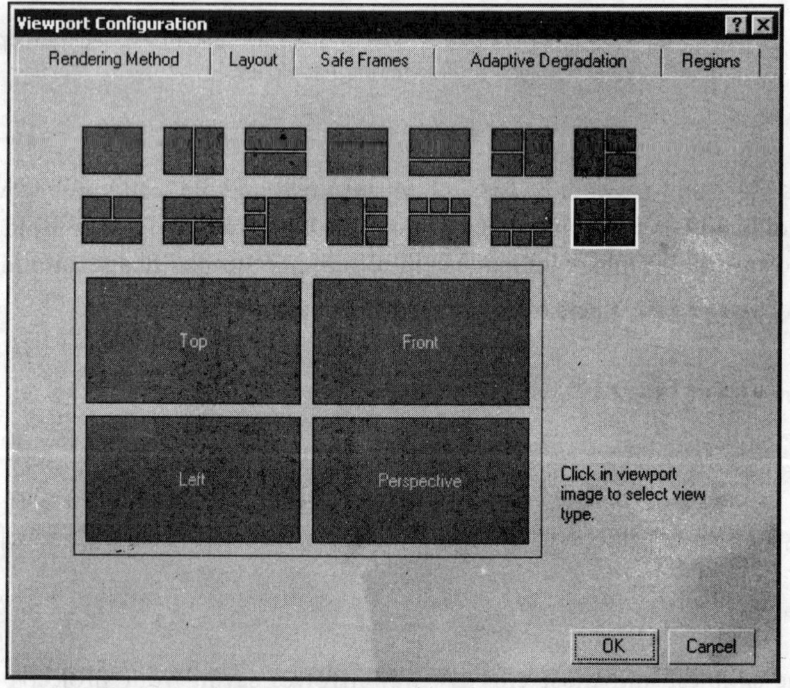

Fig. 1.5. The viewport configuration window

I have worked with various 3ds Max versions for ten years, and only a few times have I changed the layout. However, sometimes you might need to do this. The procedure is outlined as follows:

- ❐ Open the viewport configuration window (Fig. 1.5).

  Viewport right-click menu → **Configure** → the **Layout** tab

- ❐ Select the desired layout and select the desired view types by clicking each viewport.

Displaying Objects

Smooth
Facets + Highlights
Facets
Flat
Lit Wireframes
Bounding Box

3ds Max can display geometric objects in different ways. The main ones are the Wired and Shaded modes (Fig. 1.6, *a* and *b*). To switch between them, use the <F3> key. There are a few more display modes available in the viewport right-click menu.

The main display mode is the Shaded mode with Edged Faces (Fig. 1.6, *c*). You can enter it using the <F4> key. You should get accustomed to this mode.

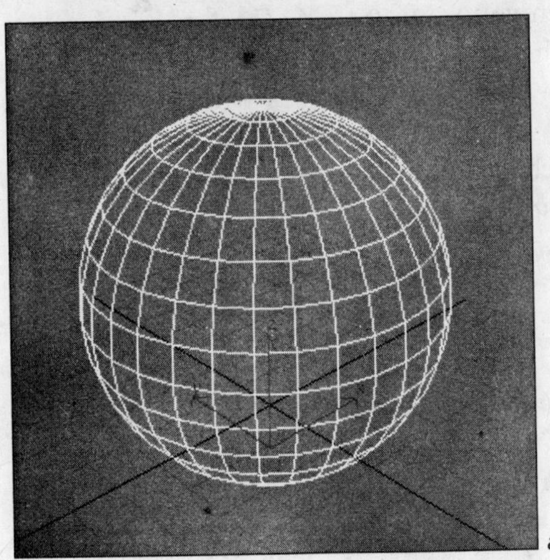
a

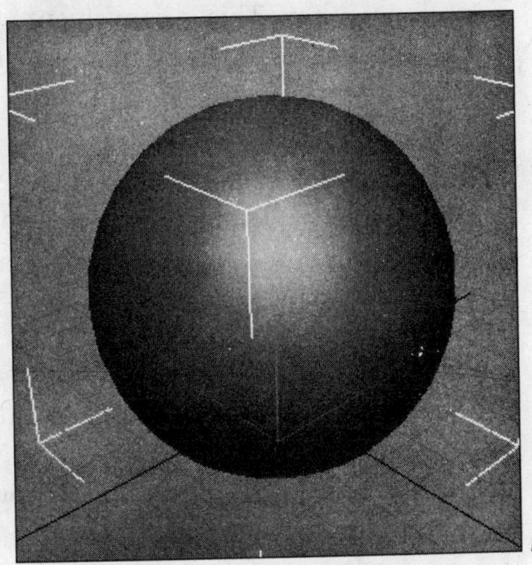
b

Fig. 1.6, *a* and *b*. The main display modes

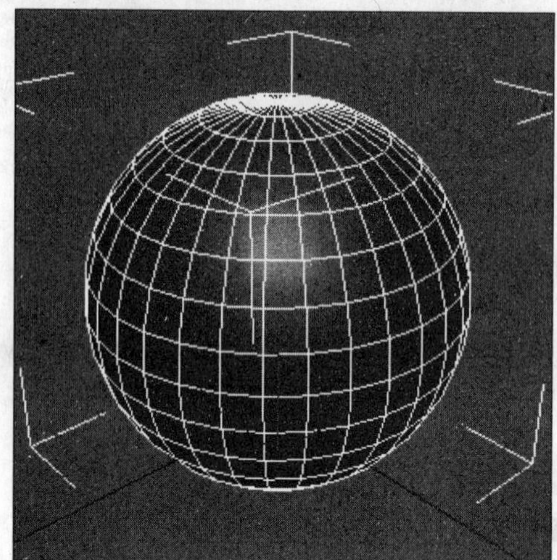

Fig. 1.6, *c*. The main display modes

Here are a few useful commands and settings that help you change the object display in the viewport.

- If you want to see all the edges, both visible and those belonging to invisible polygons, uncheck the **Backface Cull** and **Edges Only** checkboxes among the properties of the object. You can also choose to display the object as a box. This is convenient when you want to know where the object is, but it gets in the way.

  Quad menu → **Properties**

- Sometimes, you have to repeatedly switch between the display modes. In this case, you can use the **Display Floater** window (Fig. 1.7). This window also allows you to display objects by category.

  Menu bar → Tools → Display Floater

To switch quickly between the normal mode and the See-Through mode, use the <Alt>+<X> shortcut. To obtain the best quality in the See-Through mode, select the best transparency.

Viewport right-click menu → **Transparency** → **Best**

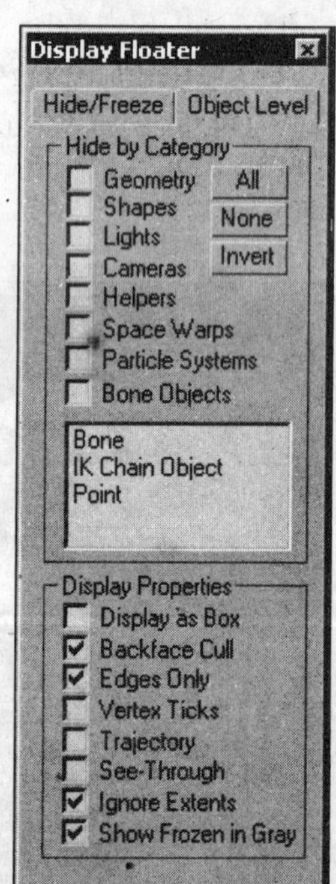

Fig. 1.7. The **Display Floater** window

- When light sources appear in the scene, the default lighting is turned off. It is inconvenient to model in such a mode, so 3ds Max allows you to turn on the default lighting.

  Viewport right-click menu → **Configure...** → the **Rendering Method** tab → the **Default Lighting** checkbox

- To speed up the display of objects in the viewport when they are moved, you can use the Adaptive Degradation mode. Unfortunately, the <O> key that enables this mode can be pressed accidentally. So, if you notice that the objects in the viewport turn into boxes during rotation, this will indicate the mode was enabled. Disable it with the <O> key.
- The Object Display Culling mode that appeared in version 7 is much more intelligent than the Adaptive Degradation and is useful when working with large scenes. To enable or disable it, use the <Alt>+<O> shortcut, and to set it up, use a special utility (Fig. 1.8). With the settings shown in the figure, if the frame rate is decreased to 20 frames per second, the distant objects are displayed as boxes.

  Command panel → the **Utilities** subpanel → **More...** → **Object Display Culling**

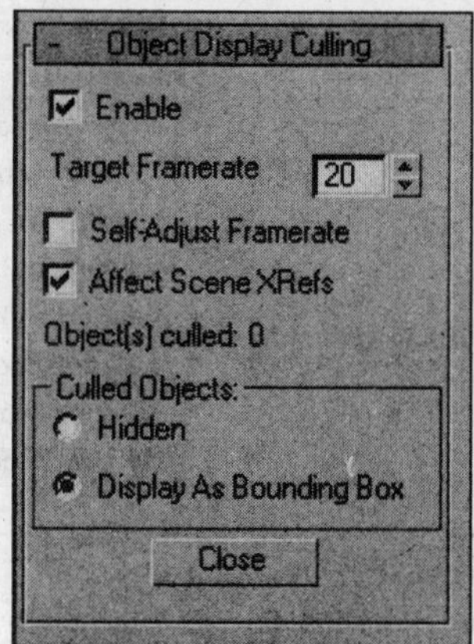

Fig. 1.8. Setting up the Object Display Culling mode

- When working with layers, the **Layer Manager** feature allows you to change the display of objects for an entire layer (Fig. 1.9, *a*). To do this, open the **Layer Properties** window by right-clicking the layer name and selecting the **Layer Properties** item (Fig. 1.9, *b*).

  Menu bar → **Tools** → **Layer Manager**

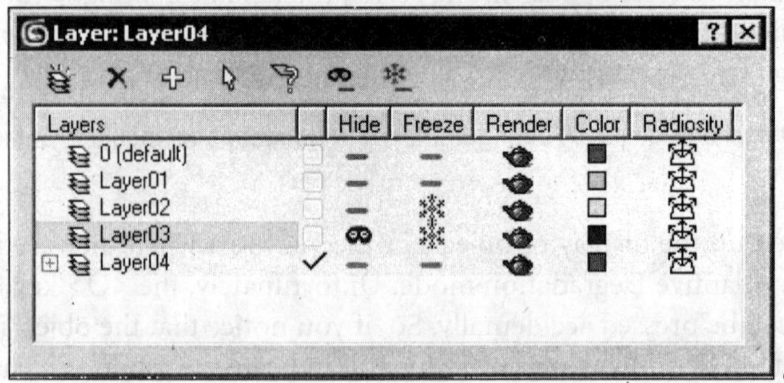

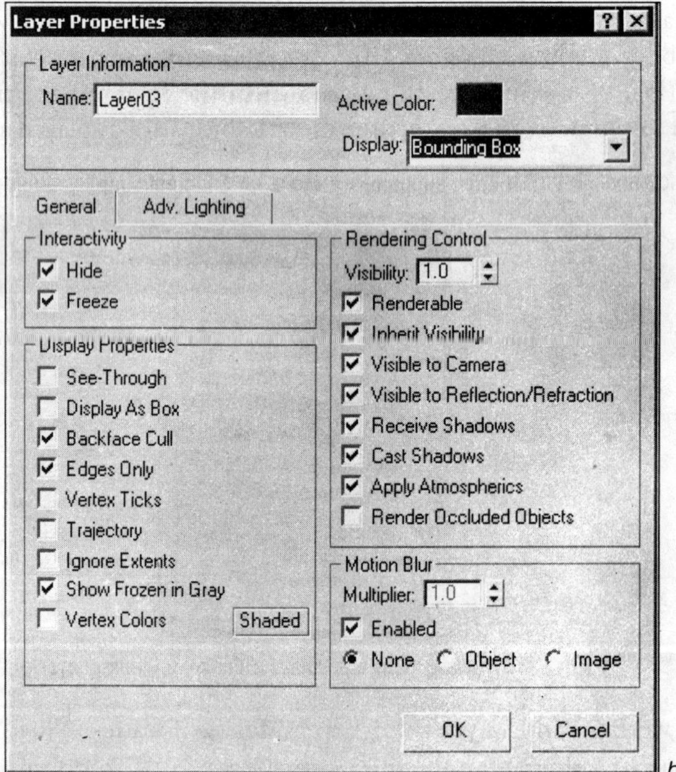

Fig. 1.9. The Layer Manager (*a*) and the Layer Properties (*b*)

Selecting a View in the Viewports

You can select a view in the viewport using the viewport right-click menu (Fig. 1.10). However, it is most convenient to use hotkeys. Here us a list of these hotkeys with brief comments.

- <T>, <B>, <F>, <L> — These keys indicate the top, bottom, front, and left views and are self-explanatory.
- <P> and <U> — These keys indicate the perspective and isometric user views. When you enable these views, the viewing angle of the current view is maintained.
- <C> and <$> (or <Shift>+<4>) — These keys indicate the camera view and the light source view. If objects of this type are missing from the scene, an appropriate warning message will be displayed. If there are several such objects in the scene, and none of them is selected, you'll be suggested to select one. In addition, the views from these objects will become available in the viewport right-click menu.

Front View
Back View
Top View
Bottom View
Left View
Right View
Perspective View
Isometric User View
Camera View

You can open the Viewports Quad Menu with the <V> key.

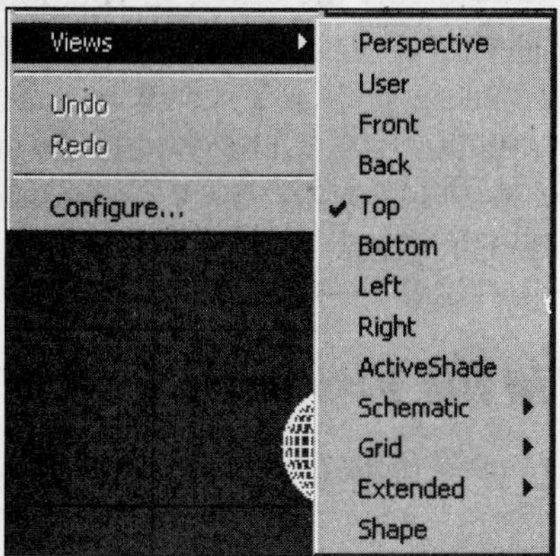

Fig. 1.10. The **Views** submenu of the viewport right-click menu

Panning the View in the Viewports

Panning the view in the viewports is done using the middle mouse button. Just click it and drag the view in the viewport. If you keep the <Ctrl> key pressed during the operation, the view will move more quickly. If you keep the <Shift> key pressed, you'll pan the view along one coordinate.

If you don't like to use the middle mouse button, or your mouse doesn't have one, you can click the **Pan** button or use the <Ctrl>+<P> shortcut.

3ds Max offers an interesting and useful feature. Move the mouse pointer to any place within the viewport and press the <I> key. The view will move so that the mouse pointer is in the center. It is convenient when the object you are creating doesn't fit into the viewport.

Rotating the View in the Viewports

Rotating the view in the viewports is useful in the final stage of modeling because it allows you to select the best angle of view. Remember that rotating the top, front, bottom, or left view switches it to the isometric user view.

When you use a three-button mouse, it is convenient to rotate the view using the middle mouse button with the <Alt> key pressed. You can use the <Shift> key to rotate the view about one axis.

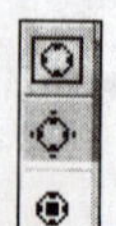

The rotation mode is enabled using the **Arc Rotate** button on the Navigation controls panel. The drop-down menu of the buttons on this panel is very important. It allows you to define the center of rotation in the viewport — the coordinate origin, the selected object (Arc Rotate Selected), or the selected sub-object (Arc Rotate Sub-object), such as a vertex or a face. Unfortunately, there is no command to select the rotation center, but you can do without it. Just select arc rotation about the selected sub-object. If no object is selected in the scene, the rotation will be done about the coordinate origin.

Zooming the View in the Viewports

Zooming commands are used most often, and there are quite a lot of them. They are the following:

- If you use a three-button mouse, you can zoom using the middle mouse button while keeping the <Alt> and <Ctrl> keys pressed. If you have a mouse with a wheel, it is most convenient to use the wheel. The zoom mode is selected using the **Zoom** button in the Navigation controls panel or using the <Alt>+<Z> shortcut. In addition, you can use the <[> and <]> keys that zoom in twice or zoom out by half.

- ❐ There is an interesting 3ds Max feature that allows you to use the current position of the mouse pointer in the viewport as a zoom point. It is up to you whether you use this feature.

  Menu bar → **Customize** → **Preferences** → the **Viewport** tab → the **Zoom About Mouse Point** checkbox

- ❐ The most frequently used command is the one that zooms all the viewports in accordance with the size of the selected object. It is executed using the <Z> key.
- ❐ The Region Zoom command is selected with the appropriate button on the Navigation controls panel or with the <Ctrl>+<W> shortcut.

Navigation in the Camera View and the Light View

Unfortunately, in these views the middle mouse button can be used only for panning. The other manipulations are done using the Navigation controls panel. In these views, the panel appears different than in the others (Fig. 1.11) and contains a few specific commands such as setting the Field-Of-View parameter for the camera or Light Falloff for the light source. To use them, click an appropriate button and execute the command with the left mouse button.

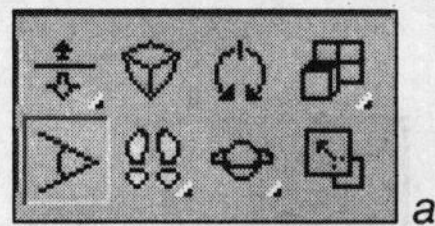

a

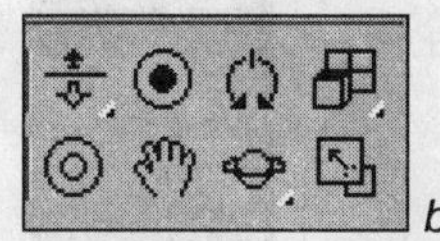

b

Fig. 1.11. The Navigation controls for the Camera view (*a*) and the Light view (*b*)

3ds Max 7 has an interesting feature that allows you to control the Camera or Perspective view using the arrow keys and the left mouse button, like in a computer game. This mode turns on automatically when you press an arrow key in the Camera or Perspective viewport. The speed of the camera is controlled with the <[> and <]> keys. The <Shift>+<Space> shortcut rotates the camera to the horizontal position. It is convenient, for example, when setting the camera in the interior.

Additional Navigation Commands

The following navigation commands are quite useful.

- **Undo View Change** allows you to return the view in the viewport to the previous state. Sometimes, this is necessary. To execute this command, use the <Shift>+<Z> shortcut (remember, the **Undo** command is executed using the <Ctrl>+<Z> shortcut).
- You can save and restore the parameters of any active viewport using the **Save Active View** and **Restore Active View** commands.

Menu bar → **Views → Save/Restore Active View**

Sometimes, you need to redraw all the viewports. To do this, use the <~>.

Coordinate Systems

3ds Max allows you to transform (i.e., move, rotate, and zoom) objects and sub-objects in several coordinate systems. Most of them are orthogonal, that is, their axes are perpendicular to each other.

You can select the coordinate system in the **View** drop-down list on the main toolbar (Fig. 1.12, *a*) or as follows: <Alt>+Quad menu → coordinates (Fig. 1.12, *b*).

Fig. 1.12. Selecting the coordinate system

View. This is the default coordinate system. It is the same in all the traditional views (i.e., top, left, etc.). The X axis is always directed to the right, the Y axis is directed away from you. In these viewports, the origin of coordinates is in the center of the viewport. In the User and Perspective views, the **World** coordinate system is used.

Screen. This coordinate system uses the viewport coordinates. The X axis is always directed to the right, the Y axis is directed away from you, regardless of the viewport.

World. The X axis is directed to the East, the Y axis is directed to the North, and the Z axis is directed to the zenith. In some cases, you may prefer this coordinate system to the **View** coordinate system. For example, when you enter numeric values in the Coordinate display, the world coordinate system is used, regardless of the coordinate system you have selected.

Local. This coordinate system is bound to the object; more precisely, to its pivot point. The top of the object doesn't need to be directed upwards. This depends on how the primitive of the object was created. When you rotate the object, the local coordinates rotate accordingly. If you want the object to be positioned according to the world coordinates from the beginning, create it in the top, user, or perspective viewport.

The situation is more complicated with sub-objects. Fig. 1.13 shows local coordinates for polygons, edges, and vertices of one object. The simplest situation is with polygons. If one polygon is selected, its Z axis is directed as its normal. When a few adjacent polygons are selected, the Z axis is directed as a vector being the sum of the normals of these polygons. Regarding edges and vertices, the Z axis for them is directed as the vector sum of the normals of the neighboring polygons. This is why it is difficult to edit multiple sub-objects in the local coordinate system. However, it is easy to edit a single sub-object.

Gimbal. This coordinate system simplifies editing animation curves when animating rotation of an object with the **Euler XYZ** controller applied. While rotation of an object in the local or parent coordinate system changes a few curves, rotation in the gimbal coordinate system affects just one curve. The axes don't have to be orthogonal. When the object is moved or scaled, this coordinate system behaves as the parent coordinate system.

Parent. If an object isn't linked to any other object, its parent object is the world, so this coordinate system is the same as the world coordinate system. However, if the object is linked to another or grouped with a few other objects, this coordinate system is the same as the local coordinate system of the parent object. The parent of the group is its gizmo. Because the object is the parent of its sub-objects, their parent coordinate system is the same as the local system of the object.

Grid. In addition to the main grid, 3ds Max creates several auxiliary grids that can be oriented in different ways. To use such a grid, you need to make it active. When you use an active grid, this coordinate system is very convenient (Fig. 1.14).

Pick. Sometimes, it is convenient to work with an object in the local coordinate system of another object. To select that coordinate system, select **Pick** in the drop-down list and click with the left mouse button. As a result, the name of the selected object will appear in the list of coodinate systems.

Unfortunately, information about the picked coordinate system isn't stored in the 3ds Max project.

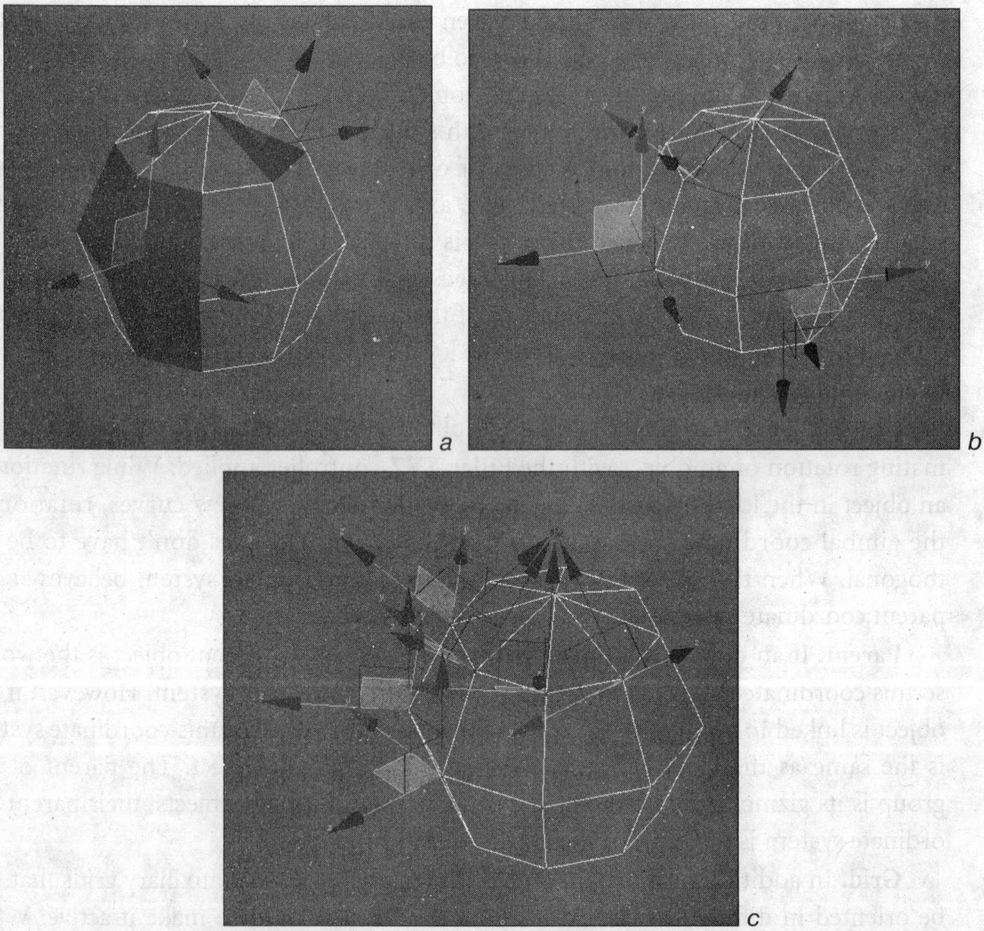

Fig. 1.13. The local coordinate systems for polygons (*a*), edges (*b*), and vertices (*c*)

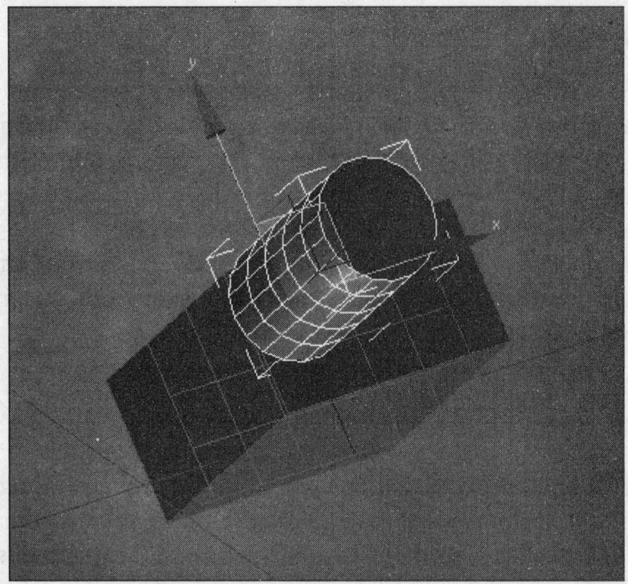

Fig. 1.14. An active grid and an object in the coordinate system of this grid

TIP

If you want the coordinate system to be the same when moving, rotating, and scaling an object (and you are likely to want this in most cases), fix the coordinate system (Menu bar → **Customize** → **Preferences** → the **General** tab → the **Constant** checkbox in the **Ref. Coord. System** group).

I should warn you about a 3ds Max feature, which is a consequence of its ideology. This feature is confusing both for novice and experienced users. If you scale an object, its local coordinate system will also change. In other words, the inch in this coordinate system can become different from the inch in the world coordinate system. In addition, this coordinate system can cease to be orthogonal. If this is crucial for your project (which is usually the case), use the **Reset XForm** command.

Command panel → **Utilities** → **Reset XForm**

Objects

The 3ds Max world is a one consisting of objects. If you want something to appear in the scene, you have to create an appropriate object. A few effects (such as mist, light, etc.) can be considered an exception. Unlike effects created after rendering, they are created during rendering. However, these effects aren't components of the scene.

Types of Objects

Objects can be divided into two categories: geometric and nongeometric.

Geometric objects are used for creating a picture using rendering. Some objects (e.g., splines) are used as basic objects when creating models, so they also can be put into this category. Particles are also objects of this type though they are often used in effects created using plug-ins such as Sitni-Sati AfterBurn.

Nongeometric objects are light sources, cameras, and various auxiliary objects that aren't used when creating shapes. There are a few exotic objects among them, such as screen manipulators. However, these are objects.

Pivot Points

Regardless of its type, every object has a pivot point. When talking about the coordinates of an object and its orientation, I usually mean the coordinates of the object's pivot point. However, this is not always the case, and I'll explain this later.

The pivot point can be located anywhere, and it doesn't need to coincide with the center of the object. It even can be outside the object. This fact is very useful in animation because animation of rotation and scaling uses the pivot point as a center.

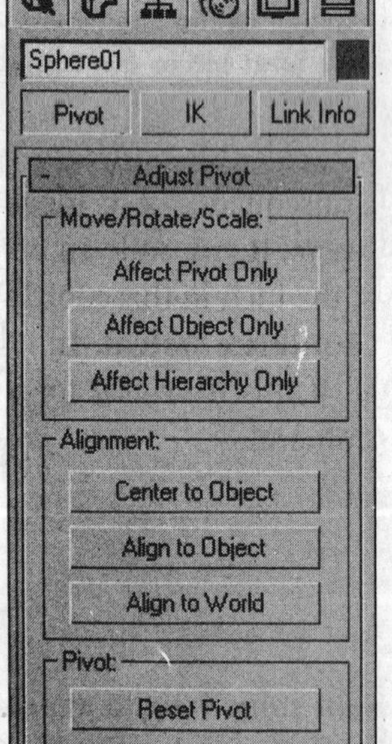

Fig. 1.15. Commands for work with pivot points

To manipulate with pivot points, use commands in the **Hierarchy** subpanel of the Command panel (Fig. 1.15).

- The **Affect Pivot Only** button enables a mode, in which the movement and rotation operations affect only the pivot point. You can place the pivot point anywhere you like and rotate it as needed. You can enter coordinates with the keyboard and use the **Alignment** commands, for example, to align the pivot points of two objects.
- The **Center to Object** button aligns the pivot point to the center of the object.
- The **Align to World** button aligns the axes of the pivot point to the axes of the world coordinate system.
- The **Reset Pivot** button undoes all the operations with the pivot point and returns it to the original position.
- The **Align to Object** button aligns the axes of the pivot point to the axes of the object.

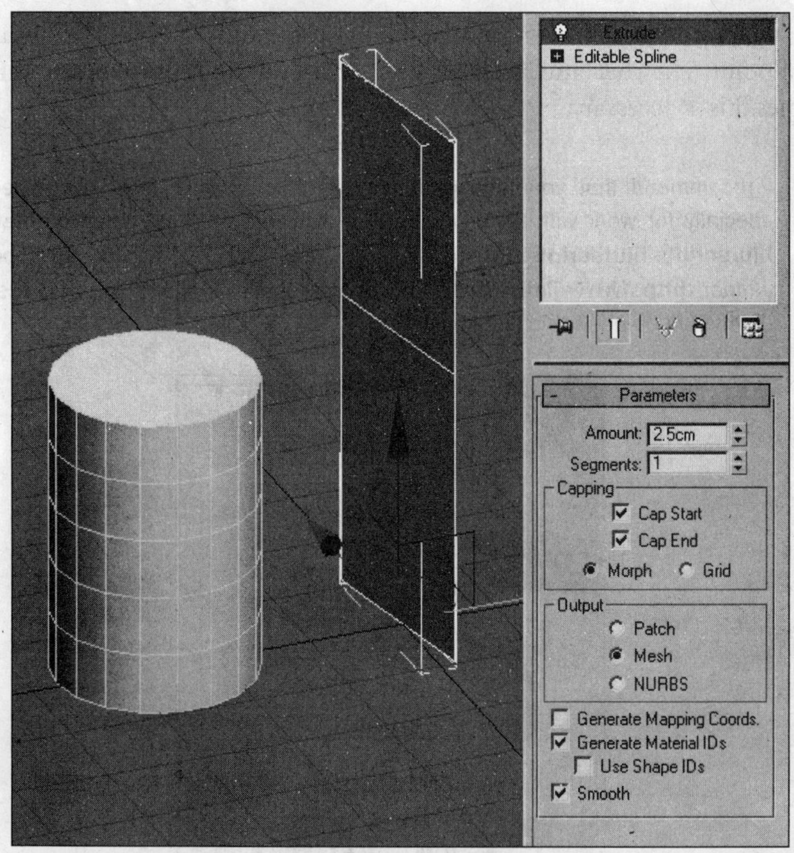

Fig. 1.16. A problem caused by disagreement between the orientation of an object and its pivot point (illustrated with the **Extrude** modifier)

The last command requires additional comments. Orientation of an object can differ from orientation of pivot point. By rotating its pivot point, you won't rotate the object. Consider an example. It often happens that the **Extrude** modifier extrudes a surface from a spline to a wrong direction (Fig. 1.16). This usually happens when the spline is made from edges of a polygonal object as shown in the figure. The local Z axes of the original object and its pivot point are directed upwards, and the resulting spline inherits this. The **Extrude** modifier extrudes the surface along the Z axis (i.e., upwards). If you rotate the pivot point, you won't obtain the desired result. The only way to deal with the problem is to rotate the "contents" of the object, for example, by rotating the gizmo of the **XForm** modifier.

The same rollout contains commands for work with an object without affecting the pivot point. They become available after a click on the **Affect Object Only** button. Sometimes this is necessary.

TIP

I recommend that you load and use the Pivot Placer script developed by Blur specially for work with pivot points. It is available at **http://www.neilblevins.com/blurscripts/blurscripts.htm** (Fig. 1.17). The **Affect Pivot** script developed by Jim Jagger (**http://www.jimjagger.com/**) is also useful. It allows you to place the pivot point of an object with a single click.

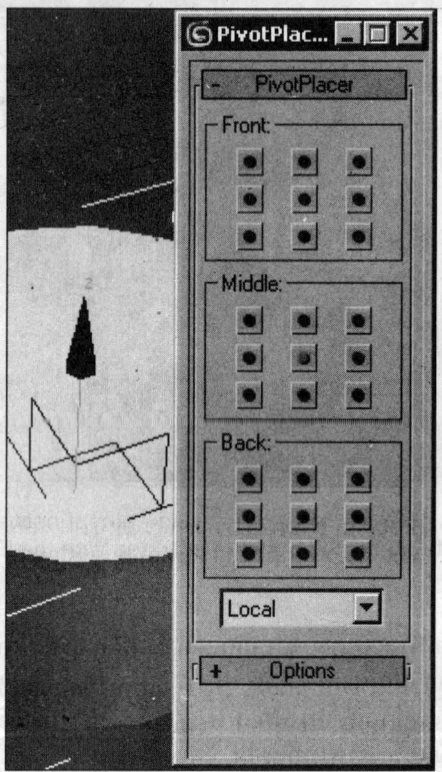

Fig. 1.17. The **Pivot Placer** interface

Geometric Objects

Because these objects are used for modeling, it makes sense to concentrate on their features and the principles behind them.

Principles for Building Geometric Objects in 3ds Max

What should you remember when you start modeling in 3ds Max?

First, there are no curves in 3ds Max. It uses broken lines consisting of segments. There are no smooth surfaces; all surfaces are built of triangles called faces. Fig. 1.18 shows circles and spheres with different levels of interpolation. You couldn't say that the middle or right objects are spheres and circles, but they are from 3ds Max's point of view. You may notice that 3ds Max tries to make them smooth, but their outlines spoil the effect.

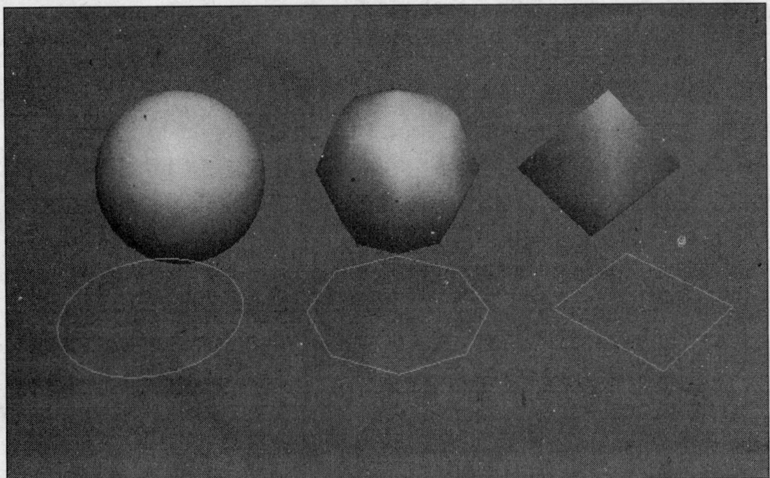

Fig. 1.18. The effect of interpolation on the appearance of objects

Why does this happen? Contemporary computers aren't powerful enough to create a realistic picture. Software developers try to abandon triangles from time to time, but the traditional algorithms still give the best rendering time-to-quality ratio.

If you want to obtain a sphere or a circle on the final image, you should take care of this beforehand. These issues are discussed later when describing examples. For now, I'd like to advise you to be guided by common-sense. When you create a video clip with the PAL format, you are likely to use a different interpolation level than when you create an A3 leaflet with the 300 dpi resolution. Models that look good in a video clip may appear unsuitable for printing. Conversely, if you create comprehensively detailed models, you'll hardly ever finish the video clip that uses them.

As in any other 3D graphics package, 3ds Max surfaces don't have thickness and are one-sided. This is done to speed the rendering. This feature might seem unusual, so you'll have to get accustomed to it and learn how to use it. It has many more advantages than drawbacks. For example, the back side of a surface is transparent for the sight and the light.

The side of a surface, whether front (visible) or back, is determined by a vector called *normal.* You might expect that it is always perpendicular to the surface, however, this isn't always the case. For a smoothed surface, the normal is computed for every point of the surface and is perpendicular to this virtual surface. In addition, the **Edit Normals** modifier allows you to change normals and create an illusion of curling when a surface is actually flat (Fig. 1.19). Though this is strange, it is quite possible.

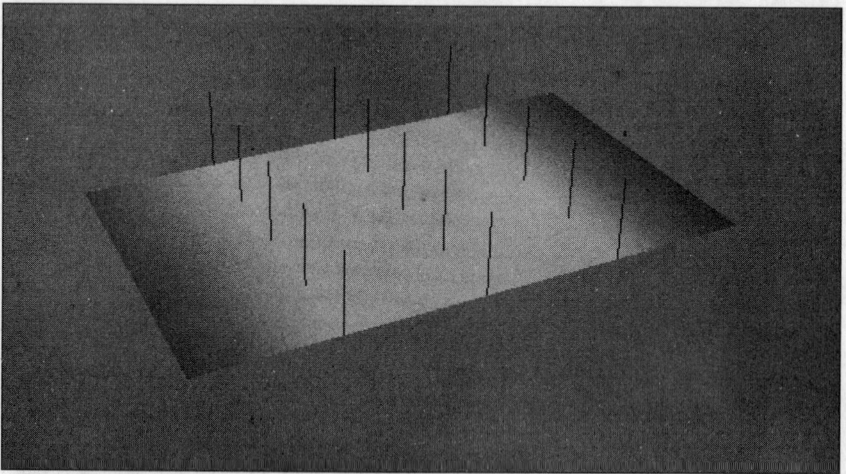

Fig. 1.19. Editing normals with the **Edit Normals** modifier

When working with geometric objects, you work with surfaces rather than volumes.

3ds Max doesn't perform a solid-body modeling, so you are responsible for the correctness of the model's topology. If you cross polygons, invert normals, or don't close a surface, 3ds Max will allow you to do so. However, the results will be unpredictable. Sometimes, this isn't a problem, but if you use algorithms for global illustration or ray tracing to create a glass effect, you are likely to obtain strange objects.

In 3ds Max, the notion of a material usually refers to how the surface reflects the light. The exceptions are a few channels. For example, a map applied to the **Displacement** channel results in creating a relief during rendering. Nevertheless, an object is empty; it doesn't contain iron or wood inside it. You can make use of it. For example, if you put a light source inside a non-transparent object, the object will glow (Fig. 1.20).

Fig. 1.20. Using the fact that surfaces are one-sided

Parametric Objects

As a rule, modeling in 3ds Max begins with creating an object called *parametric* or *primitive.* However, some primitives aren't primitive; for example, stairs, doors, and windows. So you should call them objects.

There are quite a lot of parametric objects in 3ds Max. Fig. 1.21 shows a few of them. Their common feature is that each of them is described with a few parameters, and its vertices, segments, or surfaces are inaccessible. For example, a single parameter for the circle is its radius.

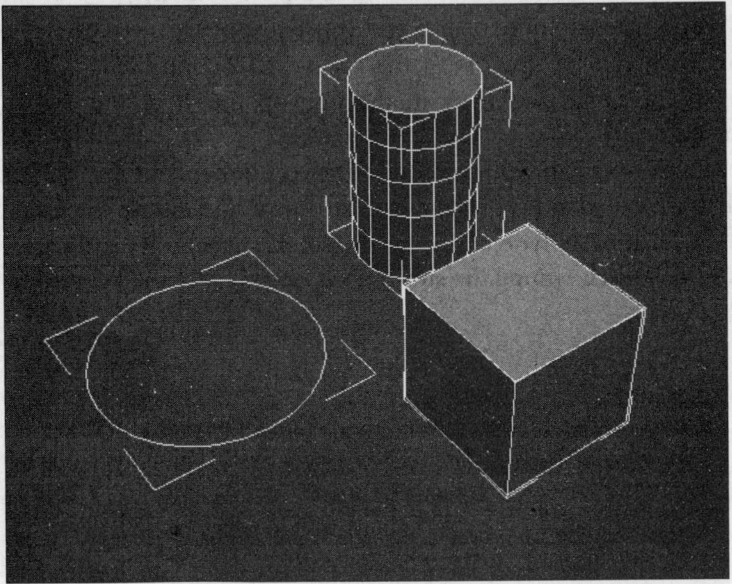

Fig. 1.21. Examples of parametric objects

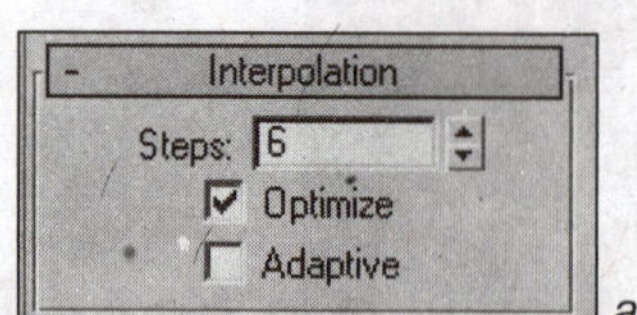

a

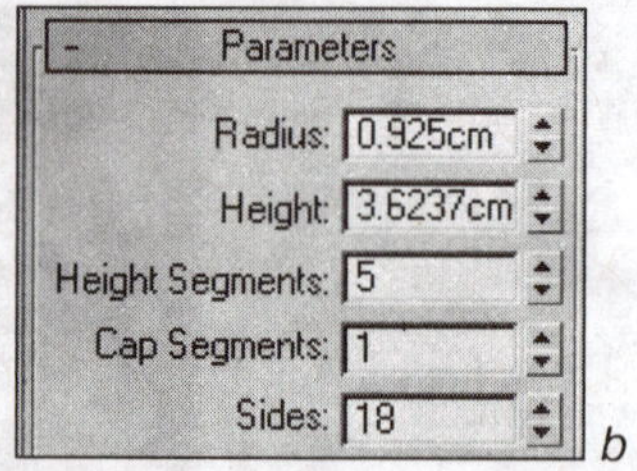

b

Fig. 1.22. Parameters that determine the complexity of an object

Each parametric object usually has one or more parameters that determine its complexity. For splines, these are parameters in the **Interpolation** rollout (Fig. 1.22, *a*), and for geometric primitives, these are the number of segments, sides, and so on (Fig. 1.22, *b*).

Remember that as long as you have the ability for setting the size of an object using parameters, you should use them. Avoid scaling parametric objects when setting their sizes!

Basic Types of Parametric Objects

Any parametric object can be converted to one of five basic types if this is possible. For example, you cannot convert a cube to the Editable Splines type, but you can convert it to the NURBS type and obtain an object consisting of six surfaces.

Convert to Editable Spline
Convert to Editable Mesh
Convert to Editable Poly
Convert to Editable Patch
Convert to NURBS

Conversion can be done with the **Convert to** commands available in the Quad menu or in the pop-up menu of the modifier stack.

After the conversion, you can access the components of the object that are called sub-objects. You can move and rotate them and execute other commands. Each basic type has a specific set of sub-objects and commands for work with them. To switch among the sub-objects quickly, use the keys from <1> to <5> on the main keypad.

NOTE

This is similar to how objects are interpreted in vector graphics packages such as CorelDraw or Xara X. After you create a circle, you cannot edit individual vertices; you should convert it to editable curves.

Remember that after conversion the object "forgets" its origin: a circle, a sphere, or a kettle. It becomes a set of vertices, edges, and so on. If you want to be able to return to the parametric object, use an appropriate modifier (e.g., Edit Poly).

Editable splines. These should be familiar to the users of vector graphics packages. They have two distinctive features. As I mentioned earlier, curves in 3ds Max are made from line segments, and their quality depends on the parameters in the **Interpolation** rollout. The second feature is that splines are three-dimensional rather than flat.

A spline has three sub-objects: a vertex, a segment, and a spline. The last one is a chain of segments.

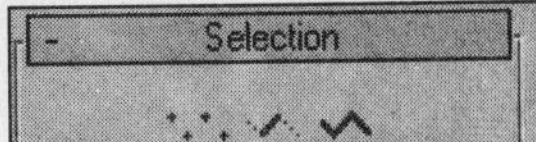

NOTE

Unfortunately, splines don't have sub-objects of the Handle type, while patches do.

Spline vertices can be of the following types (Fig. 1.23, *a*): Corner, Bezier Corner, Bezier, and Smooth. The types of segments are Curve and Line (Fig. 1.23, *b*). You select the type of vertex or segment in the Quad menu.

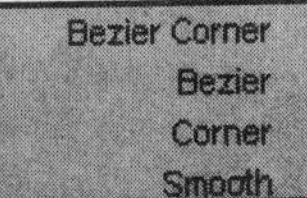

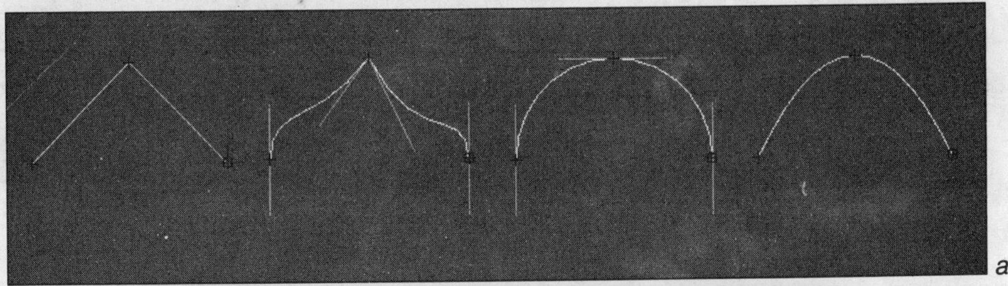

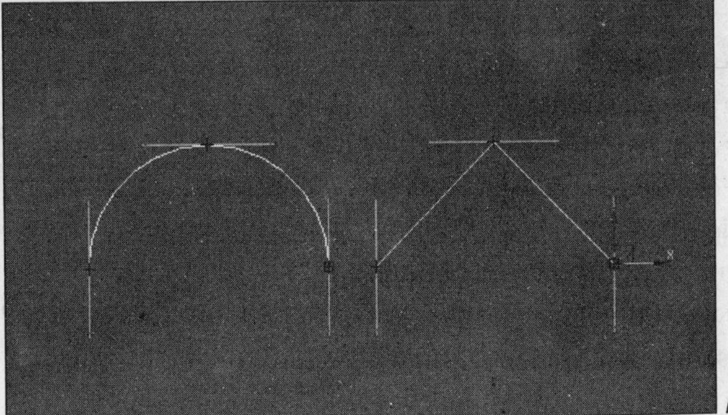

Fig. 1.23. The types of vertices (*a*) and segments (*b*) of splines

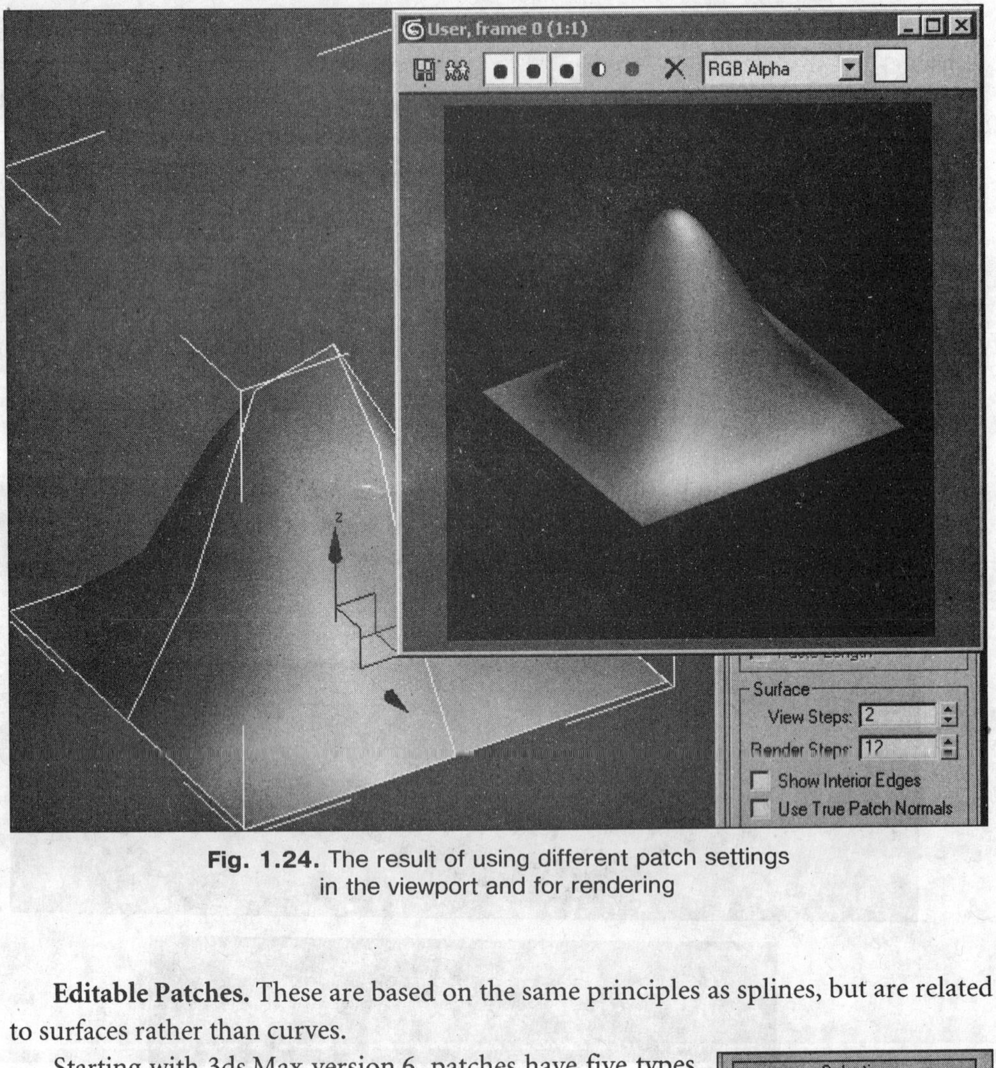

Fig. 1.24. The result of using different patch settings in the viewport and for rendering

Editable Patches. These are based on the same principles as splines, but are related to surfaces rather than curves.

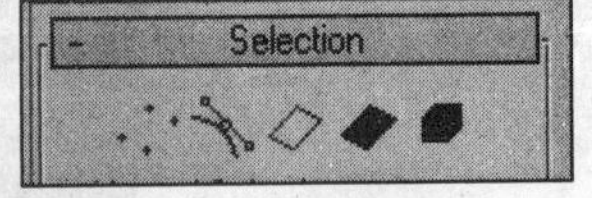

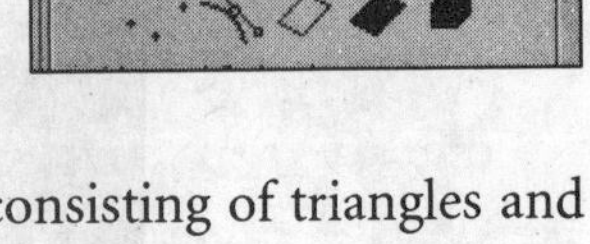

Starting with 3ds Max version 6, patches have five types of sub-objects: vertices (similar to spline vertices), Bezier handles, edges (similar to segments), patches (similar to surface segments), and elements (similar to splines).

The idea behind patches is that you work with a frame consisting of triangles and quadrangles, and surfaces are created automatically depending on the **Steps** parameter. You can use different values for rendering so that the final surface is smooth enough (Fig. 1.24).

In general, patches are a good tool, but the work with them is very labor-intensive, so I don't recommend that you use them.

- Vertices miss types that could be similar to the Corner and Smooth spline types. There is only the Corner type (similar to the Bezier Corner spline type) and the Coplanar type (similar to Bezier). With a large number of vertices, it is difficult to obtain a smooth surface. If you decide to master this modeling method, I recommend that you work with editable splines to minimize work with patches.

- The number of corners is three or four.
- Patch surfaces are regular — that is, the same number of steps is used for a large and small area. This is bad for optimization of the model.
- Tools for work with patches are scanty. In addition, mapping of complex surfaces is difficult because the new modifier **Unwrap UVW** doesn't support patches; it is intended for work with polygons.

Nevertheless, patches can be used as the basis for further modeling using polygons.

NURBS Curves and Surfaces. Non-Uniform Rational B-Splines (NURBS) first appeared in 3ds max 2. They were updated in version 2.5, and almost no changes have been made to them since then. In essence, they are similar to splines and patches, but they are based on other algorithms and equations. Unfortunately, NURBS are implemented badly in 3ds Max. You have to adjust too many parameters to give a desired shape to the surface. In addition, the viewport in the Smooth + Highlight + Edged Faces mode shows a triangle mesh; however, I would prefer isoparms (Fig. 1.25). Mathematical algorithms and other features are excellent, but because of this, NURBS require a lot of computational resources and, therefore, are too slow.

Generally speaking, this is a good tool, but the drawbacks of NURBS and the advantages of polygon modeling make NURBS almost unsuitable. An exception is a situation where you need to create a surface using a few complex cross-sections without a subsequent finishing.

Editable Mesh and **Editable Poly** (**Polymesh**). I combined descriptions of these different states of an object for a reason. At first glance, they are the same. Both have vertices, edges, polygons, and elements (Fig. 1.26). The only difference between them (besides the **Border** sub-objects) is that **Editable Mesh** has the **Face** sub-object, and **Editable Poly** doesn't. However, this difference is crucial, and describing it requires some background information.

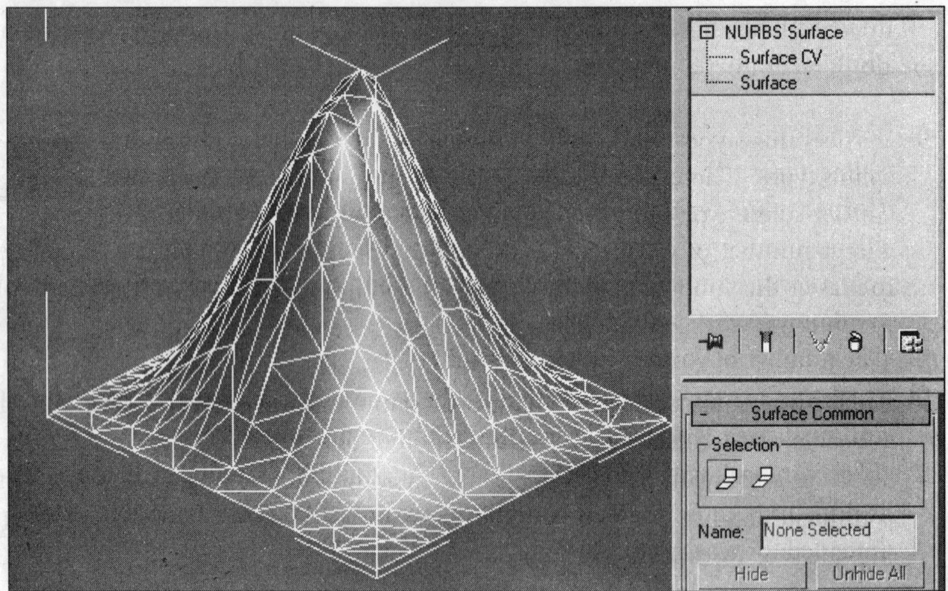

Fig. 1.25. A NURBS surface in the viewport

Fig. 1.26. Sub-objects of **Editable Mesh** (*a*) and **Editable Poly** (*b*)

In 3D Studio for DOS, only meshes were implemented. These were objects created from triangle faces. They were transferred to 3D Studio MAX almost without changes. When creating 3D Studio MAX, its developers believed that low-level modeling wouldn't be popular. This is why they focused on modifiers. However, practice shows that this type of modeling is quite useful, especially when creating models for 3D games where each triangle is valuable. Gradually Editable Mesh was becoming more and more complicated. Polygons (faces enclosed by visible edges) have appeared, and meshes became, so to speak, intellectual. For example, when a polygon was cut in earlier versions of Editable Mesh, spurious vertices appeared where the cutting plane crossed invisible edges. Starting with version 3, these are eliminated automatically though sometimes improperly (Fig. 1.27). The users have to correct the geometry from time to time, which slows their work.

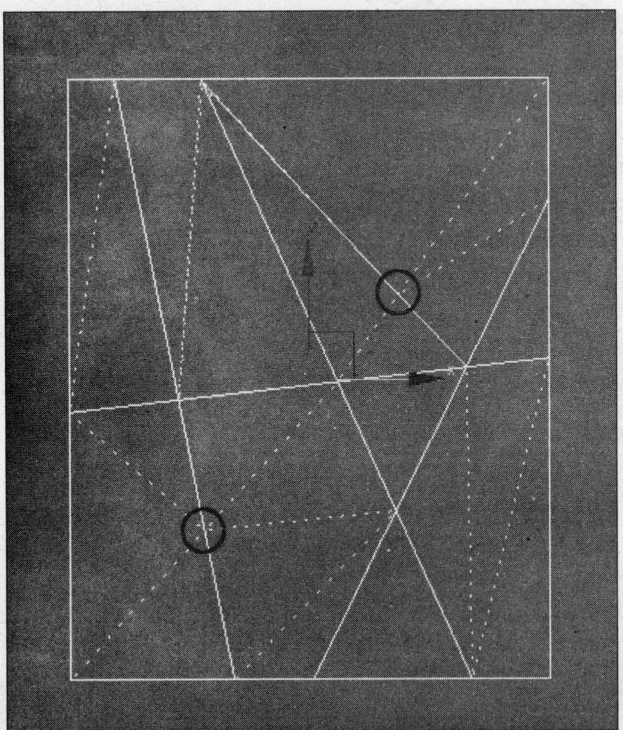

Fig. 1.27. Vertices highlighted with circles are spurious and should be deleted

Apparently, the developers decided not to upgrade Editable Mesh further. In addition, they had to maintain back compatibility so that the users could load models created in earlier versions. A file created in 3ds Max doesn't contain meshes or splines. It stores data for Editable Mesh, Editable Spline, and other plug-ins. In essence, when the file is loaded, a scene is created anew based on this data. If new algorithms were incompatible with those used earlier, the loaded scene would differ much from the original. For example, this actually happens to Boolean objects that have been implemented anew several times.

So the Editable Poly module was developed. It does the same operations as Editable Mesh, but in a different way. Triangles are hidden from the user, and there is no notion of invisible edges: Edges are present or not. During modeling, 3ds Max maintains correctness of geometry. When necessary, it adjusts the model's triangles so that it remains correct (from 3ds Max's point of view). In addition, Editable Poly watches map coordinates and does many other things hidden from the user. The cost of this is that polymesh is slower than mesh, especially during animation. However, you can easily remedy the problem. Model using polymesh and convert it to mesh for animation. This conversion is done without problems in both directions.

At the time of this publication, the tools of Editable Mesh remain the same as in version 3. The developers did their best to create tools for work with polymeshes, and succeeded. In the latest 3ds Max version, polygonal modeling is almost as good as in the acknowledged leaders, Nendo and Wings 3D. In combination with up-to-date smoothing tools (Turbosmooth), polygonal modeling is the most suitable method for creating complicated models in 3ds Max.

Modifiers

A modifier could be thought of as a procedure applied to an object or sub-objects that gives them new properties without changing the original object. You can always correct the object at the lower level.

Modifiers applied to an object are arranged in the modifier stack. I'll illustrate the work with modifiers in the stack using an example.

Fig. 1.28 shows an object with the stack of modifiers applied to it.

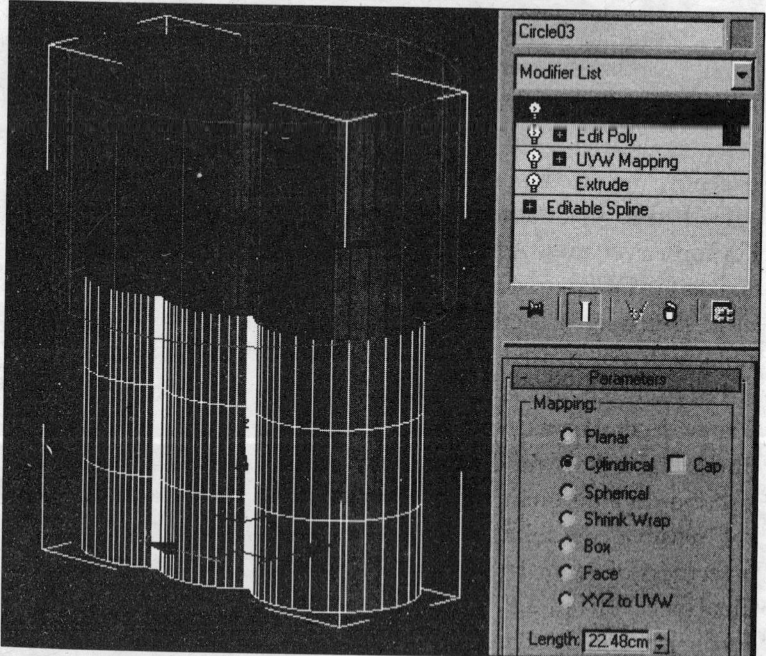

Fig. 1.28. An object and its modifier stack

Originally the object was a closed spline. This is indicated by the **Editable Spline** line at the bottom of the modifier stack.

You can apply a modifier by selecting it in a drop-down list where the modifiers are displayed in alphabetical order. It is convenient to use the **Modifiers** menu on the menu bar where the modifiers are grouped. However, to select a particular modifier, you need to know, to which group it belongs.

After the **Extrude** modifier was applied to the object, it turned into a surface. You cannot apply another **Extrude** modifier to it because this modifier is applicable only to splines and the object ceased to be a spline. If you jump down the stack and edit the original spline, the **Extrude** modifier will respond correctly to all the changes. To view the result, click the button which has a test-tube icon. (It is called **Show end result on/off toggle**).

Then the **UVW Mapping** modifier was applied to the entire object. This modifier determines how a map should lie on the object.

The **Editable Poly** modifier was then applied. It created the top polygons. After this, another **UVW Mapping** was applied. It affected only the polygons selected in **Editable Poly**. This modifier undid the action of the modifier with the same name for the selected polygons. It didn't affect the polygons that had not been selected.

It often happens that a user working with sub-objects forgets to exit this mode and tries to apply a modifier to the entire object. As a result, the modifier has no effect because usually none of the sub-objects is selected.

If you then tried to jump down the stack, you would get a warning message shown in Fig. 1.29, *a*. What problems are likely if you ignore it?

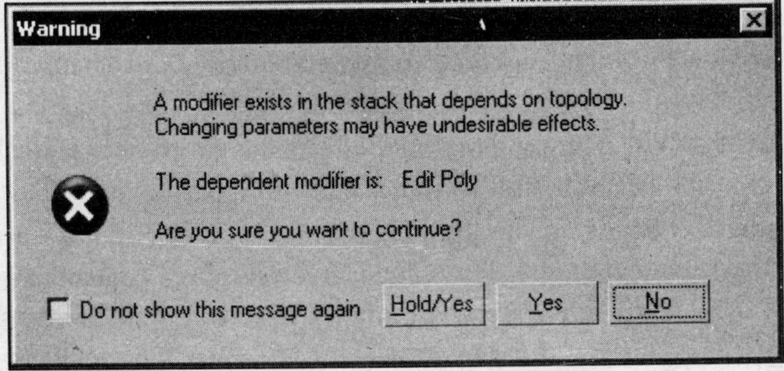

Fig. 1.29, *a*. The warning message

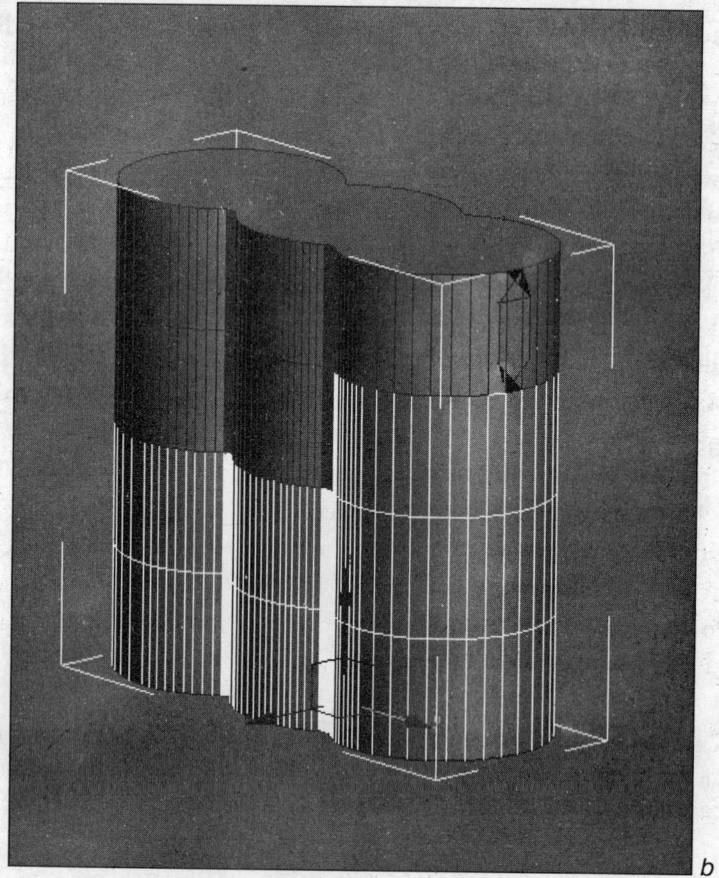

b

Fig. 1.29, *b*. The problems that could happen

I intentionally jumped down the stack and changed the number of interpolation steps from six to eight. Look at the result (Fig. 1.29, *b*). What happened?

By changing the interpolation parameter, not only did I change the number of vertices and polygons created with the **Extrude** modifier, but I changed their numeration. The lower **UVW Mapping** modifier affects the entire object, so it didn't "notice" this. However, the **Editable Poly** modifier had worked as follows: It executed the **Inset** and **Extrude** commands on the top polygon, say, polygon 123. After the numeration changed, another polygon got this number. However, the **Editable Poly** modifier was "unaware" of it. It still applied the commands to polygon 123. So you should be very careful when jumping up and down the stack and clearly understand possible results of your actions.

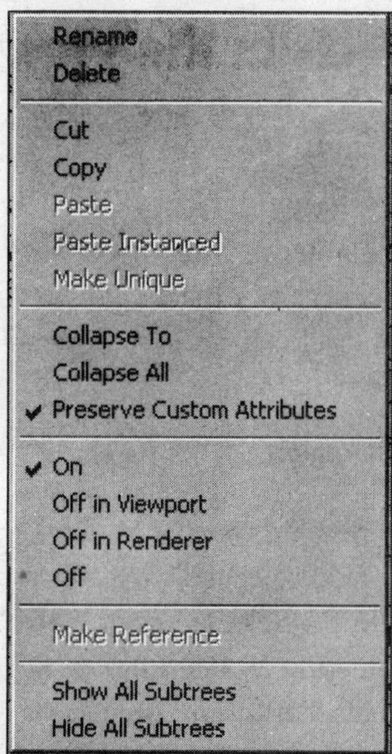

Fig. 1.30. The pop-up menu of the modifier stack

Here are a few commands for work with the modifier stack. Almost all of them are available in the pop-up menu of the modifier stack (Fig. 1.30). However, it is most convenient to click buttons on the stack.

- To delete a modifier from the stack, click the button labeled with a bin icon.
- To disable a modifier temporarily, "turn off" the lamp icon to the left of the modifier's name.
- You can drag and drop modifiers up or down the stack. However, remember that the result depends on the order of the modifiers in the stack.
- You can also drag and drop modifiers from one object to another. During the process, the modifiers are copied. If you need to move a modifier rather than copy it, press and hold the <Shift> key pressed when dragging it. If you press and hold the <Ctrl> key, you'll create an instance of the modifier. If you change parameters of one instance, the parameters of the other will change accordingly.
- To collapse the modifier stack and convert the object to one of the basic types, use the **Collapse All** command in the pop-up menu of the modifier stack. The **Collapse To** command collapses modifiers that are lower in the stack than the current modifier.

Working with Objects in the Viewports

Selecting Objects

You can select one or more objects. Selecting a single object or a sub-object is done by clicking it. To select several objects, keep the left mouse button pressed when drawing a rectangle, a circle, or an area depending on the type of selection chosen in the drop-down menu of icons.

Menu bar → **Type Selection Region**

3ds Max 7 offers you a new method of selection — with a brush. It is sometimes convenient, especially when you select sub-objects.

You can add an object to the selected ones by keeping the <Ctrl> key pressed and delete an object from the selection by keeping the <Alt> key pressed.

3ds Max allows you to select multiple objects or sub-objects using a window or crossing. With the first method, objects entirely enclosed in the selection region are selected. With the other method, objects that appear within the selection region are selected. You can toggle between these modes using the **Crossing/Window Selection** button. 3ds Max allows you to toggle between these modes on the fly. To to do this, check the checkbox and select a radio button in the application settings (Fig. 1.31).

Menu bar → **Customize** → **Preferences...** → the **General** tab → the **Scene Selection** group

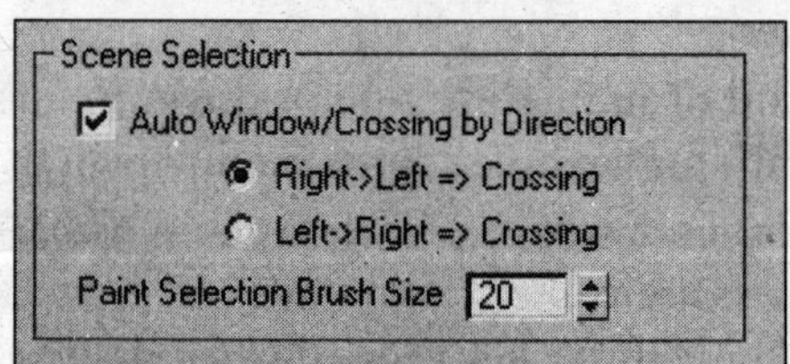

Fig. 1.31. Setting parameters to enable changing the selection method on the fly

After that, the window selection method will be chosen when you move the mouse pointer from left to right, and the crossing selection method will be chosen when you move the mouse pointer from right to left.

The parameter for the brush size is located in the same group.

3ds Max defines shortcuts that allow you to select all objects and sub-objects, unselect them, and invert the selection. These are traditional <Ctrl>+<A>, <Ctrl>+<D>, and <Ctrl>+<I>, respectively.

Moving, Rotating, and Scaling Objects

To move, rotate, or scale objects in 3ds Max, use transform gizmos (Fig. 1.32, *a*, *b*, and *c*) that have quite a few parameters (Fig. 1.32, *d*). The dialog box allows you to change the appearance of the rotation gizmo to the appearance it had in the earlier 3ds max versions (so-called Legacy R4).

Menu bar → **Customize...** → **Preferences** → the **Gizmos** tab

3ds Max allows you to select the type of operation with the hotkeys <Q>, <W>, <E>, and <R>. They correspond to the following modes: Smart Selection, Move, Rotate, and Scale. The <Q> key is also used to choose the selection method, and <R> is used to select the type of scaling (Uniform, Non-Uniform, and Squash).

Sometimes, you need to hide containers. Use the <X> key.

Fig. 1.32, *a*. Transform gizmos: Move

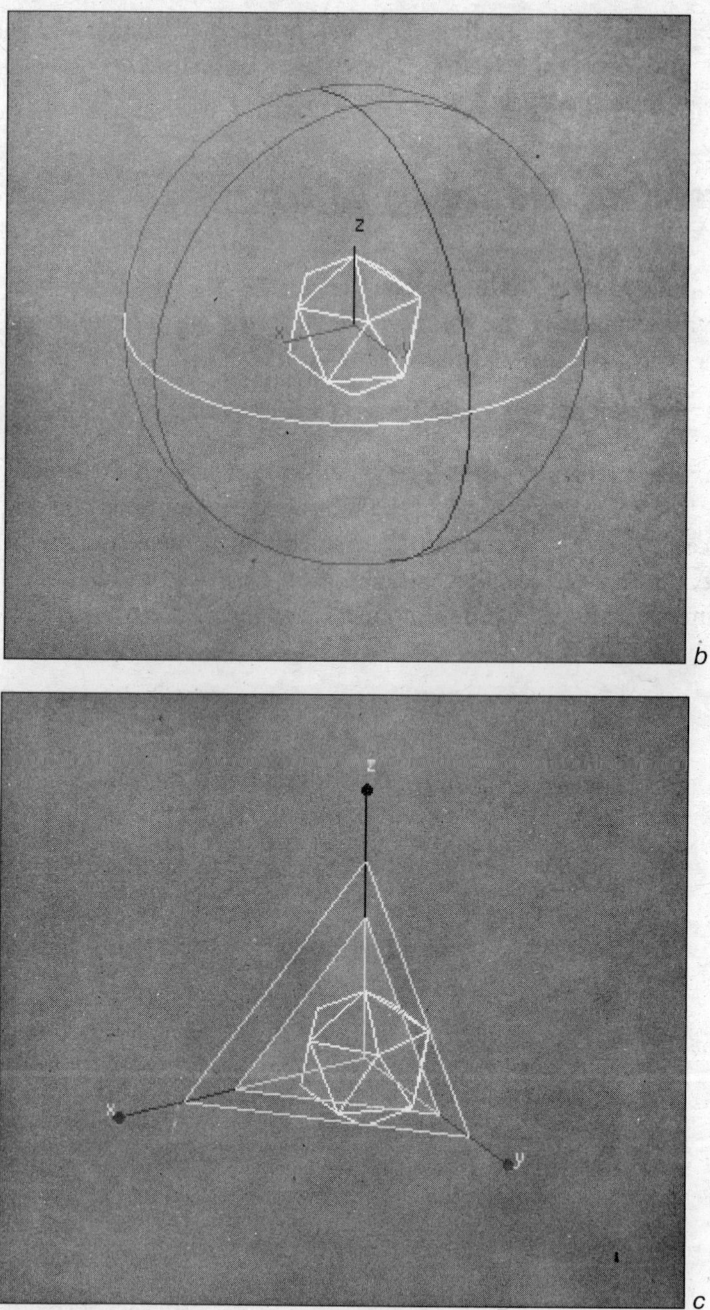

Fig. 1.32, *b* and *c*. Transform gizmos: Rotate (*b*) and Scale (*c*)

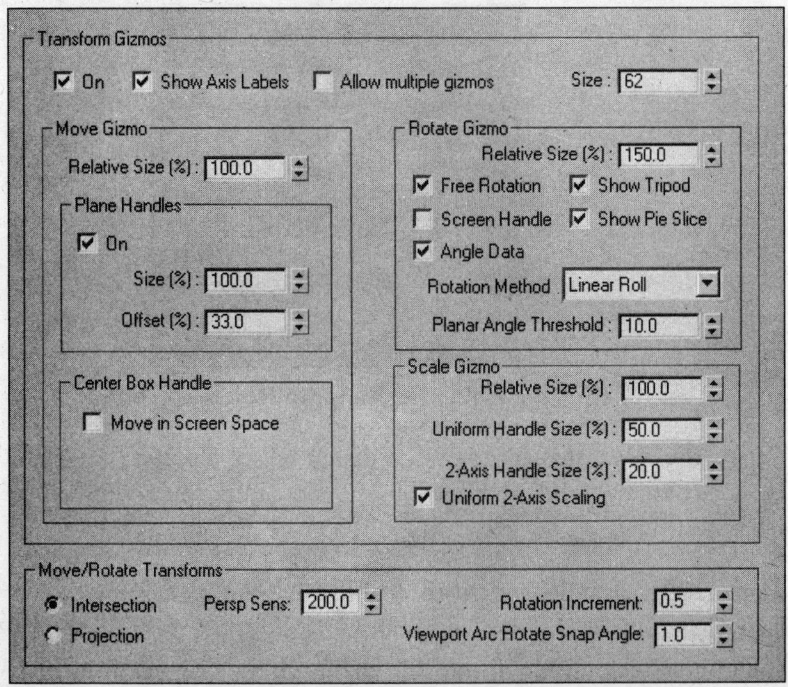

Fig. 1.32, *d*. Transform gizmos: the settings

The main toolbar misses **Restrict by Axis** buttons. Obviously, the developers hoped that the users had already remembered the <F5>, <F6>, <F7>, and <F8> keys that correspond to restriction by the X, Y, and Z axes and by the XY, XZ, and YZ planes. If you are dissatisfied with this, you can unhide the **Axis Constrains** panel (Menu bar → **Customize** → **Show UI** → **Show Floating Toolbars**). If you have enough free space on the screen, you can move this panel to the main toolbar or place it next to the main toolbar.

Select sub-objects using the <1>, <2>, <3>, <4>, etc. keys. This is true for basic types of objects, such as Editable Poly, and for modifiers. If you press a numeric key again, you'll move to the base level.

Cloning Objects

To clone an object, use the **Clone** command or just move the object while keeping the <Shift> key pressed.

Menu bar → **Edit** → **Clone**, or the <Ctrl>+<V> shortcut

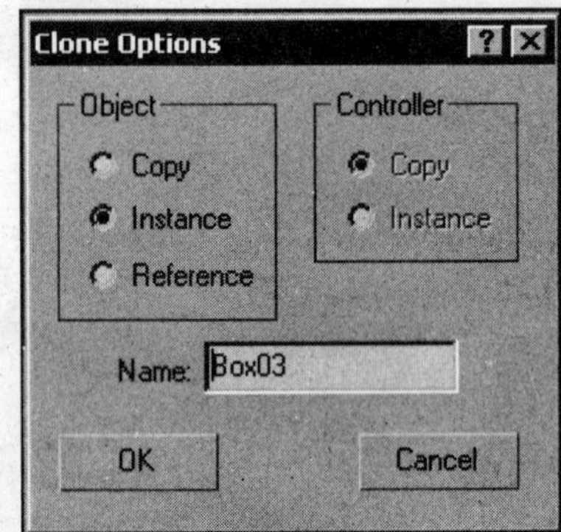

Fig. 1.33. The **Clone Options** dialog box

When you select this command, a dialog box will appear (Fig. 1.33). It will allow you to select the name for the new object. Most important, you can select the type of cloned object.

- **Copy** creates an independent copy of the object. This is clear.
- **Instance** and **Reference** create an object (or objects) linked to the original. Instance is a mutual relationship in that any change in the original or its instance (for example, low-level modeling, applying modifiers, or editing parameters), is reflected in the other object (or objects). When the Reference relationship is established, a thick horizontal line appears in the modifier stack. The modifiers below this line behave in the same way as with the Instance relationship (like the **Bend** modifier in Fig. 1.34). The modifiers above the thick line affect only the reference object. You can drag modifiers above or below the line, and the relationship will change accordingly.

The link can be broken with the **Make Unique** command in the pop-up menu of the modifier stack or with an appropriate button. The link is broken with the **Collapse All** command or the **Convert to...** command. The **Collapse To** command doesn't break links and converts the object to a basic type.

3ds Max offers you a few commands that allow you to create clones in accordance with a particular rule.

The oldest, most powerful, and least convenient tool is **Array** (Fig. 1.35, *a*). Its inconvenience is in that you cannot change the view in the viewport when the **Array** window is open. The **Preview** button that appeared at last allows you to deal with the problem to some extent.

Menu bar → **Tools** → **Array**

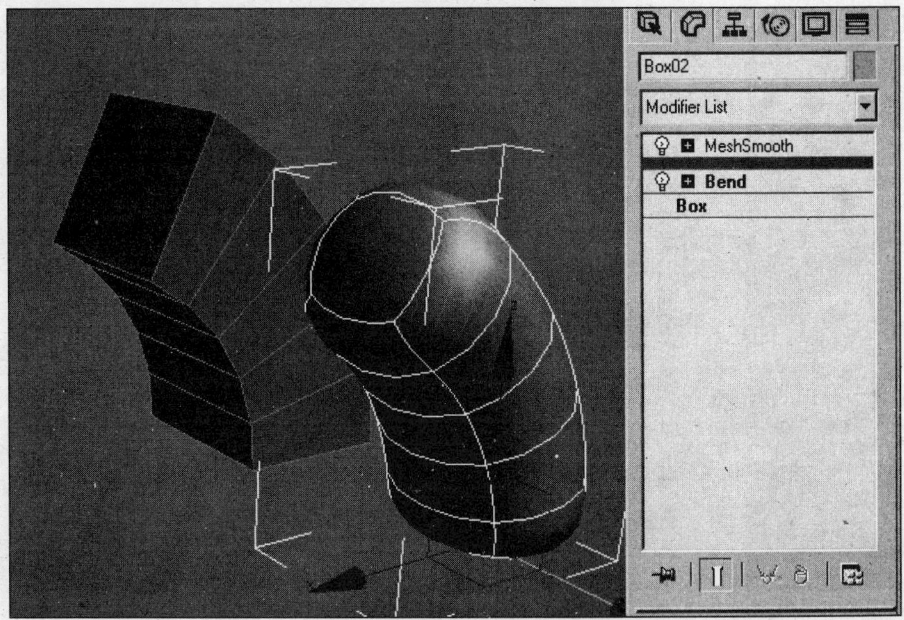

Fig. 1.34. Objects linked with the Reference relationship

To place objects along a path or using points, use the **Spacing Tool** (Fig. 1.35, *b*). It has many interesting settings; for example, you can place objects at a certain distance between their centers or edges.

Menu bar → **Tools** → **Spacing Tool**

A new tool, **Clone and Align**, allows you first to place simple objects (in Fig. 1.35, *c*, these are Dummies) and then place the desired objects with one click according to the positions and orientations of the objects placed first. Unfortunately, there is no option like **Replace**.

Menu bar → **Tools** → **Clone and Align**

Finally, there is an exotic but powerful method that involves creating animation snapshots. Naturally, it is called **Snapshot** (Fig. 1.35, *d*). To obtain snapshots, you have to animate the object first (in the figure, the position and scaling are animated).

Menu bar → **Tools** → **Snapshot**

I suggest that you visit **www.scriptspot.com**, where you'll find many interesting scripts including those intended for object cloning.

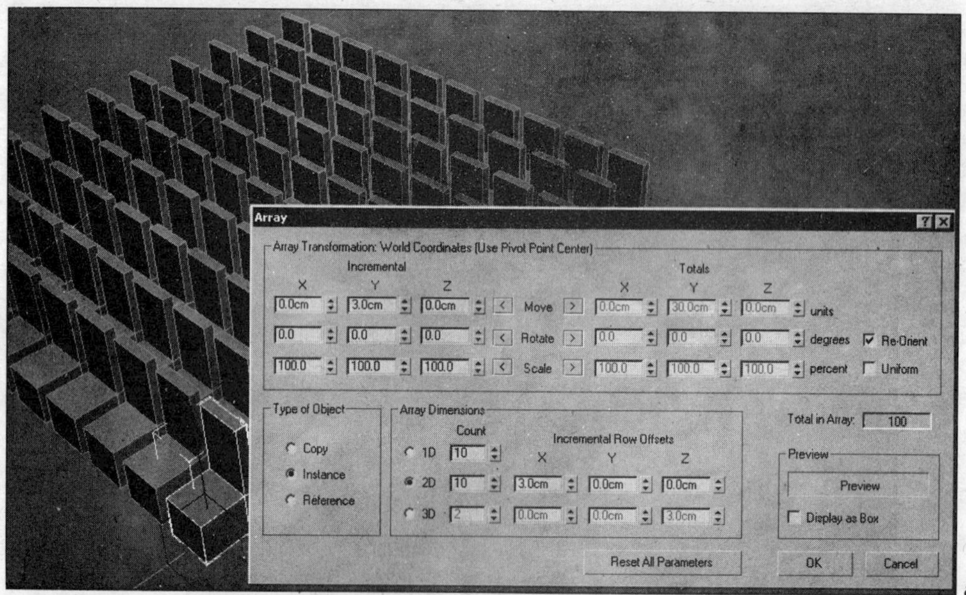

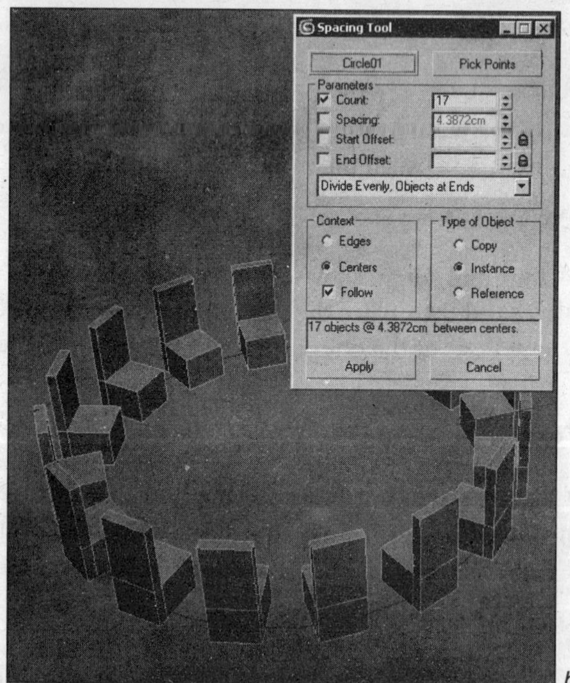

Fig. 1.35, *a* and *b*. Tools: **Array** (*a*), **Spacing Tools** (*b*)

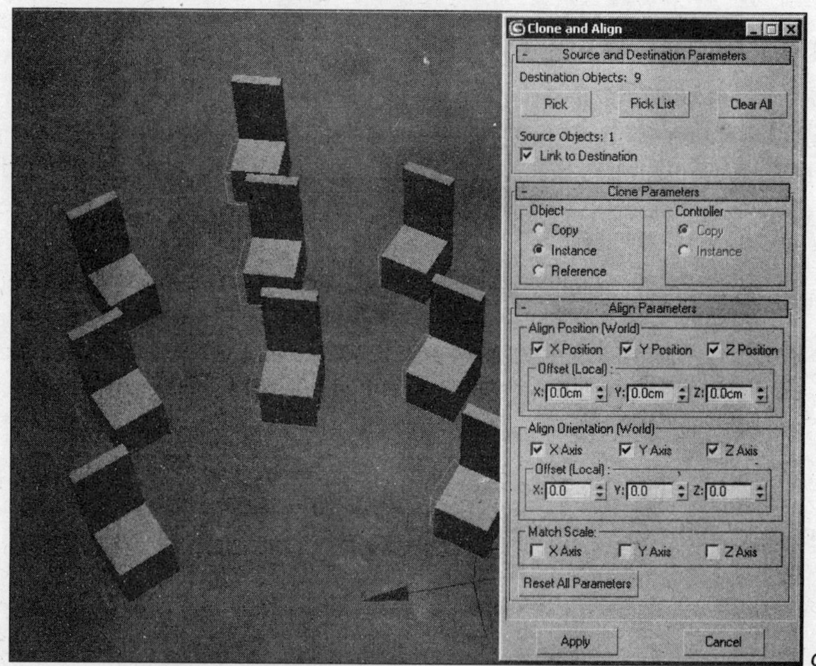

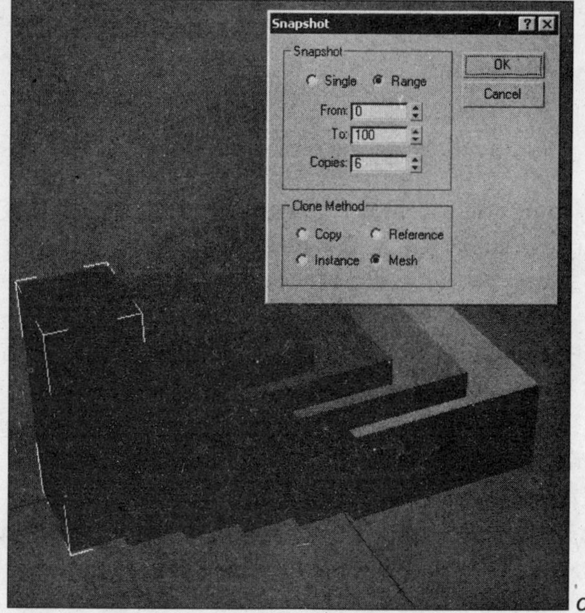

Fig. 1.35, *c* and *d*. Tools: **Clone and Align** (*c*) and **Snapshot** (*d*)

Numeric Parameters

In 3ds Max, most of the parameters can be entered as numbers into appropriate input boxes. All these boxes have special controls called spinners. You can use them either by repeatedly clicking them the required number of times, or by moving the mouse pointer up or down while keeping the left mouse button pressed.

When executing certain commands, for example, **Extrude** applied to a polygon of an **Editable Mesh** object or **Fillet** and **Chamfer** applied to a vertex of an **Editable Spline** object, you only should drag the spinner. If you click one of its arrow buttons, the command will be executed with a default step. The next click will execute the same command.

If you want the mouse pointer to remain next to the spinner, check the **Wrap Cursor Near Spinner** checkbox (Fig. 1.36).

Menu bar → **Customize** → **Preferences...** → the **General** tab → the **Spinners** group

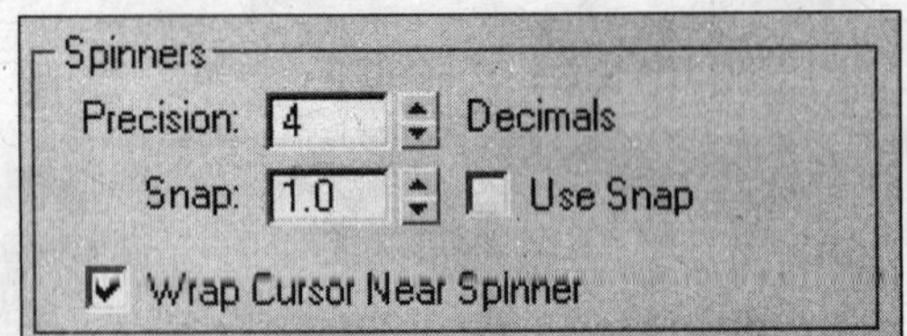

Fig. 1.36. Wrapping the mouse pointer near spinners

To change a numeric parameter quickly, keep the <Ctrl> key pressed while skimming through the values. The <Alt> key allows you to obtain greater precision for floating-point values. By right-clicking the input box, you can set the minimum parameter value.

The input boxes allow you to perform addition and subtraction. For example, if you need to increase the current value by 10 units, type r10 into the parameter's input box (r stands for *relative*) and press <Enter>. To decrease a value, use the r- prefix, for example, r-10. You can divide an integer by another integer — for example, 360/5. Unfortunately, other operations are impossible.

3ds Max has a calculator that allows you to enter numeric expressions into its input box. You can call the calculator with the <Ctrl>+<N> shortcut when the mouse pointer is in the input box of a parameter (Fig. 1.37). The syntax of the expressions is similar to that in the Expression Controller. For more details, see the user's manual.

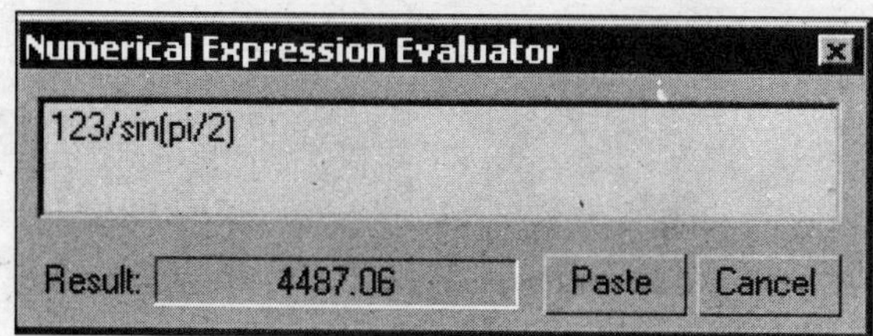

Fig. 1.37. The built-in calculator

A nice feature of 3ds Max is that it converts measuring units. For example, if you work with millimeters and need to enter a value in inches, enter the value with the units specified explicitly, for example, 8". 3ds Max will convert the value automatically.

Unfortunately, the calculator doesn't support conversion of units.

Transform Centers

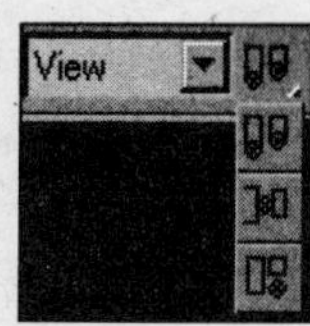

In 3ds Max, a *transform center* determines a point, about which rotation or scaling of a selected object (or objects) should be done. Select the transform center using the drop-down menu of items on the main toolbar. To skim through the transform centers, you can assign hotkeys to them (Fig. 1.38).

Menu bar → **Customize** → **Customize User Interface**

Fig. 1.38. Assigning hotkeys to transform centers

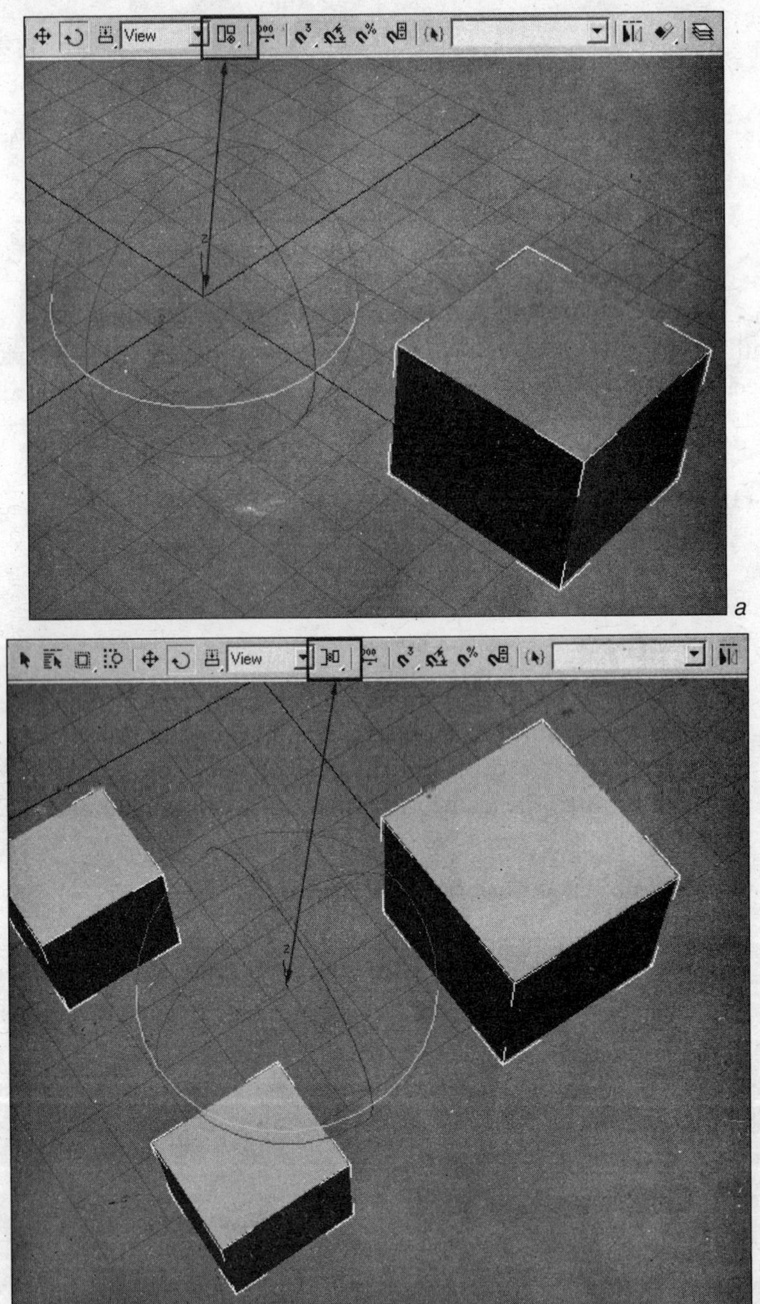

Fig. 1.39, *a* and *b*. The transform centers

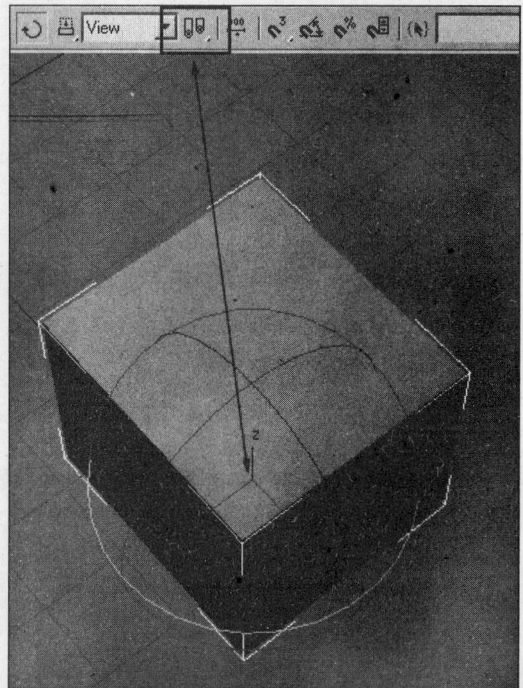

Fig. 1.39, *c*. The transform centers

Transform Coordinate Center. Depending on the coordinate system, this can be the screen center, the coordinate origin, and so on. In other words, this is the origin of the current coordinate system (Fig. 1.39, *a*).

Selection Center. The transform center is the center of a 3D shape built on the geometric centers of the selected objects (Fig. 1.39, *b*).

Pivot Point Center. For objects, the transform center coincides with their pivot points (Fig. 1.39, *c*). For sub-objects, this is not the case. As a rule, the centers of the selected sub-objects are used.

Chapter 2

Modeling and Graphic Presentation of Designed Objects

This chapter describes methods for modeling designed objects. All projects presented here were completed by students of Moscow State Institute of Electronic Technology who majored in Industrial Design. These are the students' term projects supervised by qualified professors. Each project was done during one semester and complies with aesthetic, ergonomic, and technological standards. These are are good examples from a professional standpoint.

My participation in these projects was minor. I just modeled them using the materials presented to me by the students and professors. In each case, I used a method, which was the most suitable in my opinion. I selected the projects in order to demonstrate various modeling methods.

When working on the projects, the students did their best to create beautiful pictures; however, they didn't think much about the presentation of the designed objects. It isn't enough to design a beautiful thing; you need to demonstrate how good it is. For some projects, I describe methods of simple animation that present the objects well. Novice users often neglect animation.

If you professionally use Computer-Aided Design/Computer-Aided Manufacturing (CAD/CAM) software packages, you might be disappointed in the inaccurate approach to modeling. Althrough 3ds Max bears family features of Autodesk's products, you shouldn't require the accuracy of CAD/CAM packages from the application intended for creation of photo-quality pictures and video clips. At the same time, you should be as accurate as possible during modeling, otherwise you will obtain inappropriate results. It's wise to find a compromise between a constructor's accuracy and an artist's freedom.

This chapter is divided into a few sections devoted to modeling, illumination, creating and applying materials, rendering, and animation. I believe this will be a good source of reference.

Preliminary Settings

Before you start working, you should make a few settings based on the following reason:

- Because the projects include few objects, it would make little sense to use layers. Layers are discussed in *Chapter 3*, which is devoted to modeling the interior and rendering.
- Starting with version 6, 3ds Max comes with a rendering module called *mental ray*. It has a greater variety of features for obtaining photorealistic images than the built-in renderer, so it would be best to set the module as a default renderer. In addition, you should make mental ray extensions available to objects and materials.
- There are about a dozen parameters and settings that are worth using.

You can make settings quickly by using a convenient command that switches among the default interfaces: **Custom UI and Defaults Switcher**. Select this command, then the **Max.mentalray** initial setting, and the UI scheme you like best. Confirm your choice with the **Set** button (Fig. 2.1). This window gives you comprehensive information on the settings.

Menu bar → **Customize** → **Custom UI and Defaults Switcher**

Restart 3ds Max.

If you use a low monitor resolution (below 1280×1024), I recommend that you don't use the large toolbar buttons set by default in 3ds Max since they take up too much place on the screen. To switch to small toolbar buttons, open the **Preferences** window and uncheck the **Use Large Toolbars Buttons** checkbox.

Use Large Toolbar Buttons

Menu bar → **Customize** → **Preferences** → the **General** tab

Restart 3ds Max so that the new settings come into effect.

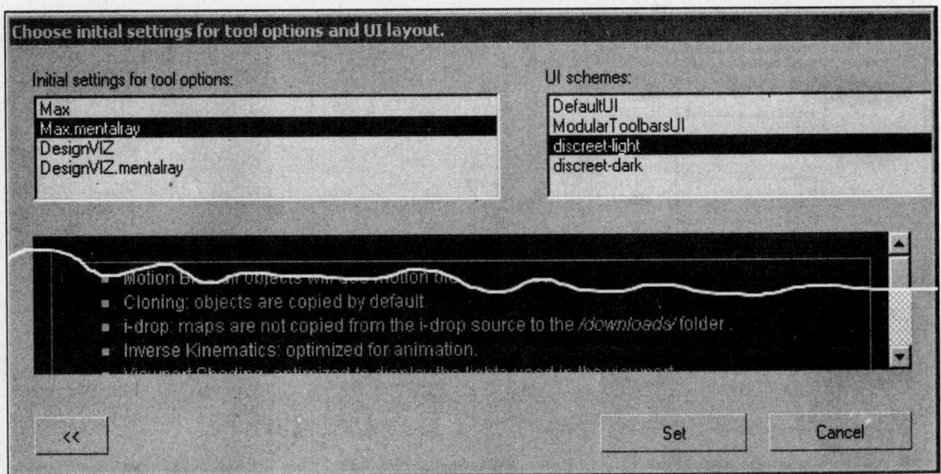

Fig. 2.1. The dialog box for choosing initial settings and UI layout

Be sure to copy the Projects folder from the CD-ROM to your hard disk. You will repeatedly need the contents of the CD-ROM, so it would be best to have them on hand.

Now, you are ready to start working. You may begin with any model. However, if you are a novice user, I recommend that you begin with the first one. When describing it, I focus on technical details. In the following models, I concentrate on commands and buttons to a lesser extent in order not to get distracted from the main topic, which is creating a project.

Modeling

A Bathroom Wall Shelf

In this project, you'll create a simple model of a wall shelf for a tooth brush, a toothpaste tube, and a soap bar. The shelf was designed by Yulia Reznikova supervised by Anna Zhiryakova. A fragment of the draft project is shown in Fig. 2.2.

Although the shelf consists of two parts, I suggest that you model it as a complete entity because no animation is intended. If you want to show the joint between the parts, you can always draw it on the final image using a bitmap editor. This would be a normal approach.

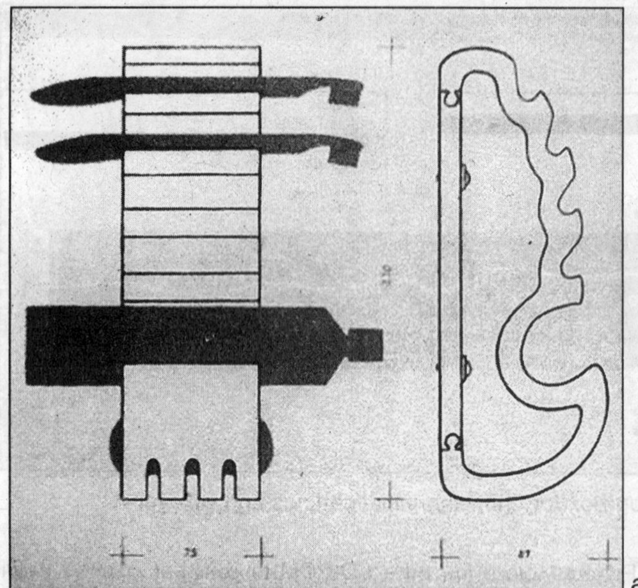

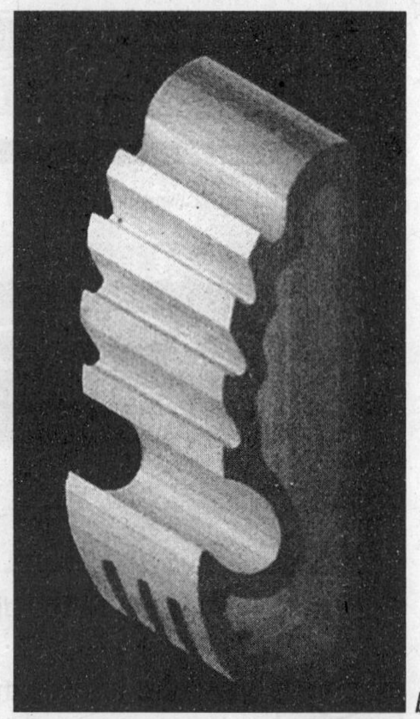

Fig. 2.2. The fragment of the draft project

This example will teach you how to model using curves with extruding. In addition, you'll have to use Boolean (logical) operations to cut holes from the bottom of the model.

Obtaining a photorealistic image isn't a goal of this project, so the result will be relative. I will skip many important issues discussed in the next sections when modeling other objects.

This project is the only project in the book that is oriented to novice users. I concentrate on manipulating with objects, rendering, and so on. In the following projects, I do this to a lesser extent.

Setting System Units

Before you start modeling, you should set system units. This is necessary for a few reasons. First, it is convenient. However, you can use the default system units (inches) if you wish. If you use the same system units in all your projects, this will save you from scaling objects when you transfer them from one project to another.

The second reason is a special one. Many processes such as global illumination, dynamics of solid and resilient bodies and cloths, and others rely on complicated algorithms. If scaling is incorrect, it can give unpredictable results. Although 3ds Max users perform many operations by eye and then correct results, you shouldn't begin with incorrect settings.

By what considerations should you be guided when selecting system units? Remember that 3ds Max has certain restrictions on precision. Don't choose millimeters when creating a model of a high building. You'll encounter many problems.

For this project and the other projects in this book, I suggest millimeters as the most suitable system units (Fig. 2.3, *a*).

Menu bar → **Customize** → **Units Setup** → the **System Unit Setup** button

Select millimeters in the drop-down list.

When setting system units in this dialog box, two issues are particularly important.

First, check the **Respect System Units in Files** checkbox if it is unchecked. This will allow you to put the system units in the files you load into correspondence with those used in the current project, and avoid scaling.

Second, set the precision of measurements. To do this, try to find the maximum size of the scene. Enter a deliberately large value as an approximate size of the scene into the **Distance from Origin** window and hit the <Enter> key.

For example, enter 2,000 (i.e., two meters) for this project.

Make sure to hit the <Enter> key, otherwise the settings won't take effect.

3ds Max can perform automatic conversion of system units. For example, if you enter 2,000, 3ds Max will understand these are millimeters. If you enter 2 m for two meters, 3ds Max will automatically convert this to millimeters.

Don't change the system units ever after. They should be set at the beginning of the project.

After you click the **OK** button, you will return to the system unit setup dialog box. These units will be displayed, and you are free to choose any units. 3ds Max will display these units, but work with millimeters. I don't think it would make sense to choose units others than millimeters (Fig. 2.3, *b*).

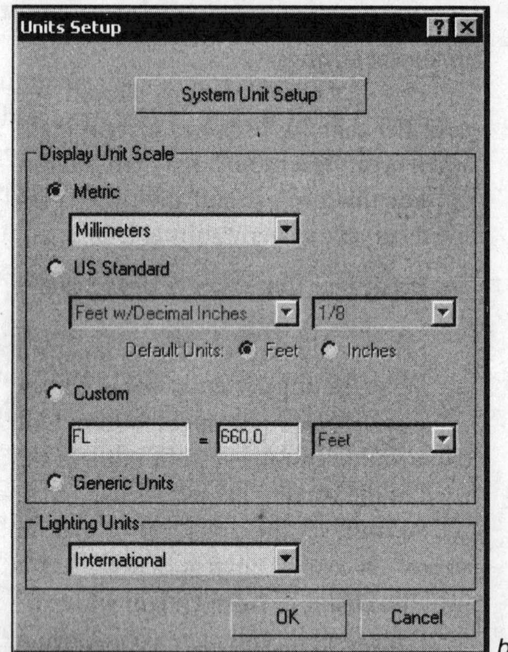

Fig. 2.3. Setting system units

If you don't want the values to have the mm suffix, select **Generic**. When entering a value, you won't have to specify the units explicitly; 3ds Max will make it for you.

Set the grid spacing to 10 mm (Fig. 2.4).

Menu bar → **Customize** → **Grid and Snaps Settings** → the **Home Grid** tab

You can hide or show the grid with the <G> key (G for *grid*).
Save the project at this stage. Name it, for example, Model1.

Menu bar → **File** → **Save**

Try to save each project in an individual folder created on the disk beforehand. You can do this in the **Save** dialog box, which is a standard Windows dialog box. During your work, it is advisable to save intermediate copies of the project. Do this in the **Save As...** dialog box by clicking the **+** button. As a result, you'll obtain files Model1-01.max, Model1-02.max, and so on. This will guard you against problems if 3ds Max crashes. In addition, this will allow you to return to an earlier variant if necessary. Methods for recovering a project are comprehensively described in *Chapter 1*.

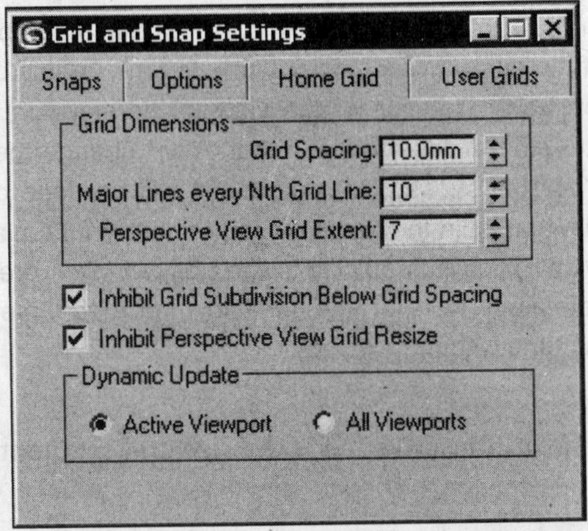

Fig. 2.4. Setting the grid spacing

Using an Image as a Background

I suggest that you do not use complicated 3ds Max features such as various snaps and alignments when you model this object. All of them are used in the next projects. You won't be able to use DWG or AI files because they aren't available — the project exists only in a "hand-made" form. That is, it was drawn on paper without the use of a computer, and a carton mockup was made.

However, I don't advise you to model by eye. Load an image in 3ds Max and outline it.

3ds Max allows you to load a background image and display it in the viewport, but it won't be convenient in this case. It would be best to use a 3ds Max feature that displays images loaded as maps and applied to objects.

- Move to the left view by clicking with the left mouse button on any point within it. Maximize the viewport. To do this, move the mouse pointer to the crossing of the viewport boundaries (the mouse pointer will take the shape of four arrows), click and hold the left mouse button, and drag so that the current viewport becomes larger.

❒ In the left view, create a plane of any size.

Menu bar → **Create** → **Standard Primitives** → **Plane**

Click anywhere within the viewport and drag.

Watch the current view by checking its name in the upper left corner of the current window from time to time (in this case it should be **Left**). Rotation of the view in the viewport (done with <Alt>+<the middle mouse button>) will change the view to **User**, and all subsequent operations will be done on the home grid, that is, in the top view, rather than on the plane of the left view. To switch quickly to the desired view, press an appropriate key (<L> for the left view) or open the view selection menu with the <V> key.

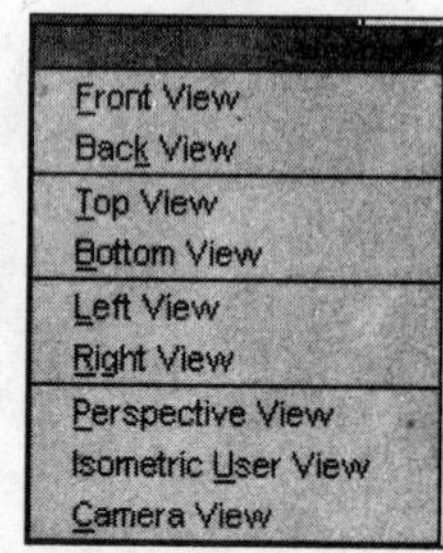

Enter the Modify mode and specify the size and segments of the plane (Fig. 2.5).

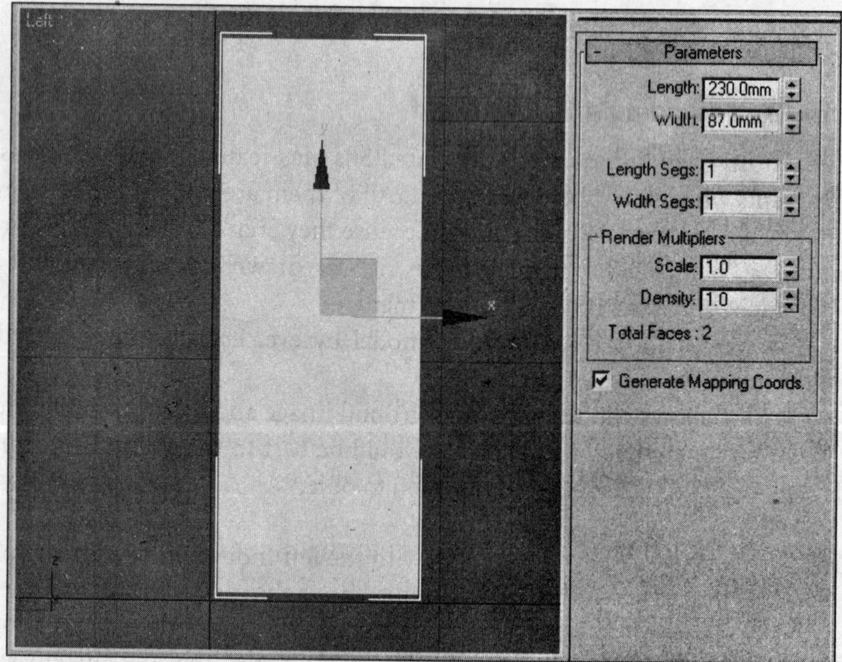

Fig. 2.5. The parameters and position of the plane

Set the plane size in accordance with the object size (230 × 87 mm). Don't scale the plane because you'll never obtain precise dimensions.

Set **Length Segments** and **Width Segments** to one.

Check the **Generate Mapping Coordinates** checkbox. You'll need this parameter when mapping the image applied to the plane.

Move the plane so that its lower left corner is as close to the origin of coordinates (the crossing of thick grid lines) as possible. Adjust the size of the view in the viewport to the size of the plane (with the <Z> key).

Fig. 2.6, *a*. Applying an image to a plane

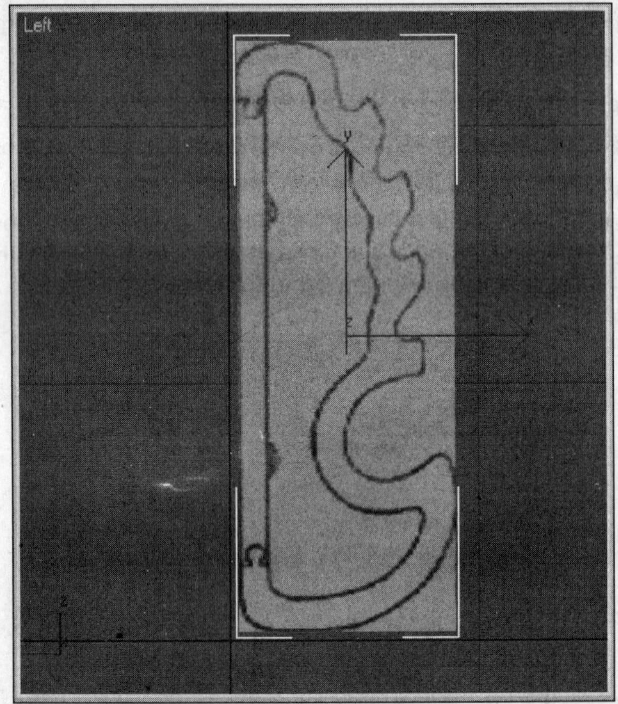

Fig. 2.6, *b*. Applying an image to a plane

- ❒ Select the shaded display mode for the objects in the viewport (with the <F3> key). The same key is used to select the wire mode.

Now, you need to apply the bitmap image from the file containing the outline of the object to the plane. You can do this in various ways, but I'll suggest the most effective.

TIP

If you haven't copied materials from the PROJECT folder on the CD-ROM to your hard disk, do this now.

- ❒ Open the built-in **Asset Browser** (Fig. 2.6, *a*).

Command panel → the **Utilities** tab → **Asset Browser**

- ❒ Open the Projects\Project1 folder and drag-and-drop the image from the Model1-left.tif file to the plane. It will immediately appear in the viewport (Fig. 2.6, *b*).

NOTE

Be advised that you cannot apply a map to an object (the image from the file is a map in this case). The drag-and-drop operation you performed started a complicated process. A material was created, the map from the file was applied to the material's Diffuse channel, and the material was applied to the object. In addition, the material is displayed in the viewport. Work with maps and materials is described in further detail later.

Freeze the plane so that it is displayed, but doesn't get in the way. Before freezing the plane, tell 3ds Max to display the image on the plane.

Quad menu → **Properties** → the **General** tab→ the **Display Properties** group → uncheck the **Show Frozen in Gray** checkbox

Show Frozen in Gray

Quad menu → **Freeze Selection**

It's important to add a few words about the background image and preparing it.

Because it isn't precise (it was made from a digital photo), I recommended that you set the plane size to the object size. I cut the image in a bitmap editor exactly to the object size. I usually fill in background images with a semi-transparent color so that objects are visible against them. The reason for this is that vertices in 3ds Max are white by default, and white against white isn't easy to see.

When preparing images, remember that 3ds Max isn't as powerful as modern 3D accelerators, many of which can display maps with a resolution of 2048 pixels or more on one side. So the largest size isn't necessarily the best. If you try to apply a very large map to an object in 3ds Max, you are most likely to see a senseless medley of pixels. The maximum size of a map correctly displayed in the 3ds Max viewport is 512 × 512 pixels. If your map is larger, scale it to an appropriate size after you create a backup copy of it. This restriction relates only to real-time display in viewports; for rendering, you can use an image as large as you like.

Creating an Outline. Variant 1

Now, you need to draw a curve outlining the image. Many users make the mistake of trying to outline an image on the first attempt. I have been using 3ds Max for many years, and I have never managed to do this at once. I suggest that you to do this in two stages. First, create a rough outline with a broken line, and then edit it.

- ❒ Maximize the left view. To do this, you can use the <Alt>+<W> shortcut (W for *wide*).
- ❒ Scale the viewport to the plane size. To do this, use the mouse wheel. If your mouse doesn't have a wheel, use the <Ctrl>+<Alt>+<the middle mouse button> shortcut.

- ❐ Start the curve in the lower left corner and move counter-clockwise. This direction is positive in 3ds Max.

  Menu bar → **Create** → **Shapes** → **Line**

Click the left mouse button, release it (don't drag), and move the mouse pointer to the next vertex.

To draw a strictly vertical or horizontal line, press and hold the <Shift> key.

TIP

Fig. 2.7 shows how many vertices you should create. I made the plane invisible, but you don't need to do this. If you accidentally create more vertices (or less), don't worry. You'll be able to correct this later.

When you return to the starting point, answer **Yes** to the **Close Spline?** question.

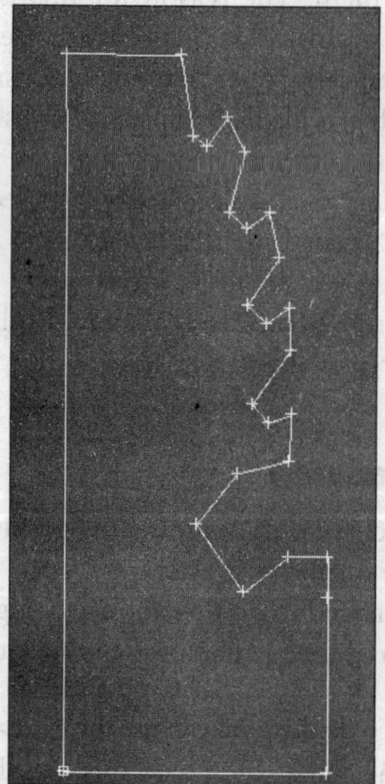

Fig. 2.7. A dummy for the model

What problems can you encounter when outlining? The most frequent problem is that you have to put a vertex outside the screen. Don't try to move the view with the middle mouse button or scale it with the mouse wheel. Creating the curve will end instantly. Use the <I> key to move the view and the <[> and <]> keys to scale.

If creating the curve is interrupted, start a new curve where you ended the previous. Your subsequent actions are described in the next paragraphs.

I simulated a situation where creating the curve was accidentally interrupted. As a result, I have three curves (Fig. 2.8, *a*). These are three different objects. To be able to edit them as one object, you should unite them. The procedure is standard for all types of objects in 3ds Max. It is as follows:

- Select any curve, say, **Line01**.
- Enter the Modify mode and attach the other objects to the selected one.

Quad menu → **Attach**

Left-click the other curves.

To finish, right-click.

Now, this is one object. However, you haven't finished. You need to weld vertices to close the outline. Even if it seems that the vertices are welded, this can be not the case. Vertices can overlap or be in the same point, but they can still not be welded. You can control this visually; all the vertices should look like crosses, and only one vertex, the first one, should look like a square.

- Enter the automatic welding mode.

Command panel→ **Geometry** rollout → check the **Auto Welding** checkbox

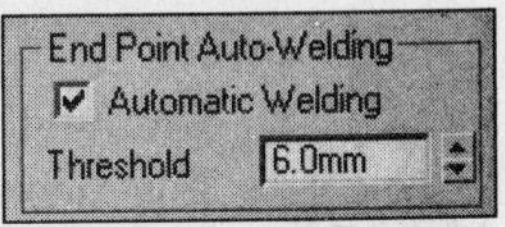

- Scale the image. Focus on the problem vertices, select one of them, and drag it to the other by grabbing the rectangle of Transform Gizmo (Fig. 2.8, *b*). The vertices will weld together.

If the vertices coincide, you can simply select both with a rectangle and execute the **Weld Vertices** command.

Quad menu → **Weld Vertices**

To delete vertices, use the <Del> key; and to add them, use the **Refine** command.

Quad menu → **Refine**

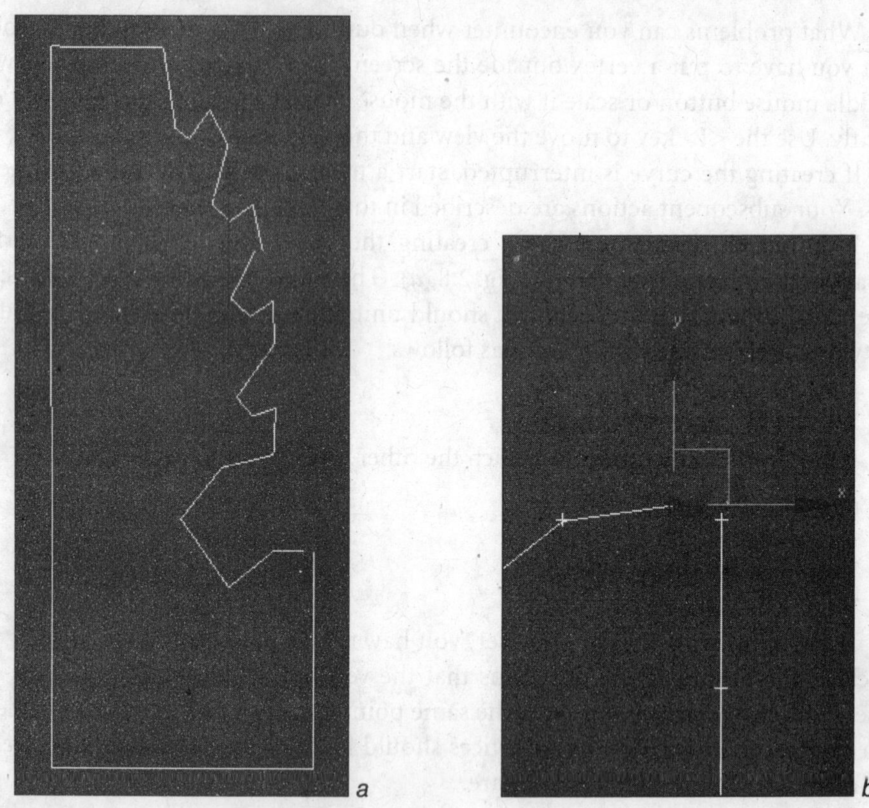

Fig. 2.8. Automatic welding

NOTE

Like **Attach** and many other commands, the **Refine** command is a batch command. This means it will execute until you interrupt it with the right mouse button or the <Esc> key.

Now, you should smooth out the angles so that the curve fits the image. To do this, use the **Fillet** command.

Command panel → the **Selection** rollout → **Vertex** or the <1> key

The **Geometry** rollout → **Fillet**

You can do this in several ways. Click the **Fillet** button and smooth out the angle at each vertex individually, or select a few vertices and smooth out all their angles simultaneously (to select multiple vertices, press and hold to <Ctrl> key), or enter radii into the input box to the right of the button.

Novice users often misuse spin controls. Don't click them! A click creates a fillet with a very small radius. Drag spins while keeping the left mouse button pressed.

Makes fillets on the rear and front sides (Fig. 2.9, *a* and *b*). To make fillets in cavities, you'll have to move the vertices first (Fig. 2.9, *c*).

The <Spacebar> key and the <X> key can cause two confusing situations because inexperienced users often hit these keys accidentally. First, the <Spacebar> key executes the **Lock Selection** command and prevents you from selecting other vertices. To know whether the Lock Selection mode is on, look at the appropriate button in the status bar. The second problem is that "arrows disappear." That is, the Transform Gizmo is switched off by accidentally hitting the <X> key which toggles the gizmo.

So you have obtained an outline like that in Fig. 2.9, *d*. It has too many unnecessary vertices. Some of them are close to each other, and you should weld them. To do this, select the pairs of such vertices and execute the **Fuse** and **Weld** commands. The first moves the vertices to one point, and the second welds them. Fig. 2.9, *d* illustrates this.

Finish the outline thoroughly. If necessary, move the vertices and change the curvature with Bezier handles. Some vertices can be deleted. I added two vertices to the front side using the **Refine** command. The result of my work is shown in Fig. 2.9, *f*.

You'll need to change the types of some vertices. To do this, select the desired vertices and select a type in the quad menu.

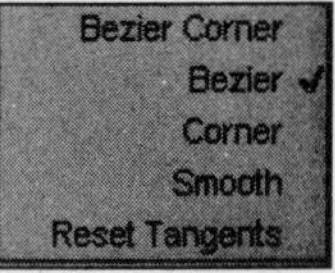

There are four vertex types in 3ds Max. Corner and Smooth vertices don't have handles, while Bezier and Bezier Corner vertices do. The difference between them is that Bezier vertices are smoothed, and their handles are tangents to the curve. As for Bezier Corner vertices, they can have corners. I prefer Smooth vertices. They aren't so capricious; although, they require certain skills. Try to use them.

Editing Bezier curves in 3ds Max is very inconvenient. First, there is no Handle sub-object type. To be more precise, it was introduced in 3ds Max 6 for Bezier patches, but it isn't implemented for curves. It is a frequent situation where you cannot move a Bezier handle because an attempt to click it results in clicking an arrow, and you move along a wrong axis. A way out could involve hiding the arrows with the <X> key. In this case, you should toggle among the axes using the <F5> and <F8> keys. The latter controls the movement on the plane.

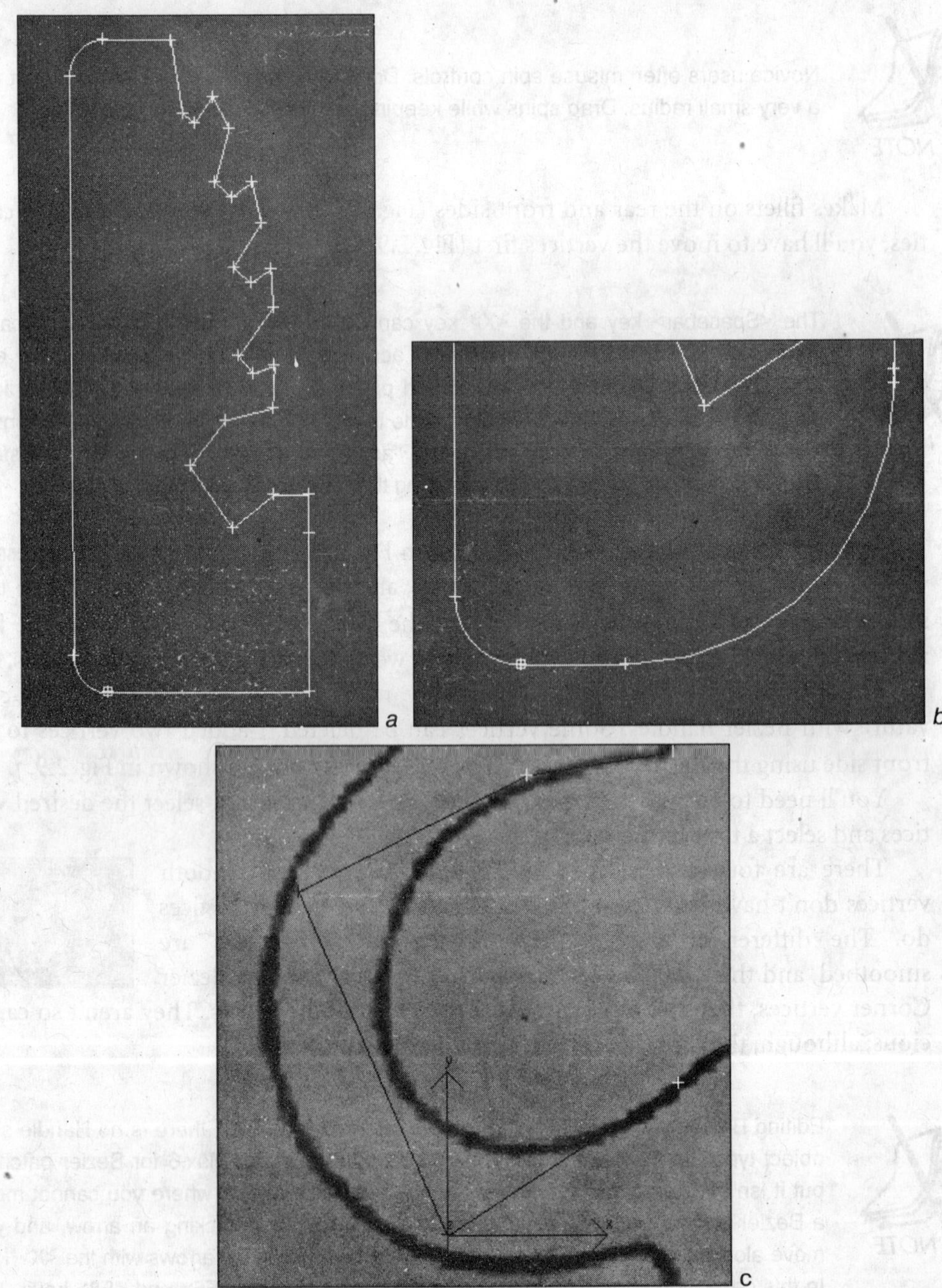

Fig. 2.9, *a–c*. Editing the outline (variant 1)

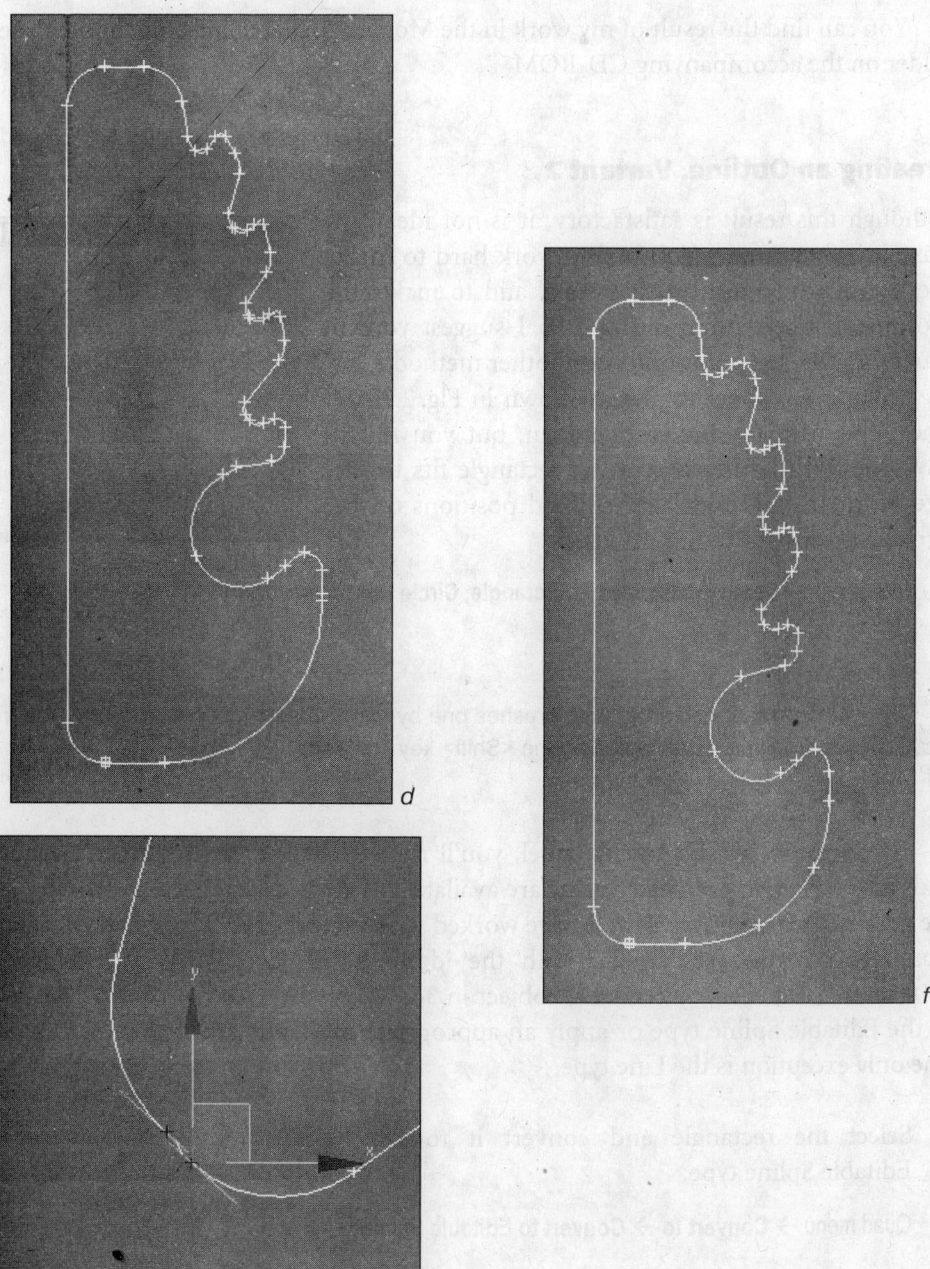

Fig. 2.9, *d–f*. Editing the outline (variant 1)

You can find the result of my work in the Model1-01(var1).max file in the Project1 folder on the accompanying CD-ROM.

Creating an Outline. Variant 2

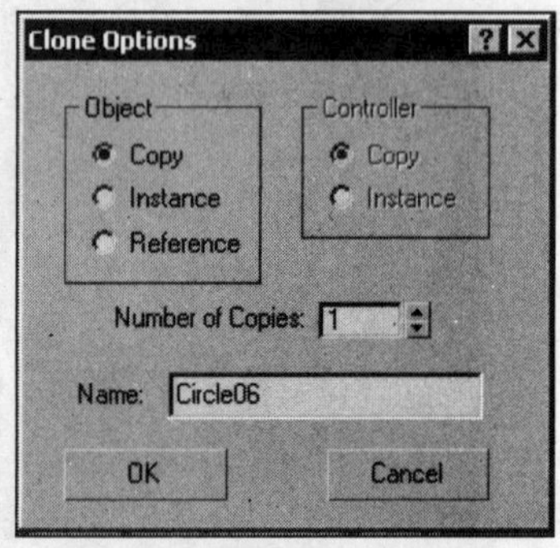

Although this result is satisfactory, it is not ideal. At least, it isn't accurate. You had to work hard to make the cutouts for tooth brushes equal and to make the toothpaste tube cutout and arc. So I suggest you to start from the beginning and use another method.

First, create a few splines as shown in Fig. 2.10, *a*. The plane with the image is hidden, but you might have guessed that the size of the rectangle fits to the size of the model, and the radii and positions of the circles correspond to the cutouts.

Menu bar → **Create → Shapes → Rectangle, Circle**

TIP

Don't create holes for tooth brushes one by one. Create just one and copy the circle by dragging it while keeping the <Shift> key pressed.

If you move to the **Modify** panel, you'll notice that the vertices aren't available, and only numeric parameter values are available. This is normal because these objects are parametric primitives. If you have worked with vector graphic applications such as CorelDRAW, you are familiar with the idea. As in CorelDRAW, to access the "internals" (i.e., sub-objects) of an object in 3ds Max, you need to convert the object to the Editable Spline type or apply an appropriate modifier, Edit Spline in this case. The only exception is the Line type.

Convert to Editable Mesh
Convert to Editable Poly
Convert to Editable Patch
Convert to NURBS

- ❒ Select the rectangle and convert it to the Editable Spline type.

  Quad menu → **Convert to → Convert to Editable Spline**

- ❒ Attach all the circles to the rectangle. You don't need to convert them.

  Quad menu → **Attach**

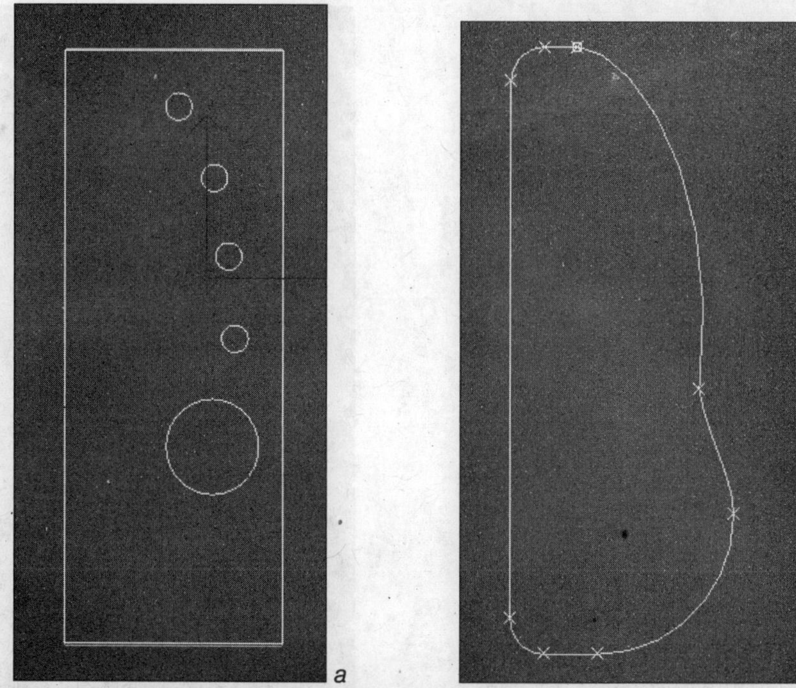

Fig. 2.10, *a* and *b*. Editing the outline (variant 2)

- Create an outline without the cutouts (Fig. 2.10, *b*). (The circles are hidden in the figure).
- Select the left vertices and execute the **Fillet** command.
- Make a fillet for the lower right vertex.
- Add a vertex on the top using the **Refine** command and delete the upper right vertex using the <Del> key.
- Add a vertex at the top point of the cutout for a toothpaste tube and obtain the necessary shape by moving the vertices and Bezier handles.
- Create additional lines tangent to the circles (Fig. 2.10, *c*). Don't drag, just click to create a vertex.

The **Geometry** rollout → **Create Line**

- It is likely that you'll need to move the circles. To do this, enter the spline mode (with the <3> key), select a desired circle, and move it.

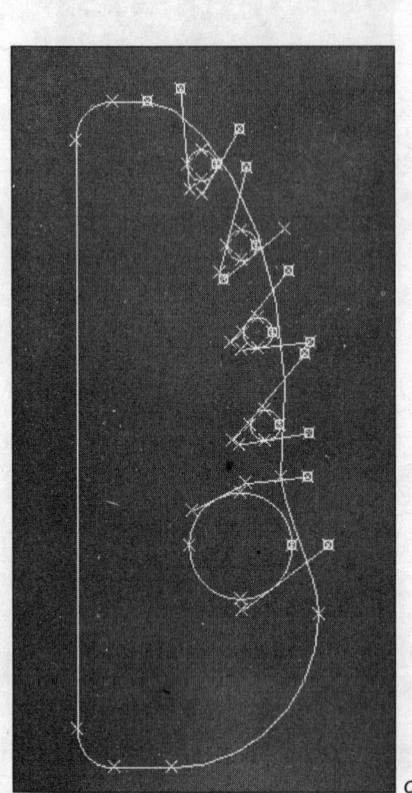

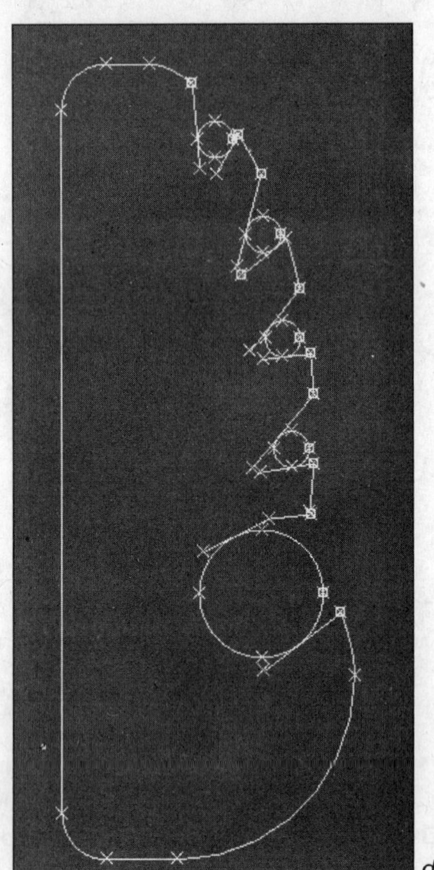

Fig. 2.10, *c* and *d*. Editing the outline (variant 2)

- In the spline mode, create cutouts and trim their curves using the **Trim** command (Fig. 2.10, *d*).

  The **Geometry** rollout → **Trim**

  Click the fragment you want to delete. It will be deleted till the nearest crossing.

  The **Trim** command works only when fragments are crossing. If you want to trim a tangent, use the **CrossInsert** command in the vertex mode (the <1> key). This command creates two vertices. Then enter the segment mode (the <2> key) and delete unwanted segments (Fig. 2.10, *e*).

- Select all the vertices and weld the coinciding ones using the **Weld** command.

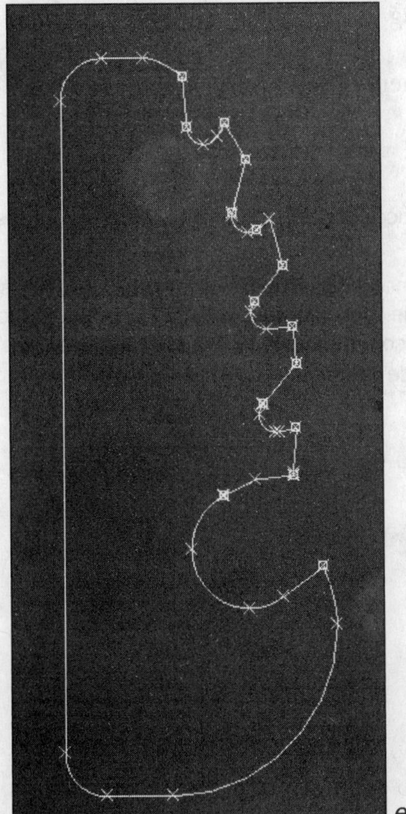

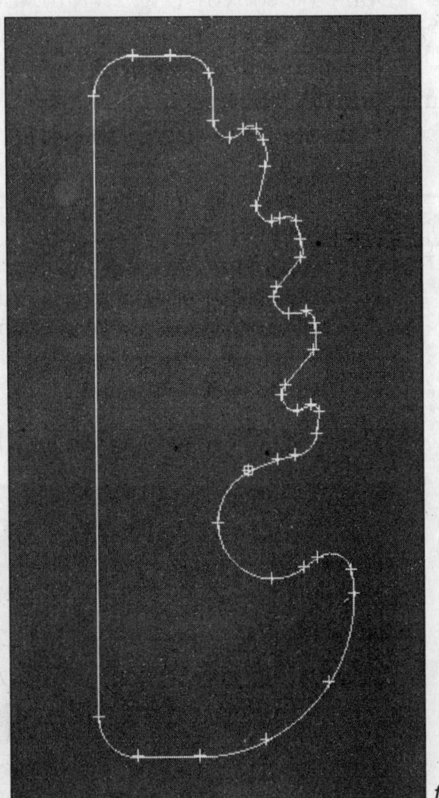

Fig. 2.10, *e* and *f*. Editing the outline (variant 2)

Now, you should look through all the vertices, delete unwanted ones, and weld some of them if necessary. You need to obtain a closed outline.

Smooth out angles with the **Fillet** command, and finish geometry. Note this outline (Fig. 2.10, *f*).

Creating the Internal Outline

Now, create the internal outline.

- Enter the spline mode (the <3> key), select the spline, and execute the **Outline** command to create the internal outline.

  The **Geometry** rollout → **Outline**

  Left-click the external outline and drag.

Don't be scared! (Fig. 2.11, *a*). Everything is all right, but this command isn't "intelligent" enough.

Delete unwanted vertices, weld some of them if necessary, and make fillets. Try to maintain the thickness of the shelf.

Make sure there are no loops (Fig. 2.11, *b*).

TIP

Sometimes, it is best to convert the vertices to the Corner type before you execute the **Fillet** command.

When there are many vertices, it is sometimes difficult to sort out, to which spline a particular vertex belongs. You can hide the external spline. To do this, select the spline and click the **Hide** button on the command panel, but not in the quad menu. These are different commands! To unhide the spline, use the **Unhide All** command on the command panel.

The result of my work is shown in Fig. 2.11, *c*.

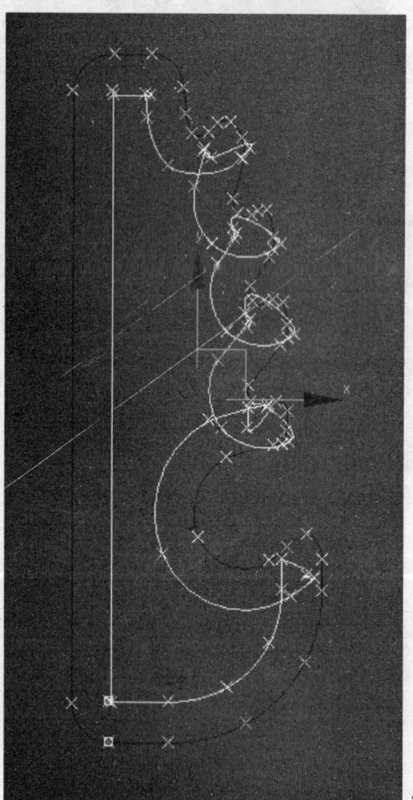

a

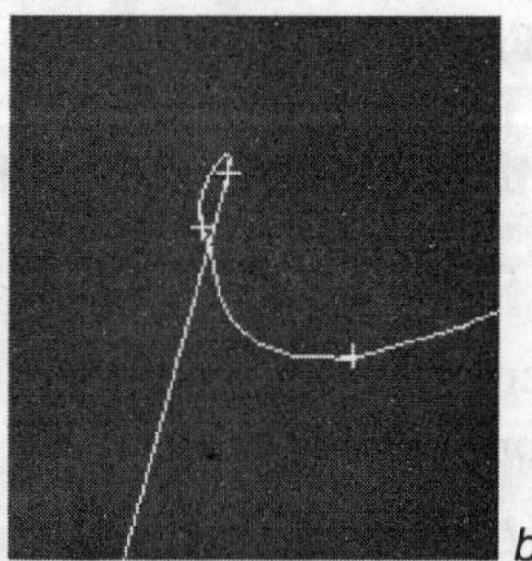

b

Fig. 2.11, *a* and *b*. Editing the external outline

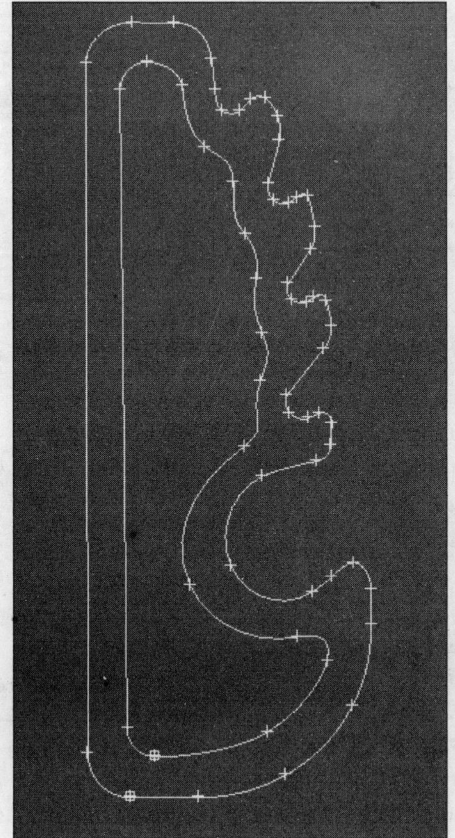

Fig. 2.11, *c*. Editing the external outline

Extruding the Outline

When the outline is ready, apply the Extrude modifier to it (Fig. 2.12) and extrude it to 75 mm by specifying this value in the **Amount** box.

Menu bar → **Modifiers** → **Mesh Editing** → **Extrude**

Don't try to obtain a required size by scaling the object along one axis. This would be a mistake.

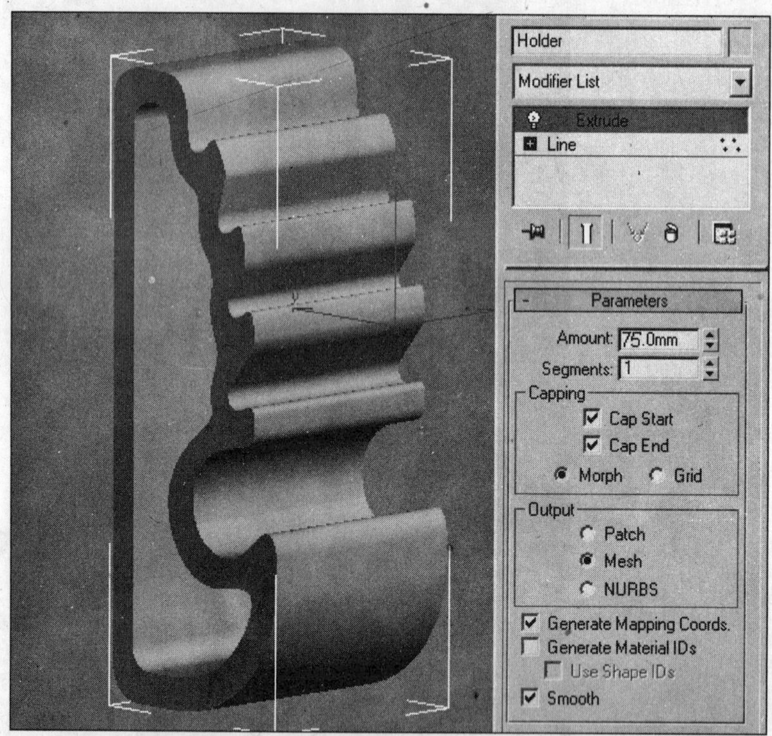

Fig. 2.12. The first stage of extruding the outline

What problems are likely? The most frequent one is a lack of surfaces on the ends. The **Cap Start** and **Cap End** checkboxes in the **Capping** group are responsible for this. If they are checked, but there are no caps, this means that the original outline isn't closed or has loops, that is, crosses itself. Jump down the modifier stack and correct the outline.

Another common problem is the presence of horizontal edges where they shouldn't be. They appear as a result of Bezier Corner vertices in the original outline. You can get rid of them by editing the outline. There is another method, which I'll describe later.

TIP

You can quickly check a spline for loops using the Shape Check utility. Proceed as follows:

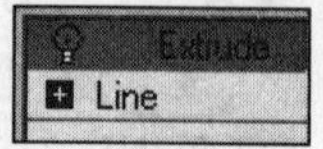

Disable the **Extrude** modifier by switching off the lamp icon in the modifier stack. This is an important step because the utility can work only with splines, and the **Extrude** modifier converts the object into a full-feature 3D object.

Move to the **Utilities** subpanel of the command panel.

Show all utilities using the **More** button and click the **Shape Check** line.

Click first on the **Pick Object** button and then on the spline. If there are self-crossings in the spline, they will be highlighted with red squares. Remember their positions. Unfortunately, the utility doesn't mark the loops in the spline.

So the model is almost ready. The result of my work on this stage is in the Model1-02.max file in the Project1 folder on the accompanying CD-ROM.

Your following actions require a preliminary discussion. Like many other 3D graphic applications, 3ds Max interpolates any curve with a broken line. Similarly, any surface is made from triangles called *faces* or *polygons*, though the latter term is not quite correct. When modeling in 3ds Max, you should clearly imagine the result. If an object is secondary, for example if the shelf is a 20 × 20-pixel fragment of the bathroom interior, you don't need to elaborate on details because the time of rendering depends on the complexity of the scene (more precisely, on the number of polygons). Conversely, if your goal is the presentation of an object, you should make it as beautiful as possible so that it doesn't look like a piece of plastic roughly processed with a file. In addition, you should size up whether this should be a finished model or an intermediate object for further editing on the polygonal level. The more complicated the object, the more difficult it is to edit it later.

To control the complexity of a model based on splines, start with the spline parameters. Everything you need is in the **Interpolation** rollout among the spline parameters. The **Steps** parameter defines the number of additional segments into which the segment between two vertices should be divided. The **Optimize** checkbox is used to avoid dividing straight segments, and the **Adaptive** checkbox turns on the adaptive mode, in which 3ds Max decides how to divide the spline. Fig. 2.13 shows a few settings of these parameters and the corresponding results. I like variant *d* best, which is default (however, this is an exception rather than a rule).

There is the **Segments** parameter among the parameters of the **Extrude** modifier. If you were not going to cut holes, I would advise you to leave one segment. However, set this parameter to four according to the number of the holes (Fig. 2.14). This will help you to avoid incorrect results when cutting the holes.

The result of my work on this stage is in the Model1-03.max file.

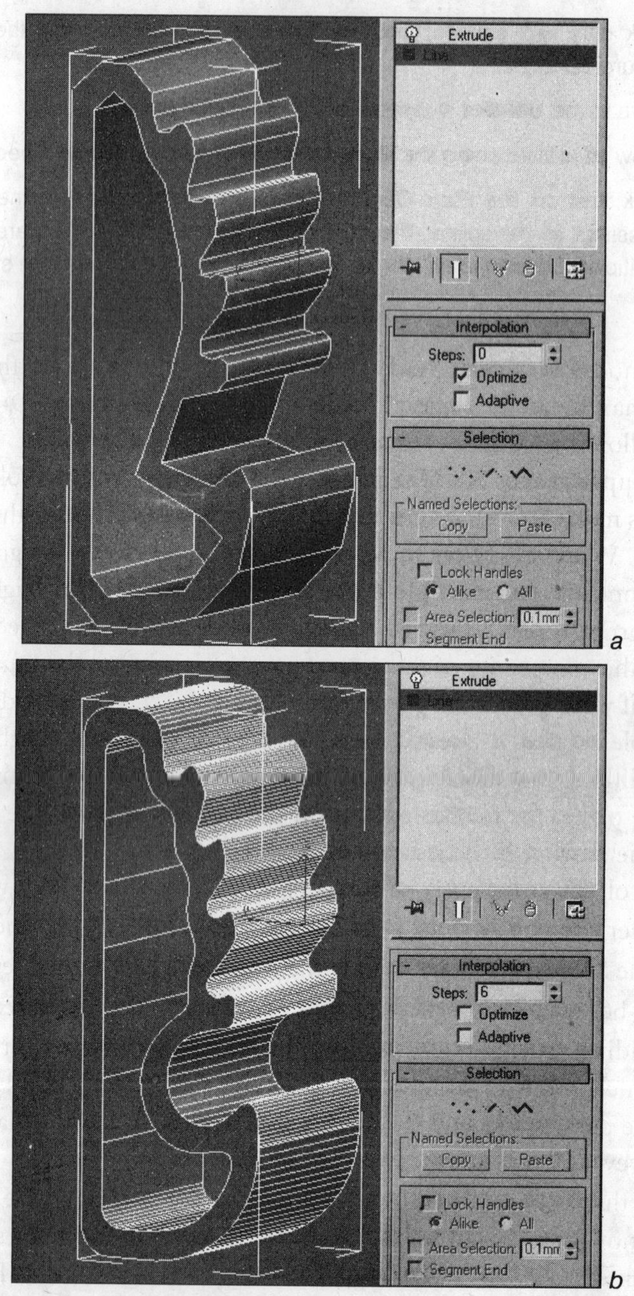

Fig. 2.13, *a* and *b*. Spline interpolation parameters and their effect on the model's final appearance

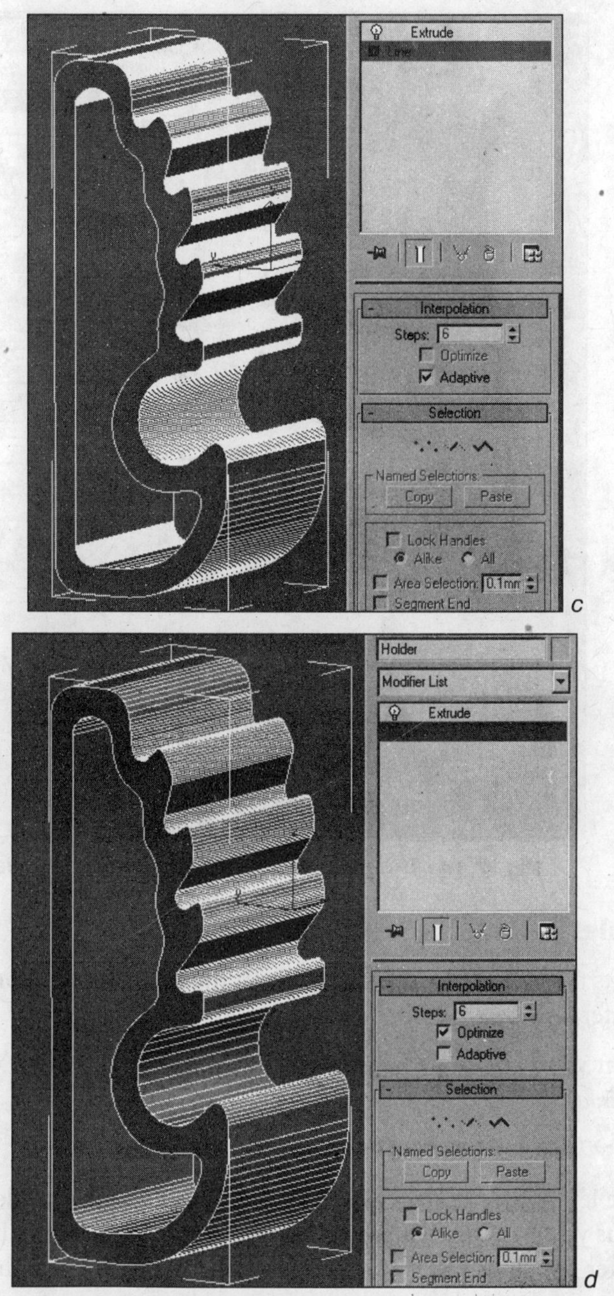

Fig. 2.13, *c* and *d*. Spline interpolation parameters and their effect on the model's final appearance

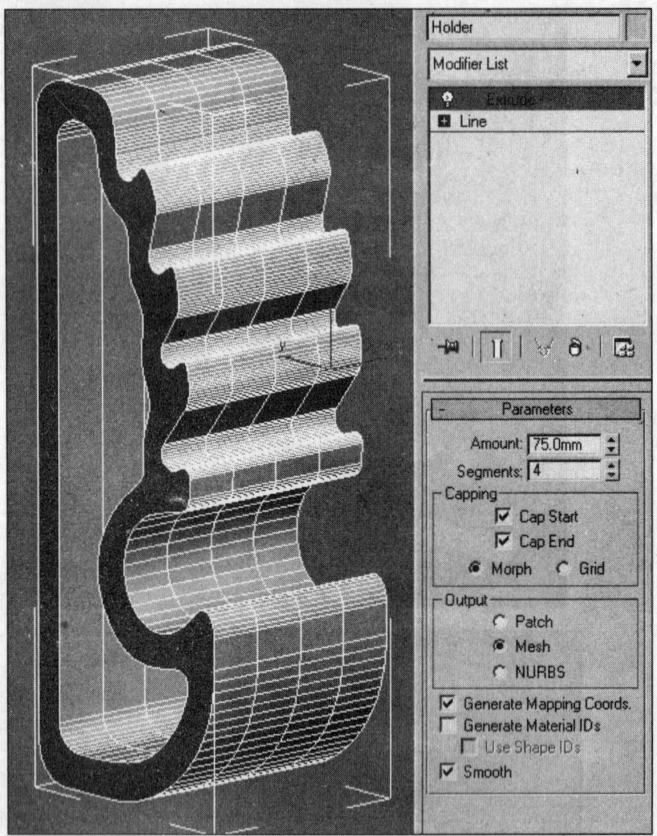

Fig. 2.14. The parameters of the **Extrude** modifier

Cutting Holes

Create objects that should be subtracted from the main object. You can use a primitive of the Chamfer Box type.

❒ In the left view, create a Chamfer Box primitive at any place with any parameters (Fig. 2.15, *a*).

Menu bar → **Create** → **Extended Primitives** → **Chamfer Box**

Click the left mouse button and drag the mouse pointer while keeping the button pressed. Thus you'll specify the length and the width. Release the button and move the mouse pointer up. Thus you'll specify the height. To fix it, click the left mouse button. Specify the size of the chamfer.

To complete creating the primitive, click the left mouse button.

How do you like the previous instruction? In addition, you have to watch the parameters. This is why I recommend that you create rough objects and then edit their parameters in the Modify mode unless you have serious reasons to create final shapes at first.

- Enter the Modify mode and specify the necessary dimensions and other parameters (Fig. 2.15, *b*).

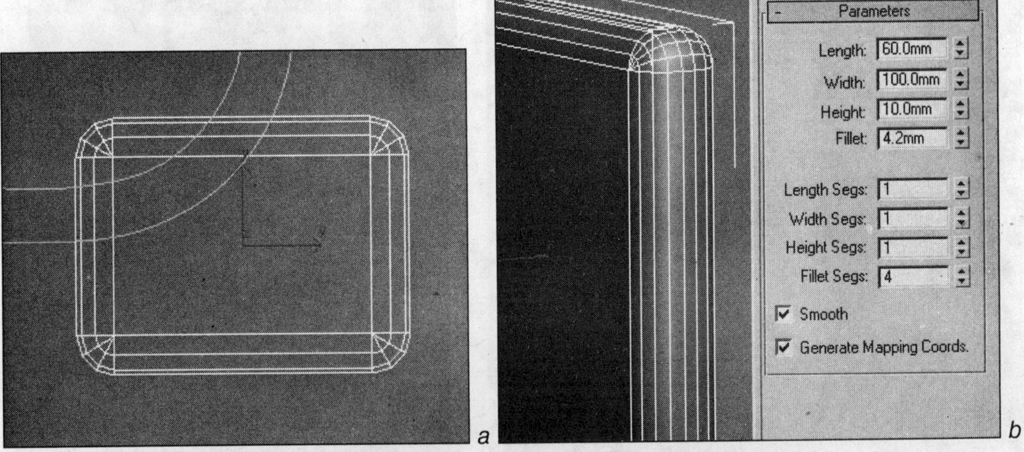

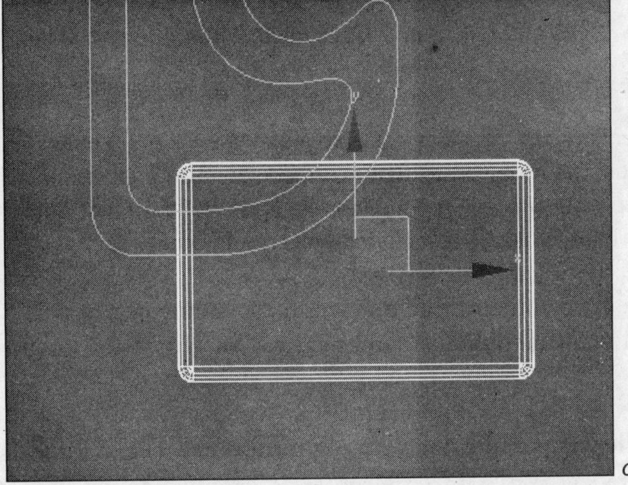

Fig. 2.15, *a–c*. Creating holes; the first stage

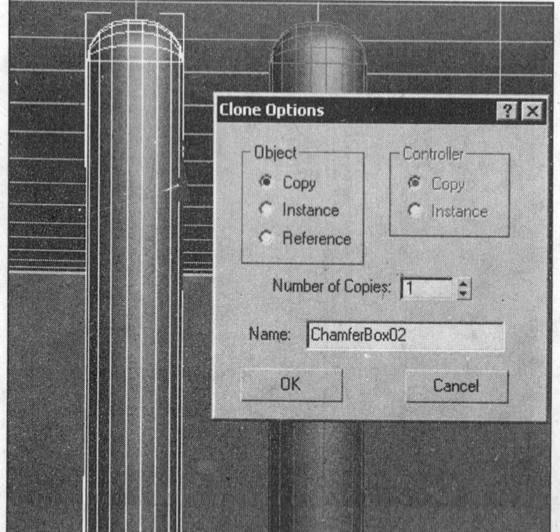

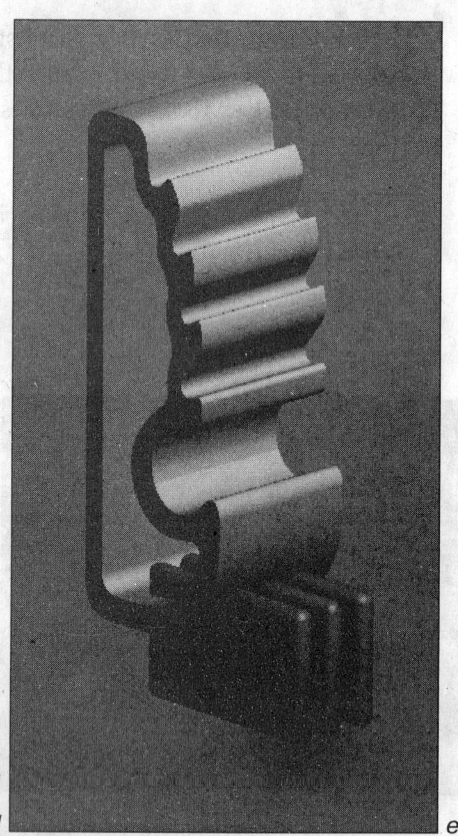

Fig. 2.15, *d* and *e*. Creating holes; the first stage

The length and the width aren't important; they can be rather large. The **Height** parameter should be set to 10 mm. I made the fillet a bit less than the height, to avoid overlapping vertices. The number of segments (the **Fillet Segs** parameter) is set to four, which is a large number for these dimensions.

Now, create two copies of the hole and place them appropriately. I think you have already noticed that the model is built by eye. Don't try to be too precise and go on in the same way.

- In the left view, place the hole object appropriately (Fig. 2.15, *c*).
- In the front view, move it to the center. Create two copies of it and place them to the left and to the right. To create a copy, move the object along the appropriate

axis while keeping the <Shift> key pressed. Select **Copy** in the dialog box and click the **OK** button (Fig. 2.15, *d*).

The result should appear as shown in Fig. 2.15, *e*.

Before you proceed, I should say a few words about Boolean (logical) operations over objects. 3ds Max doesn't implement solid-body modeling and performs operations over surfaces. There are certain rules for the Boolean operations, and you should stick to them to avoid incorrect results.

First and most important, don't use the Boolean operations when they aren't necessary. A good example is cutting holes in a cube. If you use the Boolean operations, you're likely to obtain an incorrect result. It would be best to create a spline consisting of a rectangle and circles and then extrude it.

When you cannot avoid the Boolean operations, for example, you need to cut holes from a complicated object, do this at one time. To achieve this, combine all the hole objects into one.

It is important that objects in the Boolean operations are closed shapes without loops. To check for the errors, use the STL Check modifier.

In addition, it is important that the modifier stack for the objects isn't large. Finally, you should avoid situations where one of the objects is a compound object of the Boolean type.

In 3ds Max, Boolean objects were implemented inappropriately, so it is a "very sore spot" for both the users and the developers. The module was rewritten three times. As a result, files with Boolean objects created in 3ds max versions 6 and earlier are loaded incorrectly in 3ds Max version 7.

However, in this project the use of the Boolean operations is justified. So, let's cut.

❒ Select one of the Chamfer Box objects and convert it to the Editable Mesh type. Attach the other boxes to it.

Quad menu → **Convert to → Convert to Editable Mesh**

Quad menu → **Attach**

Left-click the box. To complete the command, click the right mouse button.

Converting to a primitive type (Editable Mesh in this case) is a very important step. The object "forgets" about its origin and turns into a set of polygons. You should do this only if you are sure that you are satisfied with all the parameters. Another method involves the use of a modifier that has similar features (Edit Mesh in this case).

- Select the main object and create a compound object of the Boolean type.

Menu bar → **Create** → **Compound** → **Boolean**

- In the command panel, click the **Pick Operand B** button and then click the holes. They will be cut from the main object (Fig. 2.16) if the **Subtraction (A-B)** radio button is selected in the **Operation** group of the **Parameters** rollout.

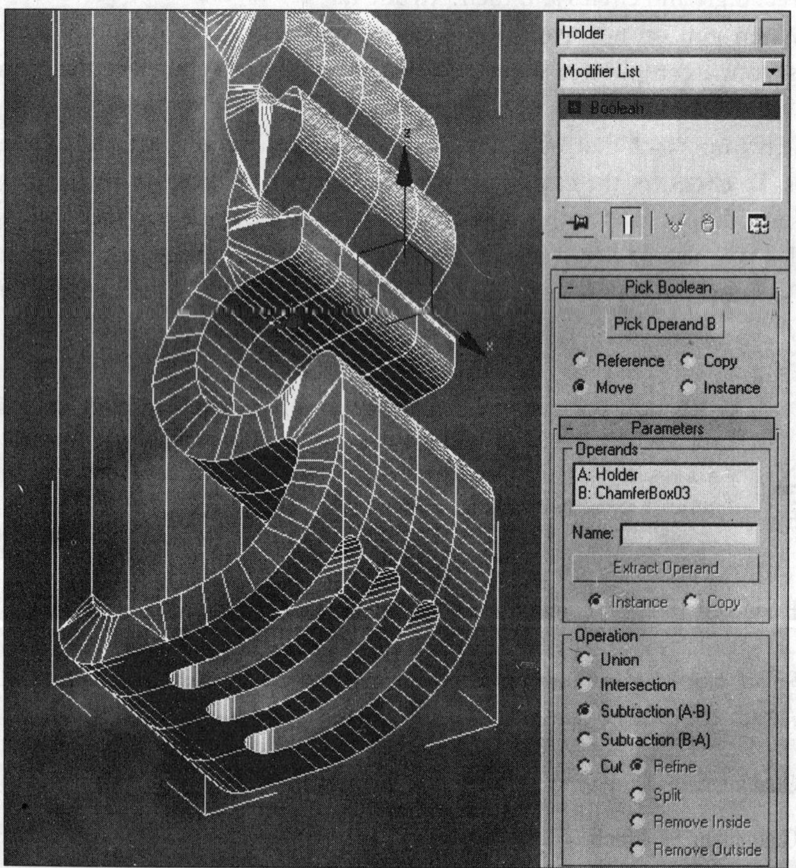

Fig. 2.16. Cutting holes

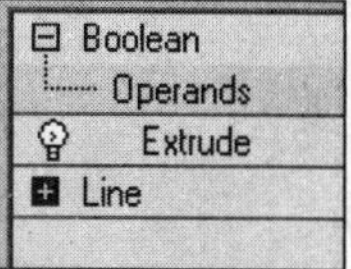

As their type implies, compound objects are based on other objects and associated with them. You can prove this by editing a sub-object. An object of the Boolean type has only one sub-object, Operands. If you select the **A** operand in the operand list, the parameters of the **Extrude** modifier and of the original line will be available in the modifier stack. This will allow you to edit the parameters of sub-objects after the compound object is created. However, it is best to set the parameters beforehand to avoid problems.

You could complete modeling on this stage, but it would make sense to perform two more operations: optimization and smoothing.

Optimization and Smoothing of the Model

In this project, optimization isn't necessary. However, when you create a series of such models, it makes sense to optimize them.

- Apply the **Optimize** modifier with parameters shown in Fig. 17, *a*. 3ds Max users don't like this modifier, because it can change the geometry and destroys mapping coordinates. However, in this particular case you shouldn't worry.

Menu bar → **Modifiers** → **Mesh Editing** → **Optimize**

In the **Optimize** group, a parameter is set that specifies angles between polygons and open edges. When angles are less than the specified values, the modifier collapses the polygons. As you see, an angle of 0.1 degrees makes the model "lighter" by 50%.

The **Bias** parameter allows you to avoid incorrect polygons. Try to set it to zero, and unpleasant creases will appear near the holes.

The **Auto Edge** checkbox allows you to hide unwanted edges that appeared as a result of the Boolean operation. You may not be satisfied with the result of this feature initially, but this doesn't matter because no edges will be visible in the final image.

Finally, you might need to eliminate a problem that is likely to appear. (At least, I encountered it.) I mean unsmoothed edges. Apply the **Smooth** modifier with parameters shown in Fig. 2.16, *b*. Don't confuse this with **MeshSmooth** and **TurboSmooth**!

Menu bar → **Modifiers** → **Mesh Editing** → **Smooth**

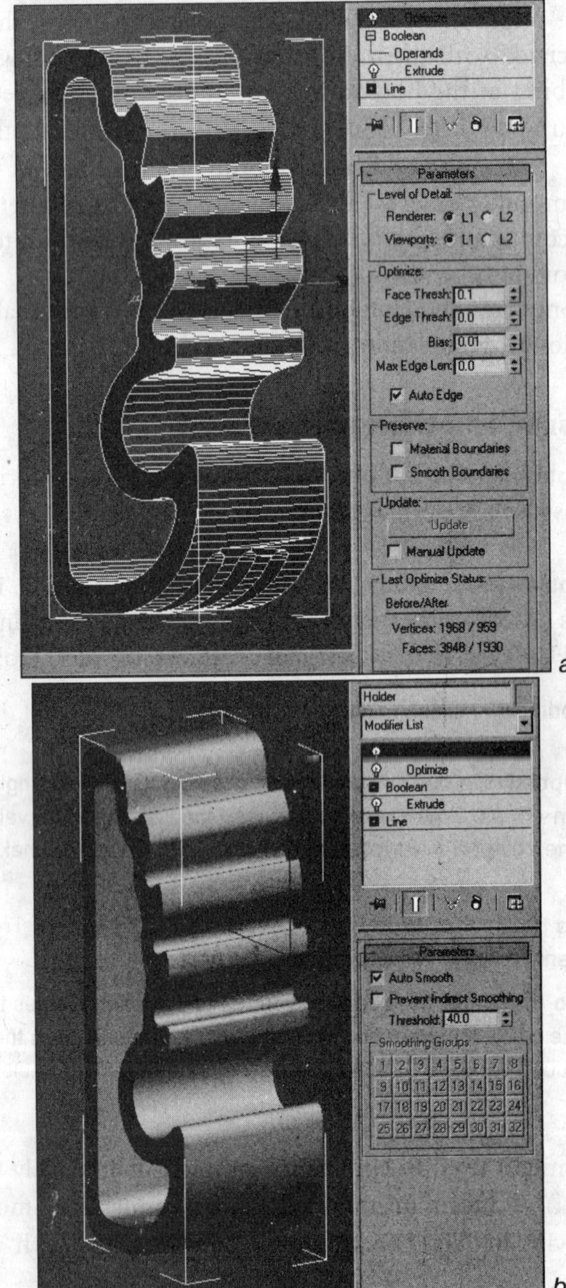

Fig. 2.17. Optimization (*a*) and smoothing (*b*) of the model

NOTE

This modifier doesn't change the geometry of a model. It just determines, which polygons will be smoothed relative to each other during rendering. The **Auto Smooth** checkbox checked and the **Threshold** parameter set to 40 degrees will give you the correct result. Save your work under the Model1-final.max name. My variant is in the Projects/Project1/ folder on the accompanying CD-ROM.

A Support Container for Stationery

This model was designed by Yulia Cherepneva supervised by Anna Zhiryakova and Valery Kuleshov. The model is simple, but quite interesting. A fragment of the draft project and the dimensions are shown in Fig. 2.18.

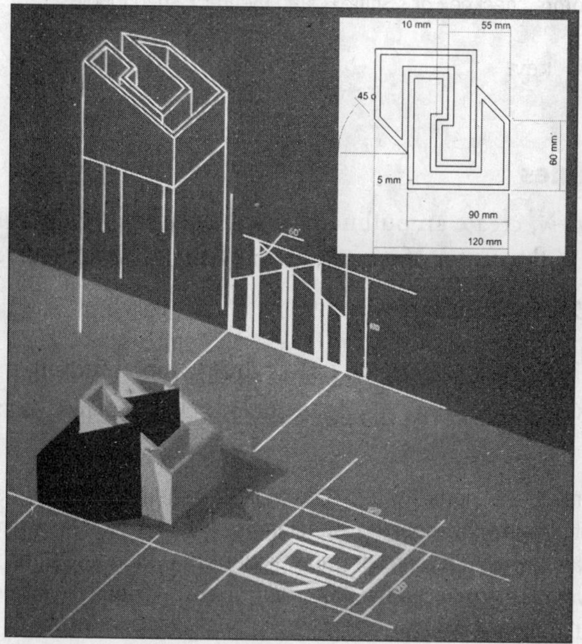

Fig. 2.18. A fragment of the draft project and the dimensions

Unlike with the previous project, here you need to take into account certain nuances necessary for a photorealistic image. In particular, you should cut chamfers on edges where necessary and show the clearance between the halves of the model. Otherwise, it would be difficult for a viewer to understand that the model consists of two parts.

- Set the system units to millimeters like in the previous project.

TIP

If you always use the same settings, you might like the following feature. Set 3ds Max as you need and save an empty scene under the Maxstart.max name in the 3DSMax7\Scenes folder. After that, every time you start 3ds Max and execute the **File → Reset** command, this file will be loaded.

❐ Set the grid spacing to 5 mm.

Home Grid User Grids
Grid Spacing: 5.0mm

Menu bar → **Customize → Grid and Snap Settings →** the **Home Grid** tab

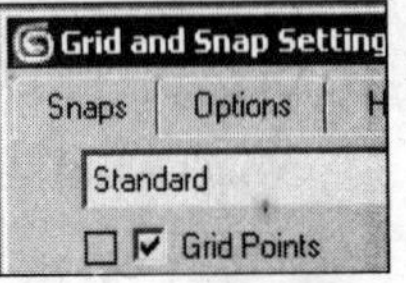

❐ Snap to the grid.

Menu bar → **Customize → Grid and Snap Settings →** the **Snaps** tab → set the **Grid Points** checkbox *or* <Shift>+Quad menu → snap toggles

Press the <S> key.

Creating Outlines

❐ In the top view, create an outline of one half of the model (Fig. 2.19, *a*). Start the broken line in the center of coordinates and move counter-clockwise.

Menu bar → **Create → Shapes → Line**

❐ Click with the left mouse button (don't drag) when building the broken line.

❐ End the broken line at the starting point and click **Yes** to close the outline.

IMPORTANT

Be careful: the home grid in 3ds Max is adaptive. When 3ds Max cannot display the set grid spacing, it switches to a greater one. You can identify the current grid spacing from the status bar. If the **Grid** value is much greater that you have specified, zoom the view in the viewport using the mouse wheel.

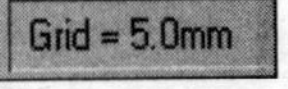

You don't like the 5-mm grid? Me neither. It would be best to create the outline on the 10-mm grid, then enter the Modify mode, set the grid spacing to 5 mm, and move the vertices to appropriate places.

If you accidentally drag the mouse pointer and create a Bezier vertex, don't worry and complete the outline. In the Modify mode, select all the vertices and select the **Corner** type in the pop-up menu.

Bezier Corner
Bezier
Corner
Smooth

Now, you are about to learn an interesting method that will allow you to edit both halves of the model simultaneously.

❒ Enter the top level of the object, that is, exit editing the sub-objects.

Quad menu → **Top Level** *or* repeatedly press the sub-object selection key (<1>, <2>, etc.)

❒ Create an instance of the model. To do this, move the model while keeping the <Shift> key pressed and select the **Clone Option** item in the **Instance** dialog box.

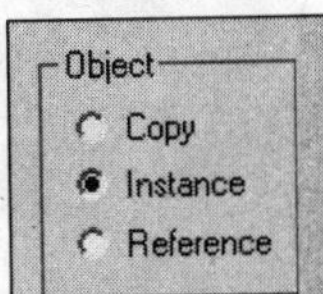

Now, these two objects are bound to each other; changing the geometry of one of them entails changes in the other. This fact is indicated in bold in the modifier stack. However, you can apply different materials to these objects.

❒ Rotate the obtained instance through 180 degrees and put it in the appropriate place as shown in Fig. 2.19, *b*.

TIP

To perform this as accurately as possible, select two snap toggles, **Grid Points** and **Vertex**, simultaneously. When moving the object, grab its vertex to snap to the grid.

Turn on the angle snap using the <A> key.

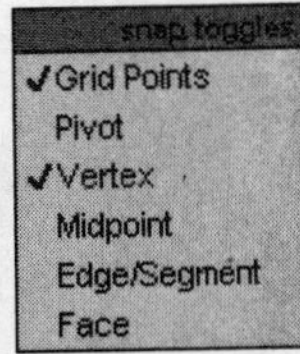

You might be tempted to cut chamfers at the moment using the **Chamfer** command. Don't rush to do this. Now, it is best to make the sides of the model thicker.

❒ In one of the halves, enter the Spline editing mode, select the spline, and create another outline 5 mm apart from the existing one. Do this with the **Outline** command.

Command panel → the **Geometry** rollout → enter "5"

IMPORTANT

If you prefer using spins, don't click the spin because an outline will appear very close to the original one. You should drag the spin. However, it is best to enter the value from the keyboard. If the second outline appears outside the first one, undo the command and enter the negative value.

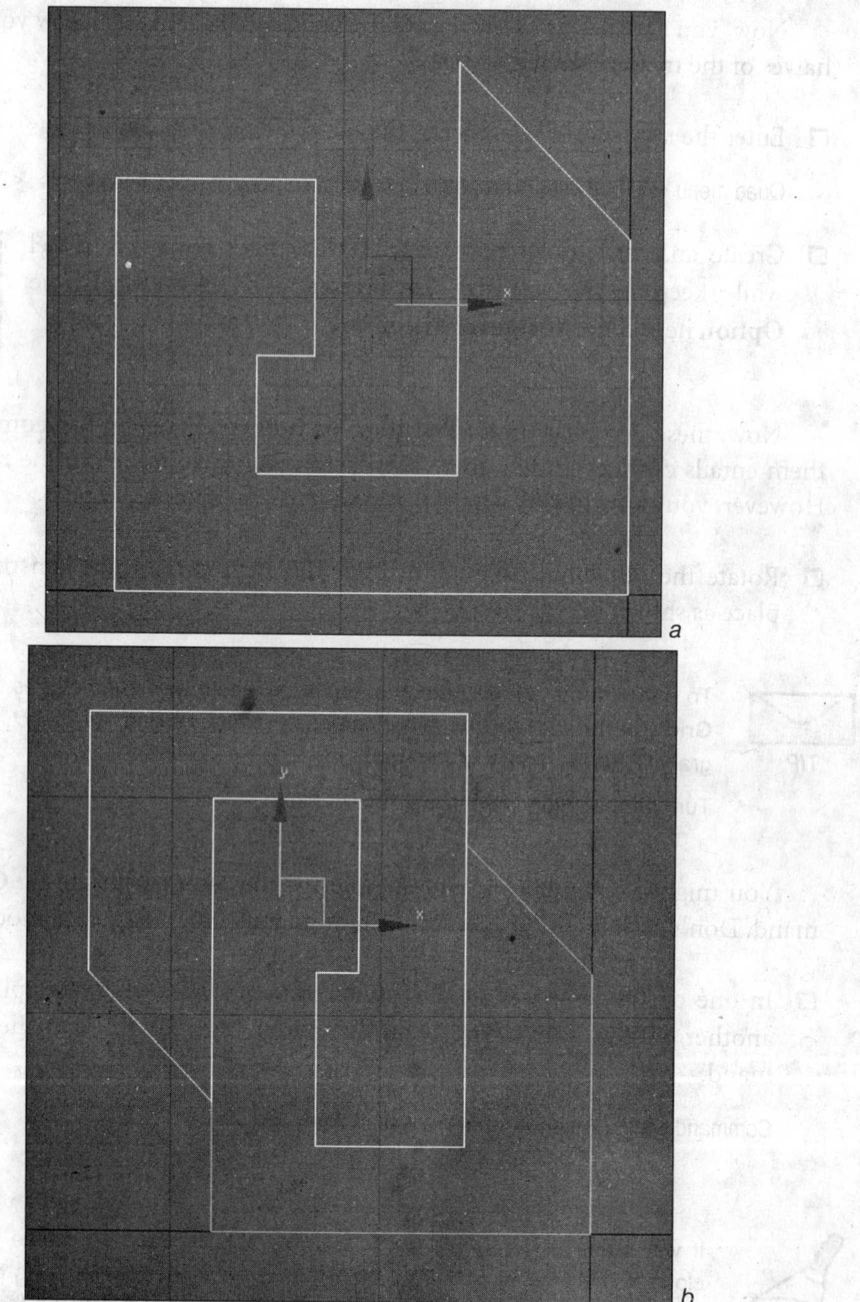

Fig. 2.19, ***a* and *b*.** Creating an outline

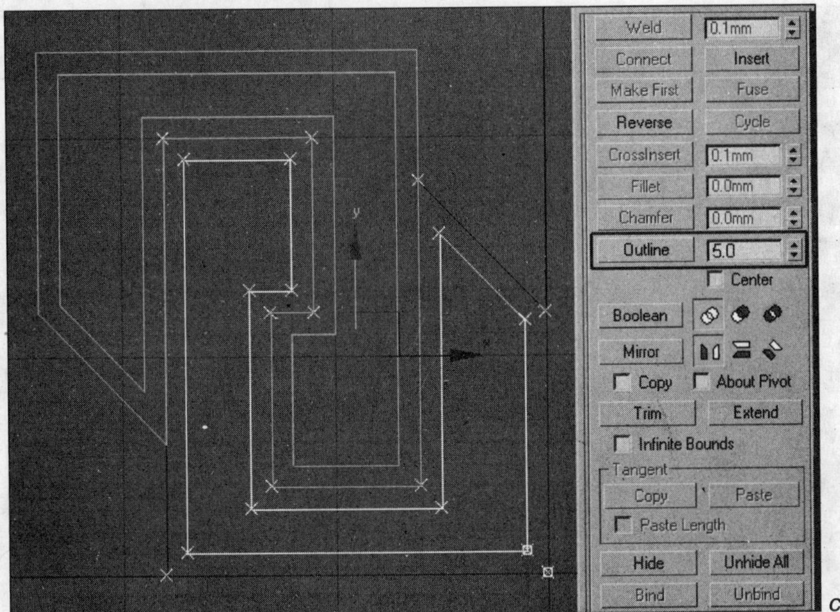

Fig. 2.19, *c*. Creating an outline

Remember, there should be a small clearance between the parts of the model. Select the outer outline (if it isn't selected) and enter a small value, 0.1 for example, into the input box.

- Select and delete the outer spline.

Now, you can use the **Extrude** modifier.

Creating 3D Geometry

- Apply the **Extrude** modifier and make the model a little higher than necessary (by 120 mm). Disable capping by unchecking the **Cap Start** and **Cap End** checkboxes (Fig. 2.20). I'll explain the reasons for this later.

  Menu bar → **Modifiers** → **Mesh Editing** → **Extrude**

- Apply the **Slice** modifier.

  Menu bar → **Modifiers** → **Parametric Deformers** → **Slice**

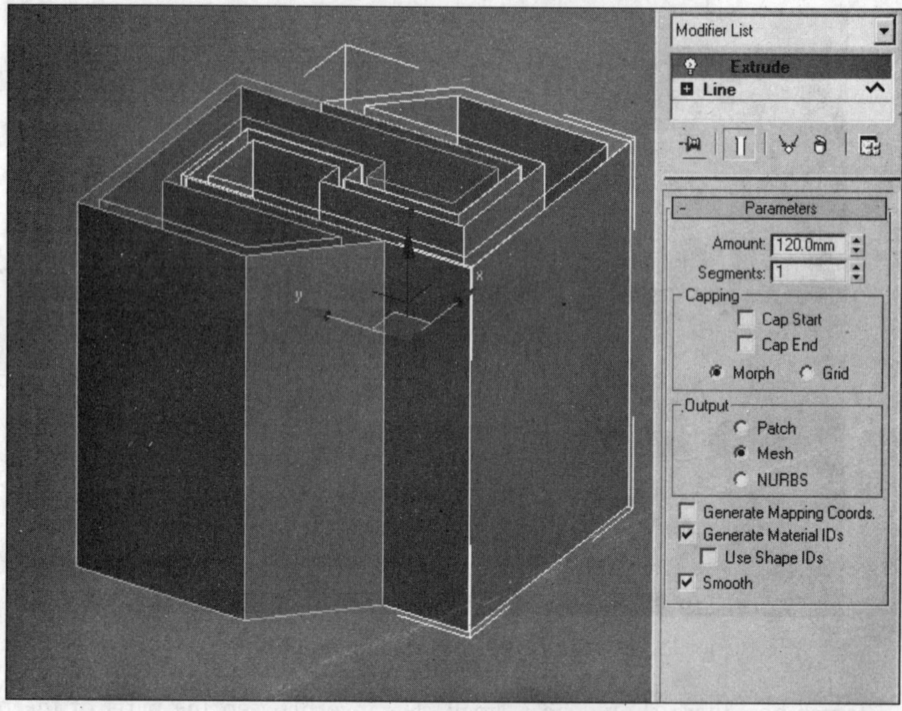

Fig. 2.20. The parameters of the **Extrude** modifier

- Enter the left view (with the <L> key) and select the **Slice Plane** sub-object of the **Slice** modifier.
- Move the sub-object vertically and rotate it through –30 degrees (turn on snap to angle).
- In the modifier's parameters, select the **Remove Top** radio button (Fig. 2.21, *a* and *b*).

Now, close up the holes and cut the chamfers. You can do this using the **Edit Poly** modifier.

- Apply the **Edit Poly** modifier.

Menu bar → **Modifiers** → **Mesh Editing** → **Edit Poly**

- Enter the mode for editing borders (the <3> key).
- Select two top borders and connect them using the **Bridge** command (Fig. 2.21).

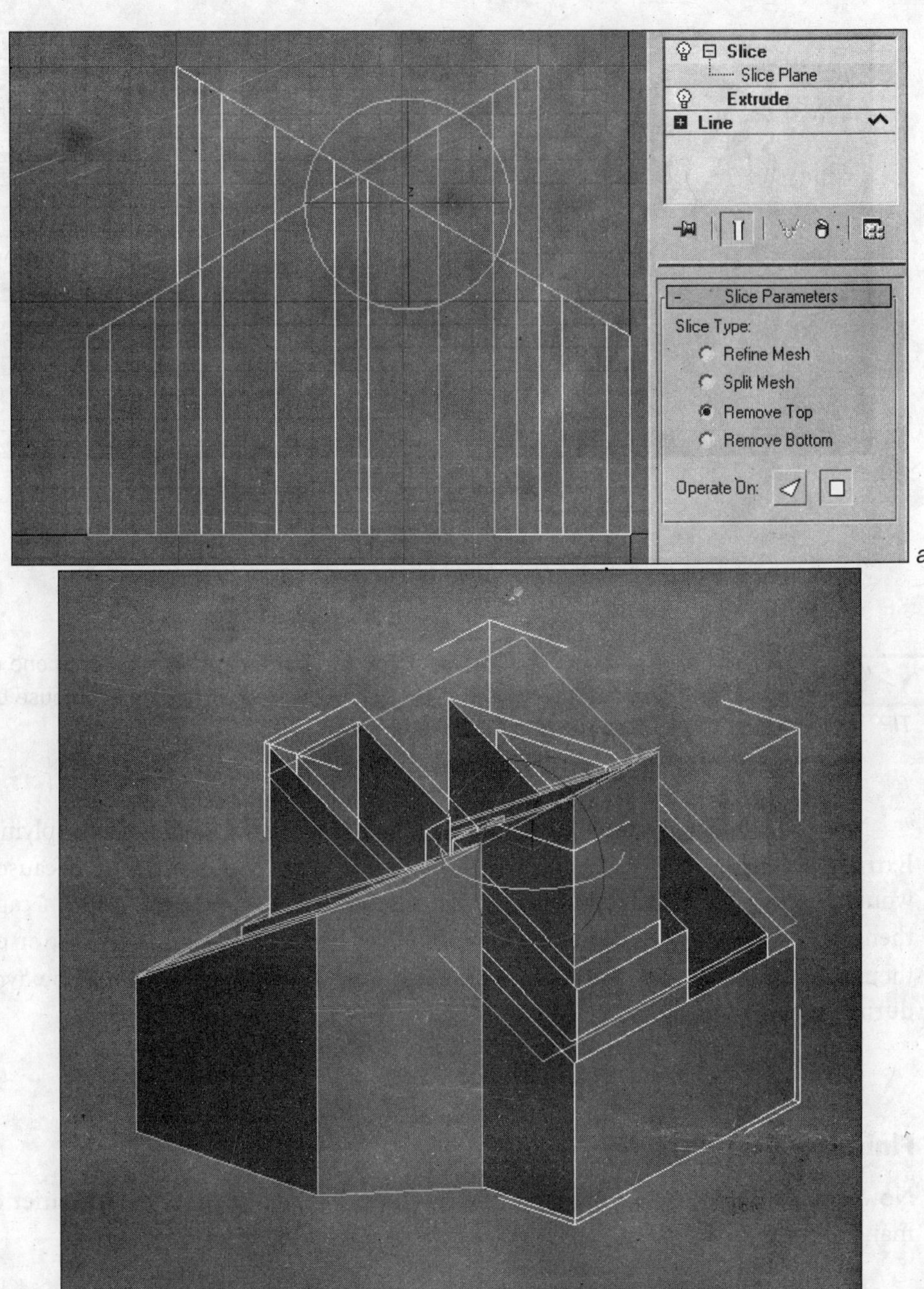

Fig. 2.21. Applying the **Slice** modifier

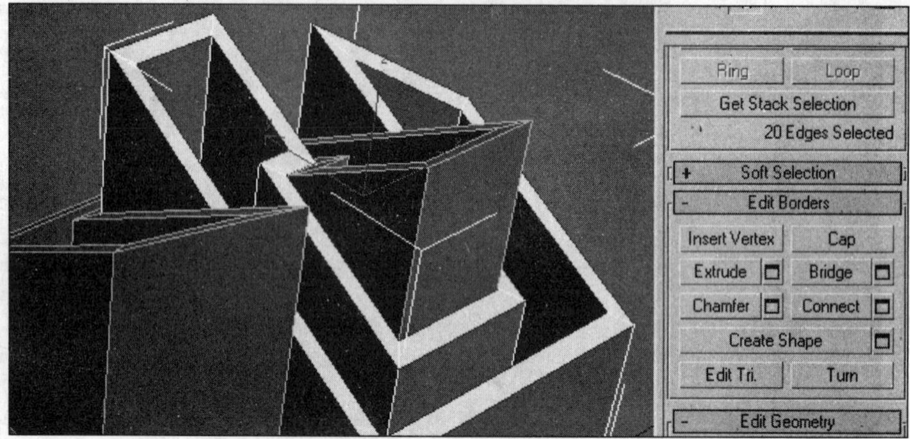

Fig. 2.22. Connecting edges

Repeat the procedure with the bottom borders.

TIP

You won't have to select the borders. Click the **Border** button, then click one of the borders, and drag the "rubber band" to the other while keeping the left mouse button pressed. Try to drag along the shortest distance.

Now, I should tell you why I advised you not to make caps when applying the **Extrude** modifier earlier. Regarding the top cap, you could make it because this wouldn't effect the editing. However, you would have to delete the bottom cap and then apply the **Bridge** command to obtain edges connecting angle vertices, or create them using the **Cut** tool. Polygons with such complicated shapes should be avoided during polygon editing.

Finishing the Geometry

Now, you only need to cut chamfers. Select all the edges and apply the **Chamfer** command to them.

- Enter the mode for editing edges (with the <2> key) and select all of them (using the <Ctrl>+<A> shortcut).

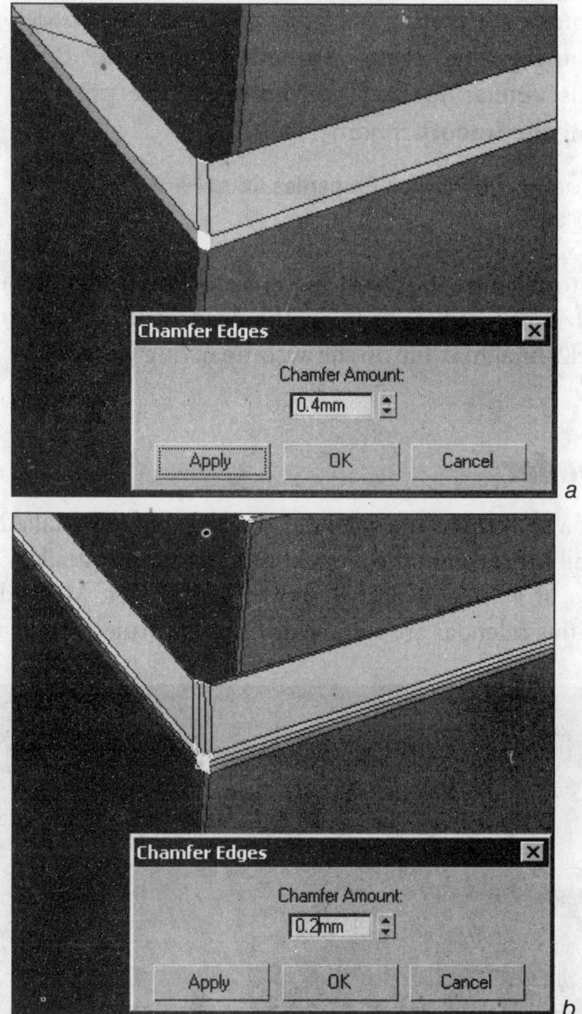

Fig. 2.23. Cutting chamfers

- Open the **Chamfer Edges** dialog box, enter 0.4 mm, and click the **Apply** button (Fig. 2.23, *a*).

  Quad menu → the **Chamfer Amount** input box

- Enter another value, 0.2 for example, and click the **OK** button (Fig. 2.23, *b*). Make sure there are no crossings because 3ds Max doesn't take care for them automatically.

- Enter the mode for editing polygons and make the model smoother using the **Auto Smooth** command. This operation is similar to that performed in the previous project using the **Smooth** modifier.

  Command panel → the **Polygon Properties** rollout → the **Smoothing Groups** buttons

Enter 20 into the input box next to the **Auto Smooth** button and click the button.

The model is finished. Save it on the hard disk. My variant is in the Projects\Project2\Model2-final.max file on the accompanying CD-ROM.

A Table-Calendar

This project of a souvenir table-calendar was developed by Lilia Morozovskaya supervised by Mikhail Morozov in the context of a term project called *"Creating a Corporate Style."* A photo of a "live" object is shown in Fig. 2.24. Methods for the creation of a 3D model of this calendar are suitable for similar projects such as a package.

Fig. 2.24. The table-calendar

Like the previous projects, this one is very simple. The main difference between them is that it has a particular map, which should be properly positioned on the surface of the model. You can achieve this using either of the following methods.

The first method involves creating individual parts of the model and assembling the model from them. You should take care of applying and setting map coordinates on the first stage.

The second method involves using a primitive, modifying it, and using the **Unwrap UVW** modifier to apply mapping coordinates.

I suggest you to try both methods so that you understand the advantages and disadvantages of each.

The First Stage. Variant 1

The image of the model was originally developed using CorelDRAW, and Lilia kindly provided me with all materials in this format. It wouldn't be wise if I ignored this fact because 3ds Max allows the users to import curves created in vector graphics applications.

First, you should prepare the file for import into 3ds Max. In an appropriate vector graphics application, delete excessive details, leaving only outlines. Set the line thickness to **Hairline** (in CorelDRAW) and remove all fillings (Fig. 2.25, *a*). Save the file in the format of Adobe Illustrator version AI88 (Fig. 2.25, *b*).

It would be good if the dimensions in the vector file were the same as in real life. Then you could avoid scaling the curves when importing into 3ds Max.

In 3ds Max, set the system units as in the previous project.

Import the Calendar.ai file located in the Projects\Project3 folder (on the accompanying CD-ROM or on your hard disk if you have copied the contents of the CD-ROM). You'll be asked two questions. Answer **Merge objects with current scene** and **Multiple Objects** (Fig. 2.26, *a* and *b*).

Menu bar → **File** → **Import**

Select the AI file type.

Your scene contains several objects, and you should assemble the model from them. However, don't rush to do this. It would be difficult at the moment. The pivot points of hexagonal caps and of each leaf are in their geometric centers and oriented in the same way. While it is all right for the hexagons, it isn't good for the leaves. If you try to rotate the leaves right now, you'll encounter a lot of problems. Therefore, you should delete all the leaves except one. This is the best way.

- ❒ Select all the leaves except one and delete them (Fig. 2.27, *a*).
- ❒ Select the snap to midpoints and turns it on (with the <S> key).

Menu bar → **Customize** → **Grid and Snap Settings** → the **Snaps** tab

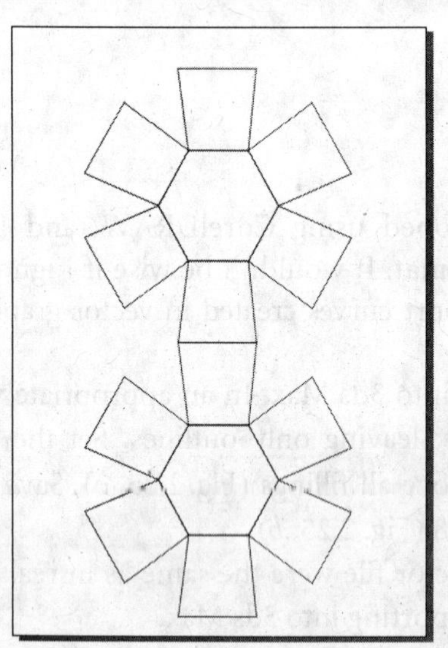

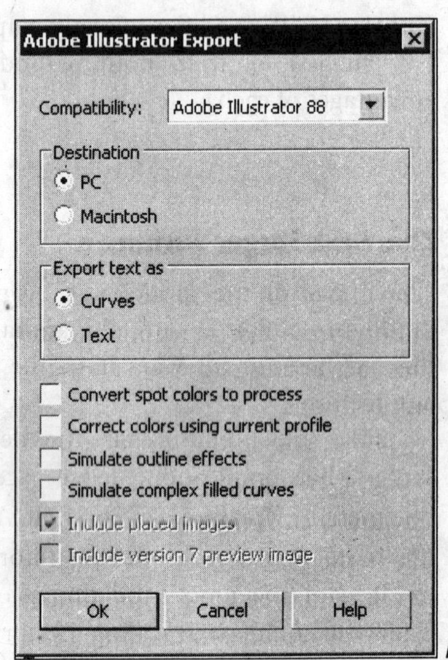

a *b*

Fig. 2.25. The vector file prepared for import into 3ds Max (*a*) and parameters for exporting in the AI format (*b*)

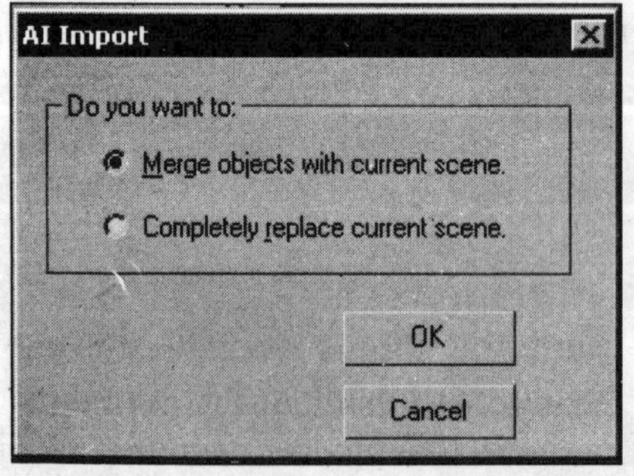

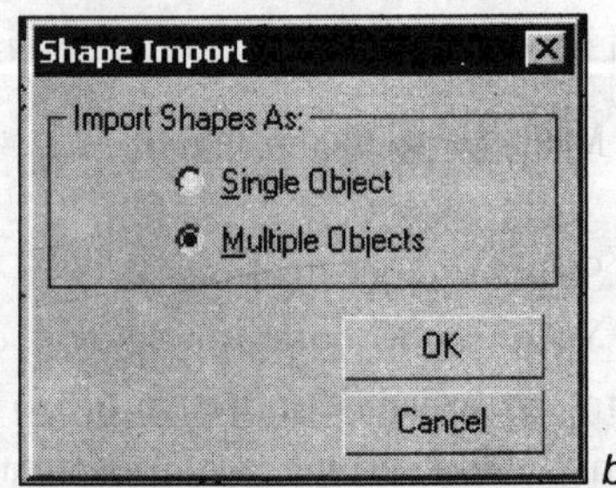

a *b*

Fig. 2.26. The import parameters

TIP

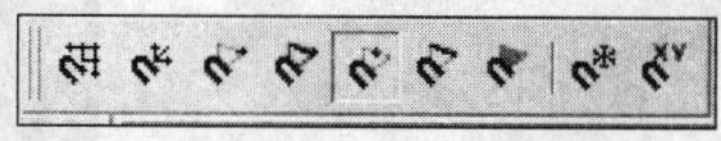

In 3ds Max 7, a new toolkit appeared. It is implemented as an individual toolbar, **Snaps**. I recommend that you drag it on the main toolbar. To do this, open all the floating toolbars (Menu bar → **Customize** → **Show UI** → **Show Floating Toolbars**), and drag the **Snaps** toolbar so that it sticks to the main toolbar. Hide the other floating command panels. Now, you can quickly toggle among the snaps.

- Select the leaf and select the **Hierarchy** toolbar in the main command panel.
- Click the **Affect Pivot Only** button. Large arrows indicating the position of the pivot point will appear in the viewport (Fig. 2.27, *b*).
- With the snap turned on, move the pivot point to the middle of the edge (Fig. 2.27, *c*). As you see, this isn't easy.
- Turn the snap off (with the <S> key). It is a good practice to do this when you don't need snaps because they often get in the way.
- Exit the pivot point mode. To do this, enter the Modify mode or release the **Affect Pivot Only** button.

Now, create copies of the leaf so that they are placed around the hexagon. To achieve this, select the hexagon's system of coordinates.

- Enter the Select and Rotate mode.

Menu bar → **Select and Rotate** or the <E> key

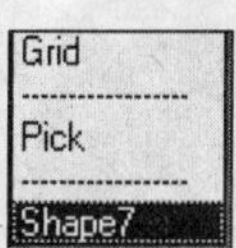

- In the menu bar, select the drop-down coordinate system menu, then the **Pick** item, and then click the hexagon. An object name (**Shape7** in this case) will appear in the coordinate system list.
- In the rotation center selection menu, select **Use Transform Coordinate Center**. Note that the rotate gizmo has moved to the center (more precisely, to the pivot point) of the **Shape7** object (Fig. 2.27, *d*).

- Turn on the angle snap (with the <A> key, or select **Angle Snap**). The default angle snap value is 5 degrees, which is alright.
- Press and hold the <Shift> key, grab the inside circle of the rotate gizmo, and rotate the leaf through 60 degrees.
- In the dialog box that appeared, enter 5 for the number of copies and click the **OK** button (Fig. 2.27, *e*).

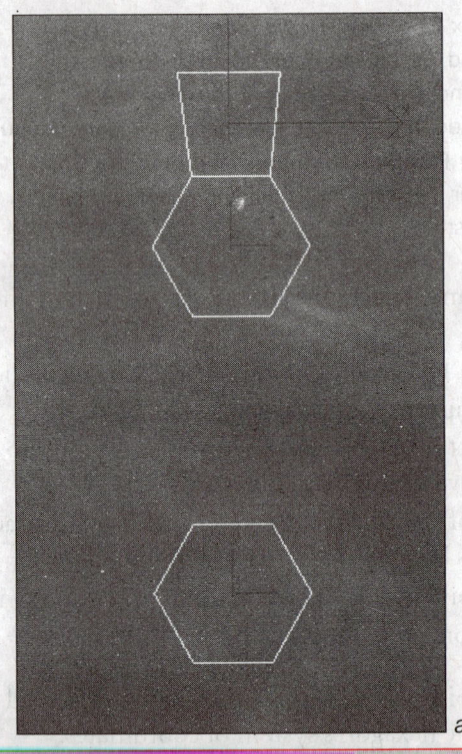

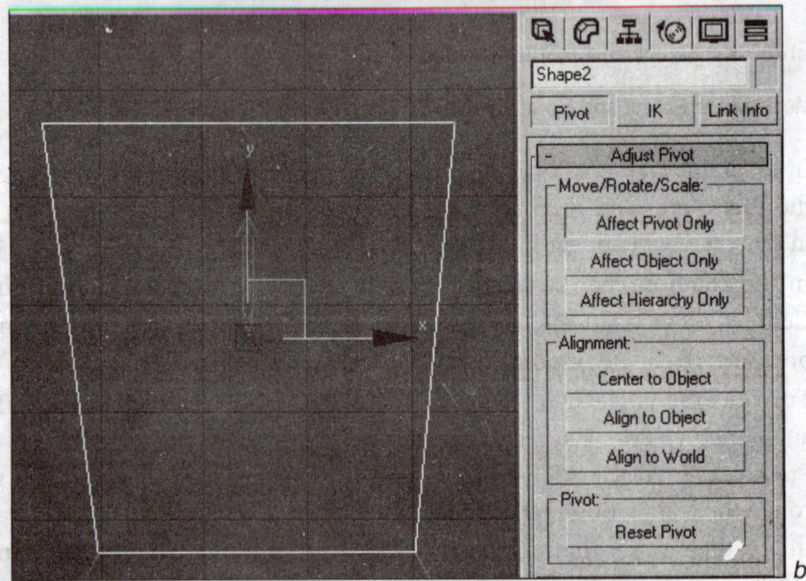

Fig. 2.27, *a* and *b*. Modeling the pattern

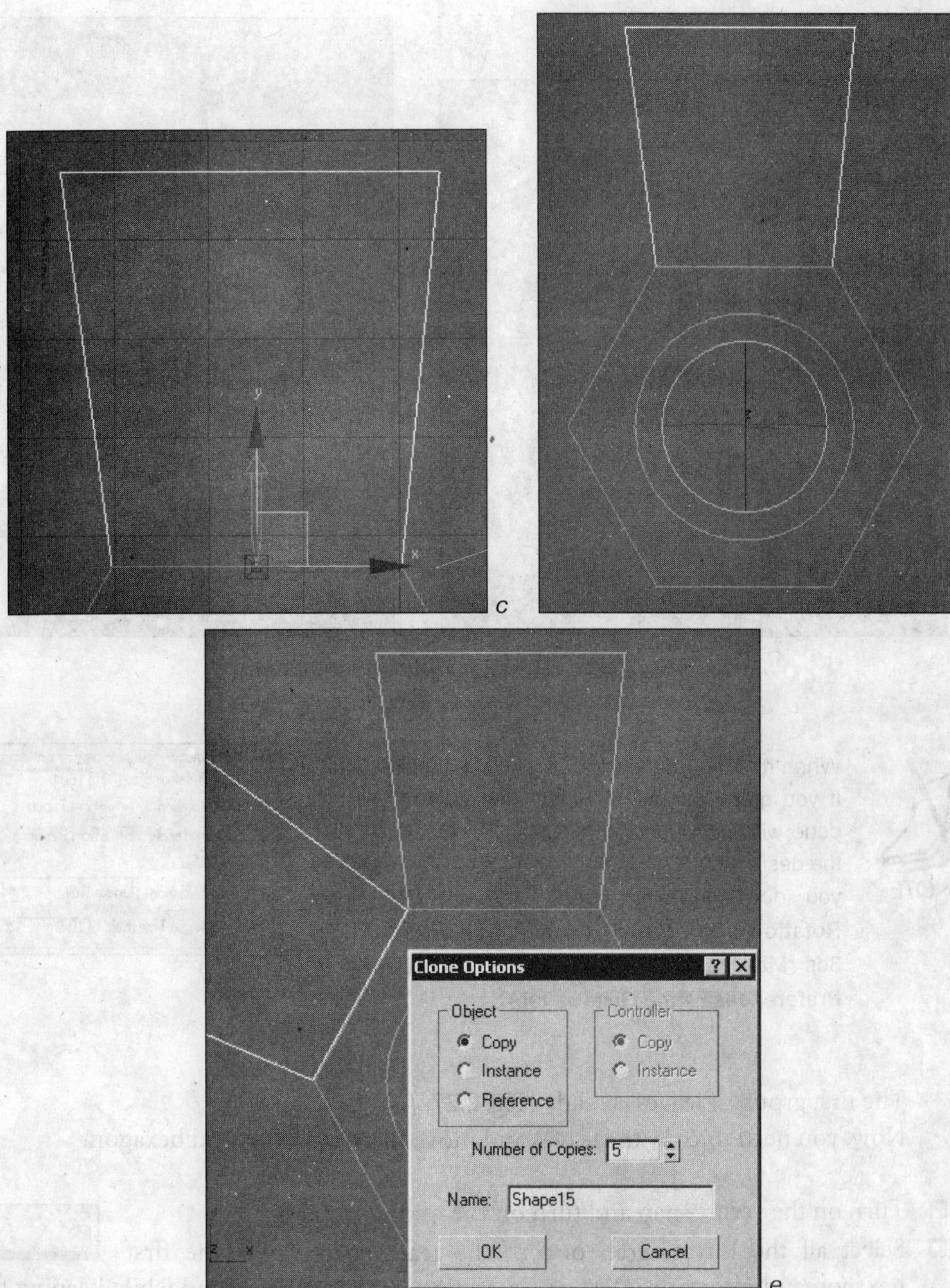

Fig. 2.27, *c–e*. Modeling the pattern

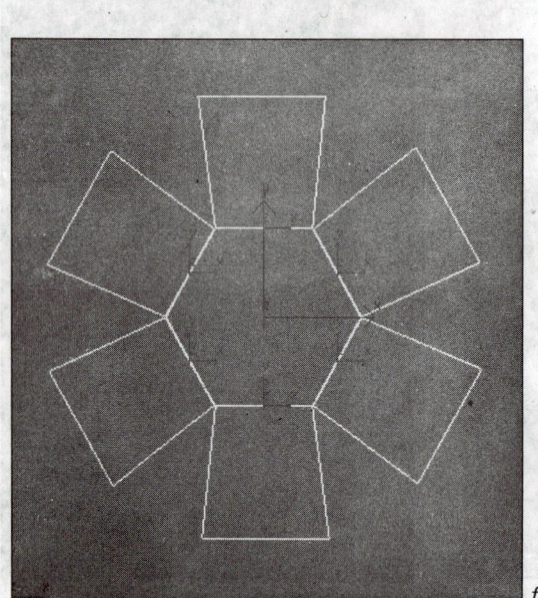

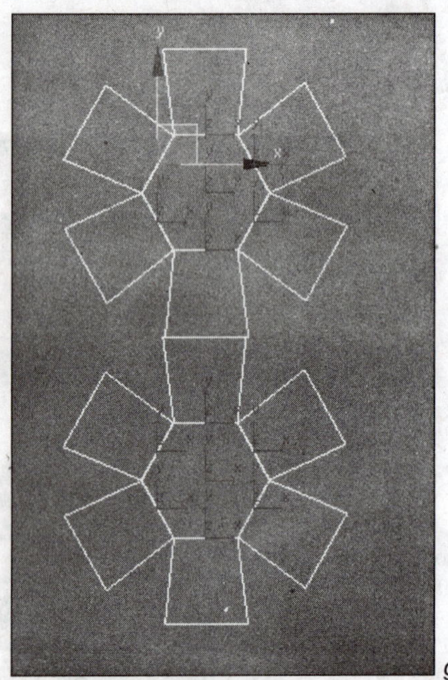

Fig. 2.27, *f* and *g*. Modeling the pattern

When rotating, make sure to grab the inside circle. If you grab the ball, the 3ds Max rotation will be done with unpredictable results. If you fail to click the desired place in the gizmo, turn off the features you don't currently need. Uncheck the **Free Rotation** and **Screen Handle** checkboxes in the 3ds Max settings (Menu bar → **Customize** → **Preferences** → the **Gizmos** tab).

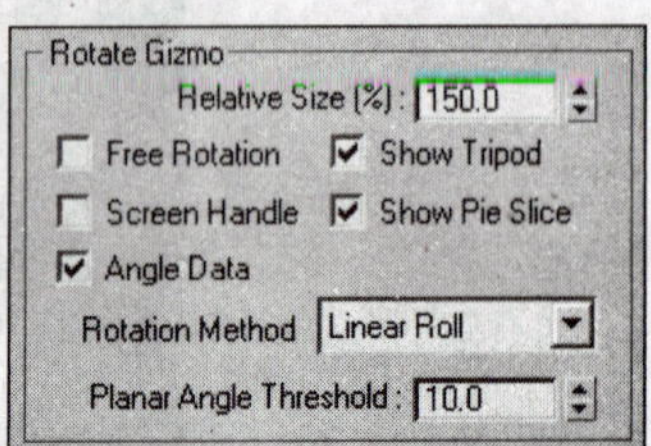

The first group of leaves is ready (Fig. 2.27, *f*).

Now, you need to copy the leaves and move them to the second hexagon.

- Turn on the vertex snap and turn off the midpoint snap.
- Select all the leaves, grab one of the leaf vertices near the first hexagon and move it to the corresponding vertex of the second while keeping the <Shift> key pressed (Fig. 2.27, *g*).

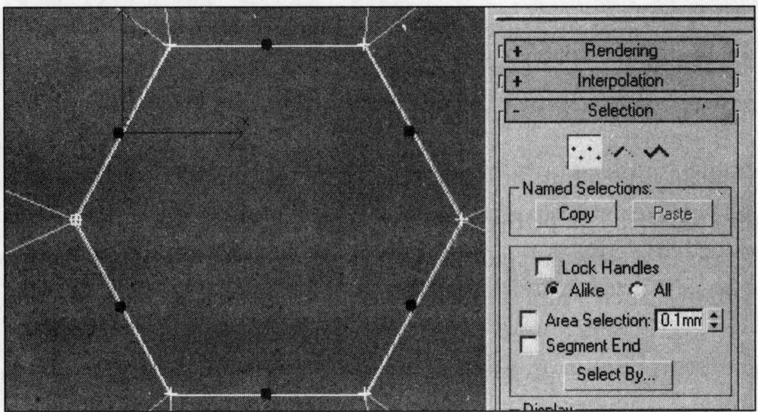

Fig. 2.28. The vertices to delete

The model is finished. A bit wry, in't it? Unfortunately, the original project isn't perfect. Don't worry, you'll make your model better a little later.

Look at the geometry. The hexagons have unnecessary vertices at the centers of the edges. Delete the vertices (Fig. 2.28).

You can proceed with the next stage.

Creating and Applying a Material

It's time to create a material, which will use the bitmap pattern as a map. You'll use the material later after you build another model using the second method.

I prepared two files that can be found in the Projects\Project3 folder. One of them, Calendar-big.tif, is quite large; in fact, its size is A4 with a 300-dpi resolution. You'll need it for rendering. However, it would be difficult to work with such a large image in the viewport because 3ds Max cannot correctly display images larger than 512 × 512 pixels. So I made a smaller file, Calendar-small.tif. You should work with it and substitute it with the first before rendering. Because the proprotions of the sides are the same in both files, the substitution won't be problematic.

Open the material editor (with the <M> key) and select an unused slot by clicking the ball.

Rename it to Calendar. It is a good practice to give objects and materials unique names when working with 3ds Max and other applications.

If you see the material editor for the first time, you might be astonished with the large number of buttons and settings. Because the developers of 3ds Max are aware of that most 3ds Max users don't need (or want) to set such a large number of parameters, they introduced a new material type, Architectural, starting with 3ds max 6.

In essence, it is a superstructure based on the Standard material that makes it easier to work with materials.

Change the material type from Standard to Architectural.

- Click the **Standard** button.
- In the **Material/Map Browser** window, double-click the **Architectural** line (Fig. 2.29, *a*). Thus you changed the material type from Standard to Architectural. The latter is much simpler than the first.

In the **Templates** drop-down list, select an appropriate preset, for example, **Paper** (Fig. 2.29, *b*). You'll be able to change the parameter later if you wish.

Apply the Calendar-small.tif file to the **Diffuse** channel as a map.

- Click the **None** button in the **Diffuse Map** line.
- In the material browser, select **Bitmap** and double-click it.

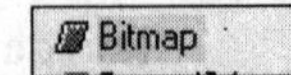

- Load the Calendar-small.tif as a map.

The material editor will work with this map. Don't change anything; the default settings are all right (Fig. 2.29, *c*).

Show the map in the viewport with the **Show Map in Viewport** button (Fig. 2.29, *c*, arrow 1 points to the button) and return to the material's parameters by clicking the **Go to Parent** button (pointed to by arrow 2). To return to editing the map, click the button with its name.

Sometimes, materials are rather complicated, so I advise you to use the **Material/Map Navigator**. It displays the structure of the selected material.

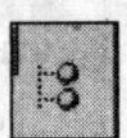

Select all the objects in the scene (with the <Ctrl>+<A> shortcut) and assign them the Calendar material by clicking the **Assign Material to Selection** button.

Nothing has happened! The material isn't displayed regardless of how many times you press the <F3> button that toggles between the shaded and wired display. This is normal, because all these objects are splines.

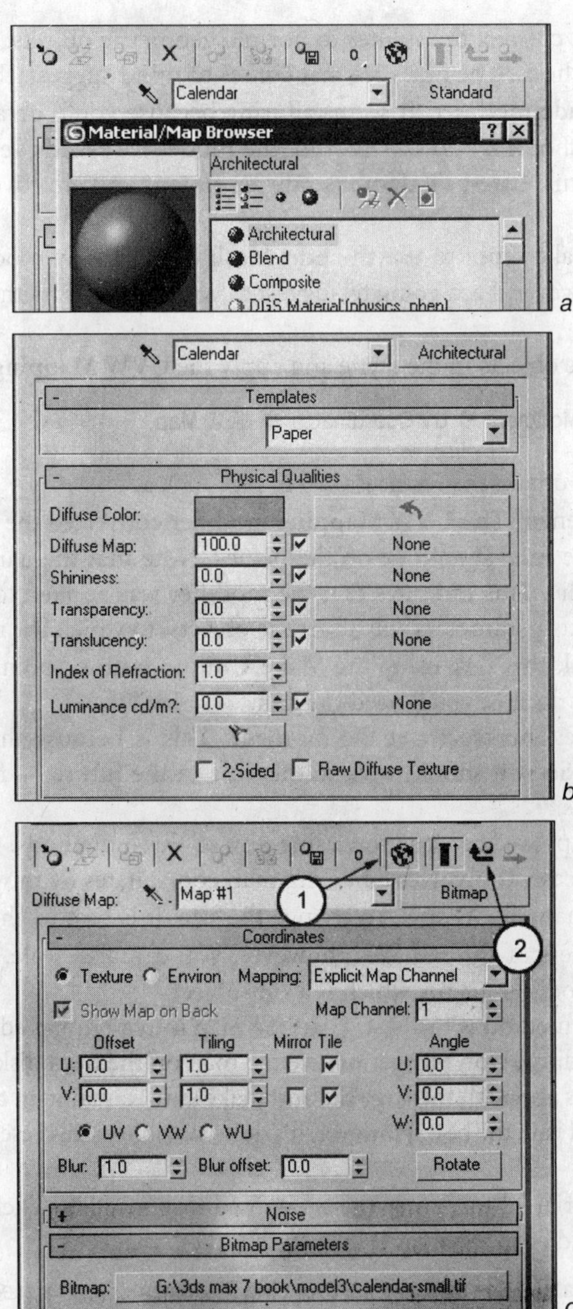

Fig. 2.29. The material for the calendar

You should convert the splines to normal geometric objects. This can be done using various methods. The first idea that comes to mind suggests that you extrude them using the **Extrude** modifier. It seems alluring because you'll obtain thickness at once. However, you shouldn't do this because the model isn't ready yet, and you would encounter problems. Later, I'll demonstrate an elegant and effective method for obtaining thickness.

It would make sense to use the **Edit Mesh** or **Edit Poly** modifier. Try this if you know now. However, I am going to suggest to you a quicker method.

❐ Select all the objects in the scene and apply the **UVW Mapping** modifier.

Menu bar → **Modifiers** → **UV Coordinates** → **UVW Map**

You should obtain the result shown in Fig. 2.30, a.

What happened? The **UVW Mapping** modifier converted the splines to planes and defined how the map should lie on the planes. Note that the name of the modifier is displayed in italic. This indicates that the modifier was applied to several objects, and any changes in its parameters will affect the objects, to which the modifier was applied. You could break this link using the **Make Unique** button (pointed to by an arrow). However, don't do this; you'll need the link.

The map lies incorrectly at the moment. This is because the original image has white margins. So you should stick to this rule in the future — for maps, use images without margins.

You can improve the situation using any of three methods. The first is the most difficult in this case. It involves adjusting map coordinates by moving the gizmo of the modifier and changing its size. To change the size, it is best to change the **Length** and **Width** parameters of the modifier; however, you can also scale. Remember to move and scale the modifier gizmo, which is a sub-object.

The second method is the best. Load the map into a bitmap editor and cut the margins using the editor. Don't forget to save the map on the hard disk and reapply it to the material. Do this also with the large file and make sure to maintain the proportions.

This method isn't the best. However, it's quite suitable in this case. Use 3ds Max tools.

❐ In the material editor, enter the bitmap editing mode by clicking the button with its name, and crop the map (Fig. 2.30, *b* and *c*).

The **Bitmap Parameters** rollout → the **Cropping Placement** group → check the **Apply** checkbox

Click the **View Image** button and crop the map while watching it in the viewport.

Because cropping is done in the relative coordinates, these settings will be kept after you substitute one file with the other.

Unfortunately, this method doesn't delete the white outlines. You might be wondering how they appeared. Remember, the bitmap image was obtained by exporting from CorelDRAW to a TIFF file, and you copied the leaves in 3ds Max. It is likely that the copied leaf is slightly asymmetric. Be aware of that inaccuracy will eventually entail problems.

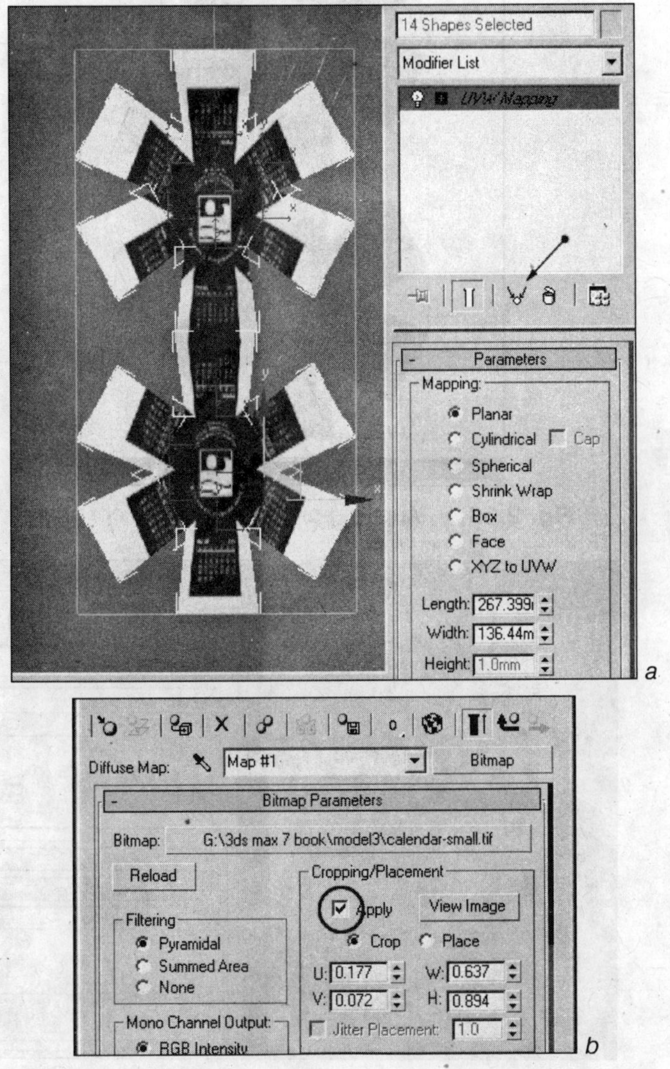

Fig. 2.30, *a* and *b*. Applying and editing map coordinates

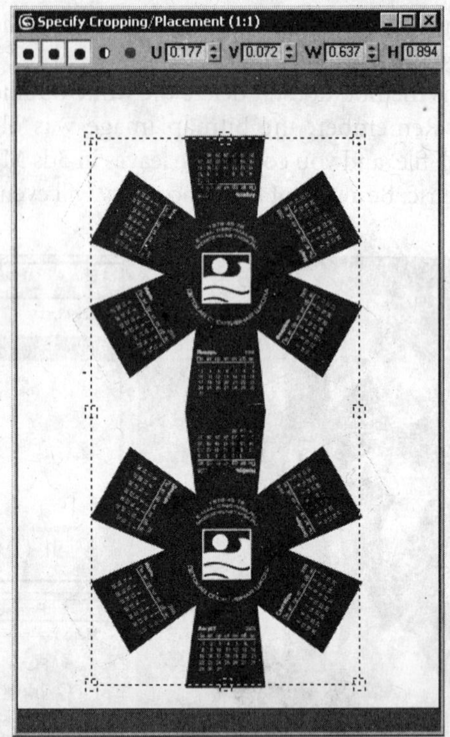

Fig. 2.30, c. Applying and editing map coordinates

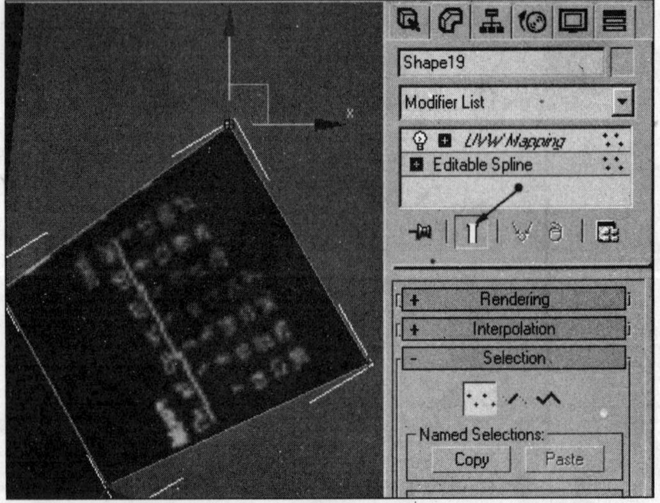

Fig. 2.31. Editing the leaf to delete the white outline

To get rid of the white segments, you can simply fill in the white background with the main color using a bitmap editor. Alternatively, you can use the following method.

- ❐ Select the leaf that caused the problem.
- ❐ Jump down the stack to edit the original outline and move the vertices slightly to eliminate the white line (Fig. 2.31). Make sure to turn on displaying the result in the stack with the **Show end result on/off toggle** button (pointed to by an arrow).

Repeat the procedure with other leaves if necessary.

TIP

To display maps in the viewport with the best quality, make the following settings: Menu bar → **Customize** → **Preferences** → the **ViewPorts** tab → the **Configure Driver** button. Despite this, you may be dissatisfied with the quality of maps in the viewport, so perform test rendering from time to time (with the <Shift>+<Q> shortcut). Now, you can make a 3D model from the pattern.

TIP

It would be most convenient to proceed with modeling in the perspective viewport or the orthogonal viewport. For the latter, rotate the view in any viewport using the following combination: the <Alt> key + <middle mouse button>.

TIP

To rotate a view in the viewport about a selected object, click and hold the **Arc Rotate** button in the viewport navigation bar. In the bar of buttons that will appear, select the lowest, **Arc Rotate SubObject**.

- ❐ Select the top cap and the top leaves and move them a little above the home grid (Fig. 2.32, *a*).
- ❐ Select the top leaves.
- ❐ Enter the mode that rotates objects in the local coordinate system about the pivot points with the angle snap on. Simply stated, do the following:

Menu bar → **Select and Rotate** (or press the <E> key)

Menu bar → select **Local** in the drop-down list of coordinate systems

Menu bar → select **Use Pivot Point Center** in the button bar to the right of the coordinate system list

Menu bar → turn on the angle snap (with the <A> key)

Rotate all the leaves through 60 degrees (Fig. 2.32, *b*). Ignore the gizmos of the **UVW Mapping** modifier. You'll get rid of them soon.

Select the bottom cap and the bottom leaves and rotate them through 180 degrees (Fig. 2.32, *c*).

Menu bar → select **View** in the drop-down list of coordinate systems

Menu bar → select **Use Selection Center** in the button bar to the right of the coordinate system list

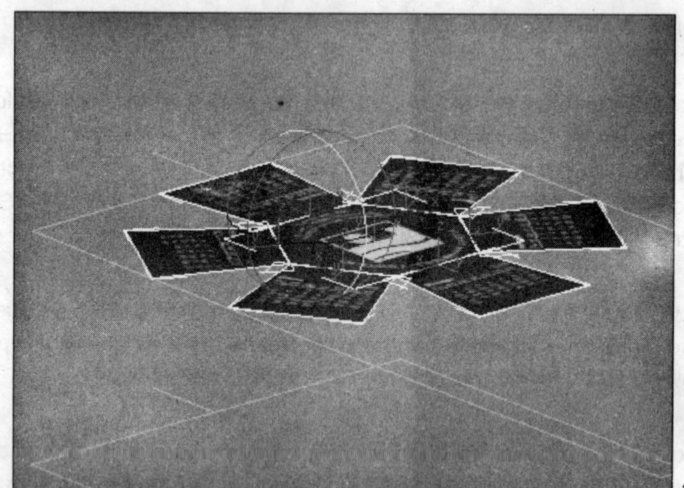

a

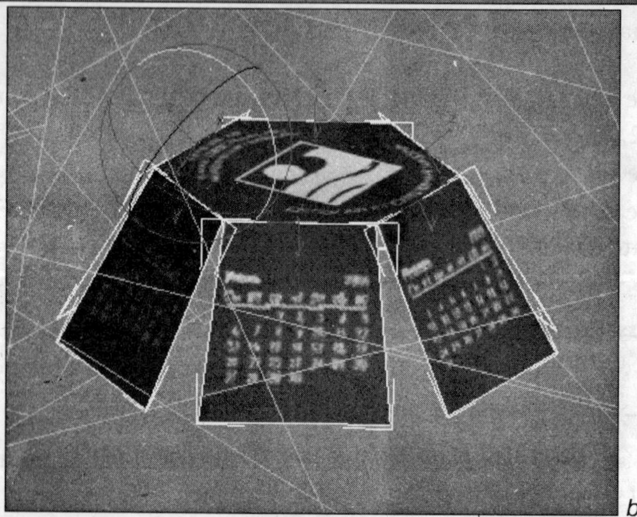

b

Fig. 2.32, *a* and *b*. The first stage (variant 1)

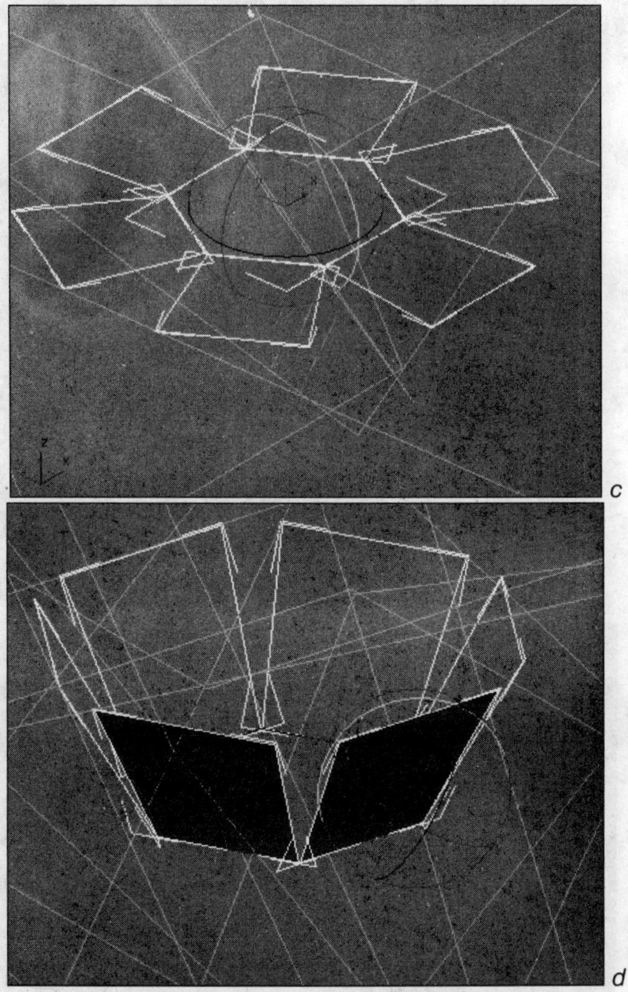

Fig. 2.32, *c* and *d*. The first stage (variant 1)

- Rotate the lower leaves through 60 degrees in the local coordinate system about the pivot points (Fig. 2.32, *d*).

You might encounter problems when selecting the desired objects. The surfaces are considered one-sided, and 3ds Max doesn't allow you to select them from the other side. Rotate the view in the viewport, feel free to look at them from below.

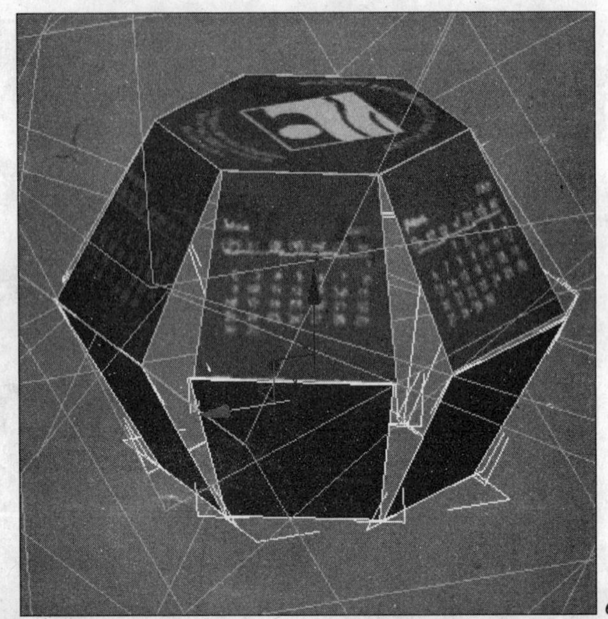

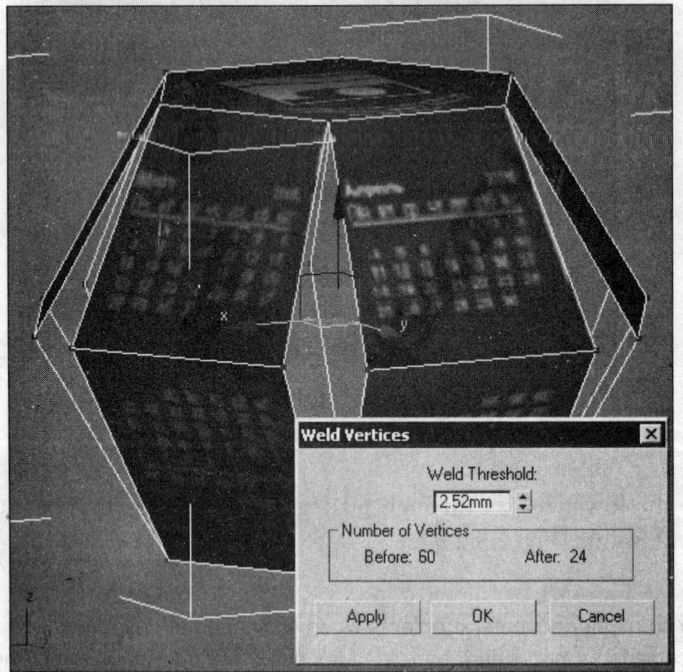

Fig. 2.32, *e* and *f*. The first stage (variant 1)

- Select all the objects of the top part (or the bottom one if you like), turn on the 3D snap to vertices, grab the angle vertex of any leaf and move all the objects to the corresponding leaf on the other part (Fig. 2.32, *e*).

Menu bar → **Select and Move** (or press the <W> key)

Menu bar → select **View** in the drop-down list of coordinate systems

Menu bar → turn on the snaps (with the <S> key)

The **Snaps** toolbar→ click the **Snap To Vertex Toggle** button (if you have made this toolbar visible; otherwise, open the **Grid and Snaps Settings** dialog box, check the **Vertex** checkbox on the **Snaps** tab, and uncheck the other checkboxes).

- Select any object (it would be best to select the bottom cap), convert it to the editable polygon type, and attach the other objects to it.

Quad menu → **Convert to** → **Convert to Editable Poly**

Quad menu → the "window" icon in the Attach line

In the dialog box that will open, select all the objects and click **Attach**.

You might be wondering why the bottom cap is the best. Its pivot point is positioned and oriented in the best way.

So you obtained one object consisting of multiple elements. To make this a complete entity, you need to weld appropriate vertices.

- Enter the vertex editing mode (with the <1> key) and select all the vertices (with the <Ctrl>+<A> shortcut).
- Weld the vertices by increasing the **Weld Threshold** parameter in the **Weld** setting window (Fig. 2.32, *f*).

Quad menu → the icon in the **Weld** line

This stage of modeling is now completed. The second stage is described later.

Save the scene. My variant is saved in the Projects\Project 3\Model3-02(var1).max file on the accompanying CD-ROM.

The First Stage. Variant 2

The previous variant would be the best if you used 3ds max version 3 or earlier. If you intended to animate the model, the previous variant would also be suitable. However, currently you're using the latest 3ds Max version, and you don't need animation, so I suggest to you another method, advanced and fast.

- Delete everything you have, leaving only the material because you'll need it. To do this quickly, simply create a new scene. The contents of the material editor won't change.

  Menu bar → **File** → **New** → **New All**

  Import the Calendar.ai file like in the previous variant.
  Select one leaf as shown in Fig. 2.33 and measure it using the **Measure** utility.

  Command panel → the **Utilities** bar → **Measure**

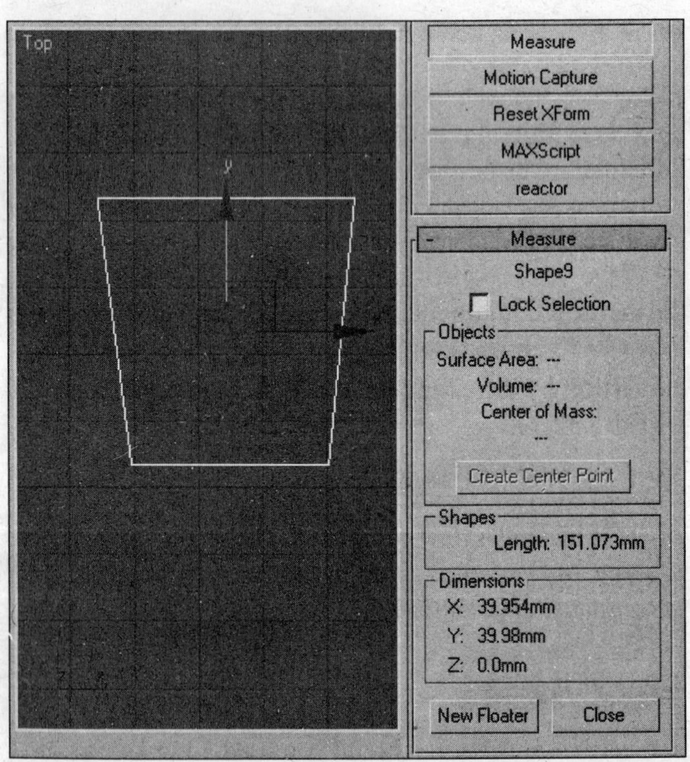

Fig. 2.33. Measuring the leaf

You can ignore the fractional parts. So the size of the leaf is 40 × 40 mm based on the greatest side.

❑ Delete all the caps except one. This will be the base.

❑ In the Modify mode, select and delete unnecessary vertices (Fig. 2.34, *a*).

❑ Use the **Bevel** modifier. Note that this modifier is missing from the menu bar, so you should look for it in the modifier list.

Shape14
PatchDeform (WSM)
PathDeform (WSM)
Point Cache (WSM)
Subdivide (WSM)
Surface Mapper (WSM)
SurfDeform (WSM)
OBJECT-SPACE MODIFIE
Affect Region
Attribute Holder
Bend
Bevel

Command panel → Modifier list → **Bevel**

This modifier is an extended version of the **Extrude** modifier. Not only can you extrude a spline using this modifier, but you also can specify bevels. All values are set in the **Bevel Values** rollout. You only need to know these values, so try to remember the school-level geometry (Fig. 2.34, *b*).

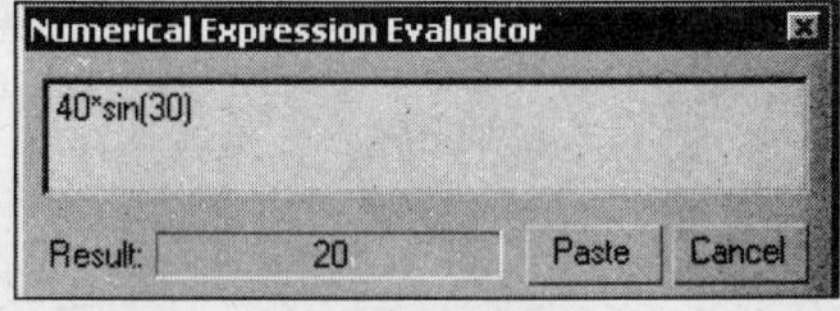

Using these considerations and the built-in calculator (which is opened with the <Ctrl>+<N> shortcut when the cursor is in the input box), you can obtain the necessary values for the **Bevel** modifier (Fig. 2.34, *c*).

Convert the model to the editable polygon type.

Quad menu → **Convert to** → **Convert to Editable Poly**

❑ Switch to the top view in the viewport.

❑ Move the model to the origin of coordinates. It would be convenient to do this by entering the move mode and typing zeroes in the input boxes.

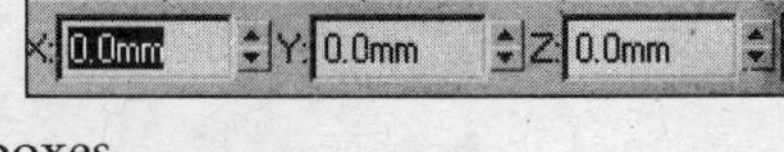

❑ Show the home grid if it isn't displayed (with the <G> key).

❑ Enter the vertex editing mode (with the <1> key) and select the vertices circularly (Fig. 2.34, *d*).

❑ Apply the **Chamfer** command to the vertices to obtain edges 40 mm long (Fig. 2.34, *e*). Unfortunately, you'll have to control this by eye, using the grid (the grid spacing is 10 mm).

Quad menu → **Chamfer**

Grab the vertex and drag it upwards or to the right.

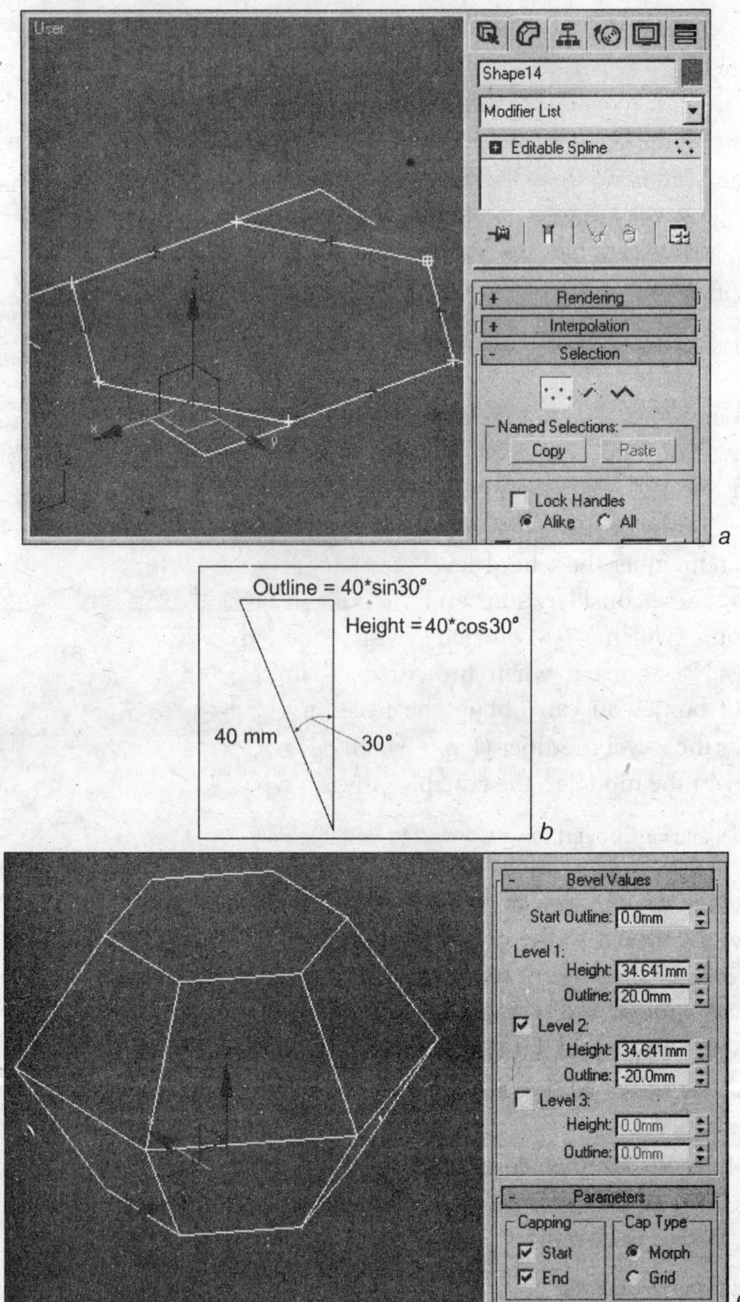

Fig. 2.34, *a–c*. Modeling the calendar, stage 1, variant 2

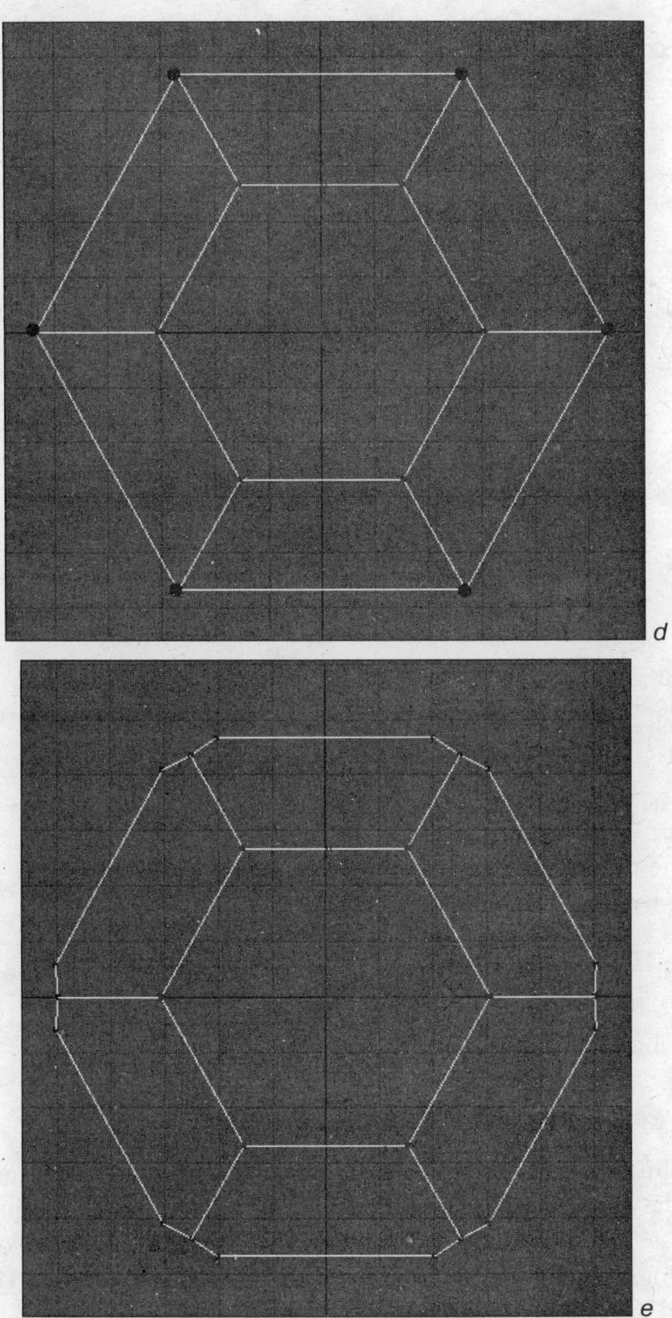

Fig. 2.34, *d* and *e*. Modeling the calendar, stage 1, variant 2

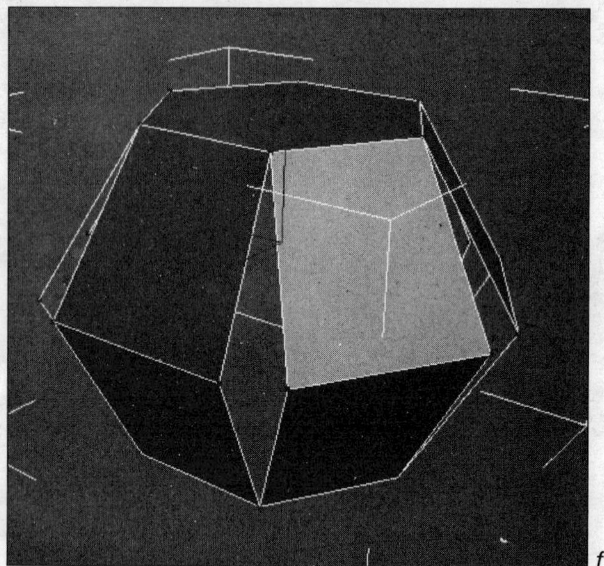

Fig. 2.34, *f*. Modeling the calendar, stage 1, variant 2

- Select the resulting polygons (with the <4> key) and delete them.
- Using the **Target Weld** command for vertices, weld the vertices to obtain the final result for the current stage (Fig. 2.34, *f*).

Quad menu → **Target Weld**

Grab the appropriate vertex and drag the rubber band to the vertex, to which you need to weld the first vertex.

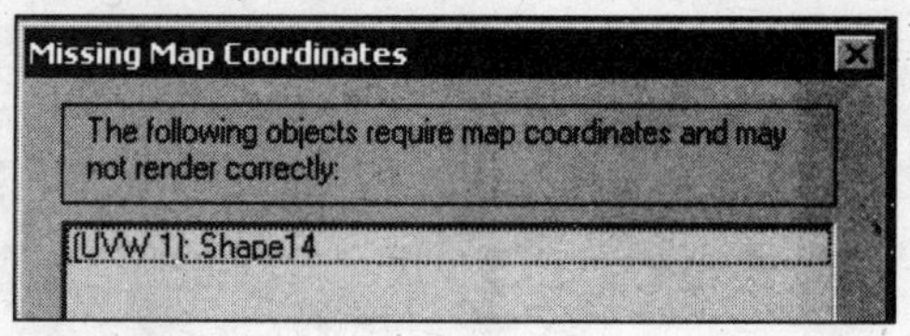

Missing Map Coordinates

The following objects require map coordinates and may not render correctly:

(UVW 1): Shape14

My variant is kept in the Projects\Project3\Model3-01(var2).max file on the accompanying CD-ROM.

Applying and Editing the Map Coordinates

Like in the first variant, it is best to apply the map coordinates right now.

Open the material editor and find the Calendar material. Assign it to the object. You won't see any map in the viewport, or you'll see it distorted. If you try to perform test rendering, you may get an error message informing you that no UVW coordinates are assigned to the object, and 3ds Max doesn't know how it should position the map over the object.

If the map and the object were simpler, you could use the classic combination of the **Poly Select** and **UVW Mapping** modifiers. By the way, you'll use this method for mapping walls in *Chapter 3*. However, in this case that method would be too complicated and tedious, so use another one that involves the **Unwrap UVW** modifier.

Exit the sub-object editing mode. The **Editable Poly** line in the stack should be unhighlighted or highlighted with gray, but not with yellow because you need to apply the modifier to the entire object. Almost all 3ds Max modifier, including **Unwrap UVW**, can be applied to a part of an object. The worst situation is where the object is in the sub-object editing mode, but no sub-object is selected. Then the modifier won't work at all.

To avoid problems when editing the map coordinates, proceed as follows. Remember, you simplified your task in the first variant by using the **Crop** feature in the mapping parameters. The **Unwrap UVW** modifier doesn't "like" this, so you should uncheck the **Apply** checkbox in the **Cropping/Placement** group among the mapping parameters of the map applied to the **Diffuse** channel of the Calendar material.

The second thing you should do relates to the map. This modifier is optimized for work with square images because 3ds Max is used for the creation of computer games. Generally speaking, you don't have to use a square map, but it is much more difficult to edit rectangular maps. This is why I prepared two maps with the "-square" suffix by widening the image so that it becomes square. In the material editor, substitute the CALENDAR-SMALL.TIF map with CALENDAR-SMALL-SQUARE.TIF.

- ❒ Use the **Unwrap UVW** modifier.

  Menu bar → **Modifiers** → **UV Coordinates** → **Unwrap UVW**

  In the viewport, you'll see the map applied to the object (Fig. 2.35, *a*).

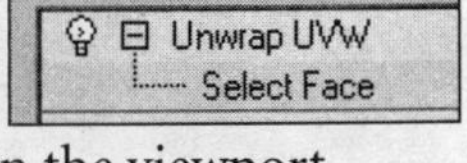

- ❒ Enter the mode for editing the **Select Face** sub-object (which is the modifier's only only sub-object). You need this mode to see, which polygon is selected in the map editor in the viewport.
- ❒ Open the map coordinate editor by clicking the **Edit** button. Be assured you'll get accustomed soon, especially if you are familiar with a vector graphics application because the tools are similar.

  Before you start editing the map coordinates, make a few settings.

- ❒ Open the Options panel with the button with the same name and set the checkboxes as follows.

- Check the **Use Custom Bitmap Size** checkbox and set the size to 512 × 512. This will improve the display quality of the map in the editor's window.
- Uncheck the **Tile Bitmap** checkbox. You don't need it, and it only gets in the way.
- If the map isn't bright enough, increase the **Brightness** value.
- Check the **Constant Update** and **Highlights Selected Verts** checkboxes. They will allow you to watch the changes in the viewport.

Close the Options panel and start editing the map coordinates.

TIP

If the selected polygons are colored with red in the viewport, and this impedes you so that you don't see the map well, disable the highlight of the selected polygons (with the <F2> key).

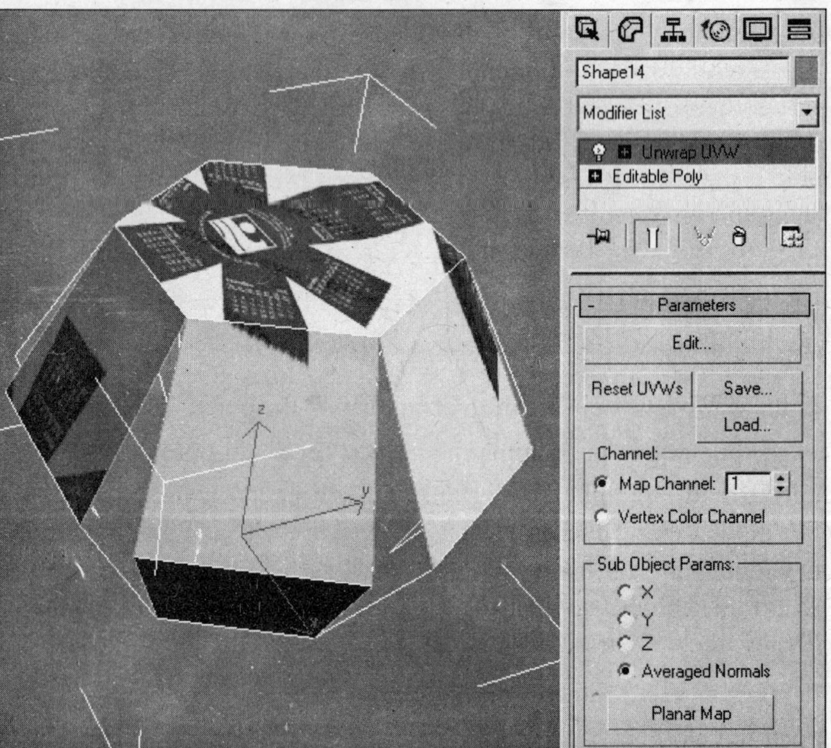

Fig. 2.35, *a*. Editing the map coordinates using the **Unwrap UVW** modifier (stage 1)

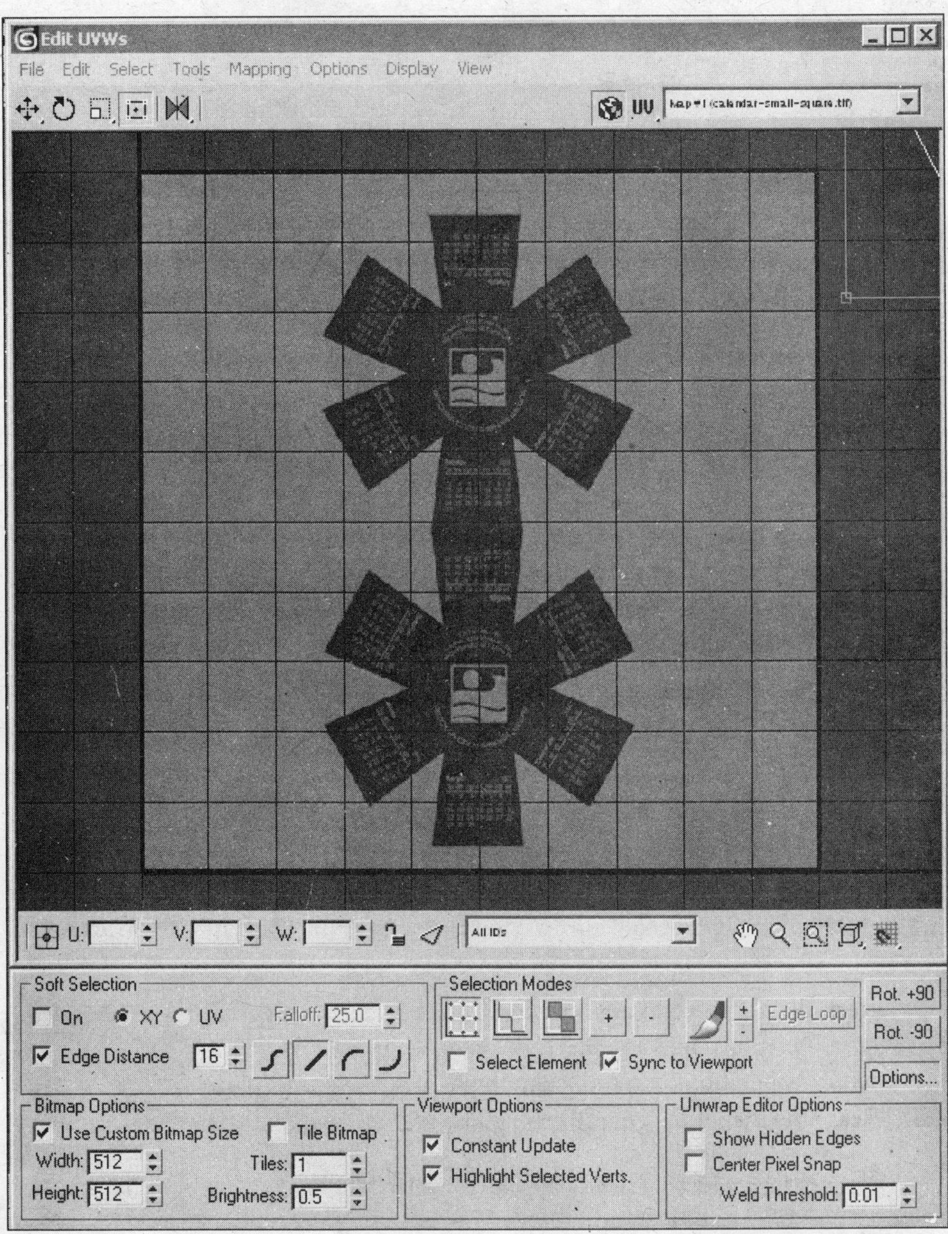

Fig. 2.35, *b*. Editing the map coordinates using the **Unwrap UVW** modifier (stage 1)

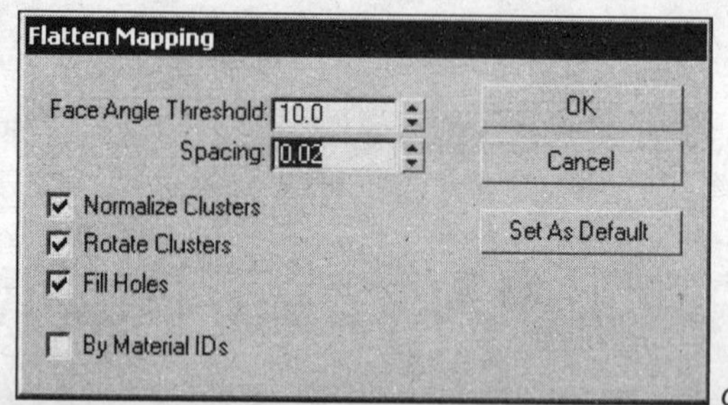

c

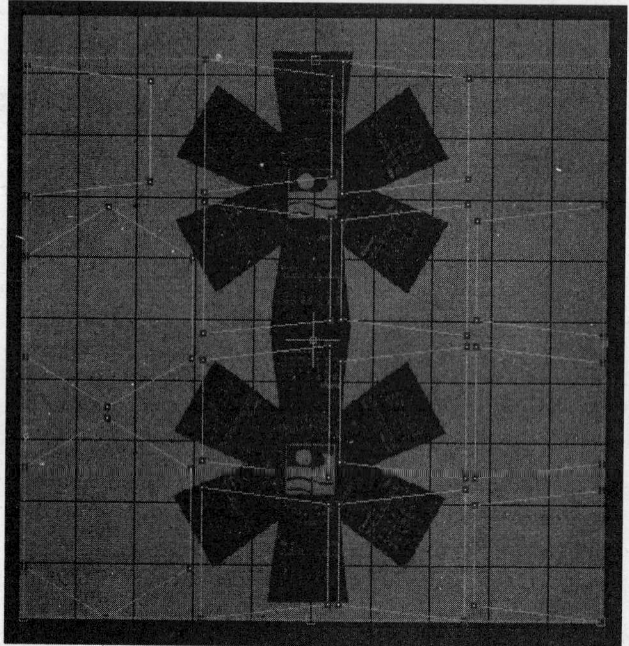
d

Fig. 2.35, *c* and *d*. Editing the map coordinates using the **Unwrap UVW** modifier (stage 1)

- Select all the polygons in the viewport, or all the vertices, edges, or polygons in the coordinate editor. These are identical operations executed with the <Ctrl>+<A> shortcut.
- "Tear" the map into separate polygons.

Map coordinate editing menu → **Mapping** → **Flatten Mapping**

Set the parameters as shown in Fig. 2.35, *c* and click the OK button. You should obtain an image like that shown in Fig. 2.35, *d*.

NOTE

The **Face Angle Threshold** parameter determines the minimum angle, with which polygons are considered flat. In this case, you need to obtain separate polygons, so the parameter is set to a very small value. The other parameters don't matter.

You can navigate in the map coordinate editor window like in the viewport — with the middle mouse button and the mouse wheel. You can move, rotate, and scale sub-objects and clusters using the **Freeform Mode** tool. How does it work? When you select sub-objects, a gizmo appears around them. If you move the mouse pointer to any point within this area, it will take the shape of four arrows: This is the move mode. If you move the mouse pointer to the middle of the gizmo edge, you'll enter the rotation mode; and if you move it to an angle, you'll enter the scaling mode.

You may edit coordinates as you like. Here is a description of how I edited them.

1. I selected all the vertices and rotated the objects through 60 degrees. To make the rotation precise, I turned on the angle snap (with the <A> key) (Fig. 2.36, *a*).
2. I moved all the objects so that one of the caps is positioned properly, and decreased all the clusters evenly along both coordinate axes. To achieve this, I kept the <Ctrl> key pressed during scaling. Test rendering in the viewport was very helpful (Fig. 2.36, *b*).
3. I entered the edge mode, selected the edges one by one, and stitched complementary clusters using the **Stitch Selected** command. Unfortunately, it would be impossible to do this after selecting all the edges (Fig. 2.36, *c*).

Quad menu of the map coordinate editor → **Stitch Selected**

4. I stitched the appropriate leaf to the edge of the lowest (in this case) leaf, then I stitched the bottom cap to the leaf stitched first, and then I stitched the remaining objects to the cap (Fig. 2.36, *d*).
5. I carefully moved certain vertices to get rid of white outlines. A very interesting feature, pixel snap, was very helpful. It is enabled with an appropriate button or the <Ctrl>+<S> shortcut.

Close the map coordinate editor.

Save your scene. My variant is in the Projects\Project 3\Model3-02(var2).max file on the accompanying CD-ROM.

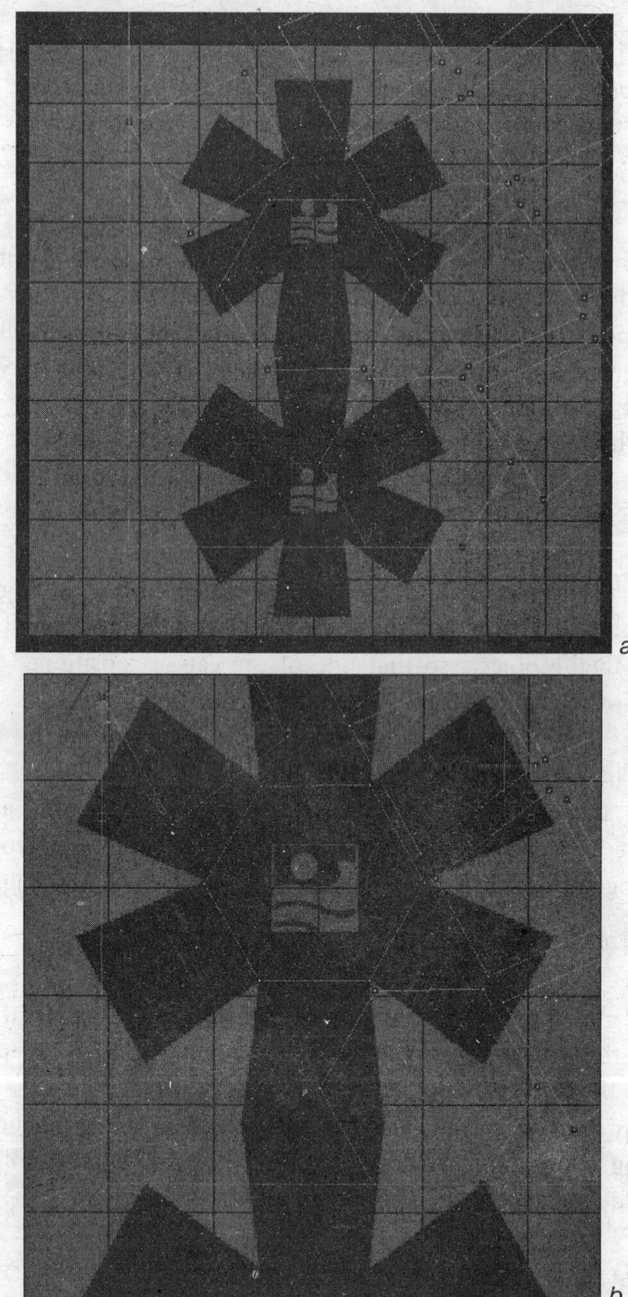

Fig. 2.36, *a* and *b*. Editing map coordinates with the **Unwrap UVW** modifier (stage 2)

c *d*

Fig. 2.36, *c* and *d*. Editing map coordinates with the **Unwrap UVW** modifier (stage 2)

The Second Stage

To continue modeling, you can use the result obtained using either of the methods. You don't need to do much on this stage. First, you should create chamfers where the paper is folded. If you did this with the previous model, you'll do this easily now.

- ❒ Apply the **Edit Poly** modifier to the model.

  Menu bar → **Modifiers** → **Mesh Editing** → **Edit Poly**

- ❒ Select edges that outline the caps. The quickest way to do this is the following: enter the polygon mode with the <4> key and select the polygons of the caps (Fig. 2.37, *a*).

- ❒ Press and hold the <Ctrl> key and enter the polygon mode by clicking the **Edge** button in the command panel. Note that the <2> key is inactive in this case. The edges belonging to the cap's polygons will be selected.

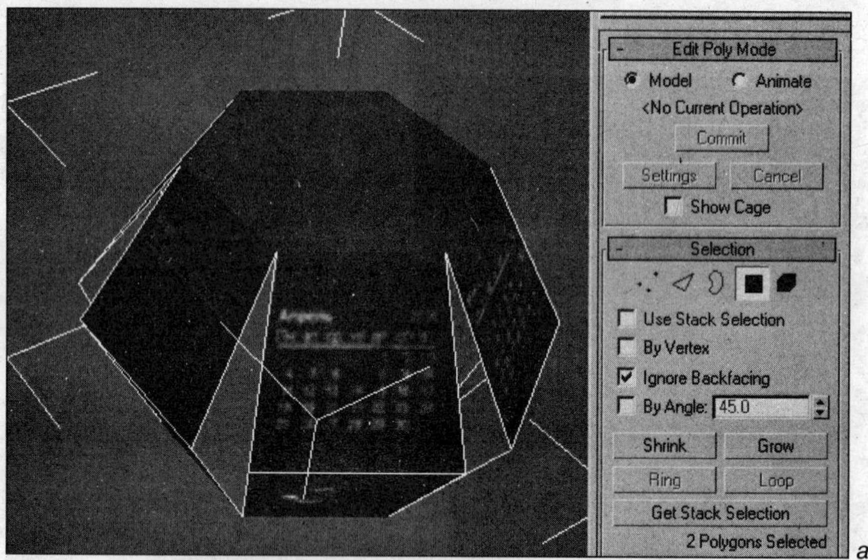

a

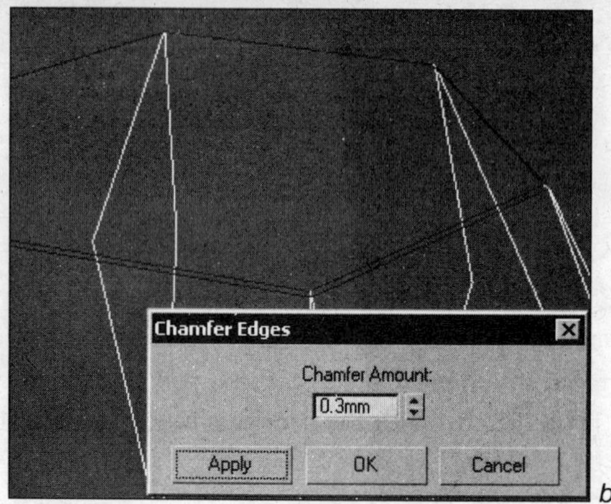

b

Fig. 2.37. Cutting chamfers

TIP

It is convenient to work when the **Ignore Backfacing** checkbox is checked.

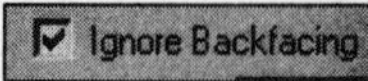

- Cut a small chamfer, from 0.2 to 0.3 mm (Fig. 2.37, *b*).

  Quad menu → the box in the **Chamfer** line

  Enter the value and click the **OK** button.

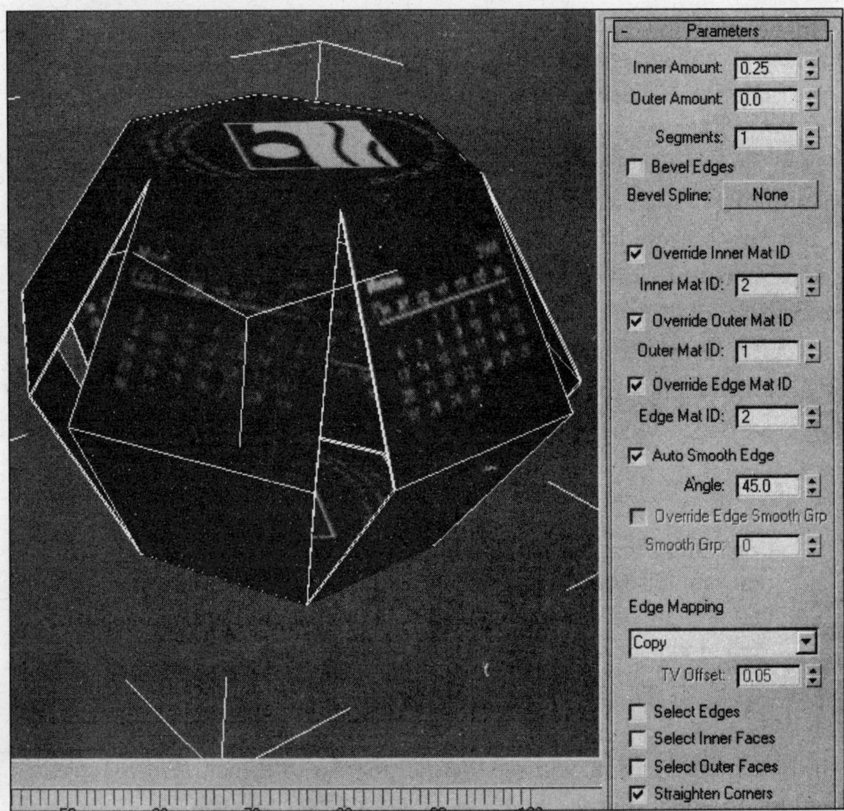

Fig. 2.38. Adding thickness using the **Shell** modifier

Now, add some thickness using the **Shell** modifier (Fig. 2.38).

Menu bar → **Modifiers** → **Parametric Deformers** → **Shell**

Set the **Outer Amount** value to zero and make the **Inner Amount** value equal to the desired thickness. However, it should be lower than the value of the chamfer cut in the **Edit Poly** modifier; otherwise, the planes will cross, which is undesirable. The **Shell** modifier doesn't allow you to eliminate this problem, unlike other modifiers such as **Bevel**. If you wish to set a greater value for the thickness, use the **Outer Amount** parameter. If you don't want to overrun the model's dimensions, use scaling.

To avoid problems with the material, set the **Override ... Mat ID** parameters as shown in the figure. Later, I'll explain why you should do this.

Check the **Straighten Corner** checkbox to obtain even thickness.

The last problem you need to remedy is that the same material is assigned to the outer, lateral, and internal faces of the object. 3ds Max sticks to the rule: One object has one material. However, the assigned material can consist of several submaterials.

❒ Open the material editor. Select the Calendar material and change its type to Multi/Sub-Object, keeping Calendar as a submaterial.

Click the button labeled with the current type (**Architectural**) and select **Multi/Sub-Object** from the list.

Select the **Keep old material as sub-material** radio button and click the **OK** button.

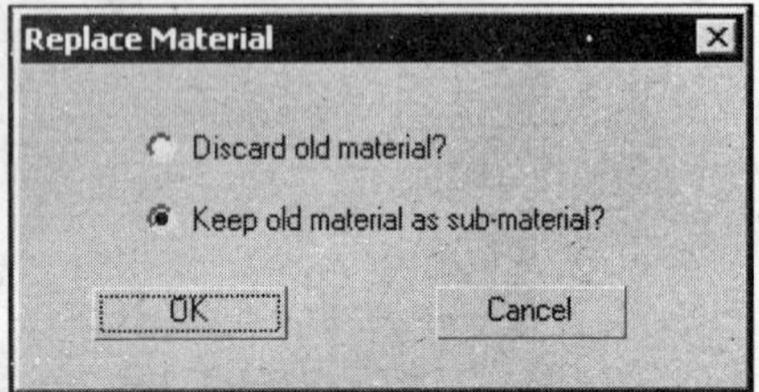

Don't worry that the map has disappeared from the viewport. This isn't a problem. 3ds Max disables display of maps in the viewport. If you wish, you can display the map by entering the material editing mode and clicking the **Show Map in Viewport** button.

In the material editor, you see the parameters of the current material type. I'll describe them in detail (Fig. 2.39, *a*).

The **Set Number** button allows you to set the number of submaterials in the material. In this case, two submaterials are enough. Click the button and type 2.

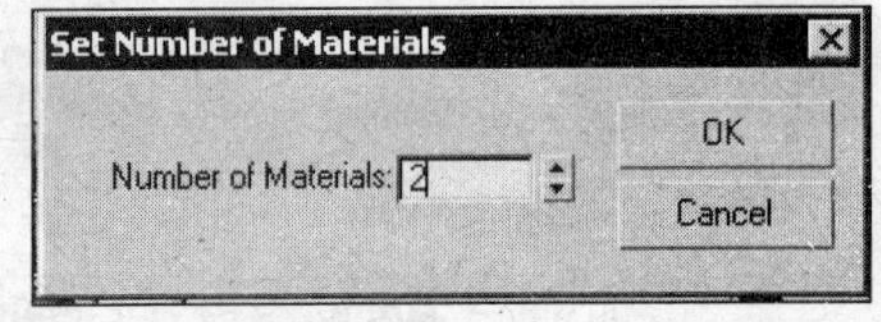

Below the button, you can see a table. Its most important elements are the **ID** and **Sub-Material** columns. Each polygon of a 3ds Max model has the **Material ID** parameter. When you applied the **Shell** modifier and set it as shown in Fig. 2.38, you actually assigned an ID equal to one to the outer polygons, and an ID equal to two to the lateral and inner polygons. If you perform test rendering now, you'll see that the map is rendered on the outer polygons, that is, on the polygons with IDs equal to one. The polygons whose IDs equal to two have a gray material. Start editing this material, change its type to Architectural, select the **Paper** preset, and make it white (Fig. 2.39, *b*). Rename this submaterial to White Paper and rename the compound material to Calendar Multi.

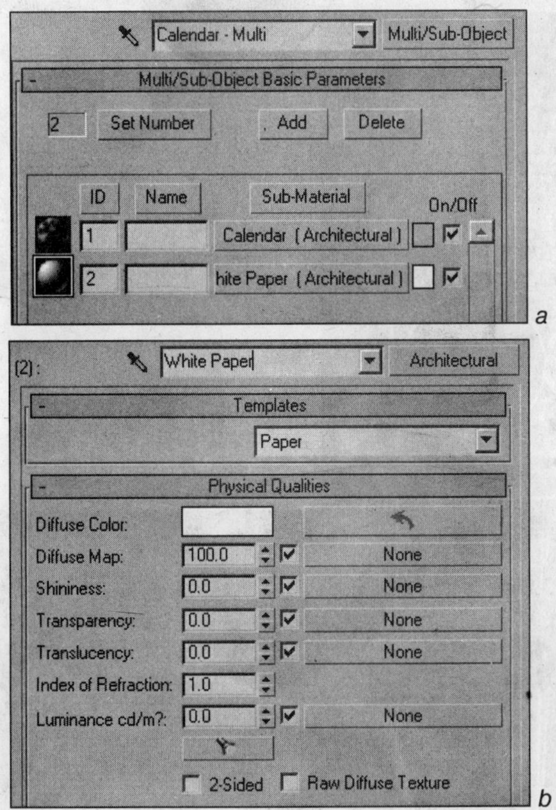

Fig. 2.39. Editing the material of the calendar

The model is finished. Save your scene. My variant is in the Projects\Project 3\Model3-final.max file on the accompanying CD-ROM.

A Container for Small Items

This is an original project of a transformer container designed and supervised by Anna Zhiryakova and Valery Kuleshov. A fragment of the draft project is shown in Fig. 2.40. Because the author of the project emphasized the appearance of the object rather than details, there is not enough information for modeling. This is why I ventured to complete the construction (Fig. 2.41). So it consists of a rod, to which the bottom container is secured, and three identical containers threaded on the rod. My draft is a result of rendering with Toon Shader. The dimensions are put using 3ds Max.

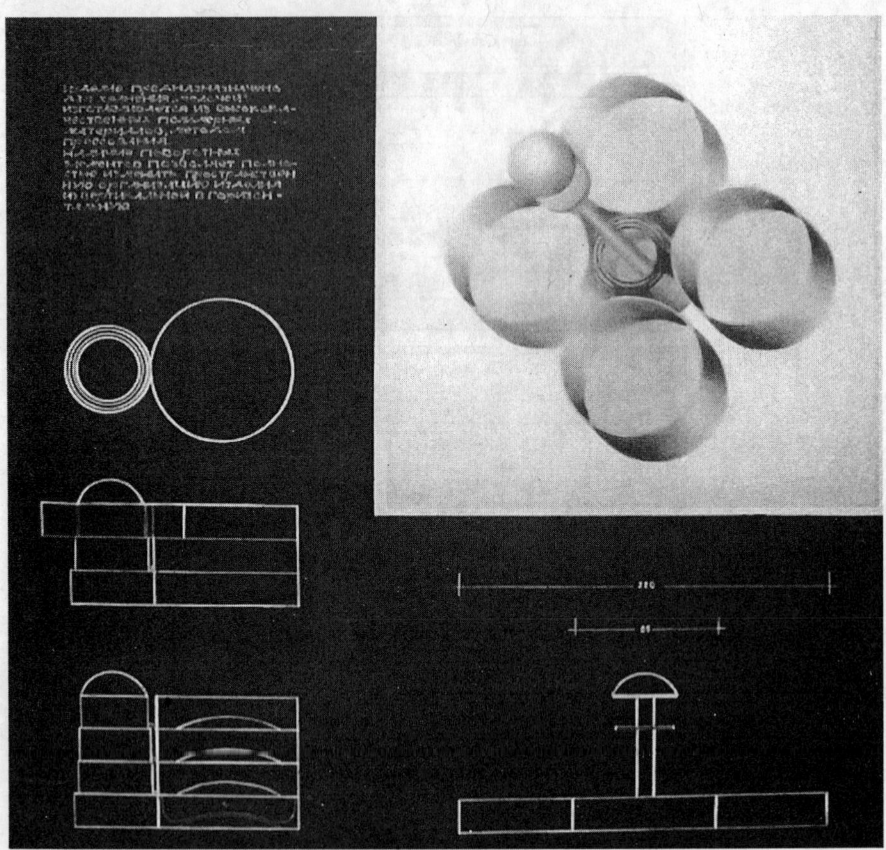

Fig. 2.40. The original draft

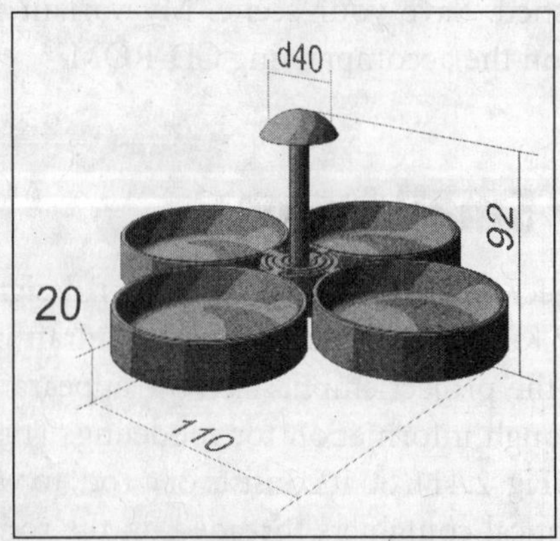

Fig. 2.41. My draft

NOTE

Like in the previous projects, set system units to millimeters and set grid spacing to 10 mm.

Modeling the Rod. Variant 1

To model the rod, you'll need to create an outline and make a surface of revolution based on the outline using the **Lathe** modifier.

In the front or left view, create three objects: two rectangles and a circle (see Fig. 2.42, *a*). Create them close to the center of coordinates.

Menu bar → **Create** → **Shapes** → **Rectangle**, **Circle**

Grid Points
Pivot

- If you turn on snap to grid, you'll be able to place the pivot points along the same axis, thus avoiding the necessity of aligning them later.
- The dimensions of the horizontal rectangle don't matter. It's only important that its top side is at the height of 80 mm.
- The radius of the circle will be set automatically if you start creating the circle in the center located at the height of 70 mm.
- Enter the Modify mode and change the width of the vertical rectangle. Set it to the diameter of the rod (10 mm). Don't change the **Length** parameter.

Parameters
Length: 130.0mm
Width: 10.0mm
Corner Radius: 0.0mm

Convert one of the objects to the Editable Spline type and attach the others to it.

Quad menu → **Convert to...** → **Convert to Editable Spline**

Quad menu → **Attach**

Enter the vertex editing mode and move the vertices of the rectangles along the vertical axis as shown in Fig. 2.42, *b*. Disable snaps for convenience.

Using the Boolean operations on splines, create an outline (Fig. 2.42, *c*).

- Enter the spline editing mode (with the <3> key).
- Select the spline of the circle.
- Enable the Boolean mode.

Command panel → the **Geometry** rollout → the **Boolean** button

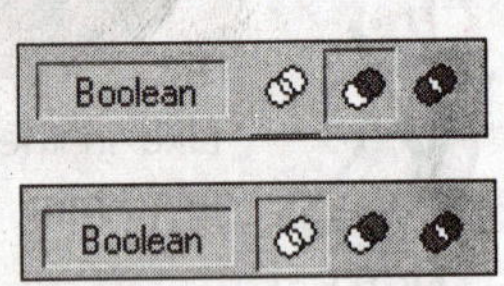

- ❐ Turn on the Subtraction operation.
- ❐ Left-click the horizontal rectangular spline.
- ❐ Switch to the Union operation.
- ❐ Left-click the vertical rectangular spline.
- ❐ Disable the Boolean mode by right-clicking on any place.

Now, you should do one important thing. Many novice modelers don't do this, thus making a mistake. If you create a surface of revolution right now, you'll obtain an imperfect result. Why? You'll obtain two coinciding surfaces rather than one, and their normals will be pointing to the opposite directions. It isn't a problem when you use a nontransparent material. However, if you use glass, the result will be awful. This is why you should rotate only a half of the outline.

- ❐ Enter the segment editing mode (with the <2> key), select the bottom segment, and halve it using the **Divide** command.

Command panel → the **Geometry** rollout → **Divide**

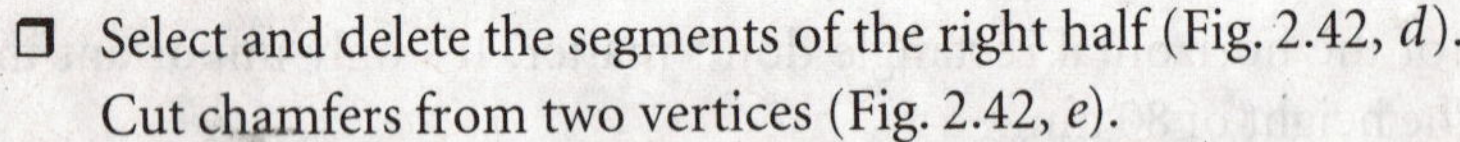

- ❐ Select and delete the segments of the right half (Fig. 2.42, *d*).

Cut chamfers from two vertices (Fig. 2.42, *e*).

- ❐ Enter the vertex mode and select two vertices.

Command panel → the **Geometry** rollout → enter 0.5 into the input box of the **Chamfer** command and press the <Enter> key.

Everything is ready for rotation.

- ❐ Select the vertex about which you want to rotate the outline. (It doesn't matter whether you select the top or bottom vertex). Apply the **Lathe** modifier with the parameters shown in Fig. 2.42, *f*.

Menu bar → **Modifiers** → **Patch/Spline Editing** → **Lathe**

NOTE

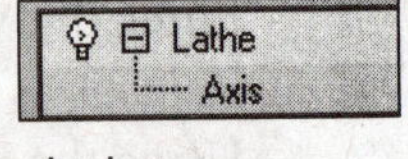

The sentence that a vertex should be selected was italicized intentionally. If you don't select a vertex, the rotation will be performed about the pivot point. You could obtain the desired result by moving the axis of rotation, but it is best to do the things correctly from the very beginning.

You should rotate the outline through 360 degrees.

The **Weld Core** checkbox checked will allow you to avoid holes at the top and bottom of the model.

To obtain a smoother surface, increase the number of the segments. It is best to use values that are multiples of four.

If your object looks wrong, that is, inside out, check the **Flip Normals** checkbox. This should eliminate the problem.

To obtain a smoother top hemisphere, jump down the modifier stack and increase the number of interpolation steps (the **Interpolation** rollout among the spline parameters).

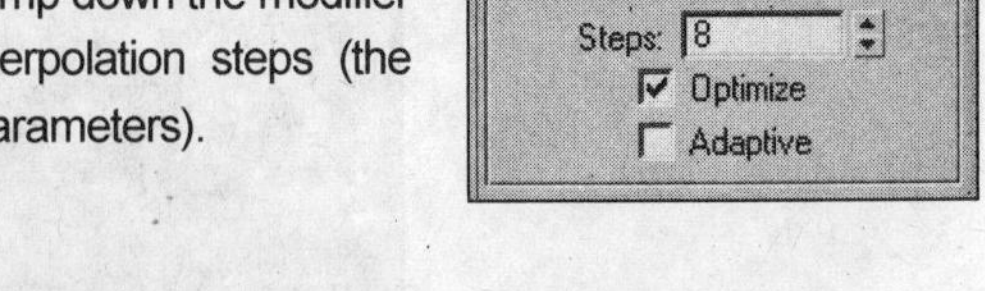

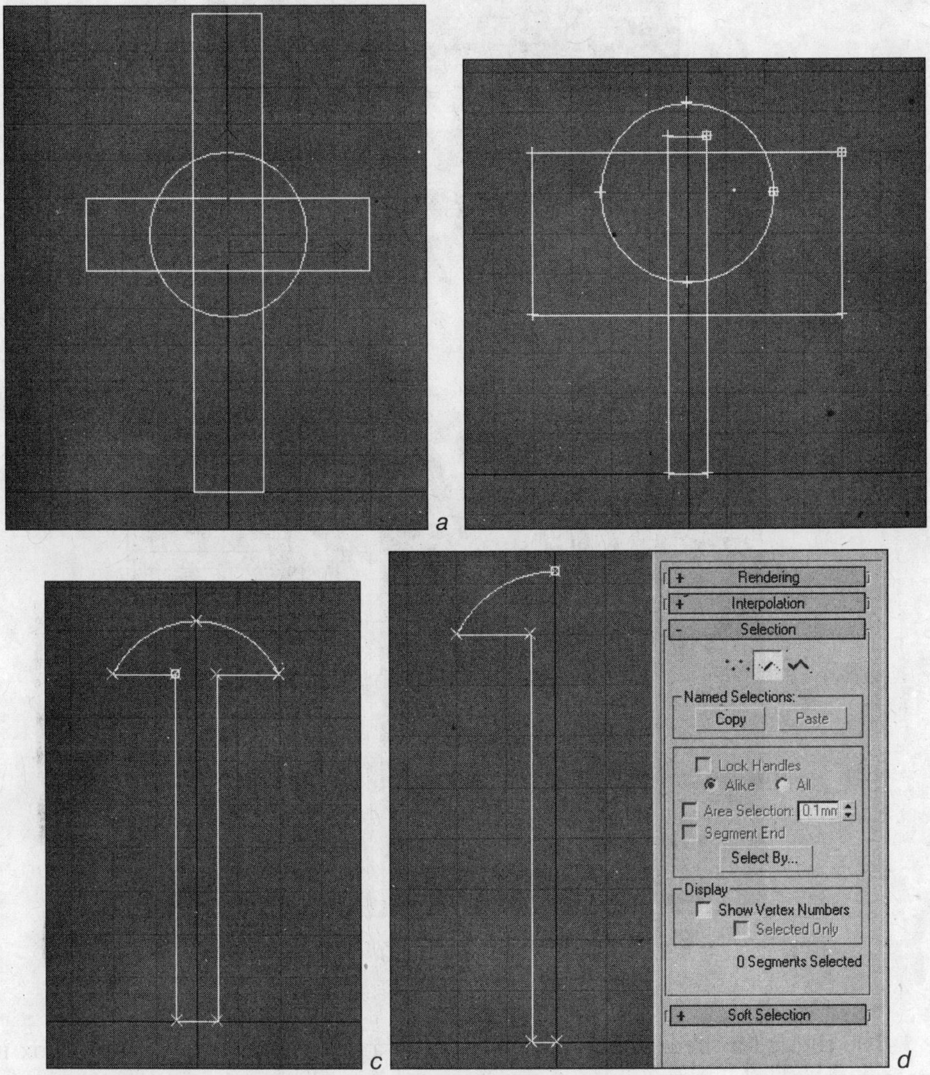

Fig. 2.42, *a–d*. Creating the rod, variant 1

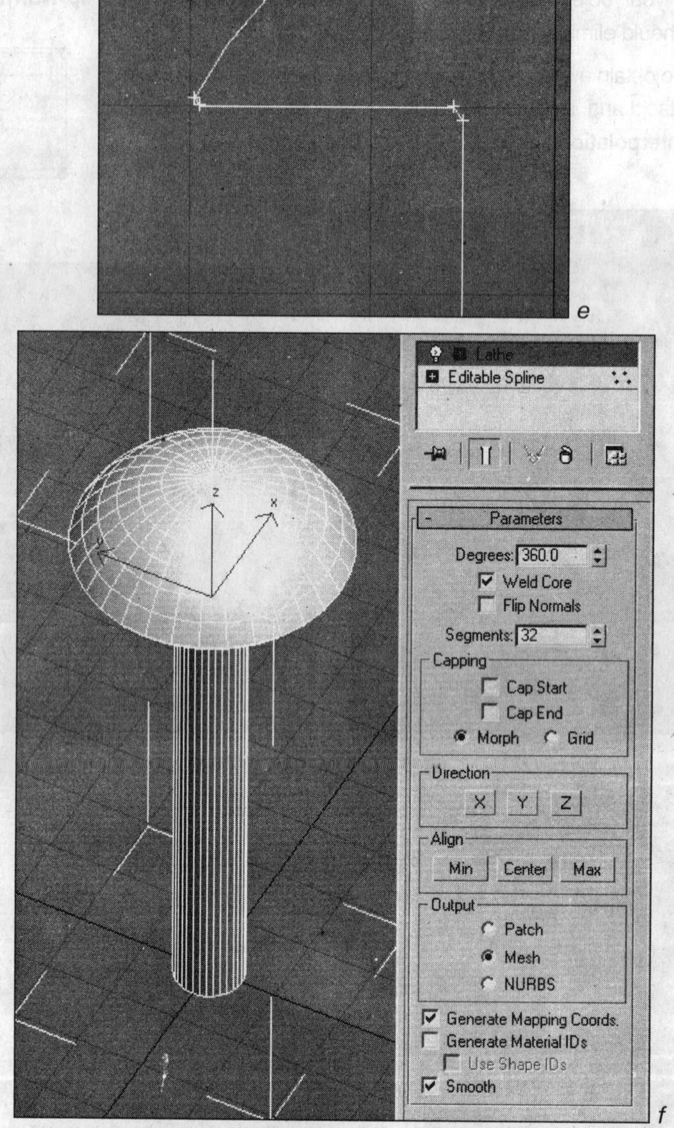

Fig. 2.42, *e* and *f*. Creating the rod, variant 1

The rod is finished. Rename it by entering a new name into the input box in the command panel and save the scene. The result of my work on this stage is in the Model4-01.max file in the Projects\Project4 folder on the accompanying CD-ROM.

Modeling the Rod. Variant 2

The previous method is universal. However, you can use a more effective method in this particular case. It took me seven minutes to create the model using it. Look how simple it is.

- Create a sphere with a required diameter and complexity.

  Menu bar → **Create** → **Standard Primitives** → **Sphere**

- Cut the bottom part using the **Hemisphere** parameter (Fig. 2.43, *a*).
- Convert the object to the Editable Poly type, select the bottom vertex, and create a 5-mm polygon using the **Chamfer** command (Fig. 2.43, *b*).
- Select this polygon and extrude it to 80 mm using the **Extrude** command (Fig. 2.43, *c*).
- Select the appropriate edges using the **Loop** command and cut chamfers using the **Chamfer** command (Fig. 2.43, *d*).

Select all the polygons and smooth them using the **Auto Smooth** command with a small angle (Fig. 2.43, *e*).

This method has one drawback: It is difficult to create a hemisphere precisely.

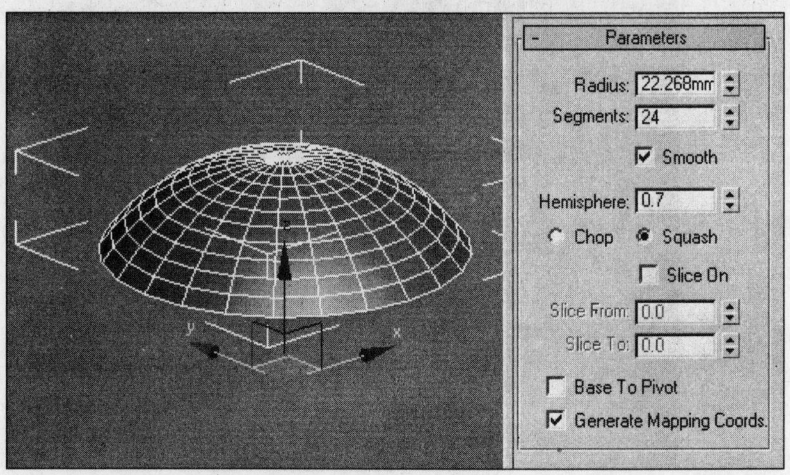

Fig. 2.43, *a*. Creating the rod from a hemisphere

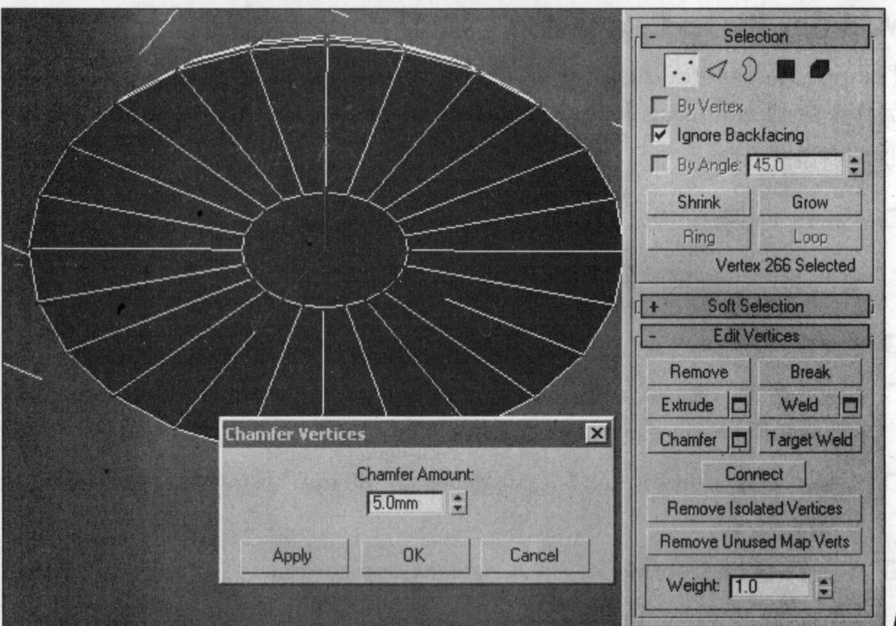

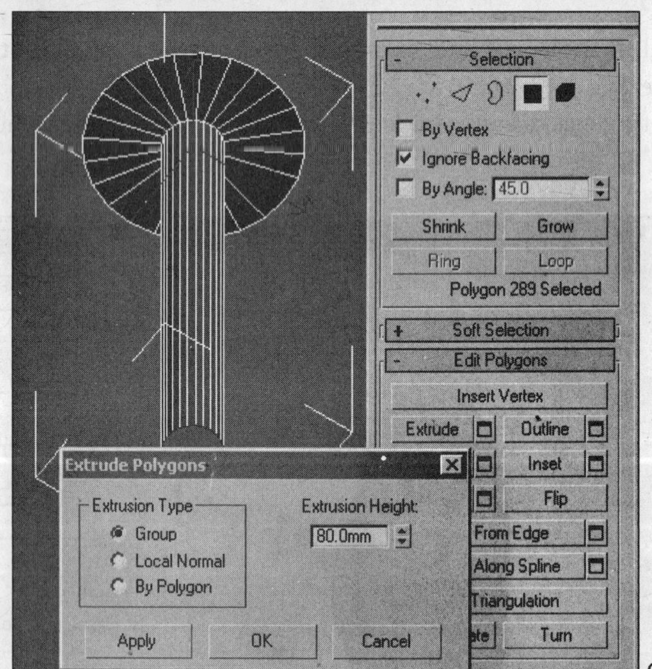

Fig. 2.43, *b* and *c*. Creating the rod from a hemisphere

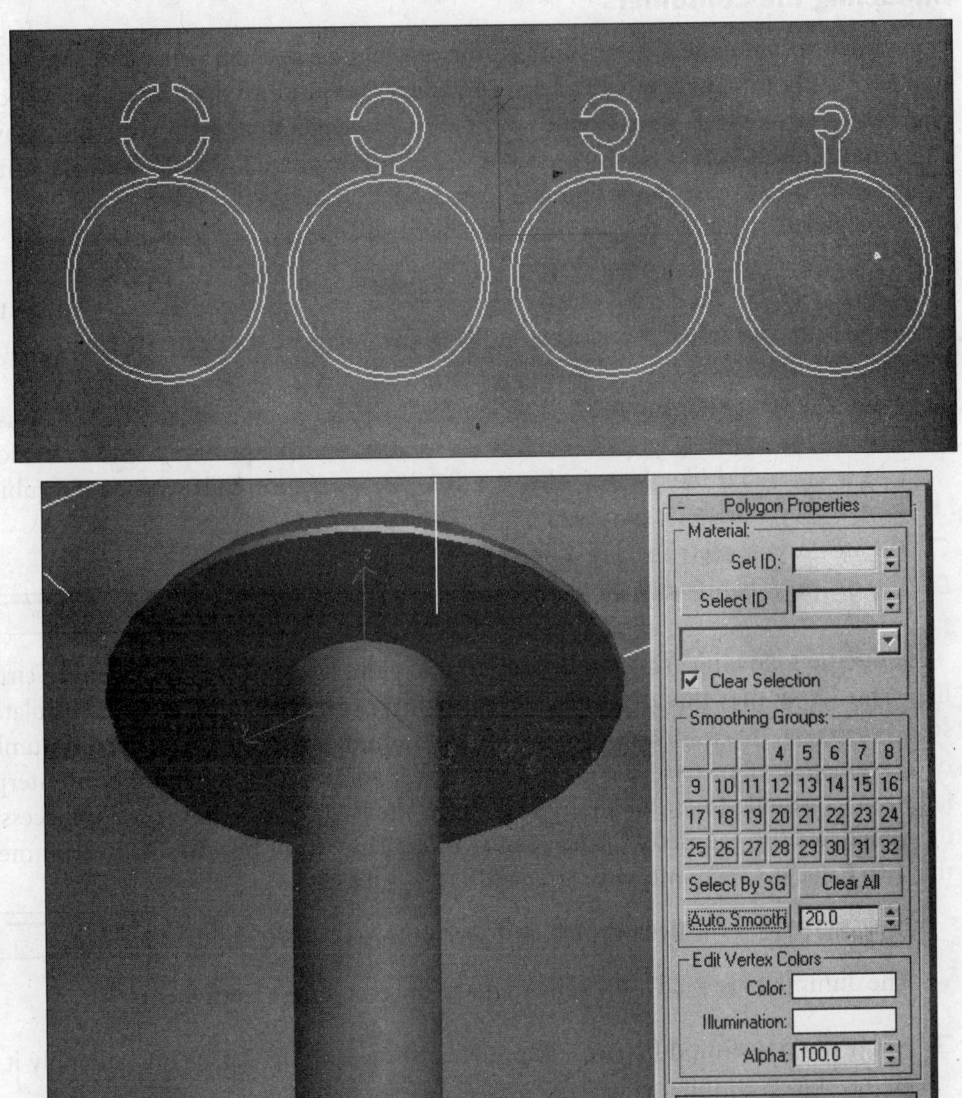

Fig. 2.43, *d* and *e*. Creating the rod from a hemisphere

Modeling the Containers

To model the containers, create four dummies from circles and rectangles (Fig. 2.44, *a* and *b*). To do this quickly and accurately, create the bottom container first, which is the base of the object. Then create copies of it by selecting all its objects and moving them along the X axis while keeping the <Shift> key pressed. Finally, remove unnecessary objects and scale other objects if you need.

Your subsequent actions are illustrated with an example of the base container.

- ❒ Convert one of the circles of the ring embracing the rod to the Editable Spline type and attach the other elements to it. Why did I choose the ring? Its pivot point is placed as necessary.
- ❒ Enter the spline editing mode and use the Boolean operations to create necessary cuts and jumpers (Fig. 2.44, *c*). It is up to you, which operations you use and in which order. I'd like to note that if a Boolean operation fails with one combination, it may work with another.
- ❒ Create the complete set (Fig. 2.44, *d*).
- ❒ Cut 0.5-mm chamfers on the sharp corners in all the objects.

Note the following. You might wish to make the circles, so to speak, more circle-like. You know that this can be achieved by increasing the number of interpolation steps. However, there are segments with small radii in this model. The default number of interpolation steps (six) is enough for them. If you increase the number of interpolation steps, you'll obtain the desired result for the large circles, but you'll unnecessarily complicate the geometry of the smaller ones. This won't be wise. So I recommend that you halve the segments with large radii (Fig. 2.44, *e*).

Command panel → the **Geometry** rollout → **Divide**

The dummies are ready. It's time to make the containers from them.

- ❒ Apply the **Bevel** modifier with parameters shown in Fig. 2.45. You can apply it to all the objects simultaneously.

Command panel → the modifier list

To make a chamfer at the top and the bottom, use all three levels of the modifier. Check the **Keep Lines From Crossing** checkbox to avoid unwanted crossings. Leave the default values for the other parameters.

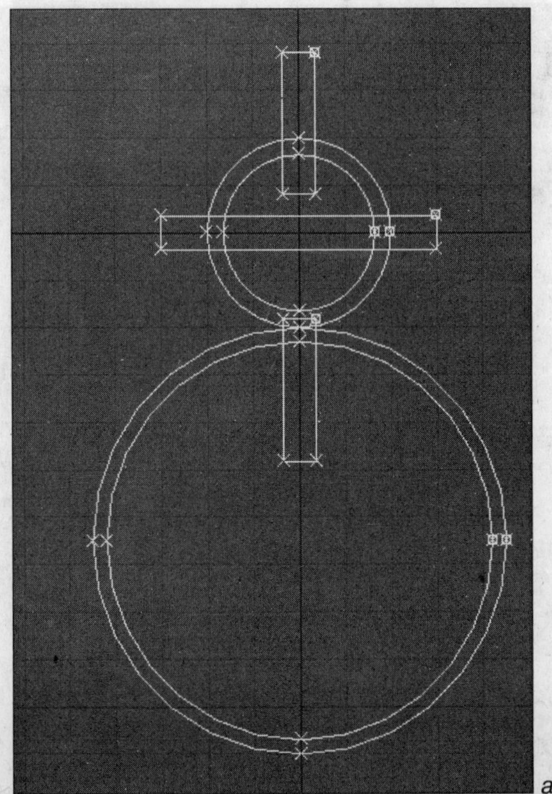

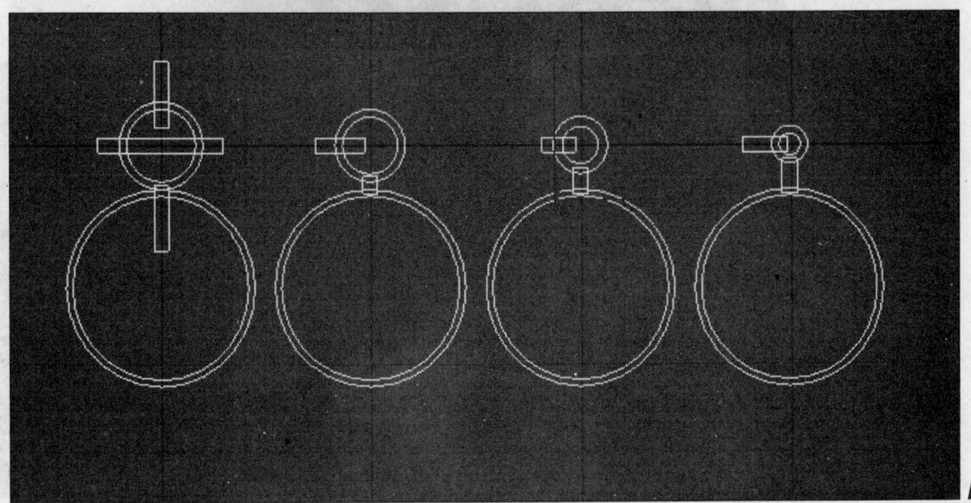

Fig. 2.44, *a* and *b*. Creating dummies for the containers

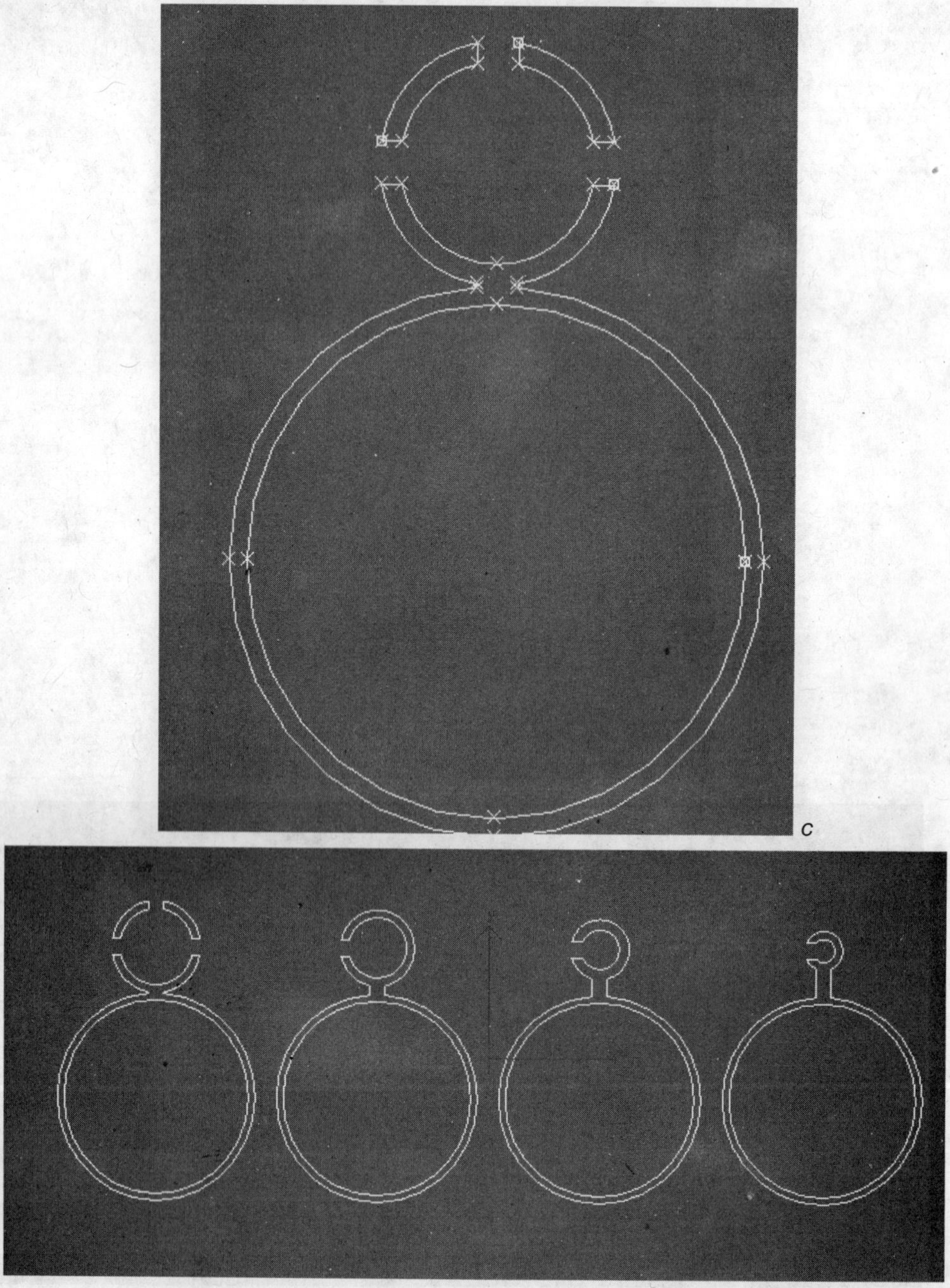

c

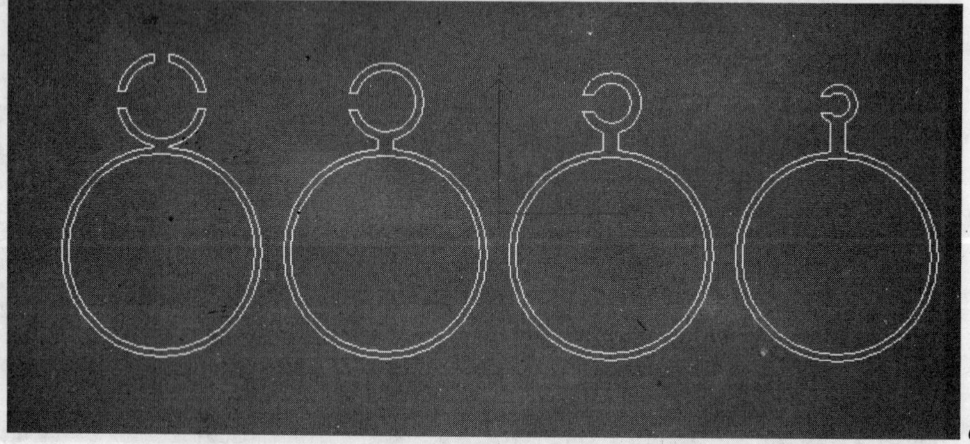

d

Fig. 2.44, *c* and *d*. Creating dummies for the containers

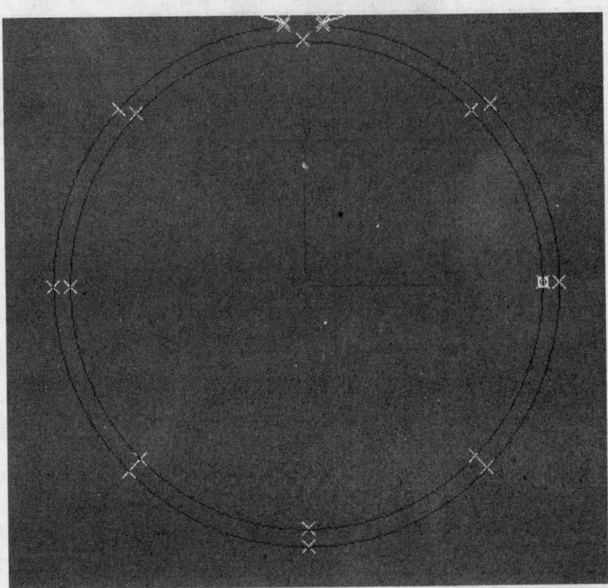

Fig. 2.44, *e*. Creating dummies for the containers

It makes sense to proceed with polygons.

- Convert the base container to the Editable Poly type or apply the **Edit Poly** modifier if you don't want to collapse the modifier stack. By the way, it is time to give the objects self-explanatory names instead of Circle01, Circle02, and so on.
- Select and delete the internal polygons of the container (Fig. 2.46, *a*). The following method will be the best. Select one internal edge, click the **Ring** button, and select all the edges circularly. Press and hold the <Ctrl> key and enter the polygon editing mode by clicking the **Polygon** button on the command panel.
- Close up the holes that appeared. To do this, select the top and bottom borders and execute the **Cap** command (Fig. 2.46, *b*).

Quad menu → **Cap**

- Select the obtained polygons and hide the others for your convenience.

Command panel → the **Edit Geometry** rollout → **Hide Unselected**

TIP

It is convenient to select polygons when the **Ignore Backfacing** checkbox is checked.

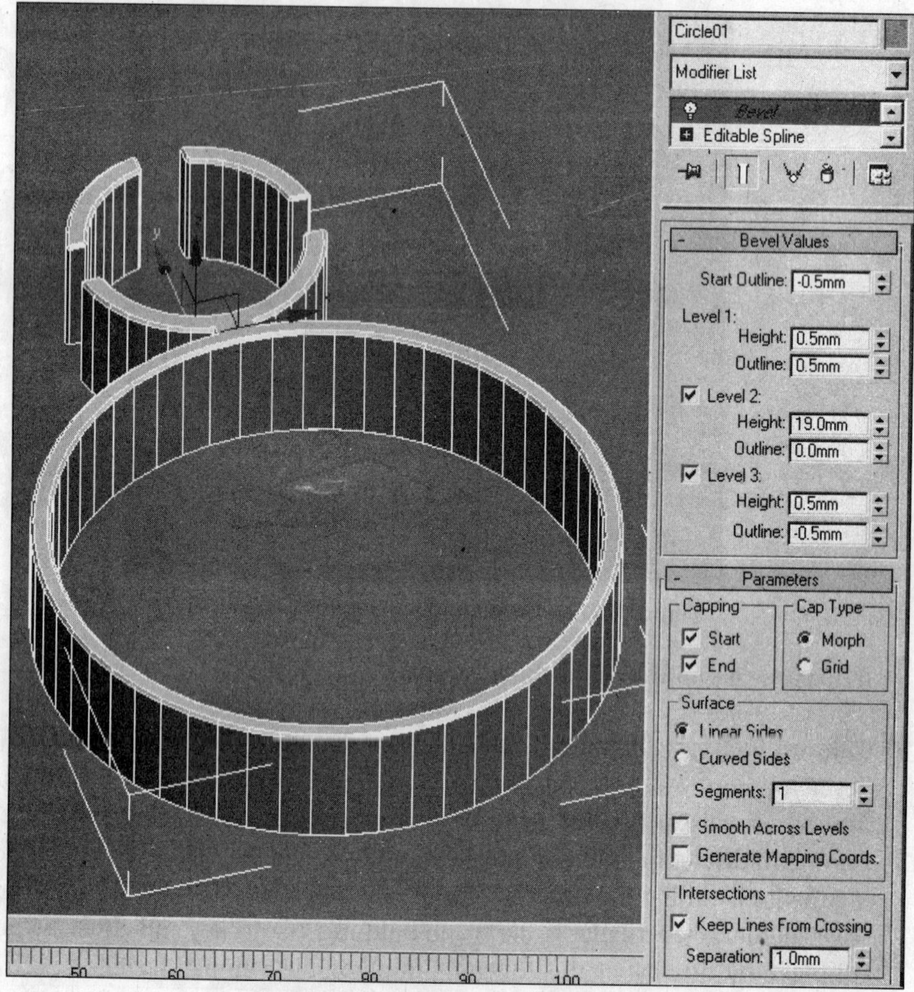

Fig. 2.45. The **Bevel** modifier parameters

- Execute the **Inset** command to add concentric edges.

  Command panel → the **Edit Polygons** rollout → **Inset**

- Collapse the central polygon to a vertex using the **Collapse** command (Fig. 2.46, *c*).

  Command panel → the **Edit Geometry** rollout → **Collapse**

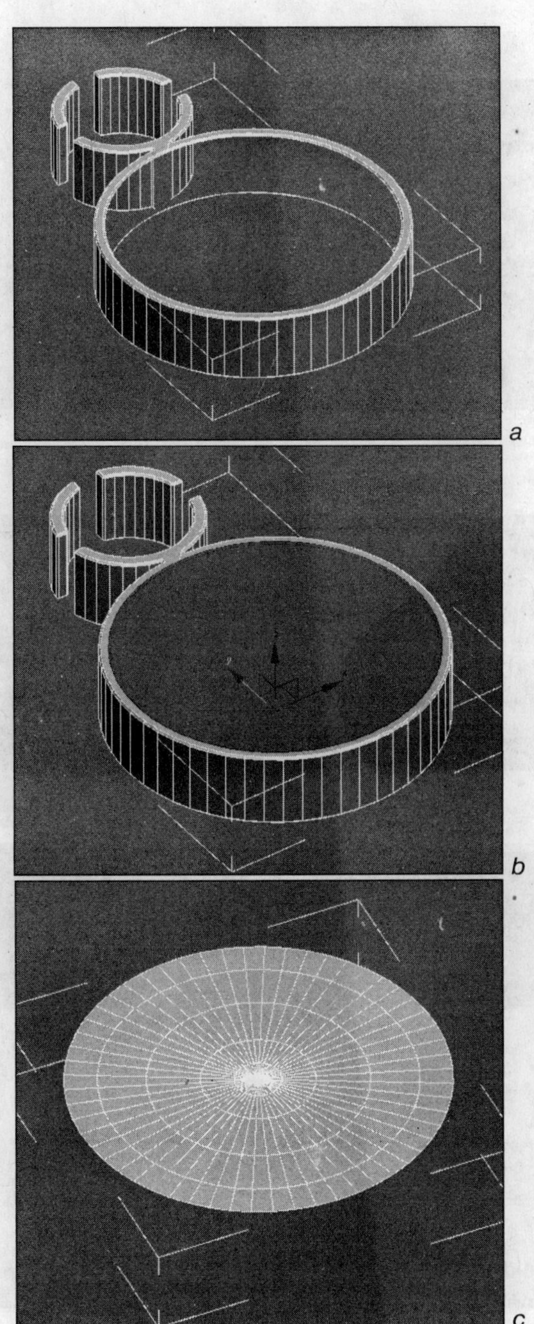

Fig. 2.46, *a–c*. Modeling cavities

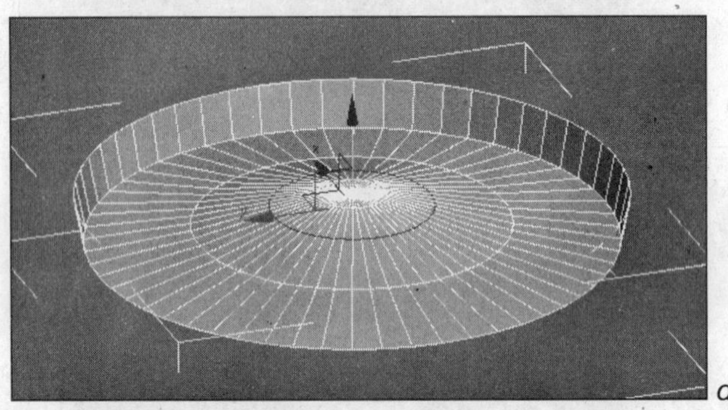
d

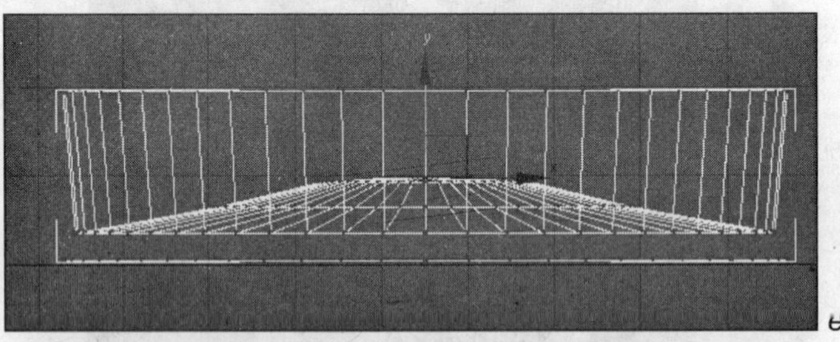
e

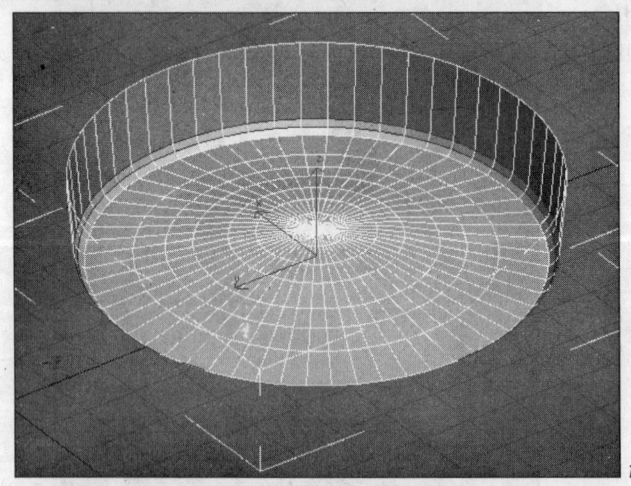
f

Fig. 2.46, *d–f*. Modeling cavities

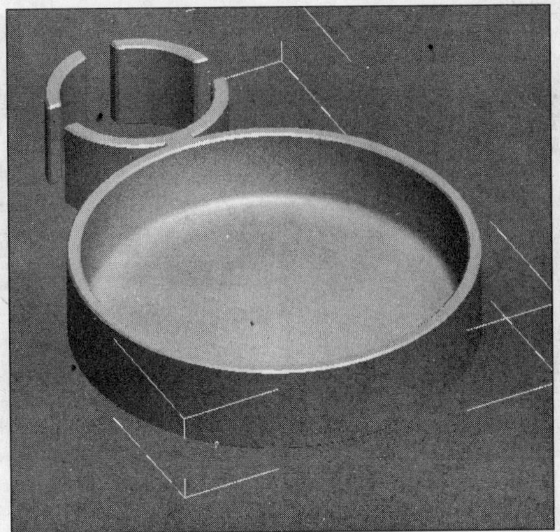

Fig. 2.46, *g*. Modeling cavities

- Create roughly the top cavity by selecting the edges with the **Loop** button and moving and scaling the edges relative to the common center (Fig. 2.46, *d*).
- Then it would be convenient to move to the left of front view. Working with the vertices, adjust the geometry by selecting groups of vertices (Fig. 2.46, *e*). Make sure to uncheck the **Ignore Backfacing** checkbox.
- Working with edges, use the **Chamfer** command to complicate the geometry where necessary (Fig. 2.46, *f*).

Process the bottom cavity in the same manner.

The model is almost finished. There is a minor problem in that the polygons of the cavities aren't smooth. Select all of them and assign them one smoothing group that isn't used in the model, 32 for example.

Command panel → the **Polygon Properties** rollout → click the **32** button among the **Smoothing Groups** parameters

- Unhide all the polygons.

Command panel → the **Edit Geometry** rollout → **Unhide All**

In my opinion, the model looks excellent (Fig. 2.46, *g*).

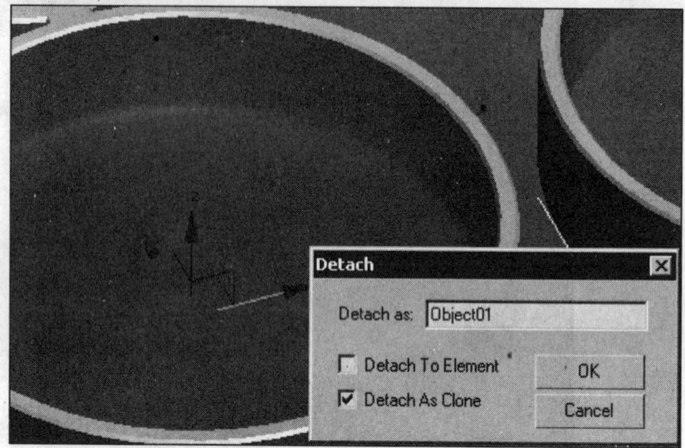

Fig. 2.47. Detaching the polygons

In reality, this model would fall into pieces. Don't worry, you'll remedy the problem later.

Now, you need to do the same with the other container. This isn't as tedious as you might think.

- Select the polygons of the cavities if you have unselected them. To do this quickly, select them by the selection group.

  Command panel → the **Polygon Properties** rollout → **Select by SG**

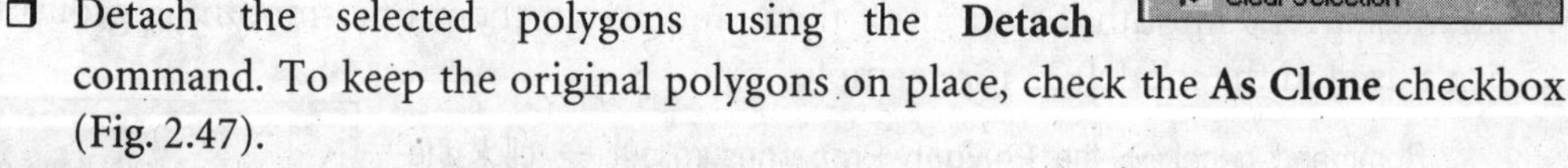

- Detach the selected polygons using the **Detach** command. To keep the original polygons on place, check the **As Clone** checkbox (Fig. 2.47).

  Command panel → the **Edit Geometry** rollout → **Detach**

You could achieve the same result if you moved the polygons along one axis, say, X, while keeping the <Shift> key pressed.

The obtained object has a very nice feature in that its pivot point is on the same place as the original object's pivot point.

- ❐ Make another container by deleting the internal polygons (Fig. 2.48, *a*).
- ❐ Align the object obtained by detaching polygons (in my project, it is called Object01) with the next container (name it Part 1) by the pivot points and all the coordinates (Fig. 2.48, *b*). To do this, use the **Align** command.

Select the Object01 object.

Click the **Align** button in the main toolbar and click the second container.

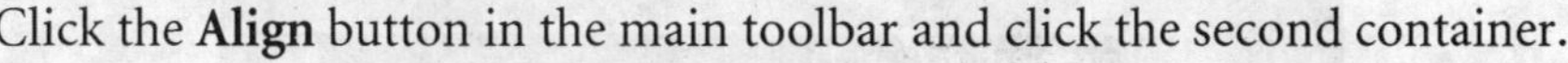

- ❐ Create a copy of the Object01 object by moving it in any direction while keeping the <Shift> key pressed. You'll need it later.
- ❐ Select the Part 1 object and attach the Object01 object to it.

Now, you need to weld vertices so that the object is a complete unity. To do this quickly, follow these steps. Select all the vertices, open the **Weld** dialog box, increase the threshold a little, and weld the appropriate vertices (Fig. 2.48, *c*).

Quad menu → the box in the **Weld** line

Repeat the same procedure for the other objects.

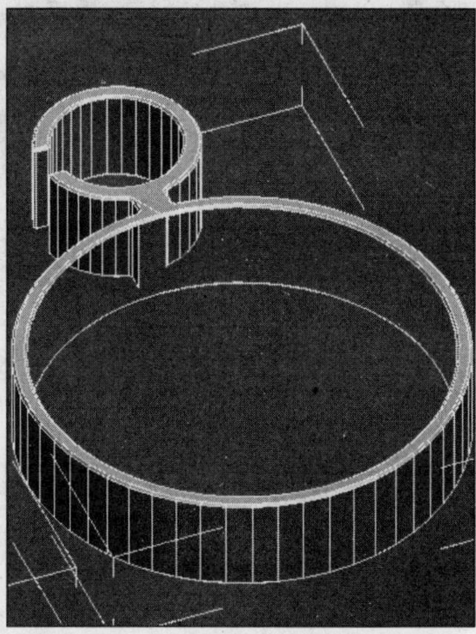

Fig. 2.48, *a*. Modeling the containers

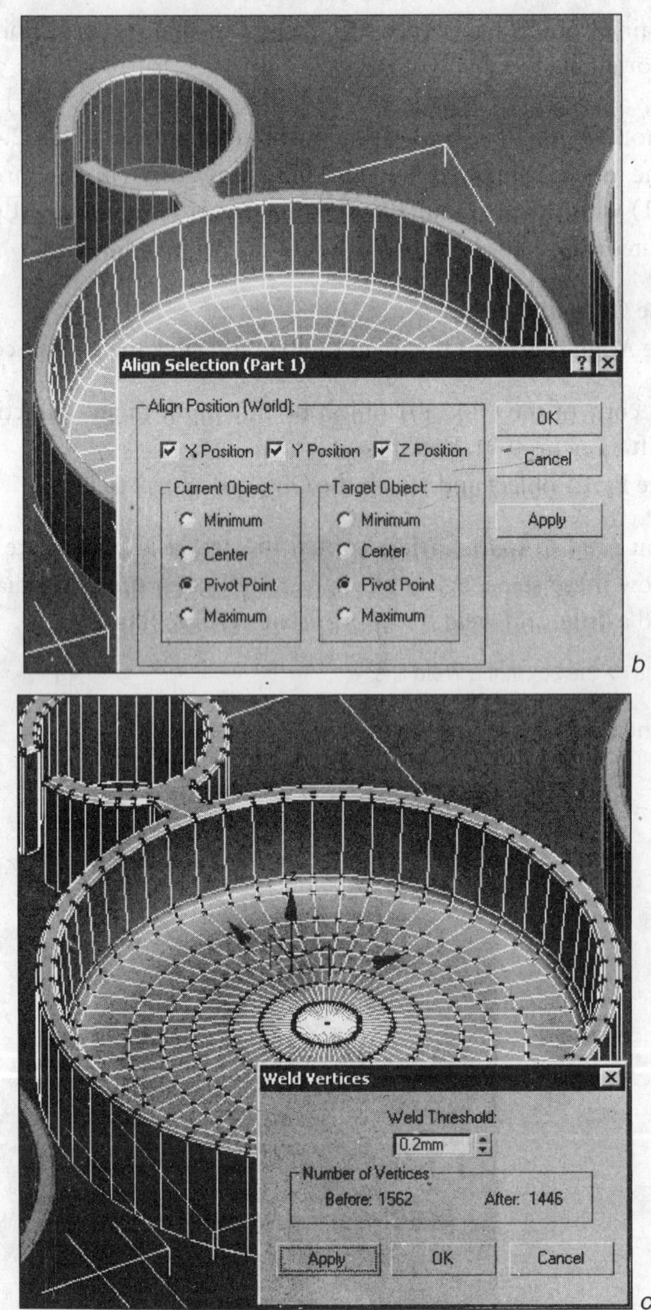

Fig. 2.48, *b* and *c*. Modeling the containers

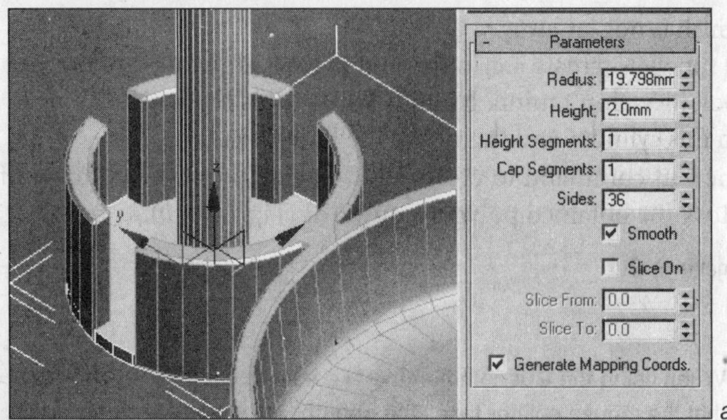

a

b

c

d

Fig. 2.49. Finishing and assembling the model

The finish is not far away.

In the top view, create a cylinder and place it at the base of the rod (Fig. 2.49). If it doesn't look nice, don't mind. Nobody will see this element.

Attach this cylinder and the rod to the Base object.

Use the **Cut** command to create additional edges at the bottoms of the other containers. Move the obtained polygons upwards (Fig. 2.49, *b*).

Quad menu → **Cut**

When using the **Cut** command, make sure to cut from a vertex to a vertex and watch that the mouse pointer takes the appropriate shape.

You may be dissatisfied with the result of this operation because the resulting polygons are incorrect. It is worth correcting them using the **Cut** command; add edges as shown in Fig. 2.49, *c*.

Finally, assemble the model (Fig. 2.49, *d*) by aligning the objects and rotating them appropriately.

Don't forget to save the model. My variant is saved in the Projects\Project4\Model4-final.max file.

A Mobile Telephone

A cutting-edge mobile telephone was designed by Alena Mahankova supervised Anna Zhiryakova and Maria Malinina (Fig. 2.50). I'm not sure how this device could be used, but it is beautiful.

At first, I wanted to perform a standard modeling procedure: creating a curve, extruding, finishing the shape using polygons, and smoothing. However, I remembered a few interesting 3ds Max features, which are undeservedly ignored by those 3ds Max users who prefer low-level modeling, which is very popular nowadays.

So here are my ideas for modeling. I suggest you to model both parts of the phone on the plane from a primitive called Chamfer Box and then give them the desired shapes using the parametric modifiers **Bend**, **Skew**, and **Taper**.

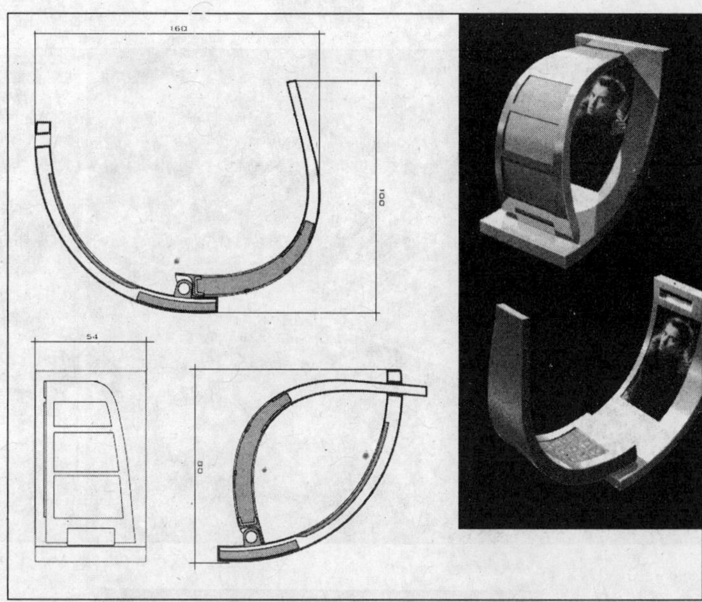

Fig. 2.50. A draft of the mobile telephone

Don't forget to set the system units.

Modeling the Base

Begin with the simplest object: the base.

- Create a Chamfer Box object with the size and settings shown in Fig. 2.51, *a*.

Menu bar → **Create** → **Extended Primitives** → **Chamfer Box**

The height and width values were taken from the project. The length was calculated using the formula 2*Pi*R/4 because this part is a quarter of a circle.

The number of steps for the length is large enough so that you can create a smooth bend. The number of steps for the width allows you to create a hollow for the display and a hole. Fillets are small, with one segment. You won't need more.

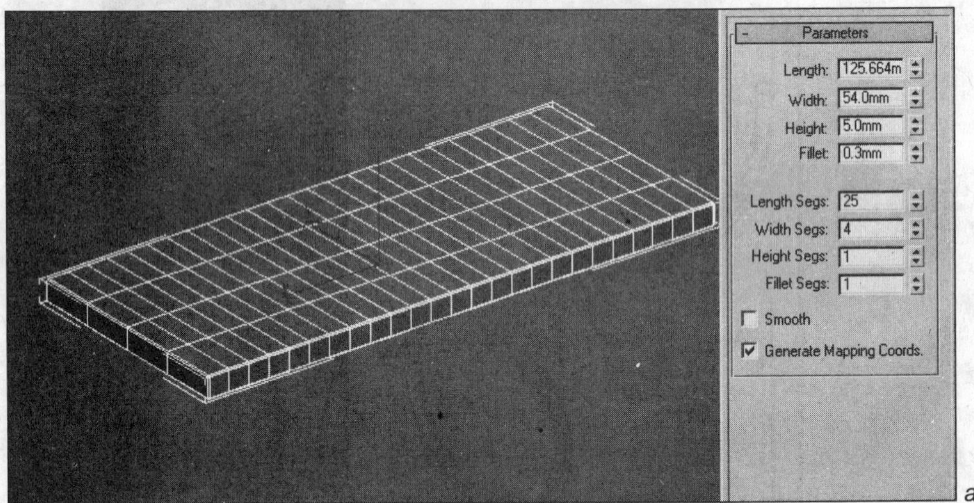

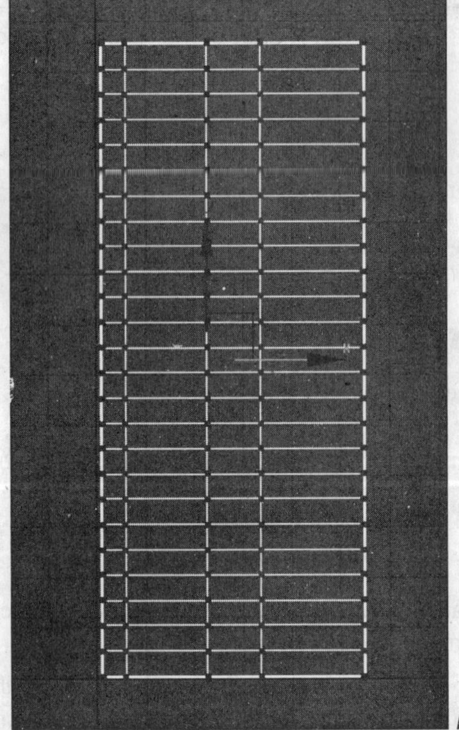

Fig. 2.51, *a* and *b*. Modeling a dummy for the phone base

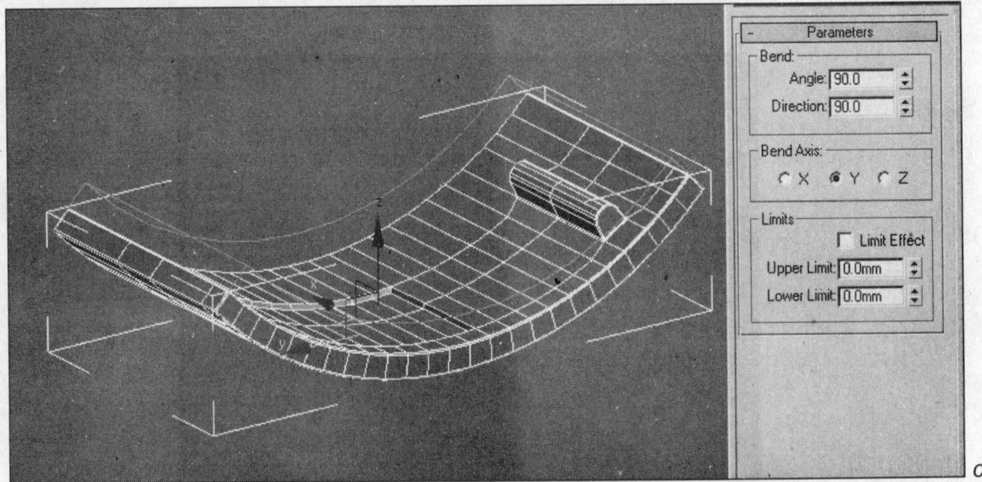

c

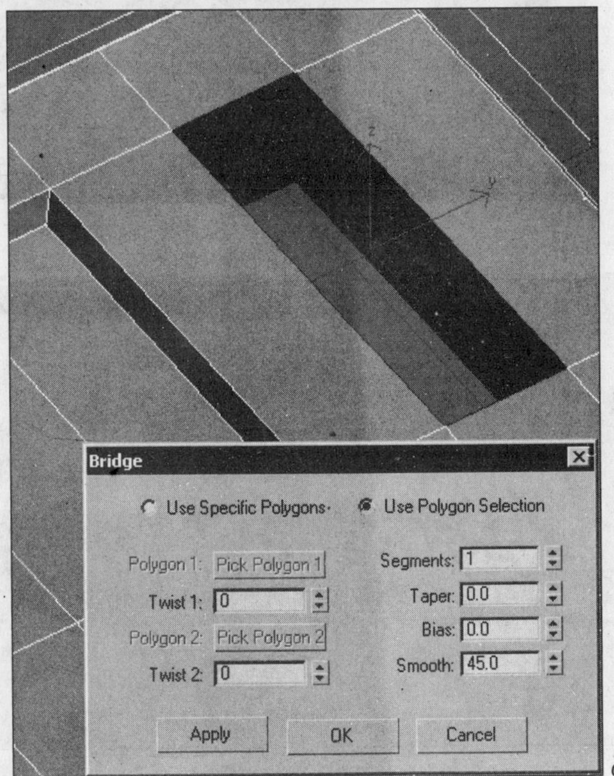

d

Fig. 2.51, *c* and *d*. Modeling a dummy for the phone base

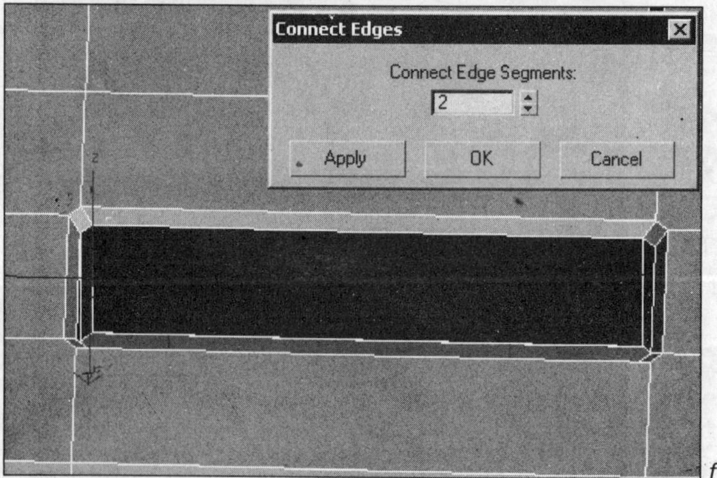

Fig. 2.51, *e* and *f*. Modeling a dummy for the phone base

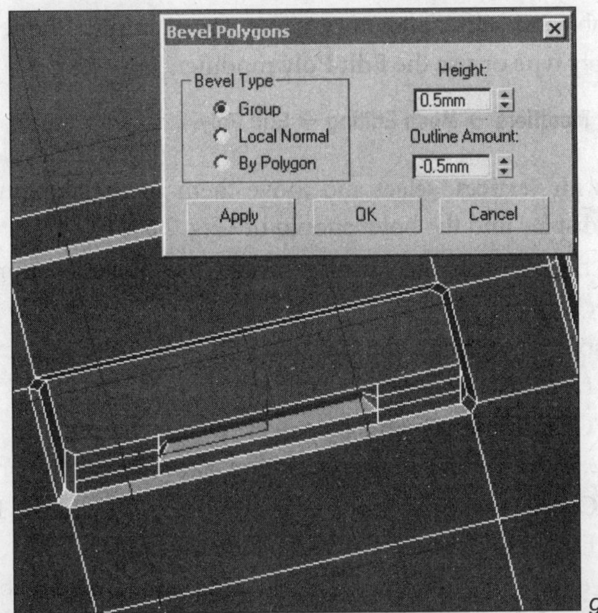

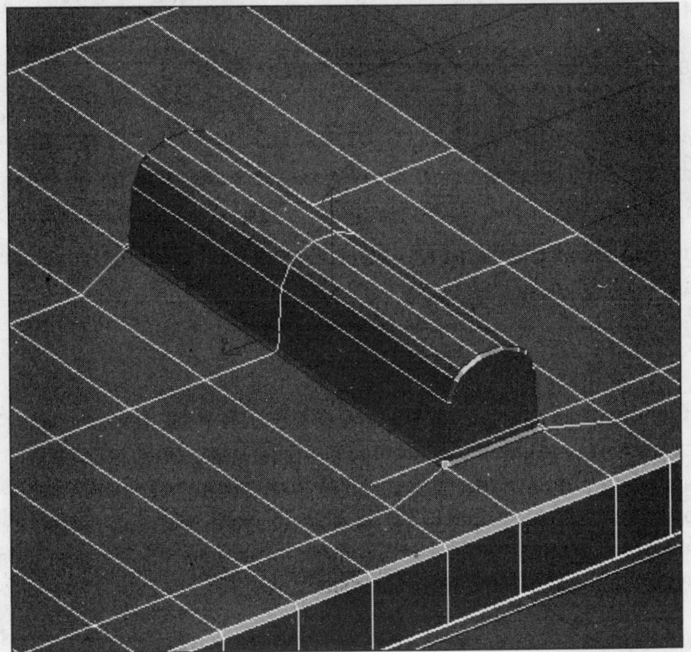

Fig. 2.51, *g* and *h*. Modeling a dummy for the phone base

- Give the object a self-explanatory name, for example, Phone-Base. Convert it to the Edit Poly type or use the **Edit Poly** modifier.

Menu bar → **Modifiers** → **Mesh Editing** → **Edit Poly**

- Working with vertices, select and move them so that longitudinal edges appear where the display and the holes should be (Fig. 2.51, *b*).
- Crèate a hollow for the display using the **Bevel** command for polygons (Fig. 2.51, *c*).
- Create a hole by selecting the polygons on both sides and executing the **Bridge** command (Fig. 2.51, *d*).
- Using the **Chamfer** command for edges, create chamfers inside and outside the hole (Fig. 2.51, *e*). Do this in one operation, simultaneously for all the edges.
- Using the **Connect** command for edges (Fig. 2.51, *f*) and the **Bevel** command for polygons (Fig. 2.51, *g*), create the lock inside the hole.
- Move the vertices, extrude the polygons, and create chamfers on the edges to make the hinge (Fig. 2.51, *h*).
- Leave the subobject mode and apply the **Bend** modifier.

Menu bar → **Modifiers** → **Parametric Deformers** → **Bend**

- Set it as shown in Fig. 2.52, *a*. If you fail to obtain the shape shown in the figure, try to adjust the **Direction** and **Bend Axis** parameters. I have worked with 3ds Max for many years, but I still don't understand the logic behind these parameters.
- Edit sub-objects of the **Bend** modifier. Move the bend center in the left viewport to the lower right corner (Fig. 2.52, *b*).

TIP

If you need to change parameters of the **Edit Poly** modifier, you can do this. However, be aware that the **Bend** modifier (like many other modifiers in 3ds Max) can be applied to a part of the object, rather than the entire object. This part is determined by a sub-object selection. To be able to work with sub-objects down the modifier stack and control the final result, insert an empty modifier such as **Mesh Select** or **Poly Select** above the **Bend** modifier.

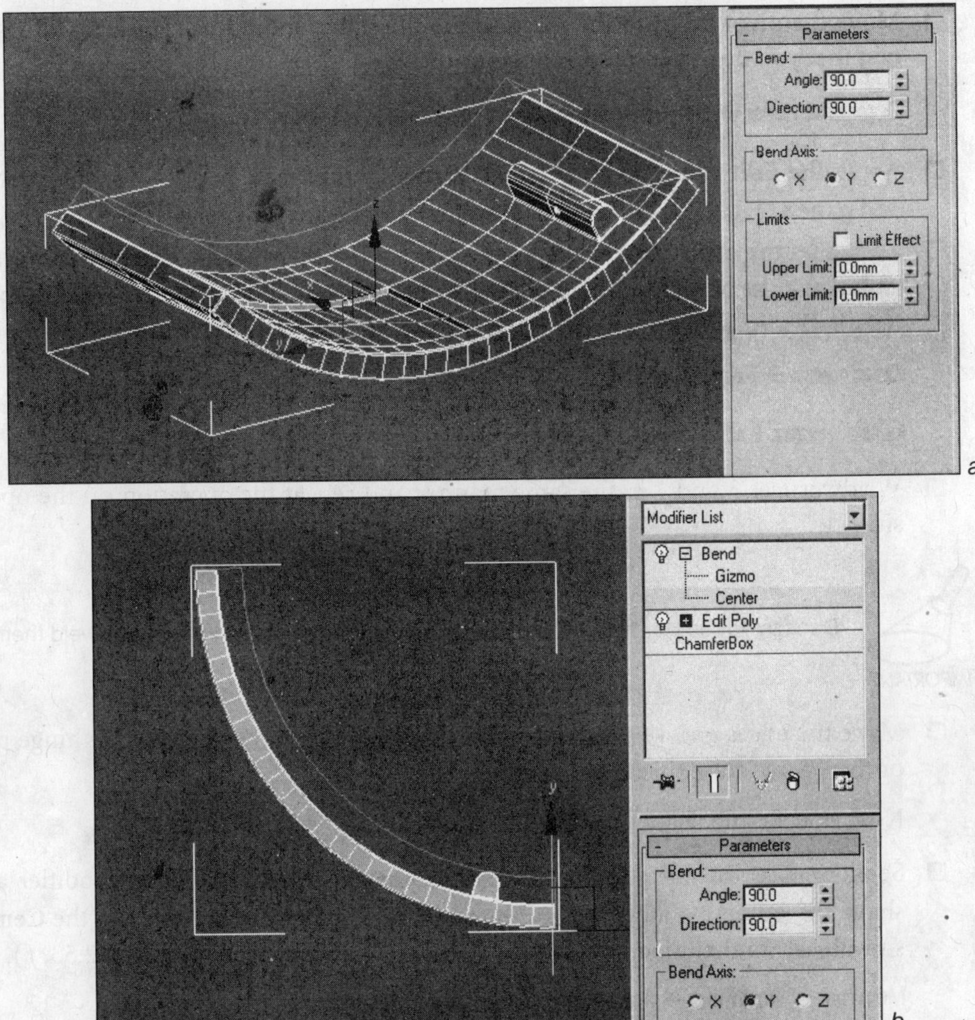

Fig. 2.52. Bending the dummy for the phone base

Modeling the Flap

The other part is modeled in the same way; however, you'll need more modifiers.

- Start modeling the Phone-Part-2 object (as I called it) by creating a **Chamfer Box** object (Fig. 2.53, *a*). I placed it to its final position because this will make modeling easier. I did this "by eye." In addition, I edited the Phone-Base object slightly.

- Move the pivot point to the place where the hinge should be (Fig. 2.53, *b*). I suggest that you don't put off this operation.

  Command panel → the **Hierarchy** subpanel → **Affect Pivot Only**

- Apply the **Edit Poly** modifier, move vertices, and create hollows for the buttons and panels (Fig. 2.53, *c*) using the **Bevel** command for polygons.
- To model the other part of the hinge, make a hollow with the **Extrude** command and adjust the positions of the edges by moving them (Fig. 2.53, *d*). Weld the vertices indicated by the numbers 1 and 2 using the **Target Weld** command.

  Quad menu → **Target Weld**

  Grab vertex 1 and drag the rubber band to vertex 2.

- Weld vertices 3 and 4 in the same manner and repeat the operation on the opposite side.

Don't try to remedy the problem just by moving the vertices. You should weld them!

- Move the edges and vertices and make chamfers (Fig. 2.53, *e*). Take the hinge part on the Phone-Base object as a pattern.

  Now, you should shape the object as needed.

- Select vertices on the side that should be skewed. Apply the **Skew** modifier and shape the model by adjusting parameters and moving the center (i.e., the **Center** sub-object) to the upper left corner (in the top view) of the object (Fig. 2.53, *f*).

  Menu bar → **Modifiers** → **Parametric Deformers** → **Skew**

- The next modifier in the stack is an empty **Mesh Select** modifier, which selects the entire object. The modifiers that follow it in the stack will effect the entire object.

  Menu bar → **Modifiers** → **Selection** → **Mesh Select**

- The next modifier, **Taper**, makes the part to taper slightly (Fig. 2.53, *g*).

  Menu bar → **Modifiers** → **Parametric Deformers** → **Taper**

- Apply and adjust the **Bend** modifier. The limits of this modifier allow you to bend only the required part of the object (Fig. 2.53, *h*).

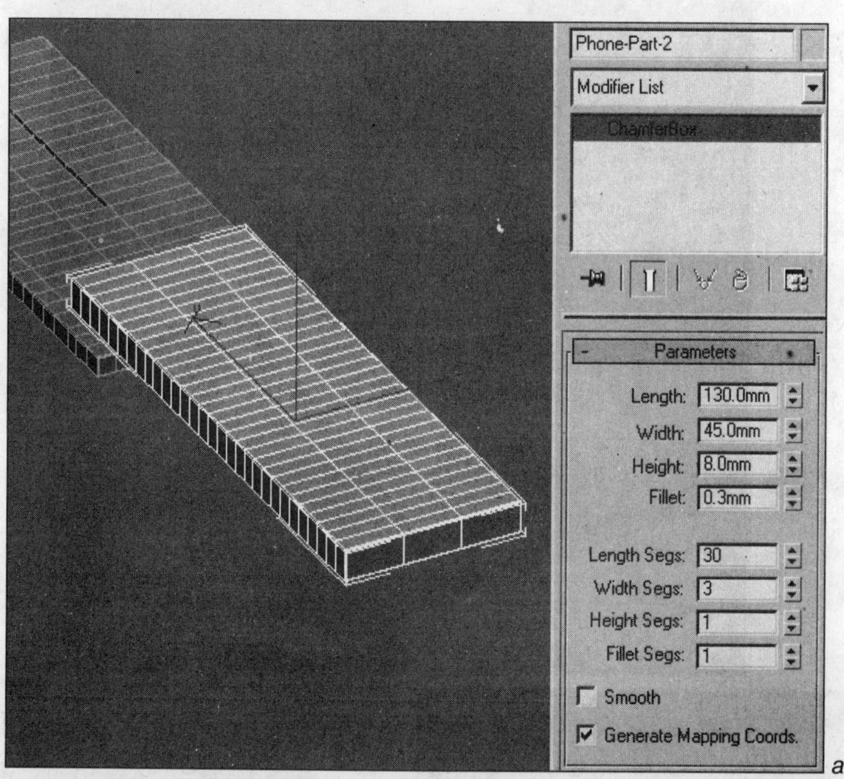

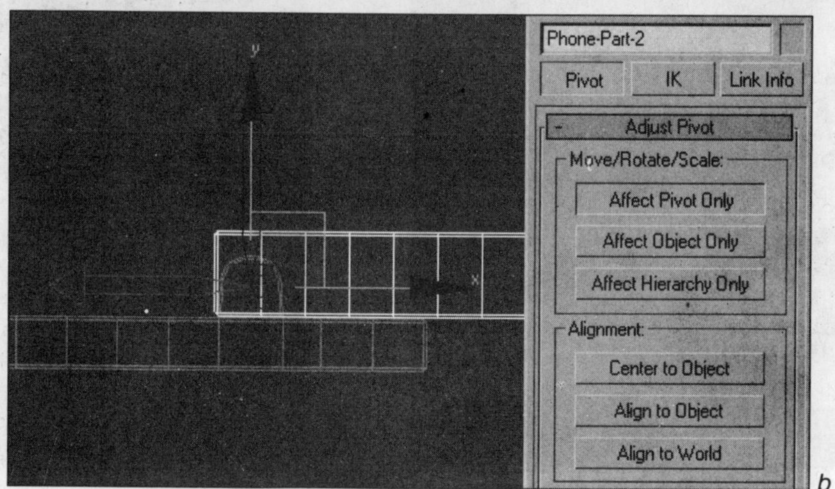

Fig. 2.53, *a* and *b*. Modeling the flap part of the phone

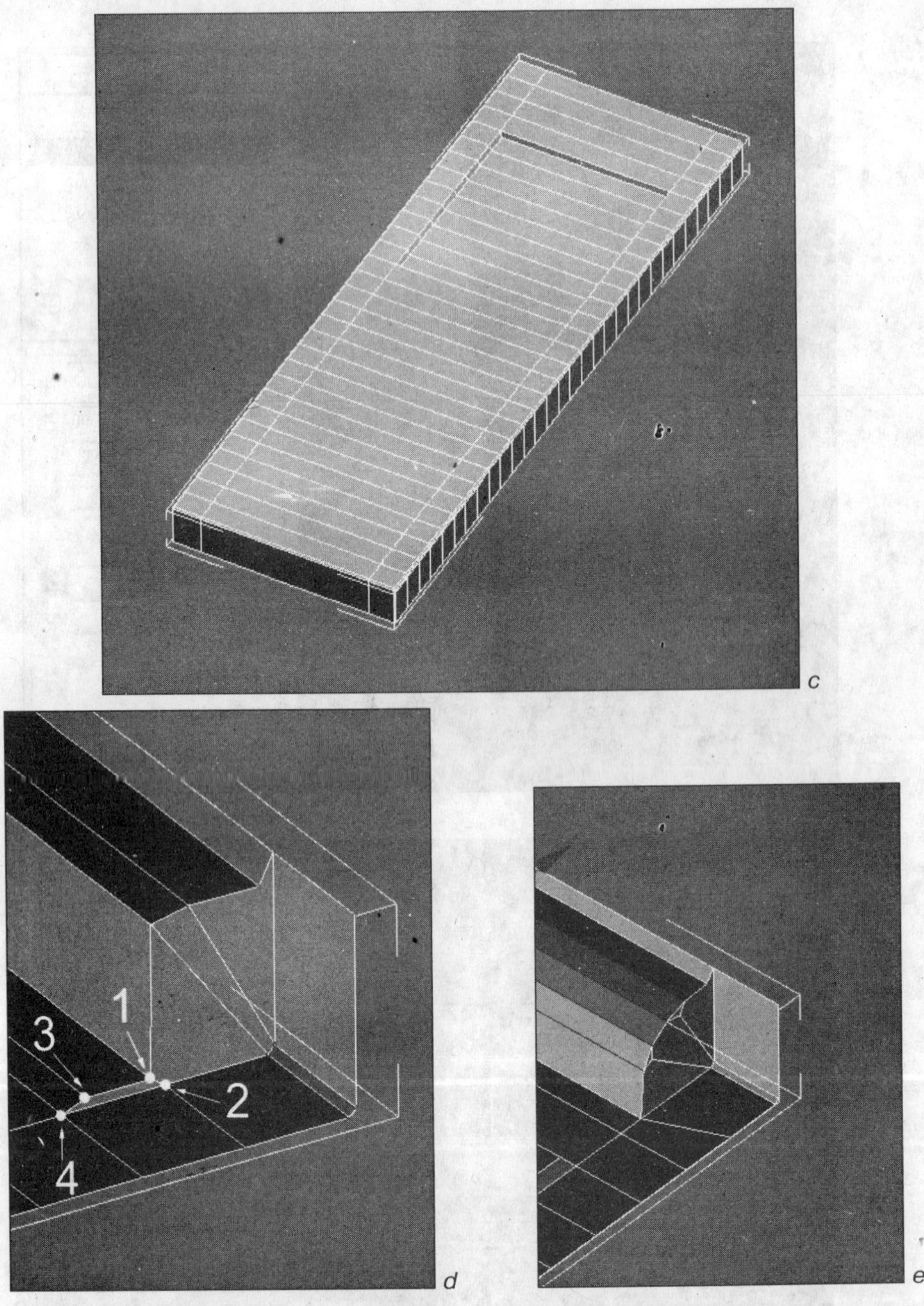

Fig. 2.53, *c–e*. Modeling the flap part of the phone

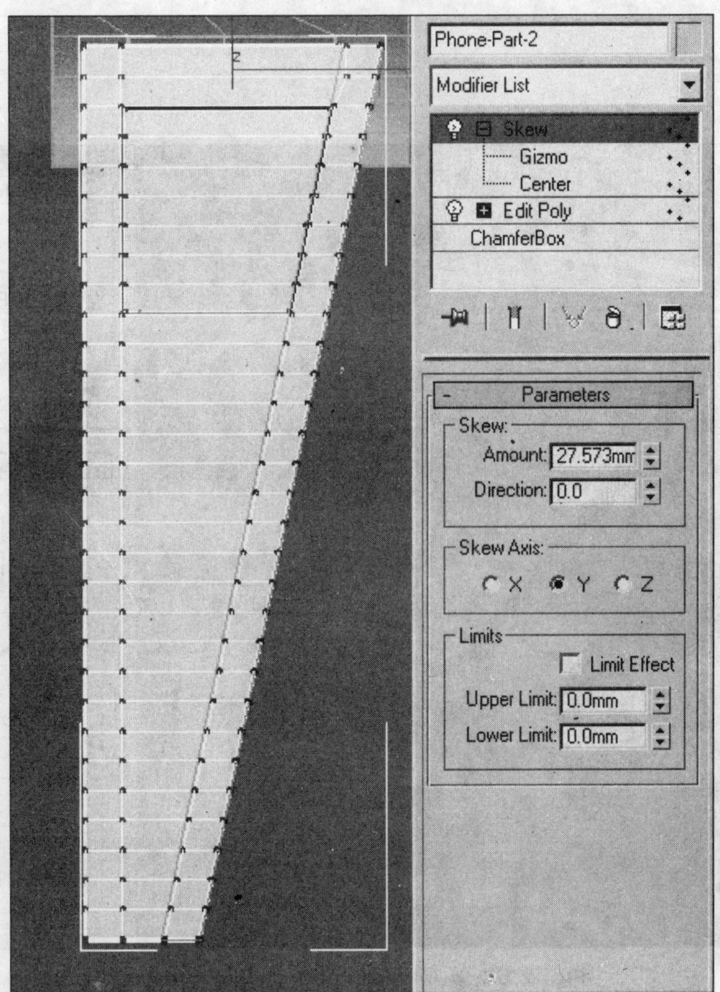

Fig. 2.53, *f*. Modeling the flap part of the phone

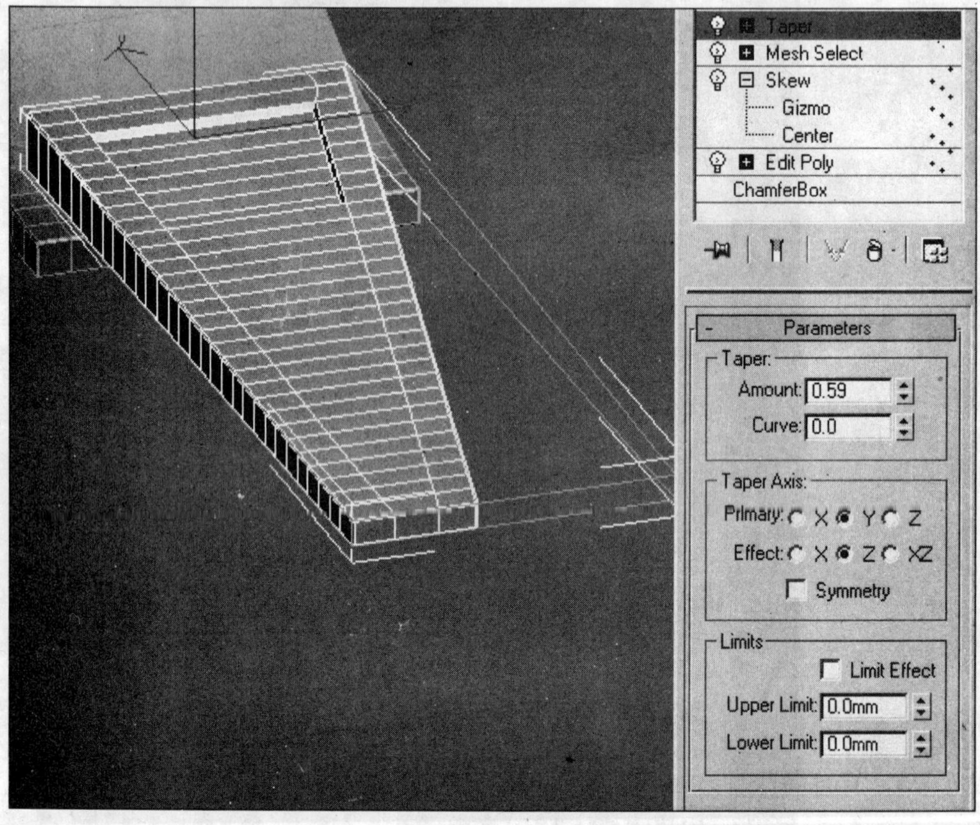

Fig. 2.53, *g*. Modeling the flap part of the phone

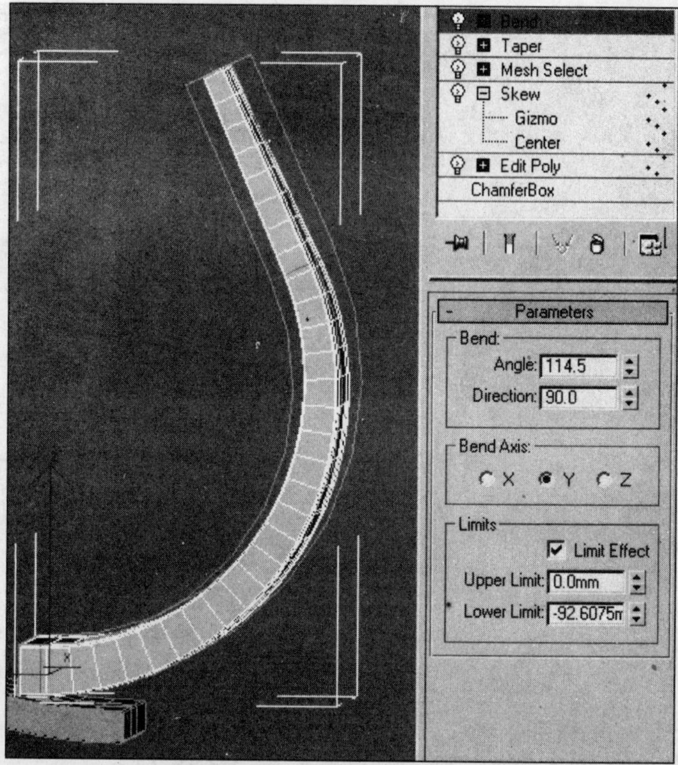

Fig. 2.53, *h*. Modeling the flap part of the phone

Finishing the Model

Rotate the object so that its sharp end is in the slot. Adjust the modifier parameters to obtain the best result. You can jump up or down the stack including the **Edit Poly** modifier involved. Don't change the vertex selection, otherwise the **Skew** modifier will work incorrectly.

You can jump down the stack to its bottom to resize the **Chamfer Box** object because you might need to change the length. Don't change the number of segments.

Don't collapse the modifier stack. You'll need to apply a map and it is convenient to do this before the parametric modifiers are applied.

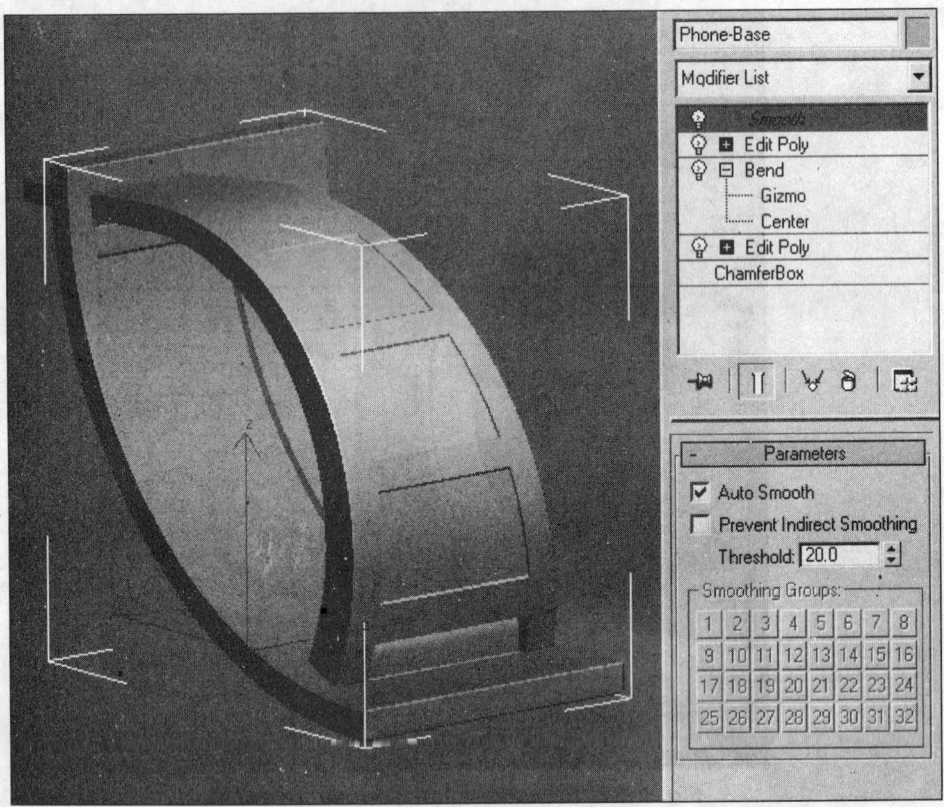

Fig. 2.54. The finished model

Finally, apply to both objects the **Smooth** modifier with the parameters shown in Fig. 2.54. The **AutoSmooth** checkbox checked and the threshold value of 20 degrees are the best choice in this case.

My variant is in the Model5-final file in the Projects\Project5 folder on the accompanying CD-ROM.

Modeling Other Objects

In this section, I'll describe modeling objects necessary for the final rendering of models created earlier. If you have already created these models, you'll easily create the objects described in this section. All of the models are located in the Projects\Misc Objects folder on the accompanying CD-ROM. As for actual objects to model, you can find them on your desk or in the bathroom.

NOTE

You should take into account the sizes of the objects when modeling.

Paper Clip

What could be simpler than a paper clip?

- Create a broken-line spline in the top view, observing the size of a paper clip (Fig. 2.55, *a*).

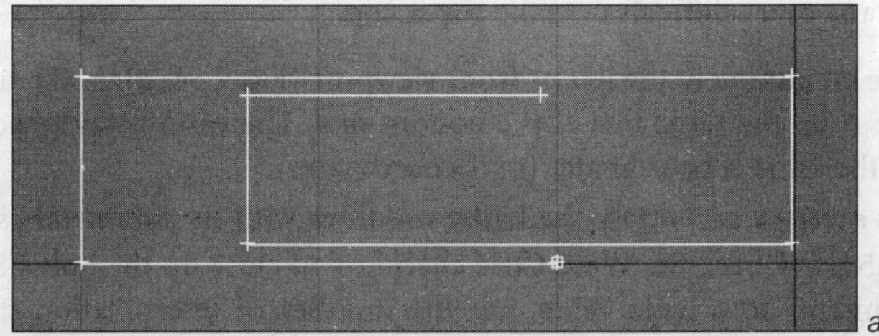

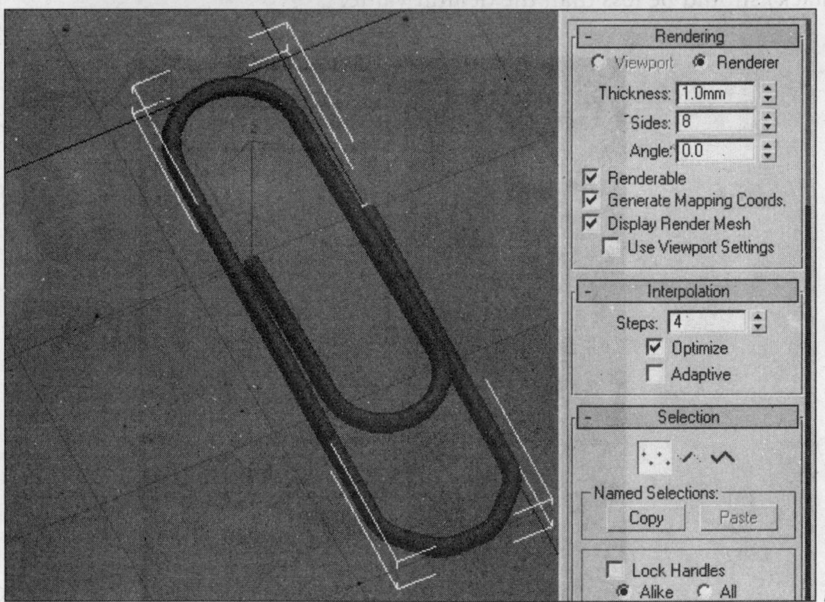

Fig. 2.55. Modeling a paper clip

- Apply the **Fillet** and **Chamfer** commands to obtain the desired shape. Weld the adjacent vertices with the **Weld** command.
- Move the necessary vertices so that the paper clip becomes nonflat.
- In the **Rendering** rollout, check the **Renderable** and **Display Render Mesh** checkboxes.

The number of sides shouldn't be large. The same is true for the number of interpolation steps.

The paper clip is ready (Fig. 2.55, *b*).

Pin

This isn't any more difficult than the paper clip.

- Create an outline in the left or front viewport (Fig. 2.56, *a*). Make sure that the top vertex is on the same line as the bottom one. The easiest way to achieve this is to enter the same X coordinates (or Y coordinates).
- Select a vertex and apply the **Lathe** modifier with its parameters set as shown in Fig. 2.56, *b*. Check the **Weld Core** checkbox to close up the holes. Set the number of segments to a large value, but the number of interpolation steps (down the stack) should be less than the default value.

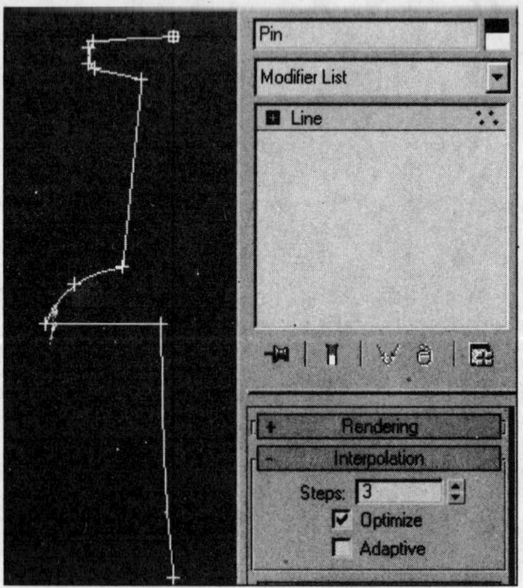

Fig. 2.56, *a*. Modeling a pin

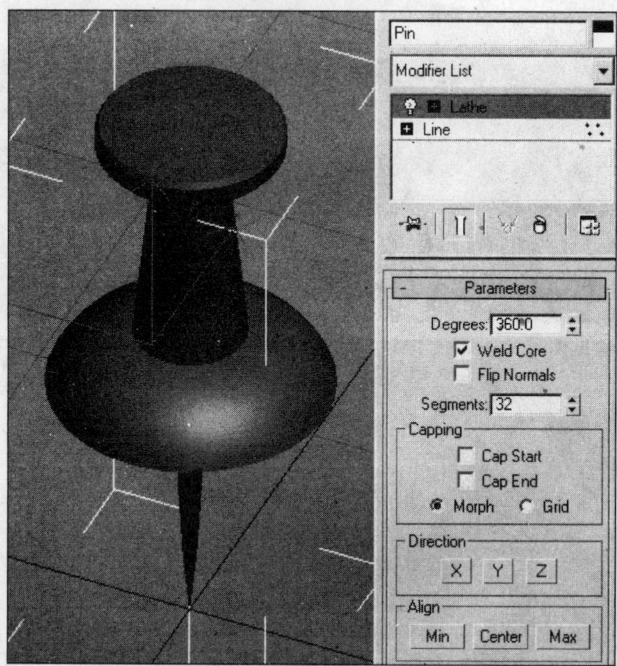

Fig. 2.56, *b*. Modeling a pin

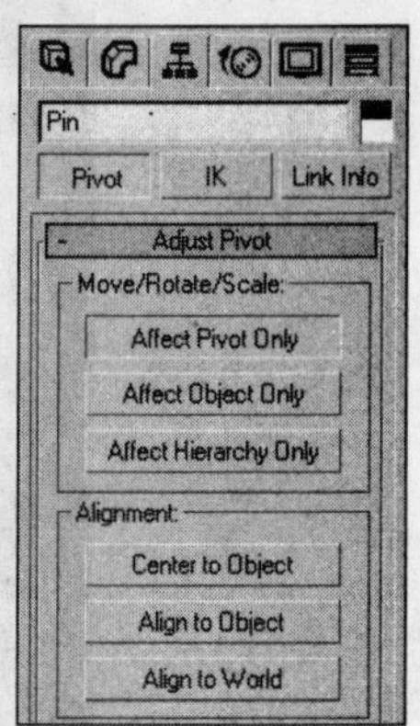

It is best to place the pivot point to the center of the object and align it to the world coordinates.

Command panel → **Hierarchy** subpanel → **Pivot** → **Affect Pivot Only** → **Center to Object**, **Align to World**

Ballpoint Pen

The first steps in modeling a ballpoint pen are the same as the pin (Fig. 2.57, *a*, *b*). I created a rectangle according to the size of a pen (15 cm long, 1 cm in diameter), converted it to the Editable Spline type, removed unnecessary fragments and added a few missing vertices (with the **Refine** command) and segments (with the **Divide** command).

If you are dissatisfied with the results of applying the **Lathe** modifier, select another rotation axis with the **X**, **Y**, or **Z** buttons.

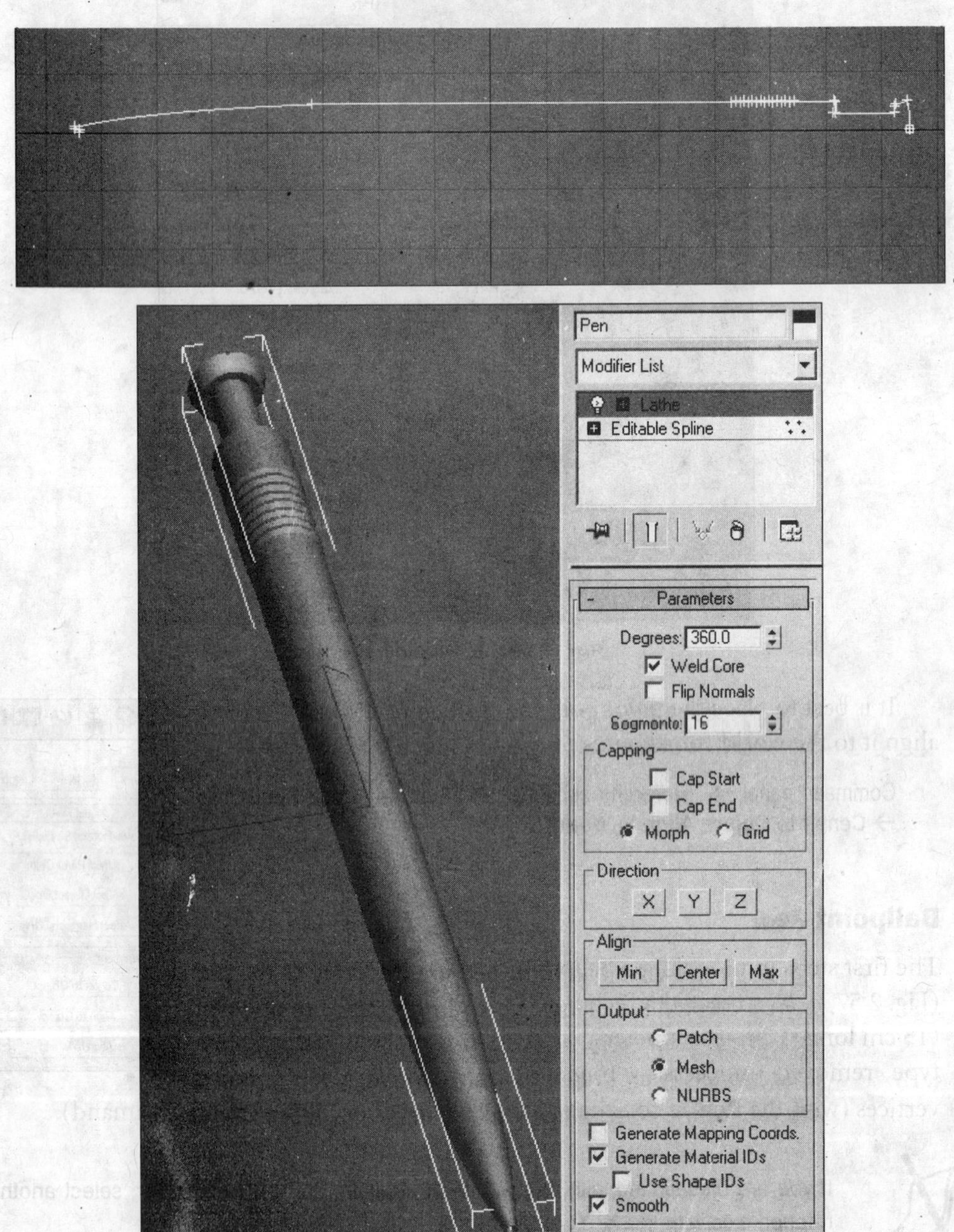

Fig. 2.57, *a* and *b*. Modeling a ballpoint pen

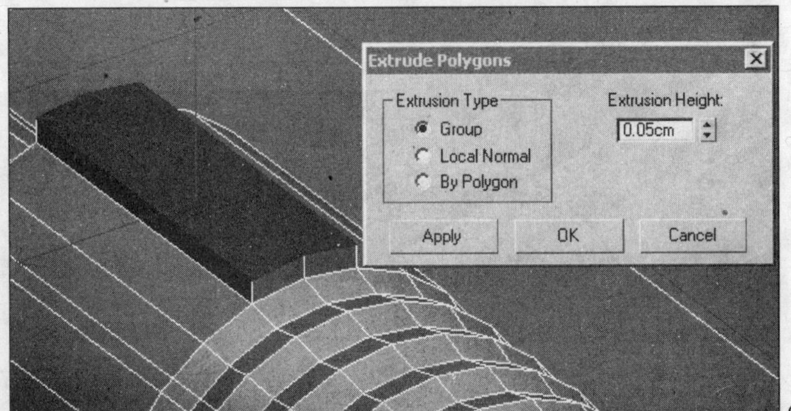

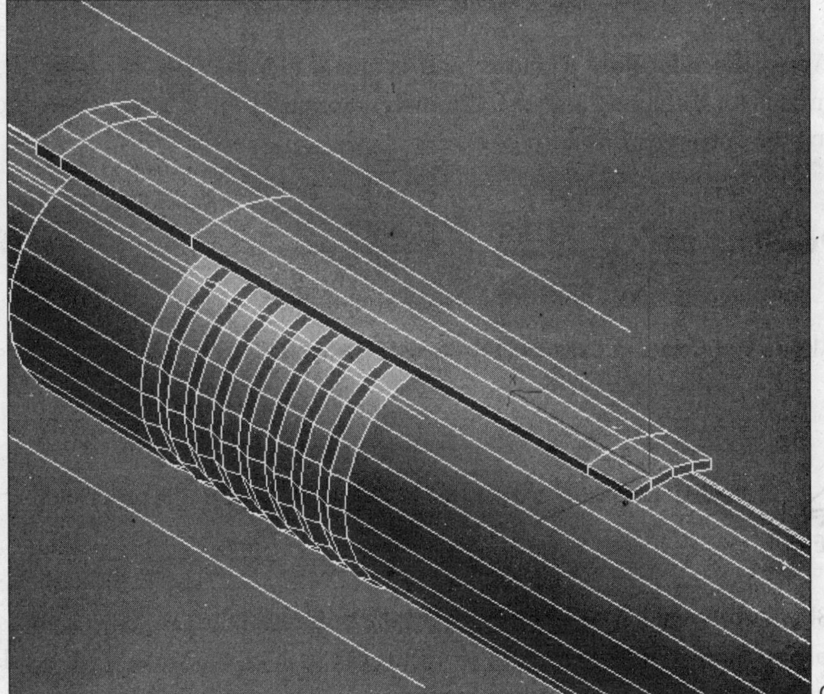

Fig. 2.57, *c* and *d*. Modeling a ballpoint pen

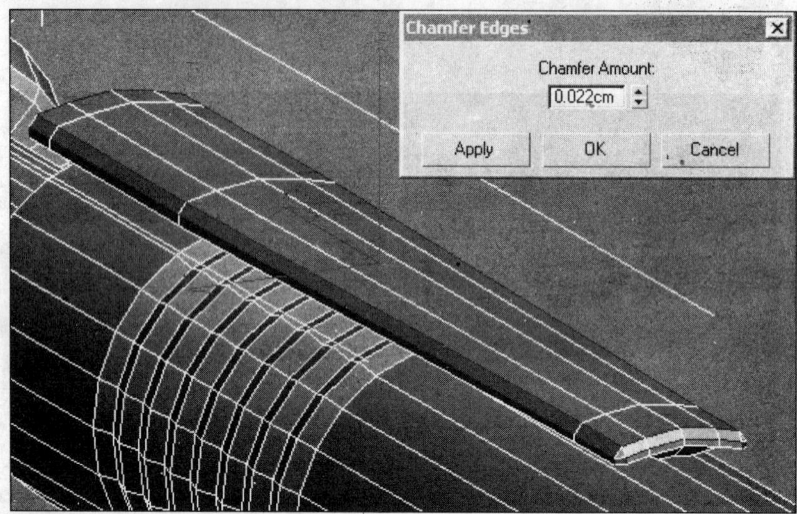

Fig. 2.57, *e*. Modeling a ballpoint pen

Apply the **Edit Poly** modifier and create a pen fastener by using the **Extrude** command for polygons and the **Chamfer** command for edges and by moving and scaling the polygons (Fig. 2.57, *c–e*).

Pencil

- Create a gengon as a billet for a pencil (Fig. 2.58, *a*).

Menu bar → **Create** → **Extended Primitives** → **Gengon**

NOTE

I created "excessive" sides to make it easier to sharpen the pencil later.

- Sharpen the pencil by applying the **Edit Poly** modifier, moving vertices, and applying the **Extrude** command to vertices (Fig. 2.58, *b*). Make a round slant at the base of the pencil (Fig. 2.58, *c*).

This pencil is somewhat rough, but it'll do as an auxiliary object. You just need to select and assign smoothing groups to the polygon (Fig. 2.58, *d*).

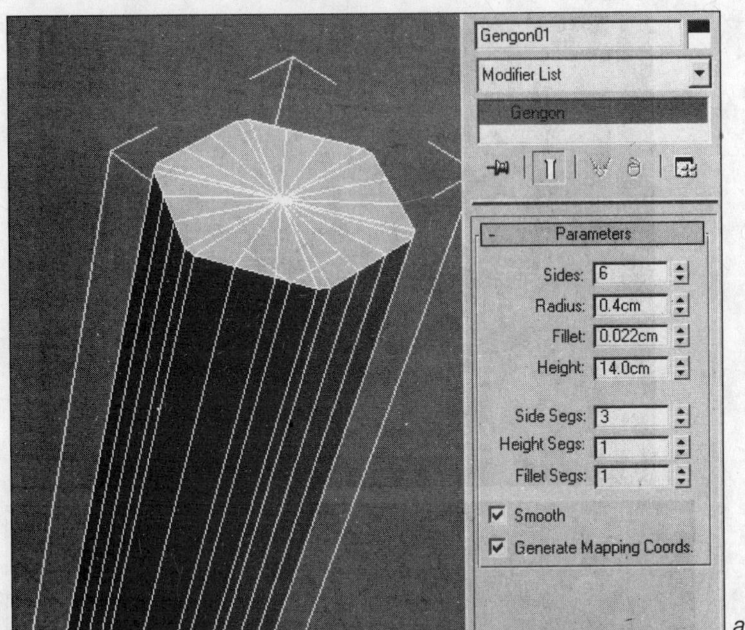

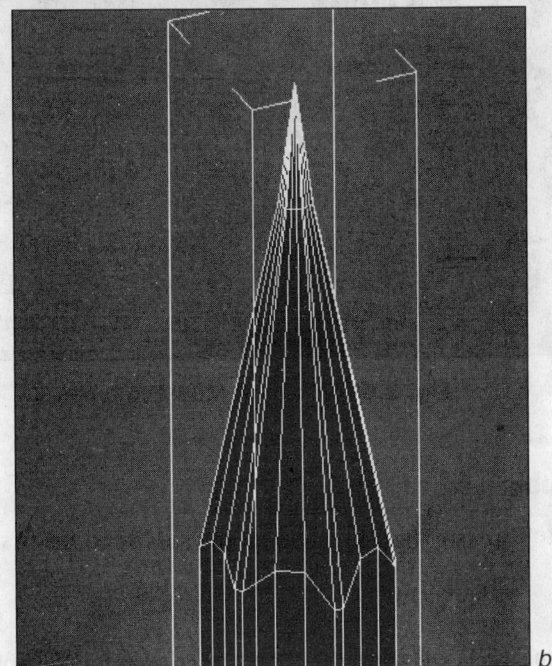

Fig. 2.58, *a* and *b*. Modeling a pencil

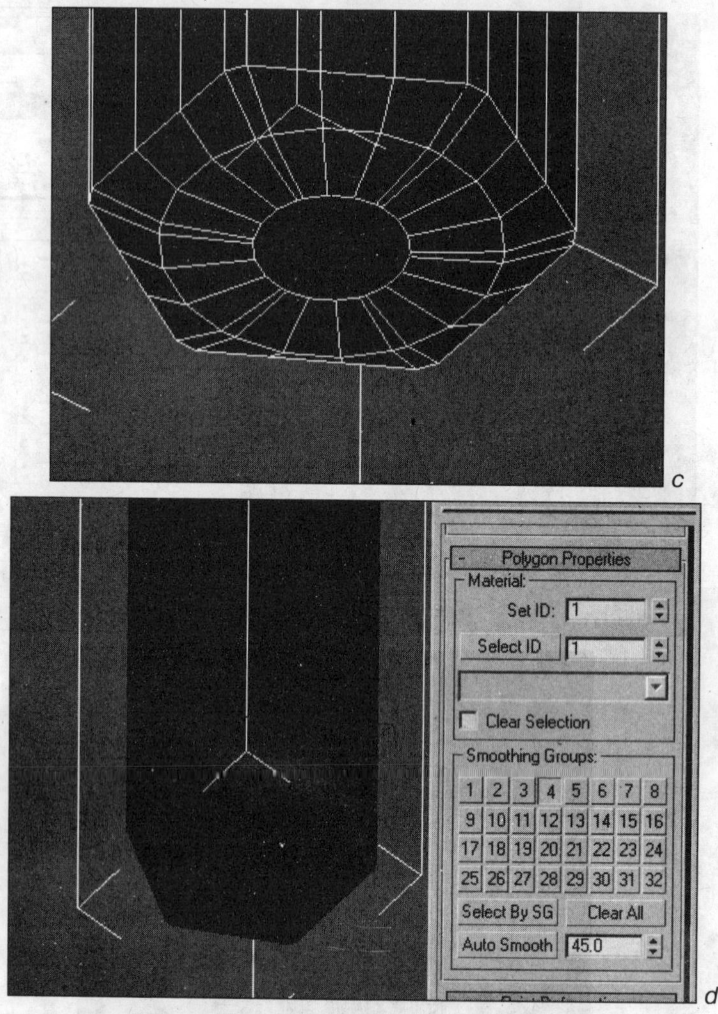

Fig. 2.58, *c* and *d*. Modeling a pencil

Toothpaste Tube

❒ To model a toothpaste tube, create a set of cross-sections first (Fig. 2.59, *a*).

TIP

Start with a circle and convert it to the type or apply the **Editable Spline** modifier to it.

- Obtain the necessary shapes of cross-sections by moving, copying, and editing the objects at the vertex level.
- Attach the objects to one of them. It is desirable that this object wasn't scaled.
- Using the **Cross Section** command, draw longitudinal splines between the cross-sections (Fig. 2.59, *b*).

Command panel → the **Geometry** rollout → **Cross Section**

- Click a cross-section and drag the rubber band to the next cross-section. Click again.
- Complete the procedure with a right click.

TIP

If you wish to obtain smooth splines, select the **Bezier** or **Bezier Corner** vertex type in the **New Vertex Type** group. When you need a corner, select **Corner**.

- Apply the **Edit Patch** modifier (Fig. 2.59, *c*).

Menu bar → **Modifiers** → **Patch/Spline Editing** → **Edit Patch**

NOTE

All necessary settings are in the **Spline Surface** and **Surface** groups.

To build a surface, 3ds Max requires that the frame consists of quadrangles and triangles. The vertices don't need to be welded, especially because this is impossible. It is only important that the vertices are in the crossing of the splines, and that the distance between the vertices is small. The threshold, under which close vertices are considered as one vertex, is set with the **Threshold** parameter.

If your model is turned inside out, check the **Flip Normals** checkbox.

The **Remove Interior Patches** checkbox prevents creating patches inside the model.

The **View Steps** and **Render Steps** parameters allow you to guess that the patches can be displayed in the viewport or rendered with various quality levels. The number of interpolation steps for splines isn't used in patches, so you don't need to worry about interpolation of the frame.

The tube is almost finished. You could work a little with the smoothing groups by selecting patches and assigning different smoothing groups to them. In addition, you could remove the patch from inside the cap (Fig. 2.59, *d*).

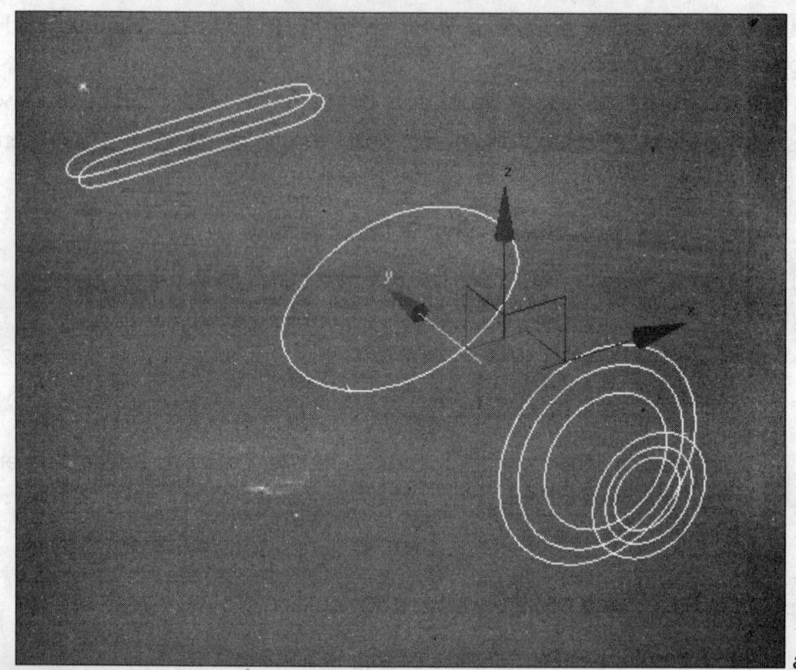

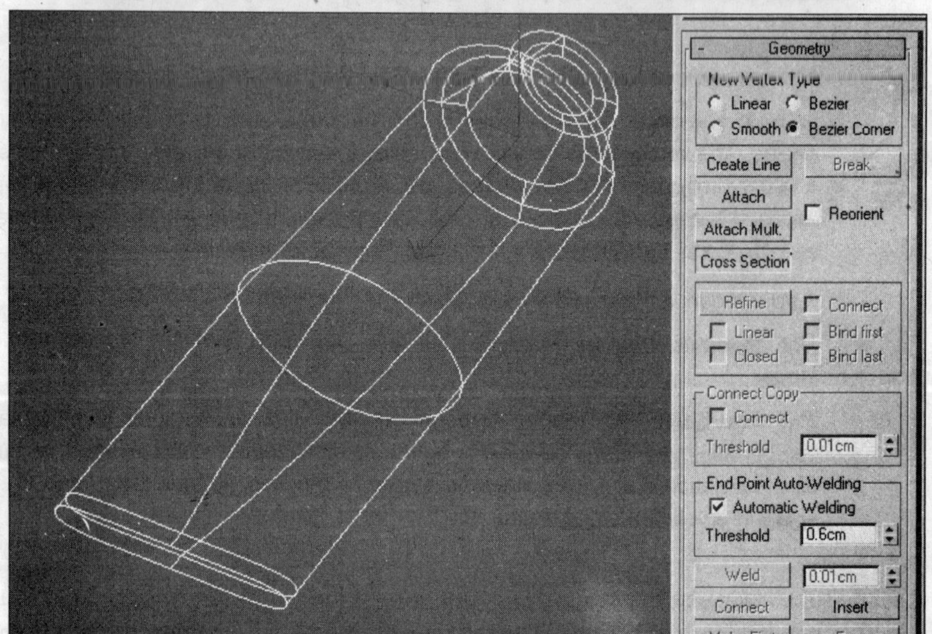

Fig. 2.59, *a* and *b*. Modeling a toothpaste tube

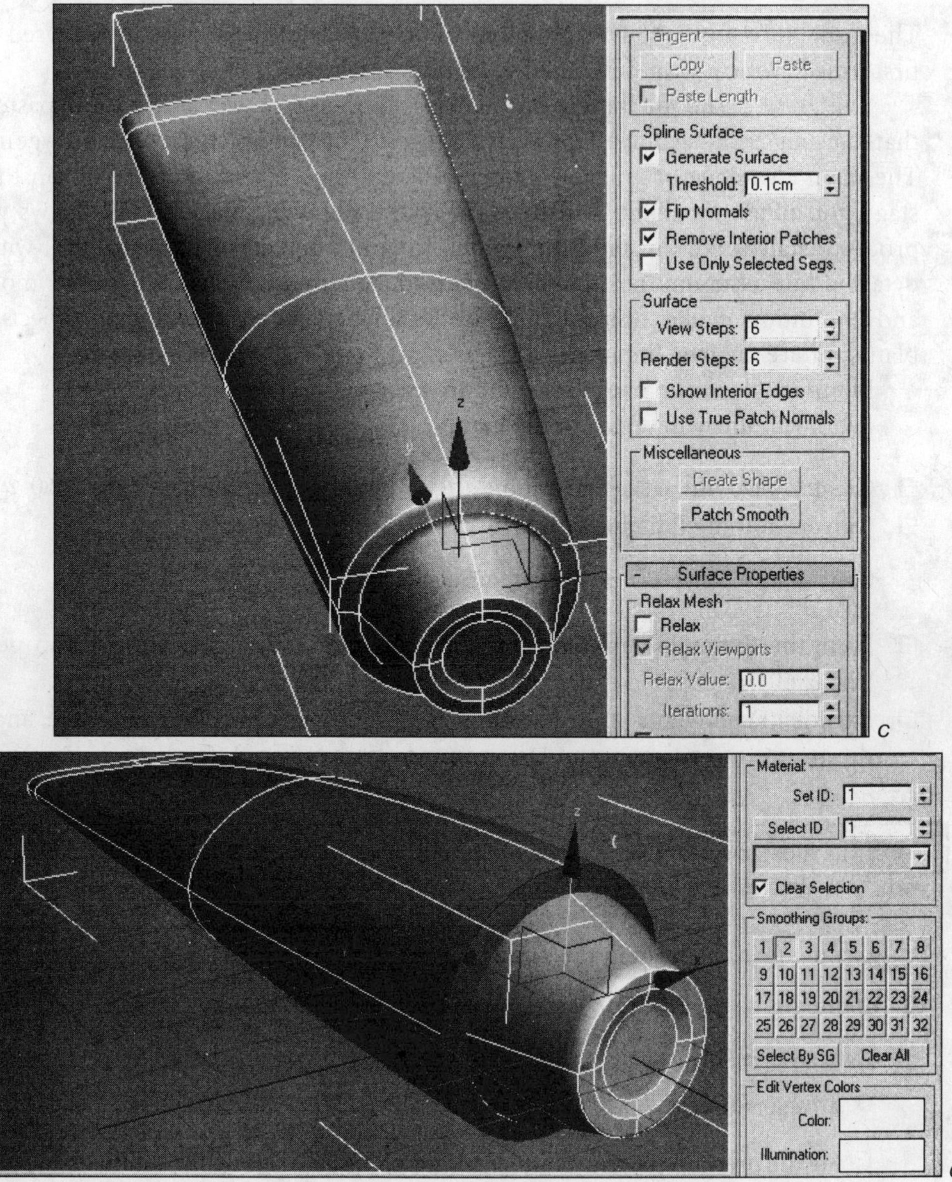

Fig. 2.59, *c* and *d*. Modeling a toothpaste tube

Modeling a Tooth Brush

The model of a tooth brush isn't going to be very detailed because it was used in the first project, which wasn't intended to be photorealistic.

You could create the handle of the brush in the same way as the toothpaste tube, that is, using cross-sections. However, I suggest that you practice at the polygon level. The main advantage of polygon modeling is that you invest much labor on the first stage, but obtain flexibility and freedom in the following stages. This allows you to process details when finishing the model. It would be very difficult to deal with tiny details if you used another modeling method. A combination of polygonal modeling and smoothing makes this method the best when you model living objects (e.g., plants) or are involved in bio-design.

I'll model the tooth brush based on my own.

Begin with the widest part of the handle.

- Create a box with a size corresponding to that of the handle base (Fig. 2.60, *a*).
- Convert it to the Editable Poly type.

Quad menu → **Convert to** → **Convert to Editable Poly**

- Using the **Extrude** command for polygons and scaling, process the top polygon (Fig. 2.60, *b*).
- Extrude the polygons of the handle forward and backward. Move, rotate, and scale the groups of vertices around the common center (Fig. 2.60, *c*).

TIP

It is convenient to do some of these operations in the left, or top viewport. Uncheck the **Ignore Backfacing** checkbox.

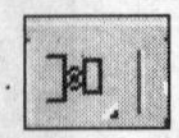

Create the brush head in the same object.

- In the top view, create a necessary polygon (Fig. 2.60, *d*).

Quad menu → **Polygon**

Quad menu → **Create**

Create the polygon moving counterclockwise while keeping the <Shift> key pressed.

- Extrude the polygon to the required height using the **Extrude** command for polygons.
- Select the **Border** and create a polygon using the **Cap** command.

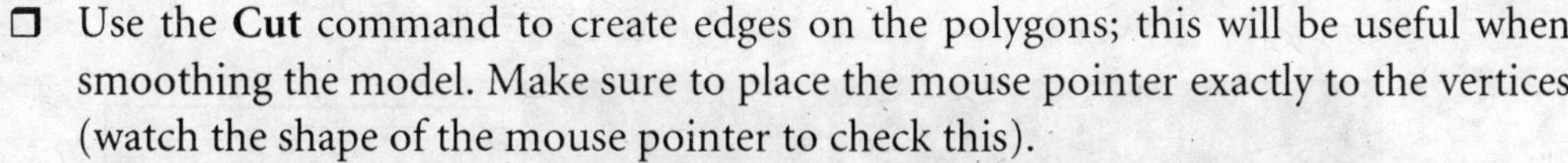

- Use the **Cut** command to create edges on the polygons; this will be useful when smoothing the model. Make sure to place the mouse pointer exactly to the vertices (watch the shape of the mouse pointer to check this).
- Use the **Inset** command for polygons to create a smaller polygon for bristle, and extrude the polygon (Fig. 2.60, *e*).
- Lift the brush head to the necessary height.
- Select appropriate polygons on the brush head and handle, execute the **Bridge** command with the parameters shown in Fig. 2.60, *f*, and give the bridge the desired shape.

Quad menu → the window icon to the left of the **Bridge** command

I won't explain the purpose of all these buttons and parameters because you'll easily figure it out. Remember that after you execute this command, you'll be able to change the model only manually. This is a modeling tool rather than a compound object.

If you now apply a smoothing modifier, for example, **MeshSmooth** or **TurboSmooth**, you won't achieve the desired result. The model will appear a little too smoothed. You could use advanced features of the modifiers, but it would be best to process the polygonal model further by making chamfers on the edges that require a small rounding radius (Fig. 2.60, *g*).

Ring Loop

Make chamfers on a few edges simultaneously. It is convenient to select them using the **Ring** and **Loop** commands. Select one edge, click the appropriate button, and observe the result. This command has no settings. If selection with the **Loop** command stops, for example, at the point, from which two edges are incident, select the next edge while keeping the <Ctrl> key pressed and try to use **Ring** and **Loop** again.

Don't leave "garbage", that is, vertices that aren't welded, but are located at the same point. Weld them using the **Weld**, **Target Weld**, or **Collapse** command.

Make sure the polygons don't cross each other. This is typical for situations when the **Chamfer**, **Bevel**, **Inset**, and some other commands are used.

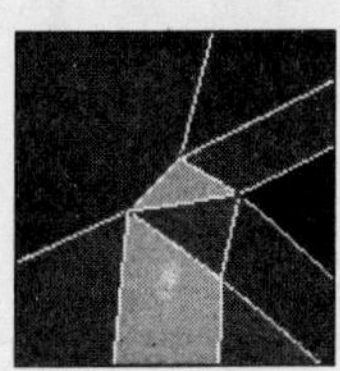

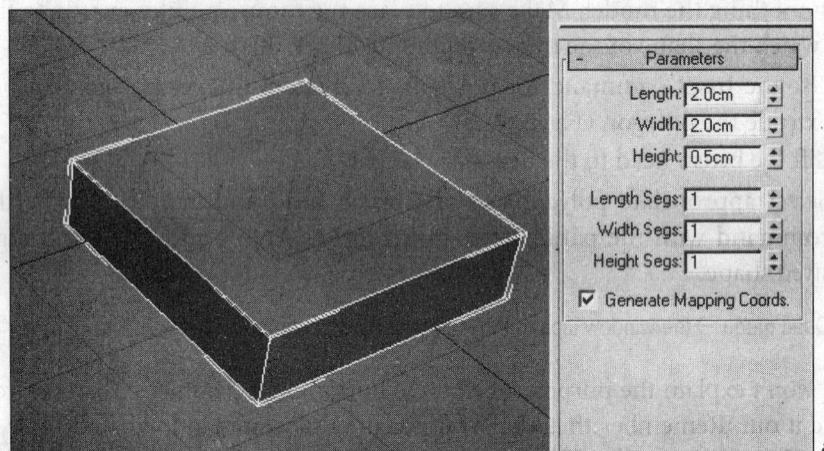

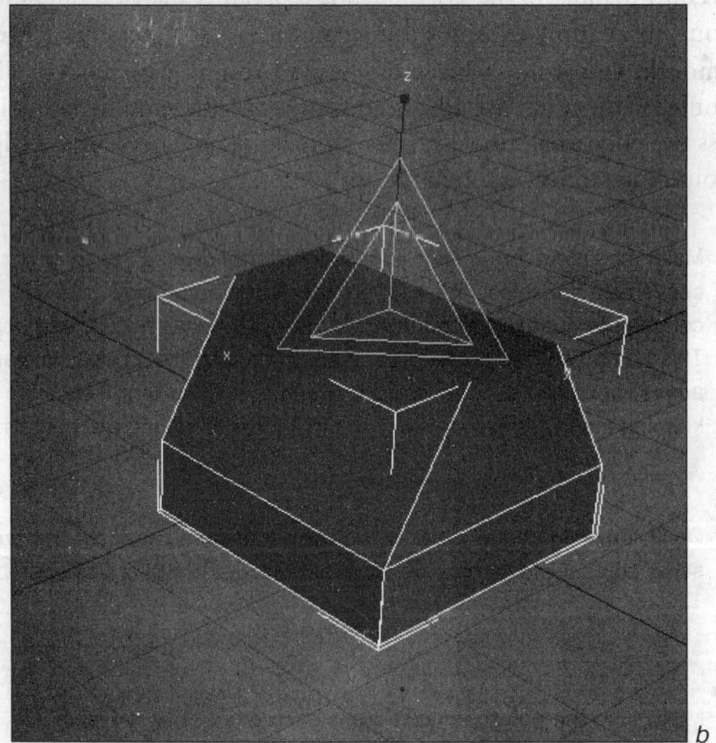

Fig. 2.60, *a* and *b*. A tooth brush

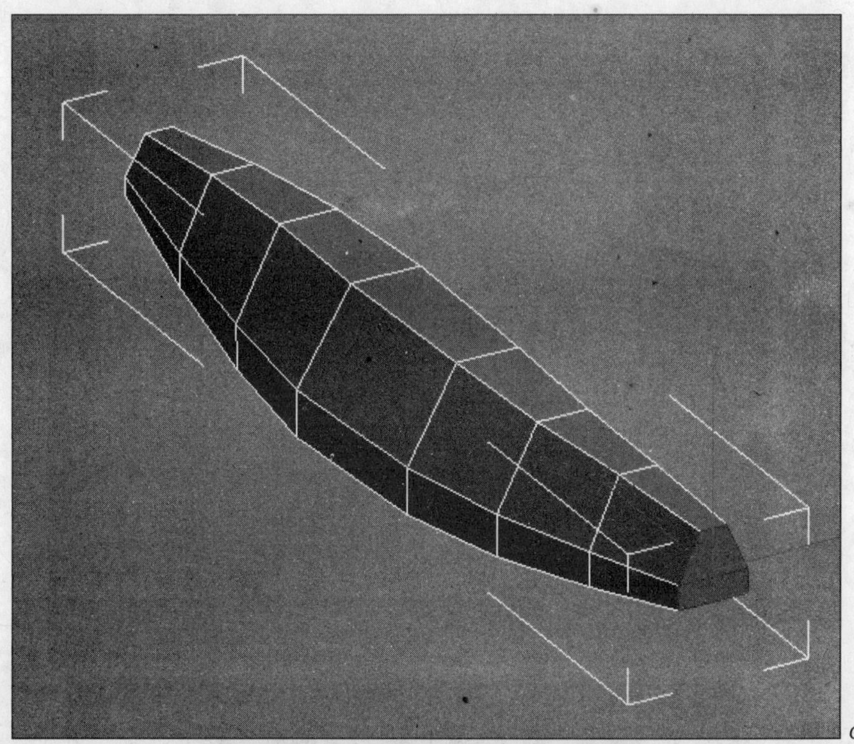
c

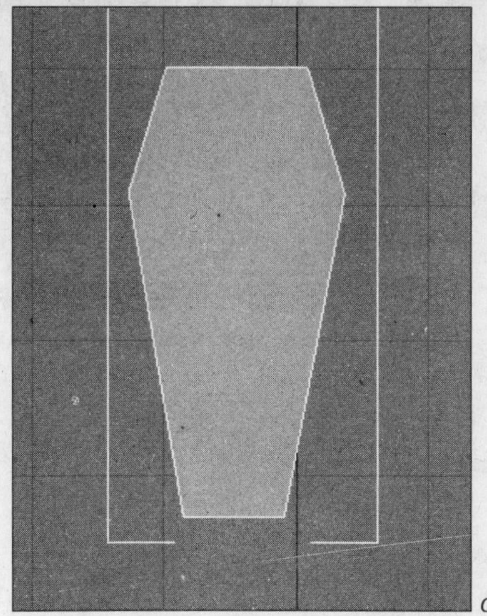
d

Fig. 2.60, *c* and *d*. A tooth brush

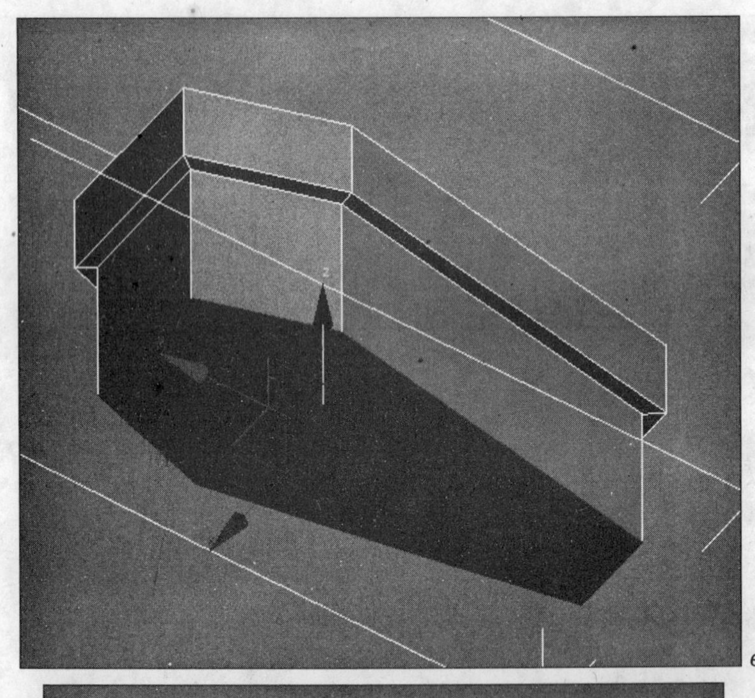

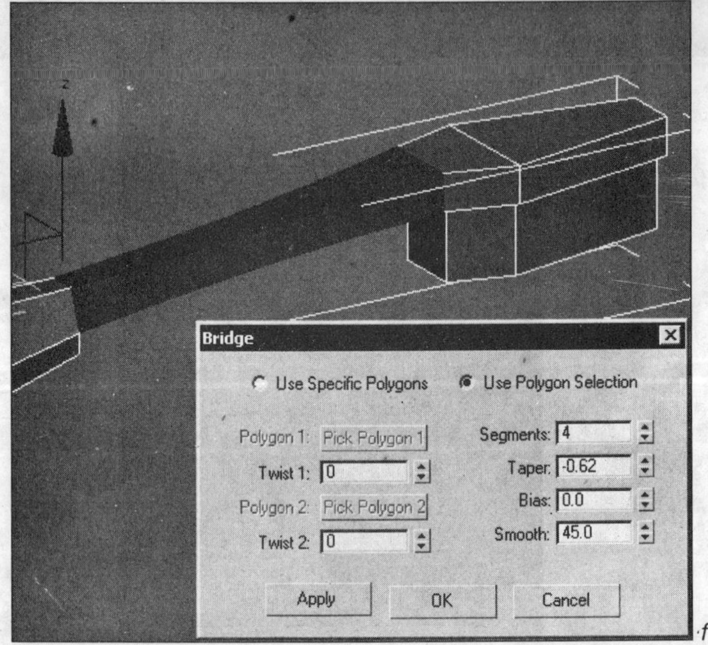

Fig. 2.60, *e* and *f*. A tooth brush

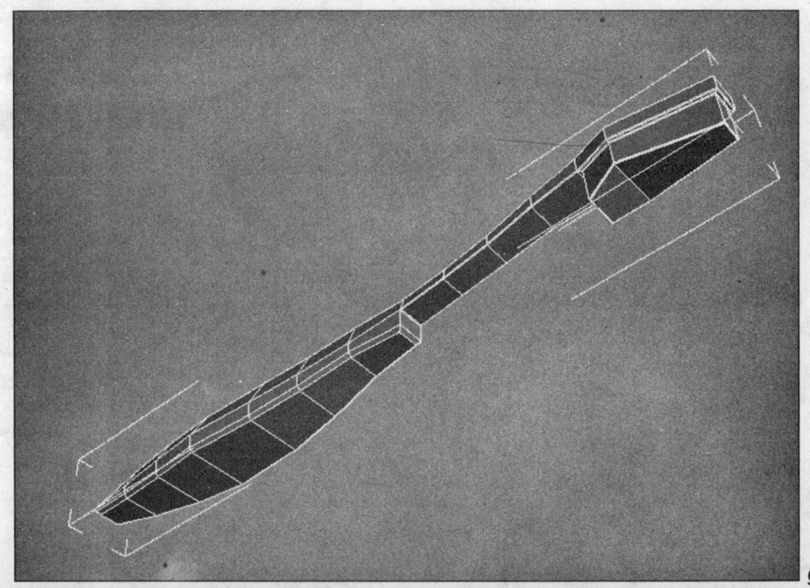

g

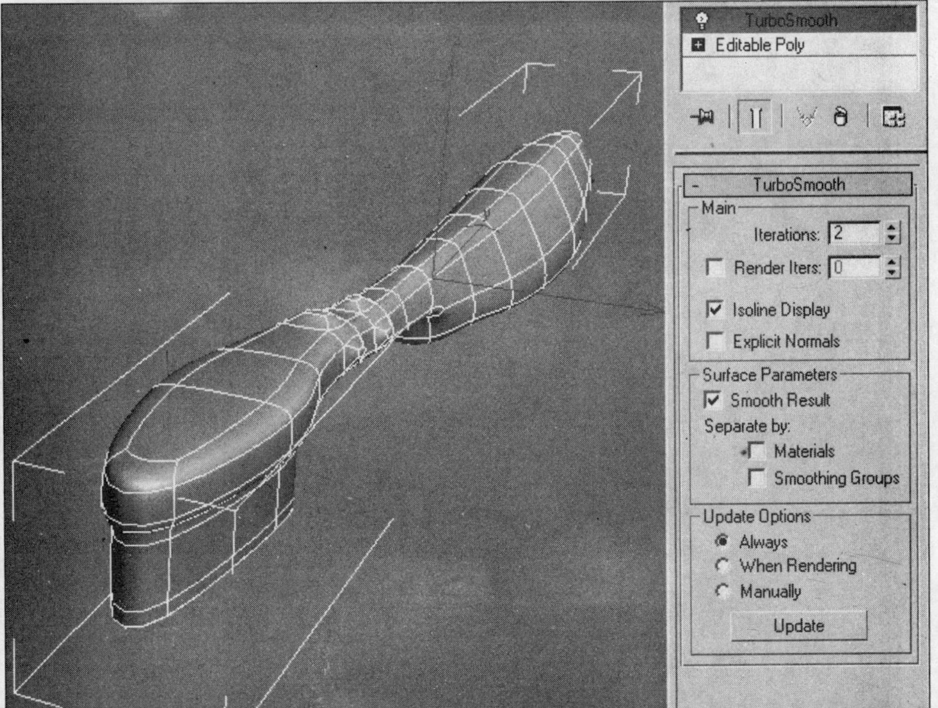

h

Fig. 2.60, *g* and *h*. A tooth brush

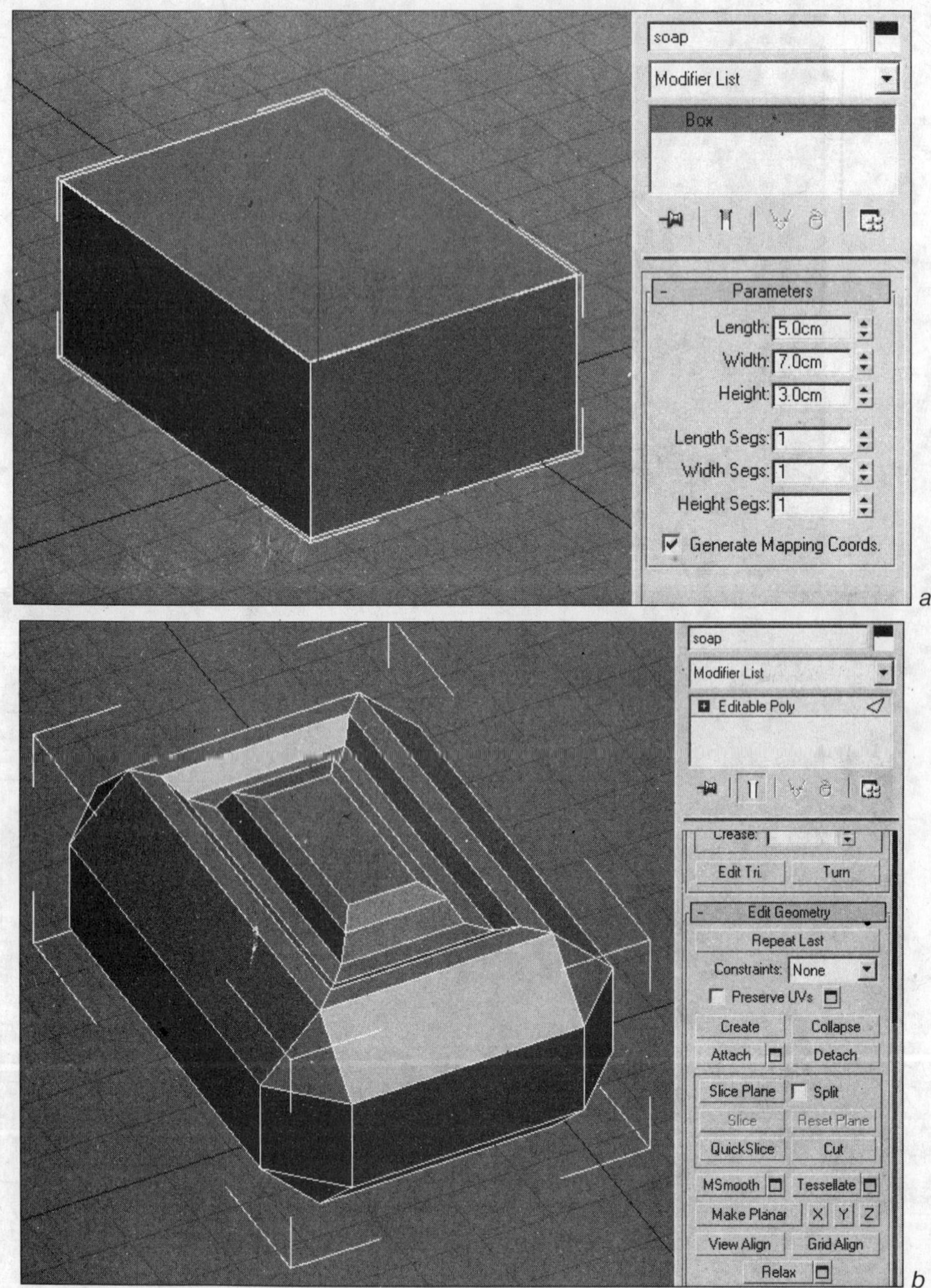

Fig. 2.61, *a* and *b*. A bar of soap

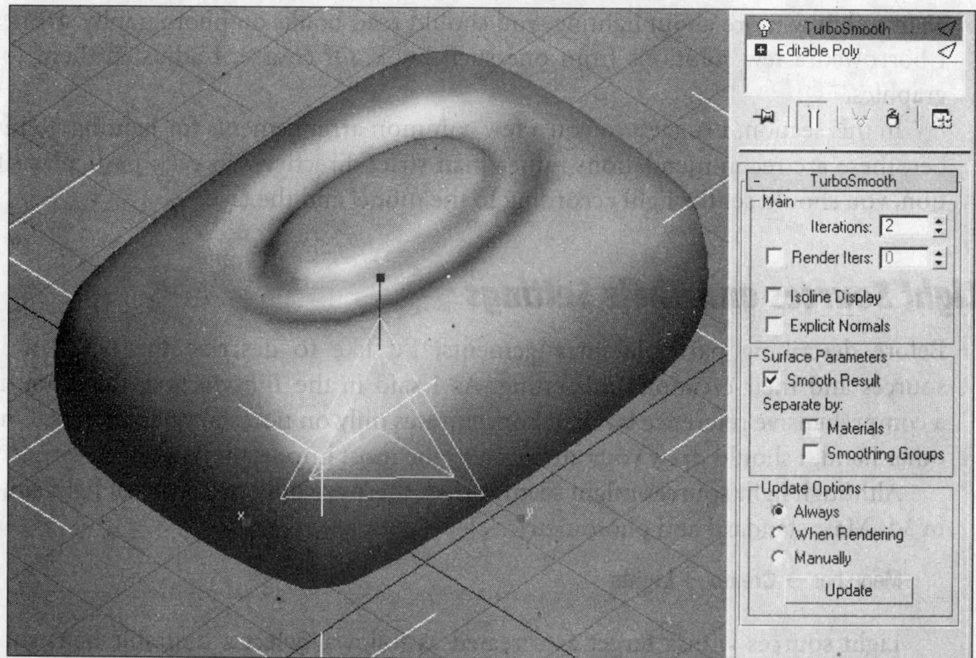

Fig. 2.61, *c*. A bar of soap

- ❒ Use the **TurboSmooth** modifier with two iterations.

Menu bar → **Modifiers** → **Subdivision Surfaces** → **TurboSmooth**.

The brush is nice, isn't it? (Fig. 2.60, *h*).

A Bar of Soap

This is easy (Fig. 2.61).

Lighting

So, the models are finished, and their geometry is good. Now, you need to render it in a manner that is appropriate for the best presentation. Lighting is the most important component of a presentation, and this is true not only for 3D graphics, but also for photography and video. The same principles are used in all these spheres, so if you want to know more about lighting, you should read books on photography. Honestly, I borrowed a few solutions from one such book. Of course, I adjusted them to 3D graphics.

In this section, I suggest to you a few common arrangements for lighting. Remember, these are recommendations rather than strict directives. In each particular situation, you should set the light according to the model and the task.

Light Sources and Their Settings

Before describing particular arrangements, I'd like to describe the types of light sources and their creation and setting. As I said in the *Introduction*, this book isn't a comprehensive reference book. It concentrates only on necessary parameters. On the other hand, I should draw your attention to the most important issues.

Although light sources might seem varied, there are only two types of light sources in 3ds Max: standard and photometric.

Menu bar → **Create** → **Lights**

Light sources with a target are created as follows. Select a desirable light source, click with the left mouse button on the viewport, and drag the target while keeping the left mouse button pressed to set the direction for the light source.

Free light sources are created by left-clicking on the viewport.

These light sources give similar results thanks to the efforts of 3ds Max developers, the standard rendering module, and mental ray. Two light sources are an exception: mental ray Area Spot and mental ray Area Omni. They work with mental ray only.

Standard Light Sources

Fig. 2.62, *a* shows examples of standard light sources (from left to right):

- Omni Light has the same light intensity in all directions. In real life, its analog is an electric bulb without a lampshade or another element that could direct the light.
- Target Spotlight has a directed light ray, which is a cone determined by the target. You can easily convert a Target Spot light source into Free Spot by unchecking an appropriate checkbox among its parameters. 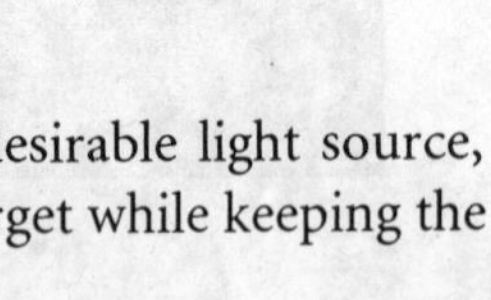
- Free Directional has a directed ray determined by a cylinder, so it would be more correct to call it *Parallel*. However, it is a dot light source. With certain reservation, its real-life analog is solar light.

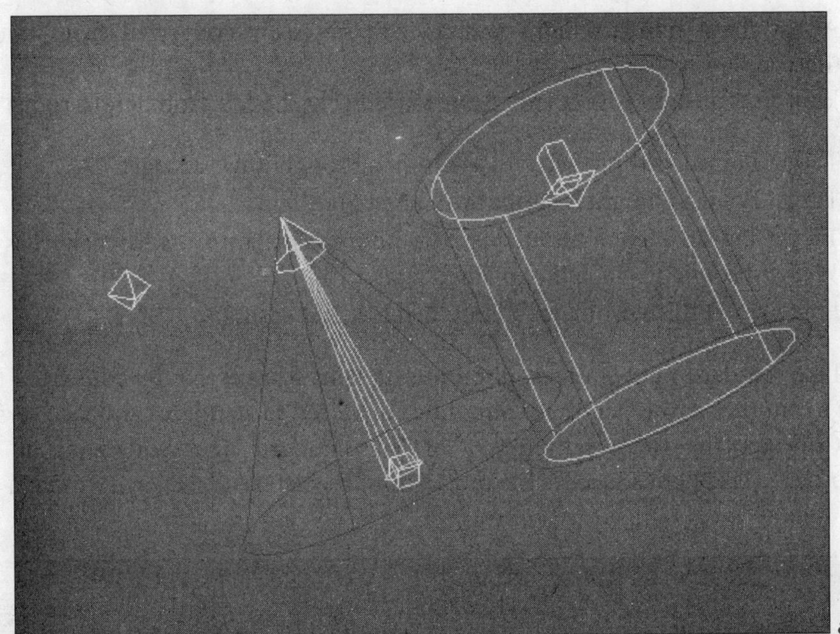

a

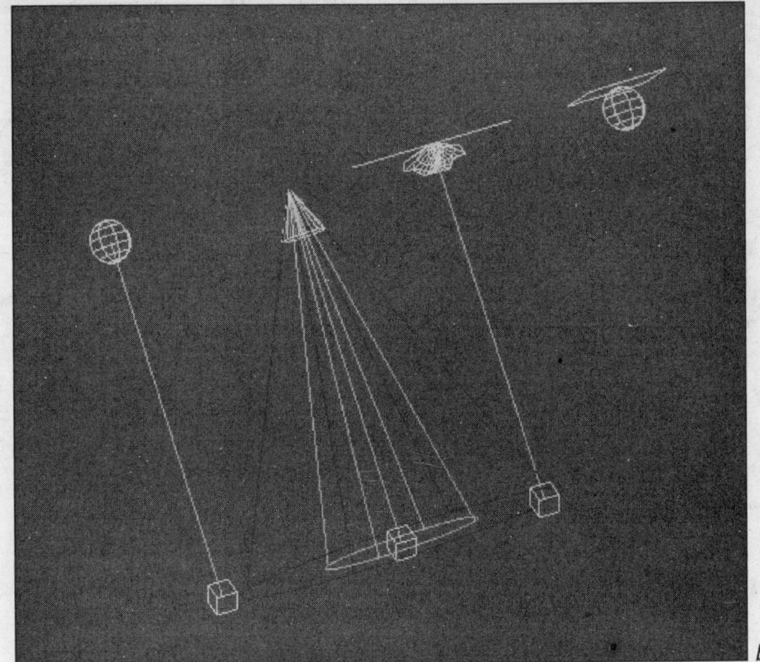

b

Fig. 2.62. Examples of standard (*a*) and photometric (*b*) light sources

All of these standard light sources can be easily converted from one type to another.

Photometric light sources are more varied (Fig. 2.62, *b*, from left to right).

- Target Point Isotropic behaves as Omni although it has a target.
- Target Point Spotlight is similar to Target Spotlight.
- Target Linear Web is an analog of a fluorescent lamp. Its intensity has a special *Web distribution*, which is explained later.
- Free Area Diffuse simulates a lamp inside a mat casing.

Like standard light sources, photometric light sources can be converted from one type to another. However, they cannot be converted to standard, and vice versa.

Consider the main parameters of the standard light source as an example (Fig. 2.63). This light source is the most popular when rendering with mental ray.

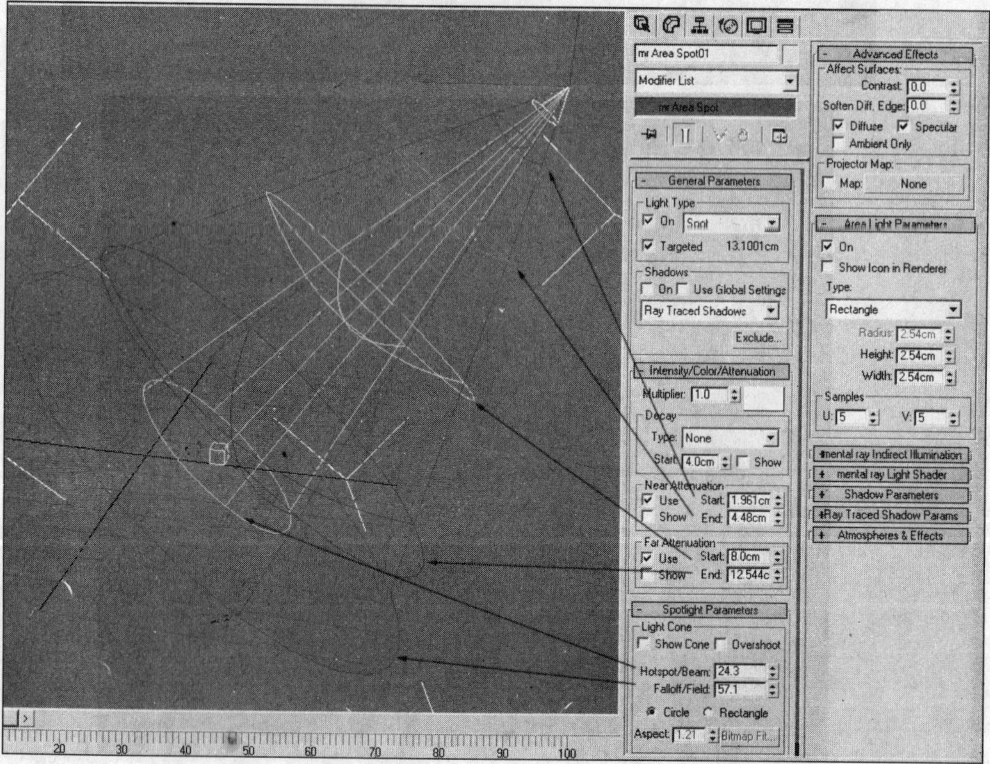

Fig. 2.63. The parameters of the mr Area Spot light source

The **General Parameters** rollout: The **On** checkbox allows you to turn the light source on and off. It is sometimes necessary to turn off all the light sources in the scene..

The drop-down list to the right of this checkbox allows you to choose among the Spot, Direct, and Omni types of the light source. Never use this control with mental ray light sources, or you'll obtain an incorrect result.

In the **Shadows** group, you can turn on shadows and select their types. Their parameters are described later. Light sources don't necessarily create shadows and you can (and should) remember this fact.

There is a small, almost unnoticeable button **Exclude** in the **Shadows** group. It opens a dialog box that allows you to exclude certain objects from being illuminated by this light source. I'll describe the use of this feature later, when looking at a particular example.

The **Intensity/Color/Attenuation** rollout: You can control the light intensity using the **Multiplier** parameter. Values that provide a normal intensity (without overlighting) are between 0 and 1.5. You can set this parameter to a negative value, and the light source will turn into, so to speak, a shadow source.

A click on the white rectangle to the right of the **Multiplier** parameter opens the **Color Selector** dialog box (Fig. 2.64). I like to use the lower right group of sliders, that is, the Hue-Saturation-Value (HSV) color model.

Is it possible to control the light intensity using color? Yes, it is. However, in my opinion it is best to use the multiplier.

By default, the standard light sources radiate light without attenuation. It would be wonderful if real-life lights possessed this feature! Unfortunately, they don't. Parameters in the **Decay** and **Attenuation** groups bring 3ds Max's light sources into agreement with the laws of the nature. However, they do this differently.

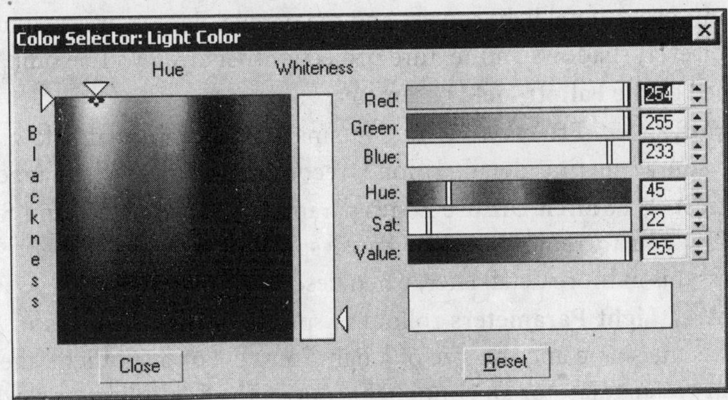

Fig. 2.64. The **Color Selector** dialog box

The **Type** drop-down list gives you three options: **None**, **Inverse** (according to the 1/R formula), and **Inverse Square** (according to the $1/R^2$ formula). Here R is the distance from the light source. The last algorithm best fits to physics laws. The **Start** parameter allows you to specify the point from the light source (remember, the light sources are points), at which the decay algorithm begins to work. This is important for ball-like lamps.

The other method (the **Attenuation** parameters) offers more options, allowing you to play certain tricks. When the parameters are set as shown in the figure, the light will behave as follows. There is no light before the **Near Attenuation Start** boundary (however, objects within this range cast shadows). Then the light intensity increases linearly up to the **Multiplier** value at the **Near Attenuation End** boundary. Then the intensity is constant till the **Far Attenuation Start** boundary. After that, the intensity decreases linearly to zero at the **Far Attenuation End** boundary. As a rule, the first two boundaries aren't used. Sometimes, they are useful, for example, for a lamp on the ceiling. Make sure to check the **Use** checkboxes, otherwise these settings won't come into effect.

You can use both methods at once but remember that **Decay** has a higher priority than **Attenuation**. Personally, I seldom use them simultaneously.

The **Spotlight Parameters** rollout is specific to a spotlight source. It sets angles of beams in degrees. Within the **Hotspot/Beam** light cone, the light has intensity determined by the **Multiplier** parameter. There is no light outside the **Falloff/Field** cone, the light intensity decreasing linearly. For Directional light sources, these parameters specify radii rather than angles. Omni light sources don't have such a rollout.

The **Overshoot** checkbox is quite interesting. If you check it, the spotlight will turn into an omnidirectional light source, and the parallel light source will turn into a "light wall." However, shadows and texture projections (if any), will be built within the area determined by the **Falloff/Field** parameter.

The **Advanced Effects** rollout contains parameters that allow you to adjust the light source in fine detail. I don't recommend that you change the values of the **Contrast** and **Soften Diffuse Edges** parameters. The **Diffuse** and **Specular** checkboxes allow you to remove an unwanted speck of light or, conversely, highlight it. I'll address this in more detail later, when describing materials.

The **Area Light Parameters** rollout is specific to light sources of the mental ray type. It sets the shape and the size of a light source. For a spotlight, the shape is either circular or rectangular; for an Omni light source, this is a sphere or a cylinder. You can control these in the viewport, but only by changing the size parameters (Fig. 2.65).

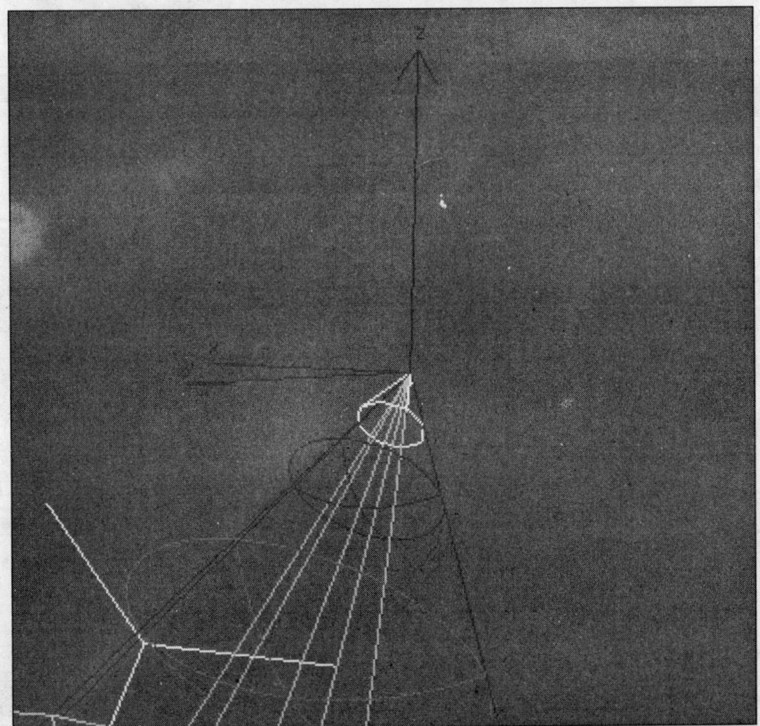

Fig. 2.65. The **mr Area Spot** light source picture in the viewport

The quality of light and shadows is determined by the **Samples** parameters. In essence, one light source is substituted with a matrix of point light sources whose number depends on these parameters. If you uncheck the **On** checkbox, an area light source will turn into a common point light source.

The **Show Icon in Renderer** checkbox makes the light source visible on the final picture.

Photometric Light Sources

Parameter of photometric light sources differ from those of the standard light sources in a few basic ways (Fig. 2.66).

First, the **Multiplier** parameter is missing, and the light intensity is specified in physical units: lumens, candles, and luxes. You can select the light color from a few presets, and you can specify the color temperature manually, in kelvins (the **Intensity/Color/Distribution** rollout).

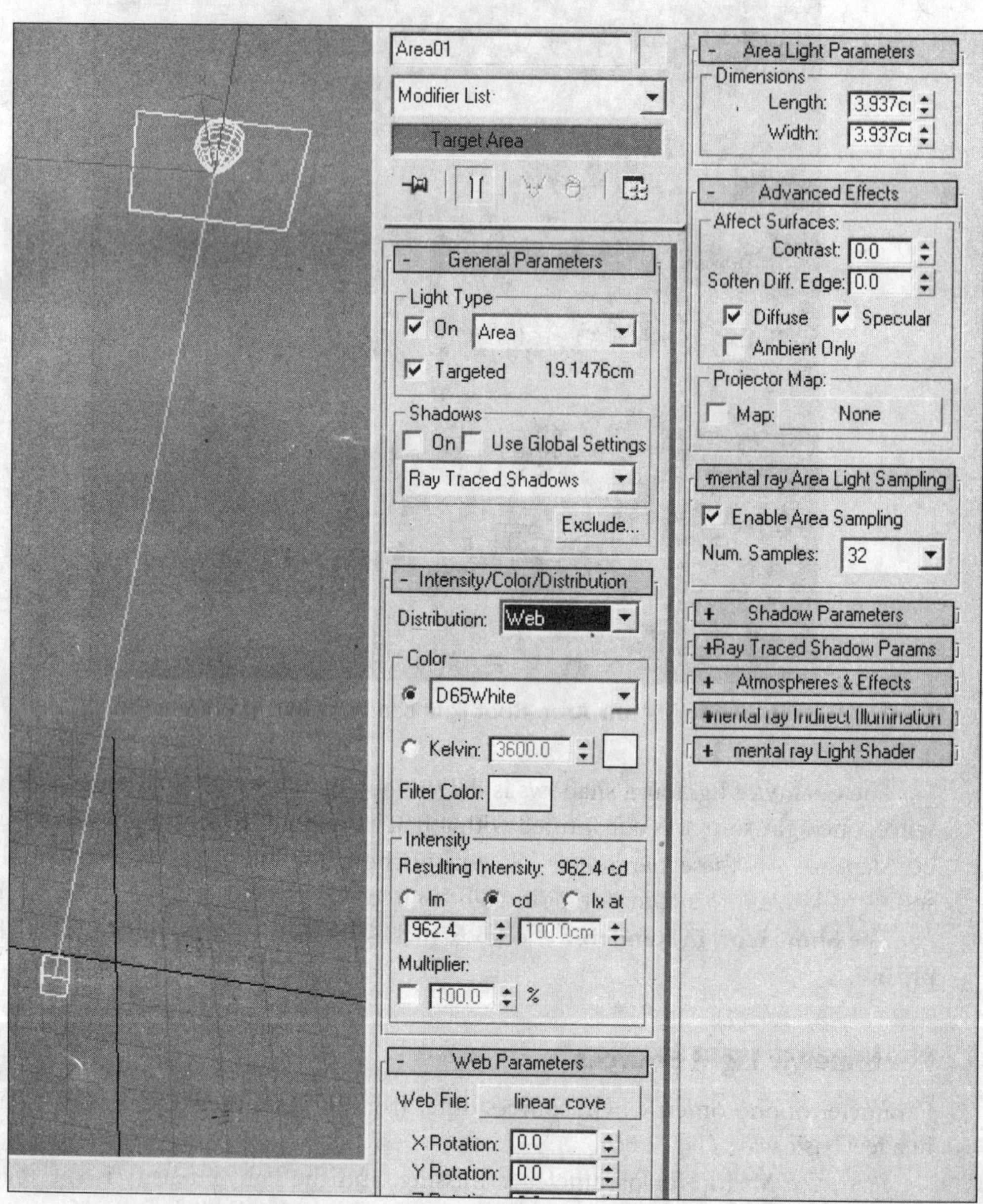

Fig. 2.66. Parameter of photometric light sources

Second, the photometric light sources miss parameters for light decay. This property is computed automatically depending on a particular light source, its parameters, and so on. Therefore, you should build a scene with the actual size of the objects, so that illumination with these light sources is correct.

In the **Distribution** drop-down list, you can select various types of light distribution. In addition to distribution types similar to those of the standard light sources, such as Isotropic (similar to Omni) and Spotlight, there are two specific types of distribution.

The Diffuse type of distribution can be selected only for the Area and Linear types of light sources. This light distribution is even within a 180-degree angle of beam.

The Web type uses an IES file that contains light distribution for the particular light source. As a result, lighting looks realistic (Fig. 2.67). You can find files with this format and other data on sites of manufacturers of light appliances. Because an IES file is just a text file, you can create your own distribution manually or using a special program, such as IES Generator 3, which was developed by Andrey Kozlov (Fig. 2.68).

Finally, there is the **mental ray Area Light Sampling** rollout for use in combination with a mental ray light source. In this rollout, you can specify the number of samples for simulation of area light sources.

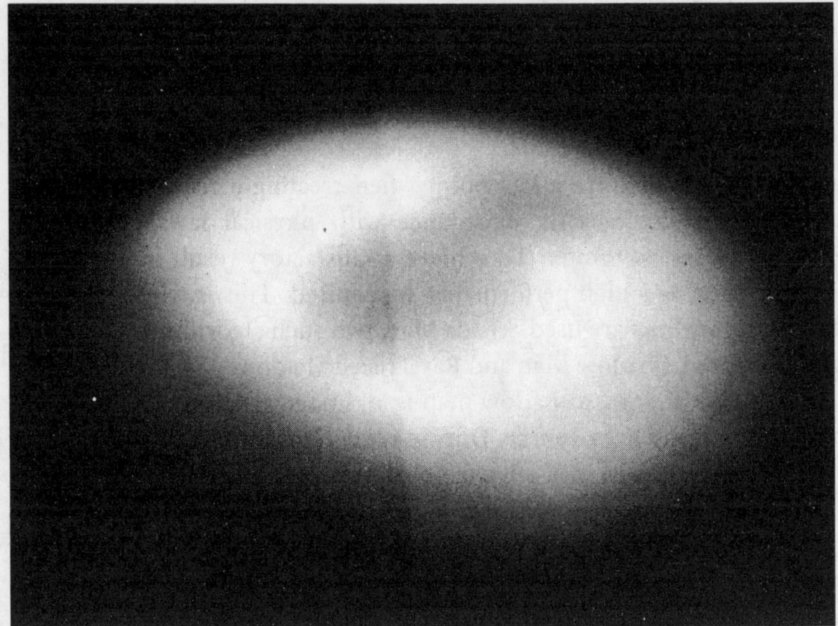

Fig. 2.67. A light spot from a source with the Web distribution type

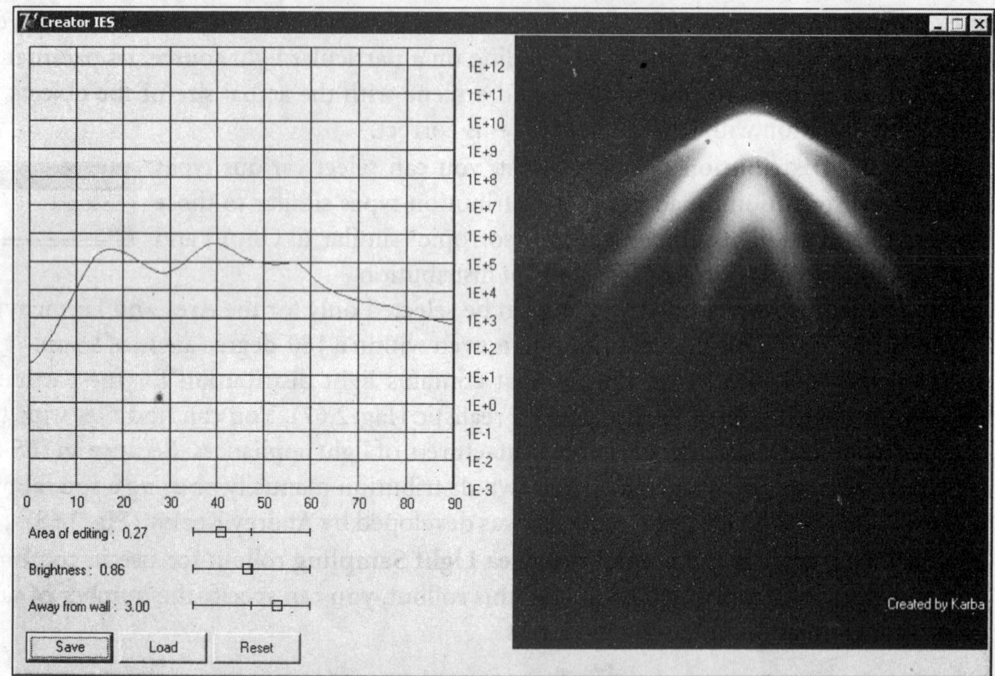

Fig. 2.68. IES Generator 3

Shadows

Shadows from objects are a key point when creating a realistic 3D image. Unfortunately, creating shadows in accordance with physical laws currently is a "back-breaking" task for computer: To achieve a satisfactory result in reasonable time, too high performance is required. This is why simplified algorithms are used. In 3ds Max, two such algorithms are implemented, Shadow Map and Ray Traced Shadow.

Adv. Ray Traced
mental ray Shadow Map
Area Shadows
Shadow Map
Ray Traced Shadows

As its name implies, a shadow map is an image generated before rendering as the projection from the light source. During rendering, the shadow map is applied to the objects multiplicatively. An advantage of this algorithm is that it builds shadows quickly. If there is no object animation in a scene, and if only the camera is animated, the shadows are built at the beginning of animation and used during it. However, the algorithm has at least two disadvantages. First, you cannot use it to create realistic soft shadows that are sharp near an object and gradually becoming less distinct as the distance to the object increases. The shadows you obtain are either sharp everywhere or not.

The second disadvantage is that such shadows take up much computer memory. When using them, carefully set the areas illuminated by the light source. Try to illuminate only the necessary areas and minimize the sky light.

Ray-traced shadows are built during rendering. When using them, you don't need to take care of the size of a shadow map because there isn't any. However, building such shadows lasts longer than building a shadow map. Although shadows obtained with this method are rather sharp, they are used for creating soft shadows.

In 3ds Max, setting shadows with light source parameters is done in two rollouts. The first one, **Shadow Parameters** is common for all types of shadows (Fig. 2.67, *a*). The main parameters are described in the next paragraphs.

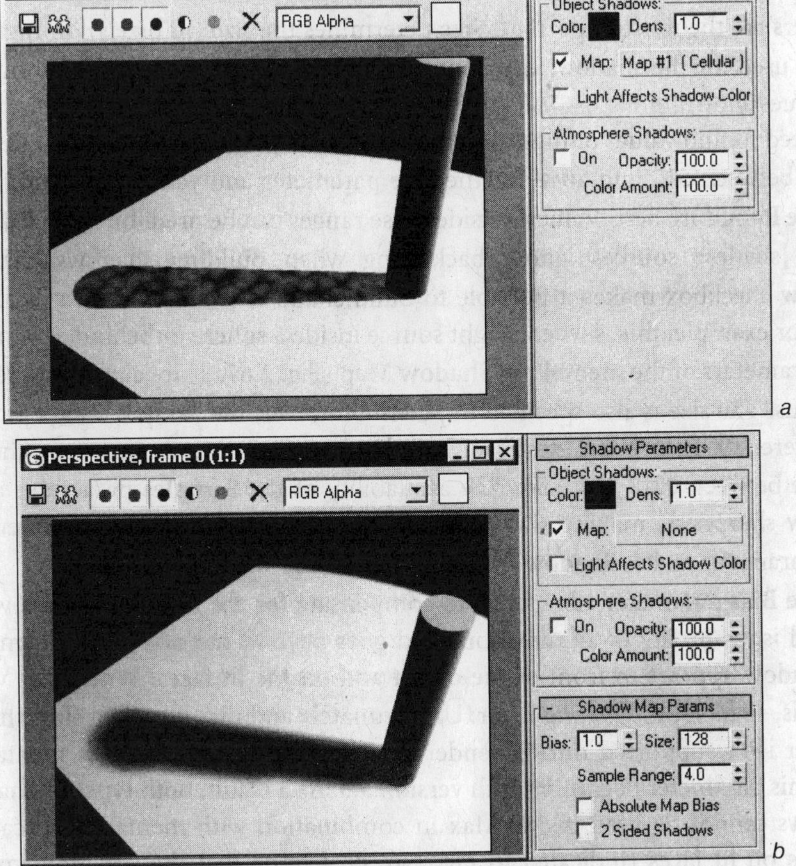

Fig. 2.67, *a* and *b*. Types of shadows in 3ds Max

The **Color** and **Density** parameters are self-explanatory. By changing these parameters slightly (I'd like to emphasize the last word), you can make a shadow less dense or give it a tint. However, don't abuse these parameters. It is best to adjust shadows using additional light sources or global lighting.

There is an interesting feature that allow you to assign a map to a shadow. You can use this option, for example, to simulate the shadow from an aquarium. This effect is set in the same way as the light spot parameters.

The **Light Affect Shadow Color** checkbox allows you to give the shadow the color of the light source. The "warm light casts cold shadows" rule adopted in painting is ignored here.

The second rollout is specific for each shadow type. Consider it more closely.

The **Shadow Map Params** rollout contains parameters for shadow maps. Two parameters are the most important. **Size** determines the size (in pixels) of the image that will be used for the shadow, and **Sample Range** determines shadow smoothing. With the values shown in Fig. 2.67, *b*, the shadow size is too small, so the shadow is blurred. You need to find values of these parameters in each particular case. As a rule, however, values between 512 and 2048 for the **Size** parameter and values between 2 and 8 for **Sample Range** are best. Values outside these ranges can be used for special effects.

All shadow sources ignore backfacing when building shadows. The **2 Sided Shadow** checkbox makes it possible to build shadows when an object is lit from the rear. For example, this is when a light source inside a sphere or behind a plane.

Parameters of the **mental ray Shadow Map** (Fig. 2.67, *c*) are almost the same as the previous. The size is also specified in pixels. However, the **Sample Range** parameter is set differently. Ignore the "mm" suffix: it has no relation to millimeters. The best values are between 0.01 and 0.04. The availability of the **Samples** parameter affects the shadow sharpness, making this property controllable. However, the absence of the **Bias** parameter makes **Shadow Map** and **mental ray** shadows unusable.

The **Bias** parameter allows you to compensate for the fact that a shadow becomes blurred isotropically in all directions and goes beyond the object. With small values, the shadow appears in front of the object and on the lit faces. With great values, the object is, so to speak, floating in air. Unfortunately and incomprehensibly, the **Bias** parameter isn't supported during rendering with mental ray although mental ray features this parameter beginning with version 3.3. As a result, both types of Shadow Map shadows cannot be used in 3ds Max in combination with mental ray because "dirt" appears on lit faces (indicated in Fig. 2.67, *c*). I hope that the situation improves in the nearest future.

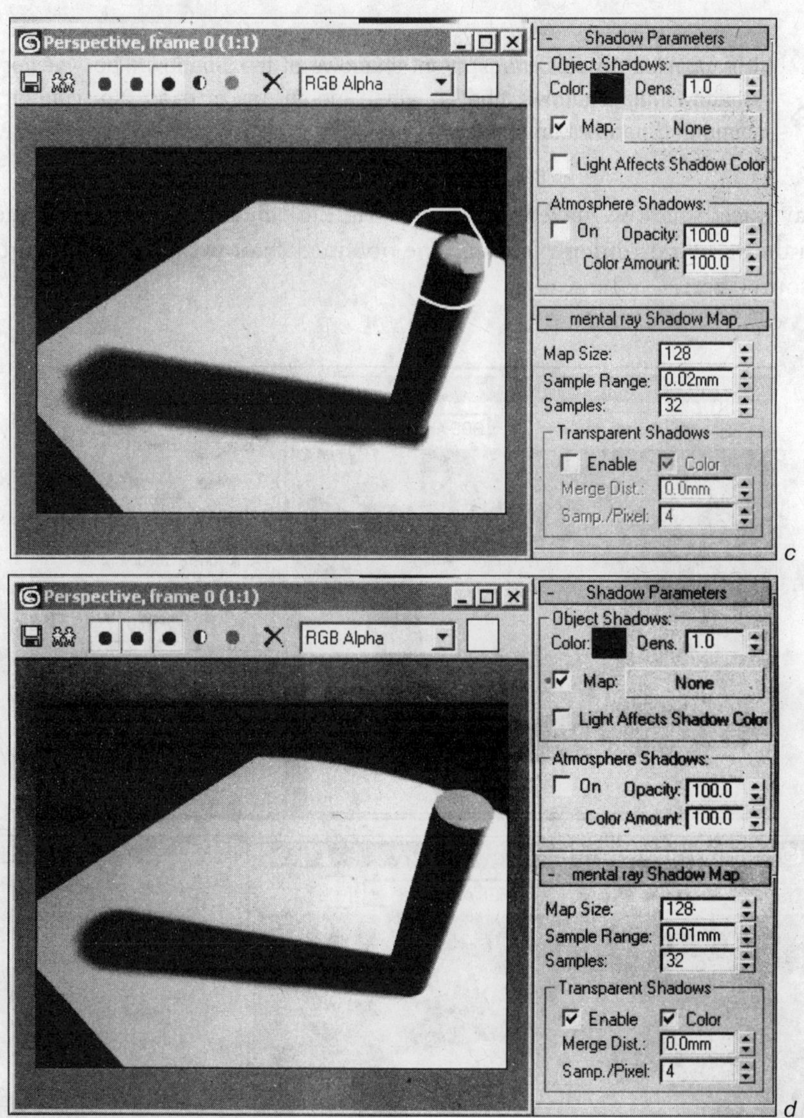

Fig. 2.67, *c* and *d*. Types of shadows in 3ds Max

Certain consolation is in the **Merge Distance** parameter in the **Transparent Shadow** group. In essence, this is bias. If you use transparent shadows, the flaws mentioned earlier disappear even with the zero value of this parameter (Fig. 2.67, *d*). like to reiterate I hope that the situation improves in the nearest future.

NOTE

It is possible to build transparent shadows of the Shadow Map type for mental ray Shadow Map shadows, that is, when mental ray is used. You cannot do this for common Shadow Map shadows.

Ray traced shadows have few settings (Fig. 2.67, *e*), and the default values are best. When the standard renderer is used, the obtained shadows are sharp regardless of the light source type.

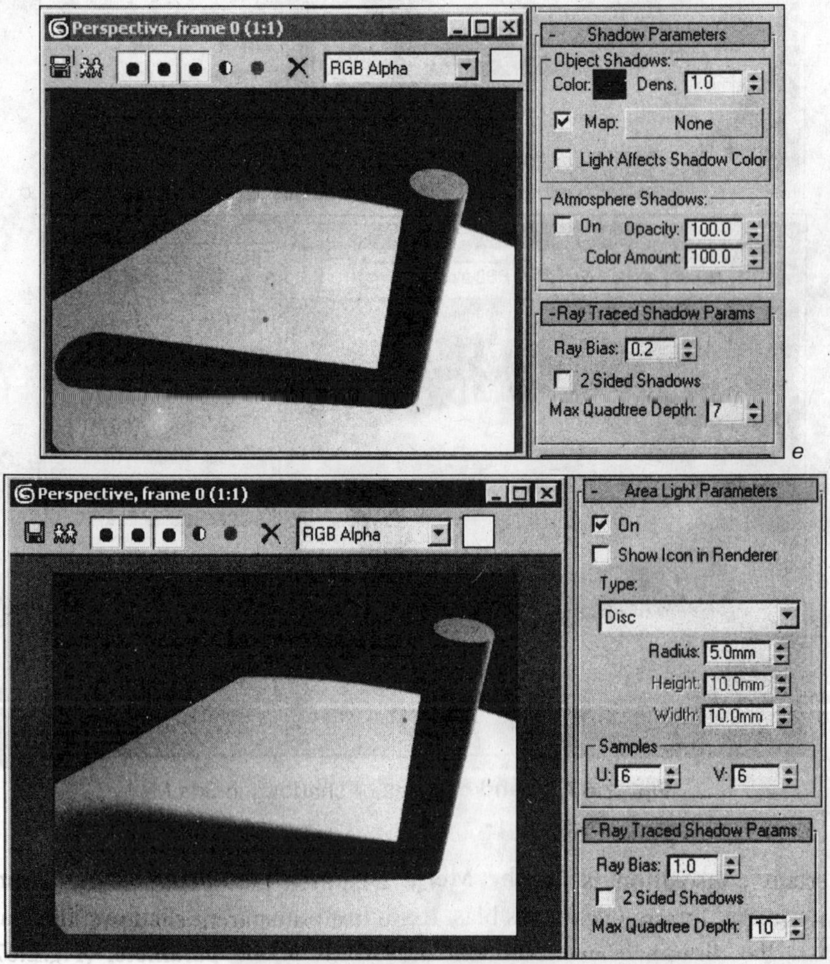

Fig. 2.67, *e* and *f*. Types of shadows in 3ds Max

The use of ray traced shadows in combination with mental ray gives an interesting effect. With the mr Area Omni and mr Area Spot light sources, you can obtain realistic soft shadows by adjusting the light source parameters in the **Area Light Parameters** (Fig. 2.67, *f*). The same is true for photometric light sources of the Area or Linear type. I recommend that you use these shadows.

As for shadows of the Advanced Ray Traced and Area Shadow types, they are specific to the standard renderer and aren't used by mental ray. During rendering, they are substituted with Ray Traced shadows and can give a soft shadow effect depending on the light source type.

The following table contains features of 3ds Max shadows depending on different renderers.

Shadow type	Default Scanline Renderer	Mental ray Renderer
Shadow Map	The borders of the shadow aren't sharp. Transparent shadows aren't possible.	The **Bias** parameter is missing. As a result, "dirt" appears on the object.
Mental ray Shadow Map	Isn't used.	The same as with Shadow map. Transparent shadows from transparent objects can be built.
Ray Traced Shadows	Shadows are always sharp. Transparent shadows from transparent objects can be built.	The same as with Default Scanline Renderer. When light sources of the mr Area, Photometric Linear, or Area types are used, soft shadows are possible.
Advanced Ray Traced	Similar to Ray Traced Shadows, but shadow border sharpness is controllable.	The type isn't supported. During rendering, it is substituted with Ray Traced.
Area Shadows	Similar to Ray Traced Shadows, but soft shadows are possible.	The type isn't supported. During rendering, it is substituted with Ray Traced.

In addition to these types of shadows, when using mental ray, you can assign a shader to an appropriate material slot. The objects with this material will cast shadows in accordance with this shader.

The Sky and the Sun

The IES Sky and IES Sun light sources are intended to make your rendering realistic. However, they aren't suitable from an artist's point of view since they are a little too "close to nature."

The best light source for simulation of the sky is SkyLight. It is among the standard light sources. However, use it with indirect lighting. When used in combination with mental ray, it won't work without indirect lighting. In the standard renderer, it can be used as a direct light source, but you'll be either dissatisfied with the result or wait for it for quite a long time. In any case, if you don't use indirect lighting, use the sky dome simulation.

Ambient Light

This light source has appeared in 3D Studio for DOS. It isn't popular now, but it is sometimes useful when you want to illuminate the scene as a whole. It doesn't cast shadows and evenly illuminates all the objects from each side. You can set it in the **Environment** window, but be careful and do not over-light the scene.

> Menu bar → **Rendering** → **Environment** → the **Common Parameters** rollout → the **Global Lighting** group

Controlling the Exposure

You can improve the result of rendering, that is, compensate for over-lighting or under-lighting, or adjust contrast or brightness by using a built-in exposure control. Although it was primarily developed for photometric light sources, you can also use it with standard ones.

> Menu bar → **Rendering** → **Environment** → the **Common Parameters** rollout

Though there are several exposure controls in 3ds Max, only one of them is used with mental ray. This is the **Logarithmic Exposure Control** (Fig. 2.68). Generally speaking, it is the most suitable for the standard renderer. It is similar to Adobe PhotoShop tools or other graphic editors. The only parameter that requires explanation is **Physical Scale**. You can use it to bring the intensity of the standard and photometric light sources into agreement. With the settings shown in the figure, one unit of the multiplier of an Omni light source equals 1,500 cd of a photometric light source with the isometric light distribution.

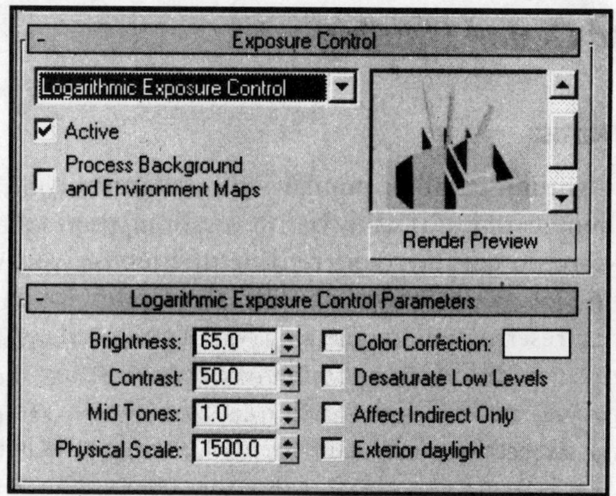

Fig. 2.68. Parameters of the logarithmic exposure control

You might ask "Wouldn't it be easier to finish the scene in Adobe PhotoShop?" It would, but only if you actually have the scene. When a scene is overlit, and the main color is white, you cannot restore missing details or can do this only roughly if you aren't in 3ds Max. The same is true for an underlit scene.

Useful Tips

Here are a few tips and warnings based on practice.

- Don't scale light sources since this will lead to unpredictable results, especially with shadows. Use the parameters only.
- Don't use color shadows unless you have to. Try to obtain the desired hue using colored light sources. The shadow colors are added when the shadows overlap, so it is likely to obtain a bright colored spot where a few shadows overlap.
- Prefer directed light sources to omnidirectional ones. This is the most economical solution. The only exception is additional light sources that cast no shadows.
- If you use omnidirectional light sources with shadows, avoid using shadows of the Shadow Map type. Otherwise, be aware that as many as six shadow maps are created for omnidirectional light sources, and the boundaries of the neighboring maps aren't necessarily close to each other.
- Try to obtain the desired result using the parameters of the light sources. Use exposure control only on the final stage, for example, to adjust the contrast, and not to eliminate defects.

Doing without Global Lighting

Preliminary Notes

Because global lighting is rather popular with designers, you might be wondering why I suggest doing without it. Is it wise to use simulation rather than check an appropriate checkbox so that the renderer does the job for you? Well, you cannot be sure it will do the job exactly as *you* need. In some cases, for example, when rendering a model for a presentation or a catalog, you don't need certain effects such as realistic reflection. In addition, computation of global lighting takes quite a long time, especially when you need a high-quality picture. Finally, arrangements described in the following subsections are valid for the latest methods (though with certain adjustments).

Virtual Photo Studio

This arrangement is used most often both on 3ds Max graphics and in photo and video shooting. Even in painting, still lives are illuminated according to a similar scheme.

I'll take the container for stationery as an example. All related files (the model, the intermediate scenes, and the result of lighting) are in the Projects\Project2 folder on the accompanying CD-ROM. The additional objects are located in the Projects\Misc folder.

It wouldn't be interesting to show an empty container. Indeed, the task of 3D graphics is to present photorealistic images. So I decided to create a simple composition to demonstrate the container, so to speak, in use, that is, with a pen and a pencil inside. By the way, the use of well-known objects is a good way to show the size of a model.

First, create a screen large enough as shown in Fig. 2.69. This is a curve bent with a large radius. The surface is obtained using the **Extrude** modifier. If the normals are directed incorrectly, change their directions with the **Normal** modifier.

Menu bar → **Modifiers** → **Mesh Editing** → **Normal Modifier**

Don't confuse this with the **Edit Normals** modifier.

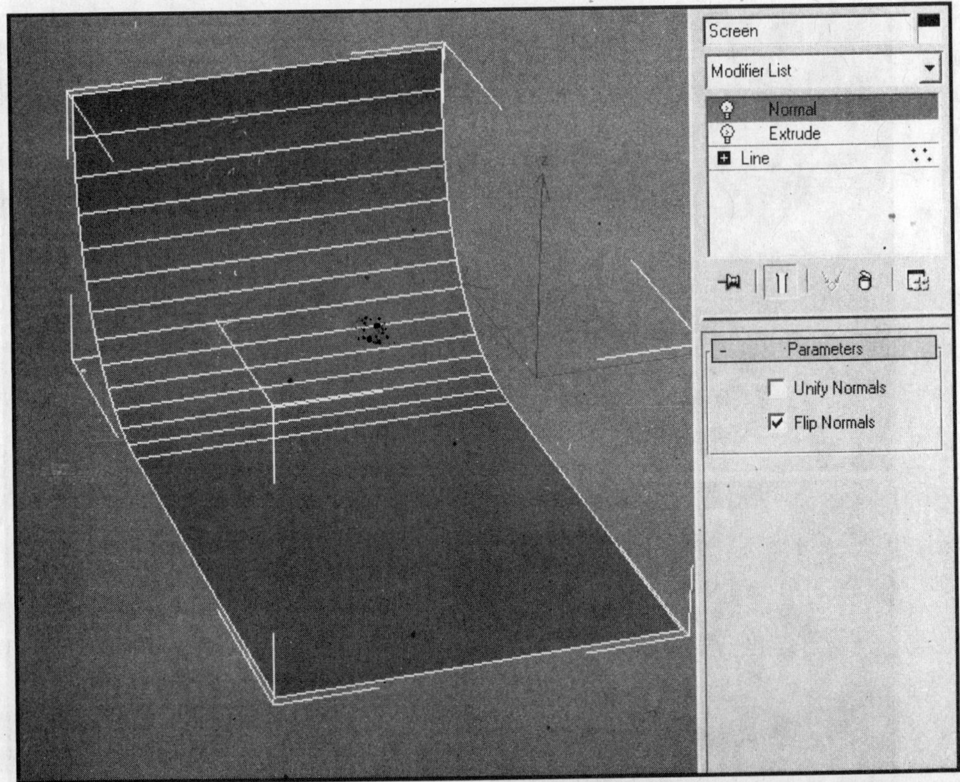

Fig. 2.69. A screen for a photo studio

- Load the necessary objects into the scene from the Model2-final.max, Pencil.max, and Pen.max files using the **Merge** command.

Menu bar → **File** → **Merge**

Select the appropriate file, select all the objects in the dialog box that will open, and click the OK button.

- Place the objects to your liking. Select the model and the auxiliary objects and group them for the sake of convenience.

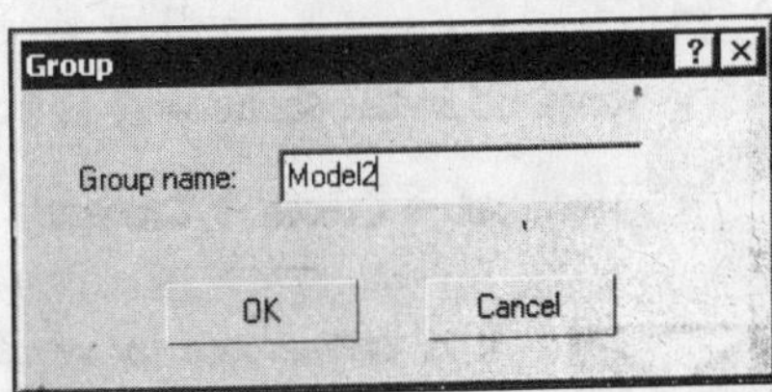

Menu bar → **Group** → **Group**, enter a group name and click the **OK** button.

- To be able to access the objects in the group, use the **Group** → **Open** command.

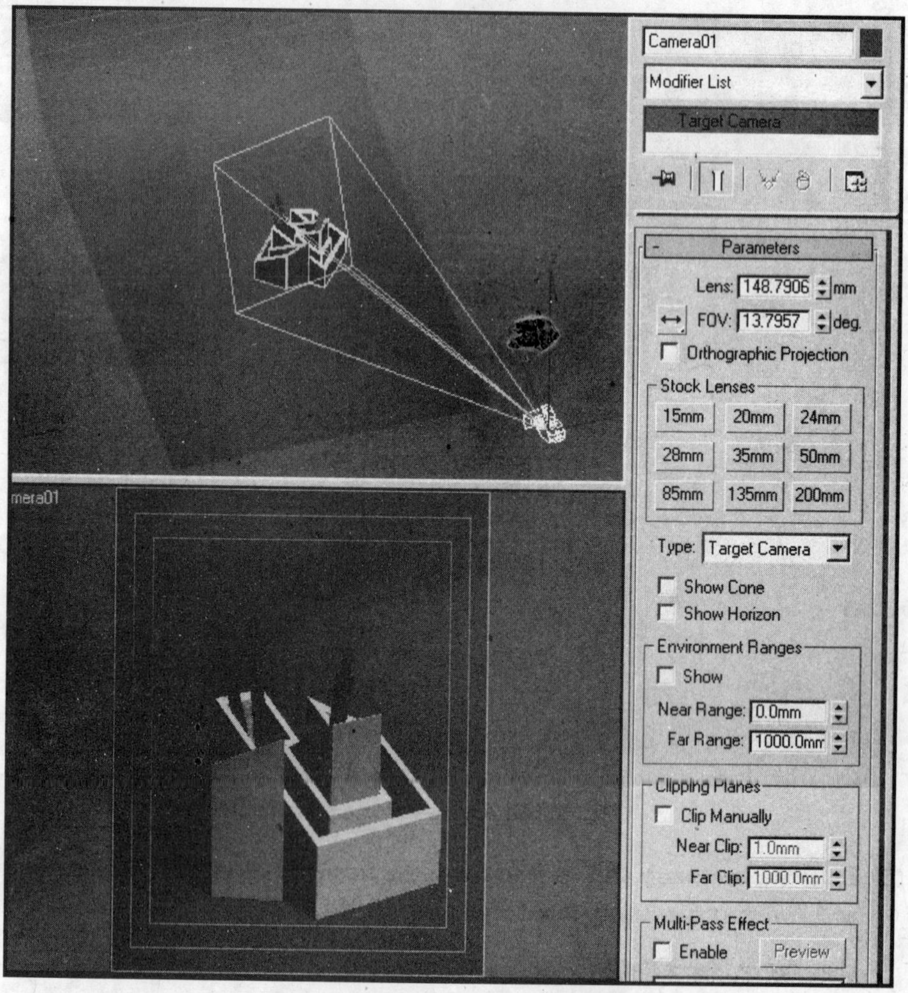

Fig. 2.70. The composition and the camera parameters

- Choose the best viewing angle. My variant is shown in Fig. 2.70.
- Create a camera. You'll use it for intermediate and final rendering. Cameras are created in the same way as light sources.

Menu bar → **Create** → **Camera**

TIP

It is convenient to adjust the viewing angle in the perspective view and create a camera corresponding to this angle by pressing the <Ctrl>+<C> shortcut. The camera should have a long-focus lens to diminish perspective distortion. However, the distortion should take place because you want a realistic image. The only parameter you need at this stage is **Lens**. Set it equal to approximately 150 mm.

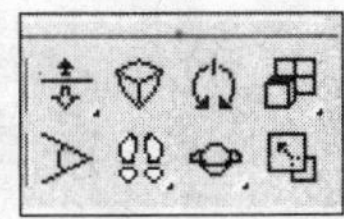

To switch to the camera view, use the <C> key. To control the camera view, use the left mouse button after you select a command among the navigation controls (this panel will change after you select the camera view). The middle mouse button is used only for panning. The main commands are **Dolly** and **Orbit.**

❐ Set the size of the final image.

Menu bar → **Rendering** → **Render** → the **Common** tab → the **Output Size** group

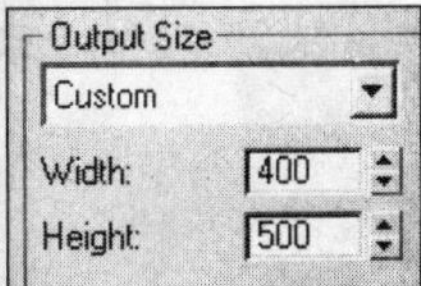

Don't make the size too large. You'll need to do test rendering repeatedly, and this shouldn't take a long time.

TIP

It would be convenient to use the safe frame (The viewport right-click menu → **Show Safe Frame**). This will allow you to control what should be present in the final picture.

TIP

You'll do test rendering many times, so remember the following two shortcuts: <Shift>+<Q> (Quick Render) renders the current viewport, <F9> (Render Last) renders the last rendered viewport.

Before you choose and assign materials, set all them as gray, and set lighting "by gray." Experienced users don't need to stick to this rule, but novice users do. If your composition looks nice without materials, it will look even better after you assign them.

❐ Select all the objects (with the <Ctrl>+<A> shortcut).
❐ Open the material editor (with the <M> key) and assign a gray material to all the objects in the scene.

Material editor → the **Assign Material to Selection** button

The result of my work on this stage is in the Project2-lighting-01.max file.

The first and most important light source you should create is called a key light. Its position and parameters and the result of rendering at this stage are shown in Fig. 2.71. Look at it closely.

Fig. 2.71, *a*. The position of the Key light

The type of this light source is mental ray Area Spot because this light source allows you to obtain soft shadows when rendering with mental ray. Therefore, the Ray Traced shadow type (indicated within box 1 in Fig. 2.71, *b*) is selected. The parameters in the **Area Light Parameters** rollout (indicated within box 2) specify a disc with a radius of 100 mm. The number of samples is large enough to obtain high-quality shadows. For test rendering, you can specify 2 × 2.

Select a warm, yellowish light color. Set its intensity (the **Multiplier** parameter) to a value a little larger than one (indicated within box 3). Remember that there will be many light sources in the scene, and the resulting light is their sum.

I selected the Inverse decay type, but this process should start behind the model (indicated within box 4).

TIP

Because there will be many light sources, you should give them self-explanatory names. For example, name the light source Area Spot as Key.

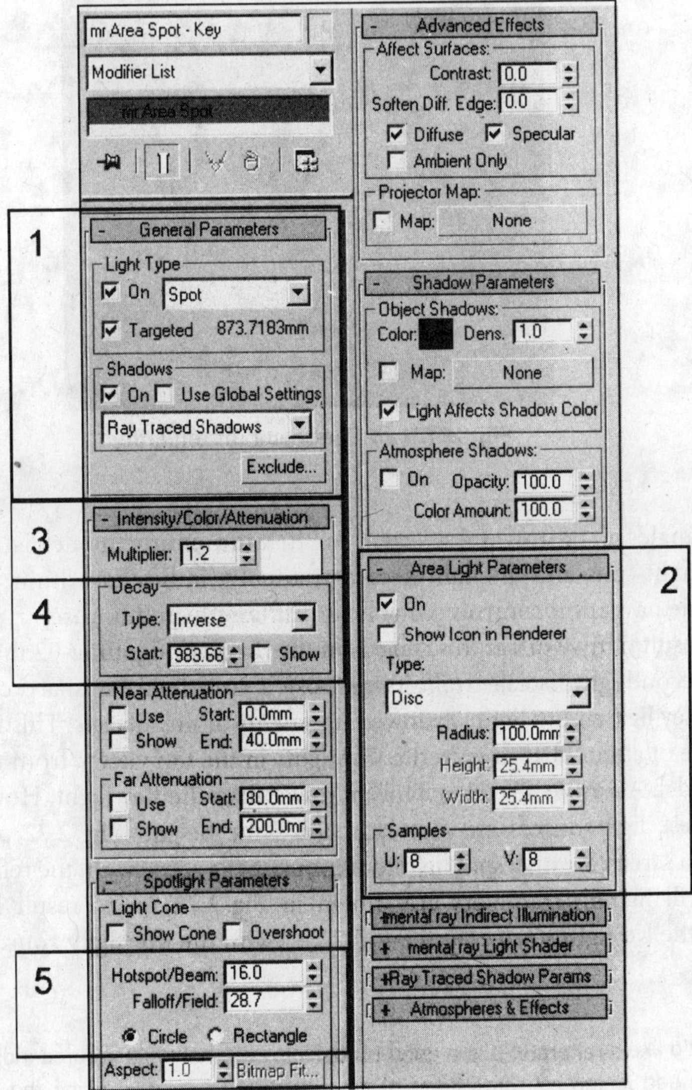

Fig. 2.71, *b*. The parameters of the Key light

Fig. 2.71, c. The result of rendering

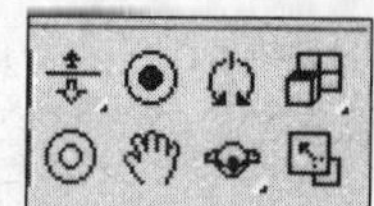

The angles of beams are selected so that the entire model is within a light cone, and the light decays gradually (indicated within box 5). The navigation controls panel looks differently in this case.

The result of my work at this stage is in the Project2-lighting-02.max file.

The second light is called *Fill.* Its purpose is to soften the sharp contrast obtained with the Key light and to light shadowed fragments of the objects. This light source is set at an angle of about 90 degrees to the Key light (in the top view), from the opposite side of the model. As a rule, it is set at a height lower than the Key light. However, in this example, these light sources are almost at the same height (Fig. 2.72, *a*). The Fill light simulates a screen lit with a spot light to illuminate the scene with the reflected light.

The Fill light's parameters are shown in Fig. 2.72, *b*, its result is in Fig. 2.72, *c* (without the Key light source) and Fig. 2.72, *d* (with the Key light source).

TIP

I'd like to reiterate: It is a good practice to set each light source individually, so you'll need to turn off the others. It is convenient to do this using the **Light Lister** tool (Menu bar → **Tools** → **Light Lister**) (see Fig. 2.73).

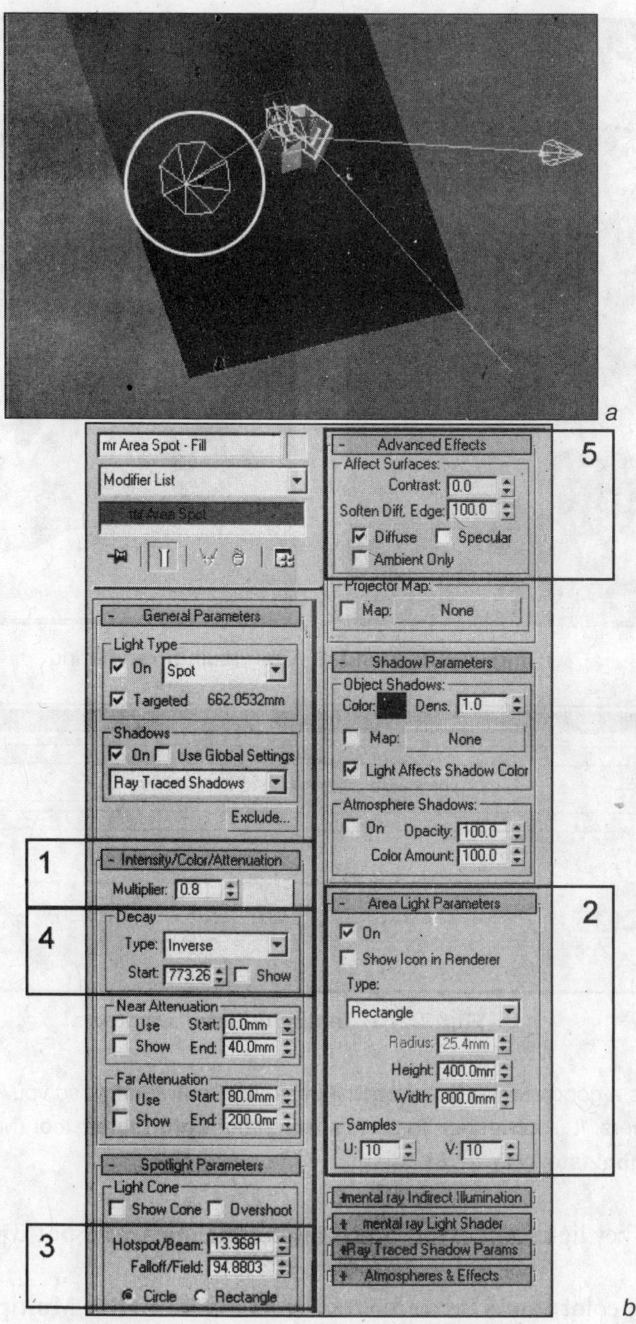

Fig. 2.72, *a* and *b*. The position (*a*) and parameters (*b*) of the Fill light

c

d

Fig. 2.72, *c* and *d*. The result of rendering

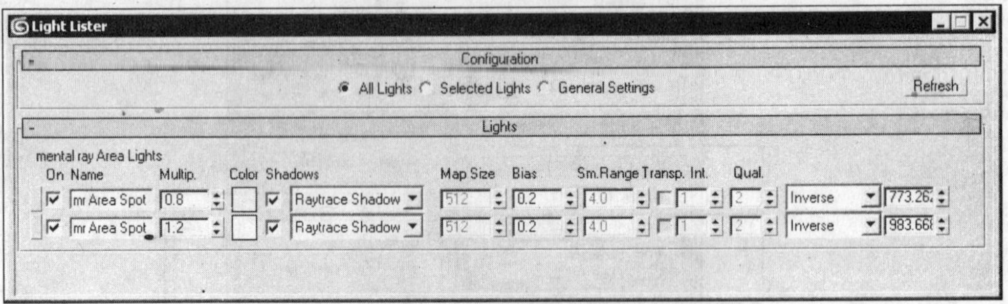

Fig. 2.73. The **Light Lister** window

TIP

It is a good practice to set each light source individually, so you'll need to turn off the others. It is convenient to do this using the **Light Lister** tool (Menu bar → **Tools** → **Light Lister**) (Fig. 2.73).

Like the key light source, this one is also of the mr Area Spot type, so name it Area Spot – Fill.

The light color should be cold blue. Set its intensity (the **Multiplier** parameter) to a value lower than one (indicated within box 1 in Fig. 2.72, *b*).

It is considered an artist's mistake when an object casts more than one shadow. You could disable shadows for this light source, but the resulting picture would be lifeless, computer-style. This is why this light source creates shadows, but they aren't sharp because the light source is large (indicated with a two), and the **Falloff/Field** is large too (indicated within box 3). You can decrease the shadow density if you wish.

I suggest that you use the **Decay** parameter. The decay process should begin before the light reaches the model (indicated within box 4).

To avoid undesired specks of light on a shining material, uncheck the **Specular** checkbox in the **Affect Surfaces** group (indicated within box 5).

The result of my work at this stage is in the Project2-lighting-03.max file.

The other light sources are positioned as shown in Fig. 2.74, *a*. Their purpose is to highlight the model's rims so that it is seen against the background (Fig. 2.74, *d*). These lights are called *rim*. I had to work hard when setting the rim lights because this model is inconvenient as regards lighting. For most models, it is enough to set one rim light somewhere behind-above-at-the-side of the model. In this case, two sources are necessary.

Look at the parameters in Fig. 2.74, *b*.

The light sources are common spotlights without shadows (indicated within box 1) and decay. Directional sources could be used as an alternative.

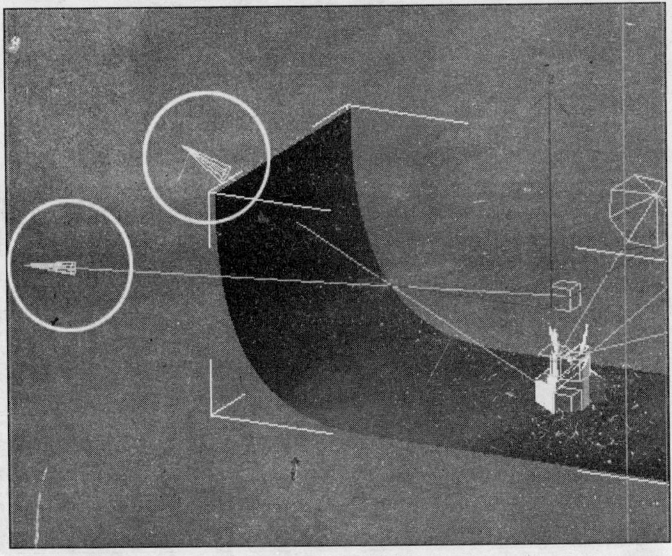

Fig. 2.74, *a*. The position of the rim lights

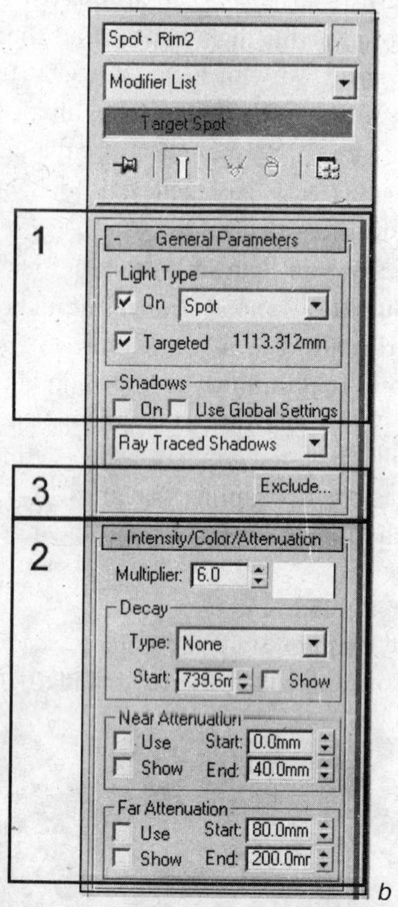

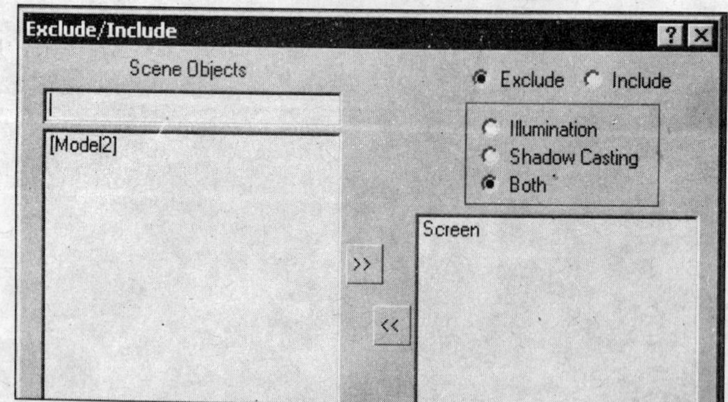

Fig. 2.74, *b* and *c*. Parameters of the rim lights (*b*). Excluding the object (*c*)

Fig. 2.74, *d*. The result of rendering

Because the light from the rim sources only touches the rims, they are rather intensive (indicated withih box 2). By the way, if the chamfers were missing from the model, these light sources would have no effect.

The left (relative to the camera) source is positioned so that its light doesn't fall on the bottom part of the pencil. Remember, sources without shadows don't have obstacles.

I used a trick natural for 3D graphics but impossible in the real life. The rim sources illuminate the **Screen** object intensively. To avoid this, exclude the screen from lighting by clicking the **Exclude** button (indicated within box 3). In the window that will open, move the **Screen** object from the left field to the right by double-clicking the object (Fig. 2.74, c).

The result of my work at this stage is in the Project2-lighting-04.max file.

I've just demonstrated to you a lighting method called *Hollywood Triangle* or a *classic three-lamp scheme.*

Sounds great, doesn't it?

What is next? You could illuminate the screen from the rear side using a spotlight whose illumination includes only this object (Fig. 2.75). The **Include** operation is preferable in this case because if you use this scheme in mass production, you'll only need to load objects.

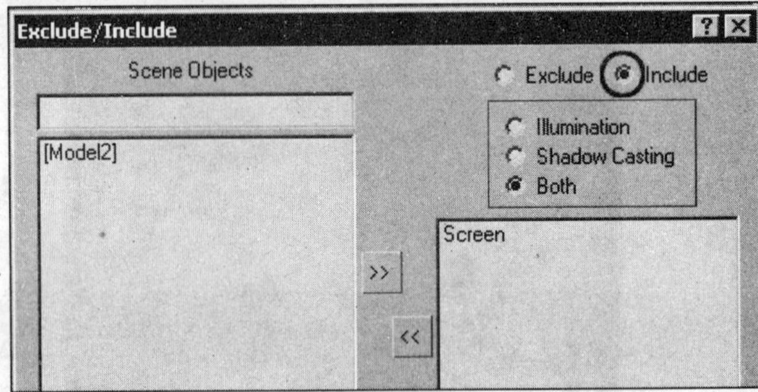

Fig. 2.75. Including the object into lighting

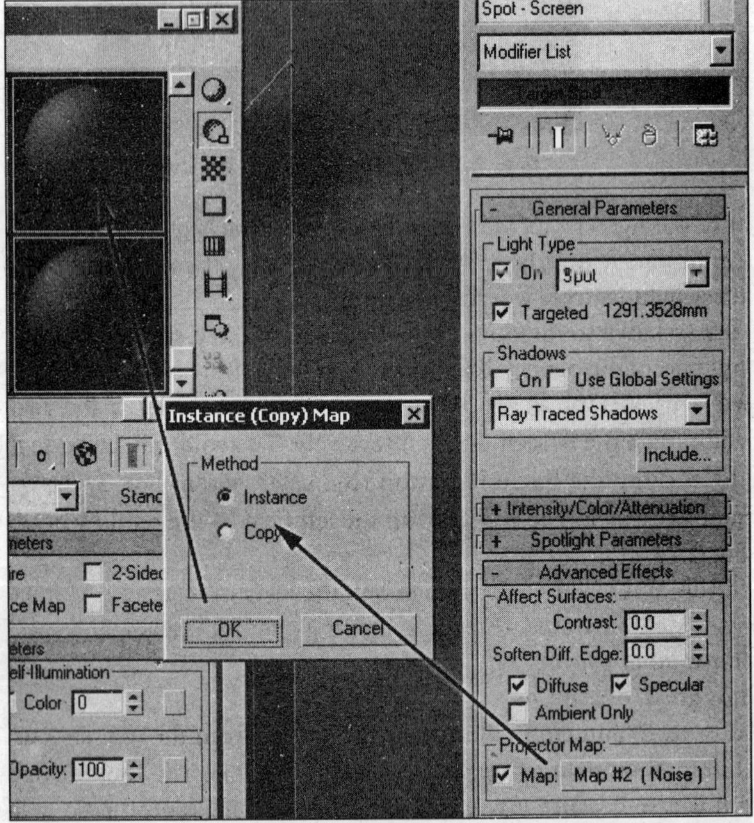

Fig. 2.76, *a*. Dragging the map to the material editor

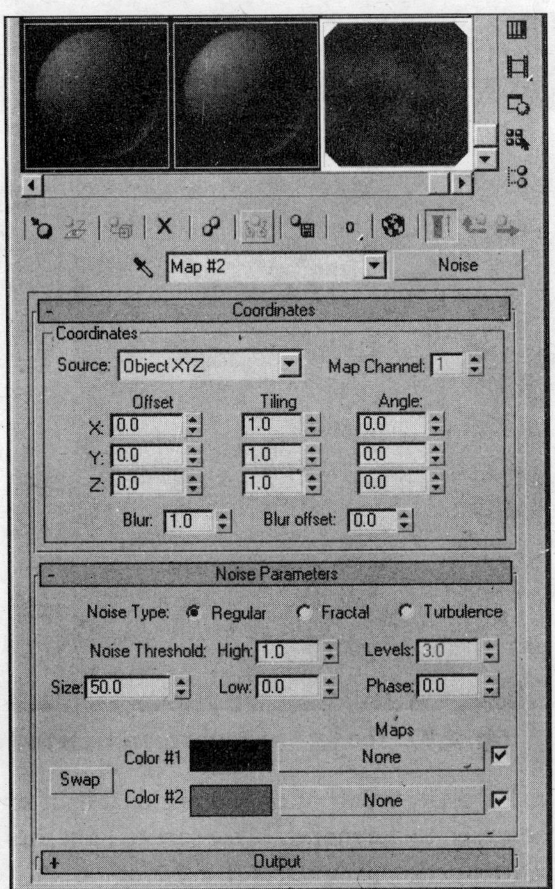

Fig. 2.76, *b*. Setting the map

The parameters of this spotlight allow you to apply a projector map.

To do this, click the **Projector Map** button in the **Advanced Effects** rollout. In the material browser window that will open, select the desired map (I used the Noise procedure map).

Then open the material editor and drag the map to any slot of the material editor. In the **Instance (Copy) Map** dialog box, select the **Instance** radio button. This will allow you to affect the projector map when setting parameters in the material editor (Fig. 2.76, *a*).

Set the map parameters as follows. Change its colors to your liking and change its size so that the final rendering shows an unclear shape colored unevenly (Fig. 2.76, *b*).

The material editor is described later in this chapter.

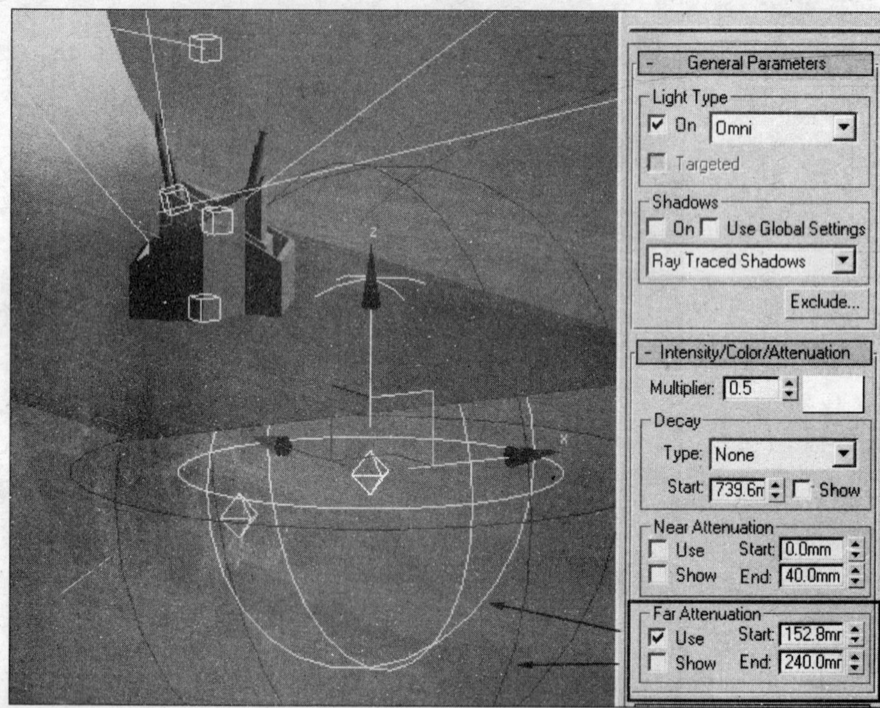

Fig. 2.77. The light sources simulating reflection

Finally, you could create a pair of omnidirectional light sources to simulate light reflection from the screen to the model. Make sure to limit their light, for example, by specifying the **Far Attenuation** parameters (Fig. 2.77).

The final arrangement and the result of rendering are shown in Fig. 2.78.

My scene is located in the Project2-lighting-final.max file.

NOTE

You used only standard and mental ray light sources. Could you use photometric ones in this arrangement? Yes, of course. However, it would be more difficult to set their parameters because these light sources are correct from the point of view of physics, so they don't have the **Decay** and **Attenuation** parameters.

This arrangement can also be used with the standard renderer. To obtain soft shadows in this case, use the Area Shadows type with appropriate settings. Be aware that these shadows are computed rather slowly, and the Quality parameter of the shadows should be doubled or even increased four times if you need high quality, especially with a fill light source.

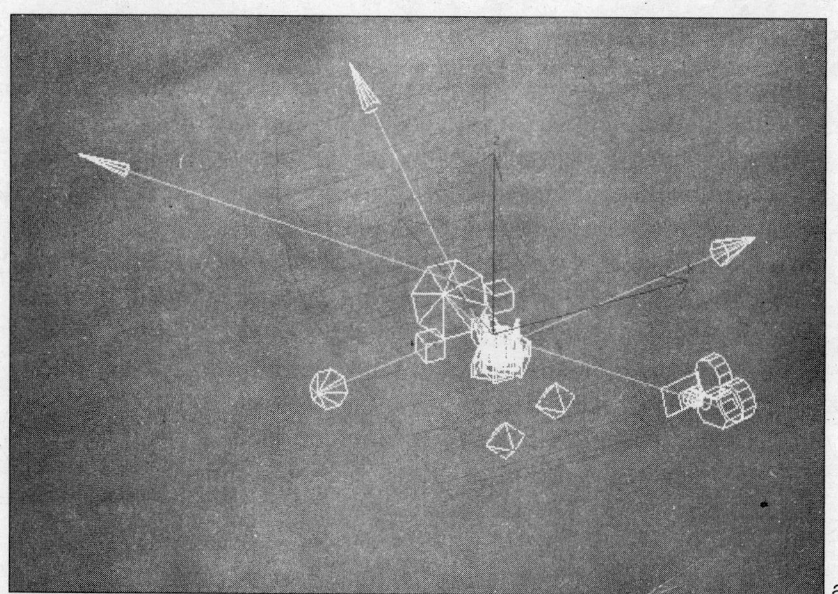

a

b

Fig. 2.78. The final arrangement (*a*) and the result of rendering (*b*)

Simulating the Sky Dome

This lighting method is currently very popular because it gives an idea of the model's geometry and materials, though the resulting picture isn't artistic.

Unfortunately, the classical variant of this arrangement works only with the standard renderer because the **Bias** parameter is unavailable for shadows of the Shadow Map type when mental ray is used. As a result, "dirt" appears on the lit surface of the model.

In the scene, the model of the container for small things should be used (the Projects\Project4\Model4-final.max file). Load it using the **Merge** command. It is desirable that the model is in the coordinates origin.

The initial scene is shown in Fig. 2.79. You can find it in the project4-lighting-01.max file in the Projects\Project4 folder on the accompanying CD-ROM. A common plane is used. Using its **Scale** parameter, you can specify scaling during rendering.

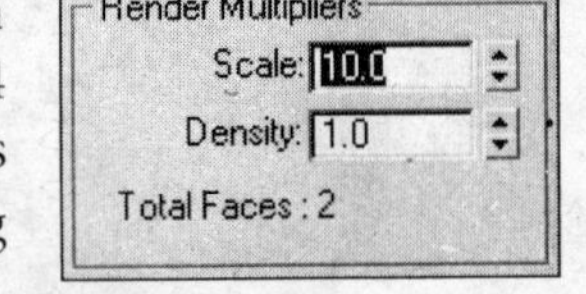

- ❐ Change the rendering module from mental ray to the standard.

Menu bar → **Rendering** → **Render** → the **Common** tab → the **Assign Renderer** rollout

In the **Production** line, click the button labeled with an ellipsis and select the **Default Scanline Renderer** item in the list. If this item is missing, the renderer is already set, and you don't need to change anything.

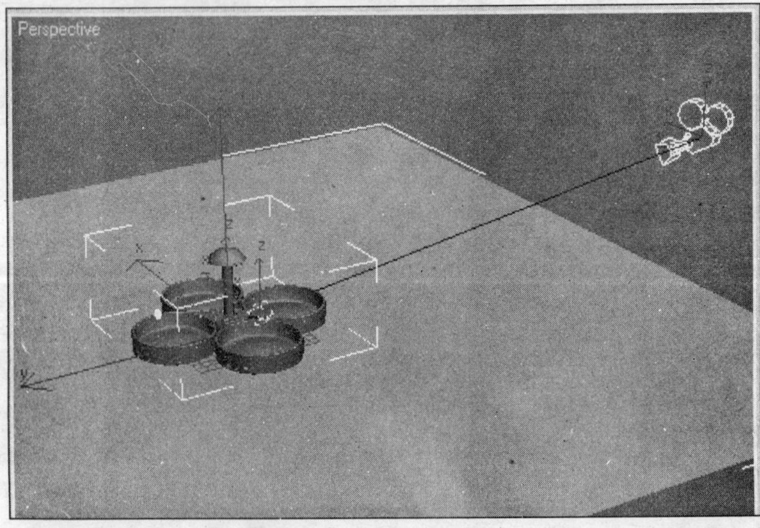

Fig. 2.79. The initial scene

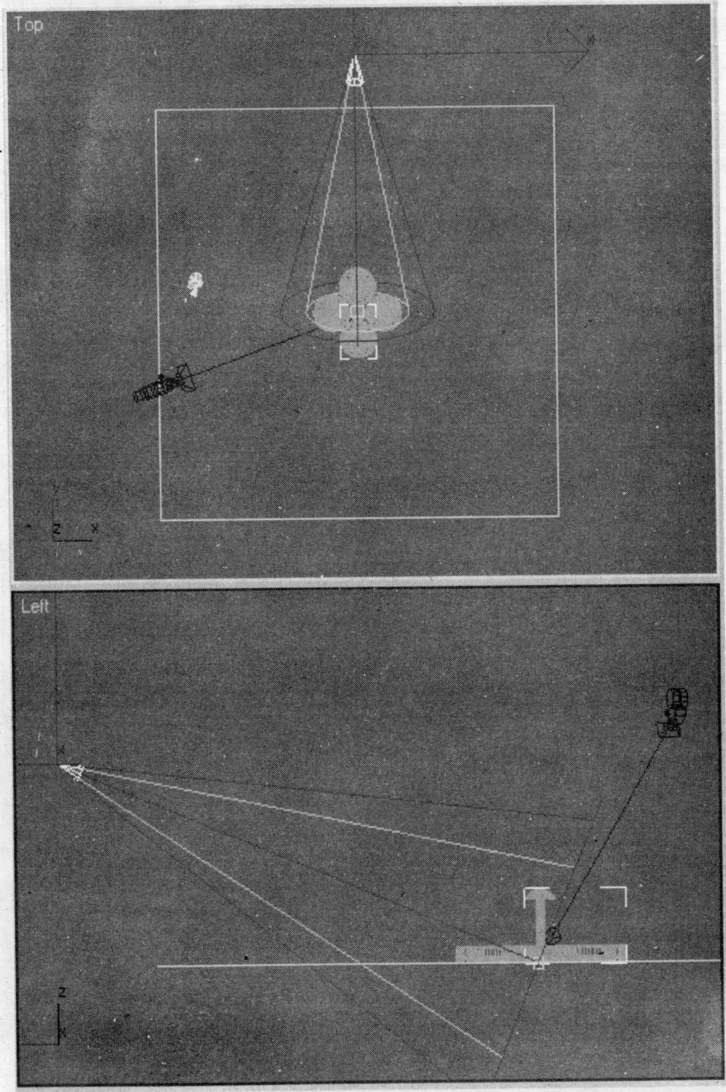

Fig. 2.80, *a*. Simulating the sky dome

- Create and set a camera and assign a gray material to all the objects.
- Create a Target Spot light source as shown in Fig. 2.80, *a*. Fig. 2.80, *b* shows its parameters.

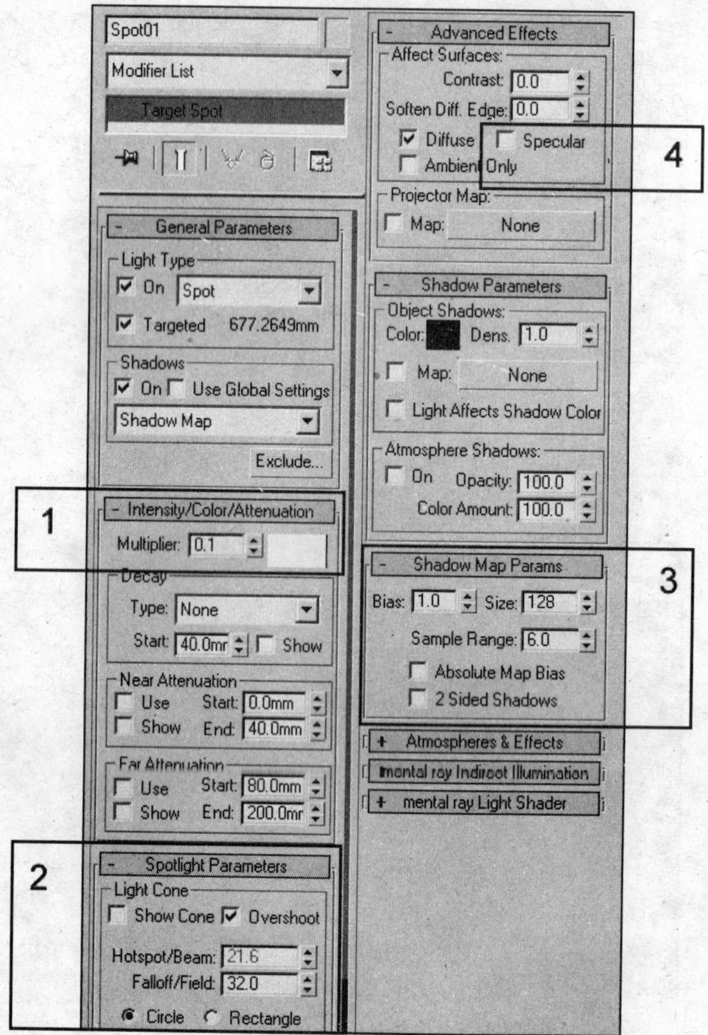

Fig. 2.80, *b*. Simulating the sky dome

Select a light-blue color of the light source. Set a small intensity because there will be enough light sources in the scene (indicated within box 1 in Fig. 2.80, *b*).

Set the angle of beam (the **Falloff/Field** parameter) so that the model is entirely within it, but don't make it too large. Check the **Overshoot** checkbox to light the plane evenly (indicated within box 2).

The shadows of the Shadow Map type should be small and shouldn't be sharp (indicated within box 3).

To avoid unwanted specks of light on shining materials, uncheck the **Affect Specular** checkbox (indicated within box 4).

- Create the other light sources by dragging this light source while keeping the <Shift> key pressed and with the **Instance** option selected. This will allow you to set the parameters of the light sources easily (Fig. 2.80, *c*). Add some chaos by moving the light sources. You can make the lighting uneven by increasing the density of light sources in certain areas. In any case, you'll need about fifty light sources. The result of this rendering should look similar to that shown in Fig. 2.80, *d*.

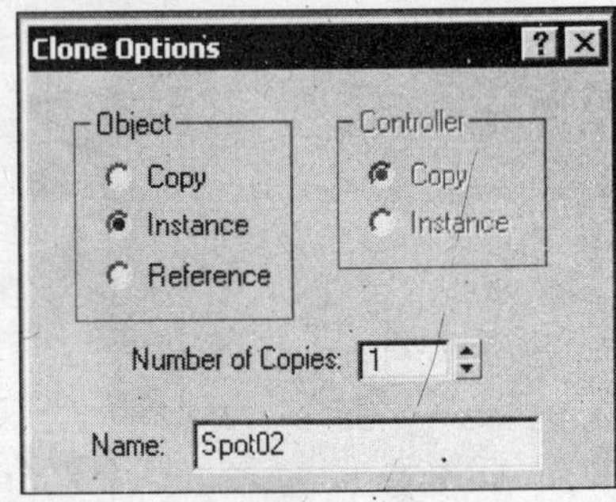

The result of my work at this stage is in the project4-lighting-02.max file in the Projects\Project4 folder on the accompanying CD-ROM.

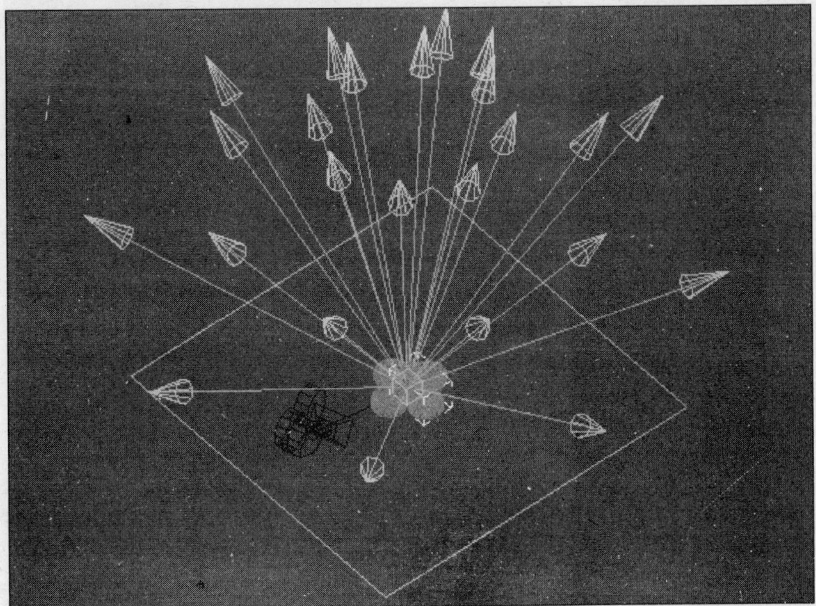

Fig. 2.80, *c*. Simulating the sky dome

Fig. 2.80, *d*. Simulating the sky dome

The first iteration is finished.

You can add a light source simulating the sun (Fig. 2.81, *a*). This should be a Directional light source with shadows of the Area Shadow type. This combination is valid for the standard renderer, but not for mental ray. The parameters of such a light source are shown in Fig. 2.81, *b*, and the result of rendering is shown in Fig. 2.81, *c*.

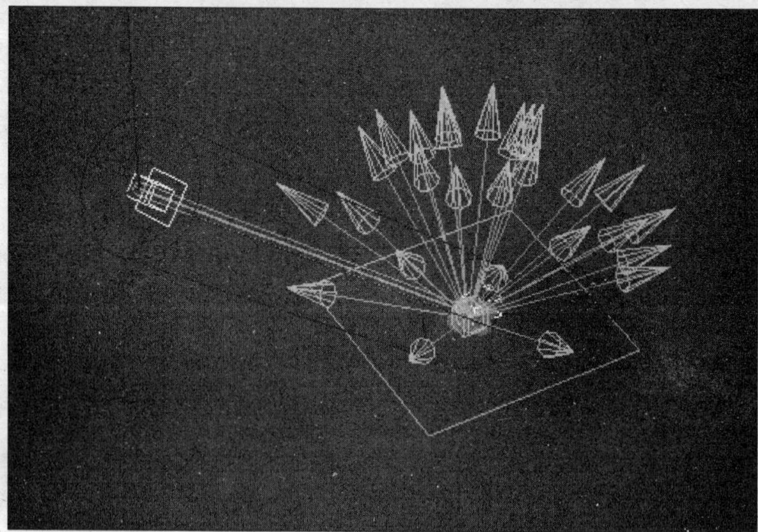

Fig. 2.81, *a*. The sky and the sun

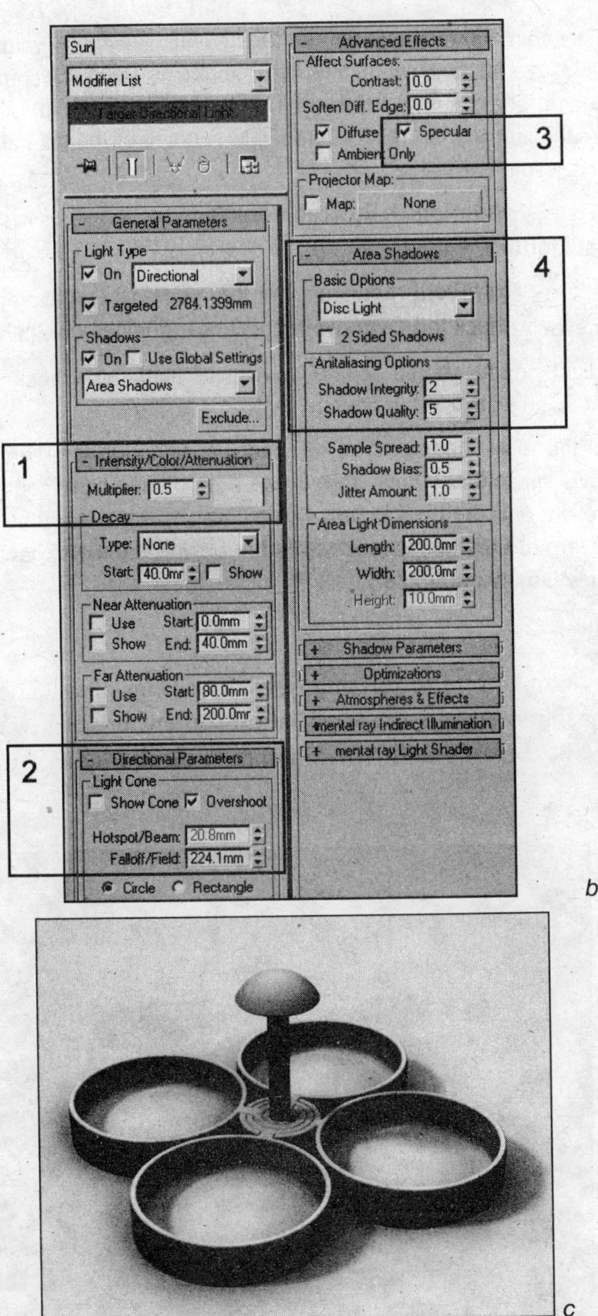

Fig. 2.81, *b* and *c*. The sky and the sun

NOTE

The light color should be warm. Set the intensity level to a value that would allow you to avoid over-lighting when this light source is used in combination with the sky dome light sources (indicated within box 1 in Fig. 2.81, *b*). You might need to decrease the intensity of the sky dome light sources or the global intensity to obtain the desired result.

Menu bar → **rendering** → **Environment** → **Global Lighting** → **Level**

Global Lighting:
Tint:
Level:
0.9

Select the **Falloff/Field** radius so that the model is illuminated entirely. To light the plane evenly, check the **Overshoot** checkbox ((indicated within box 2).

This light source should create specks of light, so check the **Affect Specular** checkbox (indicated within box 3).

Select the Area Shadows type of shadows. Although the light source is dot, these shadows simulate shadows from a free area diffuse light source. In the Area Shadows rollout (indicated within box 4), set the circle size so that the shadow becomes less sharp at a certain distance from the object. If the shadow dithers, increase the **Shadow Quality** parameter.

Finally, add light sources simulating reflections (Fig. 2.82). These should be Omni sources without shadows and with Attenuation somewhere below the plane. Their parameters should be the same as the parameters of similar light sources in the previous arrangement.

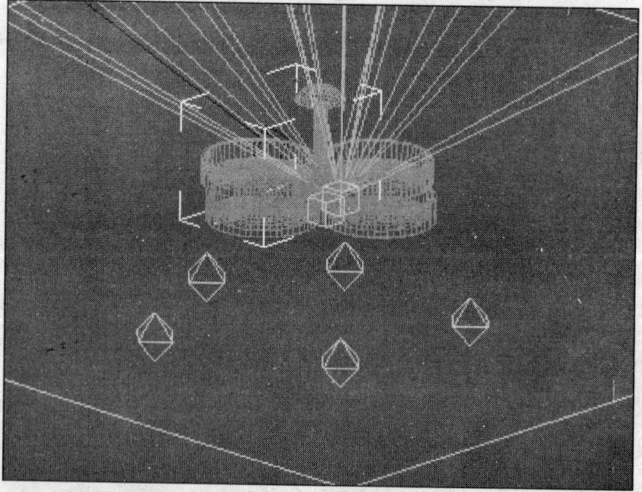

Fig. 2.82. Light sources simulating reflections

A variant of this arrangement that uses mental ray could appear as shown in Fig. 2.83, *a*. In this case, several mr Area Spot light sources with large radii are used. Shadows should be only of the Ray Traced type. A sun-simulating light source should be also mr Area Spot. In my opinion, the result is nice (Fig. 2.83, *b*).

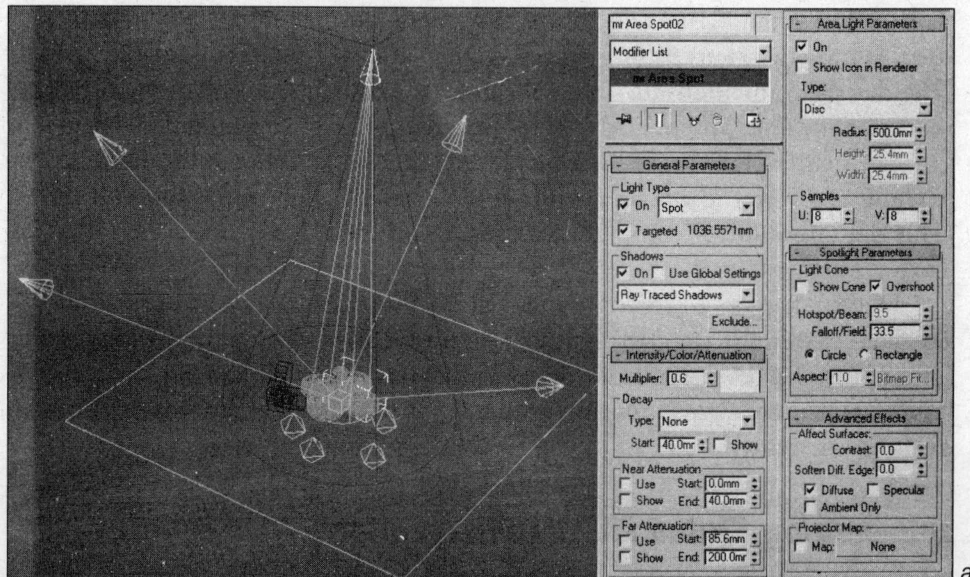

a

b

Fig. 2.83. A variant of the sky dome simulator when mr Area Spot light sources are used

There are a lot of variants of this and the previous arrangements. I suggest that you experiment with them. Perhaps, you'll find interesting solutions and use them in your future projects (unless you prefer methods described later in this chapter).

Lighting Methods That Use Global Lighting

Up to this point, I have described only methods that don't use indirect lighting. It is commonly referred to as *global lighting* although these are not the same thing. The described methods are identical for both the standard renderer and mental ray. For example, when you wanted to simulate reflections, you used additional light sources.

The lighting arrangements being almost the same, the settings described in this chapter allow you to obtain an image with realistic light reflection and refraction. This requires a lot of computation time, so you will have to sacrifice time for the sake of beauty.

In this chapter, I'll describe only the use of mental ray because the Radiosity method used in the standard renderer is suitable for interiors. Its settings and examples of use will be described in the next chapter. Although another built-in module, Light Tracer, uses algorithms similar to those used by mental ray, it is too slow, and its features are scanty.

Implementing Global Lighting in mental ray

Before I describe practical examples, I'll like to touch on a few general issues. As with light source parameters and positioning, all settings described in the following examples are just recommendations. If you are dissatisfied with the result, feel free to change the settings. All in all, people differ, and so do their monitors.

However, before you change anything, you should be aware of the results of the change. This is the topic of this section.

The effects I'm going to describe can be viewed in the everyday life. For example, these are light specks from the water on the walls and the bottom of a water poll. (The effect is called *reflective caustic*). Other examples include the following: focusing light rays as a result of refraction and reflection by a lens (*refractive caustic*), color reflexes from fruit to the white table-cloth, on which they are lying, color reflexes from the floor and the walls to the ceiling, illumination created by the light dispersed in the atmosphere and reflected from objects (global lighting), reflection of your face in a mirror, and refraction of an image by a lens. In the real life, these effects are based on the same "algorithms" described by the corpuscular-wave theory of light.

Unfortunately, the performance of contemporary computers is too low to implement these effects correctly and precisely and using a universal algorithm. This is why developers use various simplified mathematical models of physical processes to simulate these phenomena. The developers' main task is to achieve an image as realistic as possible in reasonable time.

In the following paragraphs, I'll describe the implementation of these effects in mental ray version 3.4. I won't write formulas or program code. If you wish, you can find then in the documentation for mental ray that comes with 3ds Max, in books, or on the Internet. Nevertheless, I'd like to reiterate that you should have an idea of what happens because it will help you avoid mistakes.

When I wrote this section, invaluable help was given to me by Igor Sivakov, a renowned expert in 3D graphics and an enthusiast of mental ray.

First, computation of lighting effects (global lighting and caustic), reflection and refraction of objects and images in mirrors and lenses, and building shadows from objects are three different and completely independent processes in mental ray, as well as in any other contemporary renderer. Building shadows was discussed earlier, and reflection and refraction of objects and images will be discussed later, when creating materials with relevant properties.

In this section, I'll discuss only lighting effects. Concurrently, I'll describe parameters. In my opinion, this would be the best approach.

The main parameters for setting indirect illumination are located on the **Indirect Illumination** tab on the rendering setting dialog box (Fig. 2.84).

Menu bar → **Rendering** → **Render** → the **Indirect Illumination** tab

The panel is divided into two rollouts. For caustic and global illumination, the Photon Map method is used. Its parameters are located in the **Caustics and Global Illumination** rollout which is divided into two groups, **Caustic** and **GI**. This division is intentional because caustic uses a simpler algorithm.

The third type of photons, Volume, used for creating volumetric effects is beyond the scope of this book.

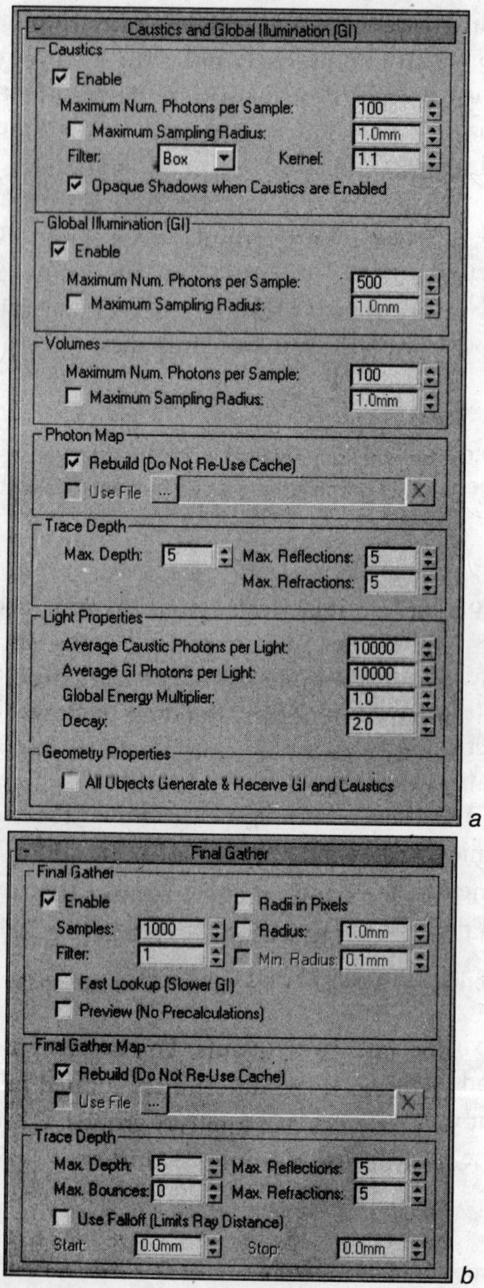

Fig. 2.84. Dialog boxes for setting caustic and global illumination (*a*) and final gather (*b*)

Roughly speaking, the photon map method works as follows.

A light source emits rays called *photons.* They have nothing in common with actual photons. The name just emphasizes that the rays are straight and carry the energy. The method of emission depends on the light source. For example, an Omni source emits the rays evenly in all directions.

Photons don't have size! 3ds Max documentation uses an incorrect term, photon radius. In fact, this parameter refers to the radius of a spot, from which the photons are taken, to obtain visual distribution of energy.

When the photons encounter a surface, it reflects them. The smoother is the surface, the fewer photons are reflected diffused, that is, the more photons are reflected in a mirror-like fashion. In other words, the following rule is observed: The angle of incidence equals the angle of reflection (Fig. 2.85). If the surface is transparent to some extent, a certain part of photons passes through it. They are refracted depending on IOR (Index of Refraction). This is true for both global illumination photons and caustic photons. The only difference is that the later are reflected only mirror-like and refracted.

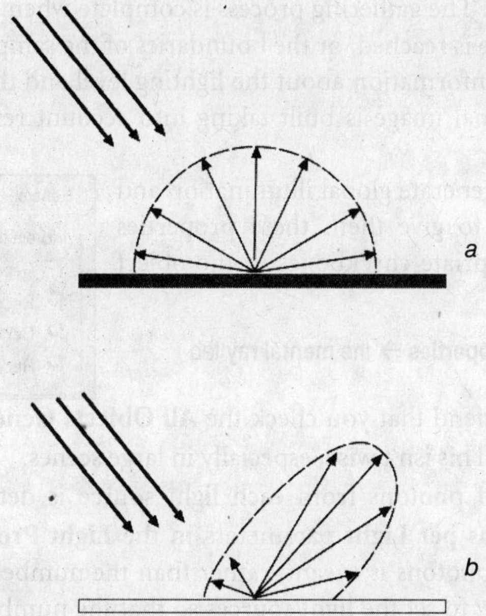

Fig. 2.85. Global illumination photons distribution from a diffuse surface (*a*) and a partly mirror surface (*b*)

Reflected (or bouncing) photons are partly absorbed or forced to disappear. The maximum number of bounces is set using the **Max. Reflection/Refraction/Depth** parameters in the **Trace Depth** group. The last parameter determines the total number of bounces. When it equals five, a photon can be reflected four times, pass through a surface once, and disappear. The greater these values, the more precise the computation of the photon map, and the lighter is the scene. However, this would require more time and memory space.

After the photons are emitted and distributed over the surfaces of objects, rendering starts. Among other operations, it gathers the photons.

In general, this process occurs as follows. The camera emits rays that scan the scene. When a ray encounters a surface, a sample (spot) is built, from which the rays are gathered. The **Maximum Num** parameters specify the maximum number of photons to be gathered for one camera ray. The greater this value, the more precise and smoother is the effect being computed: caustic pr global illumination. To limit the gathering process, another parameter is used: the sampling radius. By default, it is computed automatically. For caustic photons, it is 1/100 of the scene size, and for global illumination photons, it is 1/10. As a rule, computed values are too large, and the result is unclear. So you can set these sizes manually, using the **Maximum Sampling Radius** parameters. The gathering process is complete when the maximum number of photons per sample is reached, or the boundaries of the sample spot are reached.

After that, the information about the lighting level and the color is returned to the camera, and the final image is built taking into account refractions, reflections, and antialiasing.

For objects to generate global illumination and caustic, you need to give them these properties by checking appropriate checkboxes in the object properties.

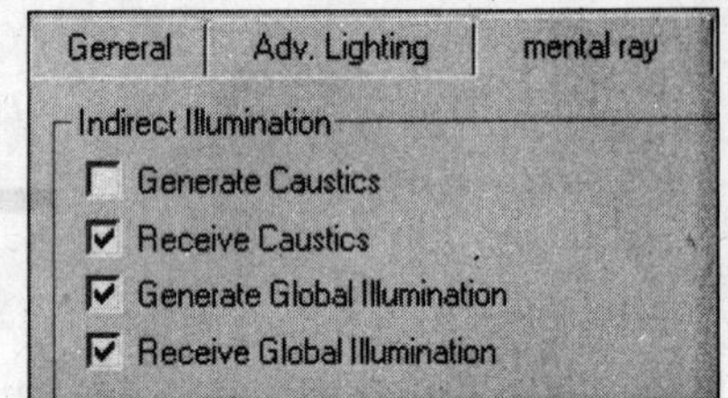

Quad menu → **Properties** → the **mental ray** tab

I don't recommend that you check the **All Objects Generate and Receive GI and Caustic** checkbox. This isn't wise, especially in large scenes.

The number of photons from each light source is determined by the **Average Caustic/GI Photons per Light** parameters in the **Light Properties** group. Here, the number of stored photons is meant, rather than the number of emitted ones. Therefore, you should try to set the light sources so that the number of photons "lost in the Universe" is as small as possible. As a rule, the default number of photons (10,000) is too large for test computation and too small for final computation. To obtain a good result, you need at least 100,000 caustic photons and from 100,000 to 100,000,000 global illumination photons. However, much depends on the scene.

For caustic photons, you can specify an algorithm and parameters of filtration. They are used to control the sharpness depending on your goals (the **Filter** and **Kernel** parameters).

The most important parameters are **Global Energy Multiplier** and **Decay**. They determine the amount of energy distributed between the photons and how the energy decays depending on the distance passed by the photons.

The **Global Energy Multiplier** parameter allows you to adjust the energy of all the light sources while maintaining the proportion between them. In addition, you can do this quickly and using a single control of the interface. Each light source has parameters for controlling energy and the number of photons in its **mental ray Indirect Illumination** rollout. Their default settings are shown in Fig. 2.86, *a*. In this case, the energy of a light source depends on its intensity. To summarize, the energy of a light source is determined by three parameters: the intensity of the light source, the **Global Energy Multiplier** parameter, and the light source's multiplier. In addition, you can change the number of photons relative to the global settings. To do this, use the multipliers. For example, you can exclude a light source from creating caustic by entering a zero into the **Global Multipliers: Caustic Photons** input box.

This rollout allows you to set the indirect lighting parameters manually for each light source, and even exclude the light source from these processes (Fig. 2.86, *b*). In this case, energy, the number of photons, and other parameters won't be related to the light source intensity and global settings.

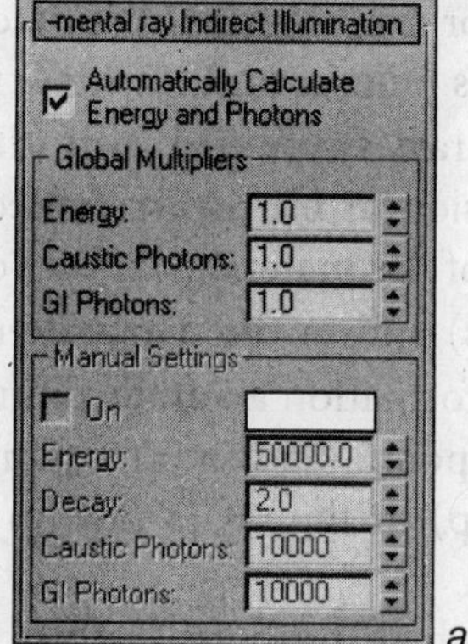

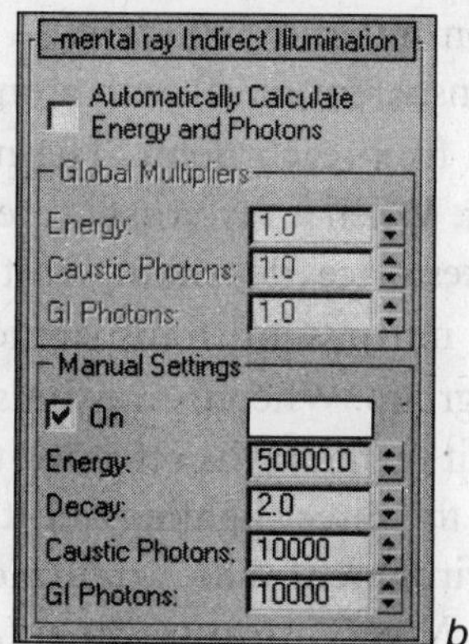

Fig. 2.86. Two variants of global illumination settings in a light source

NOTE

Global settings work correctly with photometric light sources. As for the standard ones, you need to set them individually. To simplify settings, try to avoid using different types of light sources in your scenes.

The second important parameter, **Decay**, is the power (p) in the formula $E_R = E * 1/R^p$, where R is the total distance traveled by a photon, E_R is the energy of the photon at this distance, and E is its energy when it was emitted. Therefore, a value of 2.0 corresponds to the inverse square law, which agrees with physical laws. However, this works only when the sizes of objects correspond to the real ones, and materials are set correctly.

You can (and should) compute the distribution of photons over the surface only once and then use it in the future. To do this, save it in a file in the **Photon Map** group and check the **Use File** checkbox. Alternatively, you can uncheck the **Rebuild** checkbox, but the data will be lost when you exit 3ds Max. Note that one map is stored for all photons, both caustic and global illumination.

When you use a saved photon map, object animation is out of the question. You can animate only the camera. However, you can change the radii and the number of samples. In fact, you usually need to.

The second rollout, **Final Gather**, contains parameters necessary for setting the process whose goal is to refine and improve the result of tracing the photons.

Without going into detail, this process is the following. The surface of the objects in the scene is divided into triangular elements, and *FG points* are determined. These are points used for gathering lighting information, and FG stands for Final Gather. In the process, only surfaces visible from the camera are used, unlike with global illumination and caustic photons. A hemisphere (for non-transparent surfaces) or a sphere (for transparent ones) with a one-unit radius is built around each FG point. Rays are emitted from each point. The number of the rays is specified with the **Samples** parameter. When a ray crosses the surface, diffusion or mirror-like reflection or refraction takes place, depending on the properties of the material (i.e., the combination of diffuse, mirror, and transparency components) and on the parameters in the **Trace Depth** group. When the ray finishes its way, information about the illumination of the point hit by the ray is returned to the original point. (This information is a combination of the direct lighting and the photon map). If the ray is "lost in the Universe," the Environment value is returned.

3ds Max 7.5 features mental ray 3.4, in which the Final Gather process is improved and works faster. So you can obtain a satisfactory result with small values of the **Samples** parameter. What's more, the default value (1,000) is excessive, and rendering in mr 3.4 takes longer time than in version 3.3. The best value is between 200 and 500.

Parameters in the **Trace Depth** group deserve special attention. The **Max Reflection/Refraction/Depth** parameters are related to bouncing from specular and transparent surfaces, and their essence is the same as with photons. Theoretically and practically, you could use the final gather to create caustic, but this wouldn't be the best solution.

The **Max. Bounces** parameter determines the maximum number of diffuse bounces. It was first introduced in mental ray 3.4 and is very convenient. Increasing this parameter to a value between 3 and 4 results in "softening" the scene and making it lighter. This parameter has no relation to **Max Depth**!

The **Radius** parameters determine the radii of samples, in which the gather is done. The use of this parameter and decreasing its value result in a top-quality well-detailed image, but the rendering time increases. By default (when the **Radius** checkbox is unchecked), this parameter equals to one-tenth of the scene size. You can specify radii in pixels. This is convenient in long scenes and allows you to optimize rendering time.

Like a photon map, you can save a GF map. Because it depends on the viewing angle, mental ray will rebuild it and fill in gaps if necessary. This is why it would make sense to uncheck the **Rebuild** checkbox.

The **Fast Lookup** checkbox is intended to speed up the final gather using additional information contained in the photon map. However, the result is often to the contrary.

Finally, there is a useful feature allowing you to optimize the final gather for large scenes (such as exteriors or large interiors). This is the **Use Falloff** checkbox that limits the length of rays using the **Start** and **Stop** parameters similar to the **Far Attenuation** boundaries in the light source parameters.

Global illumination and final gather can be used separately or in combination. Which method should you use and when? For interiors and closed scenes, use a combination of these methods. If you use only global illumination, you'll need a lot of photons to obtain a satisfactory result, and this might exhaust the memory of your computer. If you use only final gather, you won't obtain a desired effect: The scene will be too dark because no information about areas beyond direct lighting (e.g., areas behind a folding screen) will be available. As for exteriors and objects lit from the sky using an HDRI map, it is pointless to light them using global lighting photons.

An Arrangement with One Light Source

This example will comprehensively illustrate indirect lighting settings for an arrangement that uses one light source.

❒ Load the Project5-Lighting-01.max file located in the Projects/Project5 folder on the accompanying CD-ROM (Fig. 2.87).

I'd like to explain briefly the contents of the scene.

It simulates a show-case on an exhibition stand. The scene contains a model of a telephone on a support. The support was made from a spline using new features of 3ds Max 7.5, namely, advanced settings for spline rendering (Fig. 2.88, *a*). Then the **Edit Poly** modifier was applied to create chamfers on all longitudinal edges (Fig. 2.88, *b*). It was possible to select them quickly using the **Loop** command for edges.

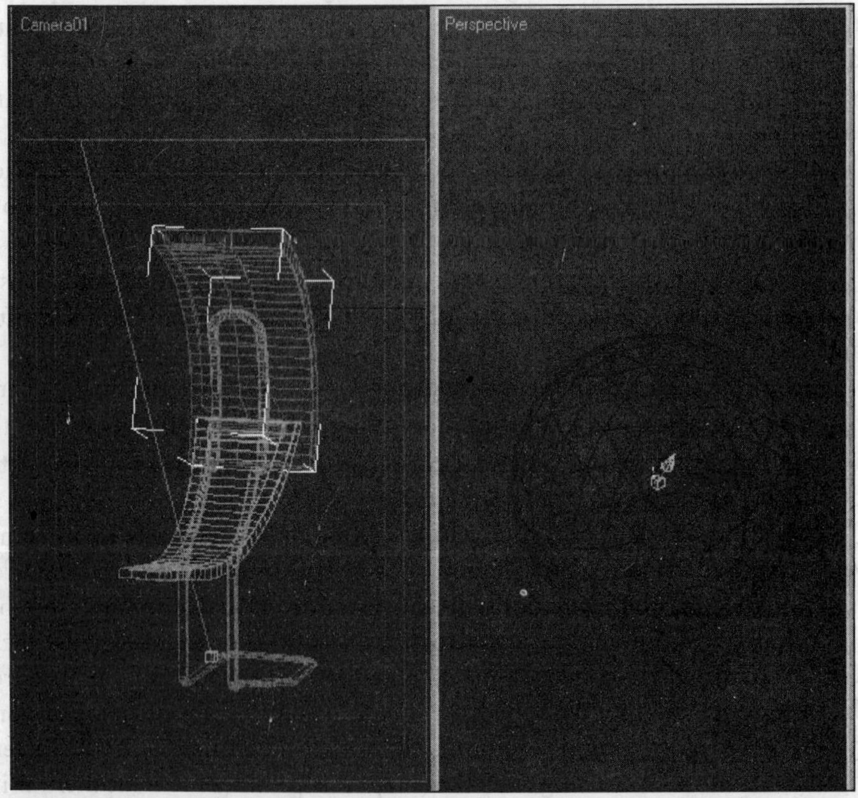

Fig. 2.87. The initial scene

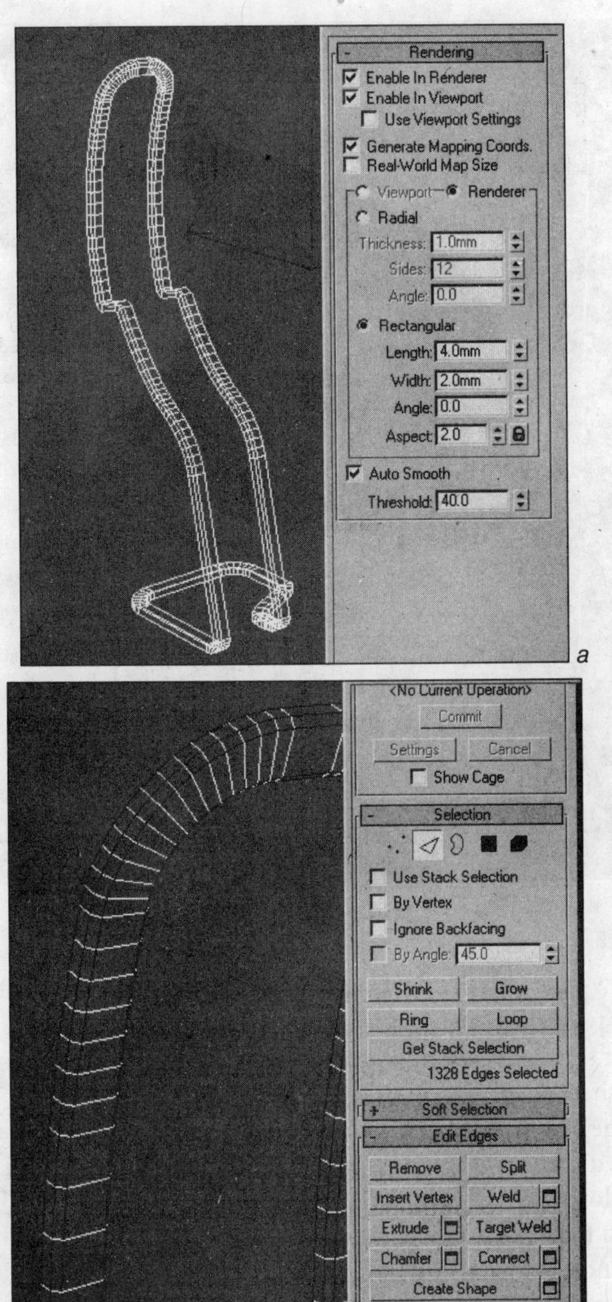

Fig. 2.88. The support

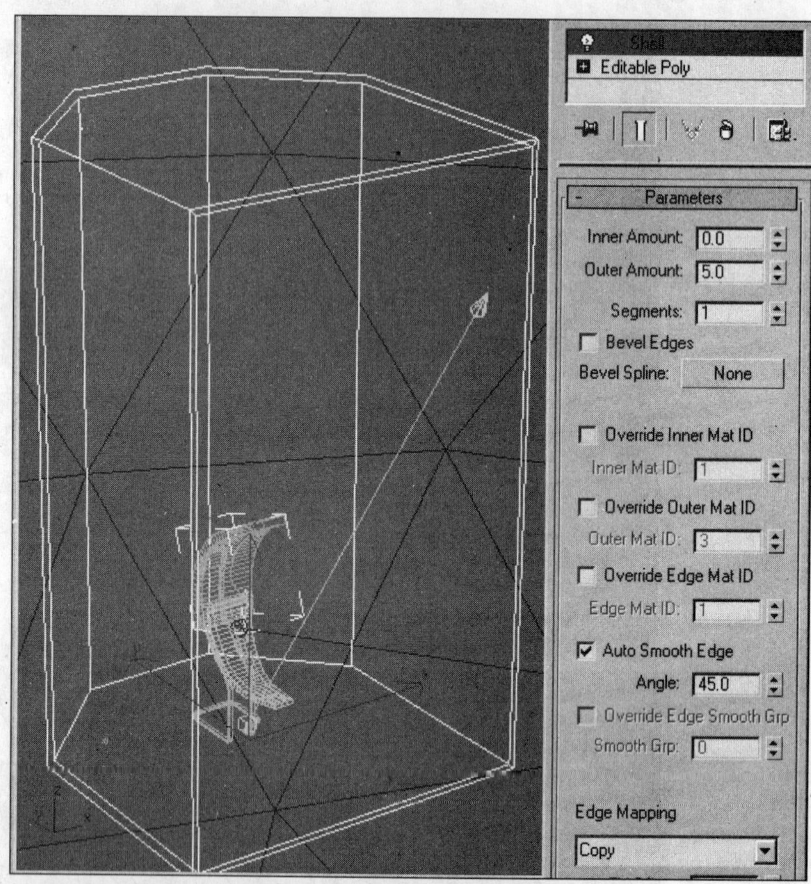

Fig. 2.89. The show-case

The show-case was made from a cube. I deleted one of its polygons, created chamfers on two edges, and applied the **Shell** modifier (Fig. 2.89).

The light source is a narrow mental ray Area Spot with Ray Traced shadows of a small diameter (Fig. 2.90).

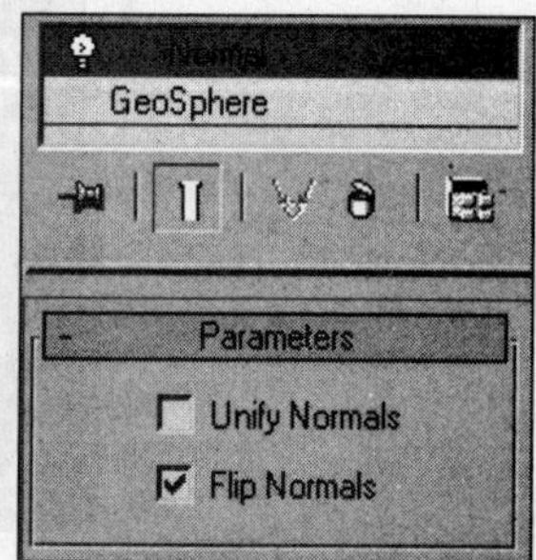

The scene is entirely enclosed within a sphere whose normals are directed inside. This is done for two reasons. First, this allows you to optimize photon tracing by preventing them to fly away. Second, a map will be assigned to the sphere, and the models will reflect the map.

The camera has a long-focus lens. It is positioned so that it can see only the model.

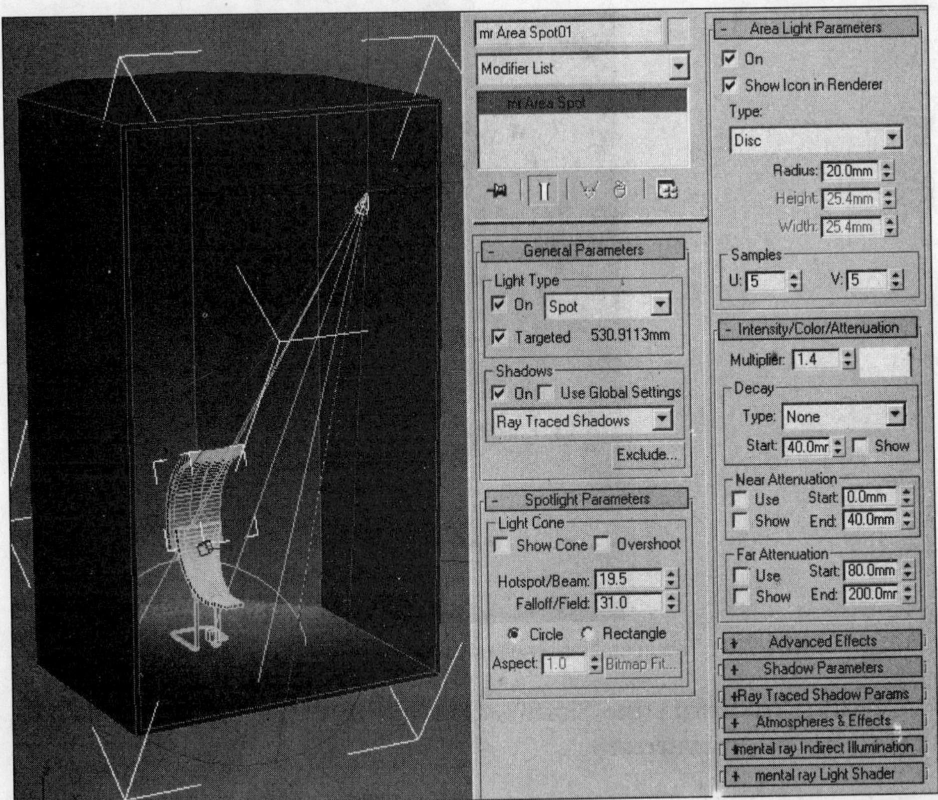

Fig. 2.90. The position and parameters of the light source

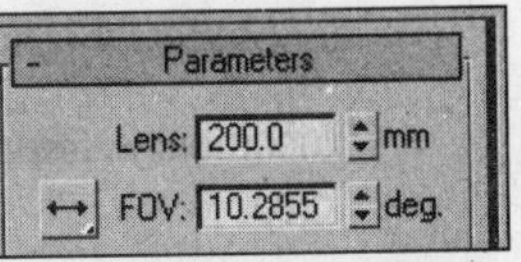

- A gray material is assigned to all the objects.
- In the properties of all objects except the sphere, the **Generate** and **Receive GI** checkboxes are checked. For the sphere, only the **Receive GI** checkbox is checked, to optimize photon map creation.

Quad menu → **Properties** → the **mental ray** tab

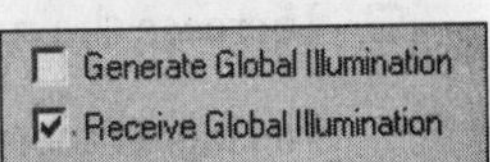

- In the rendering parameters, set the image size to 400 × 600 pixels and show the Safe Frame.

Menu bar → **Rendering** → **Render** → the **Common** tab → the **Output Size** group

The viewport right-click menu → **Show Safe Frame**

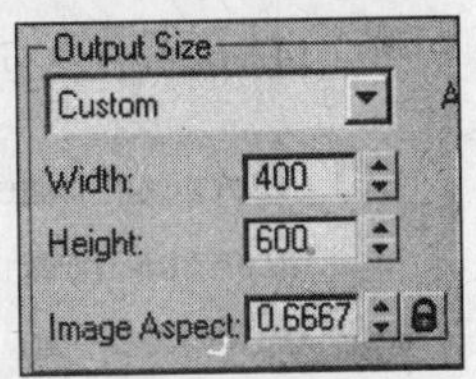

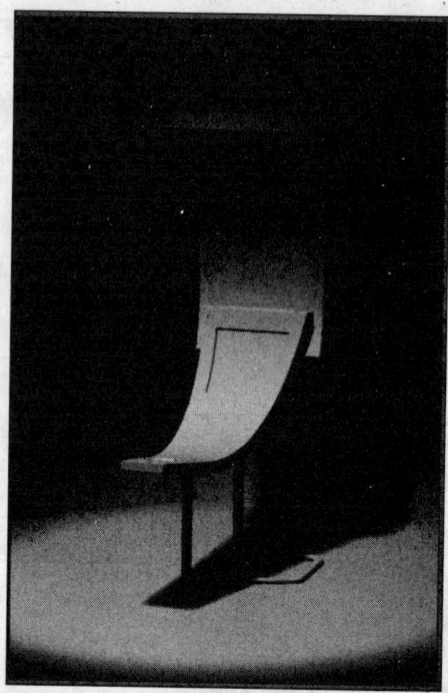

Fig. 2.91. The result of rendering the scene without global illumination

Perform rendering (the <Shift>+<Q> shortcut) (Fig. 2.91). As you might expect, it contains nothing interesting.

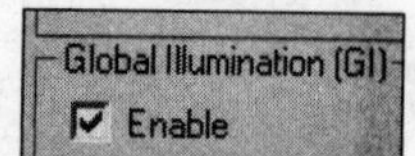

- In the rendering parameters, check the **Enable** checkbox in the **Global Illumination** group and perform rendering with the default settings. You'll notice "blotches." The number of photons is obviously insufficient (Fig. 2.92, *a*).

Menu bar → **Rendering** → **Render** → the **Indirect Illumination** tab→ the **Global Illumination** group

- Increase the number of photons to 1,000,000.

The **Light Properties** group→ set the **Average GI Photons per Light** parameter to **1000000**

However, this is not enough; the picture is disappointing.

- Decrease the maximum radius of a global illumination sample to 15 mm and increase the number of samples ten times. In addition, uncheck the **Rebuild** checkbox in the **Photon Map** group. The photon map computation takes quite a long time, so it is pointless to rebuild it repeatedly. A million photons is enough. The result is shown in Fig. 2.92, *b*. The picture is even and angles are seen, but few details are visible.

To show more details, you could decrease the sample radius, but speckles would appear. To deal with the speckles, you could increase the number of photons. Yet, this wouldn't be wise.

- ❐ In the **Final Gather** rollout, check the **Enable** checkbox. Decrease the number of samples to 100. As I mentioned earlier, the final gather algorithm was improved, and fewer samples (or final gather rays) are necessary.
- ❐ Perform rendering (Fig. 2.92, *c*).

The picture became darker. You might think the photons stopped working. This is not the case, and they still contribute to lighting. However, the final gather collects lighting from everywhere, the most information comes from outside, and it is dark there.

A possible solution to the problem is to increase the energy of photons. This isn't the best approach, but it works.

- ❐ Increase the value of the **Global Energy Multiplier** parameter twice and check the **Rebuild** checkbox in the **Photon Map** group to rebuild the photon map. You can even decrease the number of photons to 100,000 because the final gather will finish the picture.
- ❐ Perform rendering. The picture became lighter, but details aren't visible because the final gather map is not clear. To improve the image, set the final gather radius to 5 mm, decrease the number of samples to 200, and decrease the **Max Bounces** parameter to 2. Uncheck the **Rebuild** checkbox in the parameters of the photon map and final gather. In my opinion, the result is nice (Fig. 2.92, *d*).
- ❐ To get rid of the blotches completely, you can use the minimum final gather radius (ten times less will increase computation time). You might prefer to do this for the final rendering with materials.

You've spent a lot of time, with nothing to show for it.

What else can you do? First, change the antialiasing settings because the default values aren't the best.

The **Renderer** tab → the **Sampling Quality** group

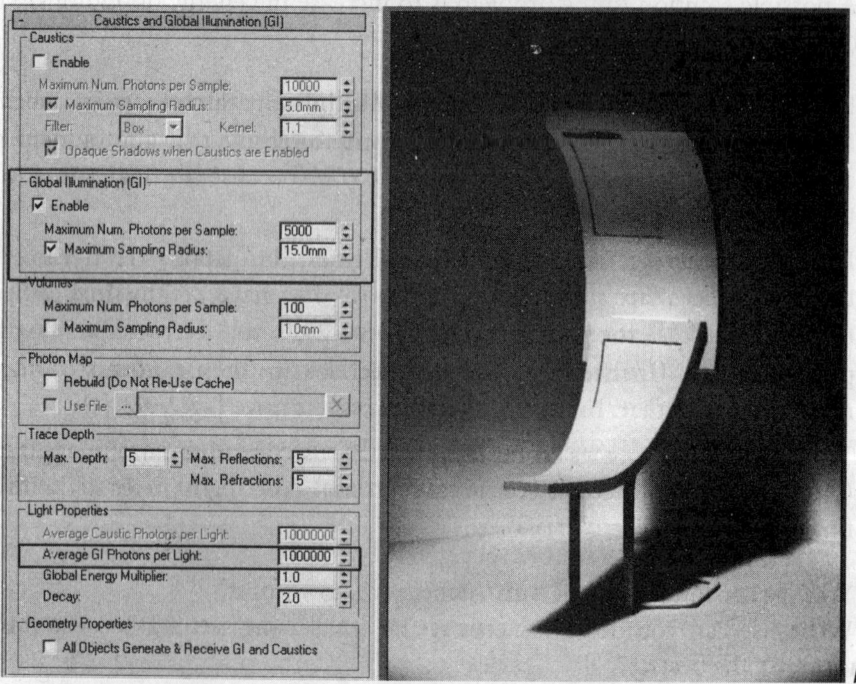

Fig. 2.92, *a* and *b*. Setting indirect illumination using one light source

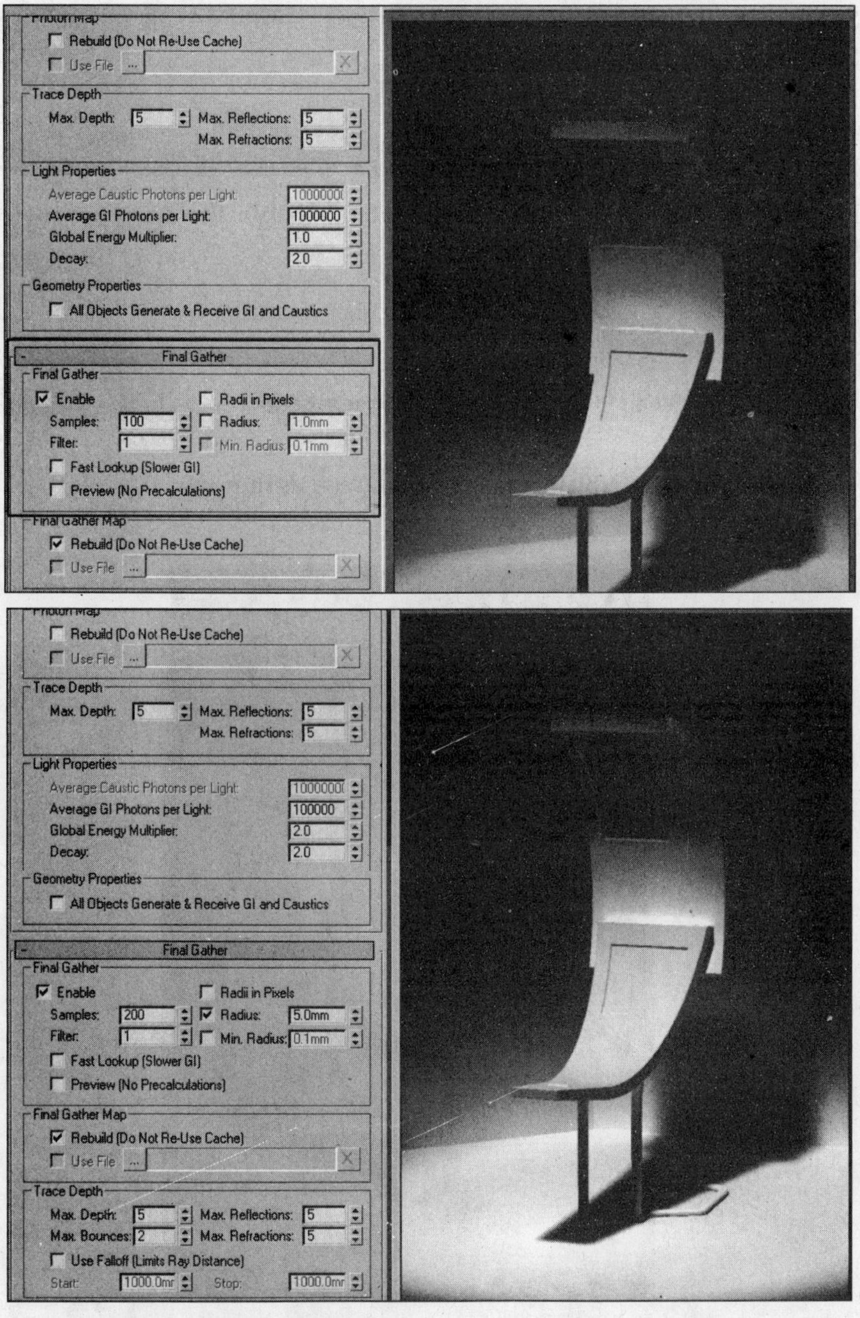

c

d

Fig. 2.92, *c* and *d*. Setting indirect illumination using one light source

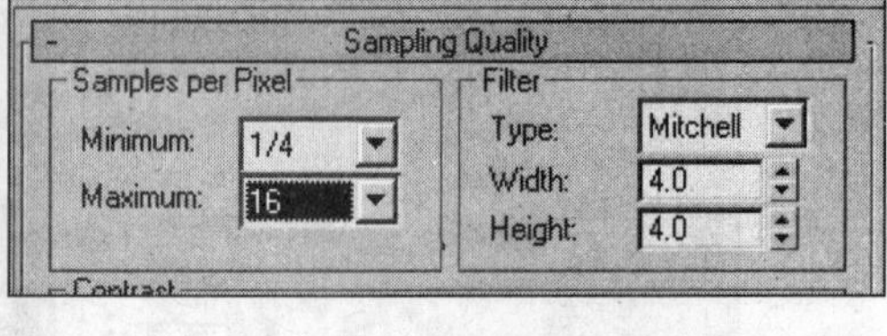

- Select the **Mitchell** type and set the **Samples per Pixel: Maximum** parameter to a value of at least 16.
- Improve the quality of the shadow by increasing the **Samples U** and **V** parameters in the **Area Light Parameters** rollout of the light source.

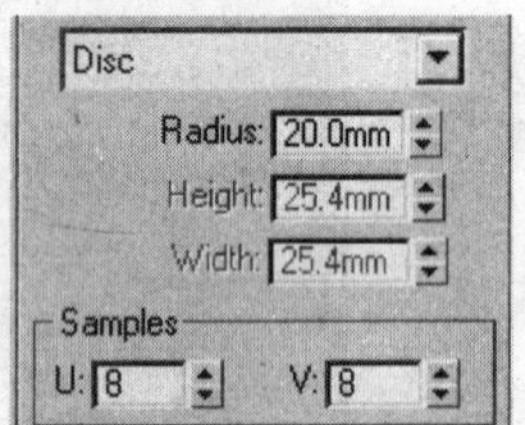

You can set the exposure if you wish. As for me, I didn't need this (Fig. 2.93).

Menu bar → **Rendering** → **Environment** → **Exposure Control**

Select **Logarithmic Exposure Control** and set it as shown in Fig. 2.94.

Fig. 2.93. The final result

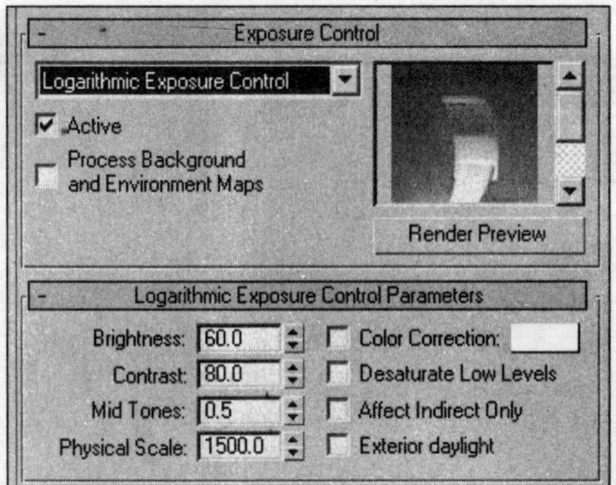

Fig. 2.94. Setting the exposure

You can find the result of my work in the Project5-lighting-final.max file in the Projects/Project5 folder on the accompanying CD-ROM.

However, you will agree that one light source is insufficient. I'm going to continue this project.

The Classic Arrangement

As I mentioned earlier, the three-lamp arrangement can also be used for indirect illumination, taking the stationery container as an example.

- ❐ Load the Project2-lighting-final.max scene from the Projects/Project2 folder on the accompanying CD-ROM.

If you have your own variant of this scene, use it.

- ❐ Delete unnecessary light sources. These are two Omni sources simulating reflection from the screen. In this example, mental ray will take care of reflection.

The scene is open, so it would be pointless to use photons for global illumination. In such scenes, you should use only the final gather.

- ❐ Turn on the final gather.
- ❐ Decrease the number of samples to 100 (Fig. 2.95, *a*). You should obtain a support filled with light (Fig. 2.95, *b*).

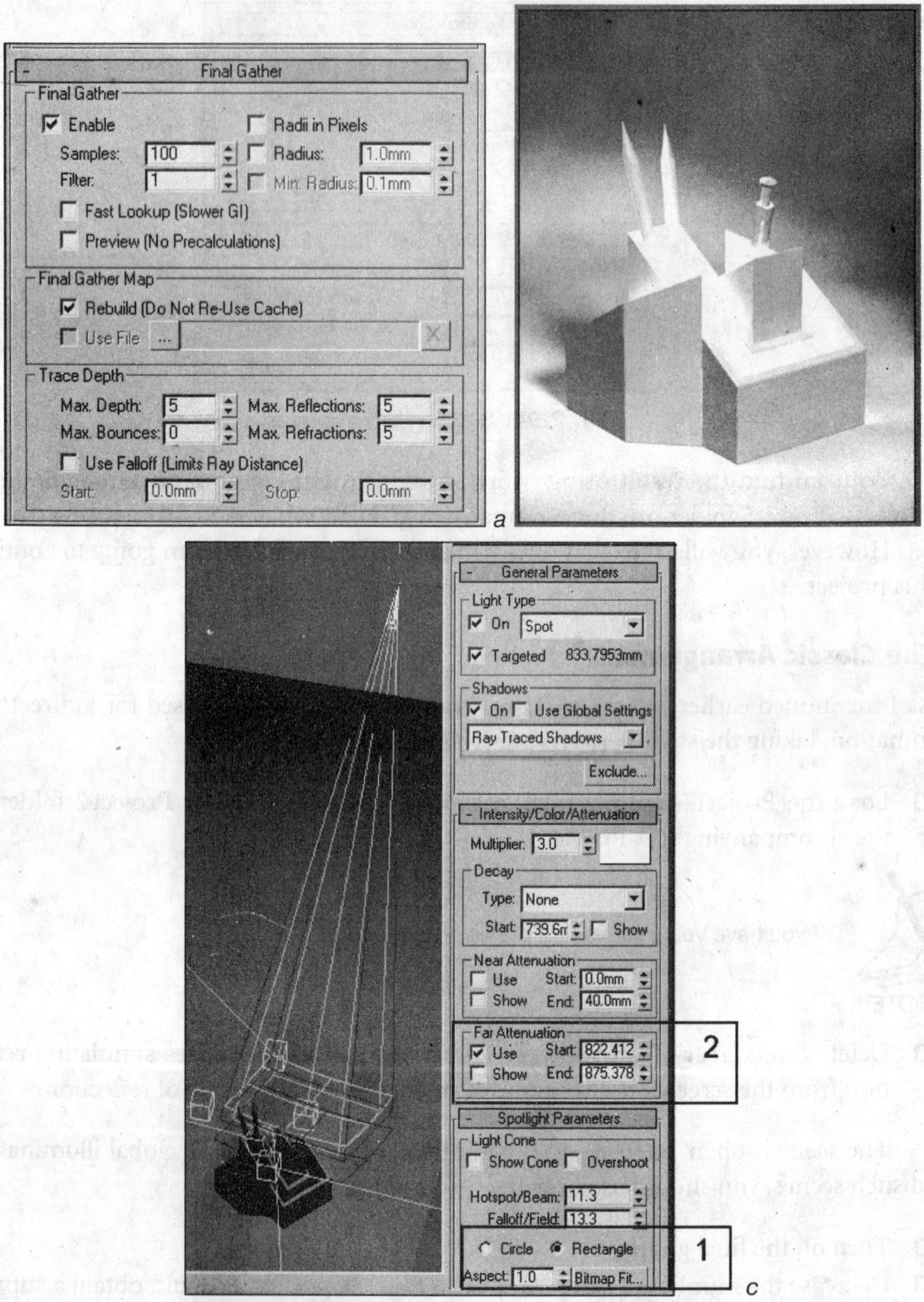

Fig. 2.95, *a–c*. Setting the classic arrangement

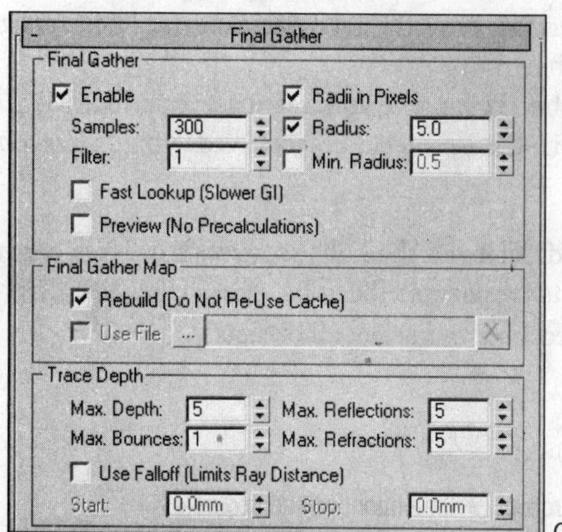

d

e

Fig. 2.95, *d* and *e*. Setting the classic arrangement

The Spot-Rim1 and Spot-Rim2 light sources that illuminate the scene from the rear side are very strong. In addition, they don't make shadows. This is why the container is so light. Unfortunately, there are no tools for limiting or locally excluding light sources from the final gather in 3ds Max. So you'll have to do a lighting engineer's job.

Fig. 2.95 shows the position and settings of one of these light sources.

NOTE

Changing the shape to rectangular (indicated within box 1 in Fig. 2.92, *c*) and moving the target of the light source allowed me to illuminate only the faces.

Setting the attenuation boundaries allowed me to exclude the internal walls of the container from illumination (indicated within box 2). Casting the shadows helped to avoid over-lighting.

Increasing the numbers of samples and bounces the sample radius (Fig. 2.95, *d*) gave a good effect. Everything is all right now! (Fig. 2.95, *e*).

The result of my work is in the project2-lighting-fg.max file in the /Project 2 folder on the accompanying CD-ROM.

Using the *SkyLight* Light Source

When describing the arrangement simulating the sky dome lighting, I intentionally mentioned that advanced methods could improve the traditional ones. The arrangement described in this section is one of them.

If you did the exercise simulating the sky dome, you can use your file. Mine is project4-lighting-skydome.max located in the Projects/Project4 folder on the accompanying CD-ROM.

- When you open this scene, select and delete all the light sources first. It is convenient to do this by selecting the objects by names (the <H> key) (Fig. 2.96). In this dialog box, check only the **Lights** checkbox and select all objects.

- Switch to mental render.

  Menu bar → **Rendering** → **Render** or <F10>

  The **Common** tab → the **Assign Renderer** rollout → the button with an ellipsis.

  In the **Production** line, select **mental ray**.

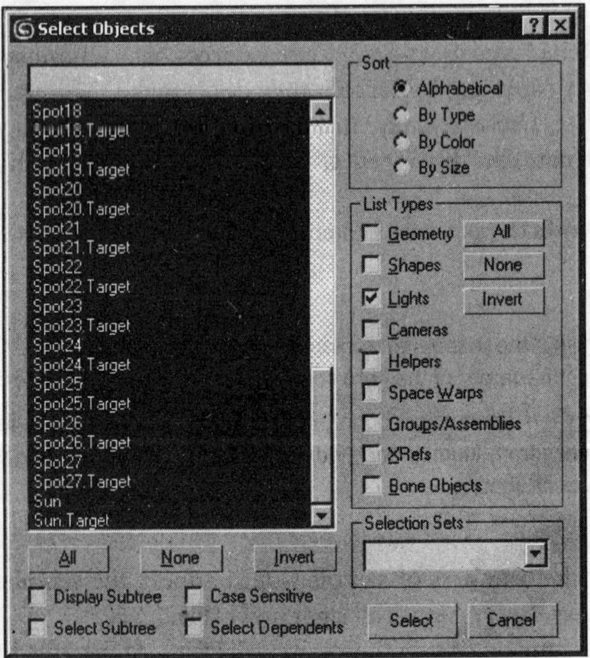

Fig. 2.96. Selecting all light sources

❐ Add the SkyLight light source with default settings to the scene (Fig. 2.97, *a*). Its position and orientation don't matter. This is just an icon.

Menu bar → **Create** → **Lights** → **Standard Lights** → **SkyLight**

Perform test rendering (the <Shift>+<Q> shortcut). You should obtain a beautiful black rectangle.

Like in the real world, SkyLight is not a direct light source. It simulates the sky and the environment light, which is the result of reflection and diffusion of the light from direct light sources including the sun. To obtain an image, you need to turn on computation of indirect illumination, more precisely, Final Gather (Fig. 2.97, *b*).

Menu bar → **Rendering** → **Render** → the **Indirect Illumination** tab → the **Final Gather** rollout

Check the **Enable** checkbox and set **Samples** to 200.

This is nice, but you can improve the result. Increase the number of samples to 500 (this is enough), decrease the sample radii, and increase the number of diffuse bounces. I obtained a satisfactory result with the settings shown in Fig. 2.97, c.

To make the picture brighter, you could increase the multiplier value of the SkyLight light source. However, you should do this only if there is only the "sky" on the picture. I suggest that you introduce a direct light source to the scene. Its position and parameters are shown in Fig. 2.97, *d*.

NOTE

I close the mr Area Spot light source to be able to build soft shadows.

In contrast to the sky, the color of the light source should be warm, and the intensity should be a bit less than one (from 0.7 to 0.8).

The type of the light source is a 100-mm circle, and the number of samples should be large enough to obtain high-quality shadows.

The **Overshoot** checkbox allows you to illuminate the entire scene and avoid a spot of light from the light source.

The result is nice (Fig. 2.97, *e*).

My scene is in the project4-lighting-sky-and-sun.max file in the Projects/Project4 folder on the accompanying CD-ROM.

IMPORTANT

Remember that the SkyLight light source cannot be used as a photon generator because it is an indirect illumination generator.

Now you're thinking about how you can improve the previous project, aren't you?

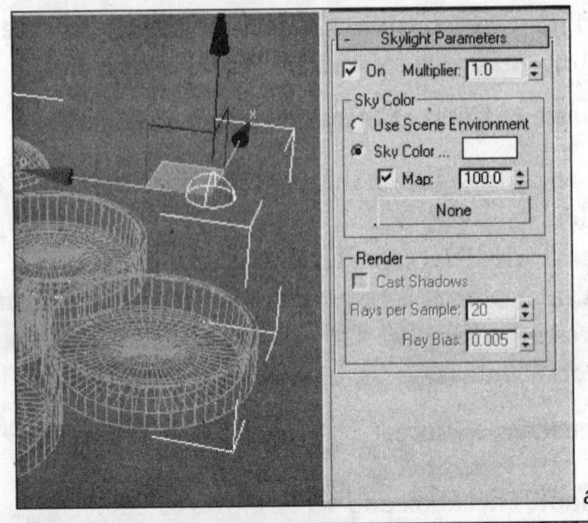

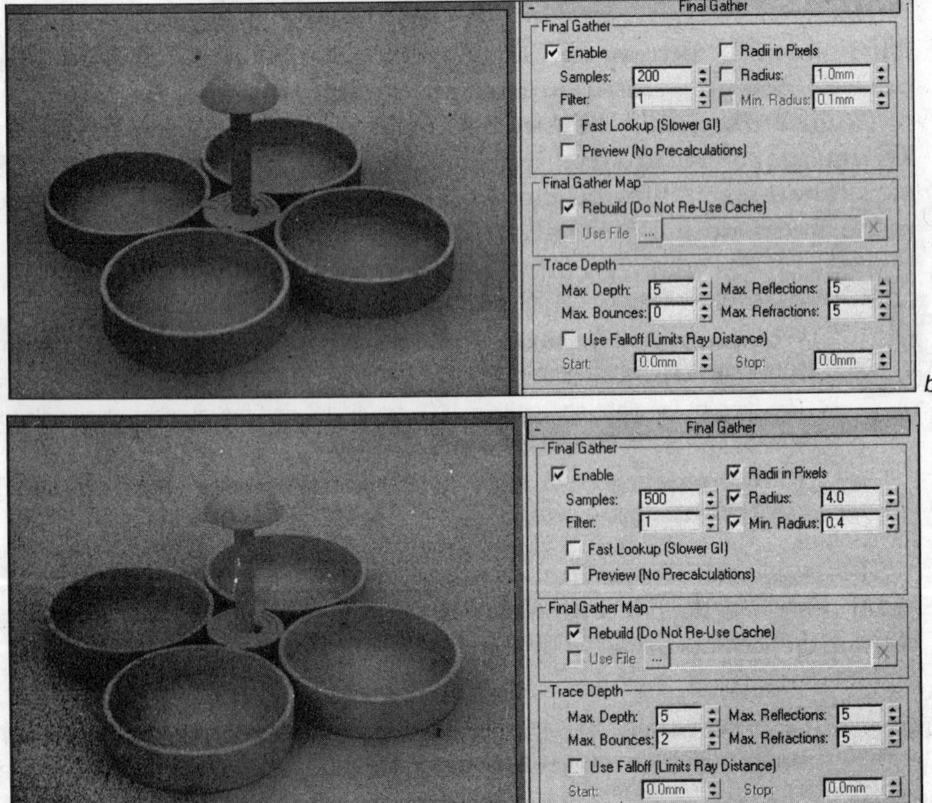

Fig. 2.97, *a–c*. Setting illumination with the SkyLight light source

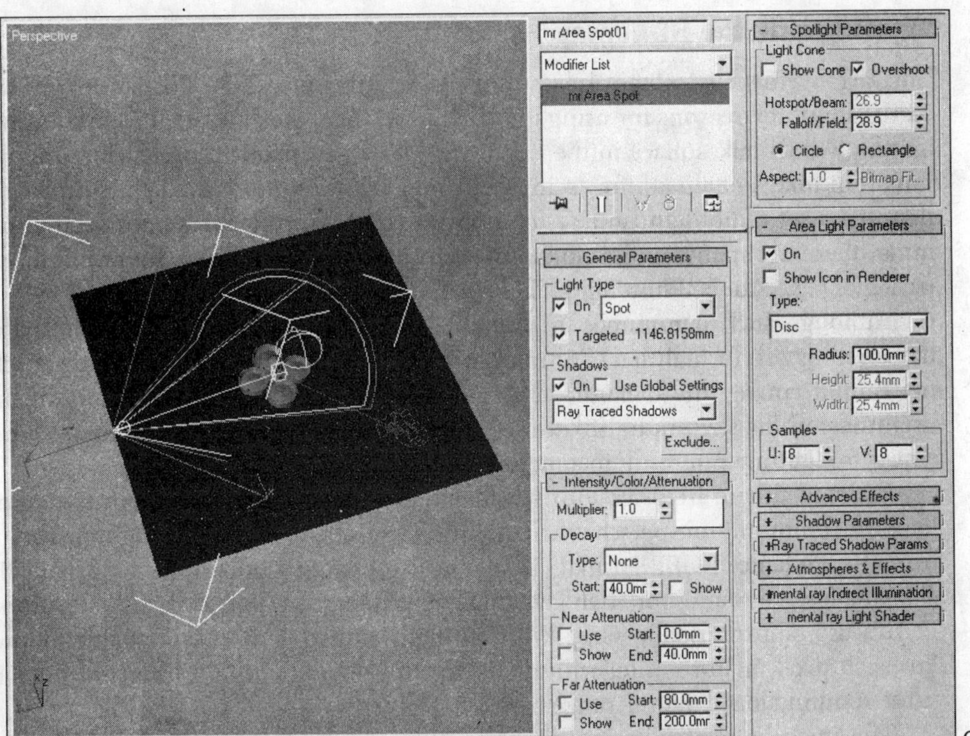

Fig. 2.97, *d* and *e*. Setting illumination with the SkyLight light source

Lighting with the HDRI Map

This arrangement is a logical extension of the previous. First, I'd like to say a few words about the reasons for using this method. When you simulate the environmental lighting (which takes place in the real world), it is reasonable to use a spherical panorama (an image obtained, for example, from a set of photos) as a light source rather than use a set of dot light sources or simply a color. For the creation of such a panorama, there are many applications, for example, RealViz Stitcher. In addition, some packages (e.g., Adobe PhotoShop CS) incorporate such tools.

Although such panoramas are suitable as an environment to create reflections, they aren't good for lighting. Common formats with a color depth of 8 bits per channel cannot convey the dynamic range of the real-world illumination, in which the brightness of the sky can be 10^{10} times greater than that of the earth. The use of such a map for lighting can result in a picture with low contrast.

Currently, there are several formats that allow you to compensate for this and other flaws of common 8-bit-per-channel and 16-bit-per-channel images. The most popular format is Radiance RGBE Format (RGBE) which became standard de facto. The HDRI abbreviation that stands for High Dynamic Range Image is usually related to this format.

It was first proposed by Greg Ward.. Roughly speaking, its essence is the following. For each pixel, it stores a logarithmic exposure value in addition to a common RGB value resulting in a dynamic range from 10^{-38} to 10^{38}.

This image is created by combining a few common photos taken with different exposure levels. Using a mirror ball, you can obtain a series of photos for creating a spherical panorama. Fig. 2.98 shows three such photos available in the hdr folder on the accompanying CD-ROM. These are files p0.bmp, p1.bmp, and p2.bmp. While taking these photos, I used a metallized plastic toy ball that wasn't a precise sample. If you need a more precise one, use a special ball, so-called light probe. However, mine will do for this project.

Fig. 2.98. Photos for creating a spherical panorama

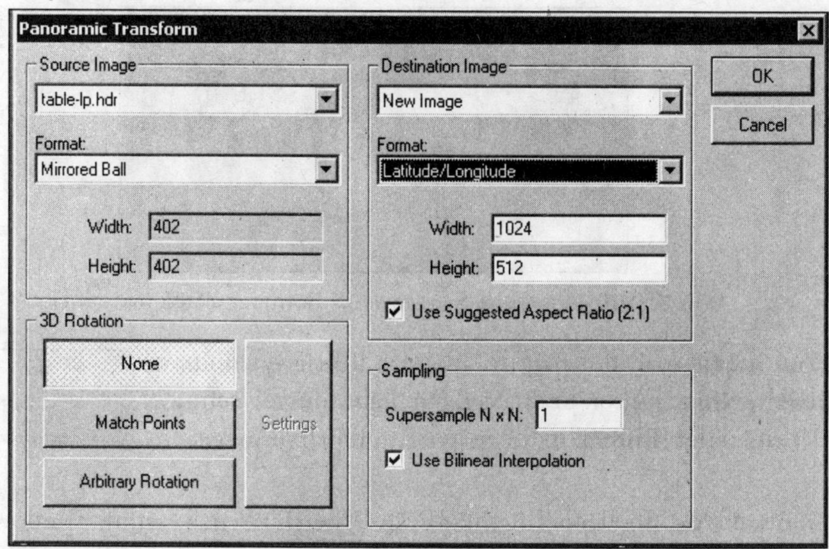

Fig. 2.99. Converting one type of the panorama to another using HDR Shop

Many packages allow you to make one HDRI photo from three photos. I used Adobe PhotoShop CS2.

Unfortunately, 3ds Max doesn't support the HDRI format as a sphere (it supports only the Latitude/Longitude format), and Adobe PhotoShop CS2 cannot do the necessary conversion. To convert the sphere to the required format, use HDR Shop developed by Paul Debevec and Chris Tchou (Fig. 2.99). You can download a free copy of this application and get additional useful information at **http://www.ict.usc.edu/graphics/HDRShop/**.

Save the result of conversion as a Radiance file (of the HDR type). My file is called table-ll.hdr.

A map of this size (or of a larger size, say, 4,000 × 2,000 pixels) is suitable for reflection, but it isn't good for lighting because such a large size can cause rendering flaws.

To decrease the size to 200 × 100 pixels and blur the image, use Gaussian Blur (Fig. 2.100). You can do this in HDR Shop or Adobe PhotoShop CS2.

I have to admit that my HDRI map is imperfect. In fact, it is terrible. Honestly, I set the exposure too freely. We will use it anyway. If the result is satisfactory, a map will give even a better result.

❒ Open the project4-lighting-sky-and-sun.max file located on the Projects/Project4 folder on the accompanying CD-ROM. Delete or turn off the mr Area Spot light source; you won't need it.

Fig. 2.100. A panorama in the HDR format suitable for lighting

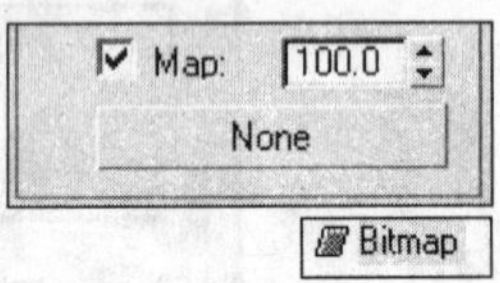

You should load this map to 3ds Max. I believe you have noticed the **None** button in the SkyLight light source's settings. Click it and select **Bitmap** in the material and map browser.

- ❐ Find and load the table-ll-light.hdr file. The HDRI map setting window will open (Fig. 2.101, *a*). The developers of 3ds Max recommend that the users load these files with a depth of 16 bits per channel. Remember the **Linear White Point** parameter value, with which the violet areas disappear.
- ❐ Open the material editor (with the <M> key) and drag the map onto any window of the material editor using the **Instance** method (Fig. 2.101, *b*).
- ❐ In the **Coordinates** rollout, change the use type to **Environment** and select **Spherical** (indicated within box 1 in Fig. 2.101, *c*).
- ❐ In the **Output** rollout, set the **RGB Level** parameter to a value equal to (or a bit lower than) the **Linear White Point** value from the HDRI map setting dialog box (indicated within box 2).
- ❐ Set **Final Gather** to small values to be able to obtain the result quickly (Fig. 2.101, *d*).

Menu bar → **Rendering** → **Render** → the **Indirect Illumination** tab → the **Final Gather** rollout

If the resulting picture is too dark, increase the light source's **Multiplier** parameter.

Now you need to obtain a nice picture, and your task will determine the best way to achieve this.

If the task implies just a smooth image, the settings shown in Fig. 2.101, *e* might be all right. The number of FG points won't be too large in this case because the default radii are equal to one-tenth of the scene radius, and the scene is relatively large. (Do you remember that the plane is scaled ten times during rendering?) The values between them are averaged, and the image is blurred.

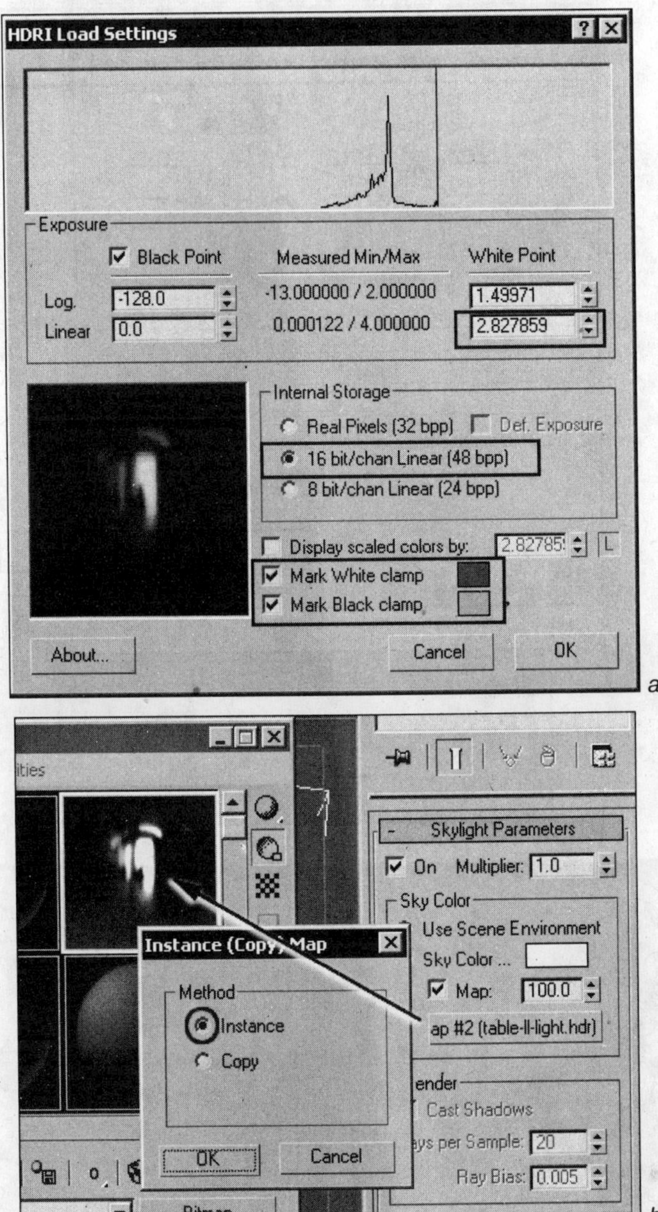

Fig. 2.101, *a* and *b*. Lighting using the HDRI map

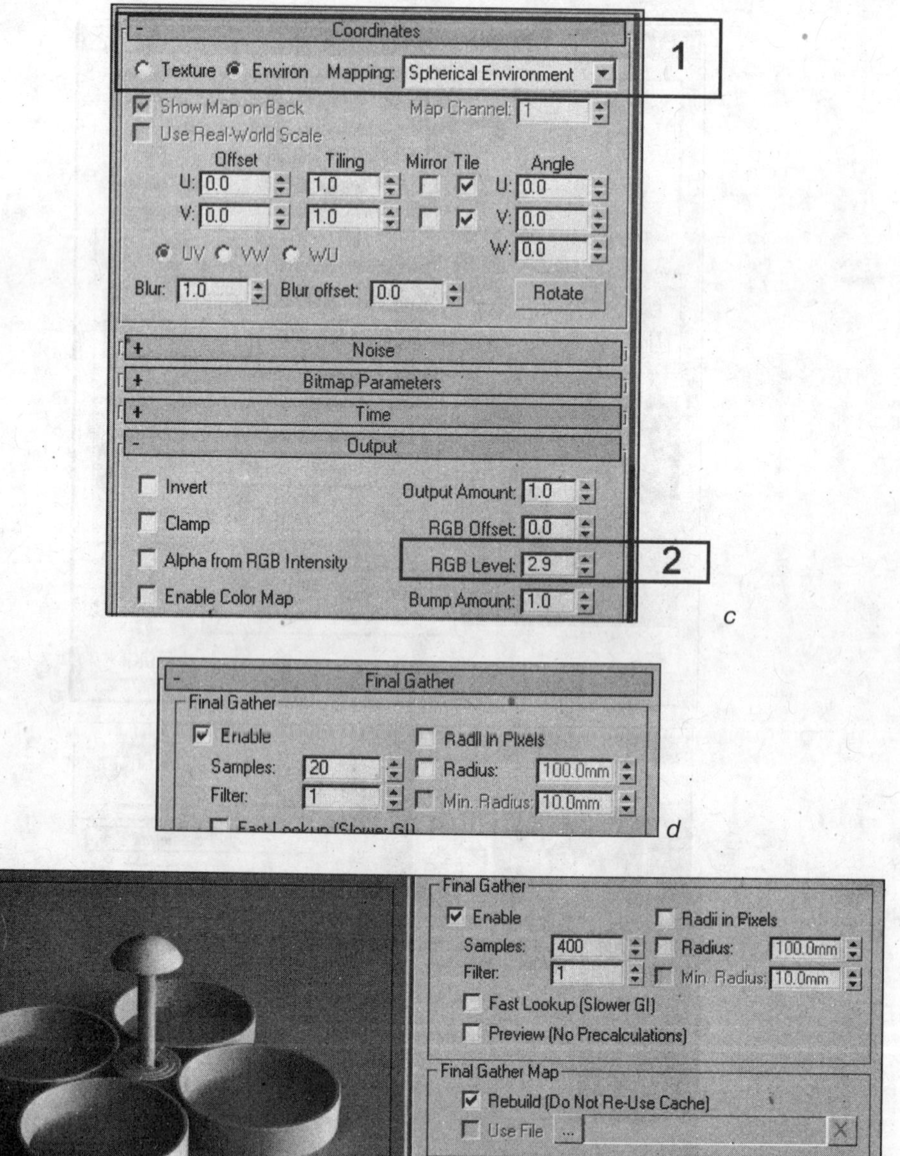

Fig. 2.101, *c–e*. Lighting using the HDRI map

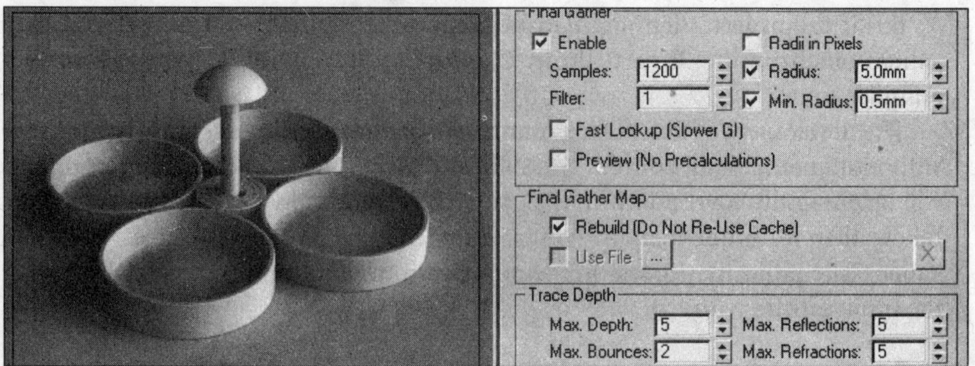

Fig. 2.101, *f*. Lighting using the HDRI map

If you need a picture with detailed secondary lighting, you'll have to limit the sample radius. Therefore, you'll have to increase the number of samples to obtain a good picture without blotches (Fig. 2.101, *f*). The computation time will increase significantly, but additional detail will appear. It's your choice.

Don't worry if you notice blotches at this stage. They are likely to disappear or, more precisely, become less noticeable after you assign materials.

Materials and Maps

Creating realistic and showy materials is one of the most important purposes of 3D graphics. This section will teach you how to create and set various materials.

I decided not to explain theory at the beginning of this section. Issues related to creating and setting materials and maps will be discussed when creating particular materials, as will methods of work with the material editor. From 3ds max version 6, the number and variety of maps and materials became enormous, and a comprehensive description of them and their use would take up a separate book two or three times as large as this one. This is because materials used in VIZ Render and in mental ray are now integrated with 3ds Max. In actual practice, many features aren't used. However, certain approaches that might seem eccentric produce showy results.

Materials for the Stationery Container

Only Architectural materials will be used in this project. This type of material first appeared in 3ds max 6. It is easier to set it than the Standard type, but its settings are less flexible than those of the Standard or Raytrace types.

Load the project2-lighting-fg.max scene with the light sources set and the final gather done from the Projects\Project2 folder on the CD-ROM, or use your file with a similar scene.

The developers of 3ds Max recommend that the users choose this type of material with photometric light sources and radiosity. According to the developers, the results will be physically correct only in that case. However, in this project you aren't going to follow their recommendation; you're using mental ray light sources and the final gather. The radiosity process isn't supported in mental ray. Let's try and see whether the result satisfies you.

Check whether mental ray is used, just to be on the safe side. To do this, open the rendering parameters window (with the <F10> key). If the **Indirect Illumination** tab is available, everything is all right. Otherwise, turn on mental ray (the **Common** tab → the **Assign Renderer** rollout).

❒ If there are groups in the scene, select and open them, or ungroup the objects. This will simplify your work.

Menu bar → **Group** → **Open**, **Ungroup**

❒ You'll need to perform test rendering repeatedly, so disable the Final Gather process temporarily.

Menu bar → **Rendering** → **Render** → the **Indirect Illumination** tab → the **Final Gather** rollout

Uncheck the **Enable** checkbox.

Yulia Cherepneva, the author of this project, intended that the container be made of plastic of a dark and light color, such as dark-blue and beige.

❒ Open the material editor (with the <M> key).

❒ Select any material slot.

❒ Change the material type to Architectural.

Material editor → the **Get Material** button

Material/Map Browser → **Browse from: New**

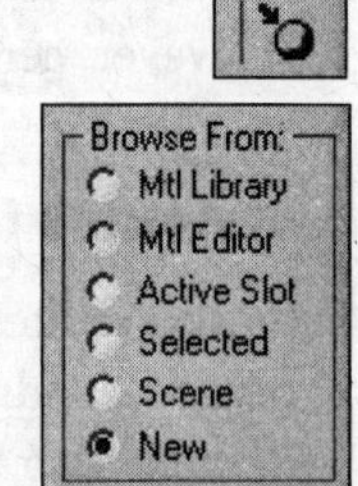

Double-click the **Architectural** line.

❒ Rename the material to Blue Plastic. Giving unique names to materials is no less important than giving them to objects.

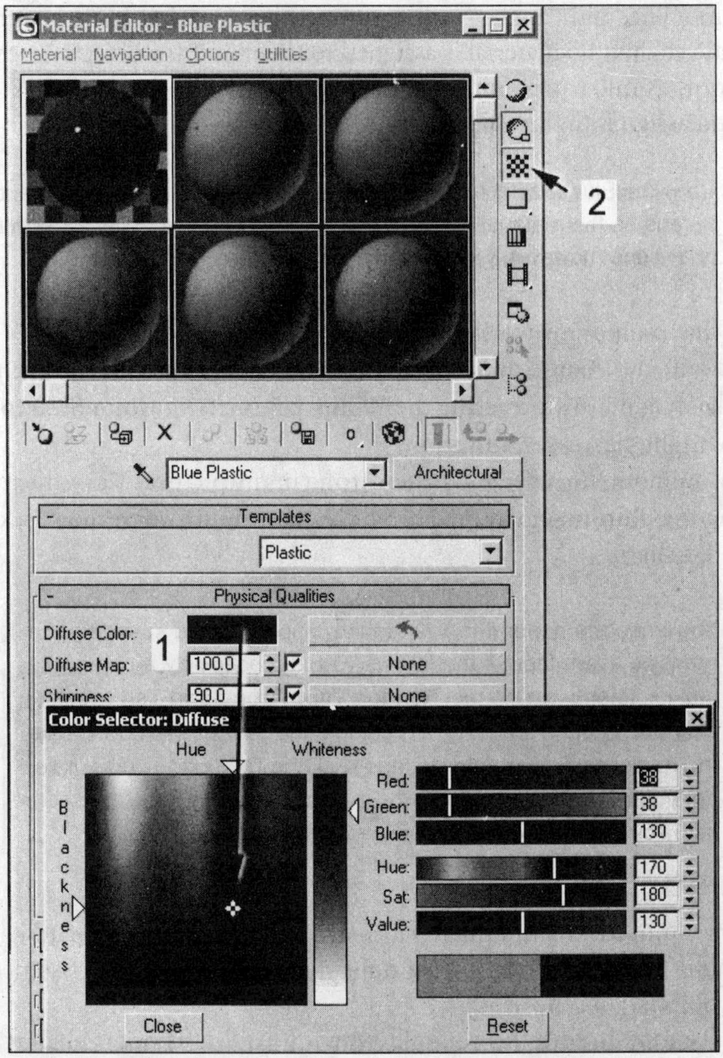

Fig. 2.102. Setting the Blue Plastic material

In the drop-down menu in the **Templates** rollout, select **Plastic** and change **Diffuse Color** to dark-blue (indicated with number 1 in Fig. 2.102).

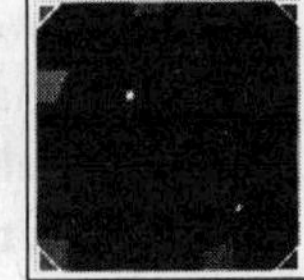

If you turn on displaying the background for this material (indicated with number 2), you'll notice that this material reflects light a little.

Assign this material to the left (in the camera view) half of the container by dragging the material onto it. In the viewport, the container will become blue, and "angles" will appear in the material slot in the material editor. These indicate that the material is assigned to the object (or objects) in the scene.

Perform a similar procedure to create a material for the other half, name it Light Plastic, and assign it to the object.

TIP

Copy the Blue Plastic material to another material slot, rename it, and set it. Be sure to rename the material because you cannot have two materials with the same name in a scene (however, you can have them in the material editor).

I like the result of my work. Do you like yours?

What can you change, and why should you change this? If the blue material is too dark, make it lighter by increasing the **Value** parameter in **Color Selector**. If the material is too bright, decrease **Saturation**.

In my opinion, the reflection is too strong in my picture. Make the material dull by decreasing the **Shininess** parameter. Notice that the shape of the speck changes, and becomes less sharp.

TIP

You'll need to perform test rendering repeatedly. To speed up the process, use a feature that allows you to render only a part of the image. (Menu bar → the **Render Type** drop-down list → select **Region**). During rendering, a rectangle will be displayed to indicate the rendering region. Adjust it and click the **OK** button in the lower right corner of the viewport. For a quick rendering, use the <F9> key. To render the entire picture, select **View**.

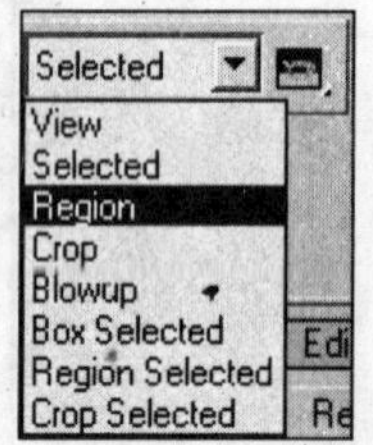

When you need to edit a material that is missing from the material editor but available in the scene (in this example, it is the gray material assigned to all the other objects), use the dropper.

If you cannot do this, for example, when the object is not visible or is inaccessible (e.g., you cannot get a map applied to a light source), click the **Get Material** button and get the material or map from the scene (Fig. 2.103).

Then you should set materials for the auxiliary objects.

The material of the screen is all right. You don't need to make it brighter because doing so would over-light the scene and require readjustment of the light sources.

The material of the pen shouldn't cause problems. This object is auxiliary, so create a material such as white plastic and assign it to the pen. Don't use the pure white color; it is too bright. Choose light-gray or, perhaps, bluish.

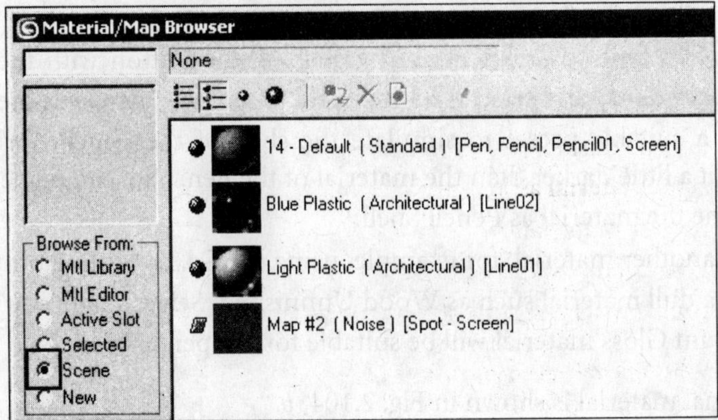

Fig. 2.103. Loading a material to the material editor from the scene

The pencils will require much time. It is desirable that the pencils are realistic, so they should have appropriate materials such as lead, wood, and varnish. In 3ds Max, only one material can be assigned to an object. If you want an object to consist of several materials, you need to use compound materials. In this case, you should use a material of the Multi/Sub-Object type. Create it.

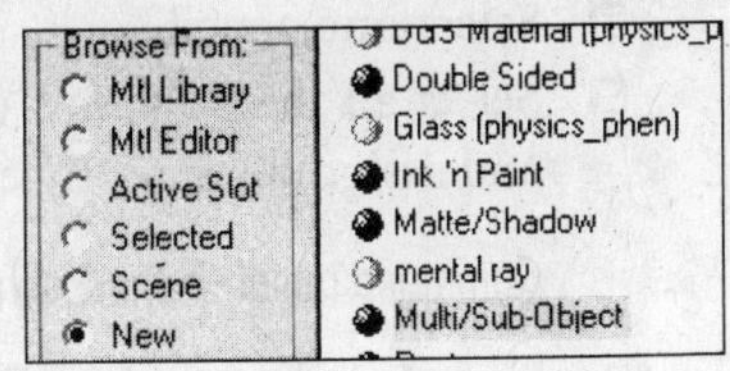

- ❒ Select an unused material slot in the material editor. Click the **Get Material** button. Set the **Browse From** radio buttons to **New** in the material/map browser, select the Multi/Sub-Object material type, and double-click with the left mouse button.
- ❒ Rename the material to Pencil.
- ❒ You'll need three submaterials, so click the **Set Number** button and enter the appropriate number.

You should obtain a picture similar to the one shown in Fig. 2.104, *a*.

Navigation in the material editor is common to all materials and maps. In this case, after you click any button in the submaterial list, you'll be able to edit this submaterial. In other words, you'll move to a lower level. You can return to the upper level by clicking the **Go To Parent** button.

TIP

It is convenient to navigate the levels of materials and maps using the **Material/ Map Navigator**.

- ❒ Go to editing the first submaterial.
- ❒ Change its type to architectural by clicking the button with the current material type (**Standard**) and select **Architectural**. Don't use the **Get Material** button!
- ❒ Select a suitable preset to simulate the shell of the pencil, for example, plastic. Make it a little darker than the material of the pen. You can make it warmer.
- ❒ Rename the material as Pencil Shell.
- ❒ Go to another material, for example, using the **Go To Sibling** button.
- ❒ Select a dull material such as Wood Unfinished. Select a light warm color for it.
- ❒ The Paint Gloss material will be suitable for the pencil core.

The final material is shown in Fig. 2.104, *b*.

- ❒ Assign the material to both pencils. You are unlikely to obtain a proper picture because 3ds Max doesn't know, which material should be assigned to particular polygons. You should tell it.

In the submaterial list of the Pencil material, note a column named ID. It contains IDs of submaterials. In the object, each polygon has its own ID. You should bring the IDs into proper correspondence.

- ❒ Select one pencil.
- ❒ Select all the polygons (using the <44> key or the <Ctrl>+<A> shortcut) and assign them an ID equal to 1.

Command panel → the **Polygon Properties** rollout → **Set ID**

Type 1 and press the <Enter> key.

- ❒ Select polygons that should be wooden and assign them an ID equal to 2 (Fig. 2.104, *c*).
- ❒ Assign an ID equal to 2 to the polygons of the core.

Repeat this procedure with the other.

Perform test rendering. Correct the materials if necessary.

NOTE

You might think the last phrase is strange. Unlike modeling and, to a lesser extent, unlike setting lighting, setting materials is a subjective process. This is why I'd like to warn you against using ready-made material libraries thoughtlessly. As a rule, almost all library materials except secondary ones need adjustment for a particular scene. In addition, in this example you should find a compromise of realism, beauty, and scientific character.

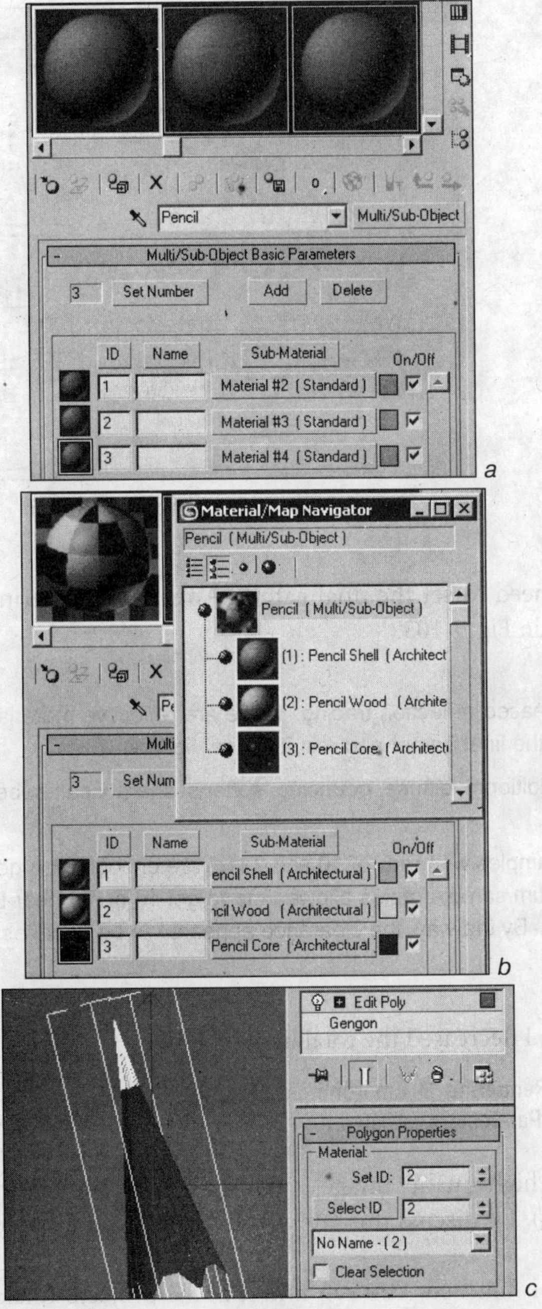

Fig. 2.104. Creating and assigning the pencil material.

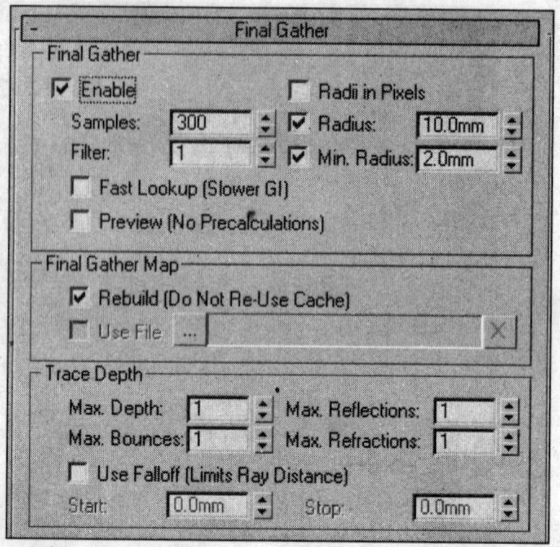

Fig. 2.105. Setting the final gather

Now, you need to set the final gather. After some experimentation, I came to the settings shown in Fig. 2.105.

I decreased reflection tracing. There are reflective materials in the scene, they slow down the final gather and result in over-lighting.

An additional diffuse bouncing softens sharp seams between the halves of the model.

300 samples with radii of 10 and 2 mm are enough for a good picture. The use of the minimum sample radius allowed me to get rid of dirt near the clearance between the halves. By the way, the clearance appeared to be unnecessary.

In addition, I decreased the total lighting level.

Menu bar → **Rendering** → **Environment** → the **Common Parameters** rollout

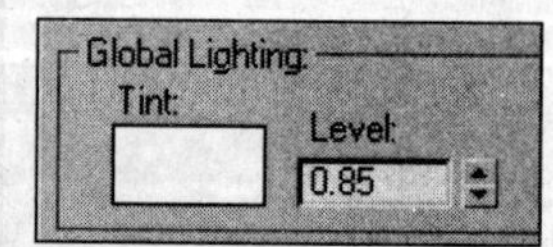

To obtain a high-quality image, I used Mitchell's antialiasing with a large sampling level (Fig. 2.106). I'll discuss this later in this chapter in a section describing rendering settings.

The project is finished. You can find it in the project2-final.max file in the Projects\ Project2 folder on the accompanying CD-ROM.

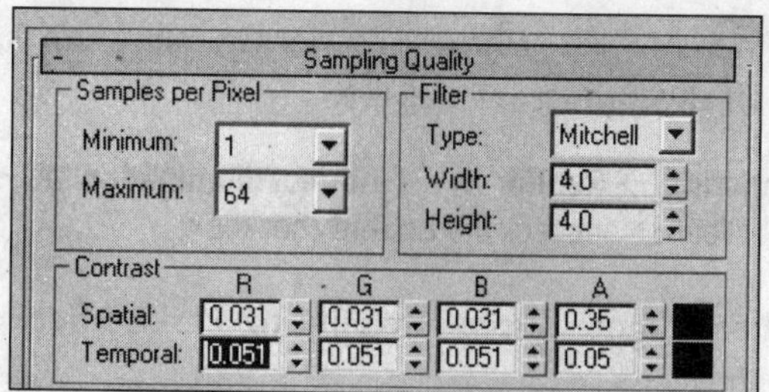

Fig. 2.106. Antialiasing settings

Materials for the Container for Small Items

The author of this project intended to use common plastic for the container. However, I used my imagination and created a model made of semi-transparent colored plastic. My goal was to demonstrate you how you should set reflection, refraction, and reflective and refractive caustics.

The initial scene shown in Fig. 2.107 is the project4-lighting-sky-and-sun.max file located in the Projects\Project4 folder on the accompanying CD-ROM.

As I mentioned earlier, you can obtain the caustic effect only with a direct light source because a SkyLight cannot be used for photon generation. Therefore, you should use a direct light source. In principle, you could obtain caustic using the final gather, but this would increase computation time significantly.

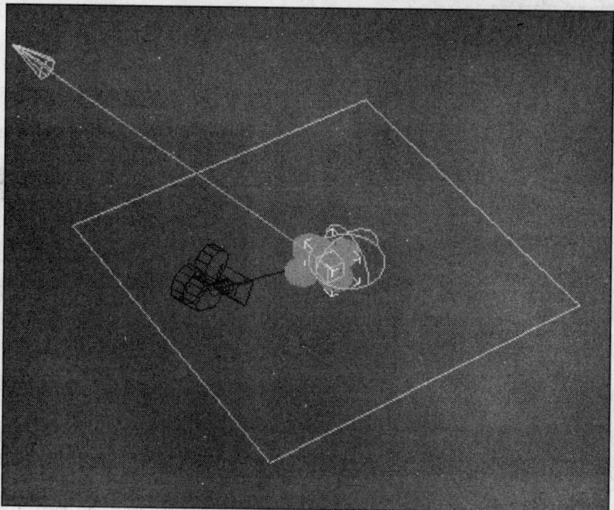

Fig. 2.107. The initial scene

- Because you'll need to perform test rendering many times, disable the final gather. This will turn off the light from the sky.

  Menu bar → **Rendering** → **Render** → the **Indirect Illumination** tab → the **Final Gather** rollout → uncheck the **Enable** checkbox

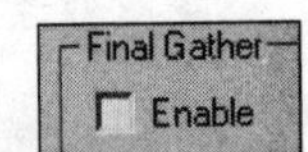

- Increase the direct light source intensity to a value between 1.2 and 1.4.

- Disable creating soft shadows by unchecking the **On** checkbox in the **Area Light Parameters** rollout.

I suggest that you use a material of the Raytrace type to simulate semi-transparent plastic. Settings of this material at this stage are the same for the standard renderer and mental ray.

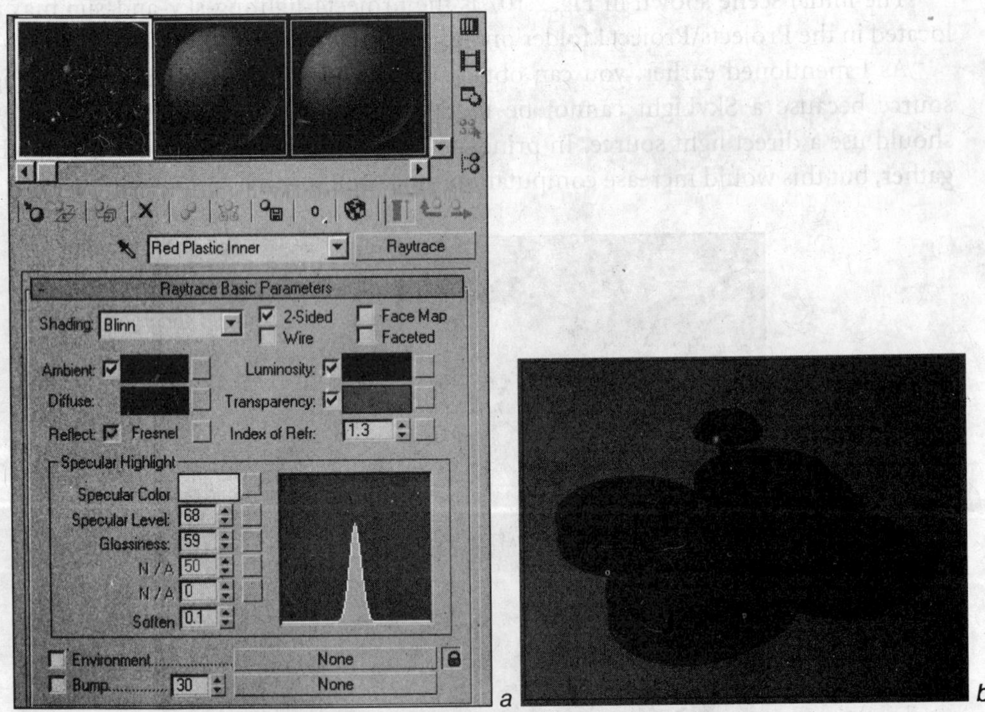

Fig. 2.108. Parameters of the material for the container (*a*) and the result of rendering (*b*)

NOTE

Why didn't I recommend an architectural material? You could use it with an appropriate preset (**Plastic** with a non-zero value of the **Transparency** parameter), but Raytrace is more flexible and offers you more setting options.

- ❒ Open the material editor (with the <M> key) and select any unused material slot.
- ❒ Change the material type from **Standard** or **Architectural** to **Raytrace**.

Menu bar → **Rendering** → **Render** → the **Indirect Illumination** tab → the **Final Gather** rollout → uncheck the **Enable** checkbox

Material/Map Browser → **Browse from: New** → double-click **Raytrace**

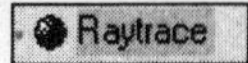

Let's simulate dark-red semi-transparent plastic. Its parameters are shown in Fig. 2.108, *a*.

NOTE

Check the **2-sided** checkbox. It controls the way the surface is treated during rendering: as one-sided or two-sided. In this example, you need a two-sided surface.

Set the **Diffuse** and **Ambient** parameters to the same dark-red color. Set the **Specular** parameter to light-red color. It is convenient to set one color and then copy it from one window to the other by dragging it as shown in the figure.

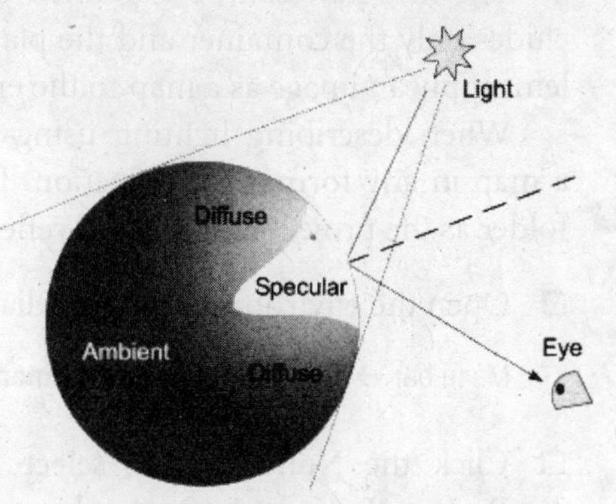

What are these colors? The **Specular** color works when the ray from a light source hits the cameras. The greater the deviance from the direct hit, the less is the effect of the specular color, and the greater is the effect of the diffuse color. In fact, the diffuse color determines the color of an object. This transition is determined with a highlight graph which is set using the **Specular Level** and **Glossiness** parameters. The **Ambient** color works when a surface is illuminated with indirect light. The **Diffuse** and **Ambient** parameters are usually set to the same value to avoid an unnatural result. I should mention that the use of the specular color and highlight graph is a simplification adopted is 3D graphics. A speck of light is just a reflection of the light source. However, light sources are dots, and it is pointless to talk about their reflection. This approach is somewhat obsolete. Contemporary renderers, including mental ray, use renderable light sources and, so to say, honest reflection with blur.

Set the **Transparency** parameter to a light-red color. In this channel, the color has two functions. Its brightness component (**Value**) determines the transparency level of the material, and **Hue** and **Saturation** control the color. Notice a checkbox next to the slot. If you uncheck it, the transparency level will be set using a digital parameter.

Set **Reflect** to the **Fresnel** value. To do this, click repeatedly the **Reflect** checkbox (unfortunately, this isn't intuitive). This will allow you to use a physically correct relation between transparency and reflection described by Fresnel's effect. In essence, reflection of all materials (not only transparent ones) usually increases when the viewing angle decreases. As a result, transparency decreases (if at all). The relation between reflection and transparency depending on the viewing angle is determined by IOR (Index of Refraction). For different types of plastic, this value is between 1.2 and 1.4. It is set in the **Index of Refraction** field.

Roughly, the material is ready. Assign it to the container's objects. It is convenient to do this by selecting them and clicking the **Assign Material To Selection** button.

Perform test rendering (Fig. 2.108, *b*).

This is nice, but there are no reflections, and shadows aren't natural.

The first flaw can be explained easily. There is nothing to reflect. The scene includes only the container and the plane, onto which you put it. To manage the problem, apply an image as a map to the environment.

When describing lighting using an HDRI map, I mentioned that you can use a map in any format for reflection. I prepared such a map. It is located in the same folder as the project and is called reflect.tif.

❒ Open the environment setting dialog box.

Menu bar → **Rendering** → **Environment**

❒ Click the **None** button, select **Bitmap**, and load the reflect.tif file from the Projects\Project4 folder on the accompanying CD-ROM.

To be able to edit the map, move it to the material editor using the **Instance** method (Fig. 2.109, *a*). Otherwise, changes made in the material editor won't result in changes in the scene.

In the material editor, change the use type to **Environment: Spherical**. Don't change the levels in the **Output** rollout (Fig. 2.109, *b*).

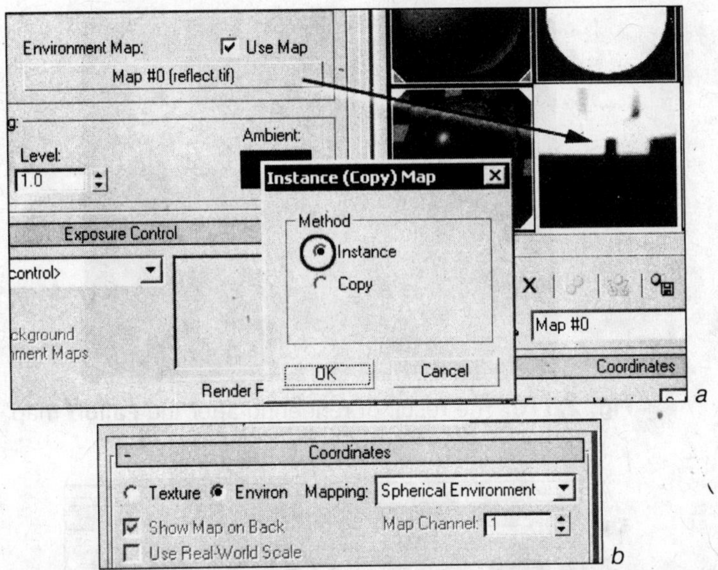

Fig. 2.109. Applying (a) and setting (b) the environment

Perform rendering. The image didn't improve much and the reflections aren't noticeable. The Fresnel method is too close to nature and not refined, so you'll have to be crafty.

- Enter the material-editing mode and click the **Reflect** checkbox repeatedly until you see the black color.
- Click a little button to the right of the black rectangle. You'll enter the material/map browser already familiar to you.

- Select the **Falloff** map.
- Don't change anything, and perform test rendering. The picture is much better now, isn't it? This is slightly dishonest, but beautiful (Fig. 2.110).

What is this map? In 3ds Max, it is one of the most powerful tools allowing you to control parameters of a material by mixing materials, maps, and so on.

- Set the map as shown in Fig. 2.111.

NOTE

The **Falloff Type** parameter set to **Perpendicular/Parallel** and the **Viewing Direction** parameter set to the camera allow you to change the color and level of reflection depending on the angle between the surface and the camera. If the angle is right (**Front**), the black color is used. If the ray is tangential (**Side**), the color specified in the second line is used. Make it light-red. Notice large buttons to the right of the color field. As you might have guessed, you can use a map rather than a color.

Fig. 2.110. The result of rendering after the **Falloff** map is applied to the **Reflect** channel

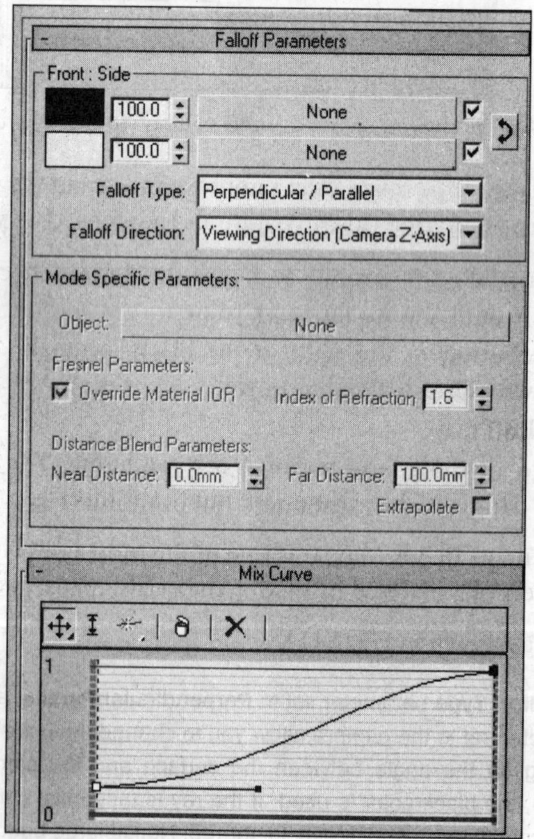

Fig. 2.111. Parameters of the **Falloff** map

NOTE

The **Mix Curve** at the bottom determines how mixing should be done. The level for **Front** is at the left, and that for **Side** is at the right. To obtain reflections also on surfaces perpendicular to the camera, I lifted the left point.

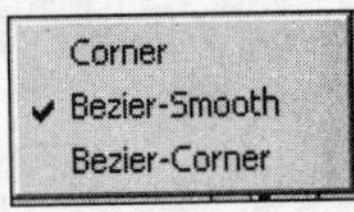

You can add a vertex to the curve using the **Add Point** button, and you can change its type with a right click.

The picture is nice. However, you don't know how these tricks will affect the next stage, creating the caustic effect.

NOTE

From now on, all the effects described are possible only if mental ray is used. The standard renderer lacks required features.

To use the caustic effect, you need to check an appropriate checkbox in an appropriate rollout of rendering settings.

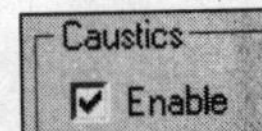

Menu bar → **Rendering** → **Render** → **Indirect Illumination** → the **Caustics and GI** rollout

An attempt to perform rendering is likely to result in an error. It is necessary to specify, which objects will generate caustic.

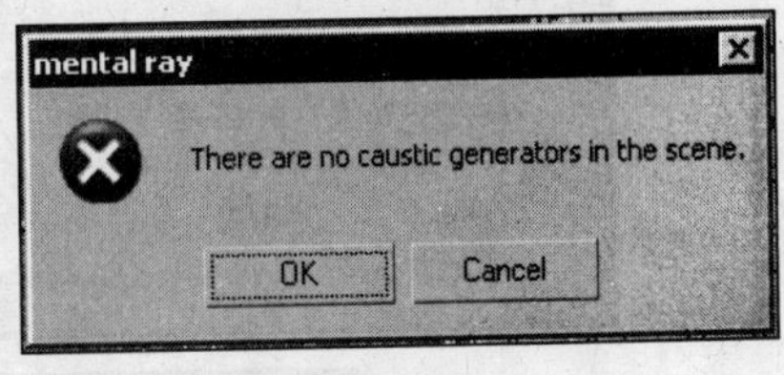

- Select objects of the container and specify that they should generate caustic.

Quad menu → **Properties** → the **mental ray** tab → check the **Generate Caustic** checkbox

This is the caustic (Fig. 2.112, *a*). Isn't beautiful, is it? Let's set it (Fig. 2.112, *b*).

- Set the radius of a sample, from which photons for the caustic will be gathered (the **Maximum Sampling Radius** parameter). This effect is local, so don't set the radius greater than 2 mm, otherwise the effect will be blurred.
- There will be many photons, so you don't need to change the number of samples. Leave 100.

Now, it makes sense to set the light source rather than make global settings.

Select the light source and set parameters in the **mental ray Indirect Illumination** rollout as shown in Fig. 2.112, *c*.

a

Caustics and Global Illumination (GI)

Caustics

☑ Enable

Maximum Num. Photons per Sample: 100

☑ Maximum Sampling Radius: 2.0mm

Filter: Box Kernel: 1.1

☑ Opaque Shadows when Caustics are Enabled

b

mental ray Indirect Illumination

☐ Automatically Calculate Energy and Photons

Global Multipliers

Energy: 1.0

Caustic Photons: 1.0

GI Photons: 1.0

Manual Settings

☑ On

Energy: 50000.0

Decay: 2.0

Caustic Photons: 1000000

GI Photons: 10000

c

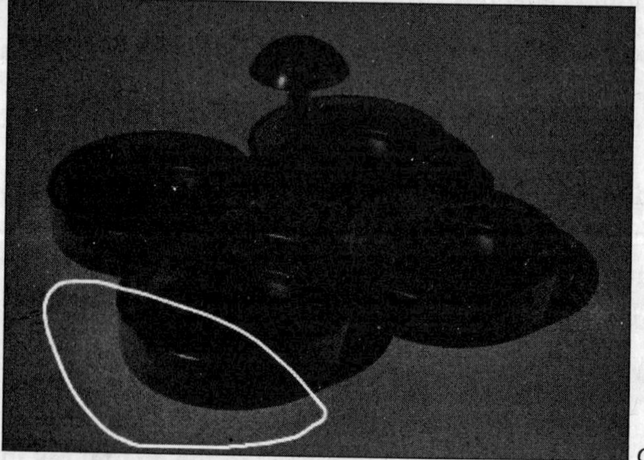

d

Fig. 2.112, *a–c*. Setting the caustic effect

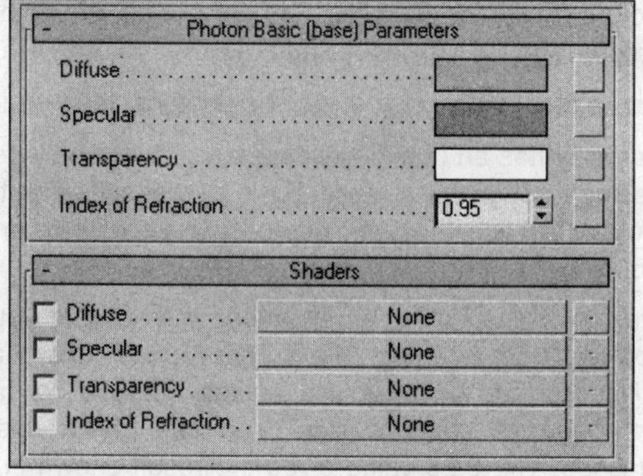

Fig. 2.112, e. Setting the caustic effect

Disable the connection to the global parameters. This is necessary so that the caustic is created independently of the light source intensity. Remember, there is the sky in the scene. It is turned off now, but after you turn it on, you'll need to decrease the light source intensity, increase its energy, and so on.

Increase the number of caustic photons 100 times.

If you don't have this rollout, use the extended mental ray. (Menu bar → **Customize** → **Preferences** → the **mental ray** tab → **Enable...**).

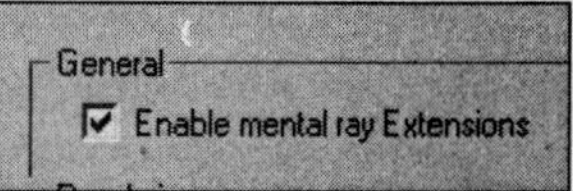

Mental ray will carefully compute distribution of photons. This will take quite a long time. One of the reasons for it is that the scene is open, and a lot of photons fly away.

Nothing happened after rendering. There's no caustic. Perhaps, the energy is insufficient. Increase its level to 150,000 units.

You can view an effect, but this is not what you wanted (Fig. 2.112, *d*). The light rings are reflective caustic. Refractive caustic is either absent or too weak, at least on my computer. This is related to your experiments with the reflection properties of the material. So keep on being crafty.

- In the material parameters, open the **mental ray Connection** rollout.
- Unlock the button in the **Photon** line, click it, and select **Photon Basic**.

Caustics and GI — Photon .... Map #8 (Photon Basic (base))

- Set the shader as shown in Fig. 2.112, *d*.

Three colors determine the color and the energy of photons. **Diffuse** relates to photons of global lighting. We don't need them.

Specular relates to the color of caustic photons. Make it light-red.

Transparency has an unexpected meaning. It not only determines the color of photons passing through the surface, but it also specifies distribution of energy between reflective and refractive caustic photons. Make it white or light-gray to decrease the energy of reflective photons in favor of refractive ones.

Finally, a trick! I set IOR to a value less than one. If you set it to an honest value (1.3), you won't get an effect of a double-convex lens, that is, you won't focus rays. This will be correct, because you actually have a concave-convex lens, and light travels through its concave side. You can check this through experimentation using glasses. The 0.95 value gives the result shown in Fig. 2.113. The only thing I haven't done yet is to increase energy to 300,000.

You can save the photon map to avoid computing it repeatedly.

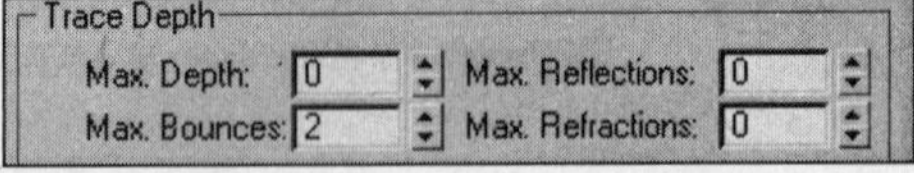

Now, you can return to the previous light source settings (set **Multiplier** to 0.7 and enable soft shadows) and enable the final gather to use light from the sky. It is desirable that you decrease the depth of reflection and refraction tracing in the final gather parameters (perhaps, zero is the best depth) and improve antialiasing parameters.

The result is shown in Fig. 2.114. Computation including the final gather took 20 minutes on my PC (Athlon XP 2800+).

Fig. 2.113. The caustic is set

Fig. 2.114. The result of final rendering

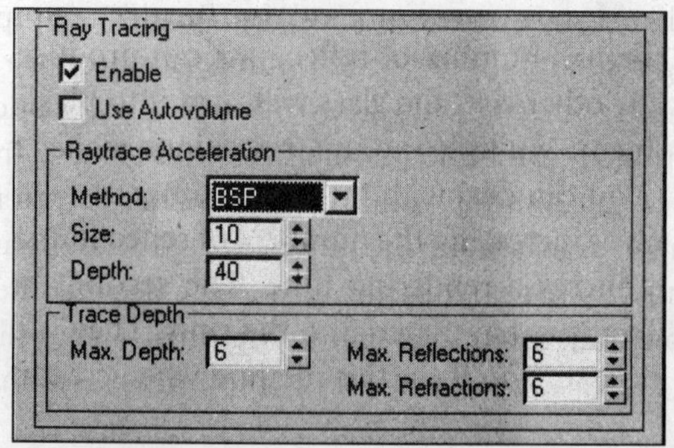

Fig. 2.115. Settings for ray tracing

How can you optimize reflection and refraction computing time? Use the settings of the ray tracer of mental ray.

Don't confuse this ray tracing with Ray Traced shadows, photons, and final gather. These are different things.

Settings of mental ray for ray tracing are located on the **Renderer** tab of the rendering settings dialog box (Fig. 2.115).

The main parameters are in the **Trace Depth** group. The **Max. Reflection/Refraction/Depth** parameters determine the path of rays from the camera if they encounter a reflective or transparent surface. For example, for the front container this will be as follows. The first outer surface makes the first refraction, the first inner surface makes the second refraction, the second outer surface makes the third refraction, and so on. Perhaps, six refractions are not enough. You can choose a small number of reflections because internal ones are also taken into account. It might appear that eight refractions and two reflections (total 10) are suitable for this example. Try these values.

The **Method** parameter determines the optimization level. The default BSP method is the best for small scenes. The **Size** and **Depth** parameters can speed up computation if you decrease the first and increase the second. However, this will be achieved at the cost of increasing the preliminary computation time and the amount of memory used. For detailed information, refer to the user's manual.

My project is saved in the Project4-Final.max file in the Projects/Project4 folder on the accompanying CD-ROM. You can find the model with the additional objects in the Project4-Final2.max file.

Finally, I'd like to give you some advice. In this example, the object is plastic; therefore, setting a small number of reflections can produce a good result. Don't do this for glass objects; otherwise, the glass will turn into plastic. However, glass objects cause another problem: Multiple internal reflections make "noise" at the rims, which doesn't look nice. You can deal with this using either of two methods. The first is extensive, and it involves increasing the numbers of reflections and refractions. However, it will significantly increase rendering time. The second method involves assigning a similar, but non-transparent material to the rims. They will look polished, and rendering time will decrease. You'll use this method when creating a glass table surface.

Materials for the Telephone Model

In this project, you'll create more complicated materials. The author, Alena Makhankova, intended for the case of the model to be made of polished metal. It offers you a more complicated task. Let the internal surfaces be made of polished metal, and the external ones be made of rough metal. The screen and the keys will have particular maps, and a material is needed for the large buttons on the external surfaces.

To avoid creating two almost identical compound materials, I suggest that you create one that contains components necessary for both objects. It is convenient to create materials and apply maps in a separate file.

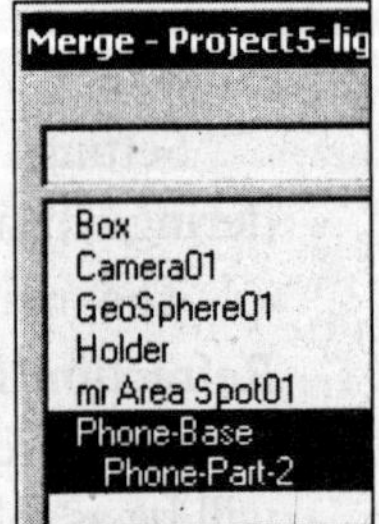

- ❒ Using the **Merge** command, load the telephone model from the Project5-lighting-final.max file into an empty scene.

Menu bar → **File** → **Merge**

Don't move the objects! They will be loaded into the original scene later.

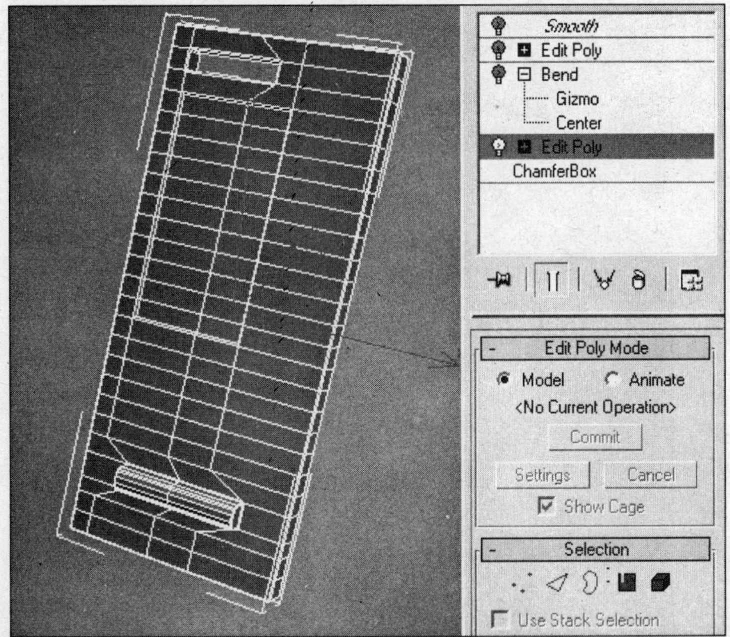

Fig. 2.116. Disabling the modifiers in the stack

Before you start creating materials, separate the polygons of the objects by assigning them IDs and apply map coordinates where necessary. (Remember, map coordinates are also known as UV coordinates).

Fortunately, the modifier stacks aren't collapsed. Otherwise, it would be difficult to do these operations on curvilinear surfaces.

- ❒ Select the Phone-Base object and hide the Phone-Part2 object.

Quad menu → **Hide Unselected**

- ❒ Disable modifiers at the top of the stack as shown in Fig. 2.116 by turning off the lamps in the lines containing the modifiers.
- ❒ Select all the polygons and assign them **Material ID** equal to one.
- ❒ Select the internal polygons and assign them **Material ID** equal to two. It is convenient to do this with the **Ignore Backfacing** and **By Angle** checkboxes checked (Fig. 2.117, *a*).

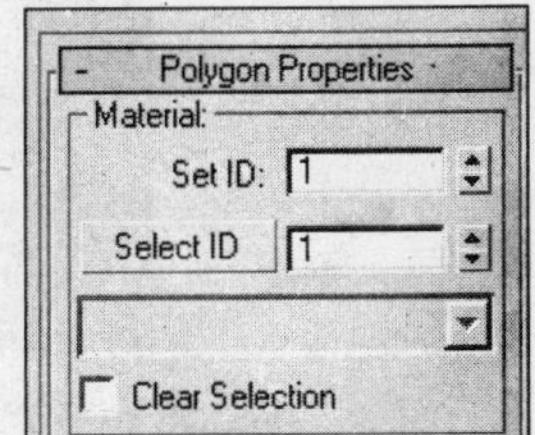

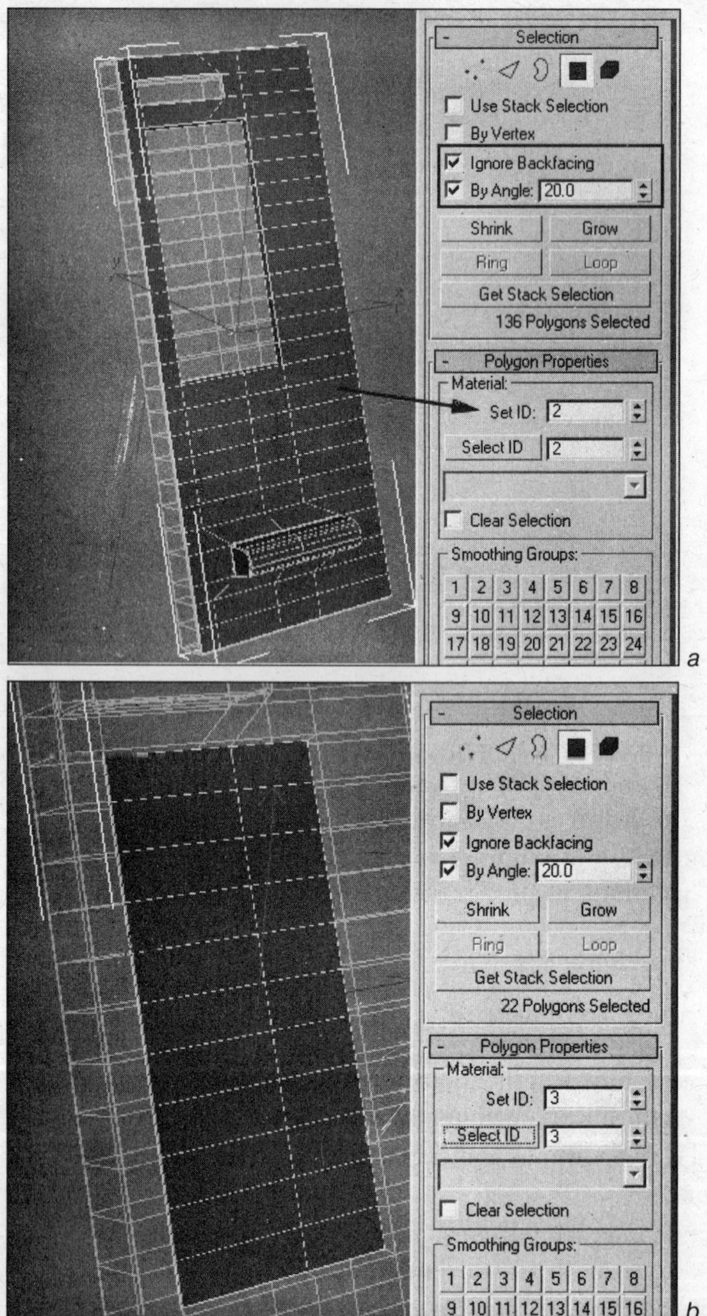

Fig. 2.117. Assigning Material IDs to the polygons of the Phone-Base object

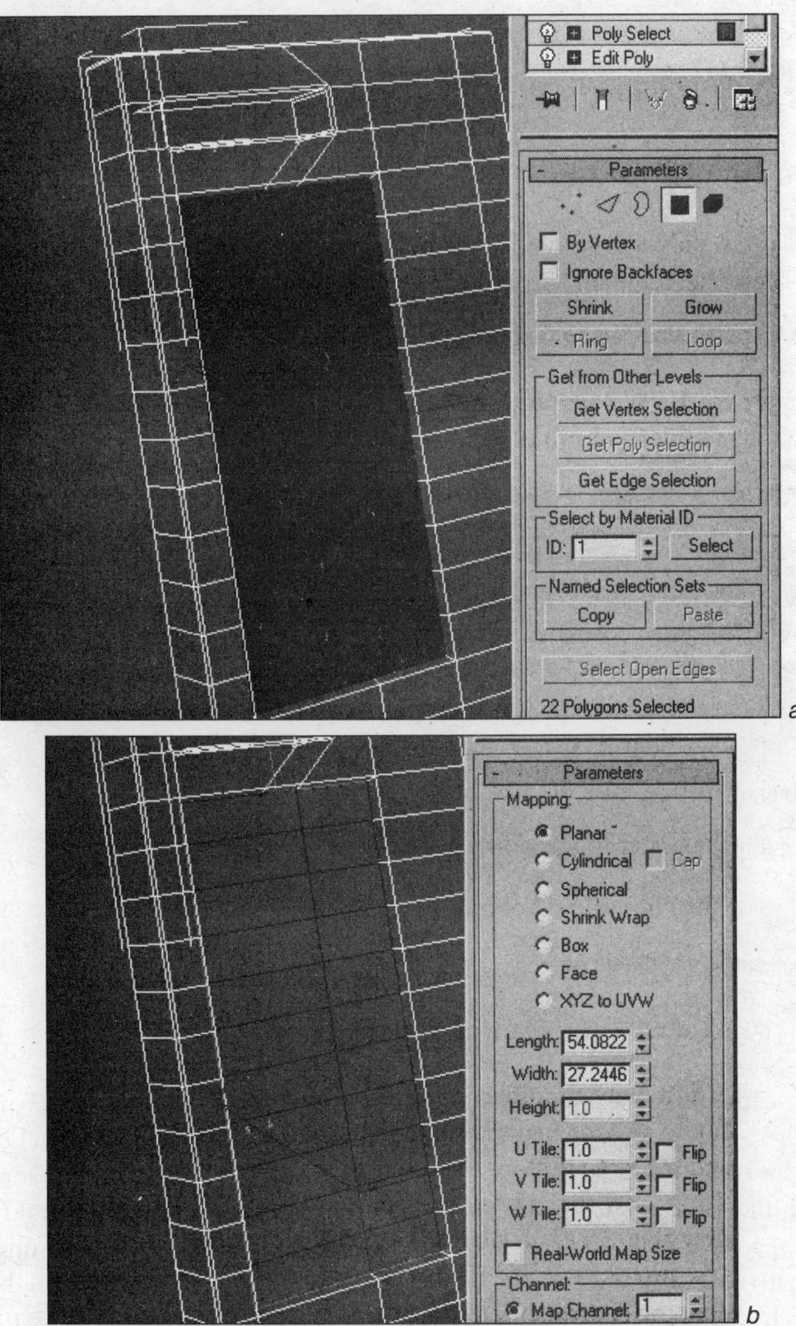

Fig. 2.118. Applying map coordinates to the polygons of the screen

- Select the polygons on the screen and assign them **Material ID** equal to three (Fig. 2.117, *a*).

Now, you need to assign map coordinates to the polygons of the screen so that the map is displayed correctly.

- Add the **Poly Select** modifier to the modifier stack and select the polygons of the screen (Fig. 2.118, *a*).

  Menu bar → **Modifiers** → **Selection** → **Poly Select**

- Apply the **UVW Mapping** modifier to the *selected polygons*. The default mapping of the modifier's gizmo is done correctly (Fig. 2.118, *b*).

  Menu bar → **Modifiers** → **Selection** → **UVW Map**

NOTE

The planar type of mapping is all right.

The gizmo should be mapped on the entire surface of the screen. If this is not the case, move, rotate, or scale it as necessary.

- Add an empty **Poly Select** modifier, because otherwise the upper modifiers in the stack will effect only the selected polygons.

  Enable the upper modifiers in the stack.

- Unhide the Phone-Part2 object.

  Quad menu → **Unhide All**

  Perform a similar procedure on this object.

- Add the **Edit Poly** modifier *above* the **Taper** modifier and assign material IDs. There should be four materials: for the external surface, the internal one, the keyboard, and the large buttons. The IDs of the external and internal surfaces should be the same, and the IDs of the keyboard and the buttons should be 4 and 5, respectively (Fig. 2.119, *a*, *b*, *c*). I skipped ID 3 because I was planning to use one material for two objects. The ID is reserved for the screen of the Phone-base object.
- Apply mapping coordinates to the polygons of the keyboard (Fig. 2.119, *d*).
- Add an empty **Poly Select** modifier.

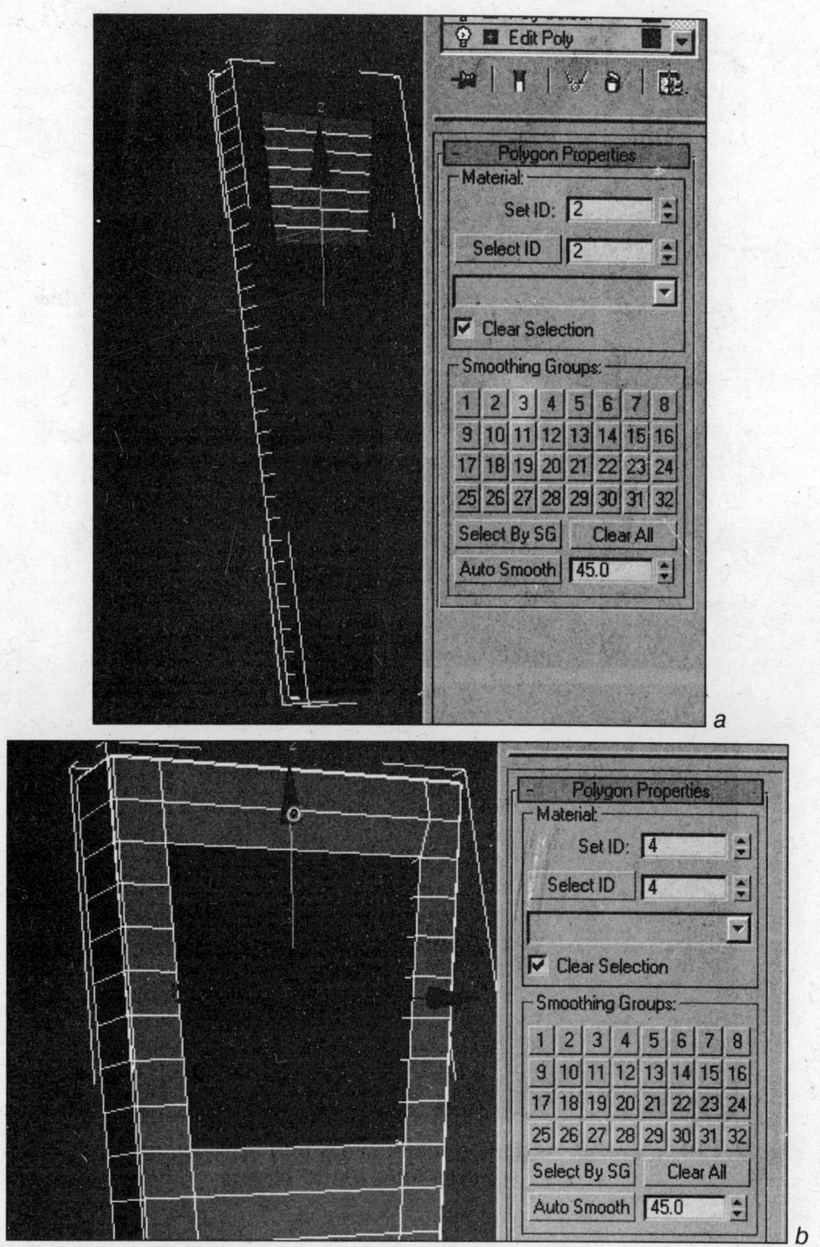

Fig. 2.119, *a* and *b*. Assigning material IDs and applying mapping coordinates to the Phone-Part2 object

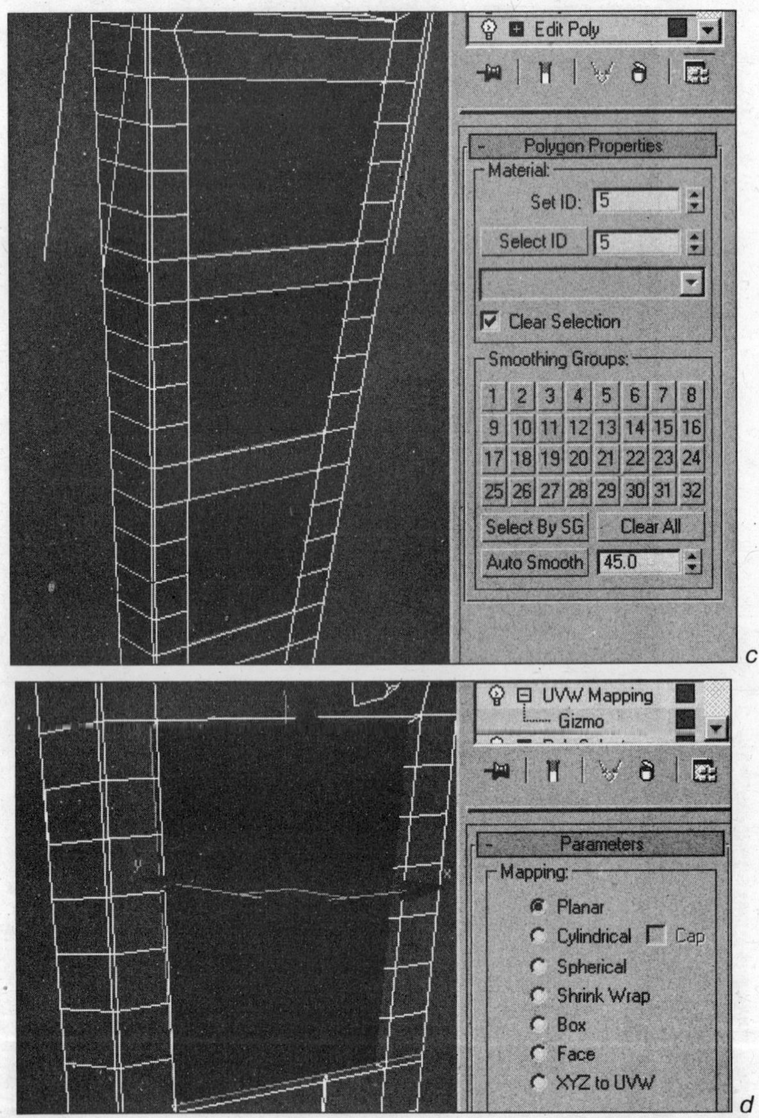

Fig. 2.119, *c* and *d*. Assigning material IDs and applying mapping coordinates to the Phone-Part2 object

Material IDs are assigned, mapping coordinates are applied. Now, you should proceed with materials.

TIP

You'll need to perform test computation many times. The main property of polished metal used here is to reflect light. However, there is nothing to reflect. You should specify the environment in the same way as in the previous projects. For the environment, choose any file, for example, stand.tif from the Projects\Project5 folder and make it a spherical environment.

I recommend that you create five materials individually and then combine them into one compound material for both parts of the telephone.

Polished Common Metal

Begin with the simplest material: metal for the internal surface. An Architectural material with the Metal Polished preset and the light-gray Diffuse color will be suitable. If you're planning to use the standard renderer, you actually have no other choice.

When used with mental ray, this material has a significant drawback: you cannot obtain blurred reflections.

However, there is an alternative for this material. The DGS shader (the abbreviation stands for *Diffuse, Glossy, Specular*) allows you to blur reflections and obtain realistic results for a vast group of materials, from various kinds of plastic to metals. Generally speaking, it is the main shader for use with mental ray. I guess that almost all 3ds Max's materials are somehow translated to DGS settings during rendering.

You can assign the shader as a material because it is available in the material list. However, it is best to use it in a mental ray material as a shader assigned to the **Surface** channel.

- Select any unused material slot in the material editor and change the material type to mental ray.
- Rename it Inner Metal.

This mental ray material is just a set of buttons, and you can assign a shader to each of them (Fig. 2.120, *a*). There are a lot of options, but you only need DGS.

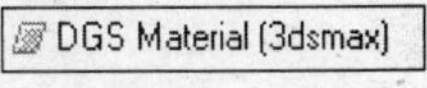

TIP

To set the material, assign it to any object in the scene. Unfortunately, reflections aren't displayed in the material slot.

The settings of the material (more precisely, the shader) are shown in Fig. 2.120, *b*.

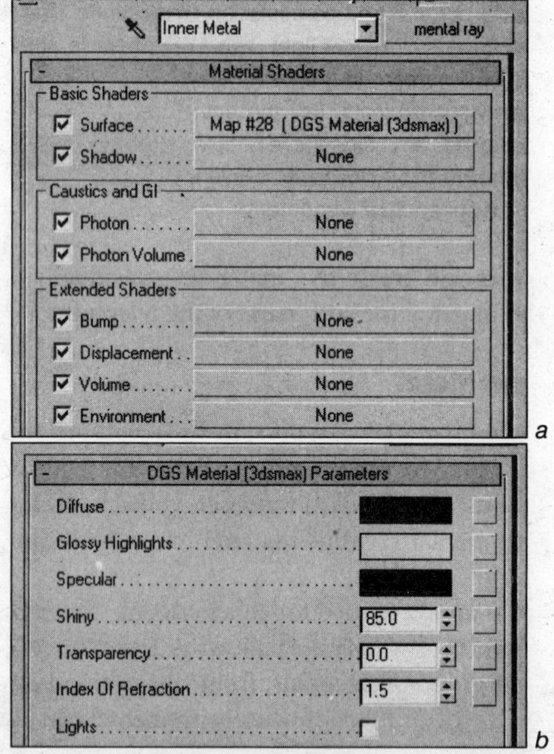

Fig. 2.120. Creating polished metal

The **Diffuse** parameter determines the material's own color. Because you're creating polished metal, you should make this parameter dark (the **Value** parameter should be little). Adjust only the **Hue** and **Saturaton** parameters.

The **Glossy Highlight** parameter determines the color and level of blurred reflections. It works in combination with the **Shiny** parameter. The greater the **Shiny** parameter value, the more glossy the surface, and vice versa. Make this color a little colder.

When blur increases (by decreasing the **Shiny** parameter), dithering takes place. Unfortunately, 3ds Max doesn't offer you tools to control this effect locally for an individual material or object. You can deal with this effect only by increasing the sampling level in the antialiasing settings (the **Samples per Pixel** parameters) and decreasing the contrast thresholds. I hope the appropriate feature appears in a future version of 3ds Max.

The **Specular** parameter determines the color and level of mirror reflections. It doesn't depend on the **Shiny** parameter.

NOTE

You should stick to the rule: "Either **Glossy** or **Specular**." Using both will result in an unnatural picture: Both blurred and mirror reflections will be seen simultaneously.

In addition, stick to another rule: "The lighter the **Glossy** or **Specular**, the darker the **Diffuse**."

To make an object with an assigned material participate in creation of global illumination and caustic, assign the **Photon Basic** shader like in the previous project. However, you can just drag the shader from the **Surface** button to the **Photon** button because DGS allows you to do so. The **Copy** method is the best in this case because when the **Specular** color in the shader assigned to the **Photon** channel is black, caustic won't be generated. Therefore, if you are planning to create caustic, you should make different settings.

Rough Common Metal

For the external surface, use the same material with slightly different settings.

- ❐ Create a copy of the Inner Metal material by dragging it to another slot and rename it to Outer Metal.
- ❐ Enter the settings of the DGS shader on the **Surface** channel.
- ❐ Set it as shown in Fig. 2.121, *a*.

NOTE

Make **Diffuse** a little lighter, and make **Glossy** darker.

Decrease the **Shiny** value to obtain blurred reflections.

- ❐ Return to editing the material and drag the shader from the **Surface** button to the **Photon** button.

You need to make the metal rough.

- ❐ Click the button in the **Bump** line in the **Extended Shaders** group and select **Bump (3ds Max)**.
- ❐ Among its parameters, click the button in the **Map** line and select **Noise**.

You'll see parameters of this map. Set them as shown in Fig. 2.121, *b*.

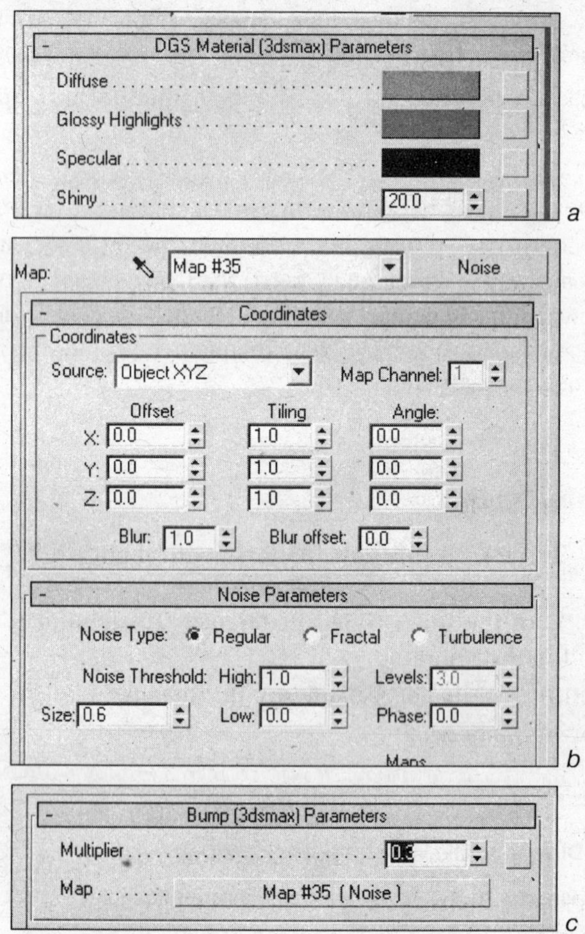

Fig. 2.121. Creating rough metal

A map of the Noise type is a so-called procedure three-dimensional map. The word "procedure" means this map is created during rendering, that is, this is actually a program creating an image according to a particular algorithm. The word "three-dimensional" and the method of application (**Object XYZ** in the **Coordinates** rollout) indicate that this map doesn't need mapping coordinates when displayed because it is applied in correspondence with the local coordinates of the object.

The size of the map is determined by the **Size** parameter in absolute units. Set it to a small value. You might think the map doesn't work, but this is not the case. You'll notice it after rendering.

❒ Jump one level up and decrease the bump multiplier to 0.3 (Fig. 2.121, *c*).

I should say a few words about the **Bump** channel. The use of this channel simulates a rough surface. It works as follows: white color indicates a bump, and black indicates, so to speak, a pit. The Bump map doesn't change the geometry of an object. If you want to change the geometry, use the **Displacement** channel.

Material for the Screen

For the screen use architectural plastic (Fig. 2.122) with textures applied to the channels **Diffuse** (Fig. 2.123), **Bump** and **Shininess** (screen.tga and screen-bump.tga).

NOTE

When a texture is used, the **Diffuse** color doesn't matter.

Maps of the **Bitmap** type from external files are used for these three channels. All maps are applied as texture (indicated within box 1 in Fig. 2.123) with Explicit Map Channel coordinates specified by the **UVW Mapping** modifiers set earlier. The map for the **Bump** channel is applied to it directly because an Architectural material allows you to control the map's level of action (indicated within box 1 in Fig. 2.122).

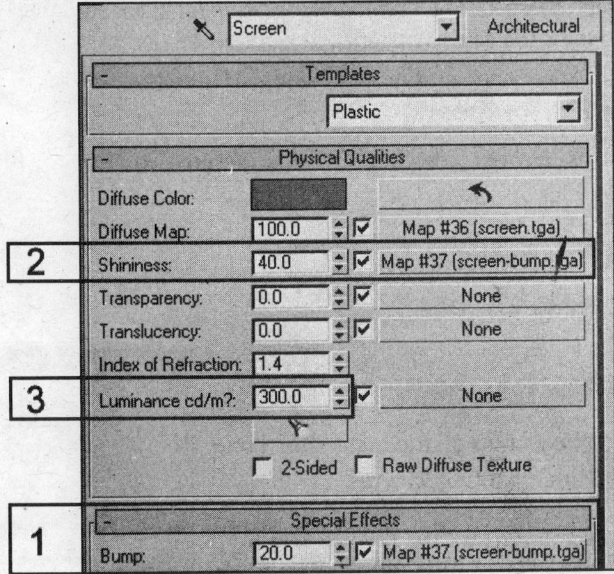

Fig. 2.122. Material for the screen

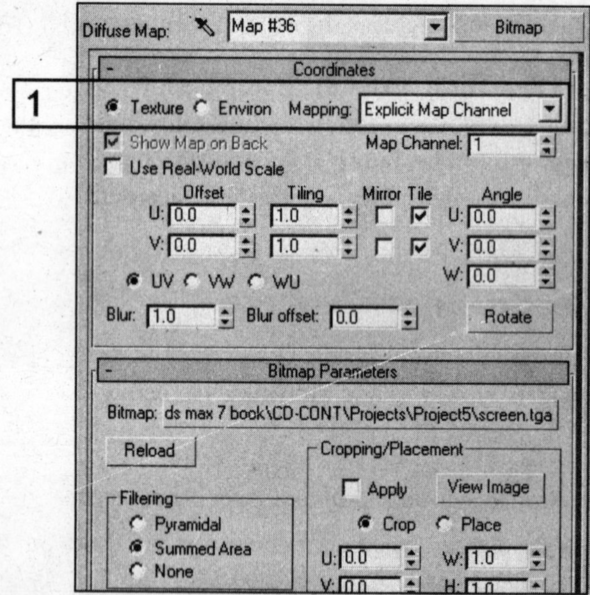

Fig. 2.123. Parameters of the map (texture) applied to the **Diffuse** channel

Application of the map for the **Bump** channel to the **Shininess** channel makes the light speck uneven (indicated within box 2 in Fig. 2.122).

A small value of the **Luminance** parameter (indicated within box 3 in Fig. 2.122) illuminates the screen material.

Material for the Keyboard

This material is almost identical to the screen material. The keyboard.tga and keyb-bump.tga files are used.

Material for the Buttons

This is simple yellow plastic.

Material for the Telephone

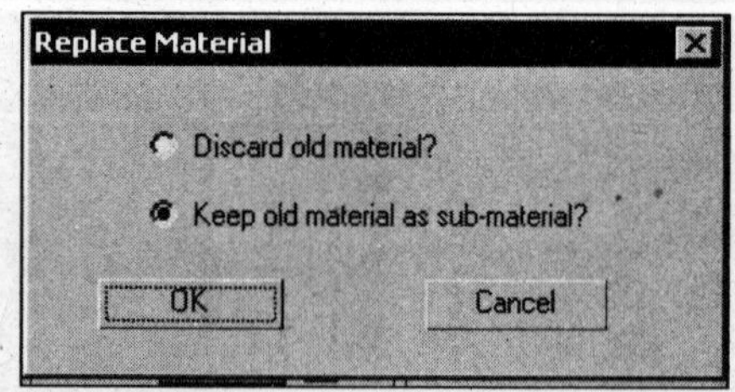

Now, you need to combine all the materials in one material of the Multi/Sub-Object type.

- ❐ In an unused material slot, change the material type to Multi/Sub-Object. You'll be asked a question. It doesn't matter whatever you answer.

- Set the number of submaterials to five.
- Using the **Instance** method, drag the materials from the slots to the submaterial buttons in accordance with the following table:

ID	Sub-Material	ID	Sub-Material
1	Outer Metal	4	Keyboard
2	Inner Metal	5	Buttons
3	Screen		

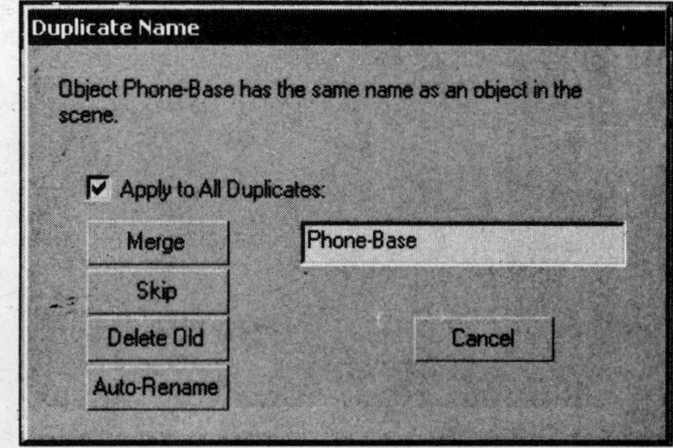

- Assign the material to the telephone model and perform test rendering to be sure that the materials are assigned correctly. The final adjustment of the materials will be done in the main scene.

Save the result of your work. Mine is in the model5-with-materials.max file.

Open the scene with lighting set previously. My scene is placed in the Project5-lighting-final.max file.

- Using the **Merge** commands, load into this scene the objects from the model5-with-materials.max file.
- You'll be asked a question concerning the objects with the same names. Answer **Delete Old** to replace the old objects with those being loaded.
- If you get a question concerning the same materials, select **Use Merged Material.**

I believe you can easily create materials for all the objects in the scene, so I'll tell you briefly what I did in my project.

Remember, there is a sphere in the scene that should gather photons flying away. You could use this sphere as the environment by applying a map to it. However, it would be best to use a screen for this purpose (Fig. 2.124).

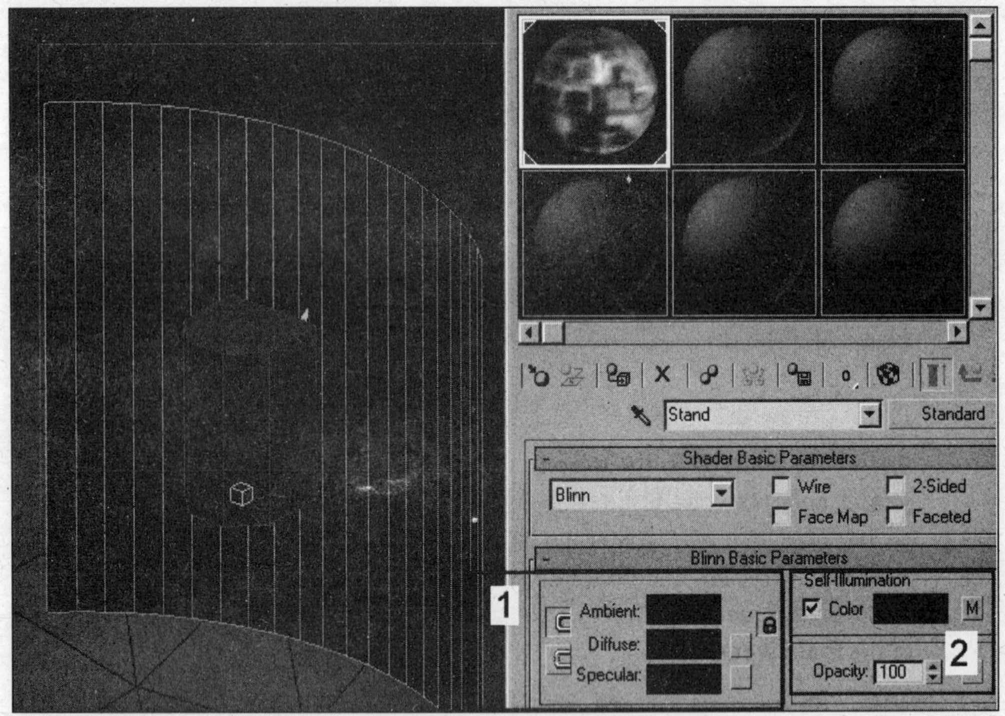

Fig. 2.124. A screen to create reflections

The screen was created from an arc using the **Extrude** modifier. When the **Generate Mapping Coordinates** checkbox is checked, the map is displayed correctly.

The material is standard. All its colors are black to avoid specks of light (indicated within box 1 in Fig. 2.124). The map from the stand.tif file is applied to the **Self-Illumination** channel. Set its blur to a value between 6 and 8 and check the **Color** checkbox (indicated within box 2).

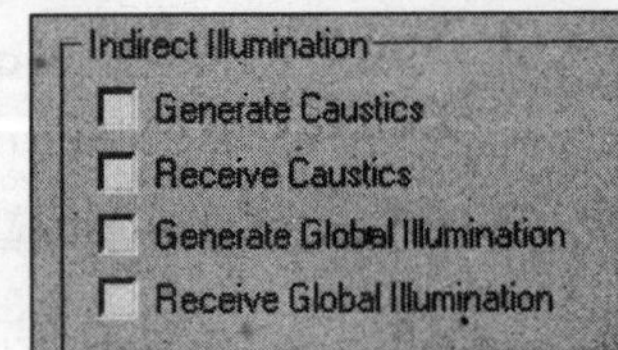

In the object's parameters, uncheck all the checkboxes on the **mental ray** tab.

The material of the show-case is a combination of architectural mirrors and a light-blue architectural material with the Ideal Diffuse preset.

The material of the support is architectural metal.

Turn on the global illumination and final gather, set antialiasing (Mitchell with parameters 1 and 16) and exposure control. Now, you can perform the final rendering.

The result shown in Fig. 2.125 was obtained as a combination of rendering to the HDR format and an element-by-element rendering with a subsequent correction in Adobe Photoshop CS2.

The meaning of the last phrase will be explained at the end of this chapter.

Fig. 2.125. The final result (is missing)

The result of my work is in the Project5-Final.max file in the Projects\Project5 folder on the accompanying CD-ROM.

Materials for Including the Model into the Environment

One of the most interesting tasks in 3ds Max graphics is inclusion of 3ds Max objects into a "live" environment, whether a photo or video. A lot of methods were developed for this purpose. The one I'm going to describe isn't the best. Why so? The use of a 3ds Max graphics package for this purpose isn't the best approach because recent advances of post-processing technologies are major. Those who have at least elementary skills in image processing will agree with me. Nevertheless, I suggest that you try this method.

An image, into which the calendar model will be included, is shown in Fig. 2.126. This photo was taken in our office. It is in the p3-back.tif file in the Projects\Project3 folder on the accompanying CD-ROM. Its size is 2,000 × 1,800 pixels.

Fig. 2.126. The photo of our office

First, you should set the perspective and create a camera.

- ❒ Start 3ds Max.
- ❒ Select millimeters as system units. This is necessary to load the model correctly and to compute lighting correctly.

Menu bar → **Customize** → **Units Setup**

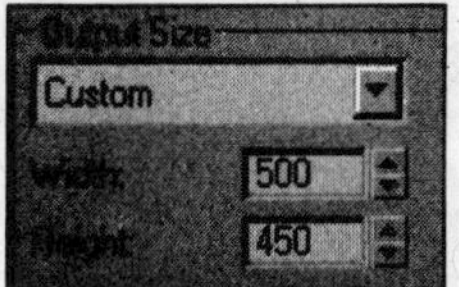

- ❐ Set the rendering size to values that are multiplies of the size of the picture you're going to use for rendering. To speed up test rendering, you may set 500 × 450 pixels.

  Menu bar → **Rendering** → **Render** → the **Common** tab

- ❐ In the perspective viewport, turn on the **Safe Frame.**

  Viewport right-click menu → **Show Safe Frame**

- ❐ Load the p3-back.tif image as the environment with the Screen type (Fig. 2.127, *a*).

  Menu bar → **Rendering** → **Environment**

  Drag the map to the material editor using the **Instance** method.

This type of environment has two features, one of which is quite useful: The image is always displayed as it is. The other feature is a drawback: This environment is reflected incorrectly, and it isn't refracted. You'll use the first feature and ignore the second because the material of the calendar is paper which won't reflect. If you needed reflection, you wouldn't be able to use this method.

To display the image in the viewport, make it a background. Remember, the environment and the background are not the same.

- ❐ Open background display settings and connect the environment to the viewport background (Fig. 2.127, *b*).

  Menu bar → **Views** → **ViewPort Backround**

  Check the **Use Environment** and **View Background** checkboxes.

- ❐ Rotate the view in the perspective viewport to align approximately the grid with the desk plane (Fig. 2.128, *a*).
- ❐ When you achieve this, create a camera (<Ctrl>+<C>) and adjust the perspective.

TIP

Use the **Perspective** feature of the navigation controls. It allows you to change the FOV (Field Of View) simultaneously with the dolly movement. This is a so-called Vertigo effect.

- ❐ Create a plane in the camera viewport.
- ❐ Load the model of the calendar (using the **Merge** command) and scale it along all the coordinates if necessary.

  The position of the model is its position on the desk (Fig. 2.128, *b*).

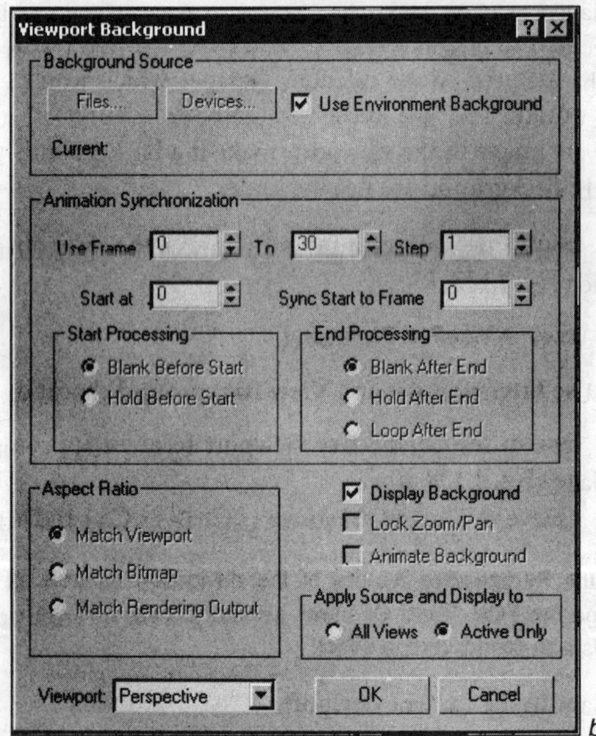

Fig. 2.127. Assigning the environment (*a*) and connecting it to the viewport background (*b*)

a

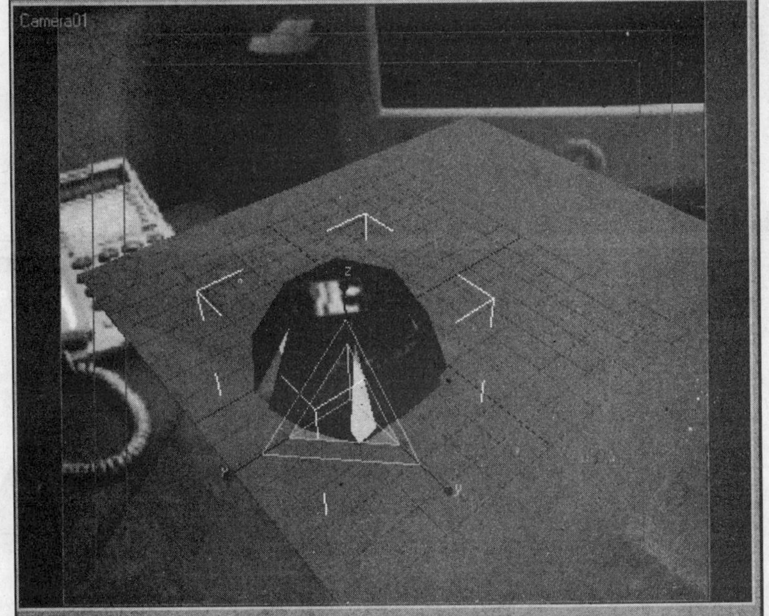

b

Fig. 2.128. Aligning the model with the photo

Now, the most interesting things will happen.

- ❒ Create a material of the mental ray type.
- ❒ Apply the **Ambient/Reflective Occlusion** shader to the **Surface** channel.
- ❒ Assign the material to the plane and perform test rendering (Fig. 2.129, *a*).

What does this shader do during rendering? The surface of an object emits rays. If they encounter an occlusion, the point that emitted them will be colored in the **Dark** color with an intensity depending on the distance to the occlusion. This somewhat resembles the final gather, that this is pure and simple trickery. The plane isn't effected by illumination, whether direct or indirect.

- ❒ Set the shader approximately as shown in Fig. 2.129, *b*.

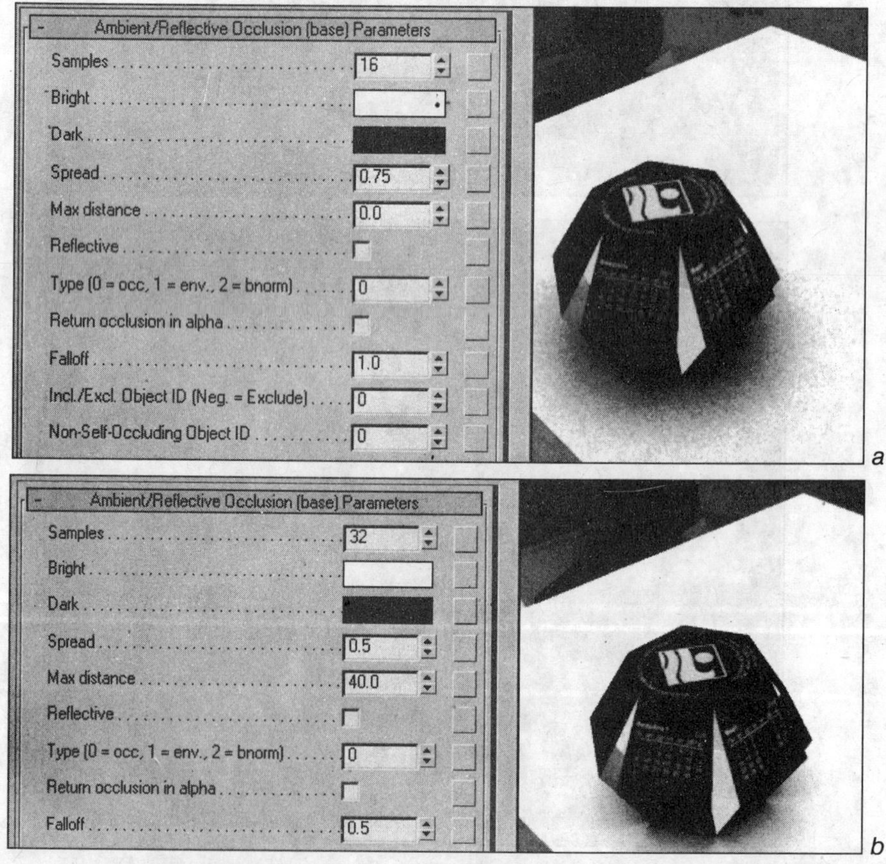

Fig. 2.129. The settings of the **Ambient/Reflective Occlusion** shader

Decrease the **Spread** parameter that controls the ray spread and set the **Max Distance** parameter.

Soften the effect by changing the **Falloff** parameter. This feature was first introduced in 3ds Max 7.5.

Increase the number of samples to eliminate dithering.

Instance (Copy) Map
Method
Instance
Copy
OK Cancel

- Drag the environment map to the **Bright** and **Dark** channels using the **Copy** method (not **Instance**).
- In the parameters of the map on the **Bright** channel, set the **Environment – Screen** type.
- In the parameters of the map on the **Dark** channel, do the same and make the map darker (the **Output** rollout, the **Output Amount** parameter).

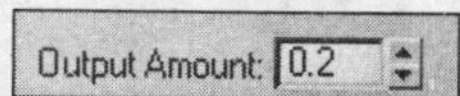

Do you like it? (Fig. 2.130)

Fig. 2.130. The result of test rendering

- Illuminate the scene with the HDRI map from the p3-ll.hdr file. You know how to do this (Fig. 2.131). This map was created at the same place and at the same time.

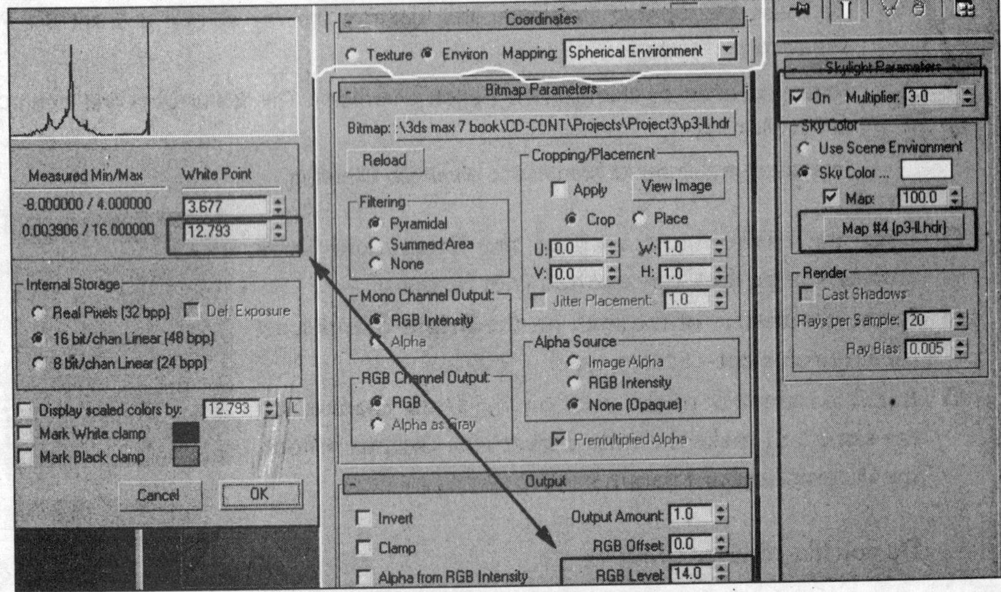

Fig. 2.131. Illuminating with the HDRI map

Fig. 2.132. The result of the final rendering

Although the light from the SkyLight light source doesn't effect the plane, the final gather collects rays from the plane. This is why the model looks natural even without reflections.

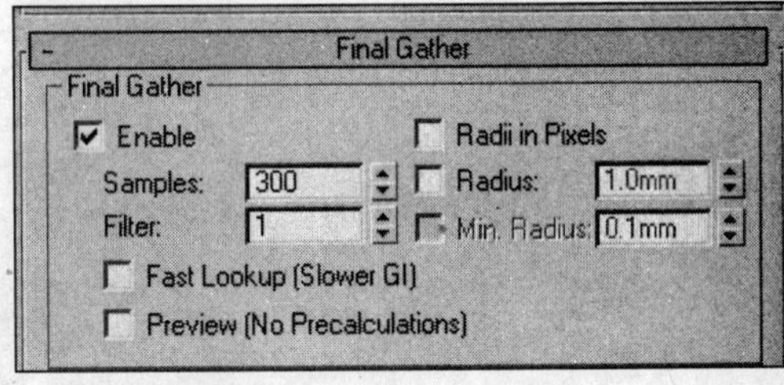

- Enable the final gather. It will be enough to specify between 200 and 400 samples.

You can try to perform rendering to the full size and with appropriate antialiasing. Make sure to substitute the small map with the large one in the material of the calendar.

Everything is all right (Fig. 2.132).

My variant is in the Project3-final.max file in the Projects\Project3 folder on the accompanying CD-ROM.

What should you do when you need reflections? You can use the **Environment** channel in the material's **mental ray Connection** rollout and apply the spherical reflection map there. It will override the global environment.

Materials for Non-Realistic Rendering

Do you remember the first project, a shelf for the bathroom? I'll use it as an example to show you how to create images in a cartoon-like style, which is currently very popular. You'll use the built-in Ink'n'Paint material and a few mental ray shaders. The result is shown in Fig. 2.133. The scene is in the Project1-final.max file in the Projects \Project1 folder on the accompanying CD-ROM. It is shown in Fig. 2.134. This figure also shows camera parameters. The most important of them is the **Orthographic Projection** checkbox checked, which disables the perspective.

The parameters of the material for the plane and the shelf are shown in Fig. 2.135, *a*. This is a material of the Ink'n'Paint type. It is suitable both for the standard renderer (for which it was developed) and for mental ray. In the latter case, rendering is much faster. In the **Paint Controls** rollout, the color and the number of grades from light to dark are specified. In the **Ink Controls** rollout, parameters for creating contours are specified.

Note that you can assign a map to each color and almost to each parameter. This gives you a lot of options for creating non-photorealistic images, for example, in the style of drawing.

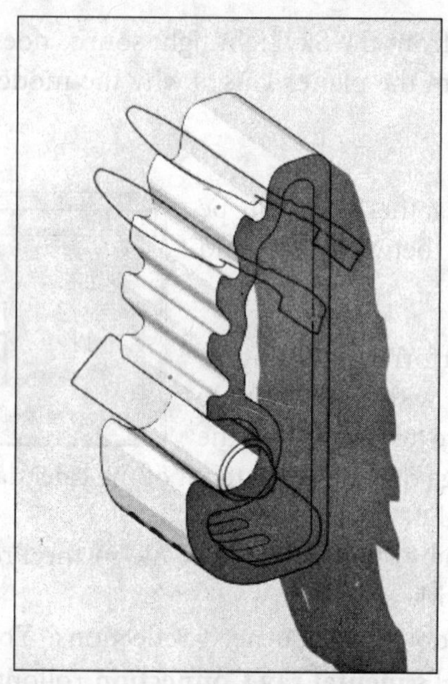

Fig. 2.133. The result of rendering

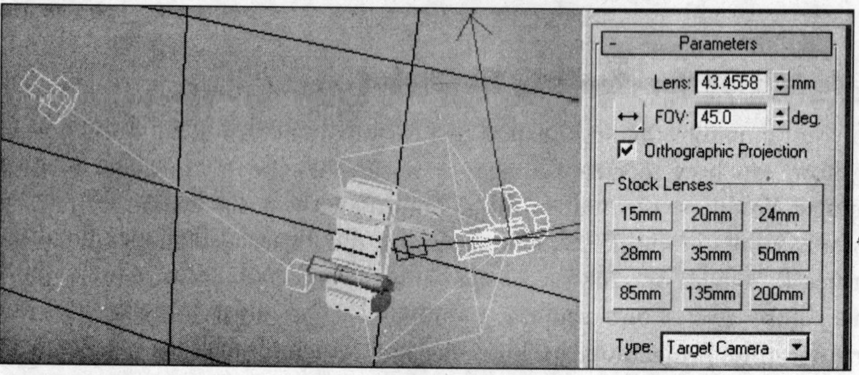

Fig. 2.134. The scene

For subordinate objects, I used a mental ray material with specific shaders (Fig. 2.135, *b*). The **Transmat** shader is assigned to the **Surface** and **Shadow** channels. This makes an object transparent and doesn't allow it to cast shadows. A **Simple (contour)** shader is assigned to the **Contour** channel. There are many shaders of this type in 3ds Max, and you can experiment with them.

- Combi (contour)
- Curvature (contour)
- Depth Fade (contour)
- Factor Color (contour)
- Layer Thinner (contour)
- Simple (contour)
- Width From Color (contour)
- Width From Light (contour)
- Width From Light Dir (contour)

However, this is not enough. For mental ray to create contours, you should check an appropriate checkbox in the rendering parameters (Fig. 2.136). If you wish, you can experiment with the shaders; just drag them to the material editor.

Menu bar → **Rendering** → the **Renderer** tab → the **Contours** group

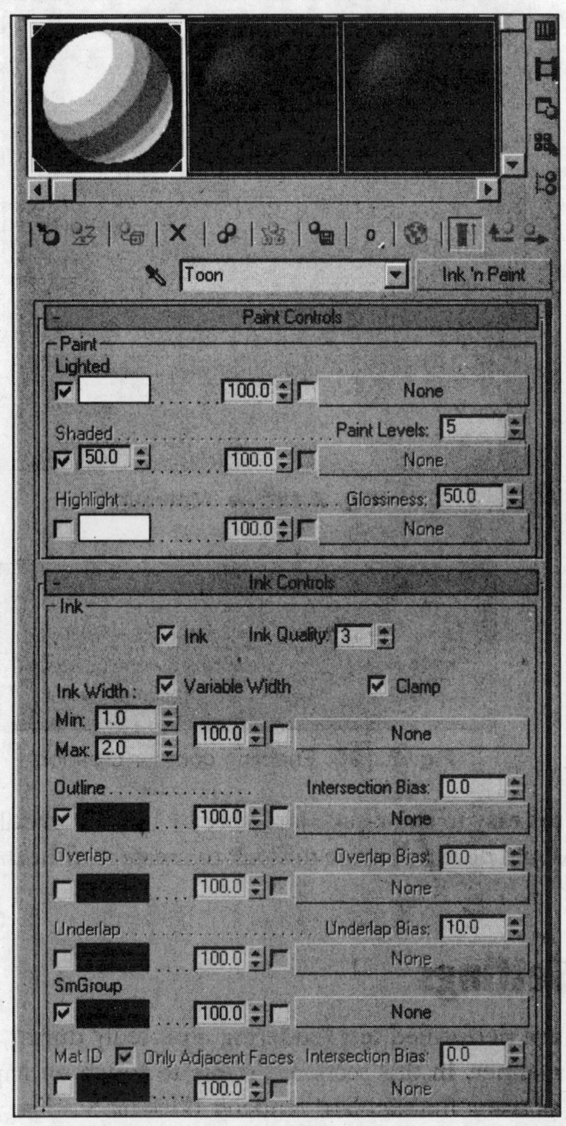

Fig. 2.135, *a*. Materials

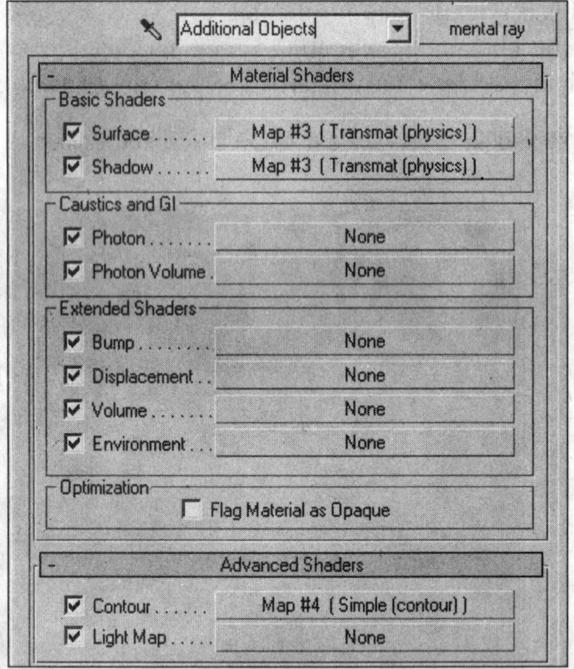

Fig. 2.135, *b*. Materials

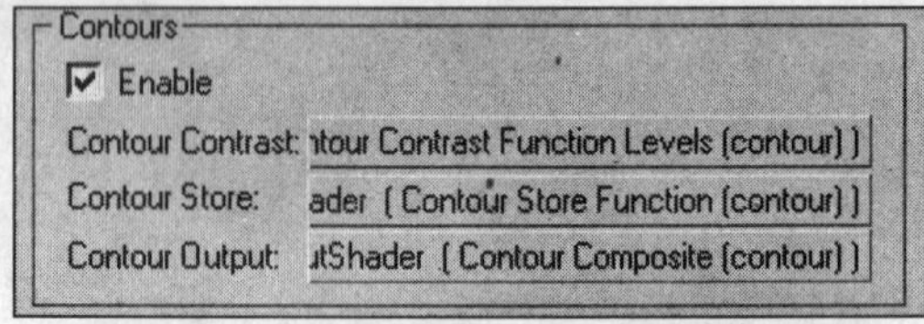

Fig. 2.136. Enabling contour creation

Of course, it is easy to draw such a picture by hand. What about an animated clip in this style? It would be much more difficult to create it without using 3D graphics.

Rendering Settings

Although you have performed test rendering repeatedly during the exercises, this was in a disorderly manner. In this section, I'd like to touch on important issues of rendering in 3ds Max using the standard renderer (Default Scanline Renderer) and mental ray. My goal is to make it easier for you to obtain high-quality images.

I'm not going to repeat material from the user's manual and various reference-books that describe the process comprehensively. Rather, I'll concentrate on issues, which are important from my point of view. I won't touch on network rendering because this is a separate topic.

Creating and Using Render Presets

You might have noticed that setting rendering parameters is a tedious task. This is why 3ds Max allows you to save and load render presets. There is a drop-down list at the bottom of the rendering settings dialog box. On the list, there is the **Save Preset** item. You can create your own presets and use them for rendering (Fig. 2.137). Note that not every parameter can be saved and loaded. In addition to the rendering parameters, environment and effect settings can be saved using this dialog box.

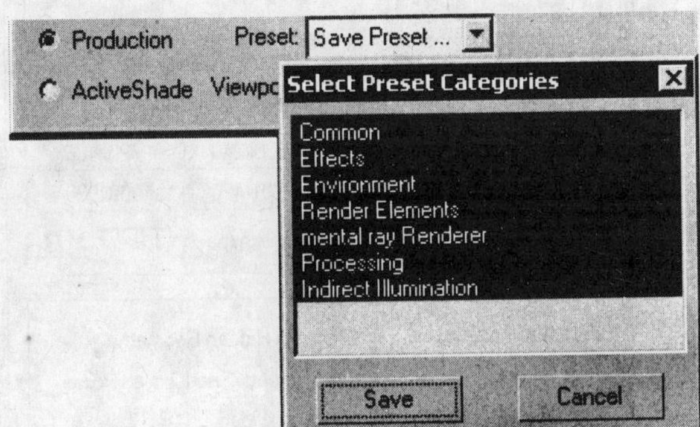

Fig. 2.137. Saving render presets

Common Settings

Settings common to all renderers are collected on the **Common** tab (Fig. 2.138).

In the **Time Output** group, you can set the time interval that should be computed. As a rule, for animation the **Active Time Segment** radio button is selected. For a static frame, the current frame is rendered.

The **Output Size** group sets the size in *pixels*. This fact is confusing to people who work in the printing industry. There is a special tool, **Print Size Wizard**, that allows you to enter the size in units familiar to those individuals (Fig. 2.139).

Menu bar → **Rendering** → **Print Size Wizard**

Checkboxes in the **Options** group allow you to enable or disable particular 3ds Max features during rendering. I'll describe just a few of them.

- The **Force 2-Sided** checkbox forces 3ds Max to treat all materials as two-sided during rendering. Sometimes, this option is useful, but sometimes you may prefer to uncheck it. Everything depends on the particular task. In any case, checking this checkbox increases rendering time.

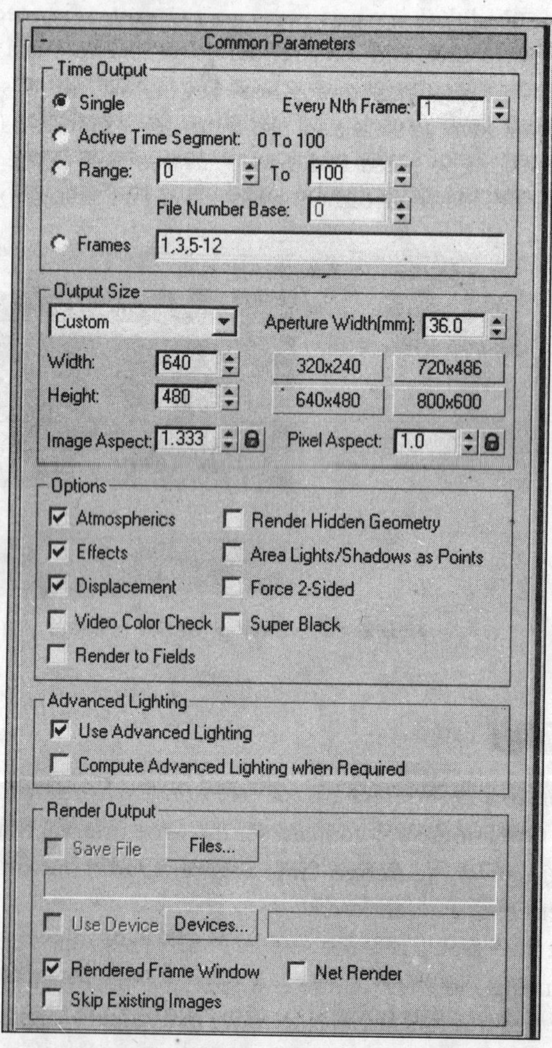

Fig. 2.138. Common render settings

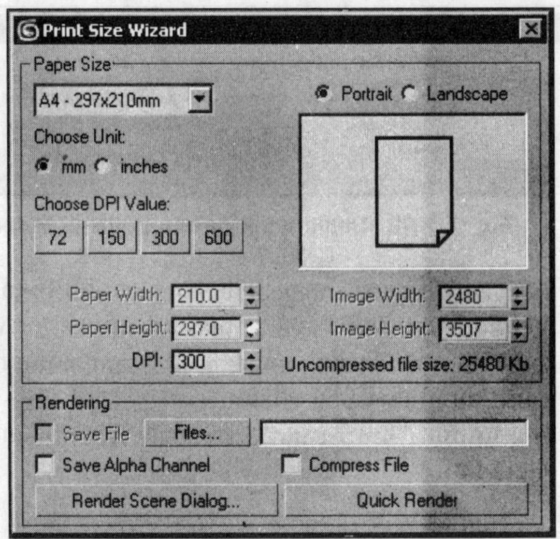

Fig. 2.139. The **Print Size Wizard** dialog box

- ❒ The **Render Hidden** checkbox allows you to render hidden objects. Remember two important points: Invisible parts of objects (such as polygons, patches, etc.) are rendered regardless of the state of this checkbox, and objects excluded from rendering using the **Renderable** checkbox in parameters of the object or a layer aren't rendered at all.
- ❒ The **Area Lights/Shadow as Points** checkbox disables soft shadows. You can use it when you need to obtain a result quickly.

The **Advanced Lighting** group controls built-in mechanisms for computing indirect illumination using the standard renderer. These parameters aren't used in mental ray.

Parameters in the **Render Output** group specify files, to which the results of rendering should be output. To save the results of rendering in a file, click the **Files** button, select or create a folder, and parameters of the file. 3ds Max has a convenient feature: If you specify the file name with an extension, the appropriate settings for this type will be selected.

There are quite a lot of available formats, but it makes sense to use only certain formats.

3ds Max saves images only in the RGB color model and its versions. The CMYK model isn't supported in output or when using maps.

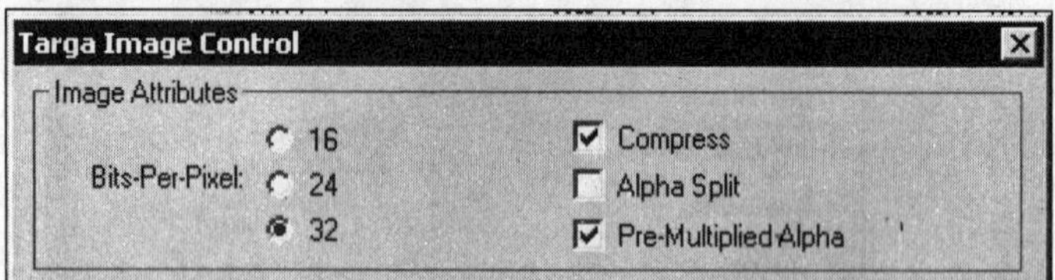

Fig. 2.140. Settings for saving in the TGA format

The Targa (TGA) and Tagged Image File Format (TIFF) formats are the most suitable for rendering when you don't need special features, or when the color depth is larger than 8 bits per channel. Both formats implement compression algorithms without loss in quality and support Alpha-channel.

When rendering to the TGA format, I strongly recommend that you set parameters as shown in Fig. 2.140.

When saving as the TIFF format, the 16-bit SGI LogL and 32-bit SGI LogLUV options are available. This is a variant that uses a large dynamic range.

Starting from version 6, 3ds Max supports rendering to the Radiance RGBE (*.hdr). In version 7, mental ray allows you to save in this format. This format is worth using in rendering because it allows you to deal with over-lighting and under-lighting at the post-processing stage. Fig. 2.141 shows the result of rendering in 3ds Max with strong over-lighting (*a*) and the result of correcting exposure in Adobe Photoshop CS2 (*b*).

The Run-length Encoded Version A (RLA) format from SGI and the Rich Pixel Format (RPF) format from Discreet allow you to use other channels in addition to the Alpha-channel. You can use these channels in your subsequent work in software packages such as Autodesk Combustion and Toxic or Adobe After Effects (Fig. 2.142).

In addition, both formats support color depths of 16 and 32 bits per channel, and, therefore, are appealing.

Here are the most important channels:

- The **Z** channel, which is a black-and-white mask, stored the "depth" of a scene. The further an object is from the camera, the darker it is. This allows you to create the effect of a mist or a focus depth on a finished picture.
- **Material Effects** and **Object ID** channels allow you to select objects in the software packages mentioned earlier and apply special effects. This is based on so-called material ID and object ID. The first is specified in the material editor, and the latter is specified in object properties.

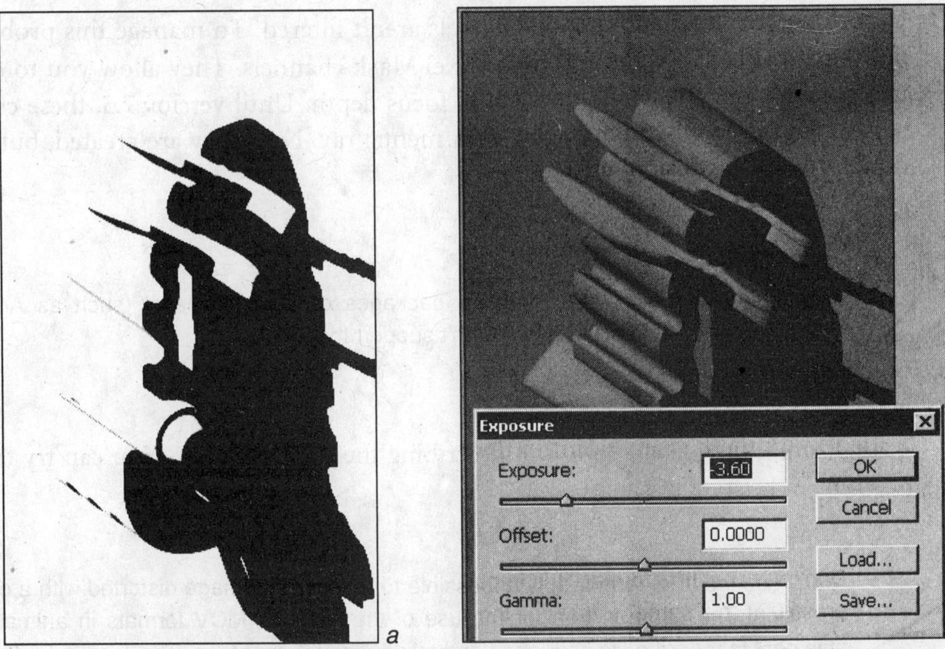

Fig. 2.141. Correcting exposure in Adobe Photoshop CS2

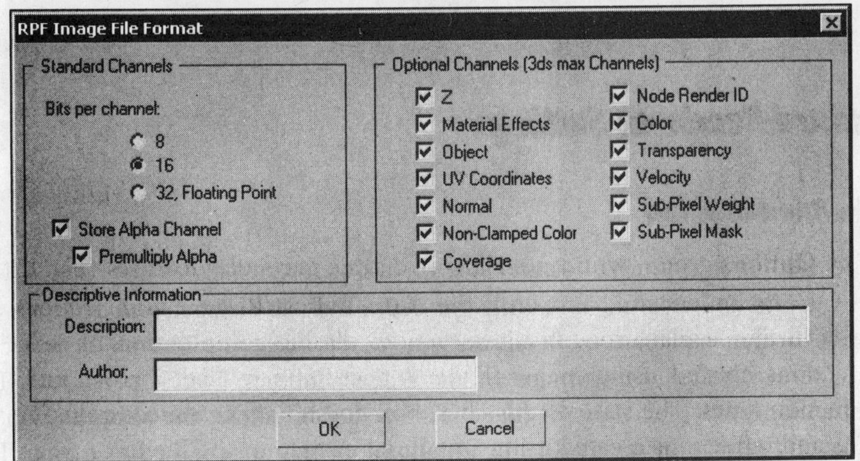

Fig. 2.142. Parameters used for saving in the RPF format

- **UV Coordinates** allows you to apply a map to a finished picture.
- The **Velocity** channel contains information on moving objects. This allows you to create a motion blur effect on a finished picture.

- Unfortunately, these additional channels aren't filtered. To manage this problem, use the **Sub-Pixel Weight** and **Sub-Pixel Mask** channels. They allow you to control precisely the effects of a mist or a focus depth. Until version 7.5, these channels weren't used when rendering with mental ray. Now they are created, but still don't provide the desired effect.

Unfortunately, most video montage packages of a middle level (such as Adobe Premiere) and Adobe Photoshop don't support these formats.

I don't think there is any point in describing the other formats. You can try them if you wish.

Don't use the JPG format. It is impossible to recover the image distorted with a compression! The same is true for the use of the AVI and MOV formats in animation. It is best to record a file sequence and mix during the montage. The reason for this is the same: You'll never recover the lost quality.

Standard Renderer Settings

The *Renderer* Tab

It the **Options** group, you can enable or disable particular features (Fig. 2.143). They are easy to understand, and only the **Auto Reflect/Refract and Mirrors** checkbox needs further explanation. It allows you to disable computation of reflections and refractions created using maps of the Reflect/Refract, Flat Mirror, and Thin Wall Refraction types. The state of this checkbox doesn't affect the computation of reflections and refractions created using a material or map of the Raytrace type. To control them, you need special parameters located on the **Raytracing** tab.

Settings for anti-aliasing are very important, and I'd like to focus on them.

In earlier versions, 3ds Max used the only algorithm, later named Area. This algorithm was quick enough, but not very good. A keen eye could easily distinguish between images produced in 3ds Max by this algorithm and the others.

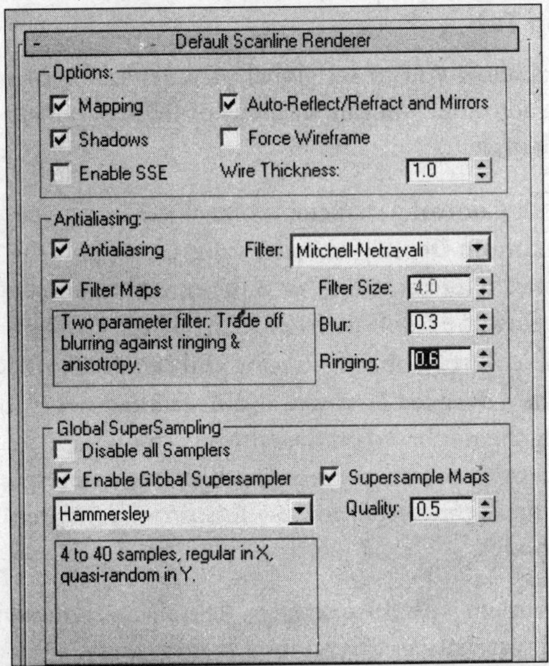

Fig. 2.143. Parameters of the **Renderer** tab for the standard renderer

Beginning with version 3, 3ds Max uses 12 antialiasing algorithms. Here are just a few of them and recommendations regarding their use.

- In my opinion, the Mitchell-Netravali algorithm gives the best results during rendering. The resulting image is live and soft and isn't too blurred. This is achieved with parameters shown in Fig. 2.143.
- The Blackman and Catmull-Rom algorithms produce very clear images. Use them for printing and when creating sprites for computer games.
- The Blend and Cook Variable algorithms are rather interesting. Their parameters have a wide ranges of values, and this allows you to obtain interesting results.

If you wish to obtain the best result using the standard renderer, use Super Sampling. It can be used globally as shown in Fig. 2.143. However, this isn't the best approach because the use of Super Sampling increases rendering time significantly. Adjust this process for the desired material in the material editor in the **SuperSampling** rollout.

Mental ray ignores these settings because it uses its own method for antialiasing.

The *Raytracing* Tab

These parameters allow you to set global parameters for materials and maps of the Raytrace type. In addition, you can set many of these parameters individually for each material and each map.

- The **Ray Depth Control** parameters control ray tracing depth. Tracing terminates when the **Maximum Depth** parameter value is reached (the total of refractions and reflections is taken into account), or if the contribution of any ray to the final pixel color drops below the cutoff threshold. Checkboxes in the **Global Raytrace Engine options** group control global ray tracing and can disable it completely. In that case, shadows of the **Advanced Raytrace** and **Area Shadows** types won't be created because building them is based on the same process.
- 3ds Max allows you to blur ray-traced reflections and refractions. Just turn on antialiasing for these processes. Because this slows down rendering many times, set this process locally.

You can experiment with these settings. Remember, however, that they don't work with architectural materials and aren't used in mental ray.

I'll describe parameters of the **Advanced Lighting** tab later, when discussing lighting in the interior.

mental ray *Settings*

When you switch the mental ray, the set of tabs changes.

You learned the **Indirect Illumination** tab while setting lighting and materials.

The *Processing* Tab

These parameters are specialized, so I'll describe the simplest ones (Fig. 2.144) especially because some of them were (and will be) used.

- The **Use Placeholder Objects** checkbox allows you to avoid rendering objects that are outside the camera's field of view. This doesn't relate to objects whose reflection the camera sees.

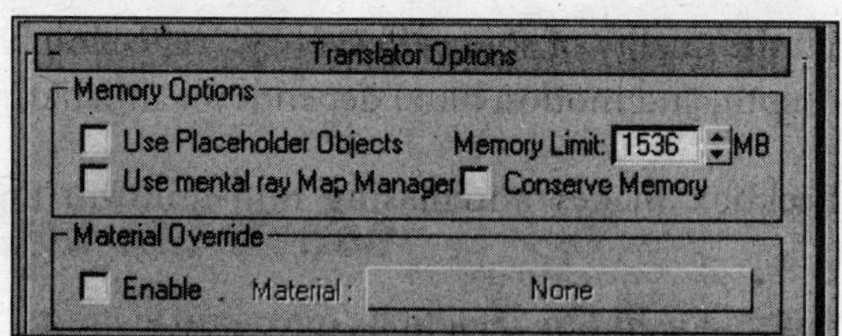

Fig. 2.144. The parameters of the **Processing** tab

- A very valuable feature allows you to replace temporarily all the materials with one material. Use the button in the **Material Override** group.

The *Renderer* Tab

Parameters on this tab are the most interesting and significant difference between mental ray and the standard renderer.

The **Sampling Quality** rollout allows you to set what is called antialiasing in the standard renderer (Fig. 2.145, *a*). In essence, it is the same, so I'll keep on using the word *antialiasing*. Feel free to find settings you like best. I'll describe those I'm using in my work.

- The default settings are suitable for a quick test rendering. As for the final rendering, I recommend that you use the Mitchell algorithm. In the **Samples Per Pixels** group, set the **Minimum** parameter to a value between 1 and 4 and set the **Maximum** parameter to a value between 16 and 64.

Don't set the **Minimum** parameter to a value less than one when using the Mitchell or Lanczos algorithm. The result will be disappointing!

- The **Width** and **Height** parameters specify the size of a sample in pixels. The default settings are the best. Increasing them will result in a blurred picture, and decreasing will result in aliasing.
- You can improve the result by decreasing the values of parameters in the **Contrast** rollout (the **Spatial** line). In most cases, the best values for each parameter are between 0.05 and 0.02. Parameters in the **Temporal** line are used to control the quality of motion blur.

Remember that the quality of some effects (e.g., reflection blur when a DGS material is used, focus depth, and motion blur) depends on antialiasing settings.

- The **Jitter** checkbox makes antialiasing non-uniform and makes the picture more natural.

Mental ray uses three rendering algorithms. The main ones are Scanline and Raytrace. The first algorithm processes direct lighting and creates shadows of the Shadow Map type. The second is responsible for all the other effects, such as indirect illumination, caustic, reflection, refraction, and Raytrace shadows. If you disable Scanline, the second algorithm will do all rendering with almost the same result. However, if you disable Raytrace, the mentioned effects will be impossible. It is normal to use both algorithms.

The Fast Rasterizer algorithm is auxiliary. It is used to speed animation rendering or, more precisely, motion blur rendering.

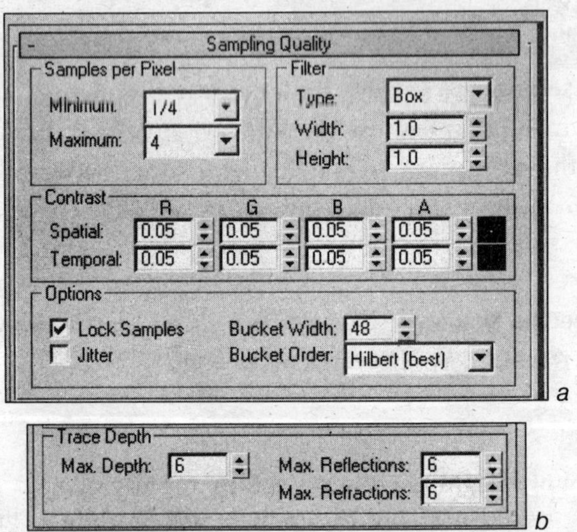

Fig. 2.145. Settings for antialiasing (*a*) and trace depth (*b*) in mental ray

The main parameters in the **Trace Depth** group in the **Rendering Algoritms** rollout are parameters, which define the depth of ray tracing for refractions and reflections (Fig. 2.145, *b*). In contrast to the standard Raytrace algorithm, mental ray misses an adaptive algorithm. When computing refractions, it considers surfaces, which a ray encounters. For example, when a ray goes through an empty glass, it undergoes four refractions, and when it goes through a glass with water, six refractions take place.

Batch Render and Managing Scene States

Two features were introduced into 3ds Max version 7.5 to simplify the automation of rendering a scene from several angles with several scene settings. Both features were borrowed from Autodesk Viz 2006.

The first feature has the ability to save and recover the scene state.

Menu bar → **Tools** → **Manage Scene States**

You can save the scene in a certain state and in certain positions. For example, Fig. 2.146, *a* shows saving the camera's position.

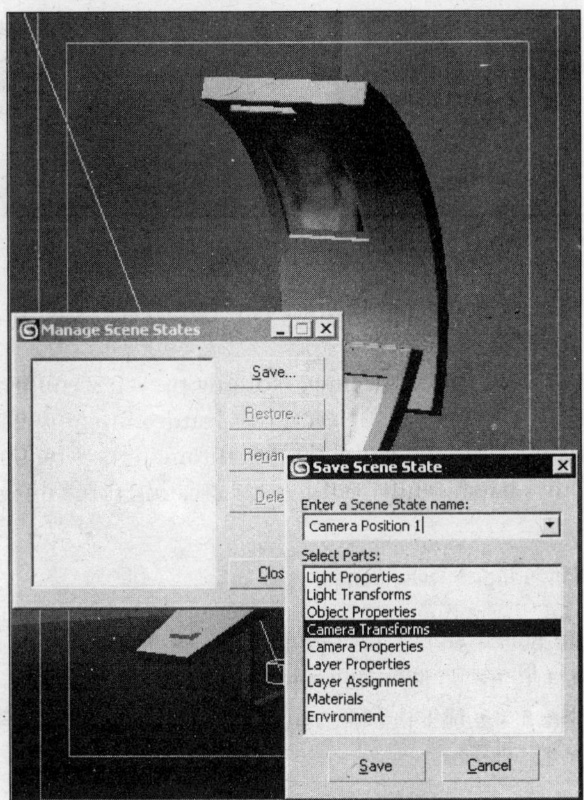

Fig. 2.146, *a*. Saving a state of the scene

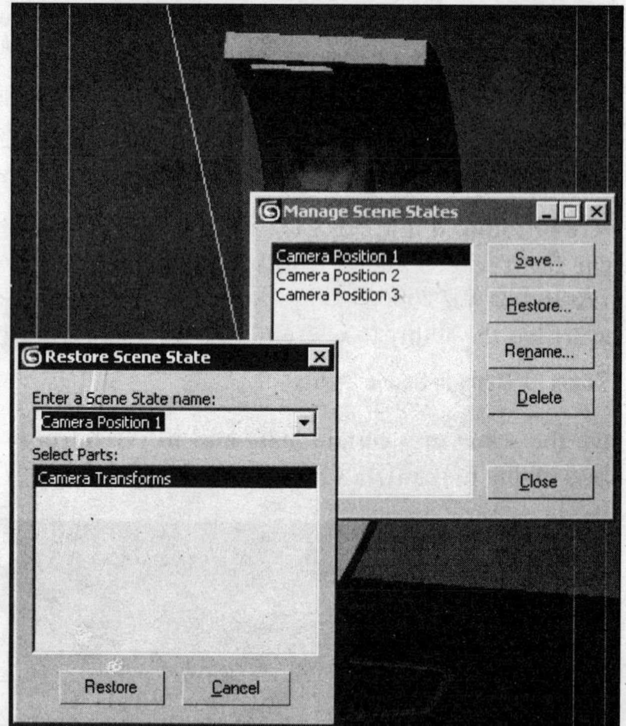

Fig. 2.146, *b*. Restoring a state of the scene

After you save a few states, you can return to any of them at any time (Fig. 2.146, *b*).

This feature in itself isn't appealing. Nothing prevents you from saving scenes and loading them when necessary. However, this feature in combination with batch rendering opens new interesting possibilities for automation of rendering.

Fig. 2.147 shows batch render settings for creating three images from three different positions.

Menu bar → **Rendering** → **Batch render**

The **Add** button adds a task to the task list. Rendering is possible only from the camera or from a directed light source, and this is all right.

Three lists at the bottom allow you to select a camera, a state of the scene, and the renderer's settings.

Everything is ready for rendering. You can start the process and go to bed.

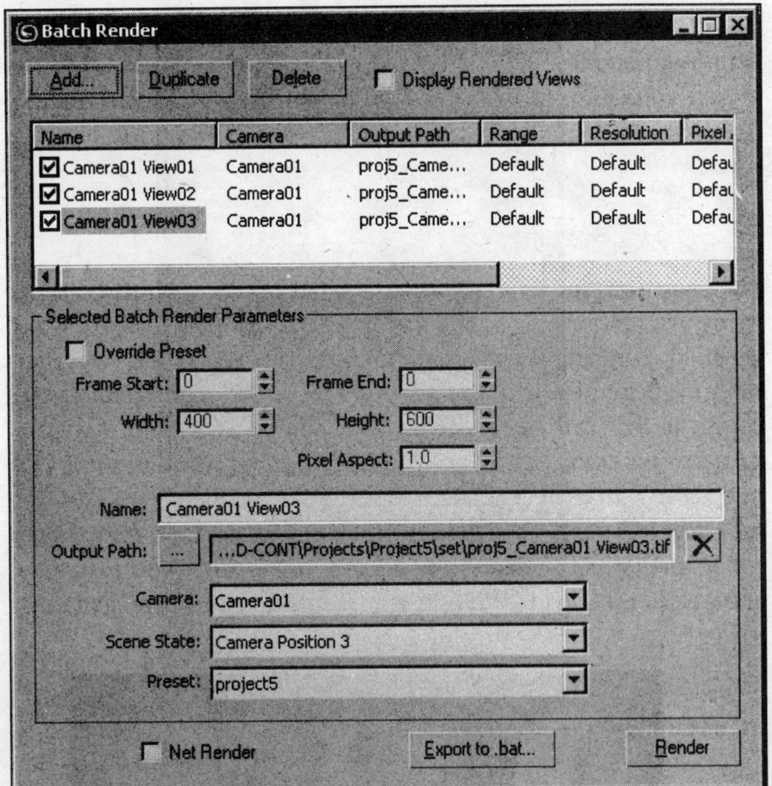

Fig. 2.147. The **Batch Render** dialog box

I'd like to mention the **Export to .bat** button that creates a batch file, which can be started from the command line without loading the graphic interface. This will save about 50 MB of memory.

Rendering to Elements

One of the most powerful tools allowing you to easily obtain photorealistic (and beautiful) images is rendering to elements. What is it? While rendering, the final image is a combination of several layers (e.g., reflection, shadows, etc.) that are computed individually. When a user obtains these layers separately and uses them as he or she likes, this is rendering to elements.

Settings for this process are on the **Render Elements** tab. Fig. 2.148, *a* shows settings I intended to use for finishing the image of the telephone model. Fig. 2.148, *b* shows a series of rendering results displayed as low-resolution images.

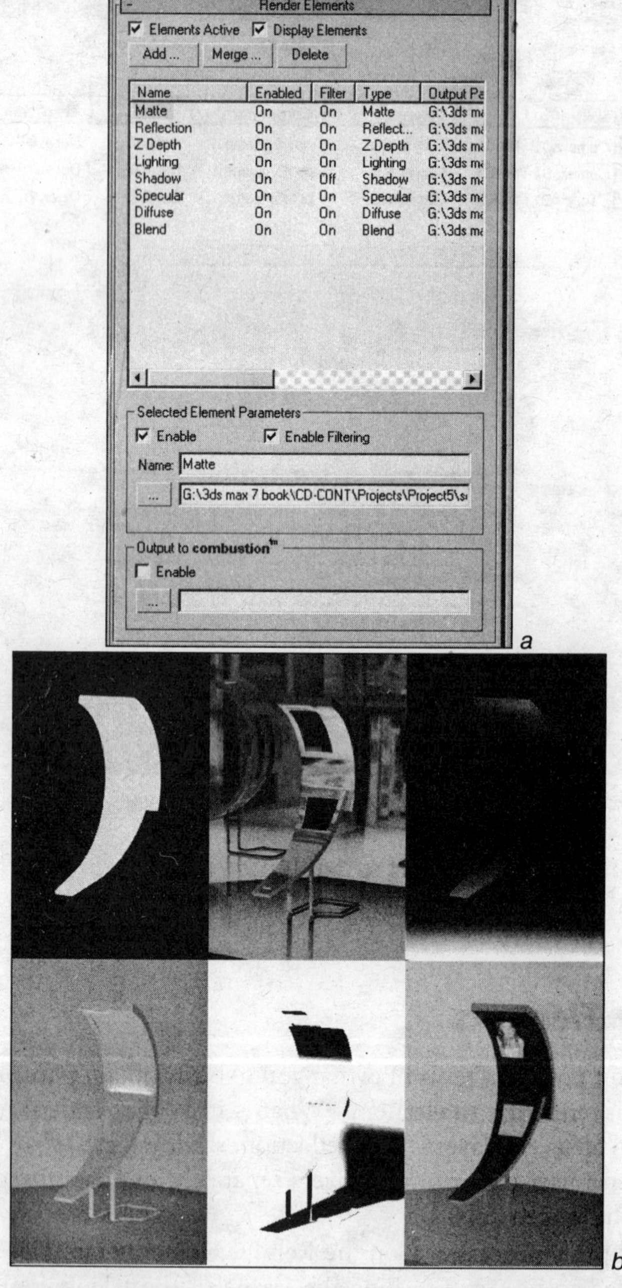

Fig. 2.148. Element settings for telephone moldel rendering *(a)* and elements obtained as a result of rendering *(b)*

The elements are added using the **Add** button. If you have already set saving to a file on the **Common** tab, names are assigned automatically.

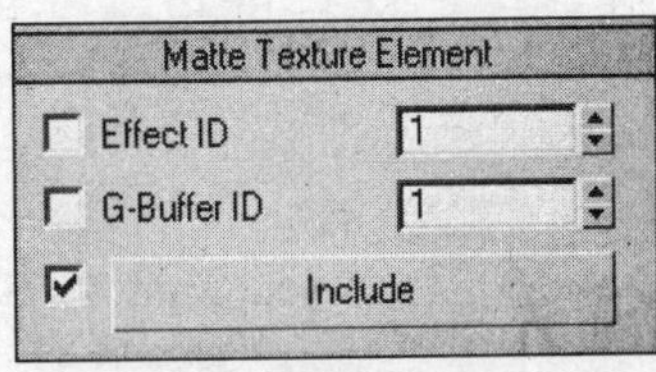

- The **Matte** element allows you to obtain a black-and-white image over the specified objects. You can specify them explicitly or using IDs. When you use a material ID, you can obtain a matte for a part of the object. You can save several such elements for different objects.
- The **Reflection** element allows you to save reflection. Using a combination of this element and a matte, you can blur or paint reflections on a particular object. This element should be applied from the top using the **Screen** method (in Adobe Photoshop).
- The **Z Depth** element allows you to record the scene depth (i.e., the distance from the camera) as a black-and-white gradient. Usually, this element is used as a matte. It has additional settings that set limits to the gradient (Z Min/Z Max). The way I did this wasn't perfect. You can set the limits using the Tape object or the camera's parameter that shows the distance to the target. It makes sense to turn on filtration for all elements.

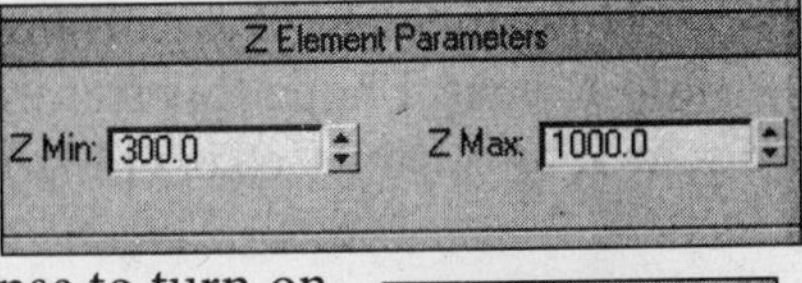

- The **Lighting** element allows you to record direct and indirect lighting and shadows separately.
- The **Shadows** element records a black picture with the alpha channel which carries information about the shadow saturation. In Fig. 2.148, *b*, you can see the result of deletion of the black color using a matte. Shadows are usually added multiplicatively from top, using the alpha channel.

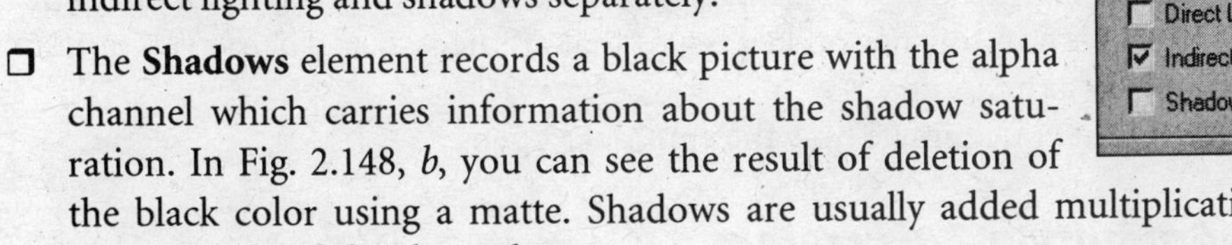

- The **Specular** element records specks of light. It isn't shown in Fig. 2.146, *b* because there are almost no specks in this scene. This element is applied from top, with a screen.

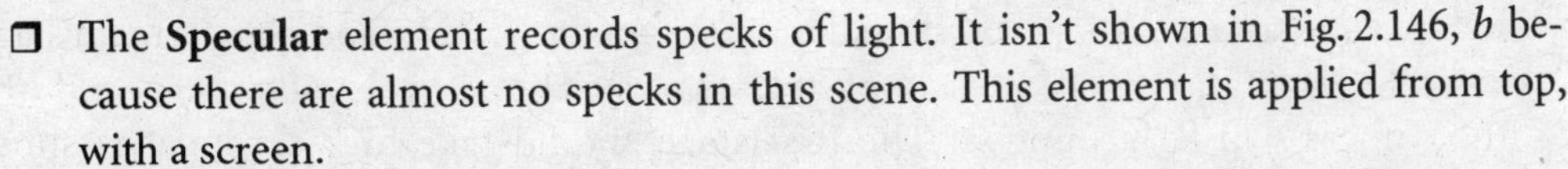

- The **Diffuse** element records the diffuse compo-nent of a material. I didn't check the **Lighting** checkbox, and this was a mistake: the picture was flat. I corrected this by rendering only this element. If I had been more accurate and had saved the photon map and the final gather map, the rendering time would have been minimal.

❒ The **Blend** element allows you to combine the channels. In fact, when all the checkboxes are checked, the final picture is output.

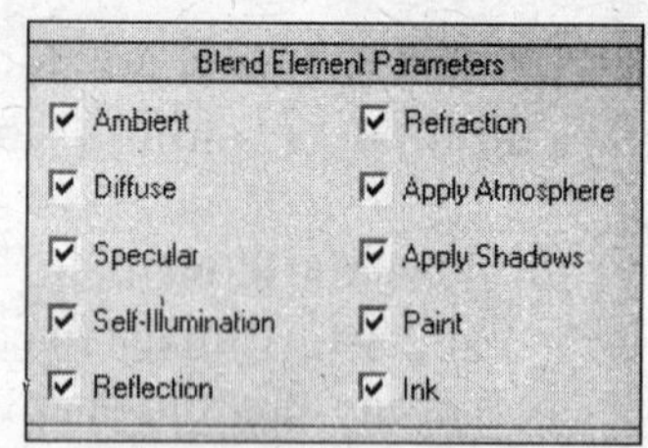

If you want to obtain the final image using mental ray, check the **Render Final Image** checkbox on the **Processing** tab or use **Blend**. On the same tab, you can set a similar process (**Render Passes**) for mental ray. This is a very powerful feature, but it is implemented in 3ds Max improperly.

Render Elements
Render Final Image

You can find the elements in the Projects\Project5\Elements folder on the accompanying CD-ROM and experiment with them.

Finally, there is an option of saving the result of rendering to elements in a file of the Combustion type (*.cws). All the elements should be saved as individual files because Combustion uses them as external Footages.

Unfortunately, it is currently impossible to save layers in a file of Adobe Photoshop format. I hope this feature will be implemented in the next version of 3ds Max, at least by buying Cebas's plug-in PSD Manager.

Animation

Although a 3ds Max designer's main task is to obtain a top-quality static picture, the ability to create simple clips for presentation that he or she modelled is not out of place.

This short section touches on key issues that are necessary when creating a simple but high-quality animation.

I suggest that you animate how the container opens.

Setting Animation Parameters

Before you start animating, you should estimate animation time and plan its main stages.

This animation will consist of two stages: The model will open, and then the camera will fly around it. The first stage should take four seconds, as should the camera's flight.

The initial scene with the model folded is in the Project4-animation-01.max file in the Projects\Project4 folder on the accompanying CD-ROM.

❒ Set animation parameters as shown in Fig. 2.149.

Animation keying and playback controls → **Time Configuration**

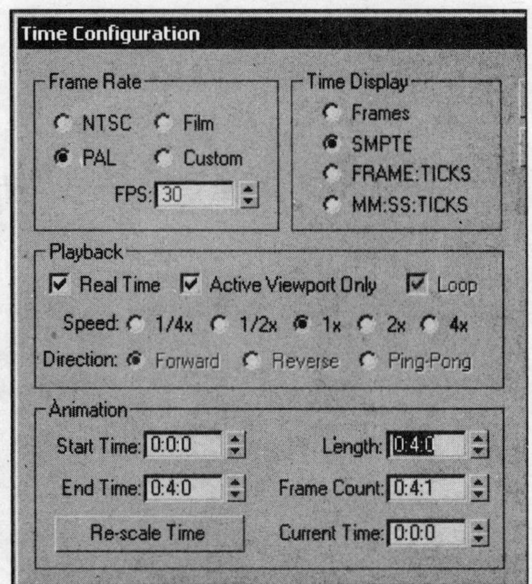

Fig. 2.149. Set animation parameters

Set the **Frame Rate** parameter to a value that conforms to the PAL standard (25 fps).

The display of the frame numbers in the SMPTE format will allow you to see them in a convenient format of *minutes:seconds:frames* (rather than fractions-of-a-second).

Set the duration of the fragment to 4 sec. It isn't wise to set it to 8 sec now; you'll be able to increase it later.

Everything is ready. You can start to create animation. The scene at this stage is in the Project4-animation-02.max file in the Projects\Project4 folder on the accompanying CD-ROM.

Animating Rotation and Motion

To make it easier to animate, ungroup all objects and then link them.

- Ungroup the objects.

  Menu bar → **Group** → **Ungroup**

- In the main toolbar, select the **Select and Link** command.
- Select the top object (Part 3) and drag a rubber ribbon to the Part 2 object while keeping the left mouse button pressed (Fig. 2.150). Note that the ribbon begins at the Part 3 object's pivot point. This is normal.

Fig. 2.150. Linking objects

- Keep on linking. Link Part 2 to Part 1 and link Part 1 to Base.
- To stop linking, press the <Q> key. The right mouse button and the <Esc> key are inactive in this situation.

Check the accuracy of links. Try to move the Base object. The other objects should move accordingly. If this doesn't happen, repeat the procedure.

You have just created a hierarchy, in which the Base object is the predecessor (parent), Part 1 is its descendant (child), and so on, till Part 3. The children in the hierarchy inherit animation of their parents. This is a useful feature, which allows you to save time when setting animation.

Create animation now.

Because you'll change viewing angles, don't create animation in the camera view. The camera is an object like the others, and all its changes will be recorded.

- Move the slider on the time line to a position corresponding to the 15th frame (0:0:15).

- ❒ Click the **Auto Key** button and rotate the Part 1 object clockwise through 90 degrees. It is convenient to turn on the angle snap (using the <A> key) (Fig. 2.151, *a*).

Note two green rectangles on the track bar. These are keys set to rotation.

- ❒ Enter the frame corresponding to the first second and move the objects 20 mm down, that is, put it on the plane (Fig. 2.151, *b*).

Two keys for movement will be set. One of them is in the zero frame. This is incorrect because the movement should start after the rotation ends.

3ds Max offers you several ways to correct this. Let's use the most advanced one.

- ❒ Open the curve editor (Fig. 2.151, *c*).

Quad menu → **Curve Editor**

A list of the parameters of the selected object is on the left. Animated tracks are highlighted in yellow.

- ❒ Select only the tracks for movement and put the initial keys to the 16th frame (Fig. 2.151, *d*).

To move the keys along one axis, keep the <Ctrl> key pressed.

TIP

Now, you should make the movements more precise.

- ❒ Select all tracks for movement and rotation and select all the keys using a box.
- ❒ Change the type of keys to linear (Fig. 2.151, *e*).

Play the animation in the viewport by clicking the **Play Animation** button. Everything is all right.

Because you created the hierarchy, you can animate the other objects by copying the animation controller from the Part 1 object to the other objects. They aren't animated now. Each of them just repeats animation of its parent.

- ❒ In the curve editor, right-click the **Transform** track and select the **Copy** item.
- ❒ In the viewport, select the Part 2 object. Its animation tracks will appear in the editor window.

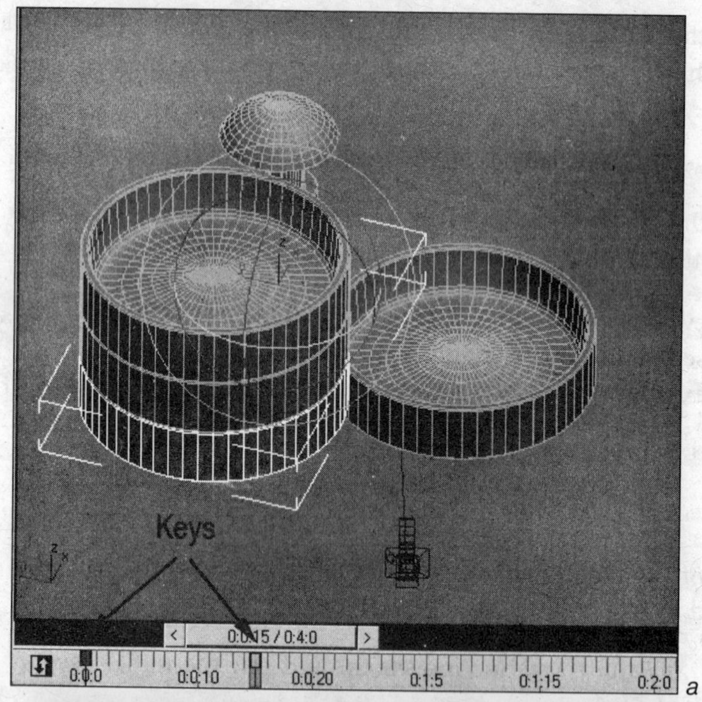

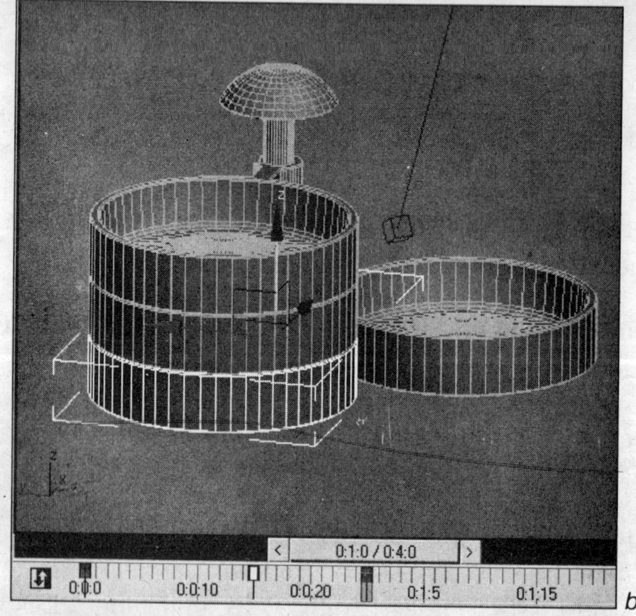

Fig. 2.151, *a* and *b*. Creating animation for unfolding the model

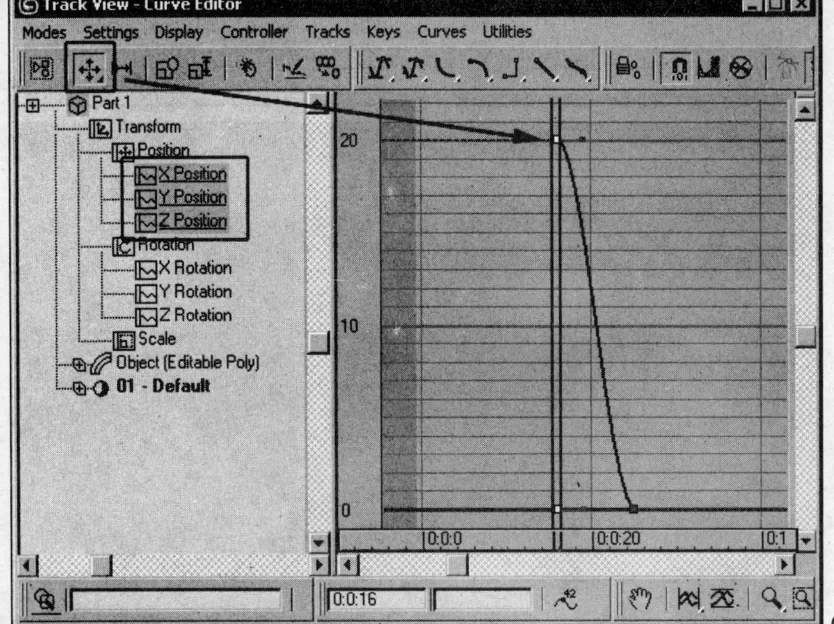

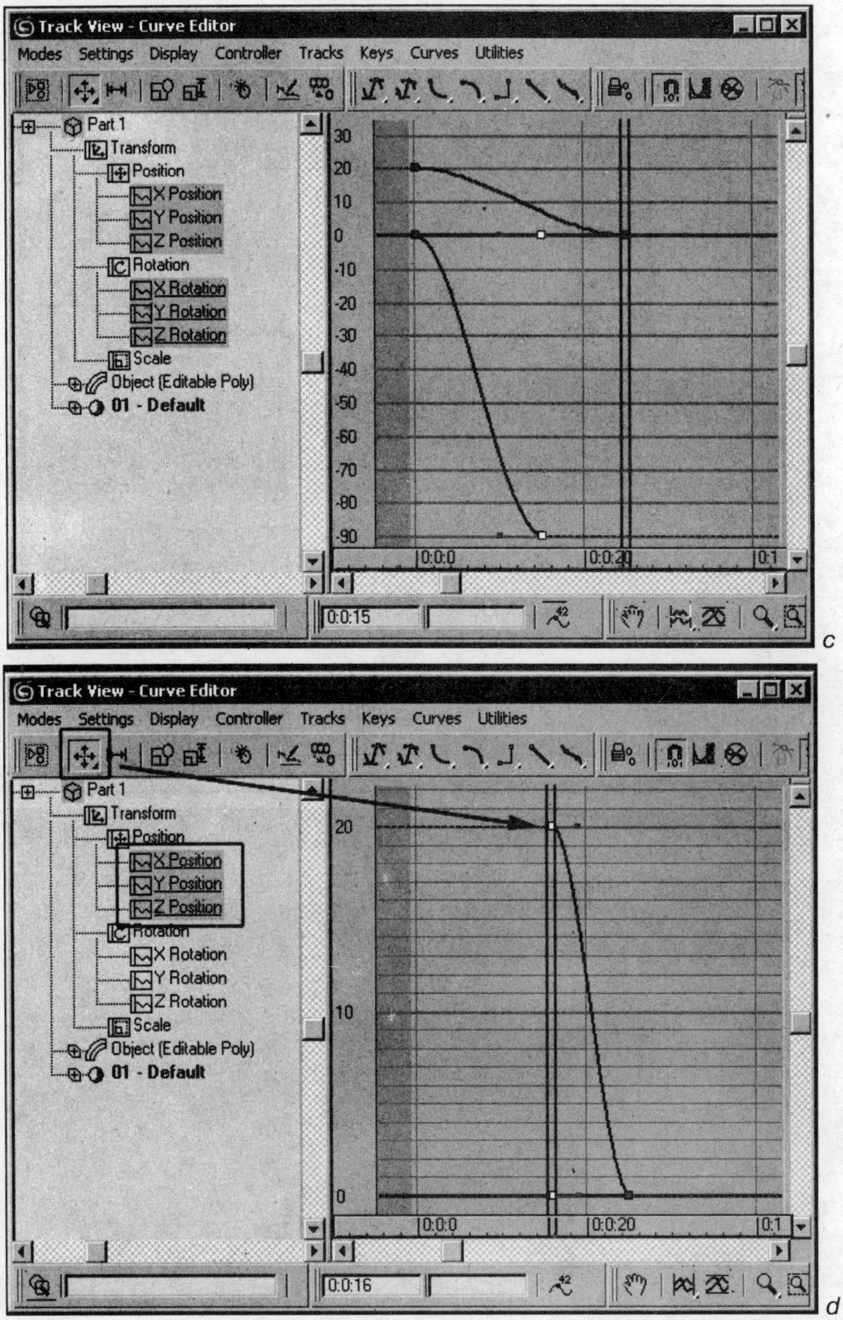

Fig. 2.151, *c* and *d*. Creating animation for unfolding the model

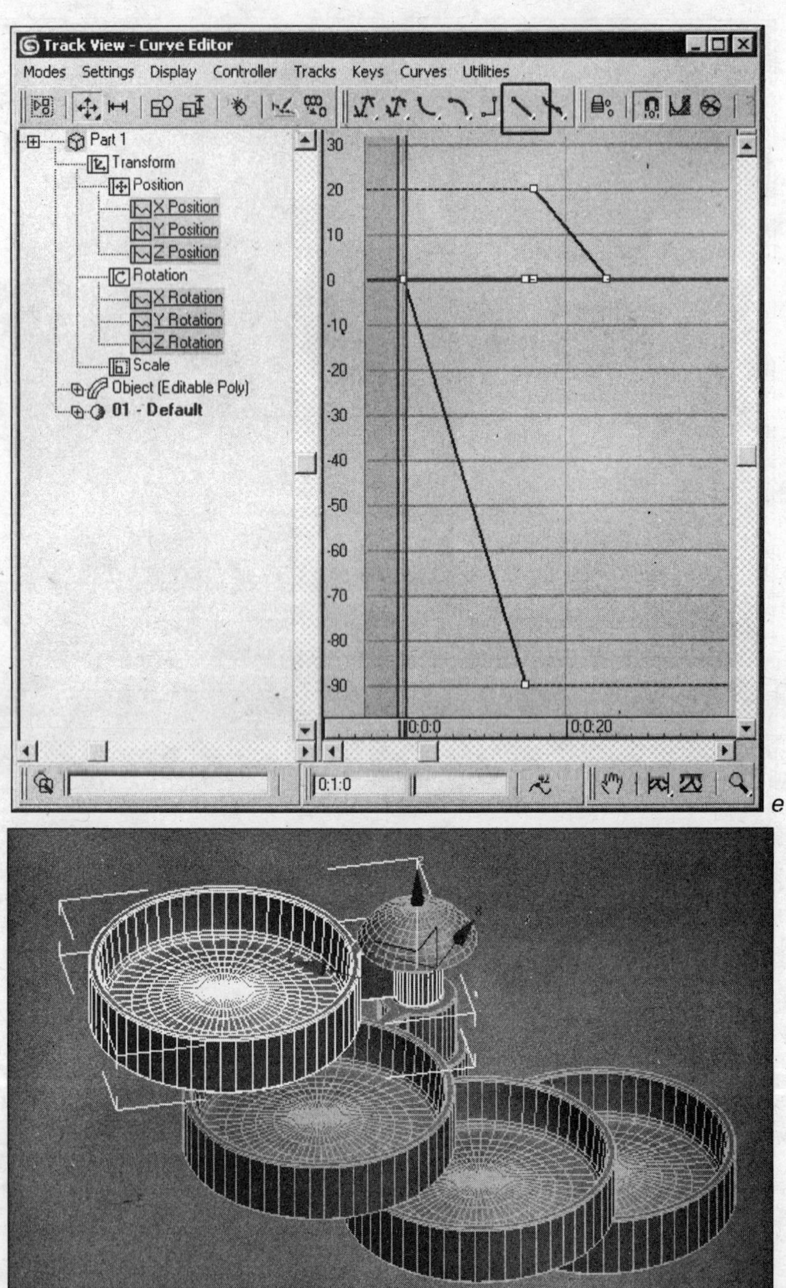

Fig. 2.151, *e* and *f*. Creating animation for unfolding the model

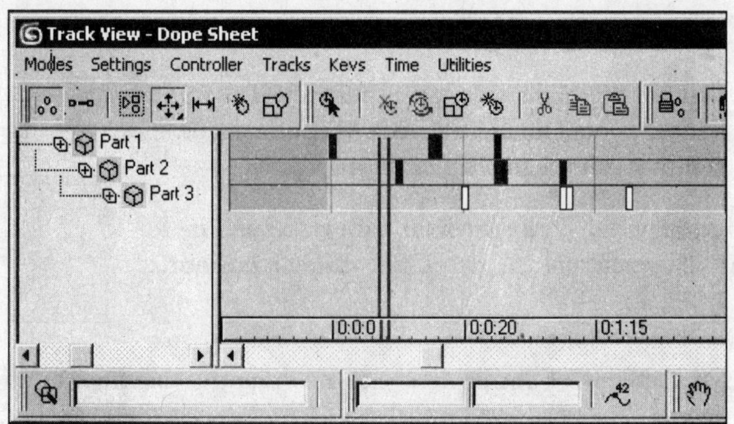

Fig. 2.151, *g*. Creating animation for unfolding the model

- Select the **Transform** track, click with the right mouse button, and paste the animation controller using the **Paste** command using the **Copy** method.

Repeat this procedure with the Part 3 object.
All the objects are moving and rotating simultaneously (Fig. 2.151, *f*).

- Select all three animated objects.
- Switch to the **Dope Sheet** mode for the sake of convenience.

The main menu of the curve editor → **Modes** → **Dope Sheet**

In this mode, the keys are displayed as lines, so it is convenient to move them along the time axis.

- Without expanding the track tree, select all the keys of the Part 2 object and move them ten frames to the right. Select and move the keys of the Part 3 object twenty frames to the right (Fig. 2.151, *g*).

The animation is ready. If you wish to speed or slow it, select all the keys on one track and scale them using the **Scale Keys** command.
My variant is in the Project4-animation-05.max file.

Animating Camera Flight

A showy flight of the camera isn't as simple a task as you might think. It is difficult to avoid unwanted zooms in and out. 3ds Max offers you many options for animation, and I suggest that you use movement along a path.

Interpolation
Steps: 6
Optimize
Adaptive

- In the top view, create a circle with a center in the point, in which the target of the camera is located (Fig. 2.152, *a*).
- Lift it to the level of the camera (Fig. 2.152, *b*).
- In the parameters of the circle, check the **Adaptive** checkbox in the interpolation parameters.
- Select the camera and make it move along the circle.

Menu bar → **Animation** → **Constraints** → **Path Constraint**

Drag a rubber band to the circle and click it.

The camera makes a full turn in four seconds, counter-clockwise, and starts at a wrong place.

You need to address three problems.

- Rotate the circle in the zero frame so that the camera is in the desired place. The camera is linked to the circle, and you can change its position only by changing the position of its path.
- Select the camera and open the curve editor (Fig. 2.152, *c*).

Only one parameter is animated. It is **Percent** that determines the location of the camera on the path.

To change the direction of rotation, change the curve type to the opposite. Move the keys horizontally so that the flight starts after a delay (Fig. 2.152, *d*).

TIP

Type values is input boxes at the bottom of the curve editor (indicated with a rectangle in Fig. 2.152, *d*). This is more precise and convenient.

To stop the movement of an object for a while, add two keys to the curve using the **Add Keys** command.

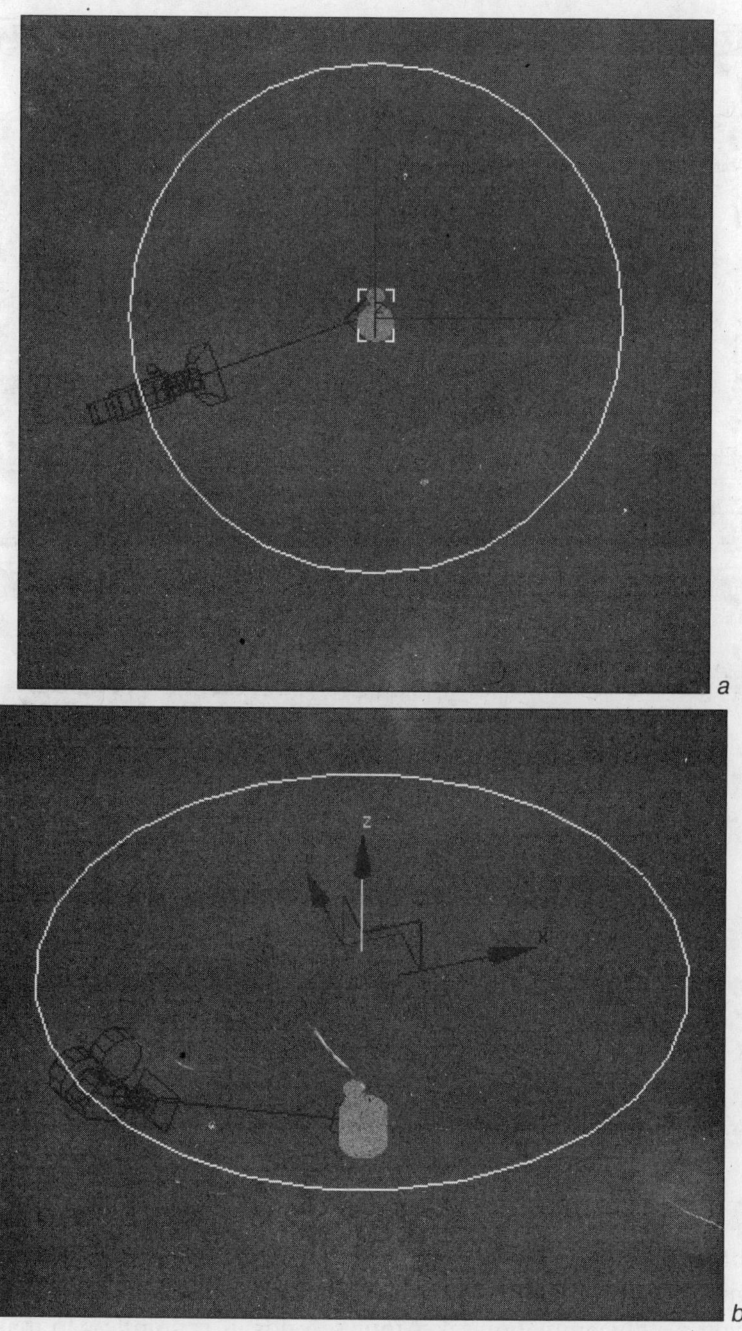

Fig. 2.152, *a* and *b*. Animating the camera flight

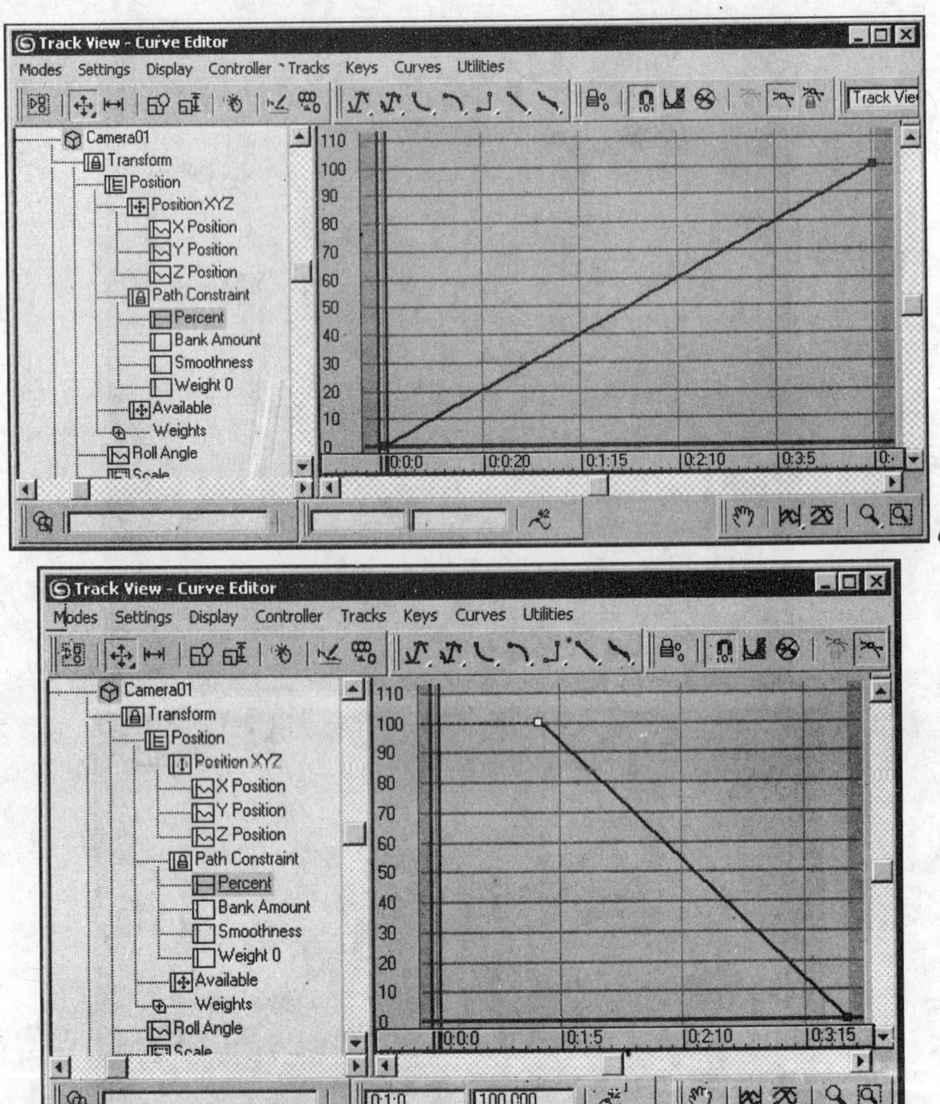

Fig. 2.152, *c* and *d*. Animating the camera flight

Another problem is that the model goes beyond the screen when the camera flies. Cope with this problem on your own. Animate the position of the camera target.

As you see, the animation takes four seconds. It is pointless to make it longer because this would break the tempo.

My variant is in the Project4-animation-Final.max file.

Here are a few recommendations concerning animation rendering.

- First, don't save the animation in an AVI or MOV file immediately. Save it in a file sequence, for example, in the TGA format. You'll be able to montage the clip later, using RAM Player built into 3ds Max, for example. Save your time!
- If you're using indirect illumination, you cannot use saved photon maps and the final gather map. You'll have to compute them in each new frame. I recommend that you save your time by sticking to the following procedure. Render until the frame, in which the animation of objects ends, and continually save the photon map and the final gather map in a file. Then use these files to render the clip starting the moment, at which the animation ends.
- You can turn on the motion blur effect to obtain a realistic animation. However, be aware that this can significantly increase computation time. To improve this effect, you'll have to increase the antialiasing parameters. This will also slow rendering.
- If you create clips often, I recommend that you master a video montage package or, better yet, a composing package (such as Autodesk Combusiton and Adobe After Effects). This will increase your performance and the quality of your animations many times.

Chapter 3

Modeling and Rendering an Interior

In this chapter, you will:

- Create an interior using drafts.
- Model and place furniture, decorations, curtains, lamps, and pictures.
- Create materials for all the objects in the scene, and assign these materials to the objects.
- Create two variants of lighting — daylight and candlelight.
- Render the interior from various angles and create a complete panorama in QTVR format.

This project was developed by Valery Kuleshov whose name should be familiar to you from previous projects. He is a Lecturer in the Design Department at the Moscow State Institute of Electronic Technology. Valery kindly gave me the materials of the project.

A draft is shown in Fig. 3.1. If you question the results of the project, look at Fig. 3.1, which displays photos of a "live" interior during the process of construction. Note that such photos are useful in your own work. The part you'll model is indicated by the thick dashed line. I will demonstrate to you only the living-room and the kitchen, since these will be enough to help you understand the main ideas.

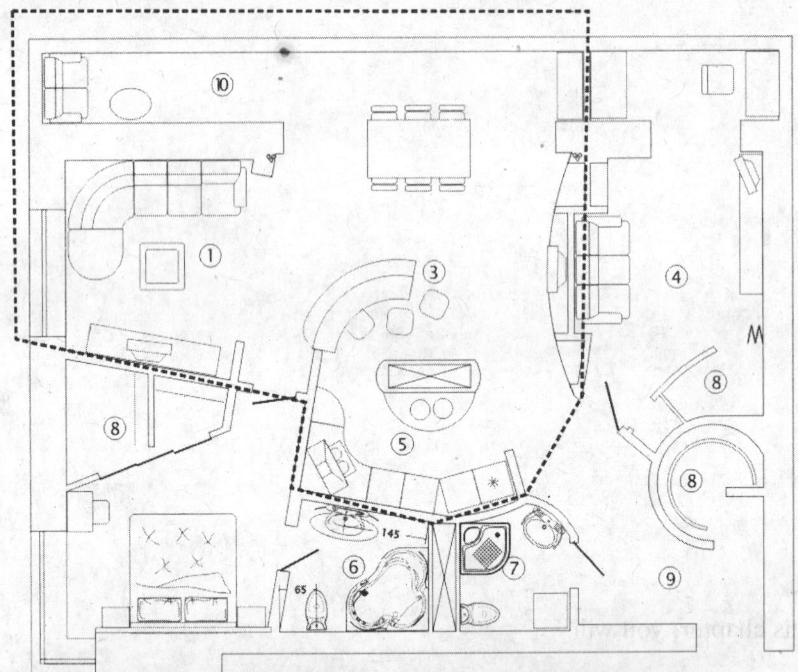

Fig. 3.1. Draft of the interior

Fig. 3.2, *a*. Photos of the interior being constructed

b

c

Fig. 3.2, *b* and *c*. Photos of the interior being constructed

Modeling

Preliminary Notes

Before you start modeling, I'd like to answer these frequently asked questions: "Why do I need to model things from scratch in 3ds Max while models created in other applications such as Autodesk Architectural Desktop are available? Wouldn't it be simpler to transfer the models to 3ds Max and use them?" Well, this is true. You should do so with certain objects in certain projects, especially since the developers of 3ds Max and Autodesk VIZ continually improve tools for interaction between the two packages. For example, 3ds Max 7.5 and VIZ 2006 support DWF format. However, such an approach would also have drawbacks. As a rule, geometry of objects exported from DXF and DWG files requires editing. An image that would work as a draft may be unsuitable for rendering since 3ds Max is used primarily for obtaining a photorealistic picture. Conversely, imported objects are often overloaded with details. For example, a detailed door handle can take up an area of 3 × 5 pixels on the final image. However, you can use a simpler model in this case. In addition, imported objects often have overlapped surfaces and vertices that are not welded. This leads to incorrect results in rendering, especially when you use global illumination algorithms. Materials require further elaboration, and in addition, it is difficult to apply amps correctly because of the flaws in the geometry of the objects.

Valery created this project on CorelDraw and 3ds Max by choice. So there are no DXF models.

It's important to remember that 3ds Max isn't a CAD package, although it allows you to model with high precision. The result of your work in 3ds Max is a beautiful picture or a video clip rather than design documentation. However, you shouldn't model sloppily since the result will be flawed. If you have a signed design documentation, don't try to improve it during modeling. The model should comply with the specification. You can take away a wall that gets in the way, but only if nobody notices it. By the way, Valery warned me not to try improving his project.

Setting 3ds Max

It the previous projects, the scenes were arranged without much order from an engineer's point of view. In this project, this would be unacceptable because the scene should include many objects, and a strict classification is needed. So a few additional settings are required. You can make them quickly by using the DesignVIZ.mentalray preset. Select it using the Custom UI and Defaults Switcher (Fig. 3.3).

Menu bar → **Customize** → **Custom UI and Defaults Switcher**

Select **DesignVIZ.mentalray** and click the **Set** button at the window bottom.

Restart 3ds Max.

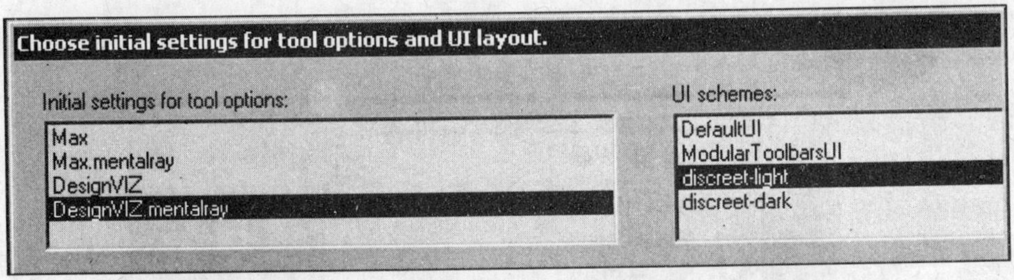

Fig. 3.3. The dialog box for the default user interface settings

In this dialog box, you can obtain comprehensive information about the current settings. I'll address just a few of them.

Unlike in the previous projects, I recommend that you use layers. This method for arranging the scene is widely used in other packages. It was introduced in 3ds max version 5 and improved in version 6. It quickly became popular with AutoCAD users because the **Layer Manager** window looks much like a similar tool in the AutoCAD family packages (Fig. 3.4, *a*). You can open this window with an appropriate button on the toolbar or with the menu bar.

Menu bar → **Tools** → **Layer Manager**

In addition to the **Layer Manager** window, you can use the **Layers** floating panel. Although it is less convenient and doesn't allow you to work with objects inside a layer, it takes up less space (Fig. 3.4, *b*). I'll tell you how to introduce it into the main interface later in this chapter.

One of the settings (Layers: all objects are created "By Layer") allows you to use the advantages of layers: You can hide, freeze, or exclude from rendering all the objects on a layer.

There are a few fine points that you should remember when working with layers:

- When a layer is created, it includes all selected objects. So if you want to create an empty layer, unselect all the objects in the scene.

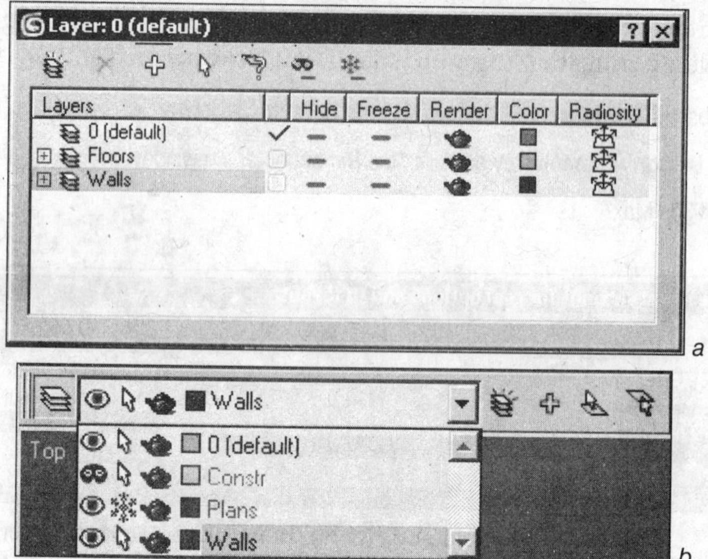

Fig. 3.4. The **Layer Manager** window (a) and the **Layers** floating panel (b)

- The layer can be active even when it is hidden or frozen. If you try to create objects in such a layer, they will be created, but you won't see them until you unhide the layer. Although this is a strange feature, it can be useful. For example, you can select an object on a frozen layer in the **Layer Manager** window and move it without unfreezing it.
- The fact that the user cannot delete a non-empty layer or an empty but inactive layer seems illogical and is inconvenient. This feature, however, is borrowed from AutoCAD. Perhaps, it is convenient for the developers.
- Loading objects from other files using the **Merge** command maintains information about the layer. That is, if an object is created in the zero layer (e.g., this is the case when layers aren't used), it will be loaded onto this layer, rather than the currently-active layer. The **Import** command loads objects onto the active layer.
- Object on a layer can be hidden or frozen individually. The **Unhide All** and **Unhide by Name** commands selected for objects in a hidden layer opens a dialog box (Fig. 3.5) that asks you to choose whether you want to unhide the entire layer (or all the layers) or just a particular object in the hidden layer. In the second case, however, the object will remain hidden because the entire layer is hidden.

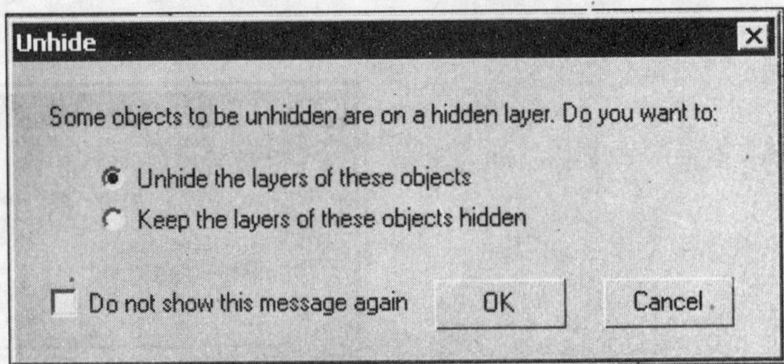

Fig. 3.5. The dialog box opened with the **Unhide All** command when there are hidden layers

- There is an interesting setting for light sources. If the layer that contains it isn't rendered, the light sources aren't rendered either. In other words, they are off. You'll use this feature by placing daylight and candlelight sources on different layers.

The default material in the material editor is Architectural. It is much simpler to set than the Standard material. In addition, the material editor includes the **Propagate Material to Instances** checkbox among its options. When checked, it allows you to assign a material simultaneously to all instances of an object.

Finally, there is an important and unordinary feature. Because many light sources are considered in interior scenes, and 3ds Max can show only the first eight light sources in the viewports, it is sometimes impossible to work in the shaded mode. This is why the default lighting is set in the viewports, just in case.

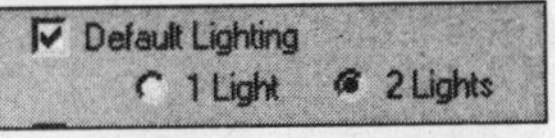

The viewport right-click menu → **Configure** → ... → the **Default Lighting** or the <Ctrl>+<L> shortcut

Setting the System Units and the Grid Spacing

Start the project by setting the system units.

- Select millimeters as system units. Set **Distance from Origin** to 10 m (Fig. 3.6, *a*).

Menu bar → **Customize** → **Units Setup** → **System Unit Setup**

- Select centimeters as displayed units (Fig. 3.6, *b*). Why? Because fewer zeroes will be displayed.

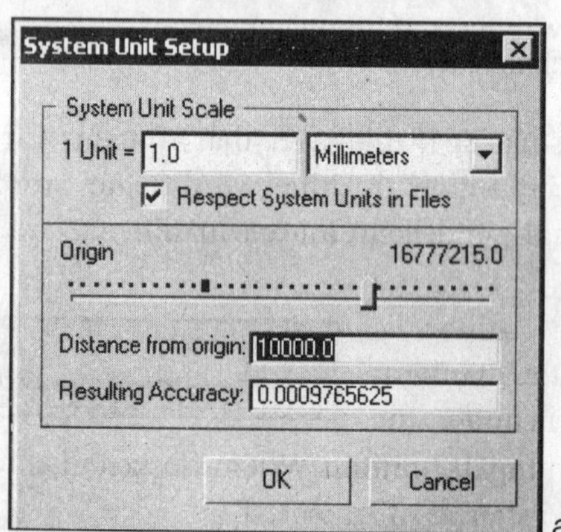

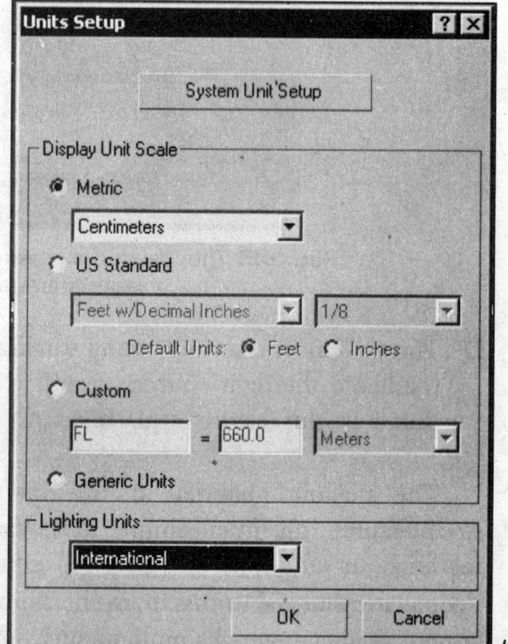

Fig. 3.6. Setting system units

Fig. 3.7. Setting the grid spacing

You might be wondering whether you can select other system units such as inches. Of course, you can. 3ds Max will automatically compute the displayed units from the system units. However, don't change them when working.

- Set the grid spacing to 10 cm (Fig. 3.7). You could do without the grid in this project, but nevertheless I advise you to set it.

Menu bar → **Customize** → **Grid and Snaps Settings**

Hide the **reactor** toolbar because you're unlikely to use it in this project. To do this, "tear off" the toolbar and hide it by clicking the cross in the upper right corner. As for the **Snaps**, **Axis Constraints**, and **Layers** toolbars, you should have them on hand.

- Unhide floating toolbars and "fasten" the **Snaps**, **Axis Constraints**, and **Layers** toolbars by dragging them to the main toolbar. Hide unnecessary toolbars.

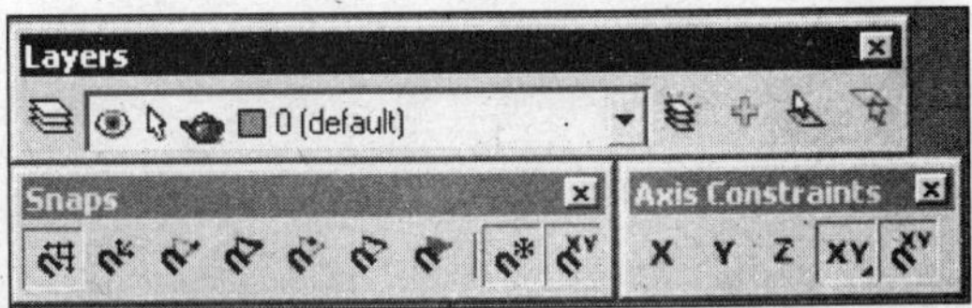

Menu bar → **Customize** → **Show UI** → **Show Floating Toolbars**

If you want to use the current interface in other projects, save it.

Menu bar → **Customize** → **Save Custom UI Scheme**

Modeling the Walls

There are several ways for modeling the walls, and a few of them are described later in this section. However, I'd like to describe the most effective and flexible method first, since it is the most suitable for this project.

Because you have a draft in the vector format, it wouldn't be wise to ignore it. You'll load and outline it using snaps.

It often happens that you have to introduce changes to a project. This is why it would be convenient to model the walls separately from the ceiling and the floor. Also, be sure to model the load-bearing walls separately from the nonloadbearing partitions. This will help you quickly re-plan the interior, which is necessary when you have many clients.

The thickness of the walls and the ceiling will allow you to avoid an undesirable effect that could take place when creating daylight lighting. I am referring to the glow that appears in the corners because shadows are created with a small bias from the object. This is especially crucial for shadows of the Shadow Map type when you use the standard renderer.

❐ Create two additional layers: **Plans** and **Walls**.

The **Layers** toolbar *or* the **Layer Manager** window→ **Create Layer**

❐ Make the **Plans** layer active. To do this, put a check in the column to the right of the layer's name in the **Layer Manager** window and select the layer in the drop-down menu of the **Layers** toolbar.

NOTE

From now on, I'll refer only to the **Layer Manager** window because it is the most convenient in my opinion. Choose the tool you like best.

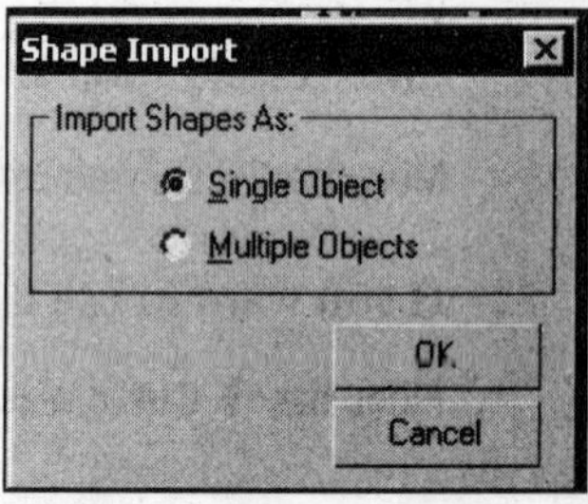

❐ Import the Walls-plan.ai file as a single object from the Chapter 3\AI folder on the accompanying CD-ROM to 3ds Max.

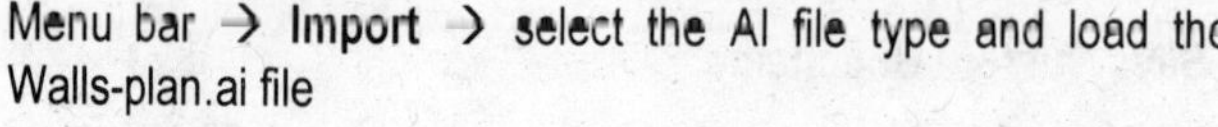

Menu bar → **Import** → select the AI file type and load the Walls-plan.ai file

Regardless of the view you used, the object will be placed horizontally.

❐ Rename the object, for example, the Walls-plan.

TIP

You can load the other files, Floors-plan.ai, Ceiling-plan.ai, and Lighting-plan.ai, if you wish. In my opinion, however, it is best to load a file before you start to model the corresponding set of objects.

These plans are drawn at scale 1:20. Therefore, you should scale them 20 times.

❐ Enter the scale mode (the <R> key) and enter 2000% into the input box at the bottom of the window.

❐ Scale the views in the viewports so that you can see the entire selected object (the <Z> key).

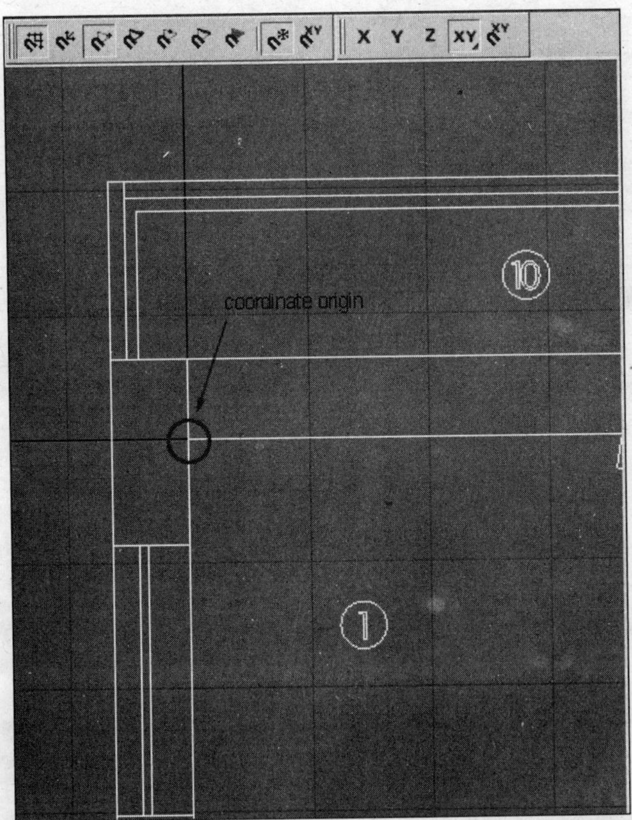

Fig. 3.8. The best position of the plan relative to the coordinate origin

It makes sense to move the plan so that one of its corners is in the origin of coordinates (Fig. 3.8). To do this, enable snaps to grid points and vertices, turn on the snap mode (the <S> key), and move the object (the <W> key) by grabbing its vertex.

- Freeze the Plans layer entirely or just the Walls-plan object, and make the Walls layer active.
- Set snapping to vertices only and enable snapping to objects.
- Enable snaps (the <S> key) and create closed splines for the walls (Fig. 3.9, *a*) and partitions (Fig. 3.9, *b*) by creating lines in the top or perspective view and snapping to vertices.

Menu bar → **Create** → **Shape** → **Line**

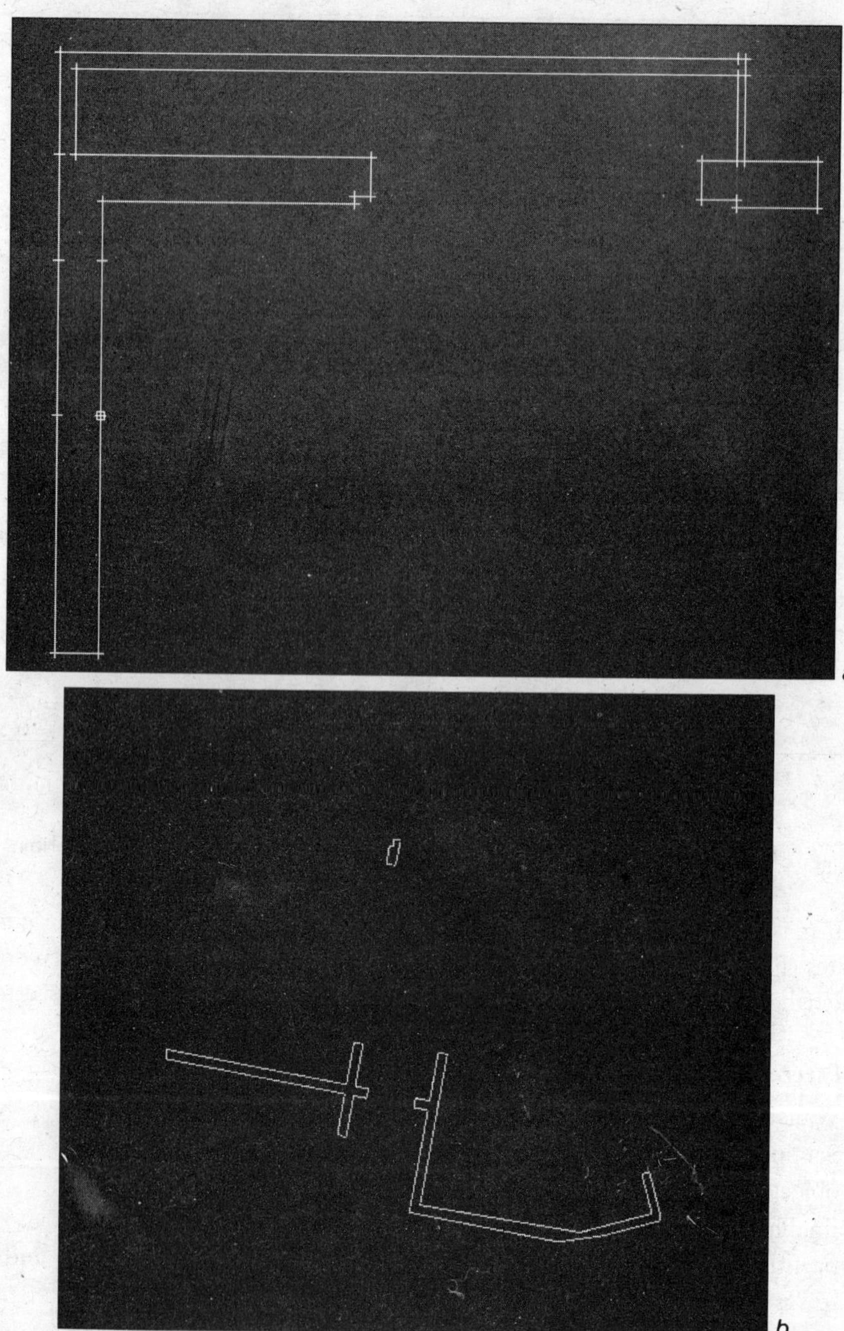

Fig. 3.9. The outline of the walls (*a*) and partitions (*b*)

Click with the left mouse button; don't drag, otherwise the vertex will change its type to Bezier. If you made such a mistake, don't stop creating the outline. You'll be able to change the vertex type to Corner in the modify mode after you open the quad menu with the right mouse button.

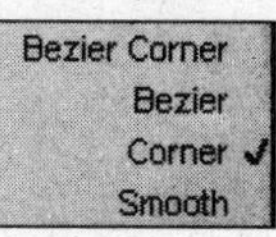

Don't forget window openings in the walls. If you didn't create them, add necessary vertices in the modify mode with the **Refine** command. Note that the kitchen wall has a decorative step, so create it.

If you go beyond the window boundaries when creating the outline, pan or scale the view using the <I>, <[>, and <]> keys. Don't use the middle mouse button. If you interrupted the line before you completed the outline, start a new line where you finished the previous. After you create all outlines, attach them to one outline and weld to vertices using the **Attach** and **Weld** commands, respectively.

It is important that the partitions touch the walls or even penetrate them. Don't leave gaps between the partitions and the walls.

- ❒ Rename the objects Main Wall # and Thin Wall #, enumerated respectively.

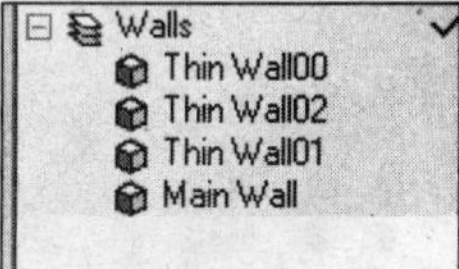

To rename multiple objects quickly, use the **Rename Objects** tool (Fig. 3.10).

Menu bar → **Tools** → **Rename Objects**

Select the objects you want to rename, enter a base name and check the **Numbered** checkbox.

- ❒ Select the Main Wall object and extrude the outlines to the height of the ceiling (3 m) with three crossing using the **Extrude** modifier (Fig. 3.11). If you do everything correctly, you'll obtain outlines for the window openings; however, at the wrong height.

Menu bar → **Modifiers** → **Mesh Editing** → **Extrude**

You can uncheck the **Cap Start** and **Cap End** checkboxes to simplify the scene. You can do this because nobody will see the top and bottom of the walls. However, if you are planning to present the room from above, without the ceiling (e.g., to show the furniture), don't uncheck these checkboxes.

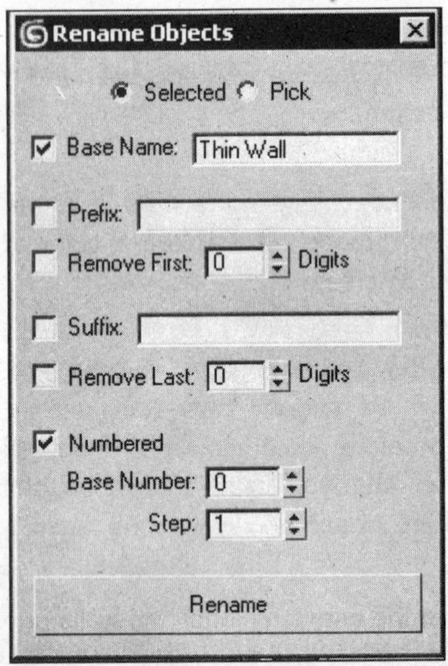

Fig. 3.10. The **Rename Objects** interface

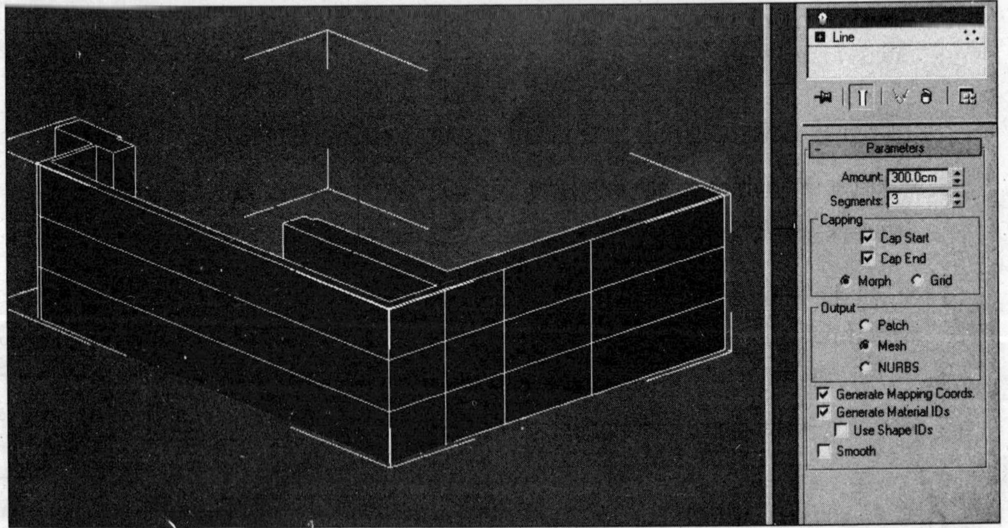

Fig. 3.11. Extruding the walls

Make the window opening.

- Apply the **Edit Poly** modifier.

  Menu bar → **Modifiers** → **Mesh Editing** → **Edit Poly**

- Select the polygons of the window opening (Fig. 3.12, *a*) from both sides, and execute the **Bridge** command (Fig. 3.12, *b*).

  Pop-up menu → **Bridge**

TIP

To avoid mistakes when selecting, check the **Ignore Backfacing** checkbox.

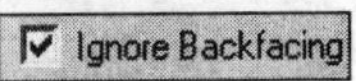

- Select the bottom polygon of the window opening, enter the move mode and enter the height above the floor (Z = 80 cm) into the input box at the bottom of the window (Fig. 3.12, *c*). Set the top polygon of the window opening to the required height (Z = 270 cm) in the same way. The window opening is ready (Fig. 3.12, *d*).

Fig. 3.12, *a*. Modeling the window opening

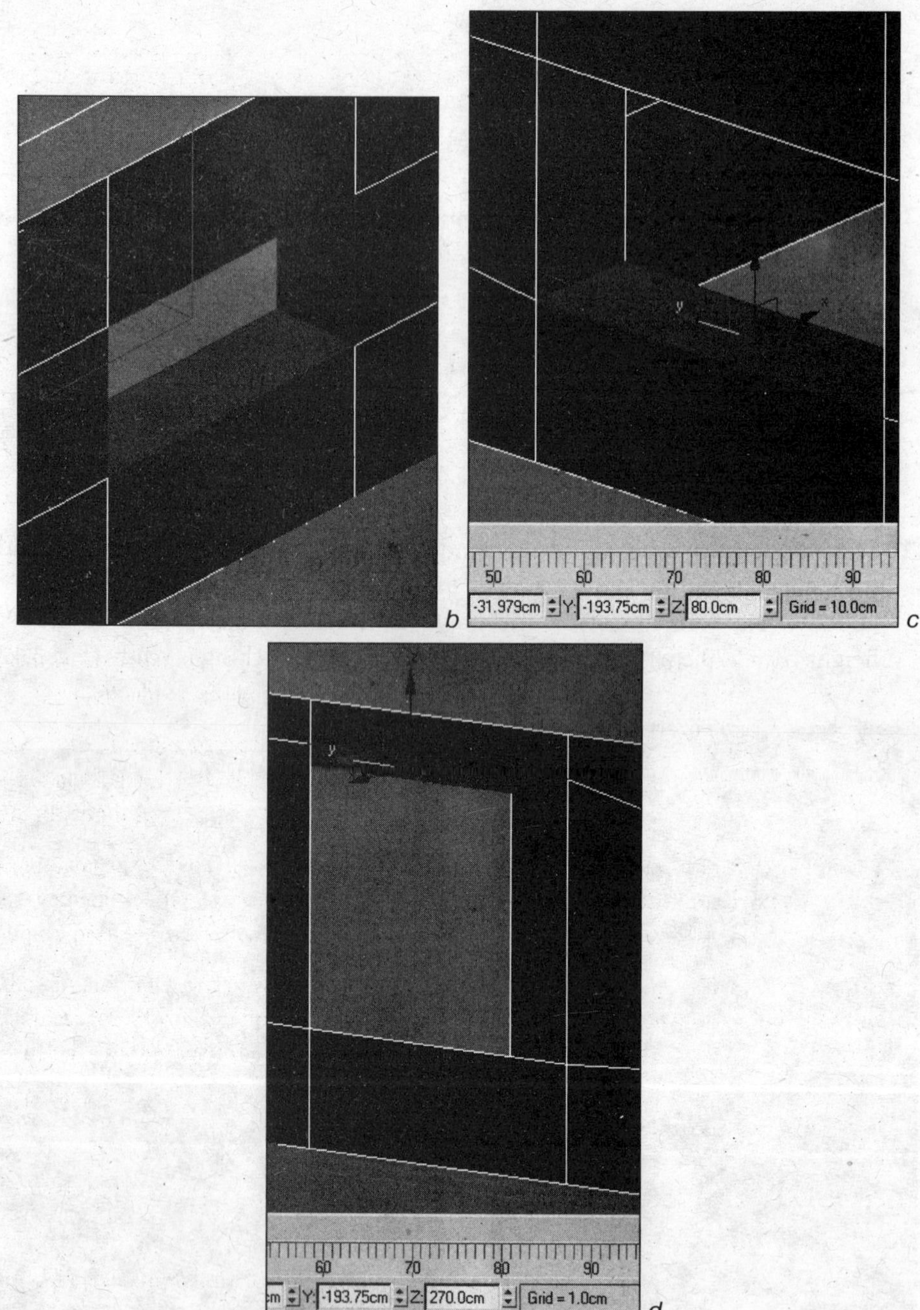

Fig. 3.12, *b*–*d*. Modeling the window opening

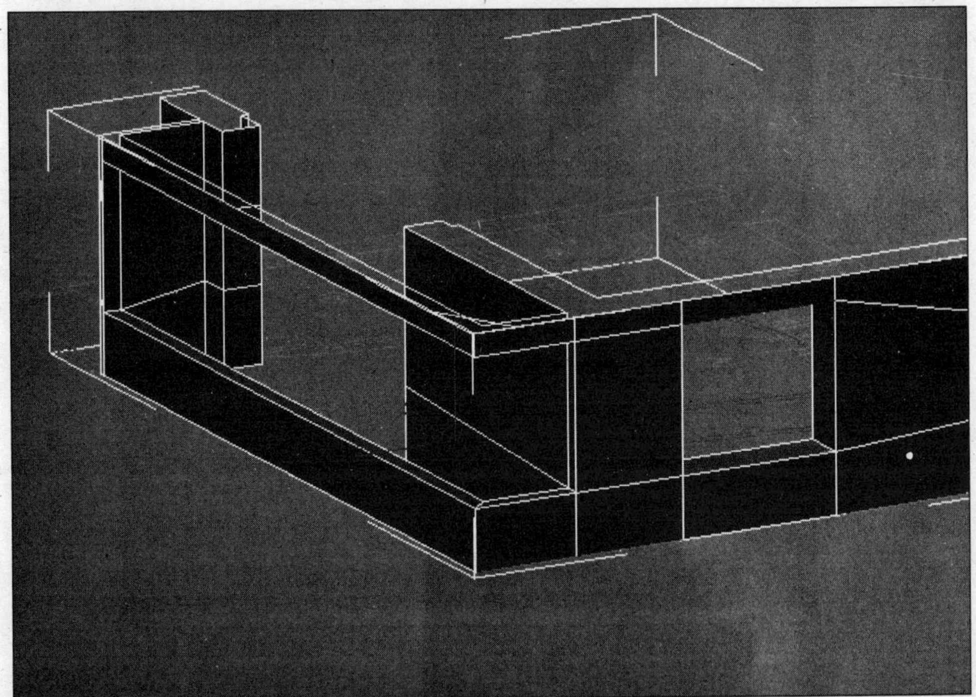

Fig. 3.13. The window opening for the loggia

- Create the window opening for the loggia (Fig. 3.13).

Apply the **Extrude** modifier to the partitions. However, use two vertical segments (Fig. 3.14, *a*).

TIP

Hide the Main Wall object using the appropriate button in the **Layer Manager** window.

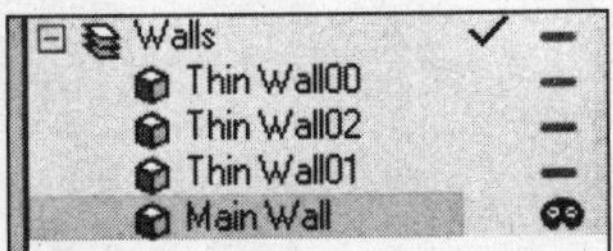

- Apply the **Edit Poly** modifier to the partition, select the necessary vertices, and specify the necessary height above the floor (Z = 137 cm). (Fig. 3.14, *b*, indicated by number 1).
- Use the **Cut** command to join the vertices at the partition top (Fig. 3.14, *b*, indicated by number 2).

a

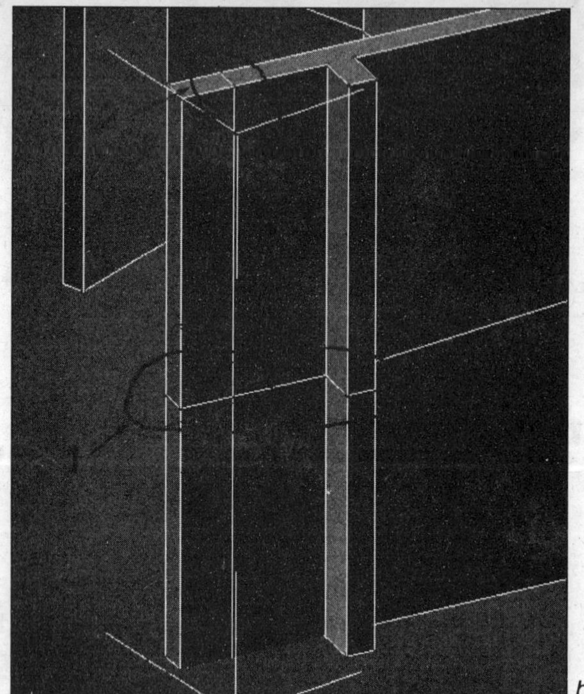

b

Fig. 3.14, *a* and *b*. Modeling the partitions

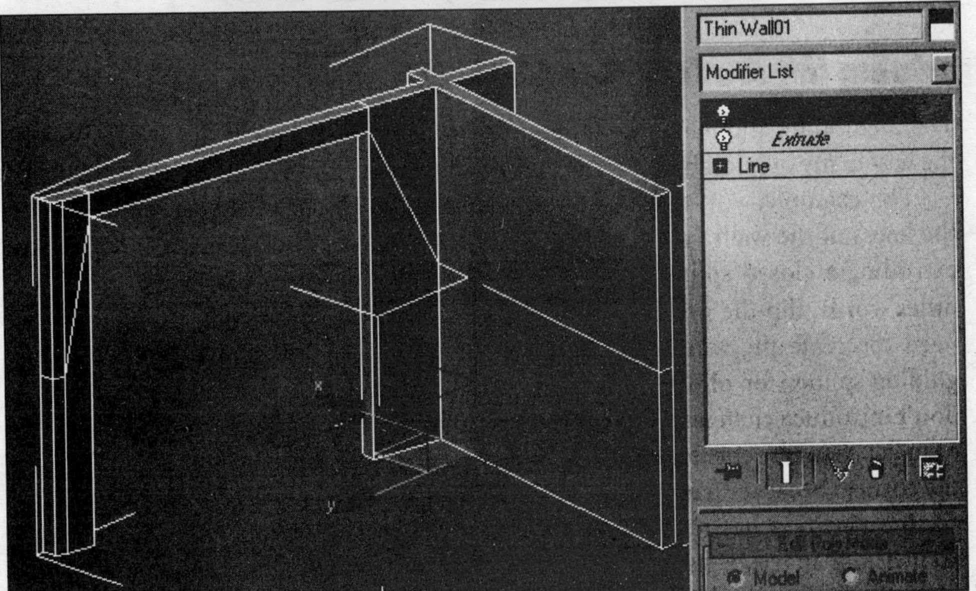

Fig. 3.14, *c* and *d*. Modeling the partitions

- Delete unnecessary polygons and create missing ones, making the round of the vertices counterclockwise (Fig. 3.14, *c*).

  Pop-up menu → **Create**

To create a bulkhead under the ceiling (Fig. 3.14, *d*), apply the **Edit Poly** modifier to one object and attach the other to it.

If you delete the **Edit Poly** modifier from the modifier stack later, the attached object will be deleted.

Lift the appropriate vertices or edges to the required length of 270 cm and join the polygons using the **Bridge** command. You don't need to select the polygons beforehand. Just select the **Bridge** command and drag the rubber band from one polygon to another.

The result of my work at this stage is in the INTERIOR_01.MAX file in the PROJECTS/PROJECT_INTERIOR folder on the accompanying CD-ROM.

Modeling the Walls: Other Methods

The method for modeling the walls and partitions described in the previous section is the best in my opinion because it is quick and precise. However, there are other methods.

For example, you can create only internal surfaces without taking care of the thickness of the walls. This is done in the same way as the exterior in *Chapter 4* — by extruding a closed spline. However, then you should turn the model inside out, in other words, flip the normals using the **Flip Normals** command. After that, you only need to create the window openings, and the walls, the ceiling, the floor, and the guiding splines for plinths and cornices will be ready. This method is suitable if you don't introduce changes to your project. However, this is rarely the case, and you have to make changes repeatedly. In addition, when simulating, the illumination appears in the corners because shadows are created with a small bias from the object.

If a partition has many decorative holes, or if window openings or doorways are archwise, it makes sense to create this partition individually. Create a closed spline with all the required holes (Fig. 3.15, *a*) and extrude it to the required thickness (Fig. 3.15, *b*). When all the walls are ready, create a room from them. Just remember that the surfaces should be coplanar and shouldn't cross.

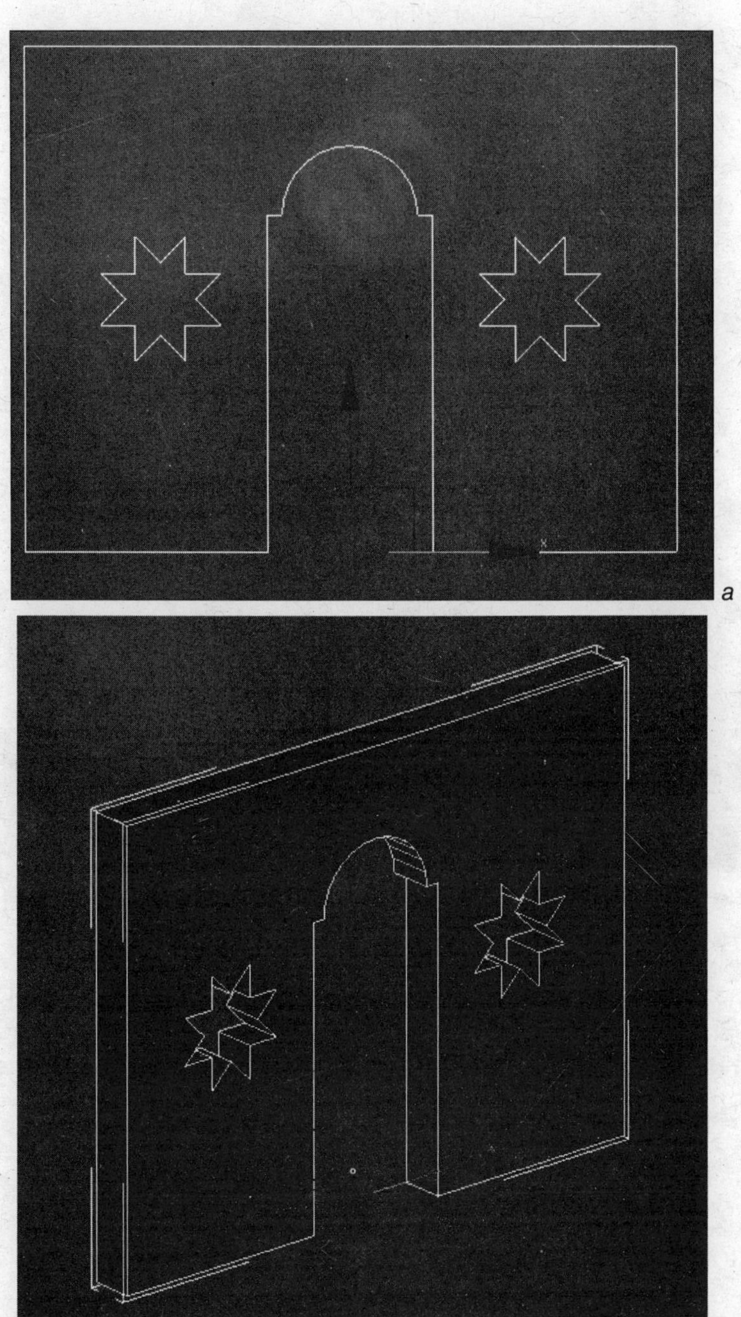

Fig. 3.15. A partition with complicated holes

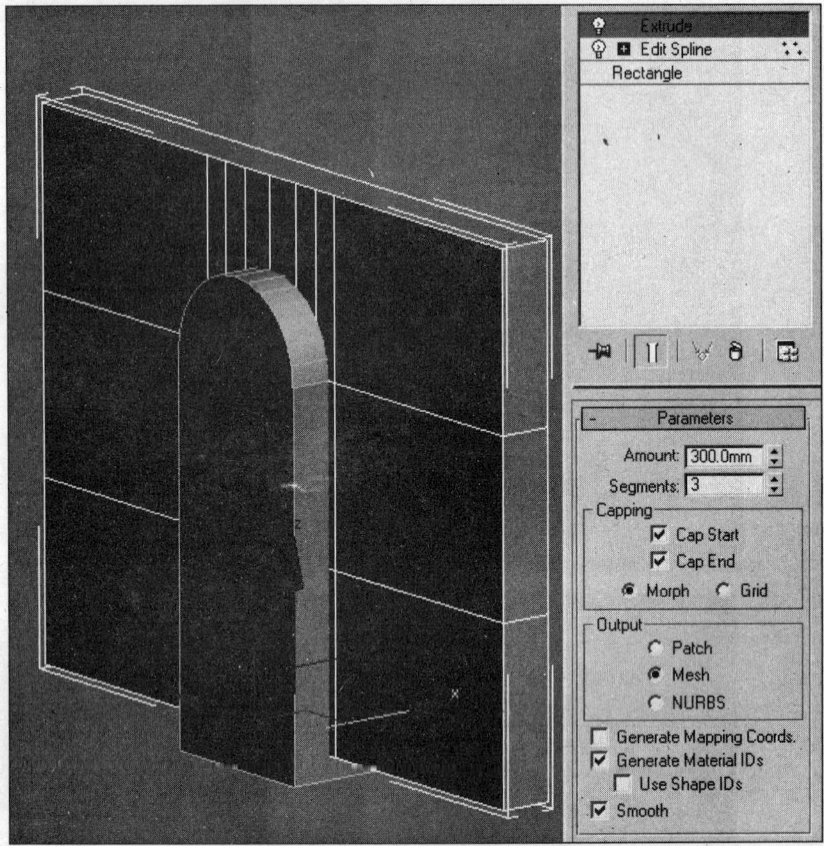

Fig. 3.16. Preparing the objects for the Boolean operations to create holes

Avoid using the Boolean operations. If you cannot do without them, try to prepare the walls geometry for the Boolean operations. For example, create a few vertices for the arch shown in Fig. 3.16 or cut the polygons using the **Cut** command. When creating several doorways or window openings, it is best to do this in one operation. Attach the objects to one of them using the **Attach** command.

Modeling a Rack with a Niche for a TV Set

The draft of this construction is shown in Fig. 17. It isn't as complicated as it seems. All the necessary information is available on this draft and on the **Plans** layer. At the beginning of this project, I promised that you would model only a fragment of the interior. However, I suggest that you model this construction completely.

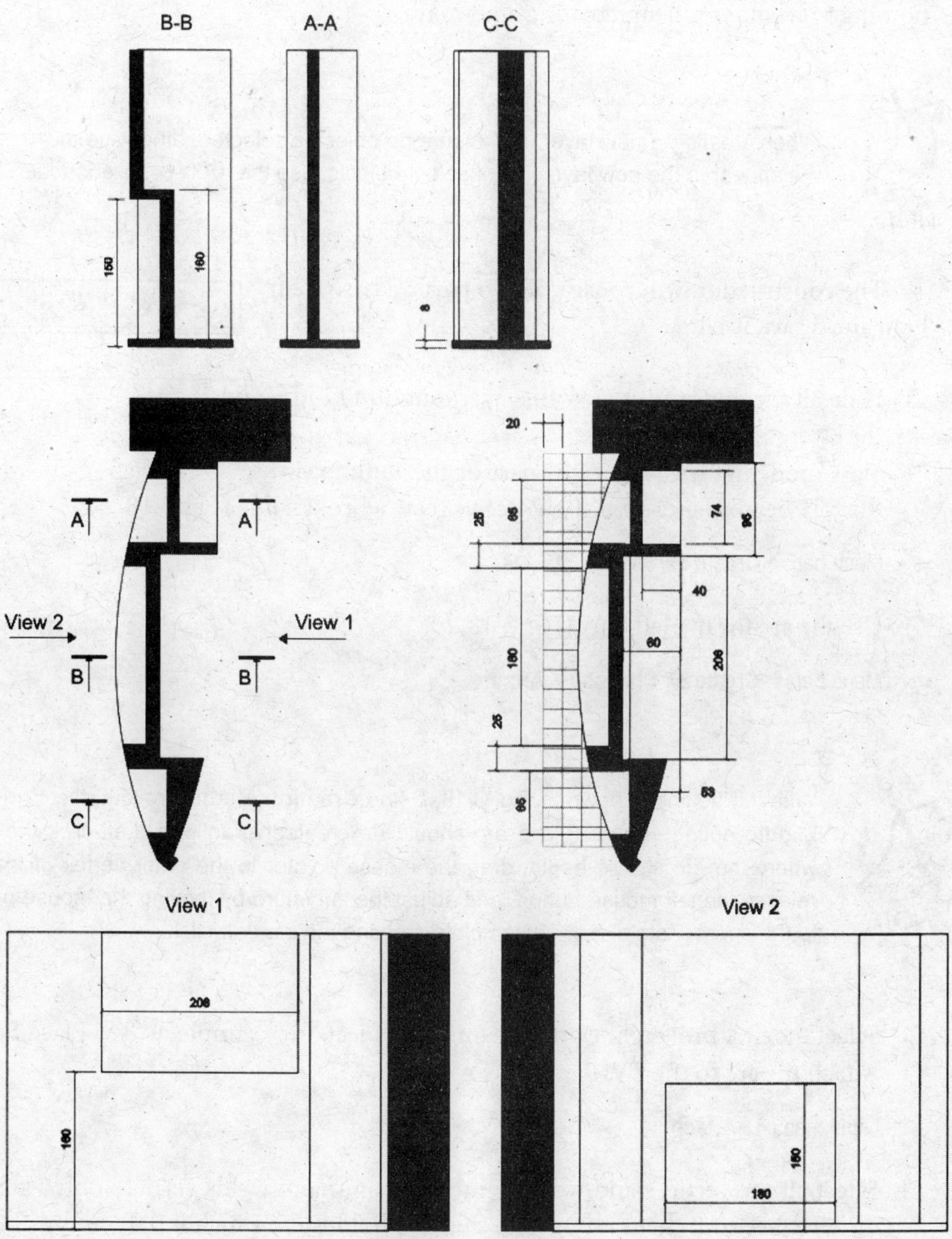

Fig. 3.17. The draft of a rack

In essence, this is a part of the wall, so you'll create it in the **Walls** layer. However, nothing prevents you from creating a new layer.

When creating a new layer, make sure no object is selected, otherwise the selection will appear in the new layer. To unselect objects, use the <Alt>+<D> shortcut.

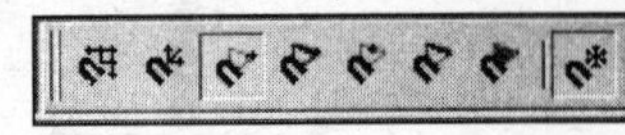

The construction will consist of two parts: a base 8 cm high and a rack itself.

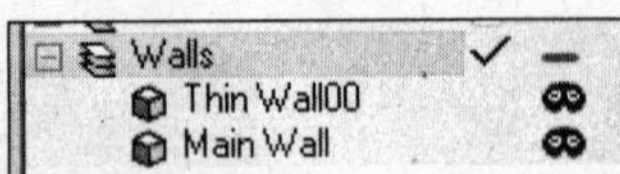

- ❒ Hide all the objects in the **Walls** layer, but don't hide the layer.
- ❒ Start modeling with the right part of the outline (in the top view). Using snap to vertices, create a broken line (Fig. 3.18, *a*).

Menu bar → **Create** → **Shapes** → **Line**

- ❒ Use the arc for the left part (Fig. 3.18, *b*).

Menu bar → **Create** → **Shapes** → **Arc**

With the settings shown in Fig. 3.18, *b* (the **Creation Method** rollout, the **End-End-Middle** option selected), the arc should be created as follows. Left-click the point where the arc should begin, drag the mouse pointer to the other vertex of the arc, release the left mouse button, and adjust the curvature by moving the mouse pointer to the appropriate place. To complete creating the arc, left-click.

- ❒ Select the first broken line and rename the object, for example, to TV-Place Base.
- ❒ Attach the arc to the TV-Place Base object.

Quad menu → **Attach**

- ❒ Select all the vertices and weld them. The command welds vertices only when the distance between them is less than the threshold value which is 0.01 cm by default.

Quad menu → **Weld Vertices**

Because you used snaps to vertices, the vertices that should be welded are positioned in the same point. When vertices fail to weld, increase the threshold of the **Weld** command (the **Geometry** rollout → a parameter to the right of the **Weld** button). However, it would be best to model as carefully as possible.

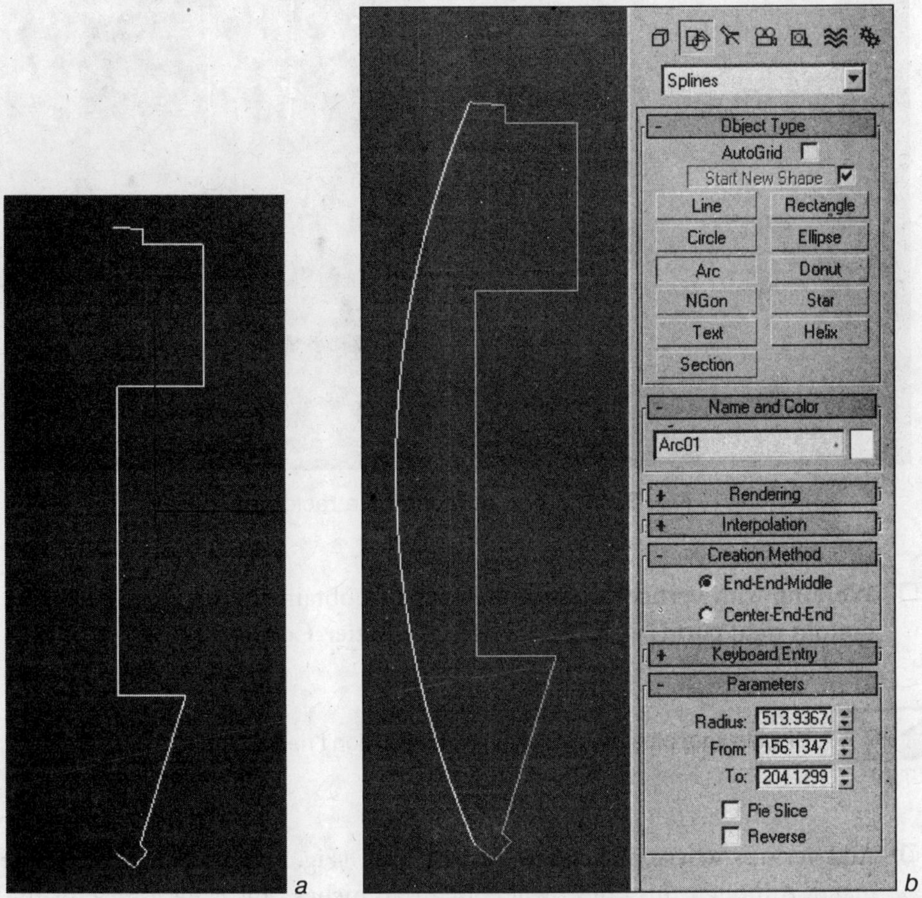

Fig. 3.18, *a* and *b*. Modeling a rack for a TV set

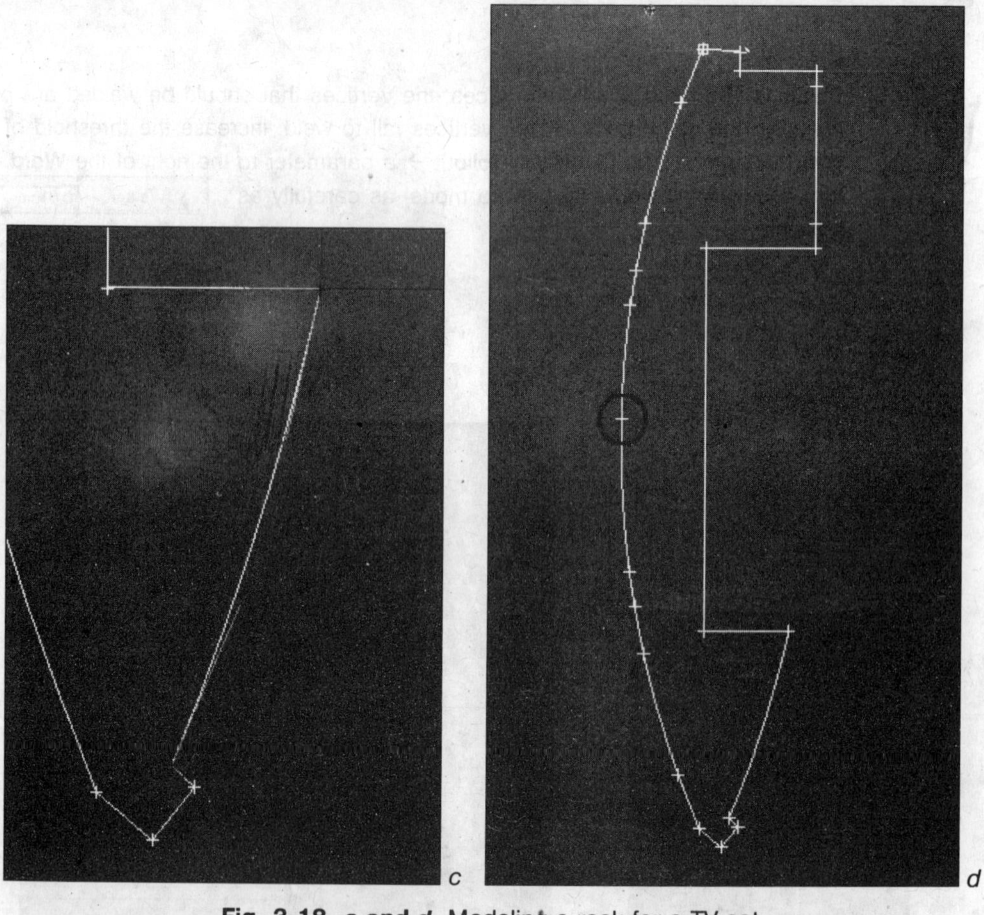

c

d

Fig. 3.18, *c* and *d*. Modeling a rack for a TV set

- ❒ Working with vertices, change their type to obtain the required curvature in the bottom right part (Fig. 3.18, *c*). I used the Bezier-Corner vertices.

TIP

Disable snapping (the <S> key) when you don't need them.

- ❒ Add vertices where niches should be placed (Fig. 3.18, *d*) using the **Refine** command. Although this object will contain no niches, this is necessary for the future alignment of the objects.

❒ Add a vertex (indicated by a circle in Fig. 3.18, *d*) to decrease the number of interpolation steps. Two steps are enough for this model.

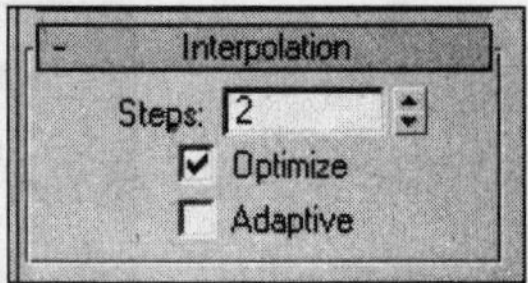

TIP

If you are dissatisfied with the fact that some segments straighten, uncheck the **Optimize** checkbox in the **Interpolation** rollout. I believe that everything should be all right even when the checkbox is checked because there are enough vertices of the Bezier type.

❒ Create a copy (not an instance!) of the object using the <Ctrl>+<V> shortcut and name it TV-Place Top.

❒ Select the TV-Place Base object, extrude it to 8 cm using the **Extrude** modifier (Fig. 3.18, *e*), and hide it.

Quad menu → **Hide Selection**

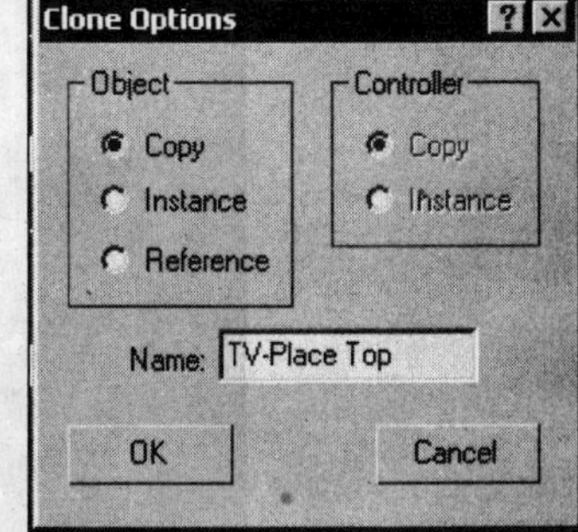

❒ Select the TV-Place Top object and, with snapping to vertices enabled, create outlines for niches (Fig. 3.19, *a*). That is, create everything except the niche for the TV set.

Quad menu → **Create Line**

IMPORTANT

When it is crucial, snap to vertices of the current outline rather than of the original outline on the **Plans** layer. Otherwise, you'll have to move vertices when welding them.

❒ Delete unnecessary segments and weld the vertices (Fig. 3.19, *b*). When vertices fail to weld, increase the threshold of the **Weld** command or use a combination of the **Fuse** and **Weld** commands for pairs of vertices. The first command moves vertices to one point, and the second welds them.

Command panel → the **Geometry** rollout → the **Fuse** and **Weld** commands

❒ Lift the object to a height of 8 cm (i.e., to the height of the base) along the Z axis.

❒ Extrude the object to 292 cm (300 – 8 = 292) using the **Extrude** modifier. Note the lugs and niches. Three segments will be enough (Fig. 3.19, *c*).

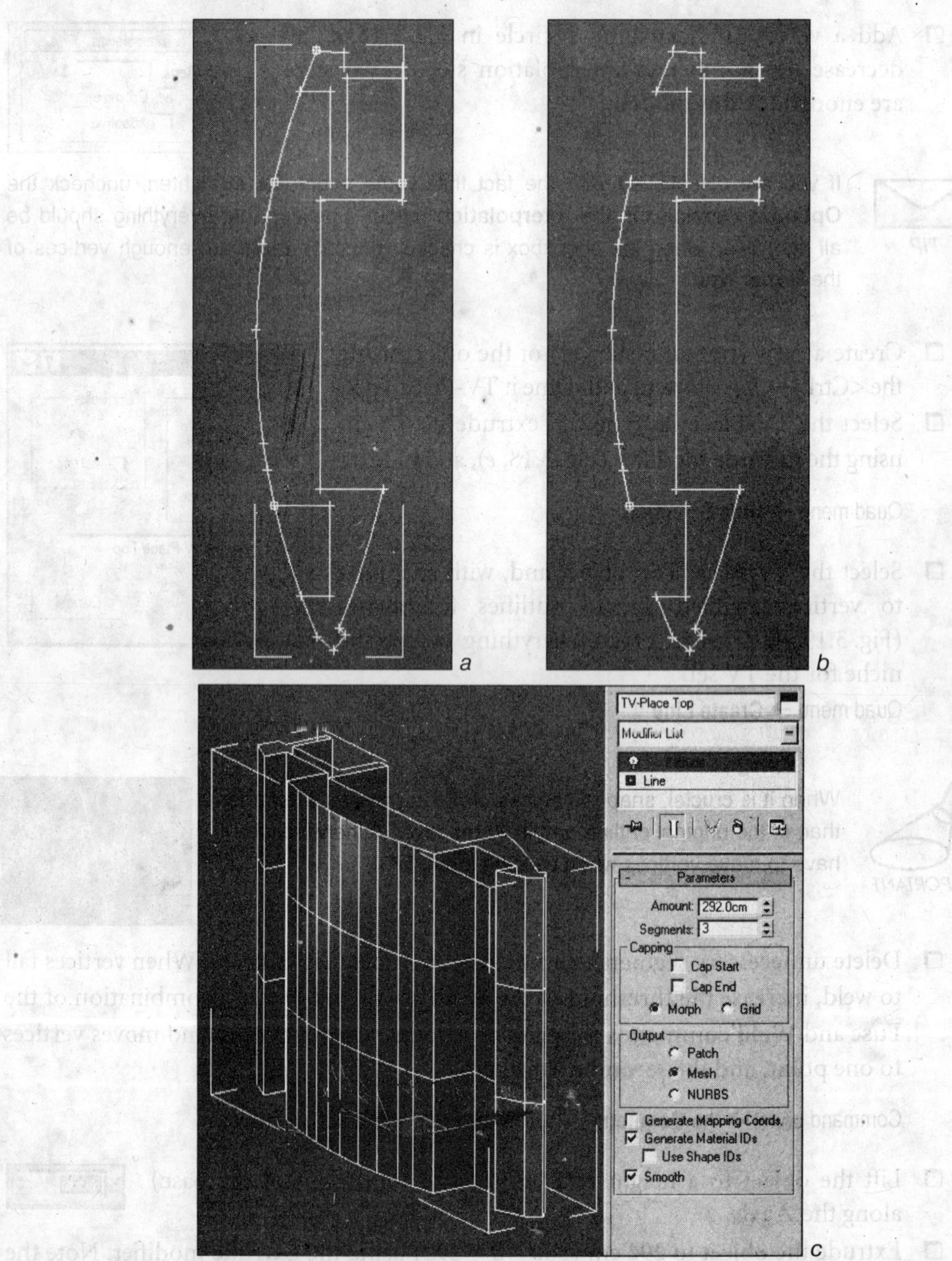

Fig. 3.19, *a*–*c*. Modeling the top part of the TV set rack

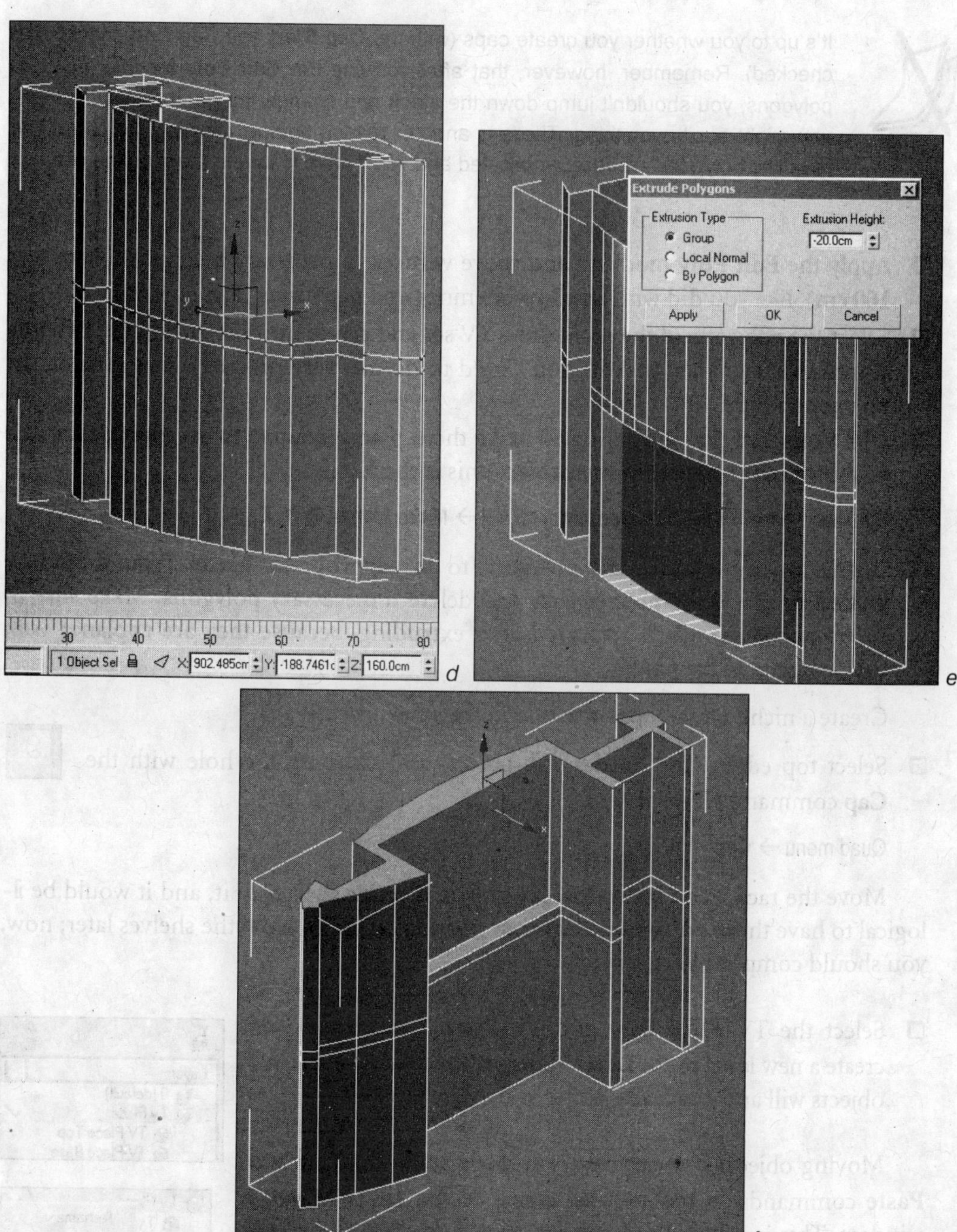

Fig. 3.19, *d*–*f*. Modeling the top part of the TV set rack

It's up to you whether you create caps (with the **Cap Start** and **Cap End** checkboxes checked). Remember, however, that after you use the **Edit Poly** modifier and edit polygons, you shouldn't jump down the stack and change the geometry. Otherwise, you might spoil everything. There is another reason against creating the caps: The resulting polygons are too complicated and you'll have to delete them during editing.

- Apply the **Edit Poly** modifier and move vertices to necessary heights (150 cm and 160 cm), like you did with window openings and partitions (Fig. 3.19, *d*).
- Select the polygons of the niche for a TV set and create the niche using the **Extrude** command (Fig. 3.19, *e*). You don't need to do this very precisely, just extrude the polygons a little.
- Don't unselect the polygons and make them planar relative to an appropriate axis as shown in the figure. In my project, this is the X axis.

Command panel → the **Edit Geometry** rollout → **Make planar, X, Y, Z**

- In the top view, move the polygons to the appropriate places (you should be guided by the Walls-plan object) and delete unnecessary polygons. Make sure to delete polygons, which appeared after extruding, because they are coplanar with the polygons of the base.

Create a niche on the opposite side in the same manner.

- Select top edges (the Border sub-object) and close up the hole with the **Cap** command (Fig. 3.19, *f*).

Quad menu → **Cap**

Move the rack to an individual layer. You'll create shelves in it, and it would be illogical to have them on the same layer as the walls. You'll model the shelves later; now, you should complete large objects.

- Select the TV-Place Base and TV-Place Top objects and create a new layer in the **Layer Manager** window. The selected objects will automatically move to the new layer.

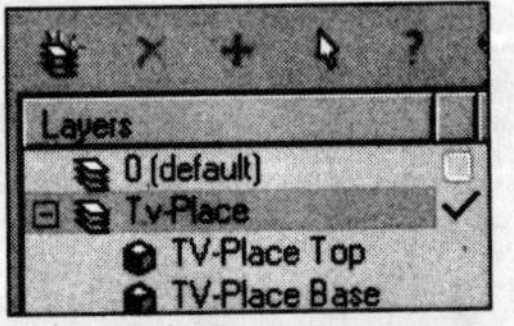

Moving objects between layers is done using the **Cut** and **Paste** commands in the pop-up menu of the **Layer Manager** window. This is a little inconvenient, but if you practice a little, it will become easier.

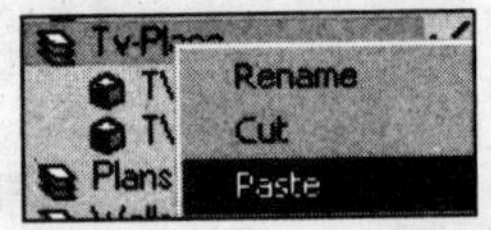

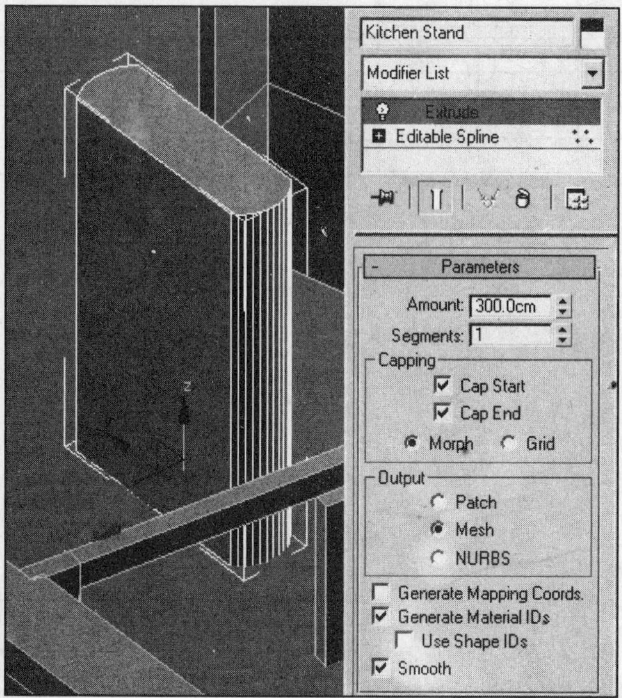

Fig. 3.20. The kitchen wall

On your own

I think you'll easily create a wall in the kitchen (Fig. 3.20) from a rectangle and two arcs. You can make it in the **Walls** layer. The other objects in the kitchen will be created later.

The result of my work at this stage is in the INTERIOR_02.MAX file in the PROJECTS/PROJECT_INTERIOR folder on the accompanying CD-ROM.

Modeling the Floor

The plan of the floors is shown in Fig. 3.21. The floor is made of three materials: a light decked parquet and two sorts of marble-like tiles. I'll describe the best method for modeling the floor. Other possible methods will be addressed later.

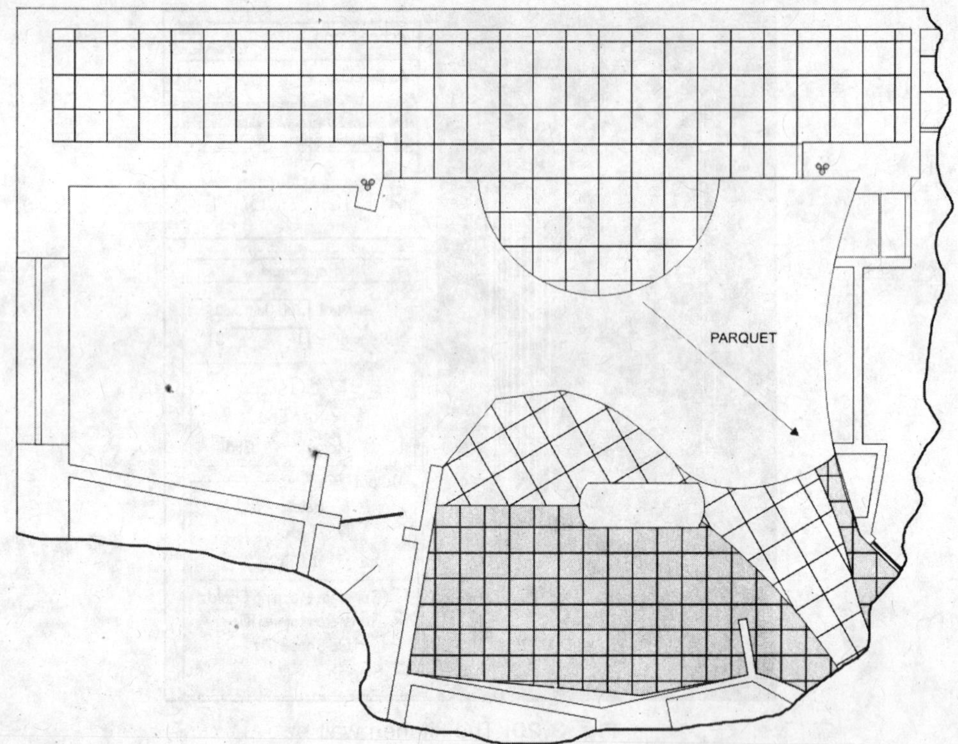

Fig. 3.21. The plan of the floors

You need to apply different materials to different parts of the floor, but maintain the integrity of the object. An ideal floor shouldn't have slots or overlapped surfaces. So I suggest that you use an interesting object type, Compound, that will allow you to achieve this goal.

Layers		Hide	Freeze
0 (default)		—	—
Plans	✓	—	—
Walls-Plan		—	—
Tv-Place			—
Walls			—

- ❐ Hide all the layers except **Plans**, unfreeze it, and make it active.
- ❐ Import objects from the FLOORS-PLAN.AI files located in the PROJECTS\PROJECT_INTERIOR\AI folder on the accompanying CD-ROM, like you imported the wall plan earlier.
- ❐ Rename the object to Floor-plan, scale it 20 times and align with the Walls-Plan object by moving it and snapping to vertices.
- ❐ Hide the Walls-Plan object and freeze the **Plans** layer.

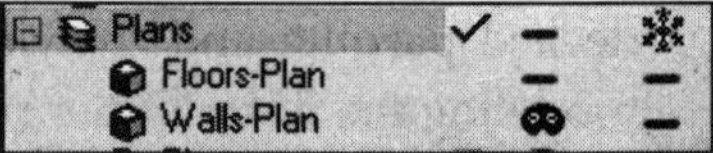

❐ Create a new layer, make it active, and name it Floors.

❐ Create a set of curves as shown in Fig. 3.22, *a*.

NOTE

In fact, there is only one curve, an arc. The others are broken lines.

Attach the curves to one of them. Although this isn't necessary, do this for the sake of convenience.

To draw a horizontal or vertical line, keep the <Shift> key pressed.

Make sure to weld the vertices where the arc touches the lines.

There are two vertices aligned with the **Fuse** command in the point indicated by a circle. You won't be able to weld them because one vertex cannot belong to more than two segments.

You don't need to be very precise in places that will be obstructed by the walls.

Change the type of vertices and move them to obtain the required curvature. Vertices of the Smooth type are suitable, but sometimes you'll prefer the Bezier type.

Set interpolation to a large value (from 8 to 10 steps).

❐ Create a plane. This will be the floor, so rename it Floor (Fig. 3.22, *b*).

Menu bar → **Create** → **Standard Primitives** → **Plane**

NOTE

Note that the curves go beyond the plane. This is important.

The **Length Segments** and **Width Segments** parameters are set to large values to avoid long and narrow triangles on the final model.

❐ Select the Floor object and create a compound object of the Shape Merge type based on it (Fig. 3.22, *c*).

Menu bar → **Create** → **Compound** → **Shape Merge**

Click the **Pick Shape** button and click the spline.

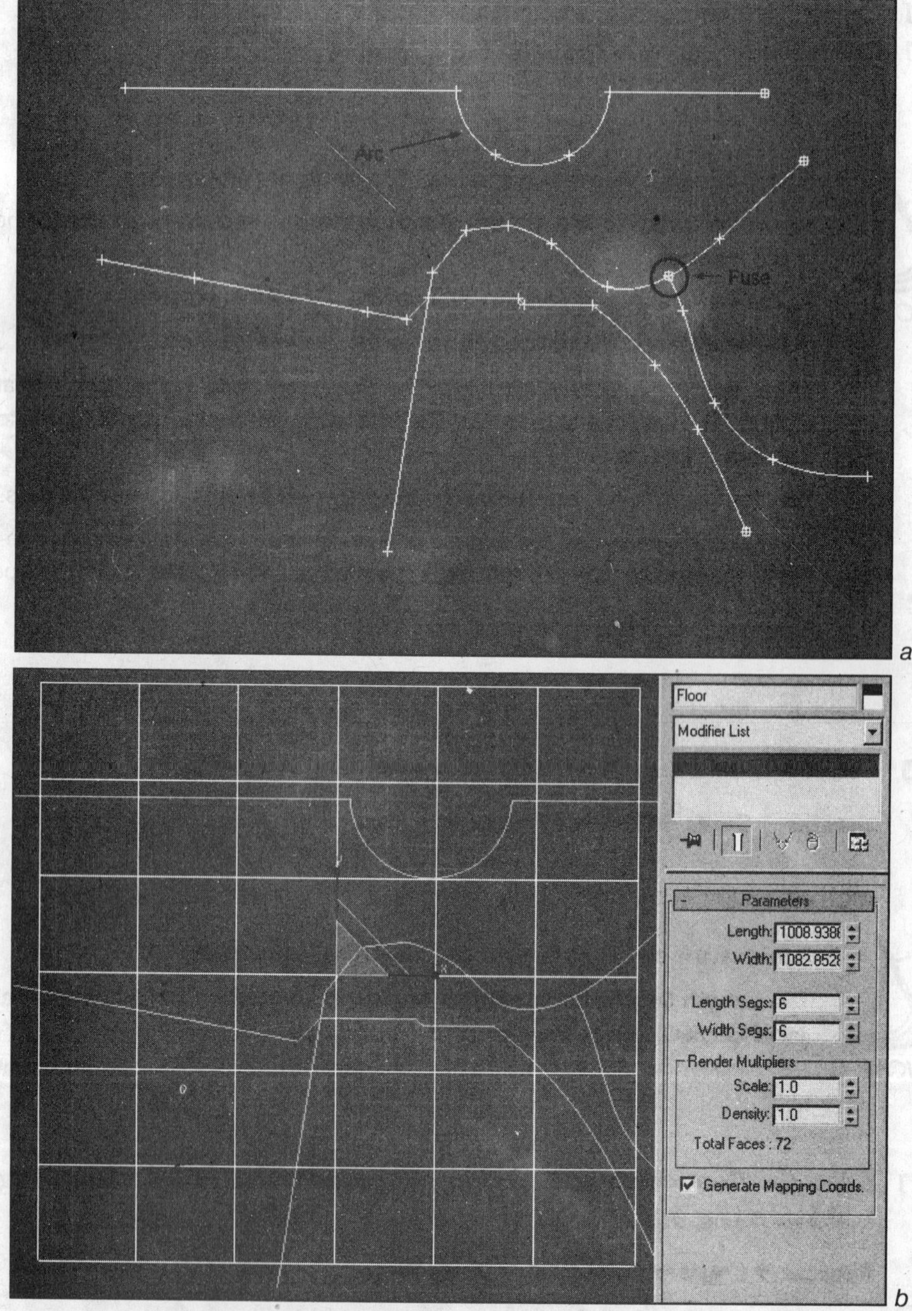

Fig. 3.22, *a* and *b*. Modeling the floor

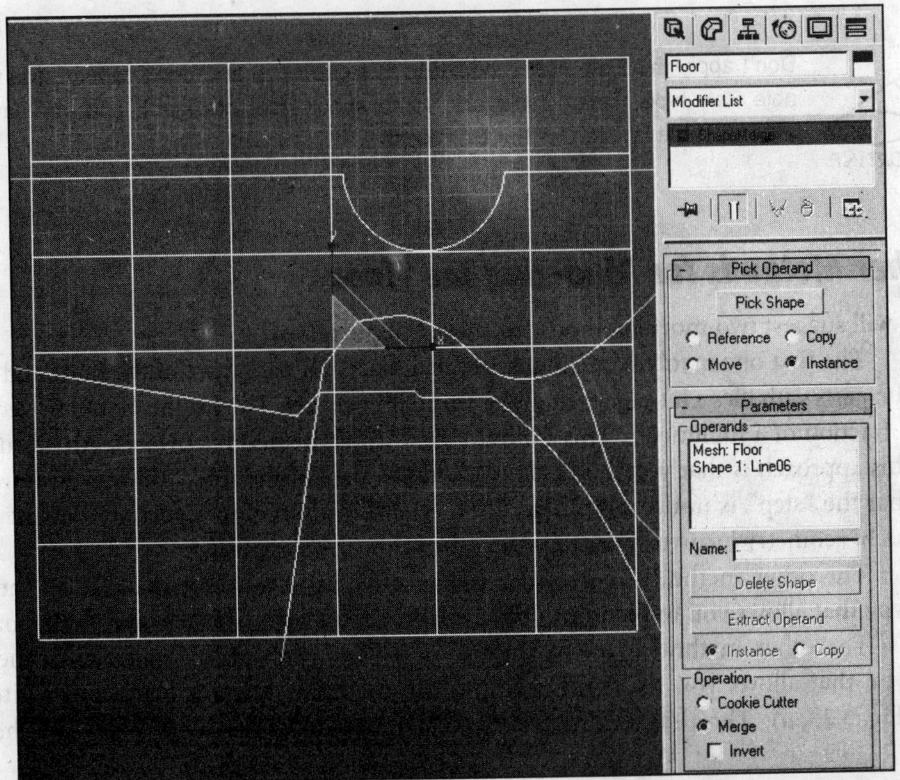

Fig. 3.22, *c*. Modeling the floor

Parameters of the Shape Merge type are similar to those of the Boolean type. However, Shape Merge can contain a few spline operands. Therefore, if you didn't combine splines into one object, you can add them with the **Pick Shape** command.

Select the Instance type to maintain the link to the original curves. Although the Shape Merge type allows you to adjust its operands, this is implemented badly.

Leave **Merge** as the operation type. The **Cookie Cutter** tool (whose name suits it very well) allows you to cut holes from a surface, but you don't need it in this project.

- ❒ Rename and hide the splines.

The geometry of the floor is ready. What are its advantages? The object is a complete entity, but it can be easily divided into polygons. Creating a material for the floor and mapping are described later in this chapter.

IMPORTANT

Don't apply the **Edit Poly** modifier to this geometry and don't convert it to the Editable Poly type. These tools are, so to speak, too intelligent, and you can obtain a undesirable result. Use the **Edit Mesh**.

Other Methods for Modeling the Floor

I will suggest two more methods for modeling this floor.

The first one involves creating separate objects for each part of the floor and placing the parts with tiles a bit higher than the part with parquet. The height should be very small, a fraction of a millimeter. This is how Valery implemented his project. An advantage of this approach is that you'll be able to change a part of the floor quickly. A drawback is that the "step" is noticeable. In addition, global illumination algorithms might process such geometry incorrectly or take too much time for computing.

The other method involves the use of a Multi/Sub-object material of the Blend type that allows you to blend multiple sub-materials using a black-and-white mask.

The other method involves the use of a Multi/Sub-object material of the Blend type that allows you to blend multiple sub-materials using a black-and-white mask (Fig. 3.23, *a*). The first sub-material affects areas indicated with black on the mask

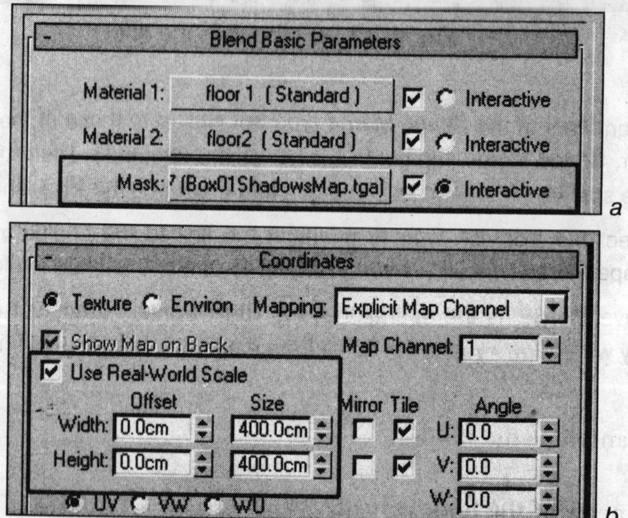

Fig. 3.23. The parameters of the Blend material (*a*), setting the size of the map mask in absolute units (*b*)

while the second affects areas indicated with white. The floor is just a plane. This method is convenient, for example, when the floor is a complicated pattern consisting of different materials such as marble with different colors. Till version 7.5, the use of this method was inconvenient because it was only possible to set tiles in the map parameters, so you would need either to adjust the sizes of tiles by eye or to distribute the map channels to different UVW Map modifiers. Now, you can set the map size in the material editor in absolute units (Fig. 3.23, *b*), and the procedure became much simpler. Remember that the mask size should be large enough so that the border between the materials is sharp. When you render to a size of 2,000 × 2,000 pixels, the mask should be at least 4,000 × 4,000 pixels.

Modeling the Ceiling

The plan of the ceilings is shown in Fig. 24. Import it from the Ceiling-plan.ai file like you imported the other plans earlier, and examine it.

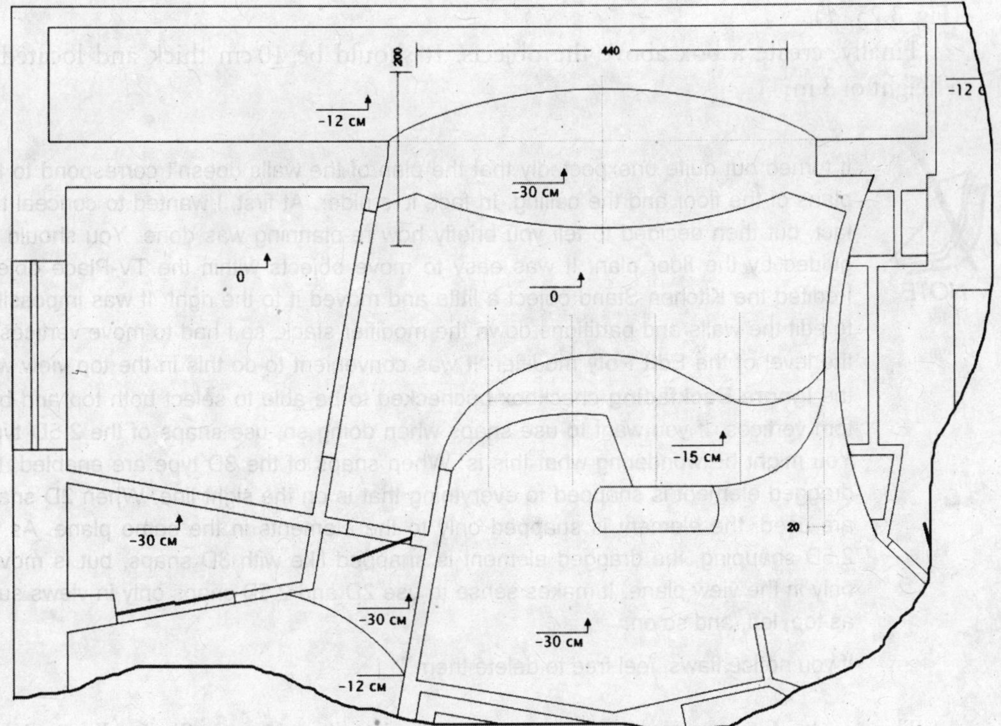

Fig. 3.24. The plan of the ceilings

The zero mark corresponds to the main height of the ceiling (3 m). You'll create the main ceiling from a cube later. The marks with negative numbers indicate downward lugs relative to the main ceiling. To create these elements, you'll need to make a few closed outlines corresponding to different heights. Fig. 3.25 shows these outlines: objects named in accordance with the levels.

The Ceiling-12 object (*a*) is just a rectangle. The Ceiling-15 object (*b*) contains many vertices of the Smooth and Corner types. The Ceiling-30 object (*c*) uses two arcs. There are lamps built into the ceiling in the corridor, so circles were attached to the Ceiling-30 object.

Interpolation for curved ceilings is quite large (from 8 to 10 steps). Note that a few lines are inside the walls. This is inaccurate, but nobody will see this. It is important that polygons coplanar with the walls shouldn't take place.

Apply the **Extrude** modifier with the appropriate (negative!) value of the **Amount** parameter to each object and lift all these objects to 3 meters along the Z axis (Fig. 3.25, *d*).

Finally, create a box above the objects. It should be 10 cm thick and located at a height of 3 m.

It turned out quite unexpectedly that the plan of the walls doesn't correspond to the plans of the floor and the ceiling. In fact, it is older. At first, I wanted to conceal this fact, but then decided to tell you briefly how re-planning was done. You should be guided by the floor plan. It was easy to move objects within the TV-Place object. I edited the Kitchen Stand object a little and moved it to the right. It was impossible to edit the walls and partitions down the modifier stack, so I had to move vertices at the level of the **Edit Poly** modifier. It was convenient to do this in the top view with the **Ignore Backfacing** checkbox unchecked to be able to select both top and bottom vertices. If you want to use snaps when doing so, use snaps of the 2.5D type. You might be wondering what this is. When snaps of the 3D type are enabled, the dragged element is snapped to everything that is on the sight line. When 2D snaps are used, the element is snapped only to the elements in the same plane. As for 2.5D snapping, the dragged element is snapped like with 3D snaps, but is moved only in the view plane. It makes sense to use 2D and 2.5D snaps only in views such as top, left, and so on.

If you notice flaws, feel free to delete them.

The result of my work at this stage is in the interior_03.max file in the Projects/Project_interior folder on the accompanying CD-ROM.

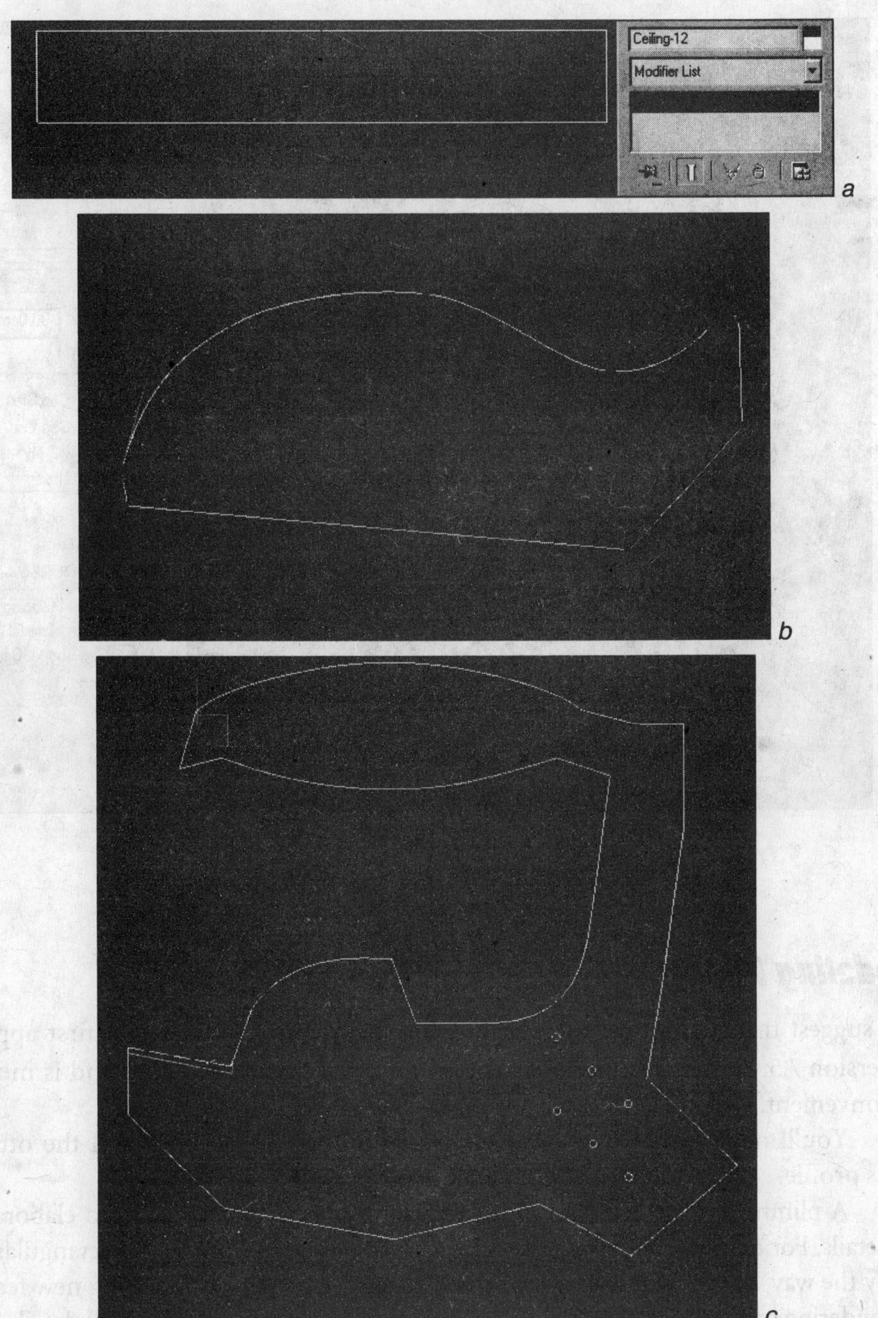

Fig. 3.25, *a–c*. Modeling the ceilings

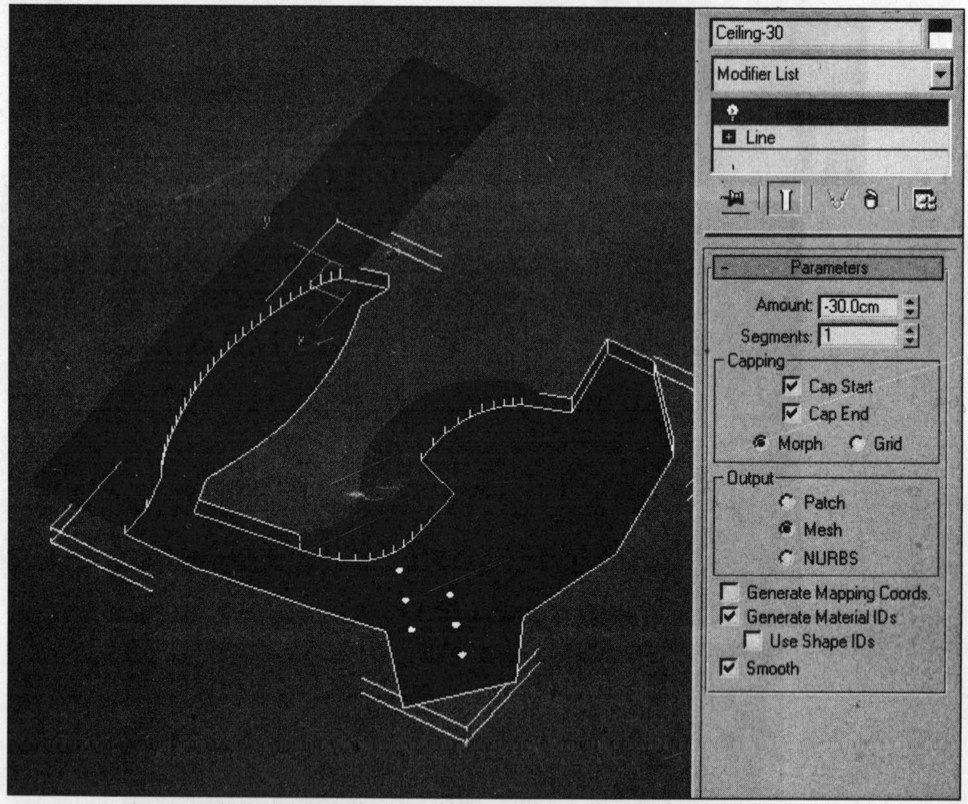

Fig. 3.25, *d*. Modeling the ceilings

Modeling Plinths

I suggest that you model the plinth using the **Sweep** modifier that first appeared in version 7.5. It is an advanced variant of the **Bevel Profile** modifier and is much more convenient.

You'll need two curves, one being the outline of the plinth and the other being its profile.

A plinth isn't the brightest detail in an interior, so it is wasteful to elaborate on its details. For example, Valery confines himself to creating plinths with rectangular profiles. By the way, currently it is very easy to create a rectangular profile using new features for rendering splines. Nevertheless, I suggest that you create a plinth with all details.

Create a new layer, name it Plinth, and make it active.

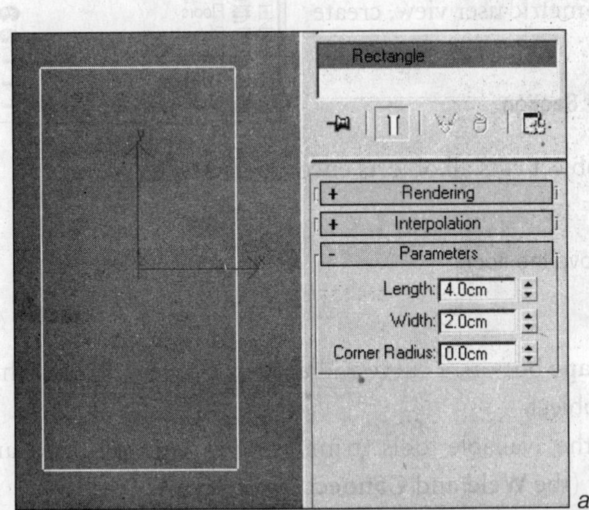

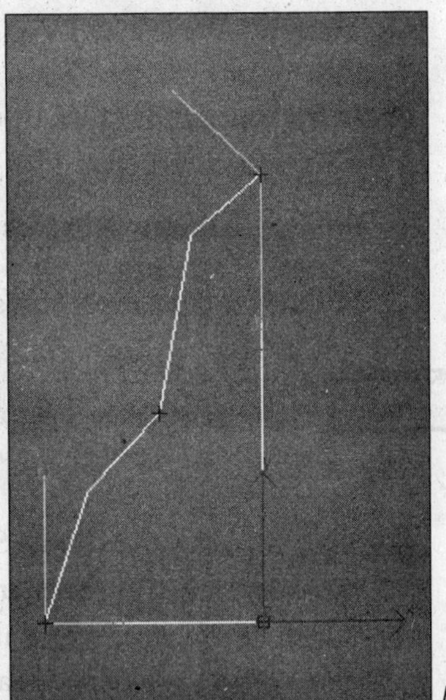

Fig. 3.26. The profile of the plinth

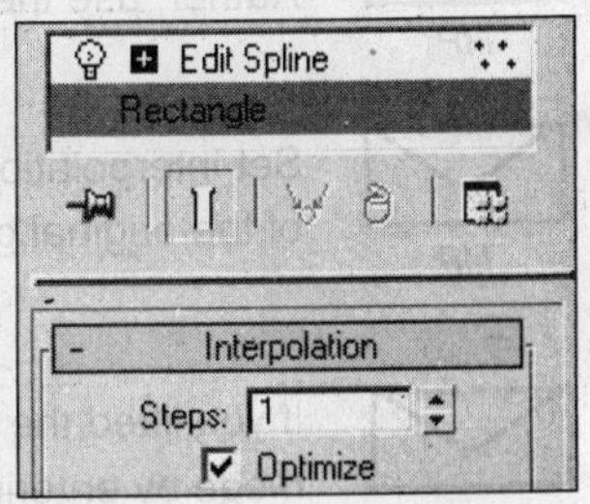

Fig. 3.26 shows the stages of creating a profile of the plinth. First, it is just a rectangle created in ant view with a particular size (*a*). I obtained the desired shape (*b*) using the **Edit Spline** modifier at the vertex level.

To simplify the final geometry, set interpolation to one at the Rectangle stack level. Because the vertex indicated with number 2 has the Smooth type, 3ds Max will make the plinth smooth during rendering.

How should you make the outline of the plinth? You can create a new outline using snap to vertices. It is important to note one fine point in this case. It is likely that the number of vertices on curvilinear surfaces (after interpolation) of the plinth will be other than the number of vertices of the walls. As a result, gaps are likely, or the plinth might penetrate a wall.

Alternatively, you can use the initial curves of the walls, which is wise. To do this, you'll need to copy them, delete all modifiers, weld, and delete excessive details. I believe you can do this on your own.

However, I suggest to you a method that allows you to make an outline when the modifier stack is collapsed, or when you import the geometry in the DWG/DXF/3DS format.

- Make the Walls and TV-Place layers visible. Hide the other layers except Plinth.
- In the top, perspective, or isometric user view, create a **Section** object (Fig. 3.27, *a*).

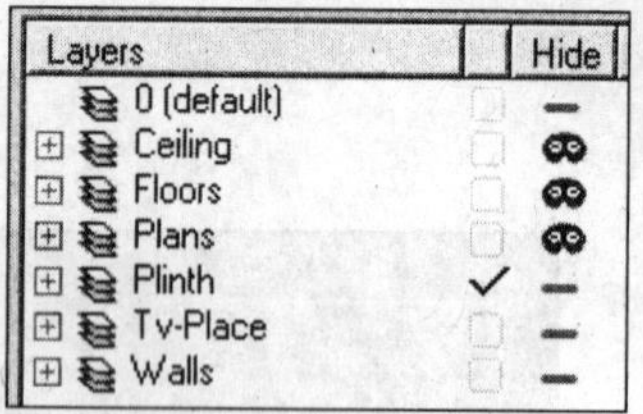

Menu bar → **Create** → **Shapes** → **Section**

With these parameters, this object cuts all objects encountered by its plane.

TIP

Lift the **Section** object above the floor.

- After you click the **Create Shape** button, a curve will appear. Name it Plinth. Then you can remove the **Section** object.
- "Clean" this curve using all the available tools (trim, remove segments, etc.) and weld vertices where necessary (the **Weld** and **Connect** commands).

TIP

It is convenient to hide all the other objects. Don't do this in the layer manager. Rather, use the **Isolate Selection** tool (Quad menu → **Isolate Selection**).

TIP

Set interpolation to zero because the vertices of the curve coincide with the vertices of the original geometry.

TIP

If you lifted the **Section** object above the floor, put the Plinth curve down in the move mode by entering zero into the input box of the Z axis.

My result is shown in Fig. 3.27, *b*.

- Apply the **Sweep** modifier to the **Plinth** object.

Modifier list → **Sweep**

NOTE

It is a new modifier borrowed from Autodesk Viz 2006. It makes it easier to create such objects, so I'll describe its parameters in more detail (Fig. 3.27, *c*).

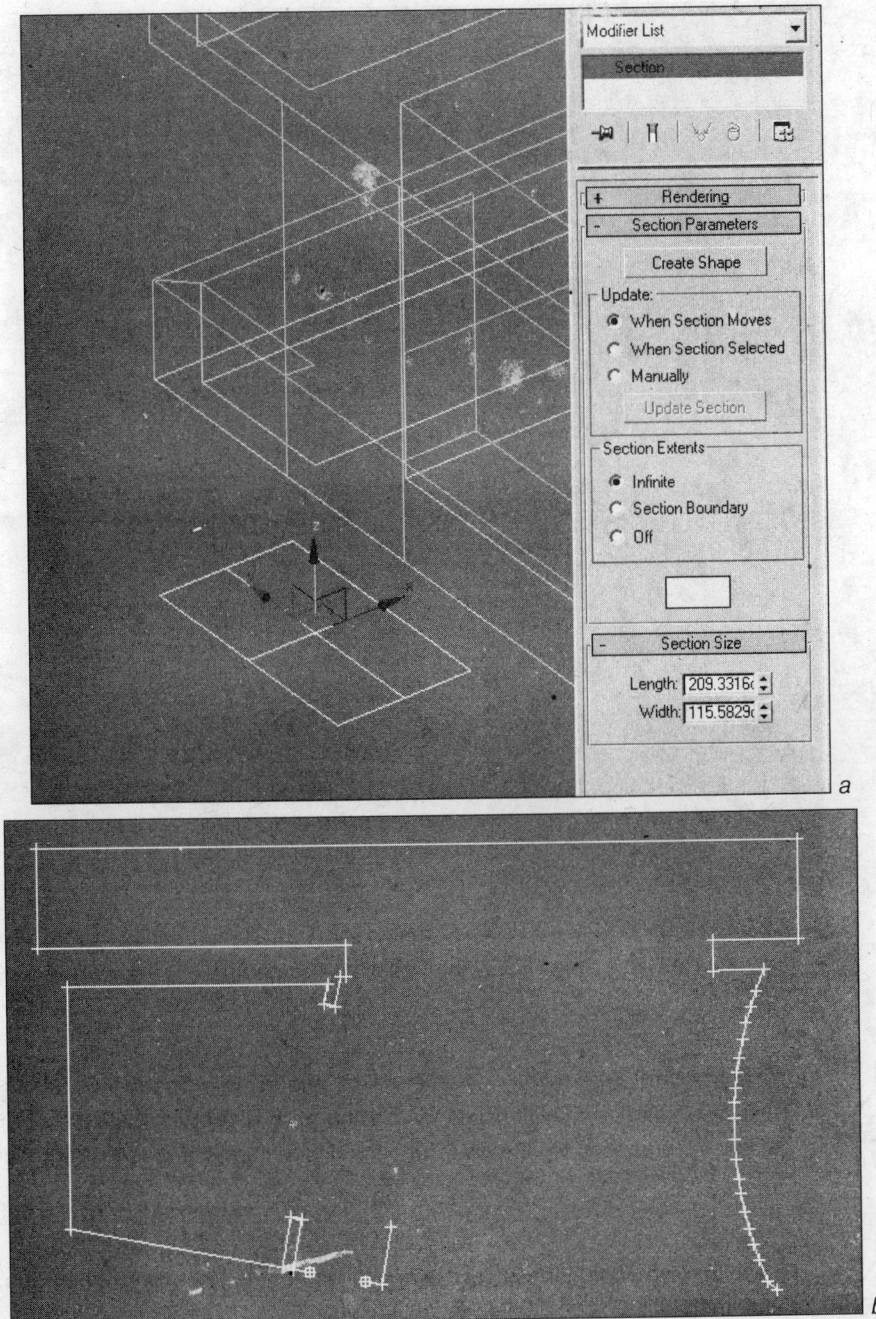

Fig. 3.27, *a* and *b*. Modeling the plinth

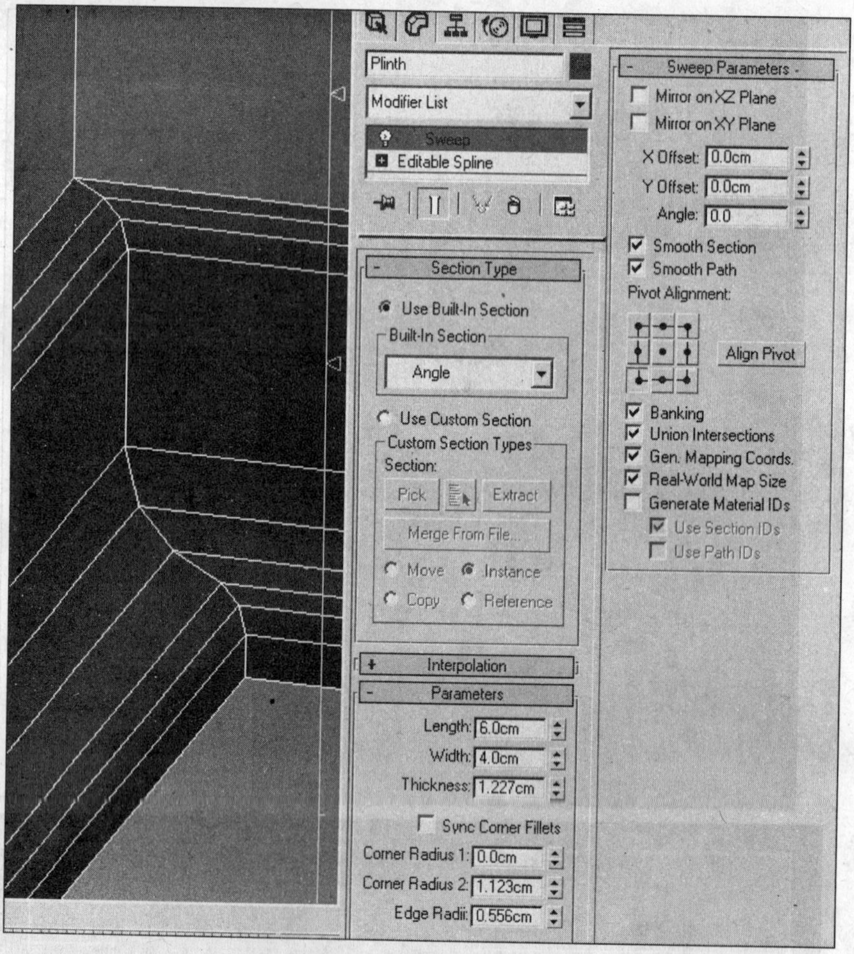

Fig. 3.27, c. Modeling the plinth

In the **Section Type** rollout, you can select and set one of several built-in sections. Their parameters are available in the **Parameters** and **Interpolation** rollouts. It took me two minutes to make the plinth with the desired profile from the **Angle** section.

In addition, you can choose your own section or a few sections. When you use the **Copy** method, you can delete the original object.

In the **Sweep Parameters** rollout, you can set the parameters of the **Sweep** modifier. All the settings are self-explanatory, and I'll comment only on the **Generate Mapping Coordinates** and **Real-World Map Size** checkboxes. If you check both, it will be very easy to apply a map to the plinth.

The **Generate Material ID** and **Use Path ID** checkboxes allow you to easily divide the plinth into several materials. Remember that the floor is compound, and you should have one plinth for the parquet and the other for the tiles.

I encountered a problem; a part of my plinth was turned inside out (Fig. 3.28). I managed it easily by jumping down the stack and changing the orientation of an appropriate spline.

Command panel → the **Geometry** rollout → **Reverse**

The plinth is ready.

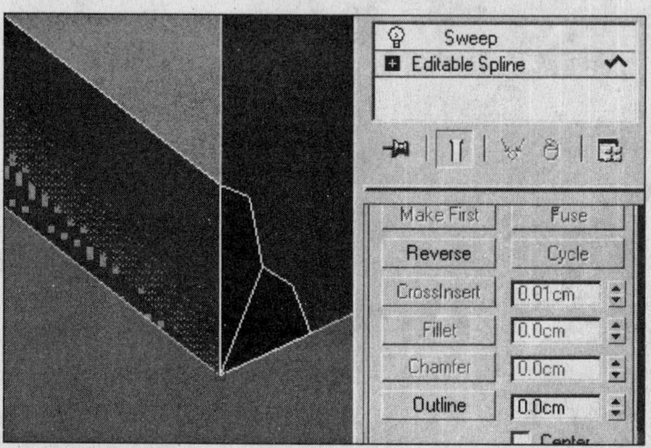

Fig. 3.28. Wrong orientation of the plinth profile

Modeling Window Frames, Glass, Sills, and Curtain Holders

The **Sweep** modifier makes it very easy for you to create simple window frames.

- ❒ Create the **Windows** layer and make it active.
- ❒ Using the snap to midpoints, create a broken line as shown in Fig. 3.29, *a*.

Fig. 3.29, *a* and *b*. Modeling the frame

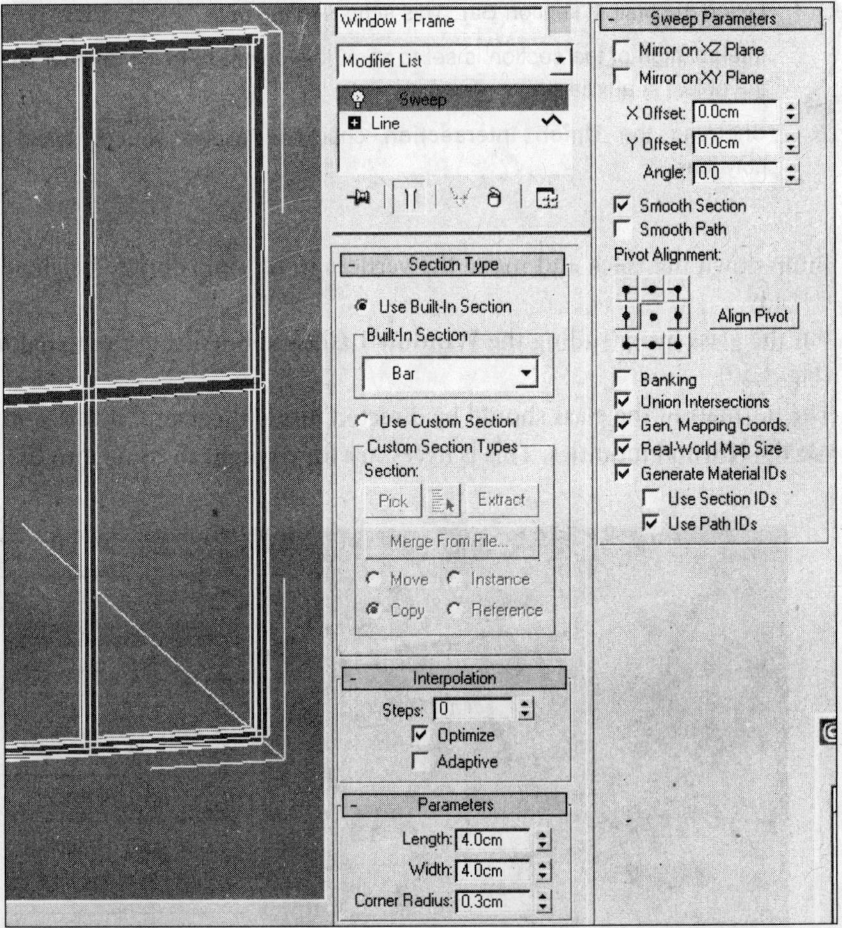

Fig. 3.29, *c*. Modeling the frame

- ❒ Copy it and name the copy Window 1 Glass. Guess why.
- ❒ Select the initial curve and rename it Window 1 Frame.
- ❒ Select the segments and divide them into equal fragments using the **Divide** command.

Divide 12

- ❒ Check the **Connect Copy** checkbox.
- ❒ Select the spline and move it along the Z axis to a certain height while keeping the <Shift> key pressed.
- ❒ Repeat this to obtain a frame of splines (Fig. 3.29, *b*).
- ❒ Apply the **Sweep** modifier and set it (Fig. 3.29, *c*).

NOTE

I used the built-in section **Bar**. This simplified the task.

Interpolation of the section is set to zero. It is pointless to set another value because the object is auxiliary.

Checking the **Union Intersection** checkbox allows you to avoid overlapped polygons.

- Jump down the stack and move the vertices to the appropriate heights. The frame is ready.
- Put the glass by extruding the **Window 1 Glass** spline using the **Extrude** modifier (Fig. 3.30).
- The normals of the glass should be directed inside the room. If this is not the case, use the **Normal** modifier. This is necessary for daylight to come into the room.

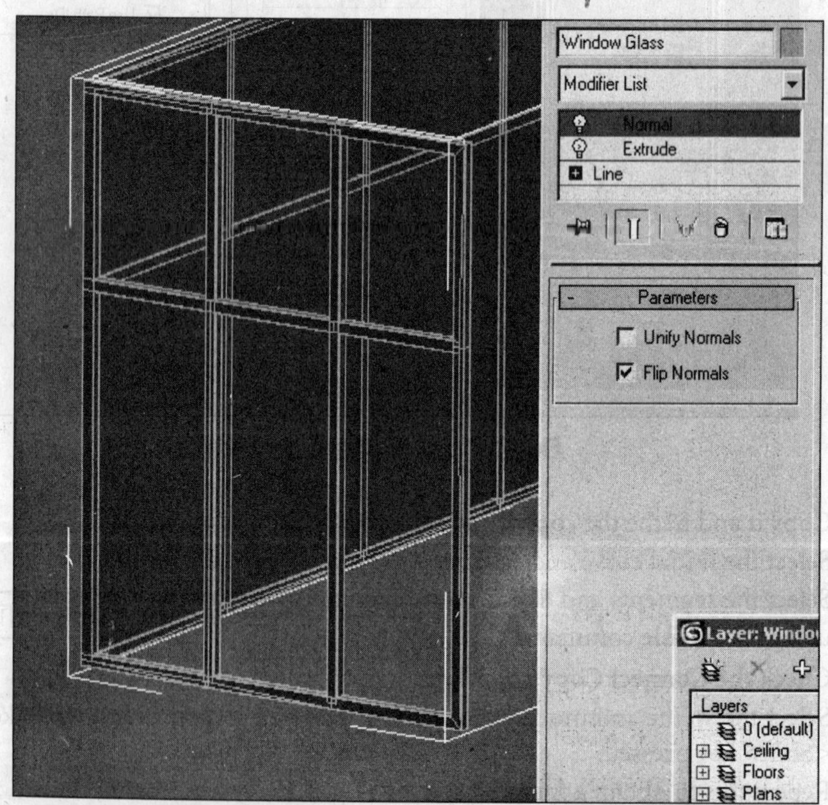

Fig. 3.30. The window glass

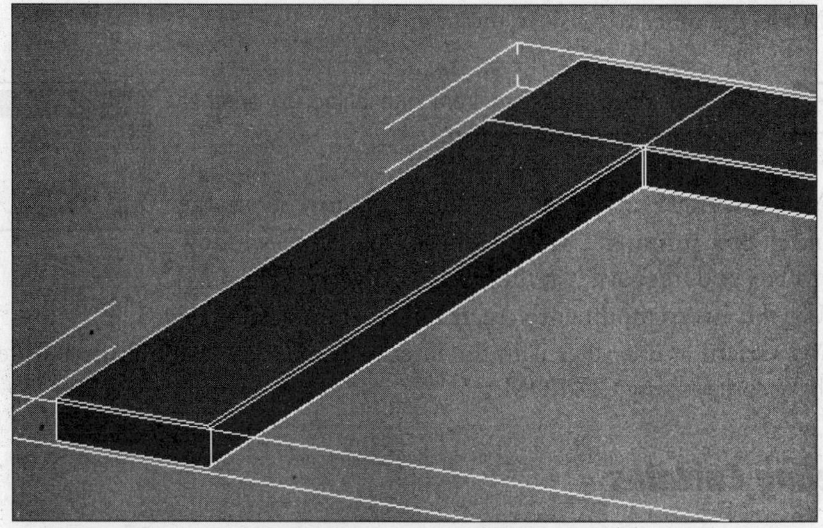

Fig. 3.31. The window sill

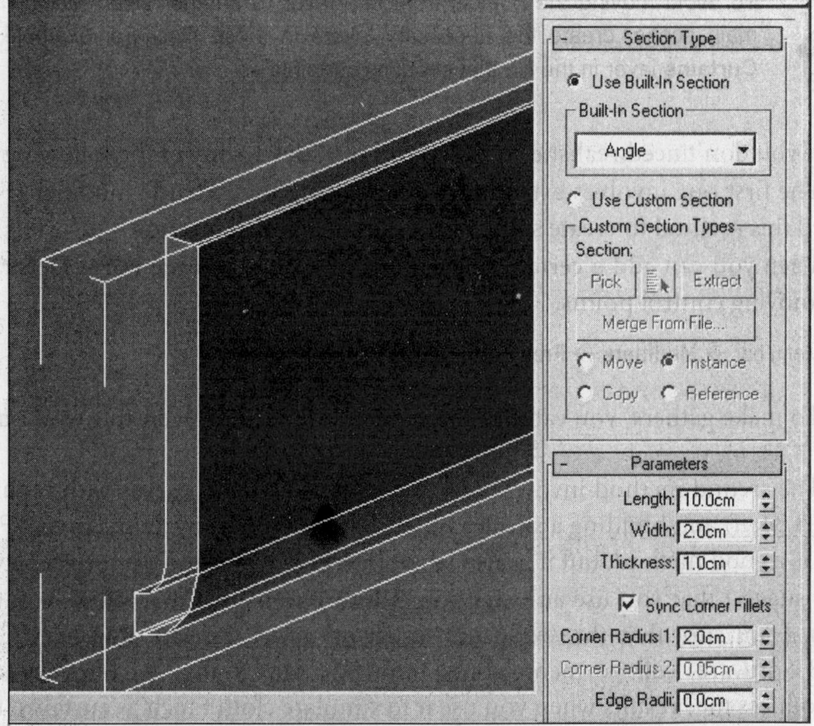

Fig. 3.32. The curtain holder

Model the other window in the same way.

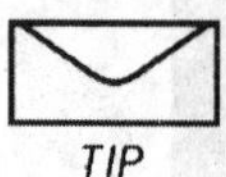

TIP

You can move modifiers from one object to another using the **Copy/Paste** method.

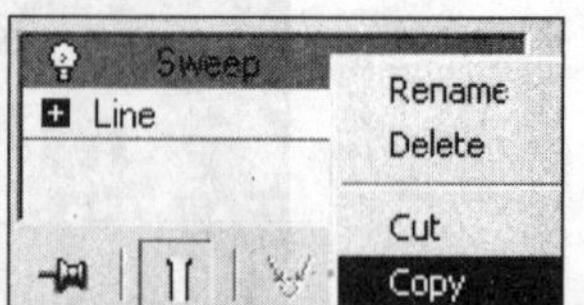

You can make a sill for the small window from the **Chamfer Box** primitive. Make a sill for the large window from a box and improve it at the level of polygons (Fig. 3.31).

Use the **Sweep** modifier to create holders for curtains (Fig. 3.32).

My variant at this stage is in the interior05.max file in the Projects\Interior folder on the accompanying CD-ROM.

Modeling Curtains

NOTE

I recommend that you model these and subsequent objects in individual files. To avoid moving the objects from one layer to another when loading them to the main scene, create the necessary layers in these files. For example, create the **Curtains** layer in the file that contains curtains.

If you don't need realistic curtains, you can stick to any of the following methods.

The first one involves extruding a spline using the **Extrude** modifier (Fig. 3.33, *a*). I used this method to create some of the curtains in this interior.

Then you can add a certain unevenness by using the **Free Form Deformer (FFD)** and moving control points.

Menu bar → **Modifiers** → **Free Form Deformers** → **FFD box**

To make gathers, you can use the same modifier; however, this won't be very easy (Fig. 3.33, *b*).

The second method involves creating a set of NURBS curves with required shapes (Fig. 3.34, *a*) and building a surface of the U-Loft type from these curves (Fig. 3.34, *b*). This is a good method, but it is also labor-intensive when you want to achieve realism.

I suggest that you use an extension (**Cloth Extension**) that allows you to simulate cloth. I am sure that this extension based on a well-known plug-in, ClothFX from Size8 Software, will be incorporated into 3ds Max 8 after its bugs are eliminated. It produces nice results when you use it to simulate cloth (such as curtains, table-cloth, flags, clothes, etc.).

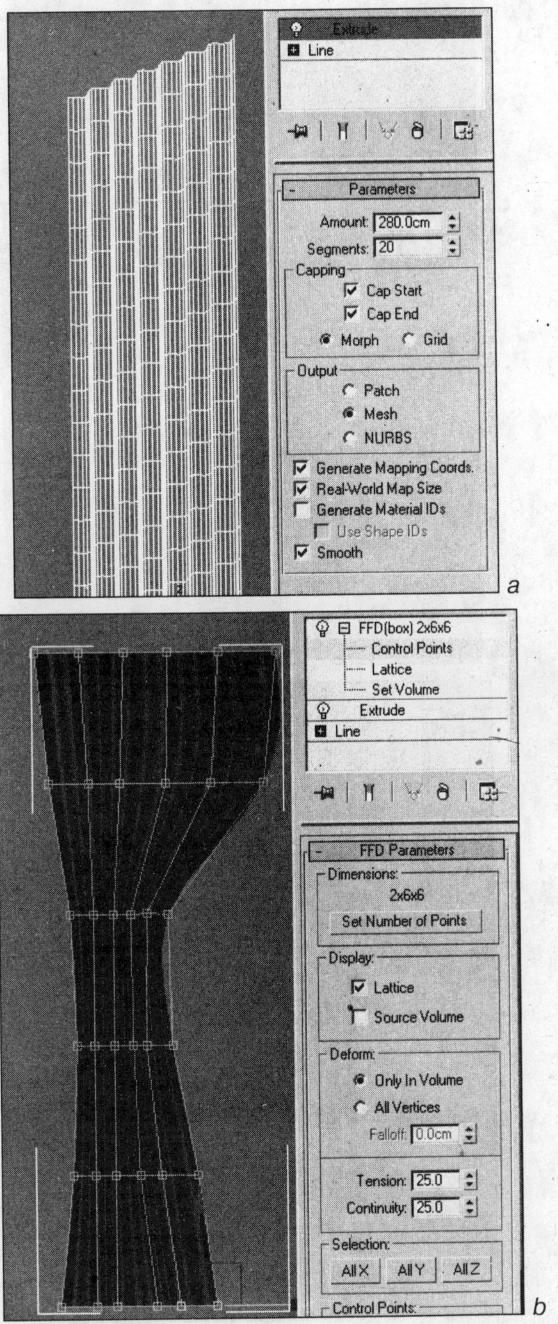

Fig. 3.33. Simple curtains created by extruding a spline

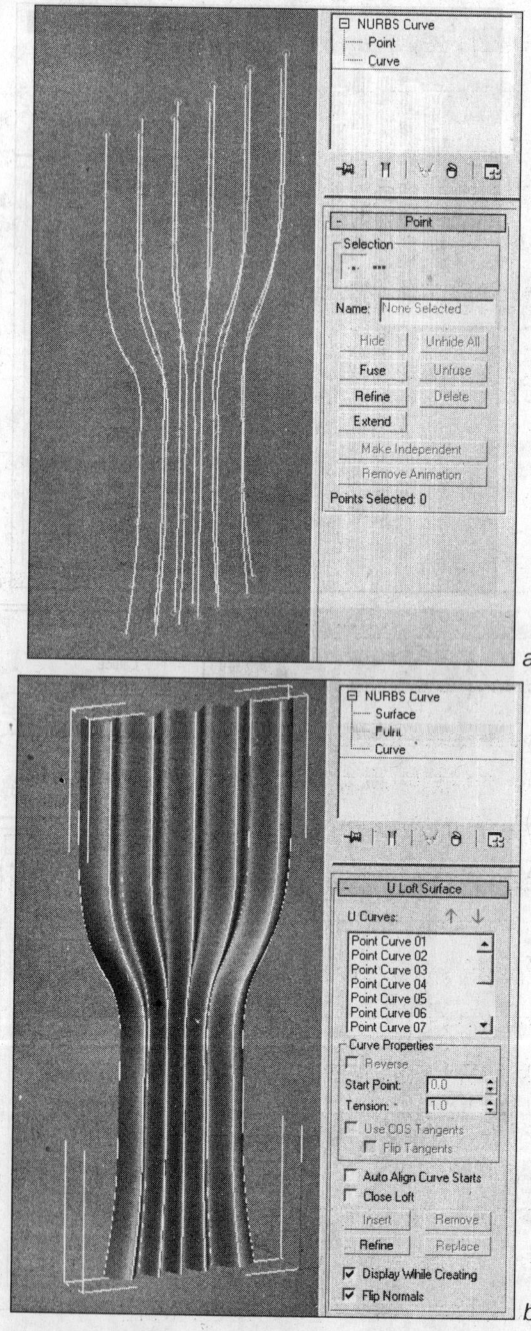

Fig. 3.34. Simple curtains created from NURBS

NOTE

Of course, to use this extension you should install it on your computer. Subscribers can receive it for free.

- In the front view, create a rectangle with a size of a cloth typically used for curtains, kind of 120 cm wide and 270 cm long. When selecting the length, remember that the cloth will stretch.
- Select the **Garment Maker** modifier in the modifier list and apply it to the rectangle (Fig. 3.35, *a*). This modifier creates a mesh of triangles based on a spline. This topology of the model is the most suitable for cloth simulation. A common plane with a rectangular mesh is less suitable because it actually consists of right triangles. Therefore, it is not even because hypotenuses of the triangles are $\sqrt{2}$ times longer than their catheti.

TIP

If you are planning to use cloth with a particular pattern, make sure to apply the **UVW map** modifier now. Check the **Real-World Map Size** checkbox to make it easier to set the map. [☑ Real-World Map Size]

- Apply the **Cloth** modifier (don't confuse it with **Reactor Cloth**).

This isn't easy. However, if you master this tool, you'll be able to create any cloth without difficulty in the future.

I'd like to describe simulation parameters available in the **Simulation Parameters** rollout (Fig. 3.35, *b*).

- The **Cloth** simulator is based on physically correct algorithms, so first you should make the system units and the units used in **Cloth agree**. It uses centimeters, and your system units are millimeters, therefore, the **cm/unit** parameter should be equal to 0.1.
- To use the Earth's gravitation, click the **Earth** button. The gravitation acceleration at the Earth's surface is 9.8 m/s^2, and it is directed downwards. This is why the value is negative. If you wish to know how the cloth will behave on the Moon or Mars, change this parameter appropriately.

Although you don't need the other parameters when creating curtains, I'll mention them briefly.

- ❒ The default settings are all right for the curtains. However, if you don't like the result, increase the **Subsample** parameter responsible for the number of intermediate computation steps.
- ❒ Checking the **Self Collision** checkbox allows you to prevent the cloth from penetrating itself. The number on this line indicates an algorithm. In simple cases such as curtains, use zero.

These weren't particularly interesting. The most interesting parameters are to come:

- ❒ Open the object's properties by clicking the **Object Properties** button in the **Object** rollout (Fig. 3.35, *c*).
- ❒ Select the **Curtain** object on the list, define it as cloth (indicated with number 1 in Fig. 3.35, *c*) and select a preset, for example, **Silk** (indicated with number 2). This is enough.
- ❒ Return to the modifier's parameters by clicking the **OK** button.

The object is a length of silk now. To check this, click the **Simulate Local** button. The object will fall beautifully without changing its shape. This is how a length of silk would fall in a vacuum.

- ❒ Reset the state of the object by clicking the **Reset State** button.

Your next task is to fasten the curtain by simulating rings. You can fasten it to the "world," but I suggest that you create a box in the front view and fasten a few vertices of the curtain to this box (Fig. 3.35, *d*).

- ❒ Enter the mode for editing **Group** subobjects.
- ❒ Select a few vertices and make a group using the **Make Group** button.
- ❒ Connect this group to the **Box01** object using the **Node** command (Fig. 3.35, *e*).

NOTE

You could fasten the group using the **Preserve** command. However, if you read further, you'll understand why I suggested another command.

- ❒ Return to the object level and click **Simulate Local**. The curtain will hang and stretch a little. If it falls, check your previous actions to locate the mistake.
- ❒ Stop the algorithm by clicking the **Simulate Local** button again and make the current state initial by clicking the **Set Initial State** button.

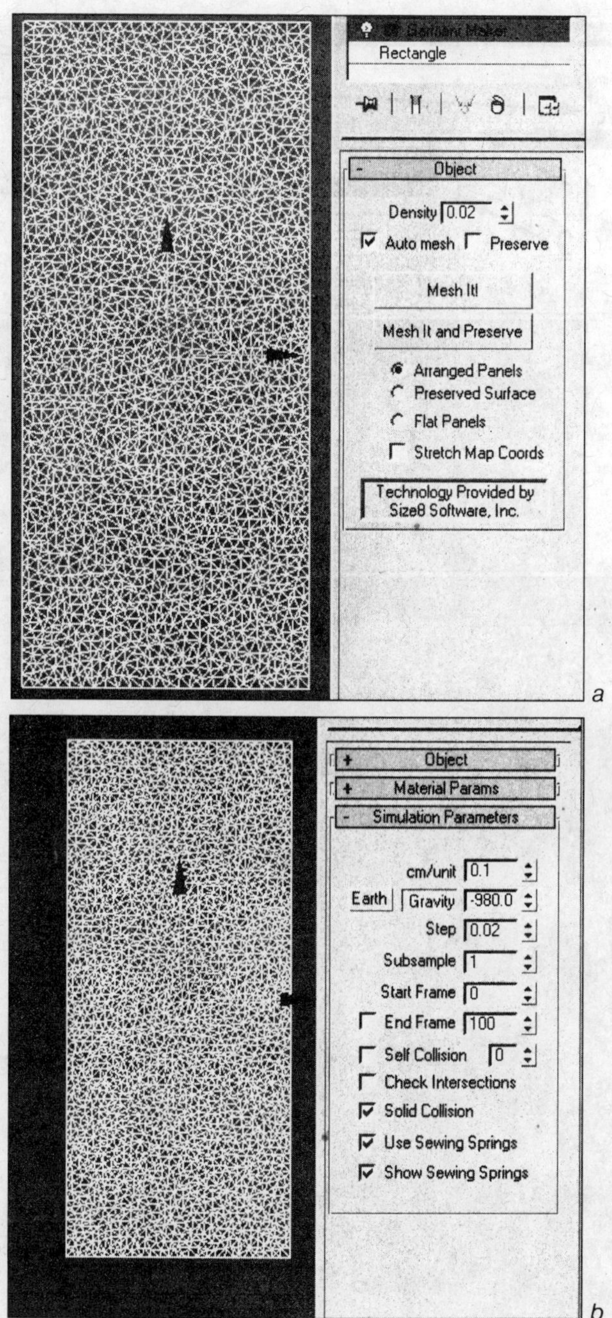

Fig. 3.35, *a* and *b*. Creating realistic curtains

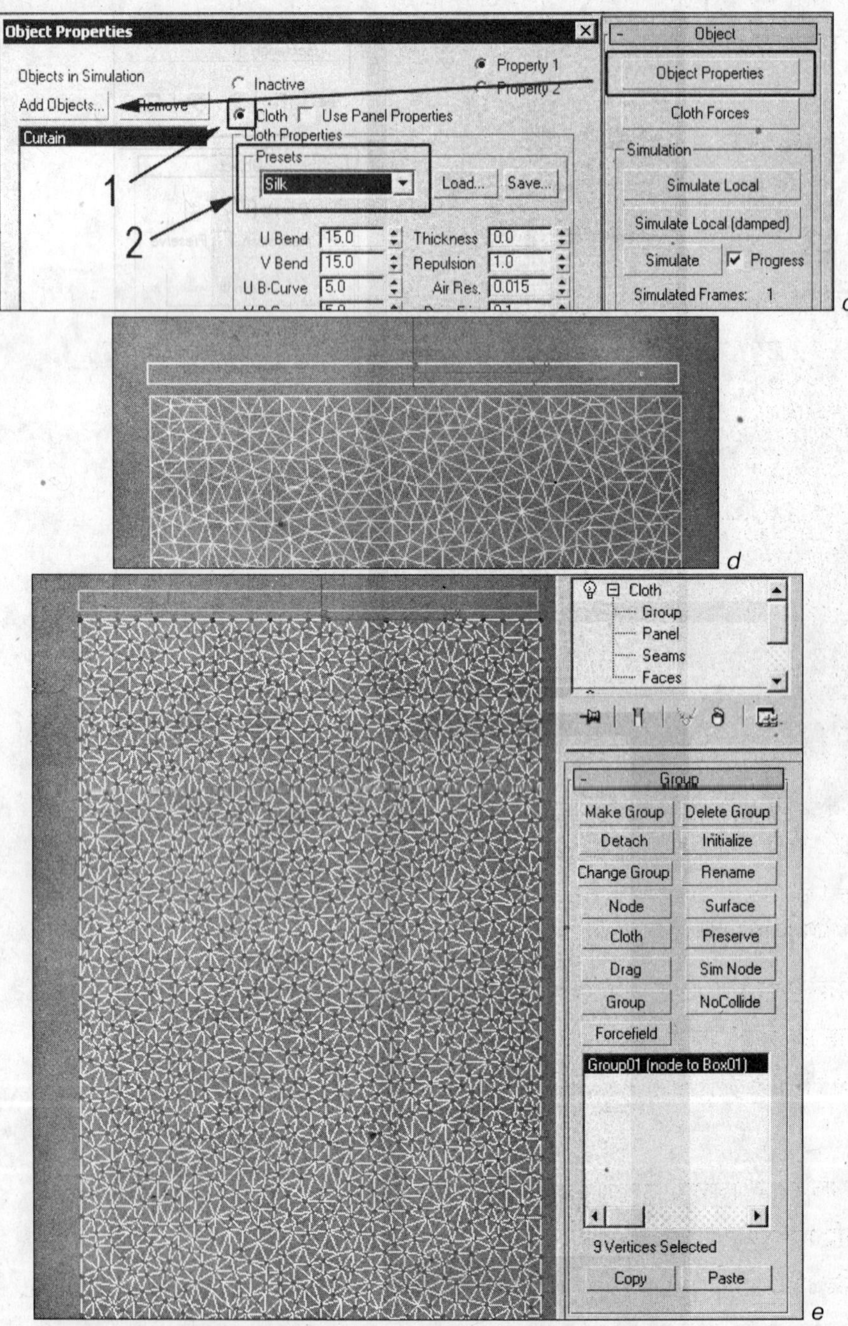

Fig. 3.35, *c–e*. Creating realistic curtains

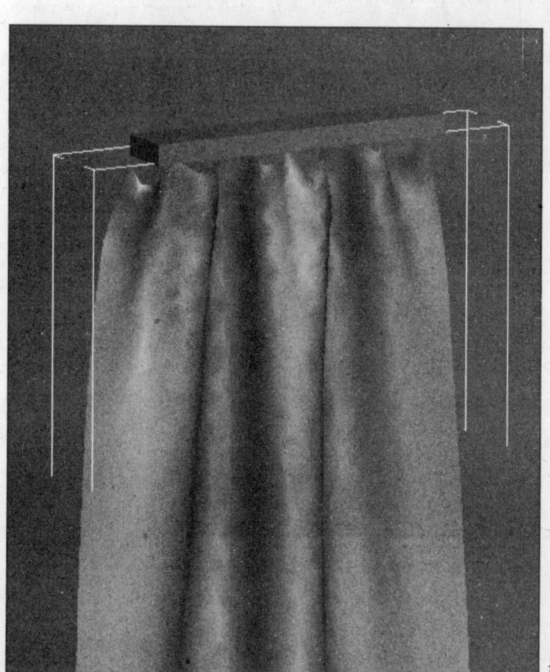

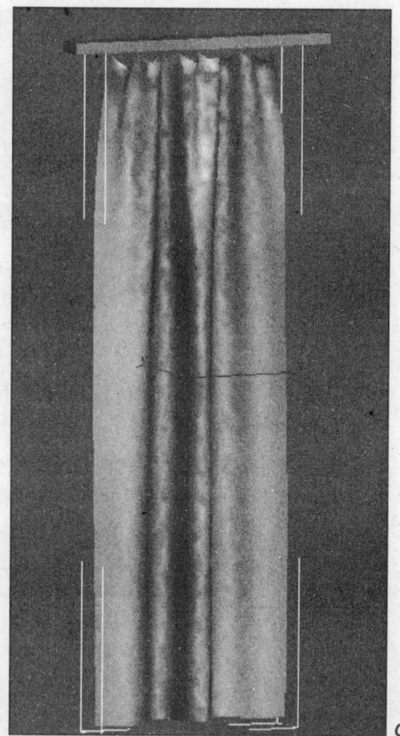

f *g*

Fig. 3.35, *f* and *g*. Creating realistic curtains

Now, you need to create gathers on the curtain. This can be achieved with animation. Unfortunately, you cannot animate vertices directly. However, you can animate the object, to which the vertices are connected.

- ❒ Move to the 50th frame, click the **AutoKey** button, and scale the box, to which the vertices are connected, by 60% along the X axis.
- ❒ Start computation using the **Simulate** button.

The result in the 100th frame is shown in Fig. 3.35, *f*.

Make the state in the 100th frame current and erase the result of simulation using the **Erase Simulation** button. Then you can return to the zero frame and start local simulation so that the curtain stretches.

Don't click the **Reset State** button. If you already did, you will have to restart the process.

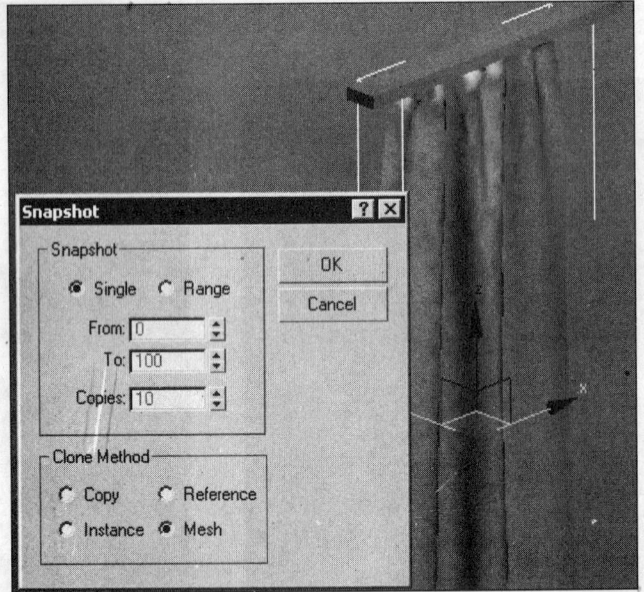

Fig. 3.36. Creating a copy of the curtain

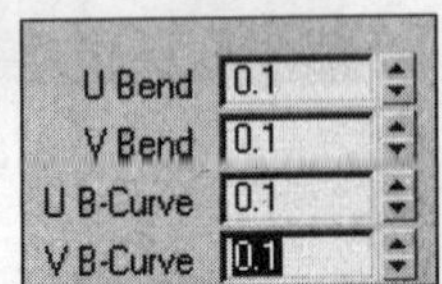

To obtain a better result, I decreased the values of the **U/V Bend** and **U/V B-Curve** parameters that determine the cloth's bending resistance. Nice, isn't it? (Fig. 3.35, *g*).

- ❒ Take a snapshot of the curtain; you'll need it later.

Menu bar → **Tools** → **Snapshot**

Select **Mesh** and click **OK** button (Fig. 3.36).

Although you don't need tied curtains in this project, I'll described briefly how you can tie them up.

- ❒ Create a **Tube** object so that it embraces the curtain (Fig. 3.37, *a*).
- ❒ Move to the 50th frame and animate the size and the position of the tube so that it tightens the curtain and moves it aside (Fig. 3.37, *b*).
- ❒ Select the curtain and add the tube as a **Collision Object** (to do this, open the parameters of the **Cloth** modifier) (Fig. 3.37, *c*).

After some computation the tube will tighten the curtain (Fig. 3.37, *d*). In the figure, you can see how you can deal with unwanted creases using the **Relax** modifier.

NOTE

It is likely that you'll need to increase the value of the **Subsample** parameter as shown in figure. Generally speaking, setting cloth is a very laborious task, so refer to the user manual.

The final variant of my curtain is in the curtain.max file in the Projects\Interior folder on the accompanying CD-ROM.

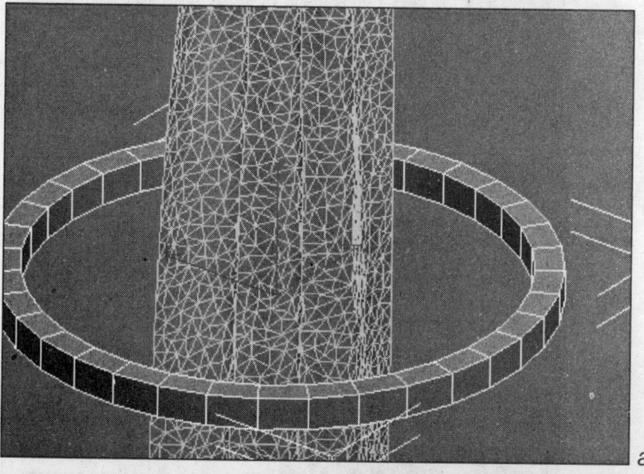

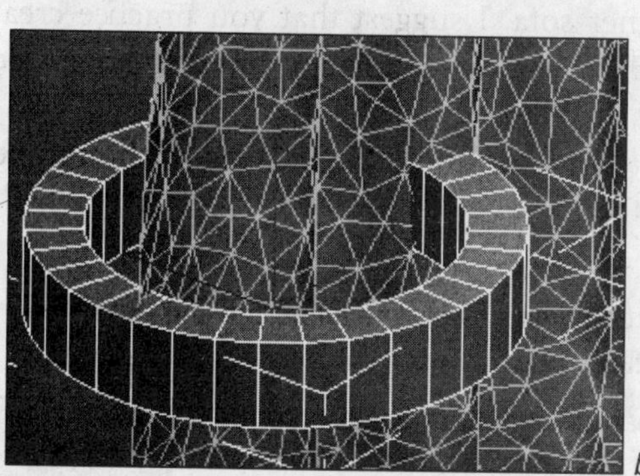

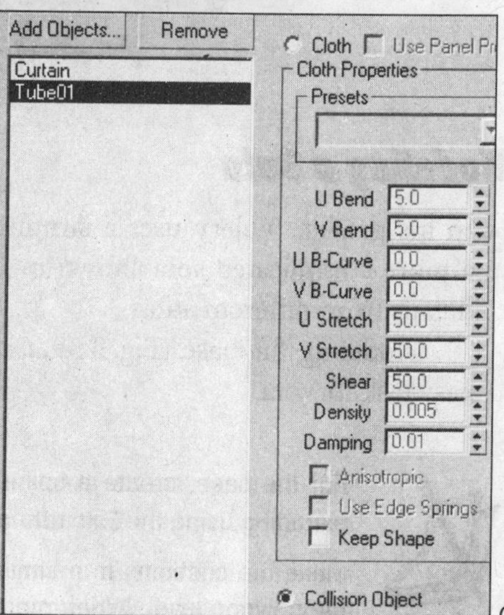

Fig. 3.37, *a–c*. Tying up the curtain

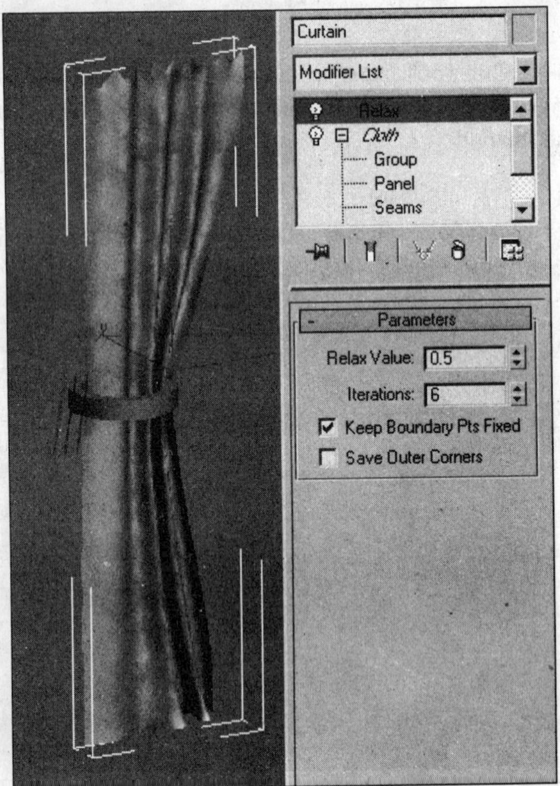

Fig. 3.37, *d*. Tying up the curtain

Modeling a Sofa

In his project, Valery uses a simple corner sofa. I suggest that you practice creating a more complicated sofa shown in Fig. 38. It isn't an actual specimen. I borrowed its details from different sofas.

Modeling the base (Fig. 3.39, *a* and *b*) and cushions (Fig. 3.39, *c*–*f*) should be an easy task for you.

For the base, create a spline by combining two rectangles, making chamfers, and extruding using the **Extrude** modifier.

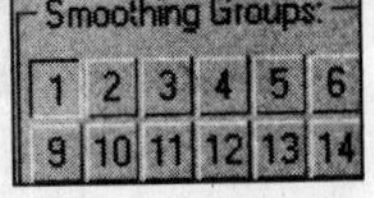

Make the cushions in a similar manner and then finish them on the polygon level. When modeling polygons, the main command at the first stage is **Chamfer** for edges. Then you should move vertices using Soft Selection. You could divide the upper polygons using the **Tesselate** command, but it is best to do this using the **Slice Plane** command so that the cushions are pressed (if you need this). Finally, select all the polygons and assign them one Smoothing Group.

It is a little more difficult to model the back. When creating it, use **Mesh Smooth**; therefore, the initial geometry is quite simple regarding the number of polygons.

Create a closed broken line to outline the number of vertices at the front and rear sides of the sofa back. Add vertices using the **Refine** command. You'll need this later.

Fig. 3.38. A model of a corner sofa

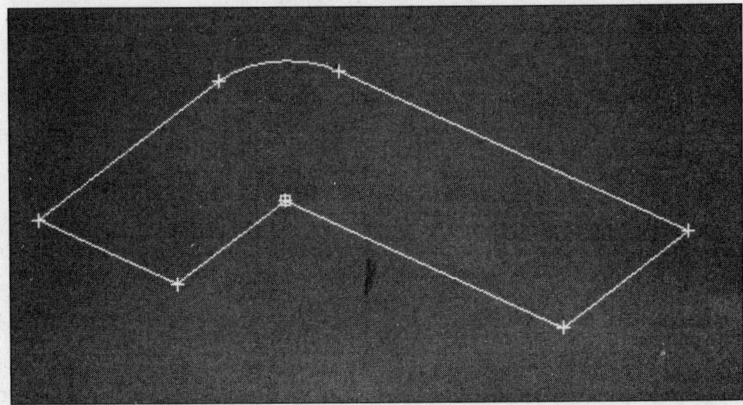

Fig. 3.39, *a*. Modeling the base and the cushions of the sofa

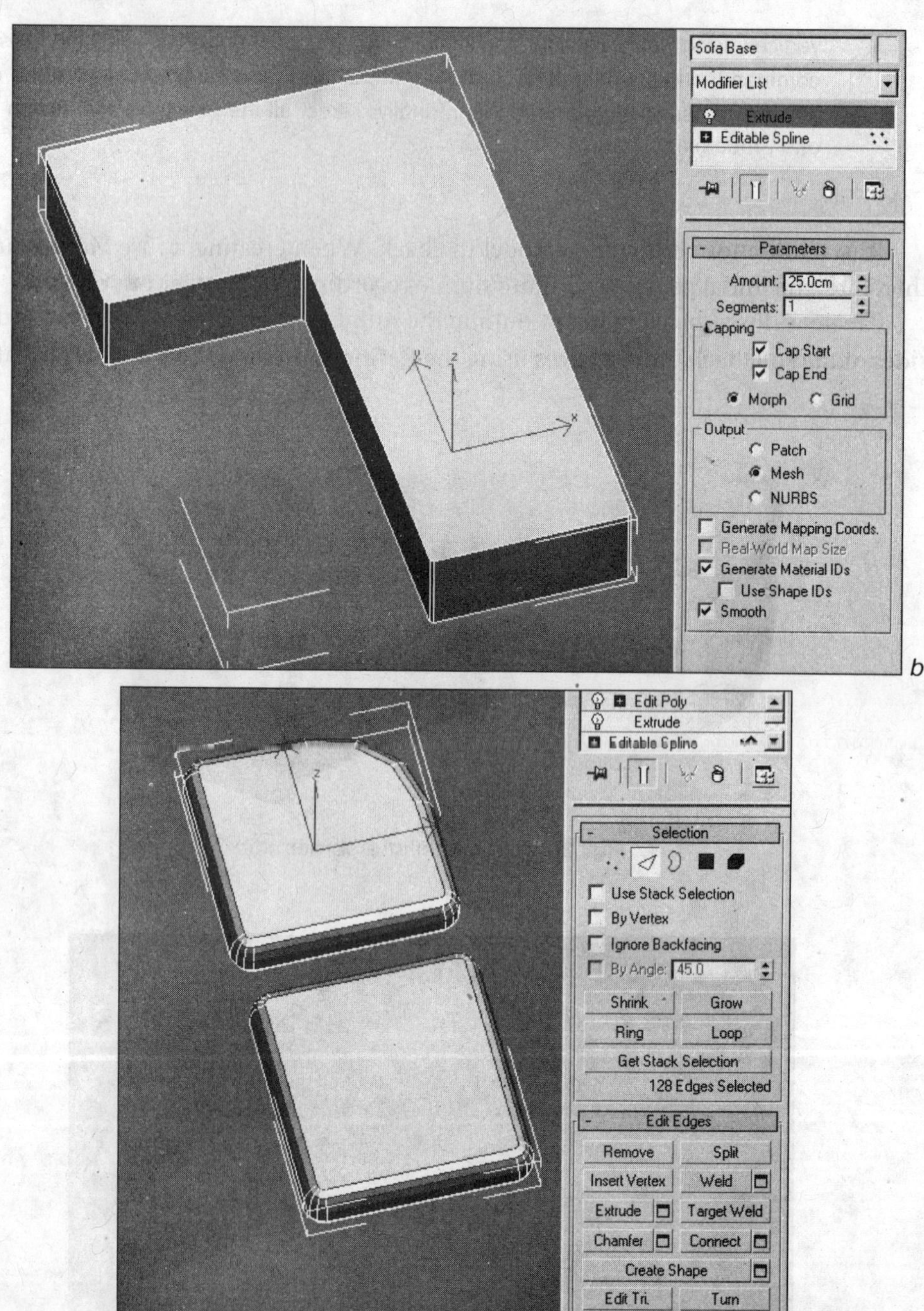

Fig. 3.39, *b* and *c*. Modeling the base and the cushions of the sofa

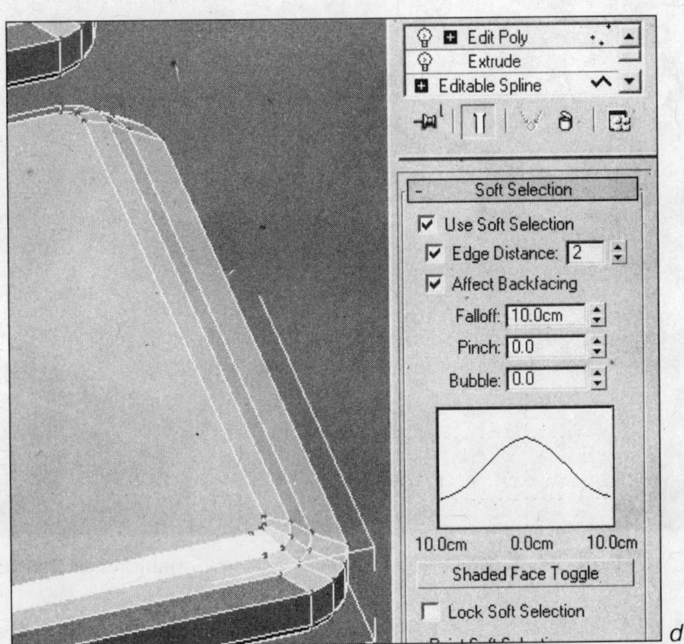

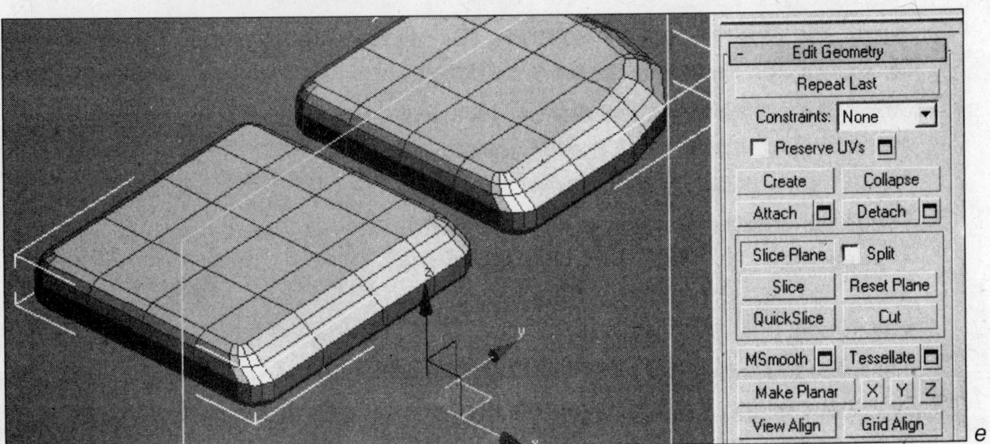

Fig. 3.39, *d* and *e*. Modeling the base and the cushions of the sofa

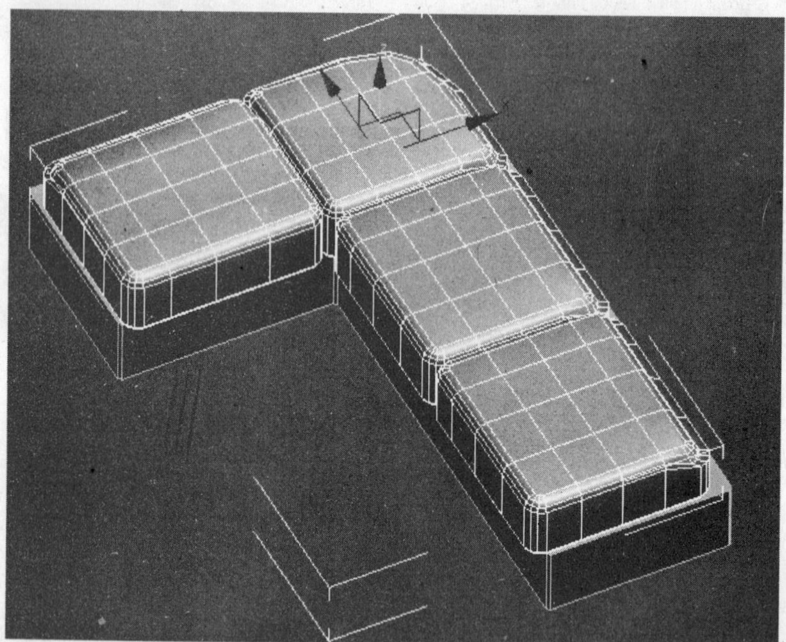

Fig. 3.39, *f*. Modeling the base and the cushions of the sofa

Extrude one section of the back using the **Extrude** modifier. Make it as long as necessary so that the central part of the section contains a head-rest (Fig. 3.40, *b*).

Use the **Edit Poly** modifier to develop the central part.

- Break the central part by selecting the vertices and scaling along one axis about the center of selection.
- Select the polygons of the central part and extrude then using the **Extrude** command for polygons using local normals.
- Select the edges and make a small chamfer. It is necessary to select this element of the back during smoothing. Otherwise, the smoothing will be too strong.

Extrude Polygons
Extrusion Type
Group
Local Normal
By Polygon
Extrusion Height
3.0cm
Apply
OK
Cancel

- Get rid of small triangles using the **Target Weld** command on vertices.
- Select the edges of the polygon on the external side of the back and make a very small chamfer.
- Cut this polygon along the vertices using the **Cut** command. This is necessary for smoothing because only quadrangular polygons are smoothed correctly.

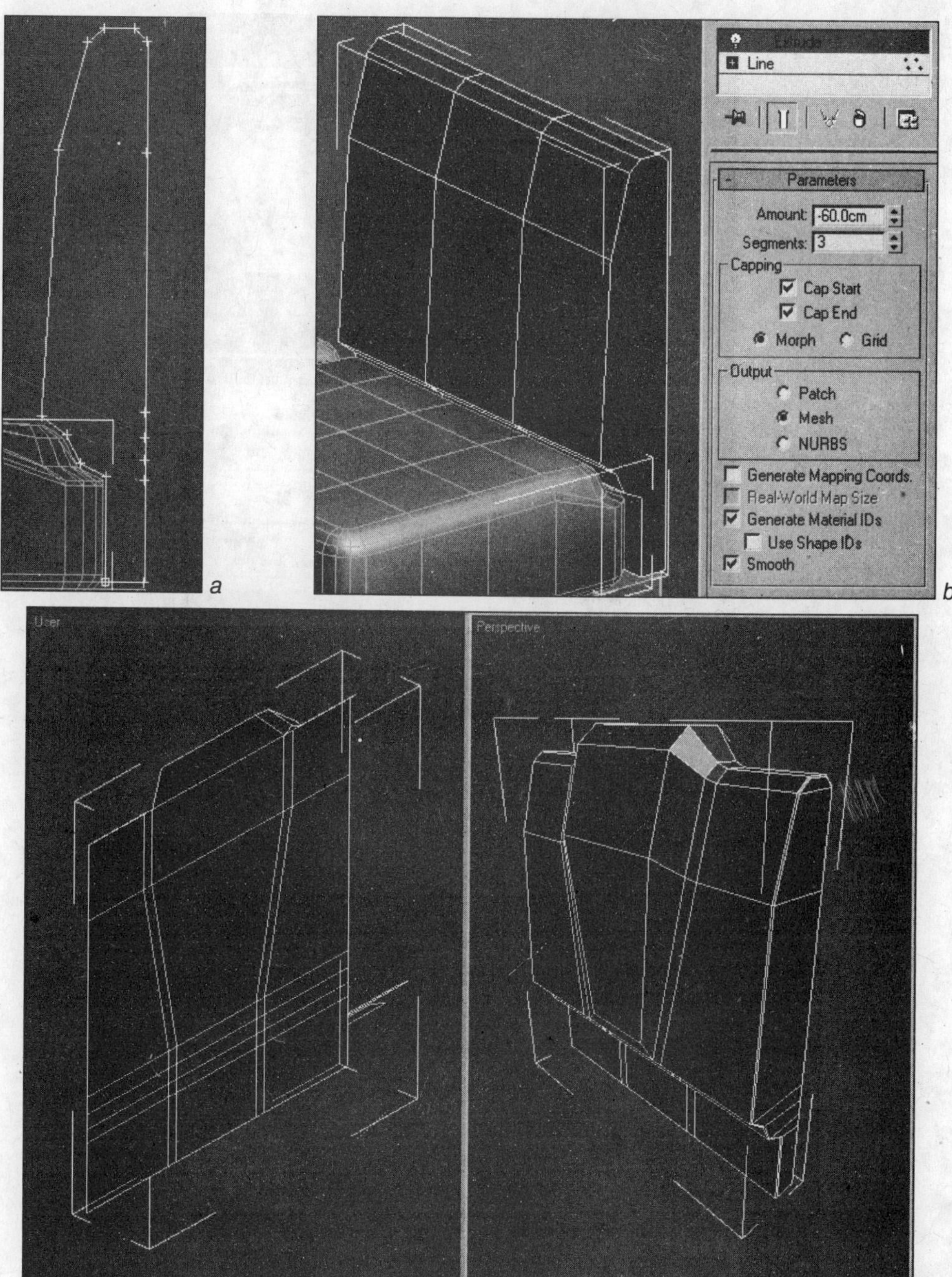

Fig. 3.40, *a–c*. Modeling the back

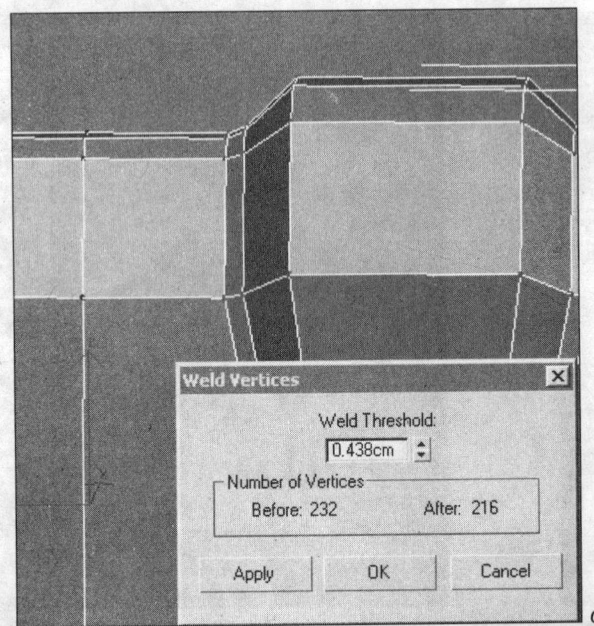

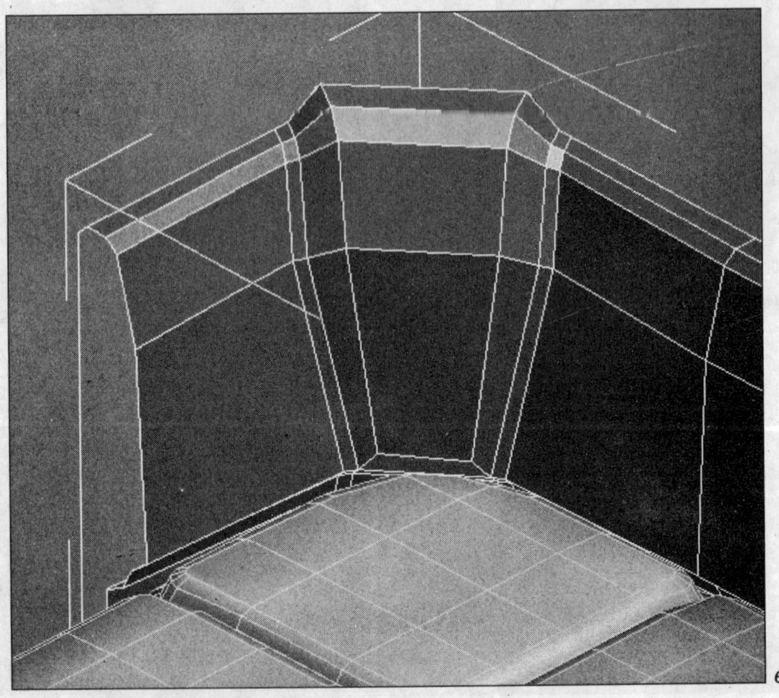

Fig. 3.40, *d* and *e*. Modeling the back

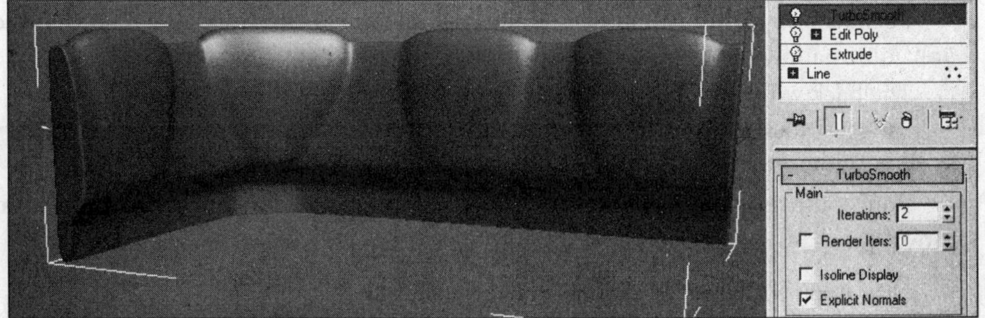

Fig. 3.40, *f*. Modeling the back

- Delete the polygon, to which the other half of the back will be connected. Also, add the bottom polygons.

One section of the back is ready (Fig. 3.40, *c*).

TIP

You can use the **MeshSmooth** or **TurboSmooth** modifier to check whether it is correct (Menu bar → **Modifiers** → **Subdivision Surfaces**).

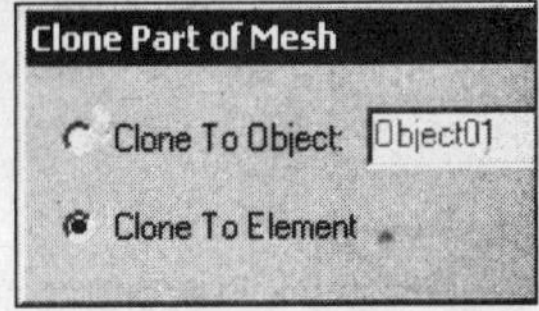

- Select all the polygons and move them so that they are at the position of the second section. When doing so, keep the <Shift> key pressed and select the **Clone to element** method of copying so that they remain the object's components.
- Remove the polygons that are between the sections, select the vertices using a window, and weld them using the **Weld** command whose threshold should be large enough (Fig. 3.40, *d*).

You'll have to work hard to rotate. I recommend that you do this in the top view as follows:

- Select the extreme vertices and rotate them around the common center through 30 degrees.
- Select the extreme vertices and the vertices of the half of the central part and again rotate through 30 degrees. Move them if necessary.
- Finally, select all vertices except those, which should be welded with the previous sections, and again rotate through 30 degrees. Obtain the best result by moving the vertices (Fig. 3.40, *e*).

I believe you can finish modeling the back on your own. A tip: You'll need to create polygons manually.

The back with two **TurboSmooth** iterations is shown in Fig. 3.40, *f*.

I suggest that you start modeling an arm from the central inset. This will allow you to choose the appropriate number of vertices (Fig. 3.41, *a*).

You could use the **Extrude** modifier, but I suggest conversion to the **Editable Poly** type.

Quad menu → **Convert To → Convert to Editable Poly**

- ❒ Make the inset using the **Extrude** command for polygons, the **Chamfer** command for edges, the **Cut** command for vertices, and the **Inset** command and movement for polygons (Fig. 3.41, *b*).

Although the top polygon (indicated with number 1 in Fig. 3.41, *b*) has many vertices, this isn't noticeable. Don't mind it.

- ❒ Select the border of the inset. To do this, use the **Border** subobject.
- ❒ While keeping the <Shift> key pressed, scale them in the plane. Move vertices in the "direct" view (i.e., front or left) to obtain a proper shape (Fig. 3.41, *c*).

I recommend that you create many vertices where indicated with an arrow.

- ❒ Extrude the border edges while keeping the <Shift> key pressed, and move vertices to obtain a proper shape (Fig. 3.41, *d*).

A few additional points.

- ❒ Create a chamfer on the front surface of the arm and on bottom edges. Move vertices to make the top chamfer larger and the bottom one smaller. This should result in a smooth change at the top, and an abrupt one at the bottom.

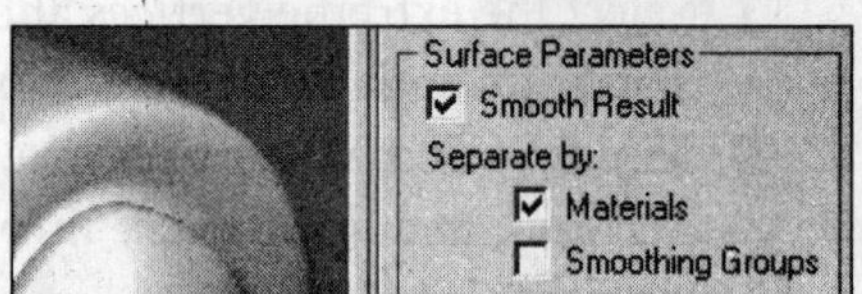

- ❒ Separate the inset and the other details of the arm into different material IDs. Set the material ID to 2 for the polygons of the inset and set IDs to 1 for the others. You need to do this in any case, and in this project you'll obtain a clear border in the **Turbo Smooth** and **Mesh Smooth** modifiers by setting the **Separate by Material** checkbox.

- To create the other arm, copy the first using the **Reference** method and apply the **Mirror** modifier. The use of **Reference** allows you to edit one object and change the other simultaneously.

The geometry of the sofa is ready. As you see, polygon editing is a laborious task, but it is worth working. However, you should be very careful when modeling.

My sofa is in the Sofa.max file in the Projects\Interior folder on the accompanying CD-ROM.

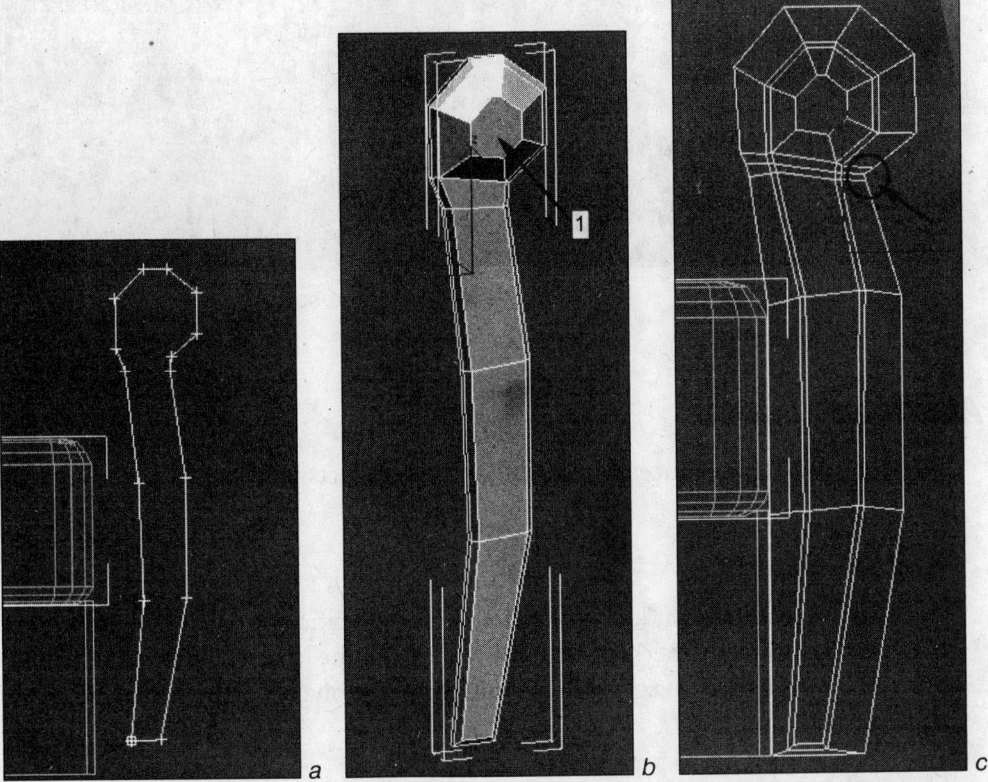

Fig. 3.41, *a–c*. Modeling the sofa

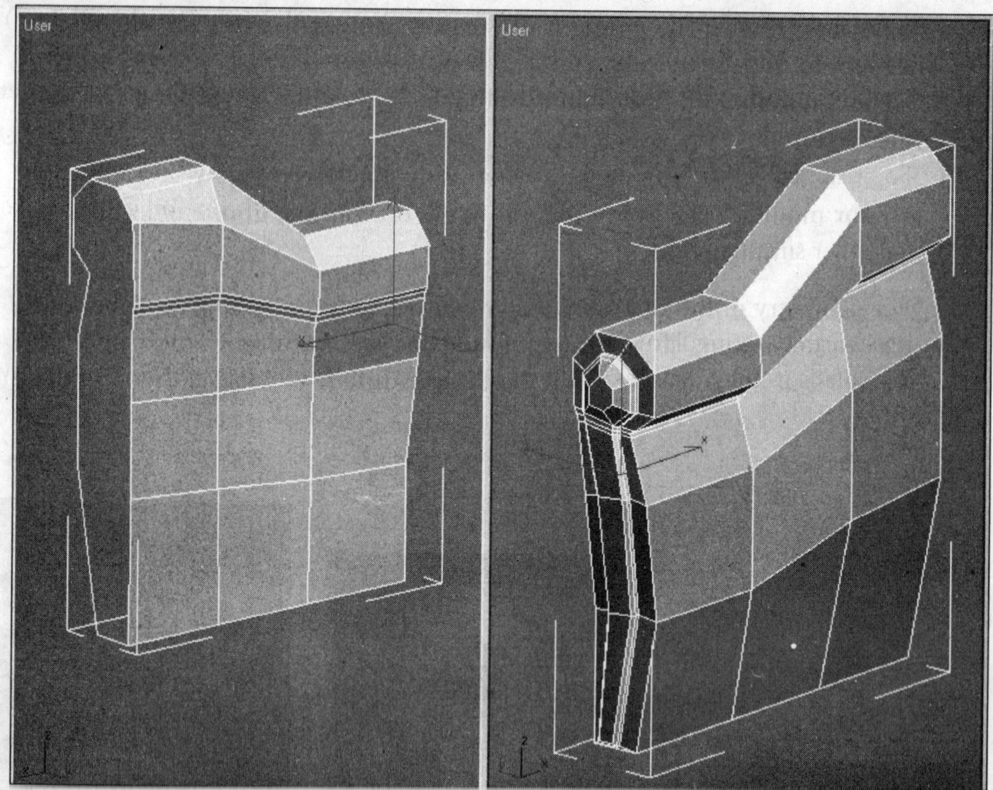

Fig. 3.41, *d*. Modeling the sofa

Additional Objects

I'd like to touch on nuances of modeling certain objects in the scene.

Modeling Chairs

There are many different kinds of chairs, and a specific approach is required in each case. In this project, the seats and the backs of the chairs can be modeled using splines, covering them with patches, and editing polygons. The frames are just sets of primitives.

- Create a set of cross-sections for the seat (Fig. 3.43, *a*). It is convenient to create one cross-section and then copy, move, and edit it.

Fig. 3.42. A draft of a chair

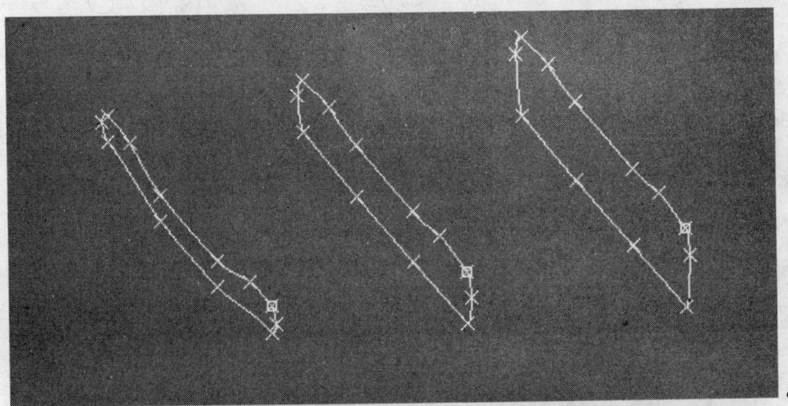

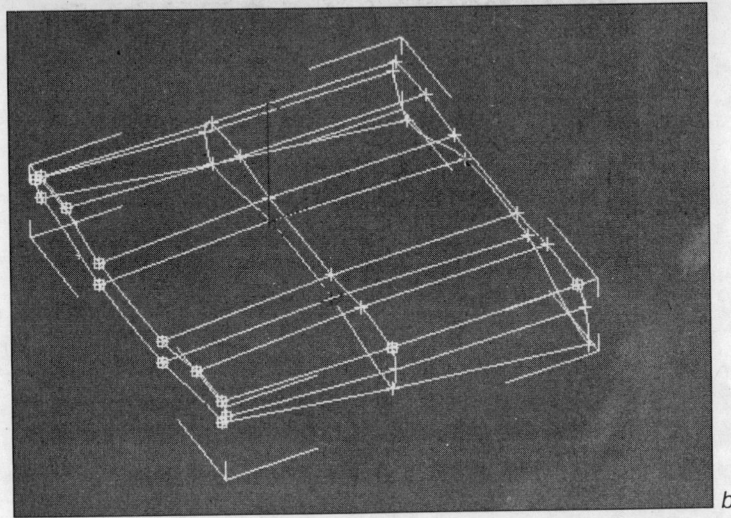

Fig. 3.43, *a* and *b*. Modeling a chair

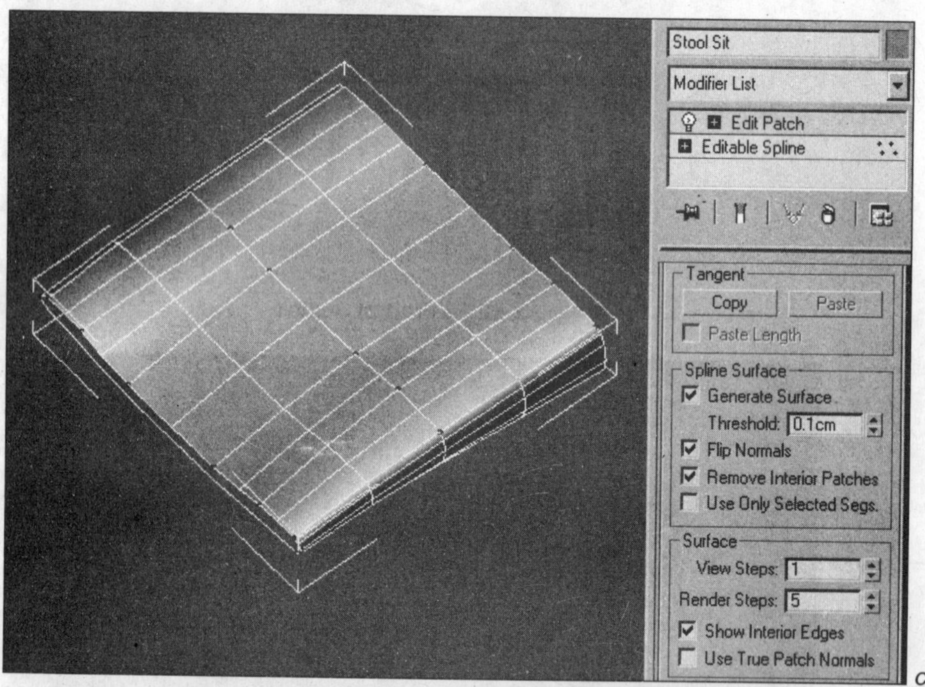

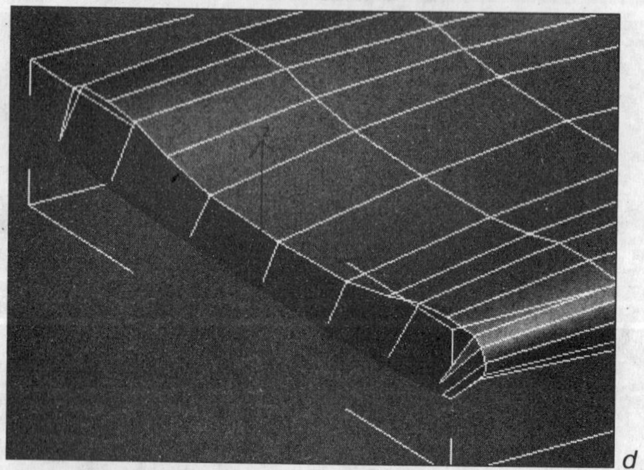

Fig. 3.43, *c* and *d*. Modeling a chair

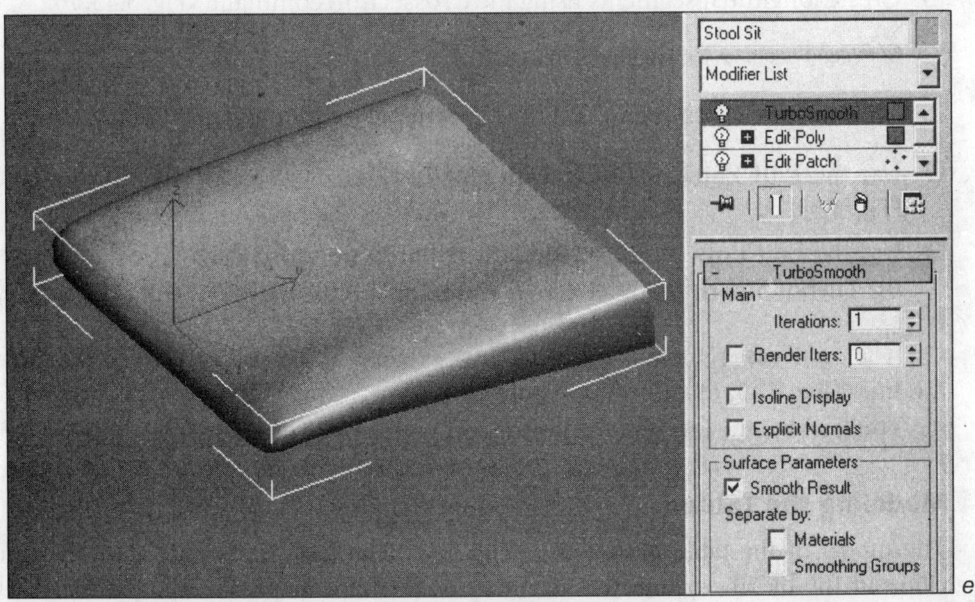

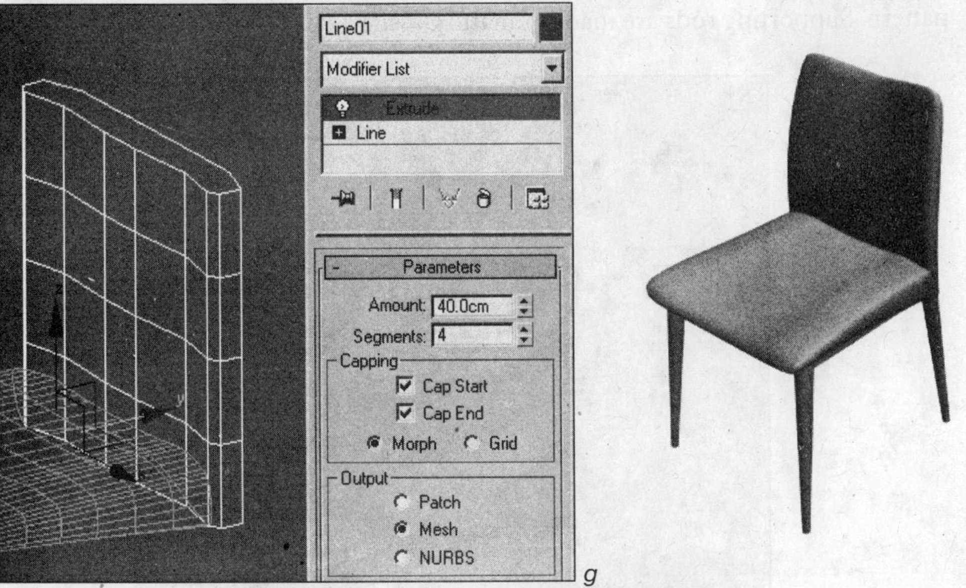

Fig. 3.43, *e–g*. Modeling a chair

- Create longitudal segments using the **Crossection** command (Fig. 3.43, *b*).

  Command panel → the **Geometry** rollout

  Click the first crosssection and drag the rubber band to the next one.

- Use the **Edit Patch** modifier with small values of steps for creating the surface (Fig. 3.43, *c*).
- Use the **Edit Poly** modifier and add required polygons (Fig. 3.43, *d*). The use of the **TurboSmooth** modifier allows you to obtain the desired result (Fig. 3.43, *e*).

It is even easier to make a back. Just extrude a crosssection using the **Extrude** modifier (Fig. 3.43, *f*) and edit the polygons.

You'll create the legs and the bottom on your own. The chair is ready (Fig. 3.43, *g*).

Modeling the Table

The model of the table is shown in Fig. 3.44. The base represents a wooden hemi-ellipsoid 100 by 50 cm, and the height equal to 5 cm. Its profile is a quarter of ellipse (30 by 10 cm). The cover is made of transparent glass of elliptical shape, having dimensions of 200 by 100 cm, 2 cm thick, with the matte central part, covered with some pattern. Supporting rods are made of matte glass.

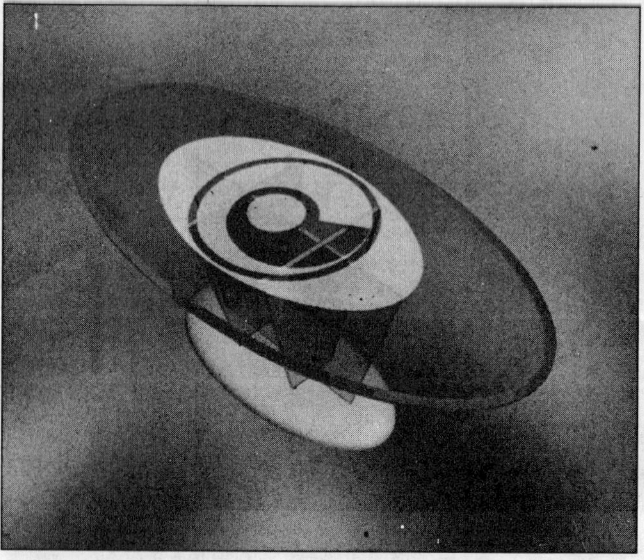

Fig. 3.44. The model of the table

I'd like to use this model to illustrate how to use the **Sweep** modifier's predecessors — the **Bevel** and **Bevel Profile** modifiers. Use them to obtain a top-quality result quickly and easily.

Start with the top of the table.

- ❒ Create an ellipse with a size of 100 × 200 cm.

Menu bar → **Create** → **Shapes** → **Ellipse**

TIP

The table should be elaborated, so you can check the **Adaptive** checkbox in the interpolation parameters.

- ❒ Use the **Bevel** modifier with parameters set as shown in Fig. 45, *a*.

NOTE

The most important parameters are in the **Bevel Value** rollout. A negative value of the **Start Outline** parameter in combination with parameters of **Level 1** makes a bevel at the bottom. A zero value of the **Outline** parameter at the second level makes a vertical surface, and the third level is used to create the top bevel.

Parameters in the **Parameters** rollout allow you to obtain an object without the top and bottom caps (the **Cap Start/End** checkboxes) and to change the profile (however, the latter feature isn't flexible enough). The **Keep Lines From Crossing** checkbox allows you to avoid crossings in internal corners.

I suggest that you use the **Bevel Profile** modifier for the table base. Unfortunately, you cannot use only the **Sweep** modifier because it cannot create caps when open profiles are used.

- ❒ Create ellipses with sizes of 100 × 50 cm and 30 × 10 cm. Apply the **Edit Spline** modifier to the second ellipse and remove all segments except one (Fig. 3.45, *b*).
- ❒ Note the vertex indicated with an arrow. Make it first. It will be used by the **Bevel Profile** modifier as reference.

Rename the large ellipse Table Base and apply the **Bevel Profile** modifier to it. Click the **Pick Profile** button and select an appropriate profile (Fig. 3.45, *c*). Something is wrong, isn't it?

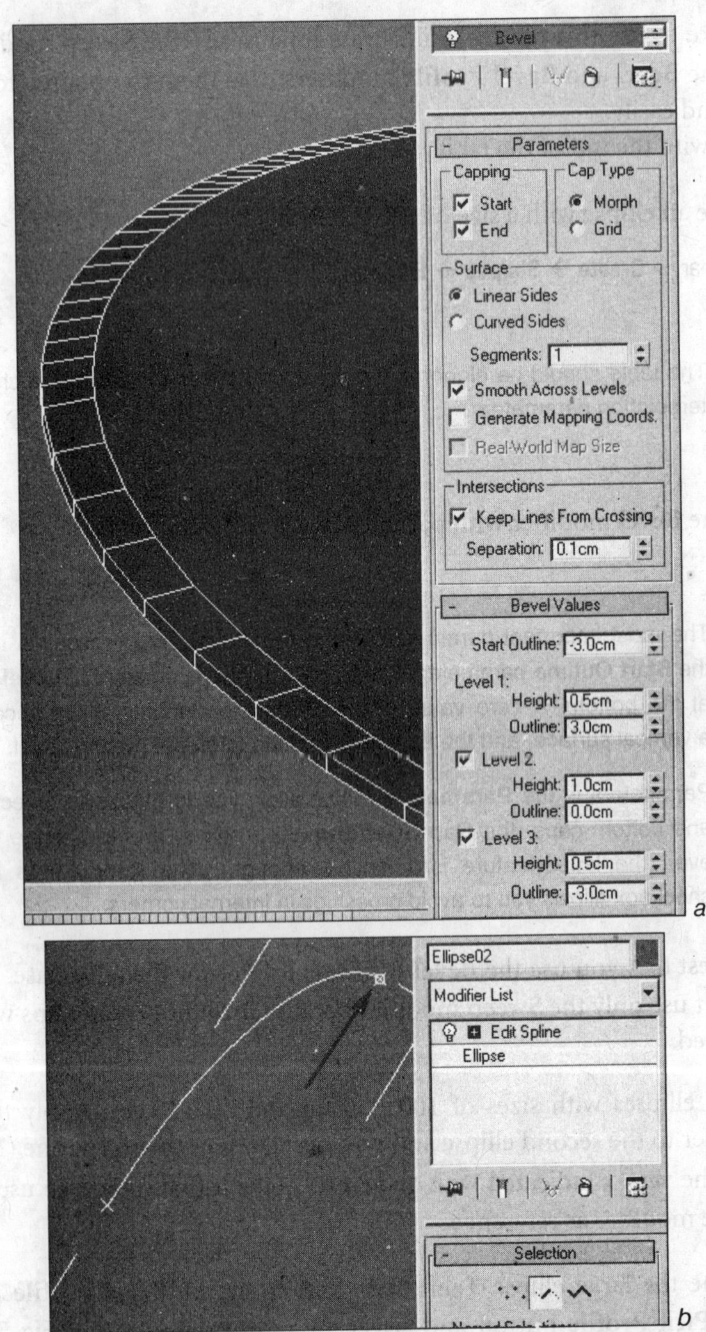

Fig. 3.45, *a* and *b*. Modeling the table

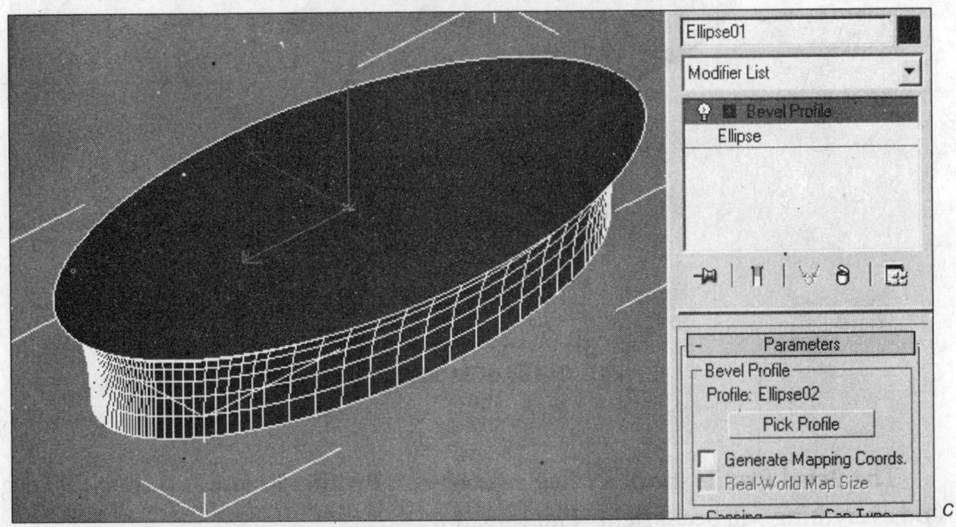

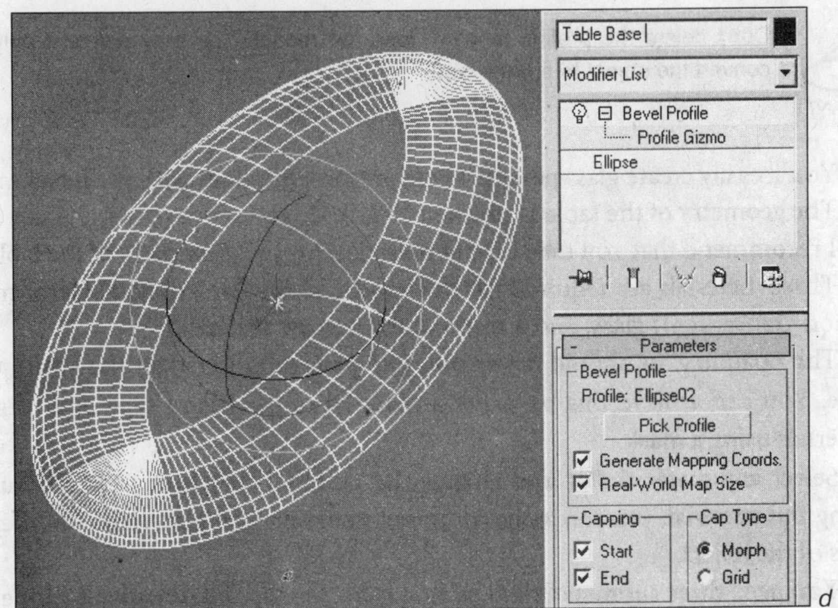

Fig. 3.45, *c* and *d*. Modeling the table

Fig. 3.45, *e*. Modeling the table

The **Bevel Profile** modifier has a subobject, **Profile**. Rotate it through 90 degrees, and everything will be all right (Fig. 3.45, *d*).

Don't delete the profile, or you'll lose the model. You may delete it only after you convert the object to a base type.

You'll easily create glass panels. These are closed splines with the **Bevel** modifiers. The geometry of the table is finished (Fig. 3.45, *e*).

I recommend that you take care of materials for the glass parts of the table.

Three materials are required for this model: clean glass, opaque (semi-transparent or non-transparent) glass, and a material for narrow surfaces.

The opaque glass should cover only the pattern rather than the entire top of the table. You can achieve this by using a material of the **Blend** type and blending two materials using a mask.

Select any material slot and change the material type in it to **Multi/Sub-Object**. Using this material, you can assign different materials (submaterials) to different polygons of the object.

You need three submaterials. The first is for the top. I'll describe it a little later.

The second submaterial is glass. It is an architectural material with the **Clear Glass** setting, and its white diffuse color should be brighter than default.

Generally speaking, the diffuse component of glass should be set to a small value (dark; ideally, black) because glass both reflects and refracts. Since settings of architectural material are simplified, traditional approaches sometimes don't work.

The third submaterial shouldn't be transparent. Let it be a greenish mirror.

The final structure of the material is shown in Fig. 3.46, *a*.

Now, let's return to the first submaterial. It is of the **Blend** type that allows either to blend two materials in a certain proportion or using a black-and white map called a mask. The black of the mask indicates areas where the first submaterial should be, while the white indicates the second submaterial (Fig. 3.46, *b*). Unfortunately, a material of this type cannot be displayed in the viewport completely. Therefore, you should adjust the position of the mask by selecting **Interactive** in the **Mask** line and clicking the **Show Map in Viewport** button in the parameters of the map.

The first submaterial is a variant of glass whose **Transparency** parameter is decreased to a value between 20 and 40. Its map is of the **Noise** type, and it is assigned to the **Bump** channel. In the settings, decrease the map size to 5.

The second submaterial in this material is glass. Link its parameters to the similar material using the **Instance** method.

Now, you should assign these materials to particular polygons.

- Select all the glass parts of the model and apply the **Edit Poly** modifier to them.
- Select all the polygons and assign them the material ID equal to 3. This is the number of the submaterial for the narrow surfaces. It is most difficult to select them, so why not to begin with them? Learn how to solve tasks in the most efficient way.
- Select the polygons on the top of the table and assign them the material ID equal to one (Fig. 3.45, *c*).
- Assign the other polygons the ID equal to two (Fig. 3.45, *d*).
- Assign the material to the objects by dragging it from the material editor.

Finally, apply the **UVW Map** modifier to the top of the table. If the position of the mask map is wrong, rotate the gizmo of the modifier through 90 degrees and click the **Fit** button.

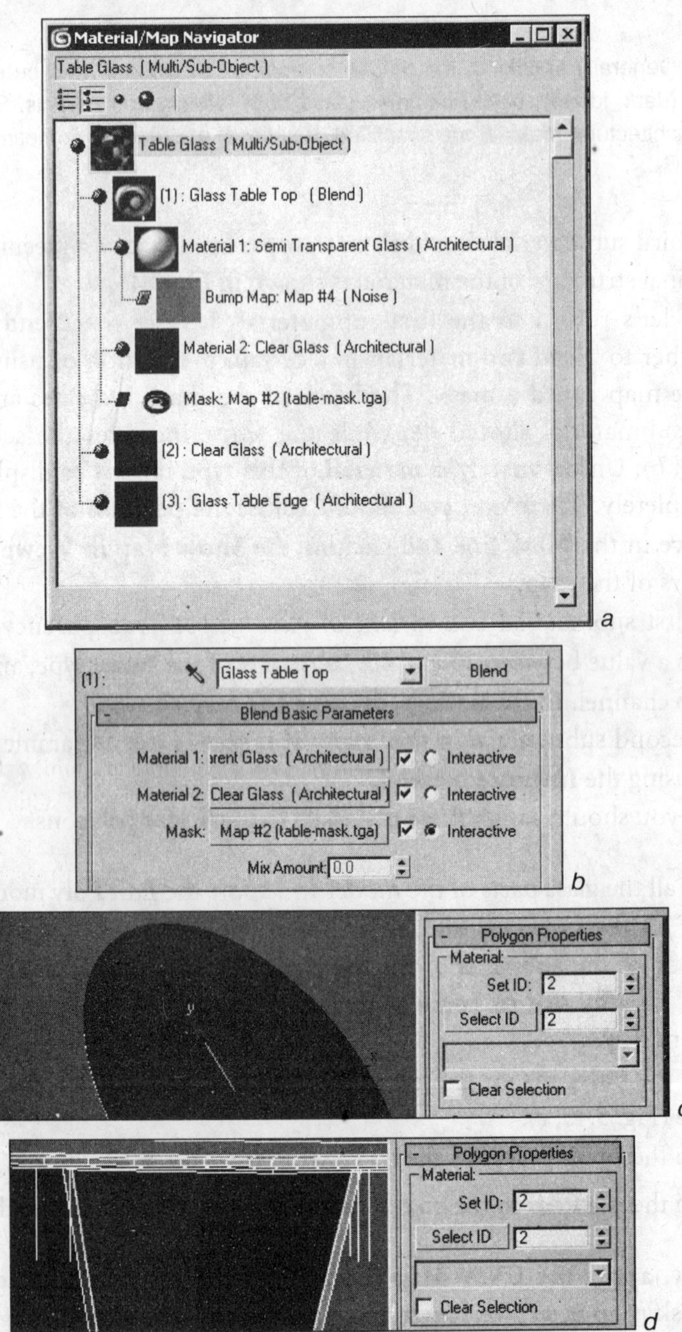

Fig. 3.46. Materials for the table

Lamps for the Living-Room

There is nothing special about these lamps (Fig. 3.47). A lampshade 50 cm long and with the maximum diameter of 6 cm is made from the **Cone** primitive with small bends at the end. The bulb and the cap are also based on primitives, and the frame is made from splines with rendering parameters set as shown in Fig. 3.48.

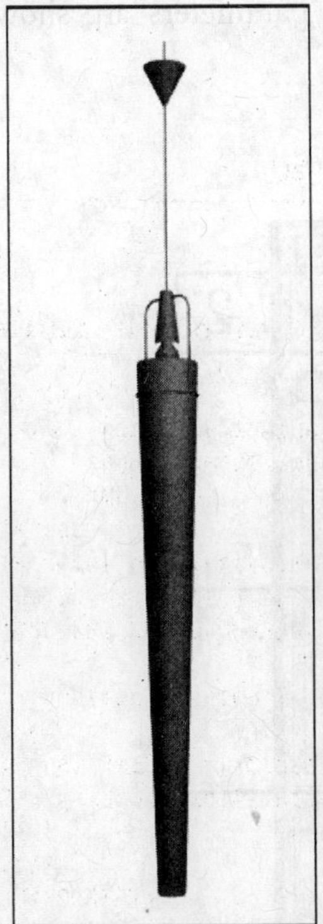

Fig. 3.47. The lamp model

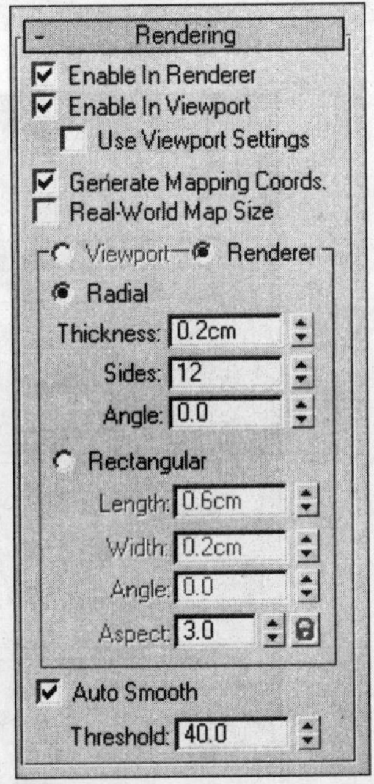

Fig. 3.48. Rendering parameters of splines for the frame

For the frame and the cable, architectural metal and architectural plastic are suitable. For the shade and the bulb, I'd like to offer you an approved approach.

It would be wasteful to assign glass to such insignificant objects. They are not worth spending computer resources. In addition, if you don't take care of the thickness of the bulb glass, the bulb will consists of a solid piece of glass. The same is true for the shade although the surface isn't closed.

Unfortunately, architectural materials don't allow you to play tricks, so use the Standard type of material.

Parameters of the material chosen for the shade are shown in Fig. 3.49, *a*. It is a standard glossy material with a sharp highlight graph (indicated within box 1) and the **2-sided** checkbox checked (indicated within box 2) so that the back face is visible. Do you remember the shade is one-sided?

The trick I mean uses two maps of the Falloff type (indicated within box 3) assigned to the **Opacity** and **Reflection** channels. Their parameters are shown in Fig. 49, *a* and *b*, respectively.

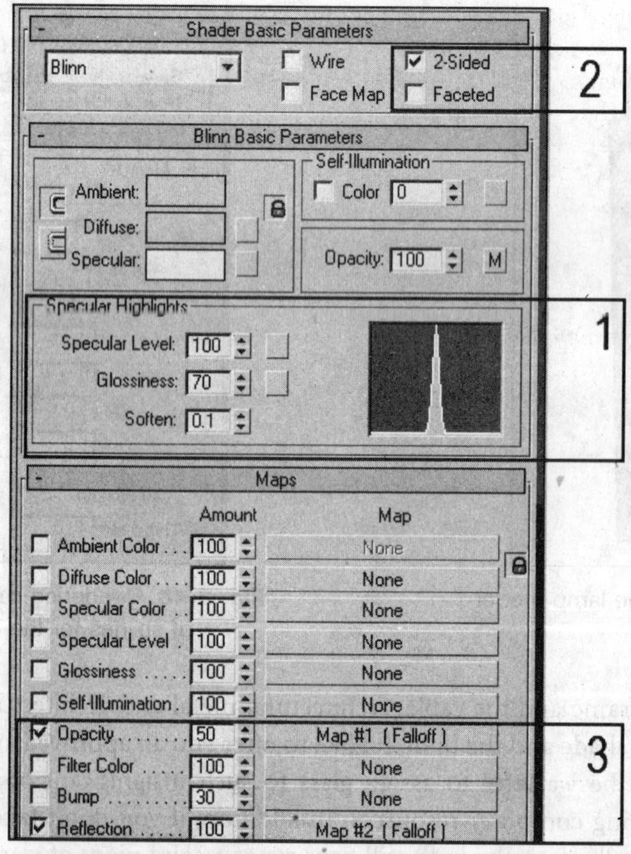

Fig. 3.49, *a*. The material for the lamp-shade

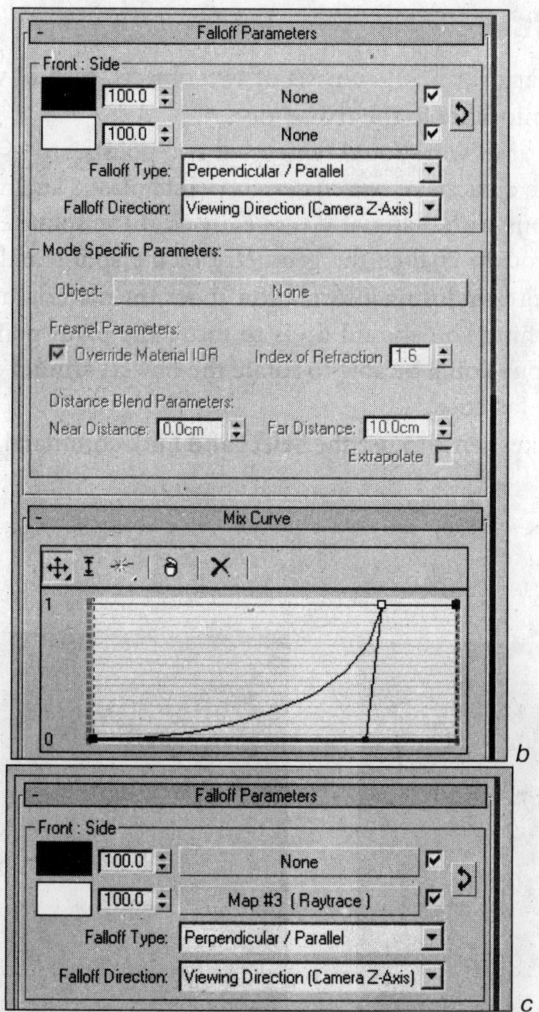

Fig. 3.49, *b* and *c*. The material for the lamp-shade

The use of the **Falloff** map with these settings changes the parameter from one to another (in this case, from the color of the map on **Front** to that on **Side**), depending on the viewing angle with the surface. For **Opacity**, the black indicates transparency, and the white indicates opacity. For **Transparency**, this is vice versa.

Using the **Mix Curve**, I make this dependence more realistic; this is non-linear.

For reflection, add the **Raytrace** map to the channel if you want to obtain "natural" reflection, or **Bitmap** as spherical environment.

Lamps for the Bar

A lamp for the bar (Fig. 3.50) consists of two objects, each of which is created by applying the **Lathe** modifier to the crossection.

This is simple, but you should remember two points.

Because the shade consists of two materials (white plastic and metal), you can separate the future polygons with material IDs as early as at the spline editing stage (Fig. 3.51). This will allow you to change the geometry of the spline and the parameters of the **Lathe** modifier without losing information about the material assignments.

The second thing you should do is to move the pivot points to the actual pivots of the construction. You'll be able to rotate the objects around each other and the rod, to which they are fastened.

Finally, it makes sense to use the **Select and Link** command to link the shade to the fastening.

Fig. 3.50. A lamp for the bar

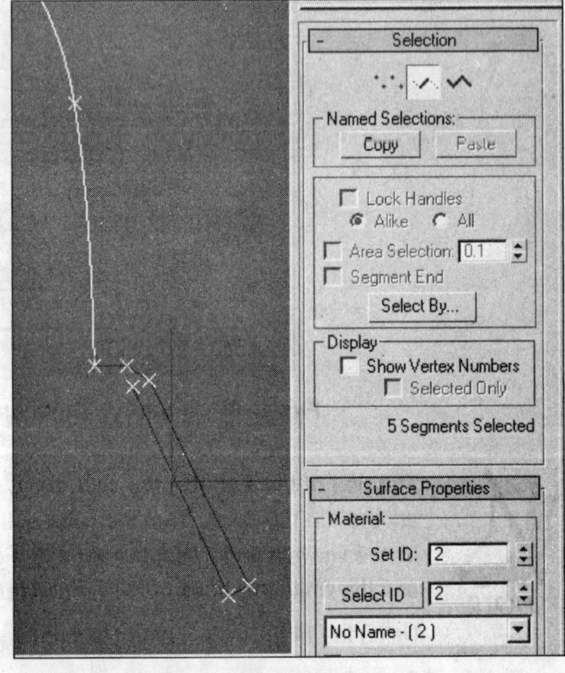

Fig. 3.51. Assigning material IDs to segments of the spline

Fig. 3.52. The positions of the pivot points

A Decoration

The stand in the center of the kitchen carries a "sandstone" decoration. You can create it using any method you like. However, I suggest that you use an interesting feature, the **Displacement** channel.

Don't confuse this with the **Displace** modifier.

A black-and-white map applied to this channel (Fig. 3.53) works much like with the **Bump** channel: The white indicates bumps and the black indicates the zero level. The difference is that **Bump** creates an illusion of roughness, while **Displacement** creates a relief. The geometry is created during rendering.

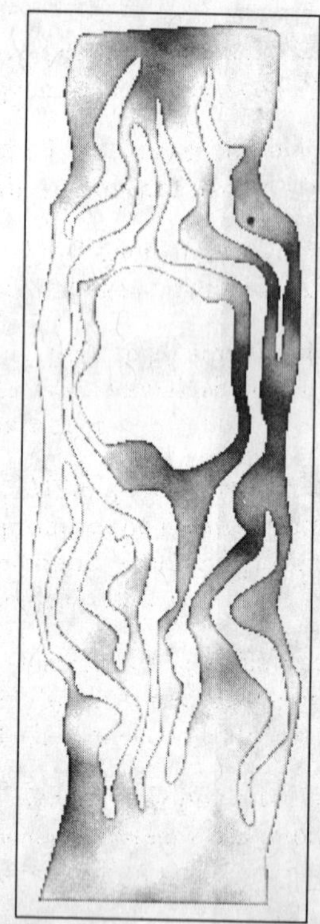

Fig. 3.53. A map applied to the **Displacement** channel

You can use the **Displacement** channel both with the standard renderer and mental ray. They are set up differently, but the first few steps are the same.

- Create a plane with the size of the decoration (280 × 100 cm).
- Open the material editor and select any material slot.
- Select the Architectural type if another type is selected.
- In the **Special Effects** rollout, assign the plate-displacement.tga file to the **Displacement** channel, and assign the material to the plane.

From now on, the settings differ. If you're using the standard renderer, you need to set the degree of surface subdivision using the **Displacement Approximation** modifier.

I obtained the result shown in Fig 3.54, *a* using the settings shown in this figure. To be honest, I don't like it.

Things differ with mental ray. In fact, everything is better. The settings for **Displacement** are on the **Renderer** tab in the render settings dialog box. These settings are global. In addition, each object has individual local settings for **Displacement** in the object properties dialog box. Fig. 3.54, *b* shows these settings and the result of rendering. This result is nice.

The degree of surface subdivision is determined with the **Edge Length** parameter. You can set it in absolute units, but it is most interesting to set it in pixels. A value of 0.5 pixel gives you a nice result with the best approximation. The **Max Displace** value marks the depth. Set it to a value greater than the **Amount** parameter value in the material's **Displacement** line.

The map you use for displacement should be slightly blurred. Otherwise, you'll see every pixel on the final image. If you wish to create bumps and hollows, draw on gray.

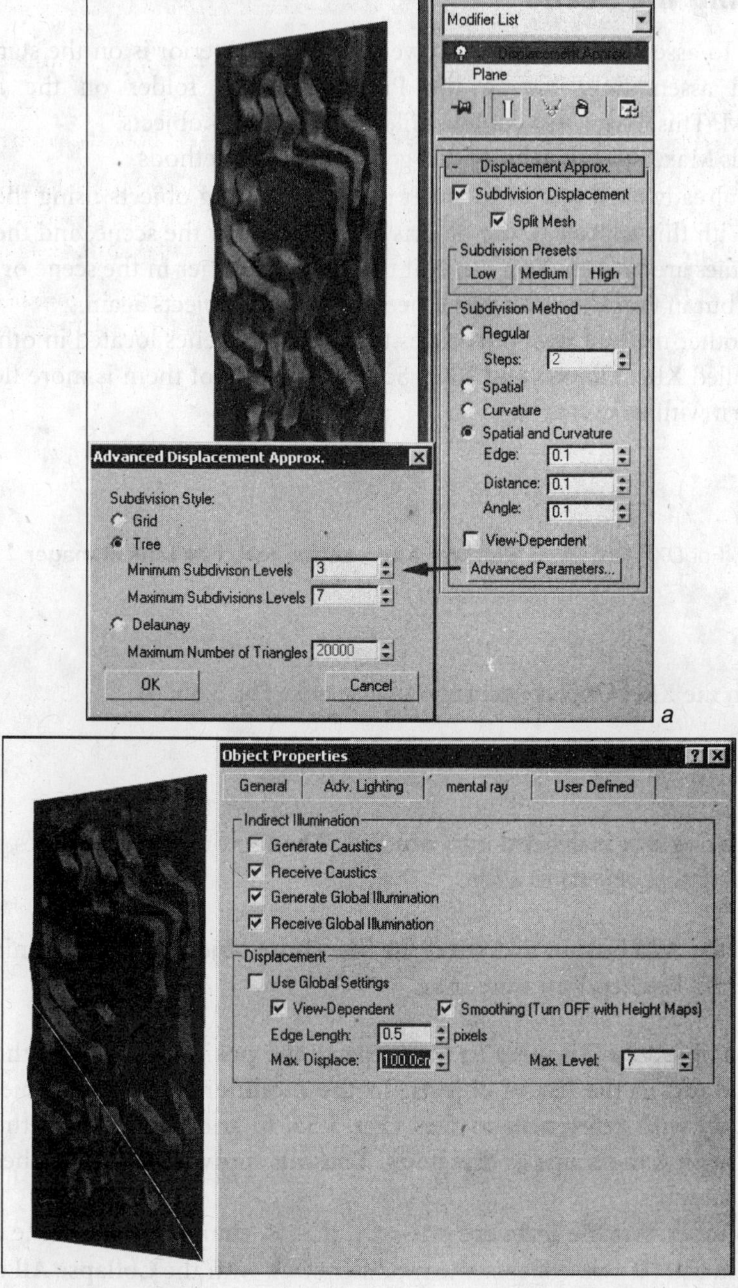

Fig. 3.54. Settings for **Displacement** for the standard renderer (*a*) and mental ray (*b*)

Assembling the Scene

It's time to assemble the scene. My version of the interior is on the stage (i.e., before the final assembling) file in the Projects\Interior folder on the accompanying CD-ROM. This folder also contains files with auxiliary objects.

In 3ds Max, you can achieve this goal using two methods. .

You already used one of them. It involved loading objects using the **Merge** command. With this approach, the objects become part of the scene, and their links to the original files are broken. You can edit these objects either in the scene or in their original files, but in the latter case you'll need to load the objects again.

The other method uses references to objects or scenes located in other files. These are so-called XRef Objects and XRef Scenes. The first of them is more flexible, and I'll illustrate it with an example.

NOTE

For DXF and DWG files, use a very similar tool, **File Link Manager**.

- ❒ Open the **XRef Objects** manager dialog box (Fig. 3.55, *a*).

Menu bar → **File** → **XRef Objects**

The dialog box is divided into two lists. The top one is a list of files, while the bottom list contains objects in a file.

- ❒ Click the **Add** button and select the file whose objects you're planning to load, for example, Kitchen Furniture.max.

These objects will appear in the scene in the position, in which they were in the initial file and in the list of objects. In the modifier stack, such objects are represented only with references to files (Fig. 3.55, *b*) and have a few other parameters that are beyond the scope of this book. You can apply modifiers to these objects and change materials.

Remember that the links are one-way, that is, changes in the scene don't result in changes in files. If you collapse the modifier stack with the **Collapse All** command, the links to the original files will be broken.

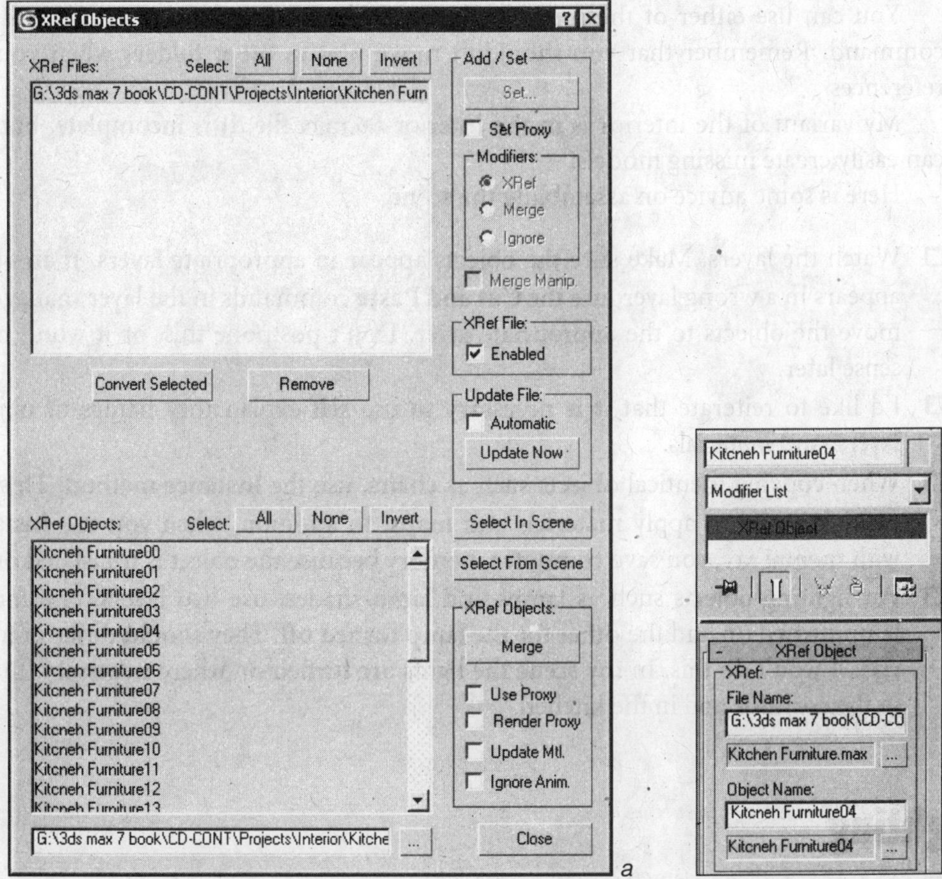

Fig. 3.55. The **XRef Objects** manager dialog box (*a*), parameters of XRef objects in the modifier stack (*b*)

Return to the parameters in the **XRef Objects** dialog box (Fig. 3.55, *a*).

- The **Update Now** button updates the objects, and the **Automatic Update** checkbox forces updating the objects every time a referred file is saved. This allows several people to work on one project simultaneously via a network.
- They can edit and update objects "on the fly."
- The **Convert Selected** button allows you to disassemble the scene to XRef objects (any objects in the scene can be selected).
- Note the **Update Material** checkbox. When it is unchecked, only the geometry of the model is updated.

You can use either of the methods, but I prefer loading objects with the **Merge** command. Remember that you shouldn't move files to other folders when you use references.

My variant of the interior is in the Interior-06.max file. It is incomplete, but you can easily create missing models.

Here is some advice on assembling the scene.

- Watch the layers. Make sure the objects appear in appropriate layers. If an object appears in a wrong layer, use the **Cut** and **Paste** commands in the layer manager to move the objects to the appropriate layer. Don't postpone this, or it won't make sense later.
- I'd like to reiterate that it is necessary to use self-explanatory names of objects, layers, and materials.
- When copying identical objects such as chairs, use the **Instance** method. This will make it easier to apply materials and maps. In addition, when you use **Instance** with mental ray, you save computer memory because the object is translated once.
- For lighting objects such as lamps and lamp-shades, use two layers: one for the lamp turned on and the other for the lamp turned off. They should differ in materials. I won't do this. In my scene the lights are turned on where necessary, that is, in the corridor and in the kitchen.

Lighting

This section describes how you should illuminate the interior with indirect illumination using both methods offered by 3ds Max: the **Radiosity** method for the standard renderer and photon maps and final gather for mental ray. In both cases, direct light (both daylight and candlelight) is set in the same way.

Setting Daylight

As I already mentioned, daylight is set identically in both cases at the first stage.

- Hide all layers except the walls, the floor, and the ceiling.

TIP

It is convenient to hide all layers in the layer manager using the **Hide All Layers** command, and then unhide the required ones.

❒ Assign light-blue to the environment.

Menu bar → **Rendering** → **Environment**

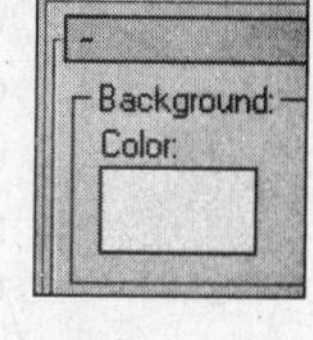

Create a few cameras and put them in appropriate places.

❒ Create a new layer, Cameras, and make it active.

❒ Create a few cameras as shown in Fig. 3.56.

Menu bar → **Create** → **Cameras**

❒ Make them free and lift them to the level of human eyes, that is, approximately 150 cm along the Z axis.

❒ In the camera views, set the cameras so that you see the required areas.

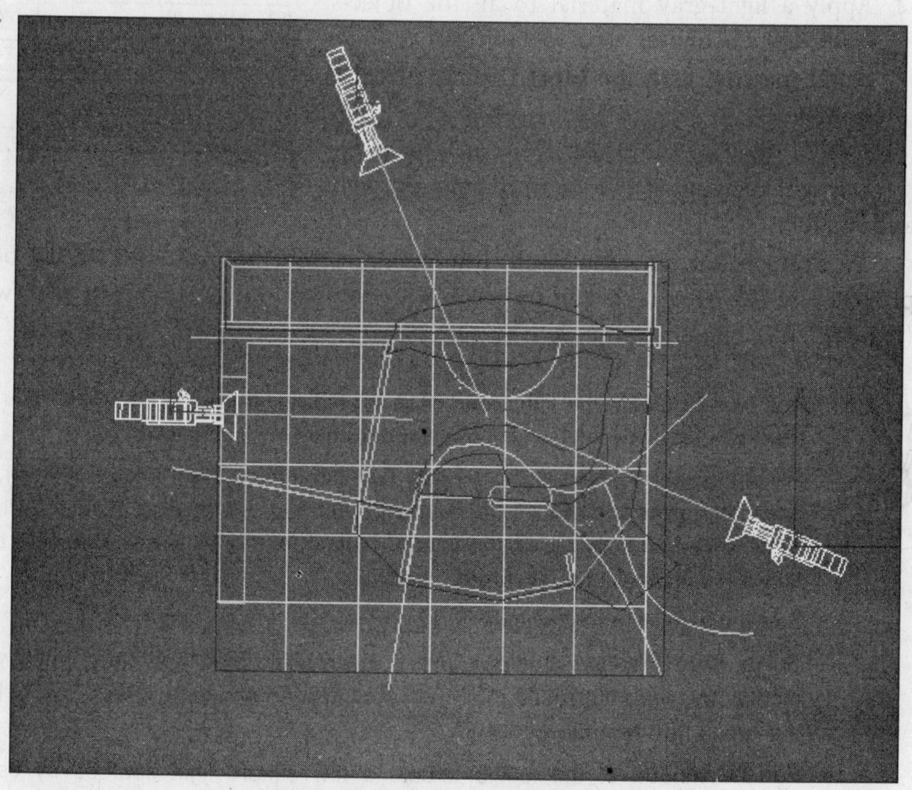

Fig. 3.56. Position of the cameras

TIP

When placing the cameras, it is convenient to use a new feature that allows you to control cameras, so to speak, in the first person. The camera position is changed using the arrow keys on the numeric keypad while keeping the <Shift> key pressed. To change the camera speed, use the <[> and <]> keys, rotate it using the left mouse button, and use the <Shift>+<Spacebar> shortcut to put the camera in a horizontal position.

TIP

Because the cameras are outside the interior, use **Clipping Planes** settings.

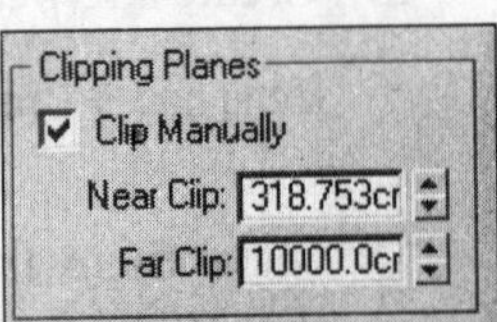

TIP

To avoid the effect of non-parallel walls (unloaded by architectors), try to hold the camera horizontally. The **Camera Correction** modifier can help a little, but it often turns into **Camera Distortion**.

❐ Apply a light-gray material to all the objects. It should be lighter than default; an architectural material with the **Ideal Diffuse** preset is suitable.

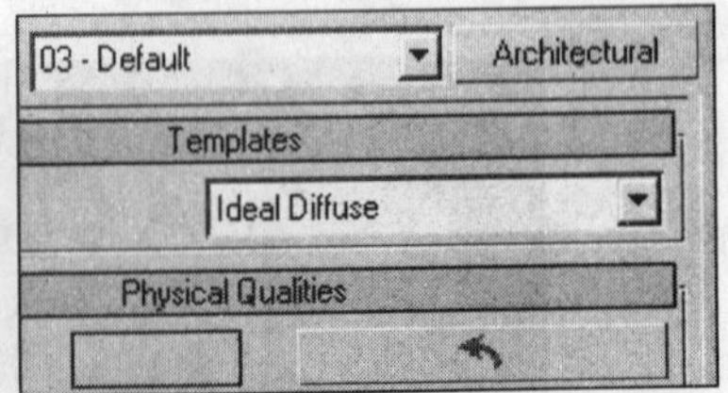

Daylight consists of two components: sky light and sun light.

To simulate the sky, you could use **SkyLight**, but this wouldn't be the best approach. Use the Area Light photometric light sources and put them in each window (Fig. 3.57, *a*).

NOTE

It is best to create the light sources in an individual layer. This allows you to turn them off quickly by unchecking the **Render** checkbox in the layer.

Place the light sources in the window opening behind the frames. However, sometimes this gives a dissatisfying result, so you can use another solution. Place the window light sources inside the interior behind the curtains and illuminate the window sills with additional **SkyLight** sources.

Select a blue color for the light.

Select **Area Shadow** shadows with a low quality (at this stage). When you use mental ray, you'll substitute them with **Ray Traced** shadows whose quality is set in the **Area Light Sampling** rollout.

For the window of the loggia, create a few square light sources by using the **Instance** method.

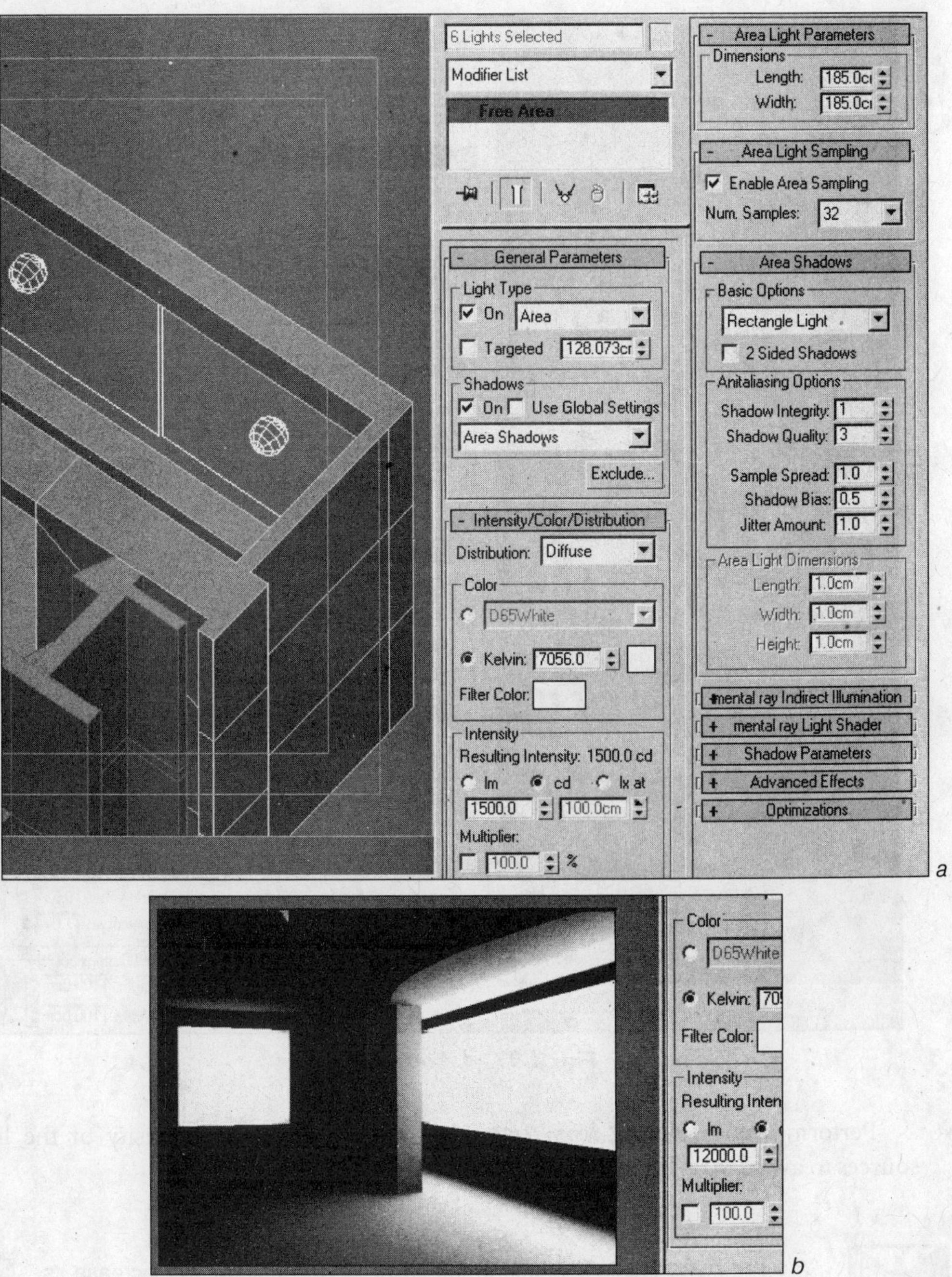

Fig. 3.57, *a* and *b*. Setting daylight

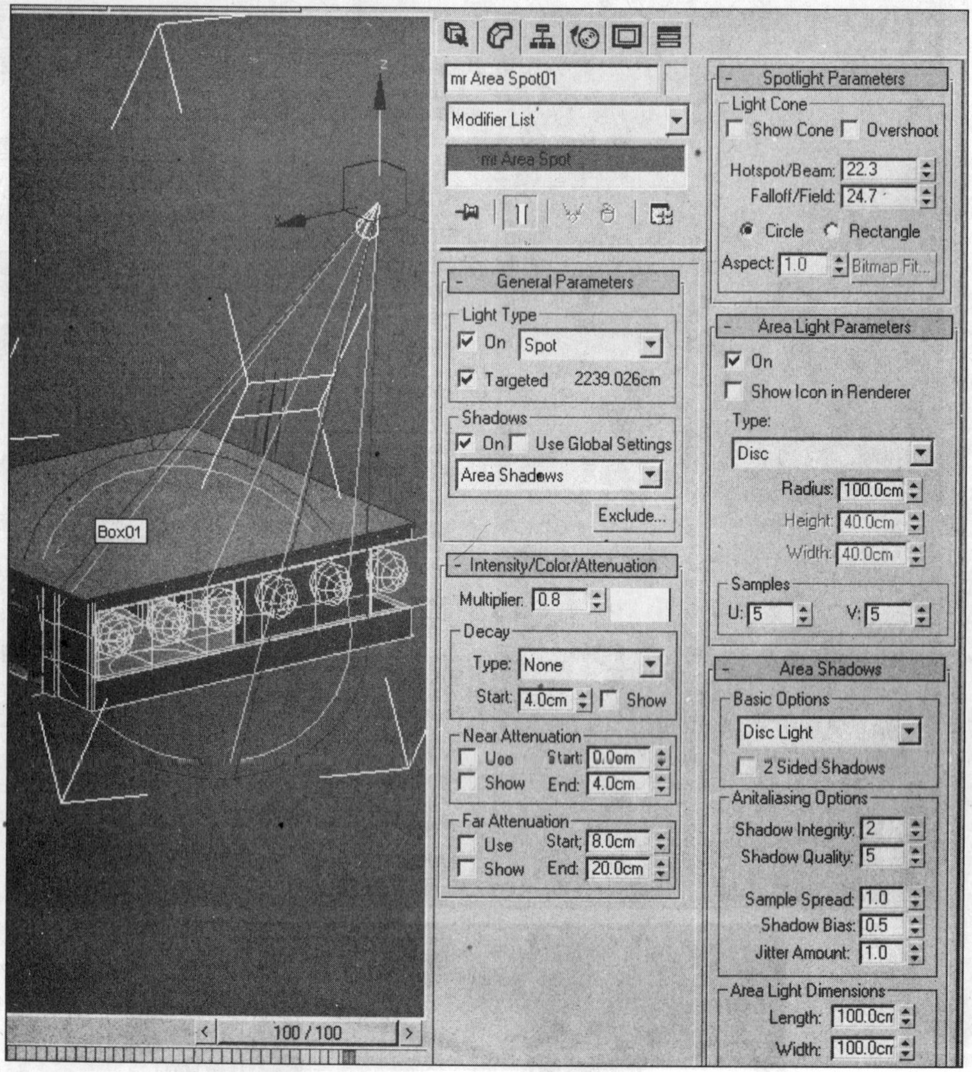

Fig. 3.57, *c*. Setting daylight

Perform test rendering from one camera and adjust the intensity of the light sources to avoid over-lighting near the windows (Fig. 3.57, *b*).

You can make the light source in the small window unique and increase its intensity relative to the light sources in the window of the loggia.

The mr Area Spot light source is suitable for sun light. Only this source allows you to obtain soft shadows both with the standard renderer and mental ray (Fig. 3.57, *c*). You can adjust it on your own. I'd like to mention that in the standard renderer, parameters of shadows are set in the **Area Shadows** rollout, and in mental ray they are set in **Area Light Parameters**. They are independent of each other.

Setting Candlelight

Candlelight will be created in three layers: light sources for the corridor, the bar, and the kitchen.

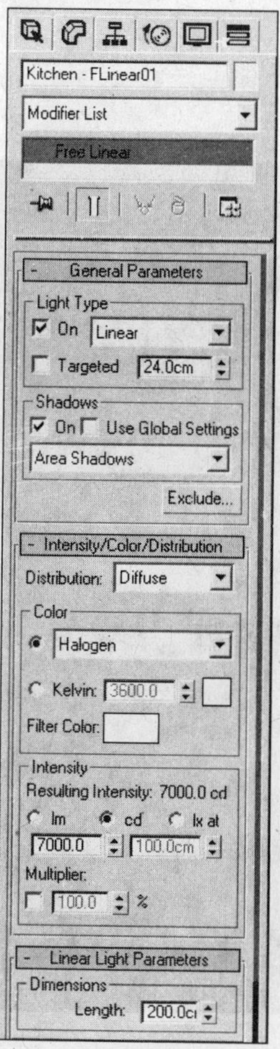

Fig. 3.58. Parameters of the kitchen light source

It is convenient to set candlelight individually, so turn off the daylight by clicking the button with a teapot icon in the layer manager.

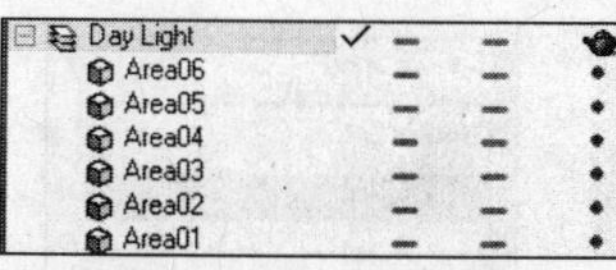

If the light sources don't turn off, open the layer and set this parameter to the **By Layer** value.

Start from the kitchen since this is the easiest. There are no lights there, and you won't go there, so one free area light source of the Area or Linear type will do (Fig. 3.58).

Photometric spot light sources are suitable for the bar (Fig. 3.59, *a*). It is convenient to place them using the **Clone and Align** tool (Fig. 3.59, *b*).

Menu bar → **Tools** → **Clone and Align**

Open the list of objects using the Pick List button and select all the lamp shades.

Delete the initial light source.

For the corridor, you can use photometric spot light sources or sources with Web distribution (Fig. 3.60). The corridor.ies file created with IES Generator is in the Projects\Interior folder on the accompanying CD-ROM.

The result of my work is in the interior-lighting.max file in the Projects\Interior folder.

NOTE

There is a small, but unpleasant problem regarding the shadows. Shadows of the Shadow Map type would be the best choice for these light sources. However, as I already mentioned in *Chapter 2*, mental ray's implementation seems to ignore them. So set shadows of the Raytrace type. I believe the problem has a solution.

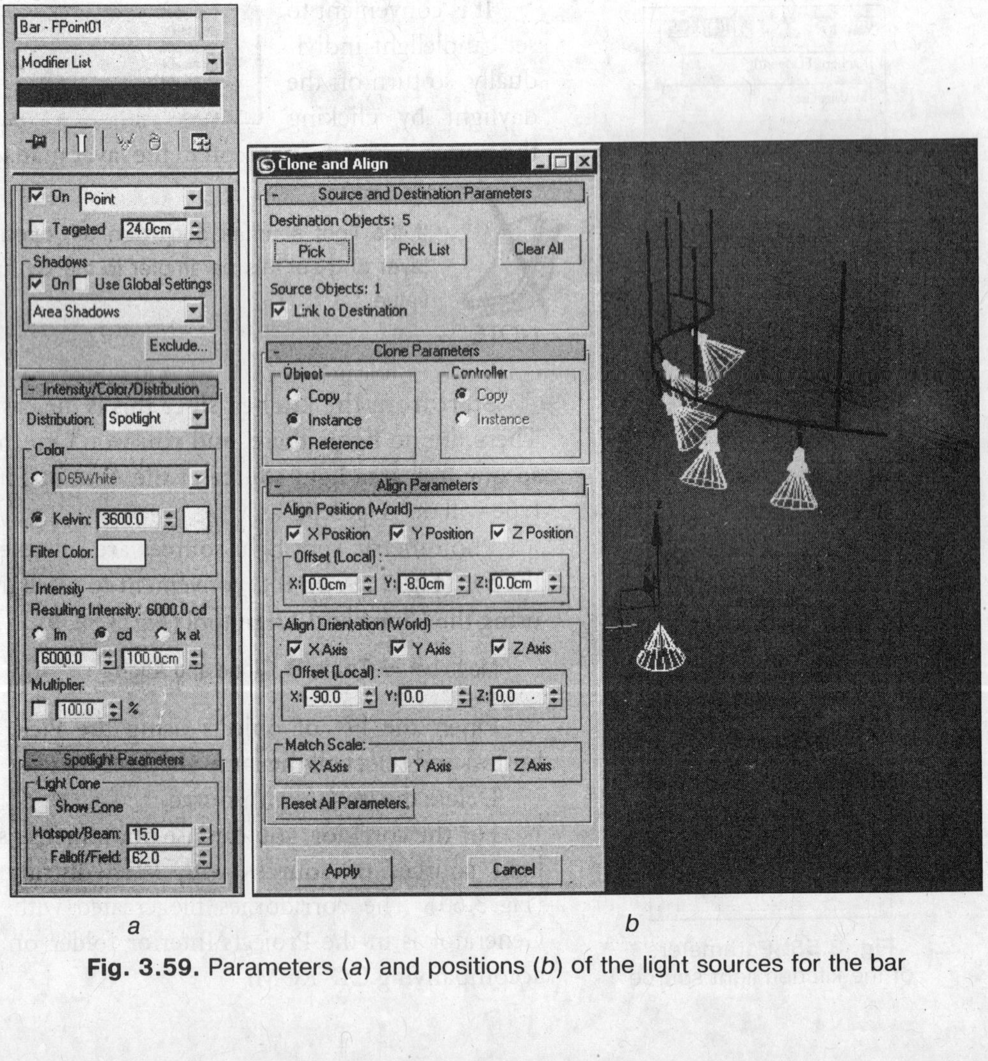

a *b*

Fig. 3.59. Parameters (*a*) and positions (*b*) of the light sources for the bar

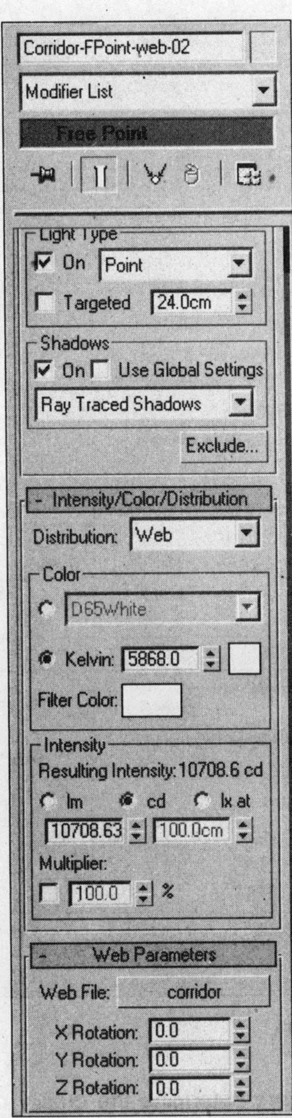

Fig. 3.60. Parameters of the light sources for the corridor

Rendering Indirect Illumination Using the Radiosity *Method*

Until version 5, there were no built-in features for rendering indirect illumination in 3ds Max. The Radiosity method that first appeared in version 5 improved the situation. A new feature, adaptive subdivision of surfaces, that appeared in version 7.5 made this process quicker and more precise. You might have noticed that I focus on the use of mental ray in this book. However, it would be a mistake to ignore Radiosity.

The essence of this method is that all the surfaces are divided into triangles during rendering, and the light energy is distributed over the triangles. A ray from a light source hits a surface element and is reflected either in all directions (if the surface is diffuse) or in a mirror-like manner (if the surface is specular). The reflected rays reach another surface, and so on. This resembles photon tracing, but uses other algorithms.

To enable using this method, switch to the standard renderer (Default Scanline renderer).

- ❒ On the **Advanced Lighting** tab, select **Radiosity** in the **Select Advanced Lighting** on the drop-down list.
- ❒ Answer yes to the question concerning the use of exposure control.
- ❒ The default settings aren't the best, so set the process as shown in Fig. 3.61 and click the **Start** button. (The figure shows the result, and **Start** is substituted with **Continue** on this button).

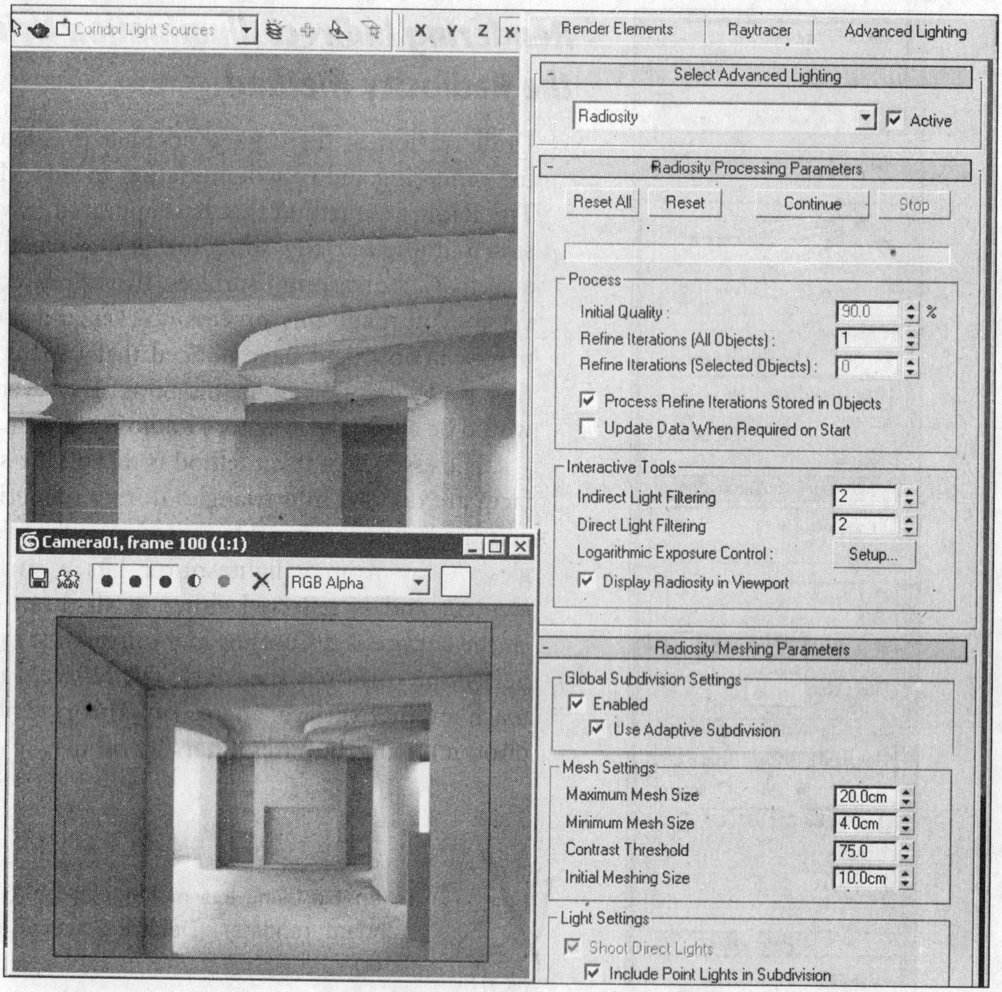

Fig. **3.61.** Radiosity settings

The **Initial Quality** and **Refine Iteration** parameters determine the quality of rendering. If you are dissatisfied with the result, increase these parameters and keep on rendering.

The **Filtering** parameters allow you to smooth the solution.

The most interesting parameters are in the **Radiosity Meshing Parameters** rollout. With the settings shown in the figure, adaptive meshing is used. First, all surfaces are divided into triangles whose size is determined by the **Initial Meshing Size** parameter. If the contrast between adjacent triangles exceeds the **Contrast Threshold** value, the subdivision is adjusted until the desired contrast is obtained, or until the **Minimum Mesh Size** value is reached. If the contrast level is too low, the triangles are merged until the **Maximum Mesh Size** value is reached.

To optimize the process, you can exclude certain objects or even layers from the Radiosity process and meshing by using local settings. You can set them (at last!) so that the objects take part in the process, so to speak, passively (i.e., only receive the diffuse energy without generating it).

Nevertheless, 3ds Max's Radiosity method is imperfect. Its main drawback is that the solution obtained with Radiosity cannot be used in rendering with mental ray although Autodesk announced that was possible.

Rendering Indirect Illumination Using mental ray

If you did exercises in *Chapter 2* on setting global illumination in mental ray, you'll easily set it for this interior. I'll touch on a few important points that will help you speed up rendering.

- Because there are many light sources, it doesn't make sense to increase the number of photons for global illumination. Leave the default value (10,000).
- You can increase the global energy value two or even three times.
- All the sources shine correctly because they are photometric. The only exception is the "sun," that is, the light source of the mr Area Spot type. For this light source to take part in the global illumination, set it manually by increasing the number of photons and the energy level and decreasing the decay. To be able to set this light source, turn off the others temporarily.
- To prevent photons from flying away beyond the scene, enclose it into a sphere with the normal directed inwards. To make the sphere invisible during rendering, uncheck the **Visible to Camera** checkbox in its properties.

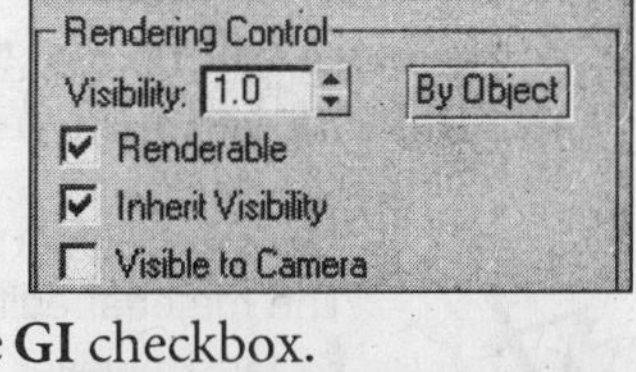

- In the parameters of the sphere, uncheck the **Generate GI** checkbox.
- Do the same for the window glass and the frames. You can do this for the curtains as well, but you don't need to. Although the normals of the glass and the curtains are directed inwards and aren't obstacles for the direct light, photons won't pass through

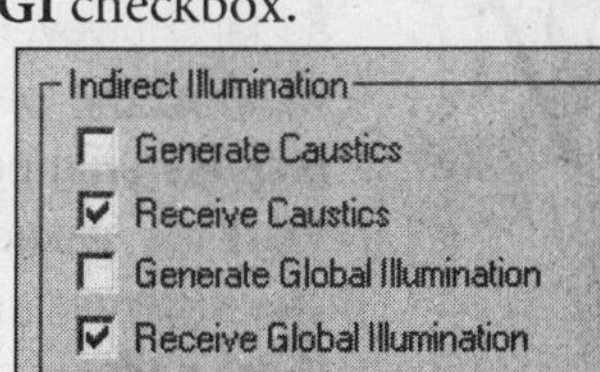

them. When you assign semi-transparent materials to the curtains, some photons will enter the room, so you shouldn't exclude them from tracing.

- Set the **Maximum Sample Radius** parameter to a value between 20 and 30 cm.
- You can try the final gather, but hide the window glass and the curtains. They are dark, and they will make the scene darker.

The result of my work at this stage is in the interior-gi.max file in the Projects\ Project_Interior folder on the accompanying CD-ROM.

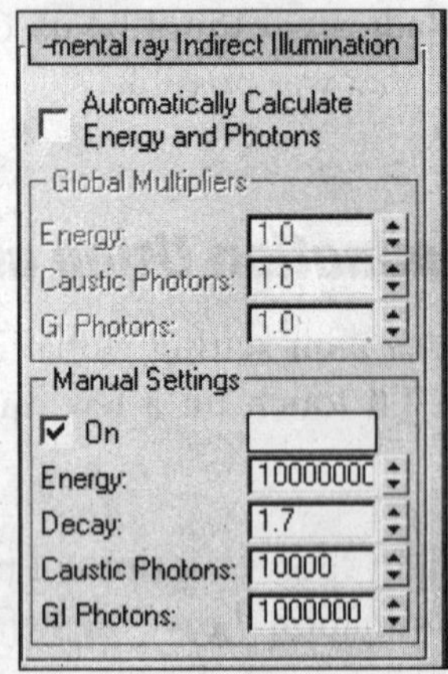

Fig. 3.62. Global illumination settings for the "sun"

Materials and Maps

In this section, materials will be created and assigned to the objects. In addition, map coordinates will be assigned to the objects. The main type of materials will be architectural with various templates.

The material editor can hold up to 24 materials and maps. This was enough for you so far. However, an interior can require many more materials. What should you do when all the possibilities are exhausted? One solution involves clicking the **Reset Map/Material** button in the parameters of the material used in the scene (Fig. 3.63). You'll be asked a question. Answer "**Affect only mtl/map in the editor slot**." The materials used in the scene will remain there. To load a material from the scene to the material editor, select it with the dropper (**Pick material from Object**).

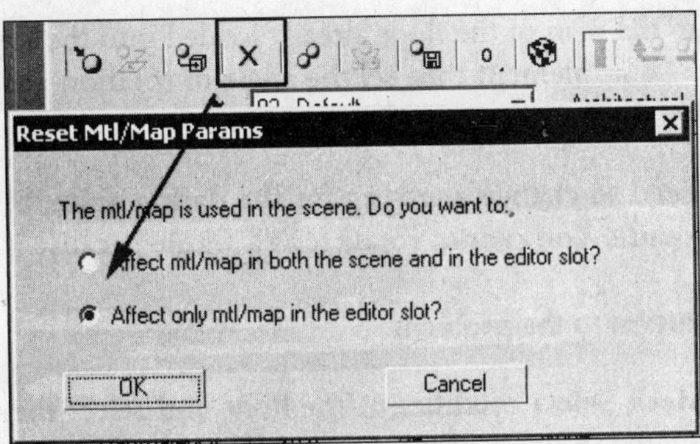

Fig. 3.63. The window that appears after clicking the **Reset Map/Material** button

Material for the Floor and Plinths

The floor consists of three different materials: parquet with deck laying and two kinds of ceramic granite, light (beige) and dark (green).

❒ Create a **Multi/Sub Object** material (Fig. 3.64, *a*).

For the parquet, use the **Wood Varnished** template and use **Stone Polished** for the granite.

In the parameters of each map, check the **Use Real World Scale** and set the size of 45 × 45 cm.

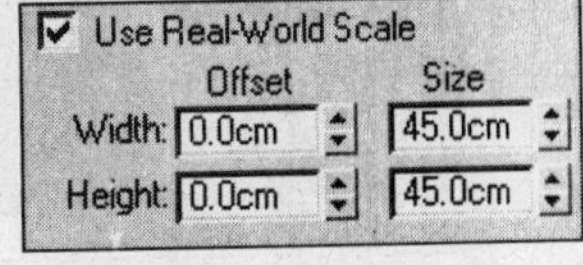

For the granite, apply a map to the **Bump** channel with the **Amount** parameter set to a value between 7 and 10.

❒ Turn on displayed materials in the viewport.

Assign the material to the floor. You won't see it in the viewport. You need to separate the materials by polygons and assign map coordinates.

❒ Apply the **Edit Mesh** modifier to the floor (make sure to use **Edit Mesh** and not **Edit Poly**).

❒ Select appropriate polygons and assign them appropriate material IDs.

You still don't see any map.

❒ Apply the **UVW map** modifier to the entire object (not to polygons!) and check the **Real World Map Scale** checkbox in its parameters. Now, the maps are visible and fit to the real sizes (Fig. 3.64, *b*). However, they lie incorrectly. Keep on editing.

❒ According to the plan of the floor already loaded into the scene, the parquet is laid at an angle. To implement this, set the angle of rotation around the W axis in the parameters of the parquet map (Fig. 3.64, *c*).

You don't need to change anything for the dark granite, but you'll have to work with the light granite. You cannot rotate it as a whole because it lies differently in different places.

Here is a solution to the problem.

❒ Apply the **Mesh Select** modifier to the floor and select the polygons whose map should be rotated.

❒ Apply the **UVW map** modifier to these polygons, check the **Real World Map Scale** checkbox and rotate the gizmo of the modifier (Fig. 3.64, *e*). It isn't easy to find the gizmo since it is small.

The floor is all right.

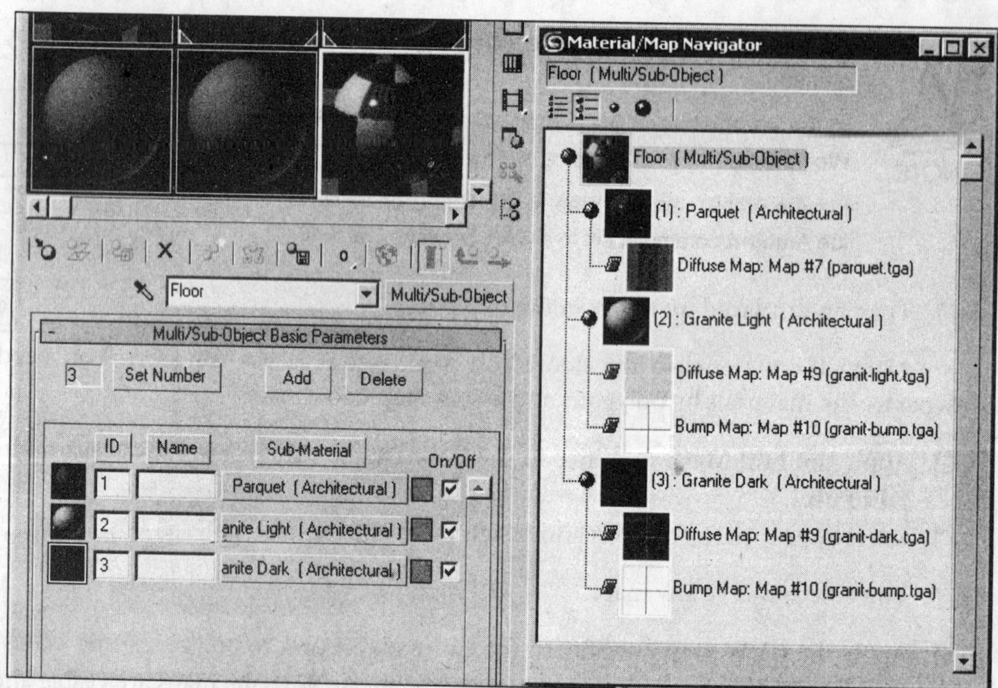

Fig. 3.64, *a*. Material for the floor

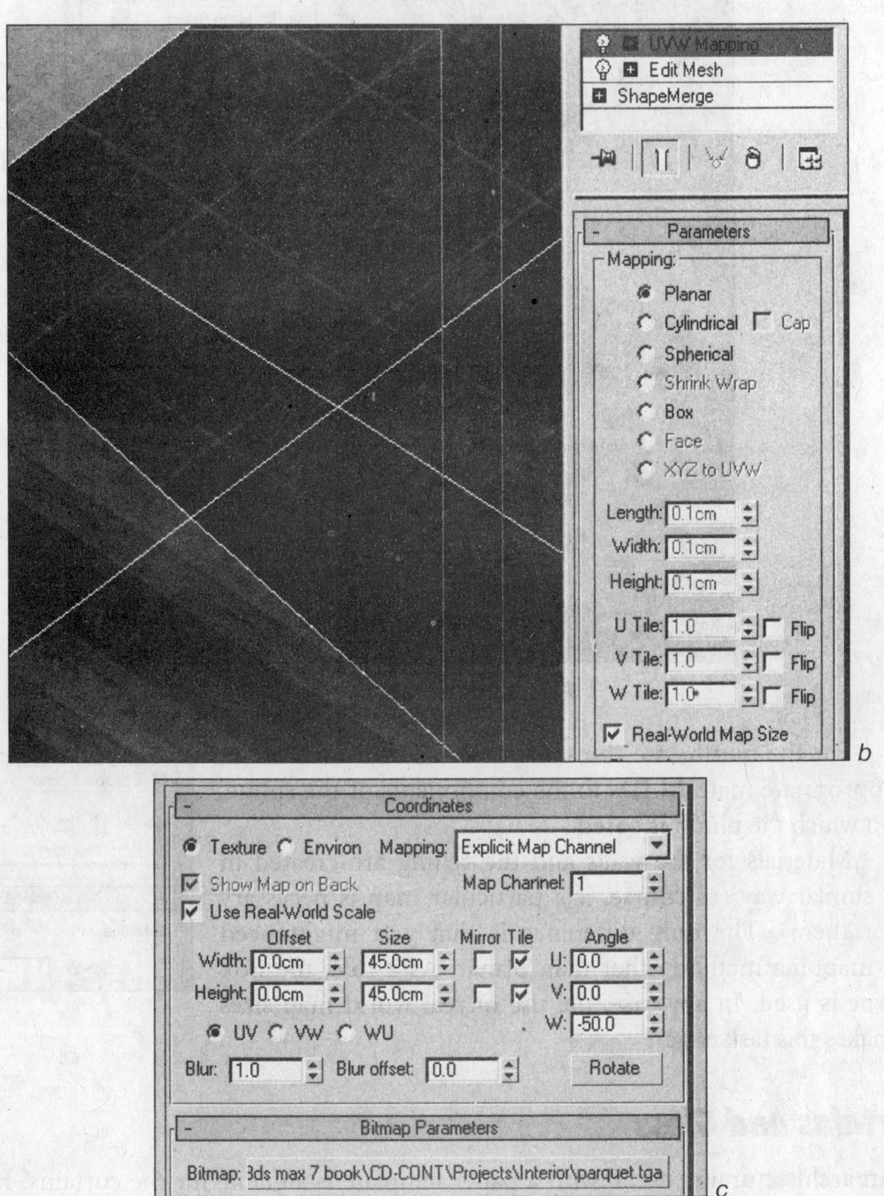

Fig. 3.64, *b* and *c*. Mapping the floor

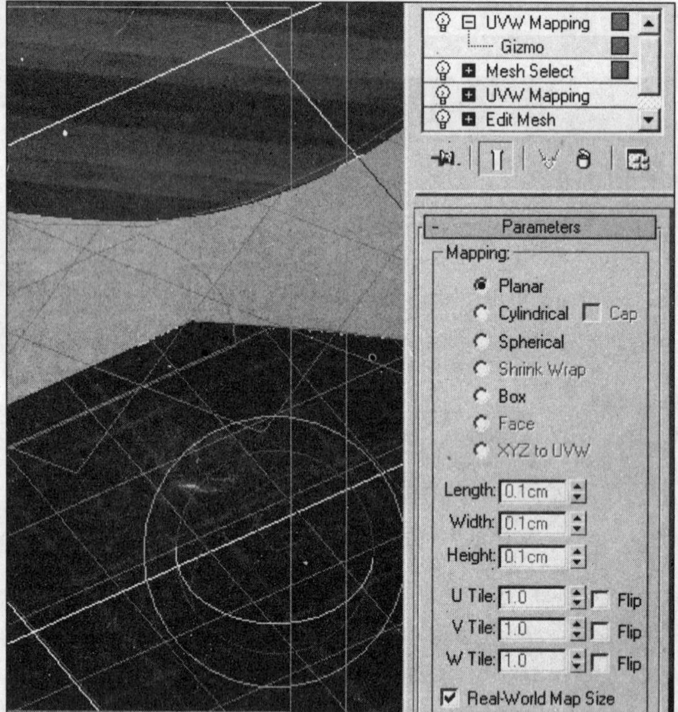

Fig. 3.64, *d*. Mapping the floor

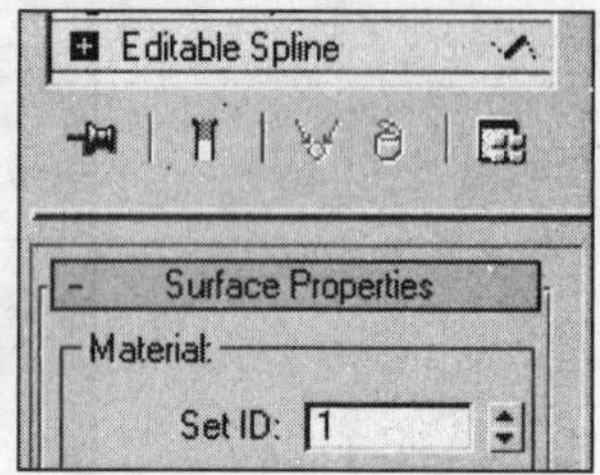

For the plinth, use the same material, but first assign appropriate material IDs to the components of the spline, on which the plinth is based.

Materials for the walls and the ceiling are created in a similar way (of course, if a particular map is necessary for them). The only difference is that you might need a mapping method other than planar. As a rule, the Box type is used. In any case, the use of real-world map sizes makes this task easier.

Curtains and Glass

An architectural material with a paper template is suitable for the curtains. However, the paper isn't a common paper; it should possess translucency. The curtains in this interior are of two kinds: one is light and transparent, and the other is dark and thick. There are no shadow curtains.

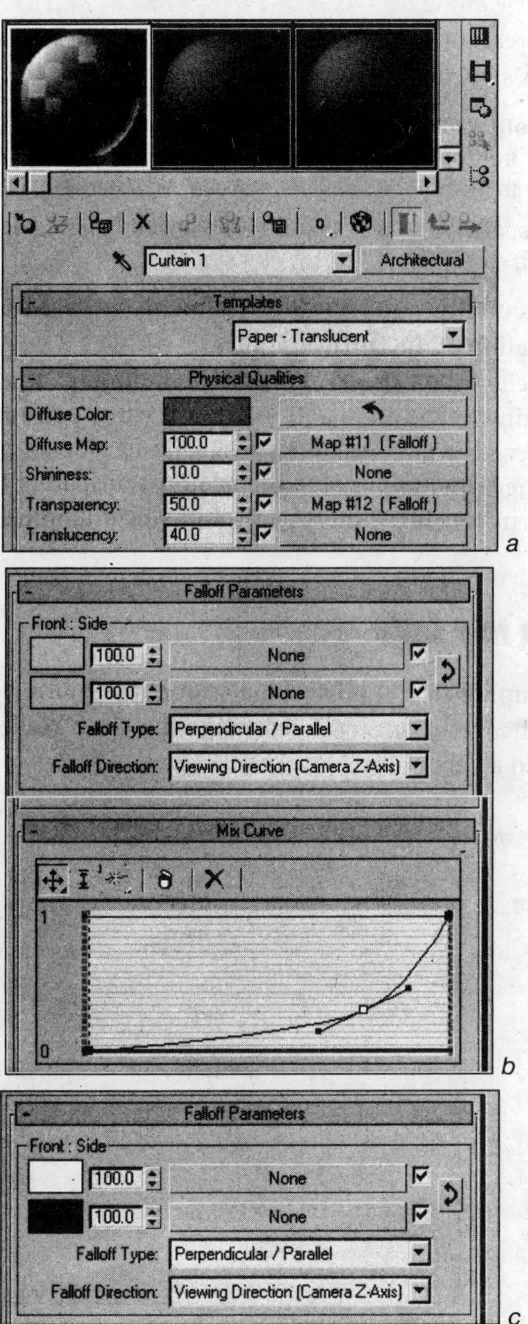

Fig. 3.65. Parameters of the material for the curtains

I'll illustrate creating the material using light curtains as an example.

Its structure is shown in Fig. 3.65, *a*.

NOTE

The **Falloff** map is applied to the **Diffuse** channel so that the color of the curtains changes from beige to violet depending on the viewing angle (Fig. 3.65, *b*). This agrees with the properties of the real curtain material intended by Valery.

The transparency is also modulated using the **Falloff** map (Fig. 3.65, *c*) to obtain the effect of a real cloth.

For the thick curtains, use almost the same material. Make it less transparent and increase the saturation of the **Diffuse** colors.

The **2-sided** checkbox deserves special mentioning. If you exclude the curtains from global illumination created with photon tracing, you should leave this checkbox unchecked. However, if the curtains participate in global lighting, you *should* check this checkbox, otherwise the curtains will be non-transparent for photons.

The same is true for the window glass, but global illumination generation isn't required for them.

The Chairs and the Sofa

A chair and sofa upholstery is a beige material of the Fabric type with the **Falloff** map on the **Diffuse** channel (Fig. 3.66). To make the cloth realistic, there is a transition from a dark hue to a light one.

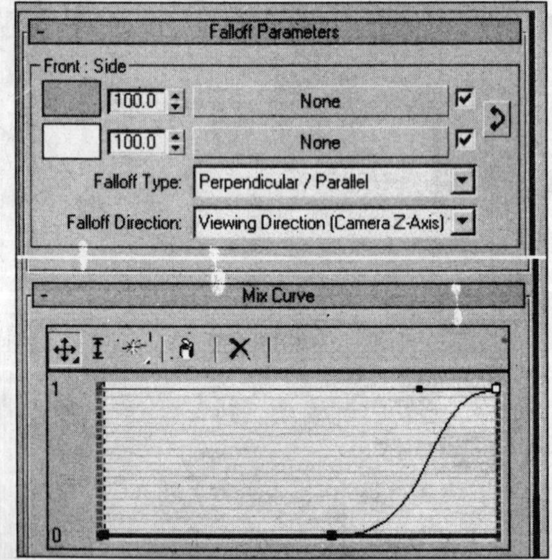

Fig. 3.66. Settings of the chair and sofa upholstery for the **Falloff** map on the **Diffuse** channel

Lamps for the Bar

The lamps for the bar already have materials. Load them into the material editor using the dropper. Because these lamps are on, you need to enter a value into the **Luminance** input box in the parameters of the plastic so that they appear appropriately (Fig. 3.67).

The other materials are either already created or can be created easily.

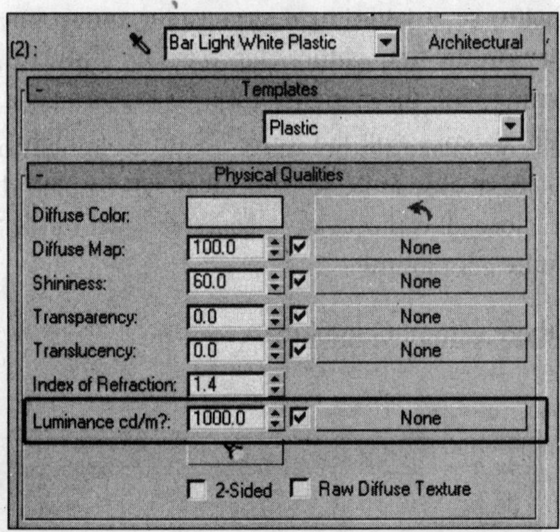

Fig. 3.67. Editing the material of the shade of the lamp for the bar

Final Rendering

The settings described in this section are just a recommendation, and the values of the parameters can be changed within a wide range.

Materials are set and assigned. The lighting is also set, and everything is ready for final rendering.

- ❑ If you render immediately, you'll be disappointed. Your white ceiling will be colored the same as the floor. To deal with the problem, minimize the color bleed for the materials of the objects that take up much of the scene. In the **Advanced**

Lighting Override rollout, decrease the **Color Bleed Scale** parameter (perhaps, to zero) for the materials of the floor, the kitchen furniture, and the curtains.

- You need to control exposure (Fig. 3.68, *b*), otherwise the final image will be too dark or contain too much contrast.
- Increase the number of photons at least five times. To avoid computing the photon map repeatedly, save it in a file (Fig. 3.68, *c*). After that, uncheck the rebuild checkbox.
- Increase the quality of antialiasing at least to the values shown in Fig. 3.68, *d*.
- If you wish, turn on the final gather (Fig. 3.68, *e*). Unfortunately, you won't be able to avoid repainting with the standard tool. Use external shaders such as **RayType**.
- You might need to replace all the sources with Area Light ones with Web distribution or with mr Area Spot sources with the inverse square decay.
- Save the scene, close all unnecessary processes, start rendering, and go to bed since this will take quite a long time.

And that's all there is to it! Good luck.

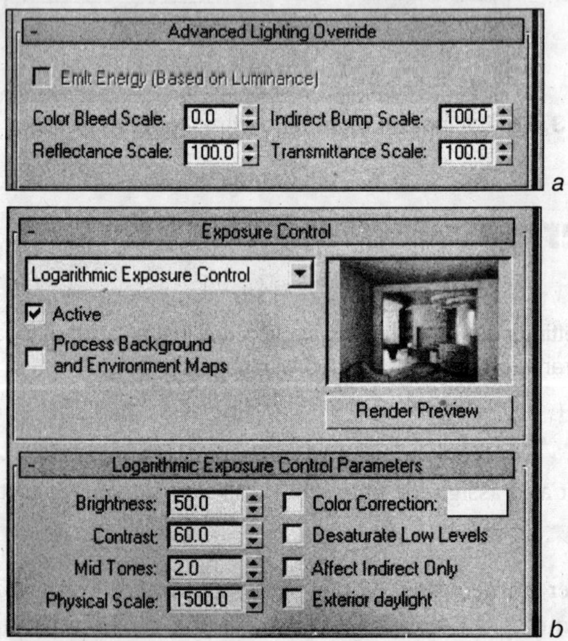

Fig. 3.68, *a* and *b*. Recommended settings for final rendering

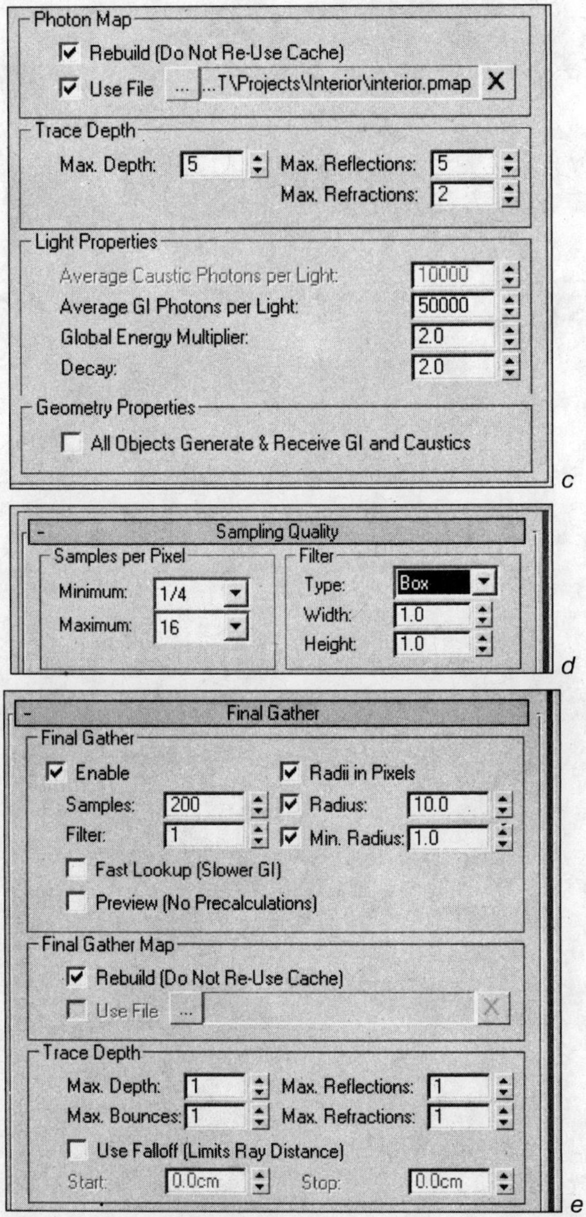

Photon Map
Rebuild (Do Not Re-Use Cache)
Use File ... ...T\Projects\Interior\interior.pmap
Trace Depth
Max. Depth: 5 Max. Reflections: 5
Max. Refractions: 2
Light Properties
Average Caustic Photons per Light: 10000
Average GI Photons per Light: 50000
Global Energy Multiplier: 2.0
Decay: 2.0
Geometry Properties
All Objects Generate & Receive GI and Caustics

c

Sampling Quality
Samples per Pixel
Minimum: 1/4
Maximum: 16
Filter
Type: Box
Width: 1.0
Height: 1.0

d

Final Gather
Final Gather
Enable
Radii in Pixels
Samples: 200
Radius: 10.0
Filter: 1
Min. Radius: 1.0
Fast Lookup (Slower GI)
Preview (No Precalculations)
Final Gather Map
Rebuild (Do Not Re-Use Cache)
Use File ...
Trace Depth
Max. Depth: 1 Max. Reflections: 1
Max. Bounces: 1 Max. Refractions: 1
Use Falloff (Limits Ray Distance)
Start: 0.0cm Stop: 0.0cm

e

Fig. 3.68, *c–e*. Recommended settings for final rendering

CD-ROM Contents

The Projects folder contains all of the required scenes and textures necessary to carry out the projects described in the book.

The Project1 subfolder contains the files for the "Bathroom Shelf" project described in *Chapter 2.*

The Project2 subfolder contains the files for the "Support Container for Stationery" project described in *Chapter 2.*

The Project3 subfolder contains the files for the "Table Calendar" project described in *Chapter 2.*

The Project4 subfolder contains the files for the "Container for Small Items" project described in *Chapter 2.*

The Project5 subfolder contains the files for the "Mobile Telehone" project described in *Chapter 2.*

The Misc Objects subfolder contains files for several projects described in *Chapter 2.*

The Hdr subfolder contains the files for creating the HDRI map.

The Project_Interior subfolder contains all files for the interior project described in *Chapter 3.*

The AI subfolder contains interior plans in the Adobe Illustrator format.

The IES Generator folder contains the IES Generator program by Alex Kozlov, intended for creating the IES-format files describing light distribution.

Index

A

B

D

E

F

N

O

P

Q

R

S

T

U

V

W

X

Z